VISUAL QUICKPRO GUIDE

AFTER EFFECTS CS3 PROFESSIONAL

FOR WINDOWS AND MACINTOSH

Antony Bolante

 Peachpit Press

Visual QuickPro Guide
After Effects CS3 Professional for Windows and Macintosh
Antony Bolante

Peachpit Press
1249 Eighth Street
Berkeley, CA 94710
510/524-2178
510/524-2221 (fax)

Find us on the Web at: www.peachpit.com
To report errors, please send a note to: errata@peachpit.com

Peachpit Press is a division of Pearson Education.

Copyright © 2008 by Antony Bolante

Editor: Rebecca Gulick
Development Editor: Anne Marie Walker
Production Coordinator: Myrna Vladic
Compositor: Debbie Roberti
Indexer: Jack Lewis
Cover Production: Sandra Schroeder

ISBN-13: 978-0-321-52634-2
ISBN-10: 0-321-52634-1

9 8 7 6 5 4 3 2 1

Printed and bound in the United States of America

Dedication

*For everyone at Kim Tom 2007's Stage 3.
Stage 3 Rocks!*

Acknowledgments

Everyone involved in creating the previous versions of this book; I hope this one does you proud.

Everyone who has let me share their lovely photos and faces.

The clever folks at Adobe Systems.

The superb book team: Rebecca Gulick, Anne Marie Walker, Myrna Vladic, Debbie Roberti, Jack Lewis, and all the good people at Peachpit Press.

Shortstack

My family, always.

TABLE OF CONTENTS

TABLE OF CONTENTS

TABLE OF CONTENTS

AFTER EFFECTS: THE BIG PICTURE

"It's the Photoshop of dynamic media."

Summing up After Effects often leads to a comparison to its more famous sibling, Adobe Photoshop. Just as Photoshop lends you precise control over still images, After Effects gives you startling command over moving images. And, like Photoshop, After Effects has established itself as one of the leading programs of its kind. But don't take the comparison too far: Judge After Effects for its unique merits.

After Effects brings together typography and layout, photography and digital imaging, digital video and audio editing, even 3D animation. You can edit, composite, animate, and add effects to each element. And you can output the results for presentation in traditional media, like film and video, or in newer forms, like DVD, the Web, or mobile devices.

In this sense, a more apt metaphor would be that After Effects is the opera of digital media. Just as Wagner sought to combine disparate forms of performance into a "total work of art"—or gesamtkunstzwerk—After Effects allows you to unite various media into a unique, dynamic whole. That may sound a bit grandiose. If it's more convenient, "the Photoshop of dynamic media" works just fine.

Because After Effects draws from so many sources, it also appeals to a wide range of users. You may want to add motion to your typography or design work. Or perhaps your interest in photography and digital imaging brought you to After Effects. Maybe you're a film or video maker who requires visual effects. Or possibly you're an animator who wants to expand your repertoire of tools. Maybe you've heard that After Effects is fun. Whatever your background, whatever your goal, you're ready to get started.

This chapter acquaints you with After Effects. It explains how After Effects works and what you'll need to get started. If you're not already familiar with the QuickStart and QuickPro series, this chapter also introduces you to the book's step-by-step, visual approach to explaining After Effects. Now, let's get to *gesamtkunstzwerk*.

The QuickPro Series

Chances are you're already familiar with Peachpit Press's QuickStart series of books. They're known for their concise style, step-by-step instructions, and ample illustrations.

As you might guess, the Pro appellation implies that the software under discussion appeals to more advanced users. After Effects is such a program. For this reason, this QuickPro guide is designed for intermediate to advanced users and assumes you have significant experience not only with computers, but also with using some form of digital media.

That said, the QuickPro series remains true to the essential QuickStart traditions. The approach still emphasizes step-by-step instructions and concise explanations. If the book looks a little thick for a "concise" guide, consider that literally hundreds of screen shots clearly illustrate every task. You don't have to be a beginning user to find a visual, step-by-step guide appealing.

Occasionally, this guide departs from the standard layout to accommodate larger screen shots, tables, or, most notably, sidebars. Sidebars set aside important background information about the task at hand. If you're already familiar with the concept, feel free to skip ahead. If not, look to the sidebars for some grounding.

Because After Effects combines assets from several disciplines—typography, design, digital imaging, animation, film, and video—it also intersects with the vast bodies of information associated with each of them. Explaining the fundamentals and background of these topics is outside the scope of this book (and even books that don't have the word *quick* in their titles). Nevertheless, this guide tries to provide enough information to keep you moving.

Adobe's CS3 Production Premium

Because After Effects brings together a range of digital media, Adobe hopes you'll use it with its other software aimed at creative professionals, known collectively as the *Creative Suite*. In fact, Adobe eschews individual software version numbers, preferring instead to state versions in terms of the suite. Hence, After Effects 8 is more commonly referred to as After Effects CS3. The collection of CS3 software tailored to the production of dynamic media is called *Adobe CS3 Production Premium*. It contains After Effects Professional, Premiere Pro, Encore DVD, Soundbooth, Photoshop Extended, Illustrator, and Flash. It also includes Bridge, Device Central, and OnLocation, and if you get the Windows package, Ultra. Attractive bundled pricing makes the Production Premium much cheaper than the sum of its parts.

As these software packages mature, they also become more integrated. Over time, it has become easier to move files from one program to another without taking intermediate steps or sacrificing elements of your work. Even the programs' interfaces have grown more consistent. However, although the landscapes are similar, the customs aren't always the same: You may find that not all shared features employ exactly the same procedures or keyboard shortcuts.

Minimum Requirements

To use After Effects, your system must meet the following minimum requirements.

Mac OS

◆ PowerPC G4, G5, or multicore Intel processor

◆ Mac OS X v.10.4.9 or later

Windows

◆ Intel Pentium 4, Centrino, Xeon, or Core Duo processor (multiple processors recommended)

◆ Microsoft Windows XP Service Pack 2 (SP2), Vista Home Premium, Business, Ultimate, or Enterprise

All systems

◆ At least 1 GB of RAM for DV; 2 GB of RAM for HDV and HD

◆ At least 3 GB of available storage for full installation of the software, plus 2 GB additional storage for optional content

◆ 1024 x 768 monitor with 32-bit or greater video card

◆ DVD-ROM drive

◆ QuickTime 7.1.5 or later to use QuickTime features

◆ Internet or phone connection for product activation

◆ Broadband Internet connection for Adobe Stock Photos and other services

✔ Tip

■ You can run After Effects CS3 on a Mac with a G4 or G5 processor, but to run many of the other programs in the CS3 Production Premium, your Mac must have an Intel processor.

Suggested System Features

Although these features aren't required, they can make working with After Effects a lot more satisfying:

Faster/multiple processors. The faster your system can make calculations, the faster it can create the frames of your animation. After Effects can render multiple frames simultaneously on systems with a multicore processor or multiple processors.

Additional RAM. The number of frames you can preview is directly related to the amount of RAM you give After Effects. The same is true for the size of the images you can work with. And you'll need a lot of RAM to run multiple programs simultaneously. Some workflows require running After Effects along with Premiere Pro, Encore, or Photoshop.

Large hard drives. Ample storage space lets you work with large, high-quality files and output longer animations. Like RAM, it seems you can never have enough drive space. Uncompressed full-screen, full-motion video, for example, consumes nearly 30 MB for every second of footage. DV footage uses a more modest 3.6 MB for every second.

Fast hard drives. Your system's ability to play back footage smoothly relies partly on how quickly information can be read from the drives. Certain high-data-rate codecs and capture devices require speedy hard drives.

Large or multiple displays. After Effects can take up a lot of screen space. A large monitor is appropriate; two monitors are luxurious.

QuickTime 7.1.5 (or later). QuickTime is Apple's multimedia technology; it's used widely on both the Mac and Windows platforms. The Pro version is well worth the modest investment. QuickTime also permits you to export movies without using After Effects' Render Queue window.

OpenGL card. After Effects can render and display frames much more quickly if you have an After Effects-supported video card that utilizes OpenGL technology. Check Adobe's Web site for an up-to-date list of recommended video cards.

Professional System Additions

Other additions can elevate your motion graphics system for working on broadcast video or film projects:

After Effects Professional. The Professional version of After Effects includes a number of additional tools geared toward professionals in video and film. See "After Effects Standard and Professional," later in this chapter.

Third-party plug-ins. A multitude of third-party developers offer software plug-in effects. Some are enhanced versions of effects already available in After Effects, whereas others are highly specialized visual or audio effects otherwise unavailable in the program. Adobe's Web site lists plug-ins offered by other developers.

Video capture/playback device. To capture or export video footage, you can add a hardware capture card to your system. Of course, you also need a deck to play and record tapes in your format of choice. Capture devices range from consumer-level gear that captures images comparable to VHS to professional cards that capture uncompressed, 10-bit video signals over a serial digital interface (SDI) connection. To use DV footage, your computer needs a FireWire or iLink connection (aka IEEE 1394 controller card) and a similarly equipped camera or deck. Some DV devices use the more common USB 2 (aka Fast USB) interface instead of FireWire/iLink. Many cards come bundled with the software you'll need to capture video, such as Adobe's own Premiere Pro.

Video monitor. *Video monitor* is really just a fancy way of saying a very good television with professional inputs and excellent color reproduction. Video monitors and computer monitors display images differently, so if your work is destined for video or broadcast, a good video monitor will allow you to judge it more accurately. To ensure accurate brightness and color, you'll need to use built-in or add-on calibration tools. A video capture device typically supports both your computer and your video monitor. With a DV configuration, you can use a DV camcorder or deck to send video to a video monitor.

Hardware acceleration. For the serious user, add-on cards offer accelerated effect rendering and can markedly decrease turnaround time on projects.

Non-linear editor. A non-linear editing (NLE) program doesn't enhance After Effects so much as complement it. After Effects is optimized for animation, compositing, and effects. But for serious editing, it can't beat a dedicated editing program such as Premiere Pro, Final Cut Pro, or Avid. Recognizing the symbiotic relationship between editing and effects, developers are eager to point out how well their NLE works with After Effects. If you haven't already committed to a particular NLE, you should consider the Adobe CS3 Production Premium, which bundles After Effects and Premiere Pro along with Adobe's other digital media production software. (See the section "Adobe's CS3 Production Premium," earlier in this chapter.)

New Features

Some of the more notable features introduced in After Effects CS3 include the following:

Shape layers. New and enhanced drawing tools not only expand the repertoire of mask shapes to include polygons and stars, but also allow you create a new kind of layer, *shape layers*. Shape layers are vector-based graphic objects that possess unique path and paint properties like the ones found in Adobe Illustrator. Shape layers make creating many graphical effects easier than ever and open up entirely new possibilities. Shape layers are covered in Chapter 14, "More Layer Techniques."

Puppet tools. The Puppet effect is a powerful yet intuitive warp effect that employs a new set of tools: Puppet tools. Puppet tools let you "pin down" certain points on a layer and move others to create natural-looking distortions and motion. Use the Starch tool to make some areas move more stiffly and the Overlap tool to give a sense of depth. You can even animate your puppet layer by recording your mouse movement in real time. Learn more about the Puppet effect in Chapter 14.

Brainstorm. The Brainstorm interface generates variants on specified parameters, letting you compare the results of different settings before committing to them. With Brainstorm you can try out small adjustments or conduct wild experimentation without disturbing your work so far. For more about the Brainstorm feature, see Chapter 7, "Properties and Keyframes."

Per-character 3D properties for text animation. After Effects' already powerful text animation features get extended into another dimension by allowing you to move and rotate individual characters in 3D space. Text layers and animation is covered in Chapter 12, "Creating and Animating Text."

Photoshop layer styles and video layers. After Effects continues to support the latest features in Photoshop, including the new Photoshop Extended. After Effects seamlessly accepts Photoshop video layers, as well as Layer Styles. You can even import Vanishing Point data from Photoshop to more easily build 3D compositions.

Flash integration. Since becoming part of the Adobe family (as part of Adobe's acquisition of Macromedia), Flash is more tightly integrated with After Effects than ever. Importing SWF (Shockwave Flash) files preserves vector-based artwork. Exported FLV (Flash Video) files maintain vectors and alpha channels, and can even contain cue points.

Clip Notes. After Effects' Clip Notes feature promotes a collaborative workflow. First implemented in Premiere Pro, the Clip Notes feature lets you export a draft-quality movie embedded into (or linked to) a PDF file. Using the free Adobe Reader software, reviewers can attach notes to timecode-specific points in the movie. When the comments are imported into the original project, they appear as markers that the After Effects artist can use to make modifications.

Export and preview for mobile devices. After Effects rendering options now encompass a wide range of formats designed for playback on mobile devices. You can test your exported movie on particular devices using Adobe Device Central (another member of the CS3 Production Premium).

Color management. In After Effects CS3, managing color is as simple as choosing a Project Working Space. After Effects maintains the color accuracy of imported files automatically.

Performance enhancements. As noted in the section, "Suggested System Features," After Effects utilizes multicore and multi-processor systems to render and preview frames more quickly, increasing your productivity. Moreover, you can export more efficiently by letting an entire network of computers share the burden.

After Effects Standard and Professional

You've probably noticed that After Effects comes in two flavors, a Standard version and a Professional version.

The Professional version, or After Effects Pro, includes all the features of the Standard program, as well as a package of extra tools and effects that address the special needs of motion graphics and effects professionals. After Effects Pro includes more sophisticated tools for controlling motion, such as motion tracking, stabilization, and automation. It also includes superior keying effects to composite footage, such as blue-screen footage. In addition, the Professional version contains more advanced warping and distortion effects, particle effects, and better audio processing effects. The Professional version also lets you work with images that contain 16 or 32 bits per channel rather than the more common 8 bits per channel.

By offering Standard and Professional versions of the program, Adobe makes it possible for you to gain admission to the world of After Effects for a relatively modest investment. Then, when your work demands it, you can upgrade to After Effects Pro. (Rest assured, if you're an After Effects professional, sooner or later you'll need After Effects Professional.)

This book covers the features and procedures common to both the Standard and Professional versions—that is, all the essential features—and refers to both simply as "After Effects" (unless pointing out a feature found only in After Effects Pro). Once you've mastered the core skills, you'll be more than ready to explore the specialized features found exclusively in After Effects Pro—such as the motion tracker, particle effects, and the motion math feature—on your own.

Television Standards

People often refer to equipment by the type of video standard it supports. Hence, it's not a *video monitor* but an *NTSC monitor*. NTSC stands for the National Television Standards Committee, the folks who develop the television standards used in North America and Japan, and whose name describes everything that meets those standards. Some have derisively joked that NTSC stands for "never the same color." But to be fair, the standard has served us well for more than 50 years, which you can't say for every technical standard that comes along.

Most of Europe uses a different standard, Phase Alternation Line (PAL). France and some countries that were formerly part of the Soviet Union use a standard called Sequential Couleur avec Memoire (SECAM).

Figure 1.1 An After Effects panel as seen on the Mac...

Figure 1.2 ...looks almost the same on a Windows system.

Mac vs. Windows

After Effects runs on both the Mac and Windows platforms. This book features screen shots from both systems).

Similarly, both Mac and Windows keyboard shortcuts and instructions are included in the text. With few exceptions, After Effects works the same on both systems, and apart from mostly cosmetic differences between the operating systems, the interfaces are also nearly identical (**Figures 1.1** and **1.2**). In the instances where a process or window differs between the two versions of the program, it's clearly noted. Otherwise, you'll find the most significant differences on the operating system level, not in the program itself.

✔ Tip

- One notable difference between After Effects (and other programs) for the Mac and Windows is the location of the Preferences command. On a Mac, choose After Effects > Preferences; on Windows, choose Edit > Preferences.

Workflow Overview

Any project, it can be argued, begins at the same point: the end. Setting your output goal determines the choices you make to achieve it. Whether your animation is destined for film, videotape, DVD, the Web, or a mobile device, familiarize yourself with the specifications of your output goal, such as frame size, frame rate, and file format. Only when you've determined the output goal can you make intelligent choices about source material and setting up a project.

That established, the typical workflow might resemble the outline that follows. However, every aspect of After Effects is tightly integrated and interdependent. Between import and output, the steps of the project won't necessarily proceed in a simple linear fashion:

Import. After Effects coordinates a wide range of source materials, including digital video, audio, bitmapped still images, path-based graphics and text, and even 3D and film transfer formats. However, it doesn't furnish you with a way to directly acquire these assets—you need a video and audio capture device, a digital still camera, a scanner, or other software packages to do that. This is not to say that After Effects doesn't generate its own graphic and sound elements; it does.

Arranging layers in time. Although it's not designed for long-form nonlinear editing, After Effects ably arranges shorter sequences for compositing and effects work. You can instantly access and rearrange layers, and use the same file repeatedly without copying or altering it.

Arranging layers in space. After Effects' ability to layer, combine, and composite images earned it its reputation as the Photoshop of dynamic media. Moreover, these capabilities extend into the 3D realm.

Adding effects. Or does "the Photoshop of dynamic media" refer to After Effects' ability to add visual effects to motion footage? After Effects offers many effects to combine, enhance, transform, and distort layers of both video and audio. An entire industry has grown up around developing and accelerating effects for After Effects.

Animating attributes. One of After Effects' greatest strengths is its ability to change the attributes of layers over time. You can give layers motion, make layers appear and fade, or intensify and diminish an effect. The timeline's Graph Editor makes it easy to focus on a property and control it with precision. The Brainstorm feature lets you try out and compare different choices.

Previewing. You can play back your animation at any time to evaluate its appearance and timing and then change it accordingly. After Effects maximizes your computer's playback capabilities by utilizing RAM to render frames, dynamically adjusting resolution, allowing you to specify a region of interest, and taking advantage of OpenGL. And as you learned in the section, "Suggested System Features," After Effects can fully utilize multicore and multiprocessor systems to optimize performance.

Adding complexity. Some projects require more complex structures than others. You may need to group layers as a single element or circumvent the program's default rendering hierarchy to achieve a certain effect. Or, you may need to restructure your project to make it more efficient and allow it to render more quickly. With features like parenting and expressions, you have the power to create complex animations with relatively little effort.

Output. When you're satisfied with your composition, you can output the result in a number of file formats, depending on the presentation media (which, of course, you planned for from the start).

Interface Overview

Before you begin exploring the program's terrain, let's take in a panoramic view.

Primary panels

Most of your work will be concentrated in three panels: the Project panel, the Composition panel, and the Timeline panel (**Figure 1.3**).

The **Project panel** lists references to audio and visual files, or footage, that you plan to use in your animation. It also lists compositions, which describe how you want to use the footage, including its arrangement in time, motion, and effects.

The **Composition panel** represents the layers of a composition spatially. The visible area of the Composition panel corresponds to the frame of the output animation and displays the composition's current frame. You can open more than one Composition panel; doing so is particularly useful when you want to compare the image in a composition to a corresponding frame in a nested composition, or view a 3D composition from different angles. It's common to call compositions *comps* and a Composition panel a *Comp panel*, for short.

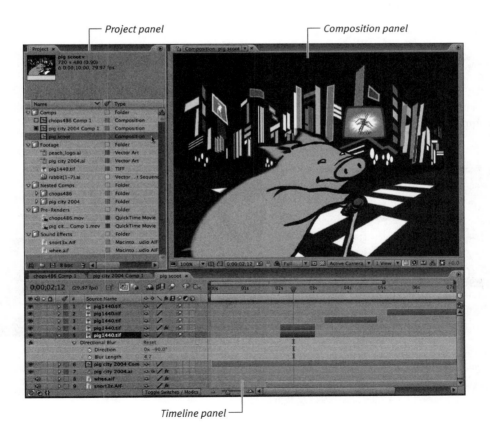

Project panel | Composition panel

Timeline panel

Figure 1.3 Your work takes place primarily in the Project, Composition, and Timeline panels.

INTERFACE OVERVIEW

The **Timeline panel** represents the composition as a graph in which time is measured horizontally. When a footage item is added to the composition, it becomes a layer. The horizontal arrangement of layers indicates each layer's place in the time of the composition; the layers' vertical arrangement indicates their stacking order. You access and manipulate layer properties from the Timeline panel.

✔ Tip

■ You can control the brightness and color of UI elements by choosing Edit > Preferences > User Interface Colors (Windows) or After Effects > Preferences > User Interface Colors (Mac).

Secondary panels

Although the Windows menu lists them in the same group as the three primary panels, you might consider the Footage, Layer, and Effect Controls panels to be ancillaries (**Figure 1.4**). The Flowchart and Render Queue panels are also among this important ensemble.

Footage panel

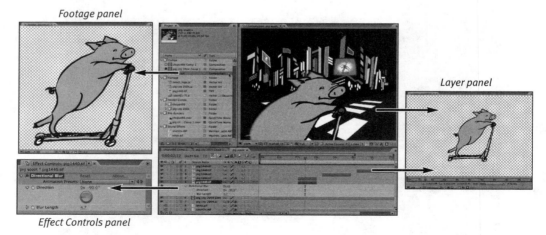

Layer panel

Effect Controls panel

Figure 1.4 The Footage panel shows the source footage listed in the Project panel. The Layer and Effect Controls panels are related to a particular layer in a composition.

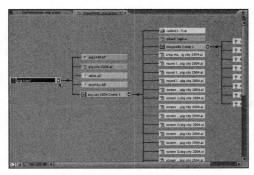

Figure 1.5 The Flowchart window helps you analyze the hierarchical structure of a complex project.

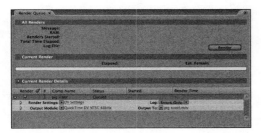

Figure 1.6 The Render Queue window lets you control and monitor the rendering process.

Figure 1.7 The Tools panel contains tools that help you perform special tasks using the mouse, as well as 3D axis buttons and a Workspace pull-down menu. (Typically, it extends horizontally across the workspace; this figure shows a more compact configuration.)

The **Footage panel** allows you to view the source footage listed in the Project panel before it becomes a layer in a composition.

The **Layer panel** lets you view each layer in a composition individually, outside the context of the Composition or Timeline panel. For example, it can be the most convenient place to manipulate a layer's mask shape. When you paint on a layer, you do so in the Layer panel.

The **Effect Controls panel** provides separate, roomier, and often more convenient effect controls than those available in the Timeline panel.

The **Flowchart panel** lets you see your project's elements in the form of a flowchart, which can make it easier to understand the structure and hierarchies of your project—particularly a complex one (**Figure 1.5**).

The **Render Queue panel** lets you control and monitor the rendering process (**Figure 1.6**).

Specialized panels

The panels listed so far—the panels you use most often—all appear at the bottom of the list in the Windows menu, below a horizontal line. Above that separator are a host of other, more specialized panels:

The **Tools panel**, as its name implies, contains an assortment of tools that change the function of the mouse pointer. Each tool allows you to perform specialized tasks (**Figure 1.7**). The Tools panel also contains buttons for changing the 3D axis and a pull-down menu for selecting a workspace.

As in other programs, a small triangle in the corner of a tool button indicates that related tools are hidden. Click and hold the button to reveal and select a hidden tool.

The **Info panel** displays all kinds of information about the current task, from the cursor's current position in a composition to the In and Out points of a layer (**Figure 1.8**).

The **Time Controls panel** contains controls for playing back and previewing the composition. By default, setting a composition's current time also sets the time in all panels related to that composition (**Figure 1.9**).

The **Audio panel** lets you monitor and control audio levels (**Figure 1.10**).

The **Effects & Presets panel** provides a convenient way to view and apply effects. You can reorganize the list, create and view favorites, and find a particular effect in the list or on your hard drive (**Figure 1.11**).

The **Character panel** provides convenient text controls to support After Effects' direct text creation feature. It includes all the controls you'd expect—font, size, fill and stroke, kerning, leading, and the like. It also includes a few you might not expect—baseline shift, vertical and horizontal scaling, superscript and subscript, and a feature to aid in laying out characters in vertically oriented languages like Chinese, Japanese, and Korean (**Figure 1.12**).

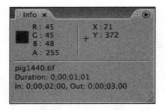

Figure 1.8 The Info panel displays information such as the current position of the cursor in a composition and the In and Out points of a layer.

Figure 1.9 The Time Controls panel contains controls to play back and preview the composition.

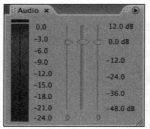

Figure 1.10 The Audio panel lets you monitor and control audio levels.

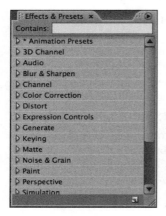

Figure 1.11 The Effects & Presets panel makes it easy to find effects and save custom presets for animation.

Figure 1.12 The full-featured Character panel lets you control the characteristics of text you create in After Effects.

INTERFACE OVERVIEW

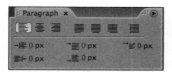

Figure 1.13 You can control blocks of text using the Paragraph panel, which lets you adjust things like alignment, justification, and indentation.

Figure 1.14 The Paint panel gives you control over After Effects' painting and cloning features...

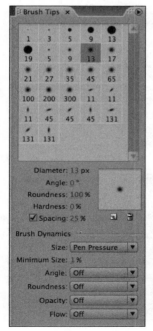

Figure 1.15 ...and its companion, the Brush Tips panel, lets you select the characteristics of the brush you employ.

The **Paragraph panel** lets you control blocks of text as you would in a word-processing or layout program. You can specify justification, alignment, indents, and the spacing before and after paragraphs (**Figure 1.13**).

The **Paint panel** gives you full control over the characteristics of paint, such as color, opacity, and flow. You can also specify which channel you want to paint onto and whether to apply a mode to each stroke (**Figure 1.14**).

The **Brush Tips panel** not only provides a menu of preset brushes, but also lets you create brushes and specify their characteristics, such as diameter, angle, roundness, hardness, and so on (**Figure 1.15**).

✔ Tip

■ After Effects' flexible interface allows you to substantially alter the appearance of each panel. Don't be distracted if a figure in this book depicts a variant of a panel that differs from the one you're using.

INTERFACE OVERVIEW

Even more specialized panels

You can open the previously listed nine panels by using keyboard shortcuts. But to open the following panels, you'll have to choose them from the Windows pull-down menu:

The **Motion Sketch panel** lets you set motion keyframes by dragging the mouse (or by using a pen stroke on a graphics tablet) (**Figure 1.16**).

The **Smart Mask Interpolation panel** (Professional only) helps you animate mask shapes more precisely (**Figure 1.17**).

The **Smoother panel** helps you smooth changes in keyframe values automatically to create more gradual changes in an animation (**Figure 1.18**).

The **Wiggler panel** (Professional only) generates random deviations in keyframed values automatically (**Figure 1.19**).

The **Align panel** helps you arrange layers in a comp vis-à-vis one another (**Figure 1.20**).

The **Tracker Controls panel** (Professional only), an advanced feature, helps you generate keyframes by detecting and following a moving object in a shot. You can use this information to make an effect track an object or to stabilize a scene shot with shaky camera work (**Figure 1.21**).

Figure 1.16
The Motion Sketch panel lets you set motion keyframes by dragging your mouse.

Figure 1.17
The Smart Mask Interpolation panel (Professional only) provides a greater degree of control when you're animating mask shapes.

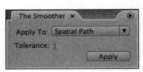

Figure 1.18 The Smoother panel helps you smooth changes in keyframe values.

Figure 1.19
You can generate random deviations in keyframed values automatically using the Wiggler panel (Professional only).

Figure 1.21 Using the Tracker Controls panel (Professional only), you can generate keyframes to follow a moving object automatically or, conversely, to stabilize a shaky image.

Figure 1.20 The Align panel helps you arrange layers.

INTERFACE OVERVIEW

Figure 1.22 This figure shows the Standard workspace.

Figure 1.23 Selecting the arrangement you want from the Tools panel's Workspace pull-down menu...

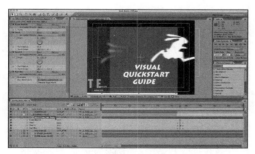

Figure 1.24 ...arranges the panels according to the workspace you choose. Here, note how the Effects workspace places the Effect Controls panel where the Project panel is located in the Standard workspace (shown in Figure 1.22).

Setting a Workspace

With so many controls at your disposal, it's clear that you must arrange the panels to suit the task at hand and change the arrangement for each phase of your workflow. Conveniently, After Effects provides several preset arrangements, or *workspaces*, optimized to accomplish particular tasks, such as animation or effects (**Figure 1.22**). Selecting the appropriate workspace from a list (or using a keyboard shortcut) opens and configures the panels you need.

When you modify a preset workspace (using methods explained in the section "Customizing the Workspace," later in this chapter), After Effects maintains the changes until you reset the preset to its defaults. You can even create your own preset workspace.

To specify a preset workspace:

◆ *Do either of the following:*

▲ Choose Window > Workspace, and then choose the name of the arrangement that corresponds with the task at hand.

▲ In the Tools panel's Workspace pull-down menu, choose the name of the workspace (**Figure 1.23**).

For example, changing from the preset Standard workspace to the preset Effects workspace opens the Effect Controls panel in place of the Project panel (**Figure 1.24**). The workspace retains any modifications you make to it until you reset the workspace.

To create a new workspace preset:

1. If you want, set the workspace that uses an arrangement on which you want to base a custom workspace.

2. In the Tools panel's Workspace pull-down menu, choose New Workspace (**Figure 1.25**).

   A New Workspace dialog box appears.

3. In the New Workspace dialog box, type a name for the custom workspace, and click OK (**Figure 1.26**).

   The current workspace becomes the newly named workspace preset.

4. Modify the workspace using any of the methods described in the section "Customizing the Workspace," later in this chapter.

To reset a preset workspace:

1. With the workspace set to a modified preset workspace (such as Standard), choose Reset "*workspace name*" (**Figure 1.27**).

2. When prompted, confirm that you want to discard the changes you made to the workspace.

   The workspace reverts to its original preset arrangement.

✔ Tips

- The Workspace pull-down menu also contains commands for deleting a workspace and for assigning a keyboard shortcut to a workspace.

- The Window menu (in After Effects' main menu bar) also contains all the commands pertaining to workspaces.

Figure 1.25
In the Tools panel's Workspace pull-down menu, choose New Workspace.

Figure 1.26 Enter a name for the custom workspace in the New Workspace dialog box.

Figure 1.27
Choosing Reset "*workspace name*" in the Tools panel's Workspace pull-down menu reverts the workspace to its original state.

Customizing the Workspace

Using the preset workspaces is convenient, not compulsory. By customizing the size and arrangement of the panels, you can optimize your workspace and your workflow. You just have to know a few things about frames, panels, and tabs.

The After Effects interface consists of an interconnected system of *panels* contained within *frames*. Unlike a collection of free-floating windows that can be arranged like playing cards on a tabletop, frames are joined together in such a way that the interface may remind you of a mosaic or stained glass. Resizing one frame affects the adjacent frames so that, as a whole, the frames always fill the screen (or, more strictly speaking, After Effects' main application window, which most users maximize to fill the screen). With frames and panels it's easy to change the relative size of each part of the interface without wasting screen space. And you don't have to worry about one window disappearing behind another.

You can also customize a workspace by taking advantage of tabs. The tab that appears at the top of each panel looks a lot like its real-world counterpart in your office filing cabinet. By dragging a panel's tab into the same area as another panel, you *dock* the panels together. When panels are docked, it's as though they are filed one on top of the other. But like physical file-folder tabs, the tabs of the panels in the back are always visible along the top edge of the stack; you click a panel's tab to bring it to the front. (The Footage, Comp, and Layer panel tabs include a lock option and pull-down menu, discussed in the section "Using Viewers," later in this chapter.)

Just as docking reduces the number of spaces in the interface's mosaic of frames, dragging a panel between other panels creates an additional space, or frame.

Finally, you can separate a panel from the system of frames, creating a free-floating window. A floating window may be useful for tasks you don't perform often or when you can move it to a second computer screen.

Because the interface's design is intuitive and common to several Adobe programs, it won't be covered in detail here. However, the particular way After Effects lets you switch among images in a single panel is described in the following section, "Using Viewers."

Using Viewers

As you work, you'll need to open numerous footage items, compositions, and layers. To prevent a frame from becoming over-crowded with tabs, the Footage, Comp, and Layer panels utilize *viewers*. (And because each layer can contain a set of effects, the Effect Controls panel also employs viewer system.)

Instead of opening in separate tabbed panels, multiple items of the same type (footage, comps, layers, and a layer's effects) share a single panel of that type (Footage panel, Comp panel, and so on) (**Figure 1.28**).

A pull-down menu in the panel's tab allows you to switch to another image, or *viewer*. For example, you can see any layer in the project by selecting it in a Layer panel's viewer menu (**Figure 1.29**).

However, you can prevent new items from opening in a viewer by *locking* the viewer. When locked, the viewer pull-down menu still works, but the panel doesn't accept new viewers. Instead, the item opens as a separate tabbed panel (**Figure 1.30**). (If another compatible panel is visible and unlocked, then new items open in it.)

Naturally, the viewer feature doesn't prevent you from using any of the methods described in the section "Customizing the Workspace"). Viewers are just another feature to help you manage your workspace and your workflow effectively.

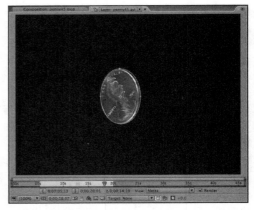

Figure 1.28 By default, all footage items open in the same Footage panel; comps share the same Comp panel; and layers share the same Layer panel.

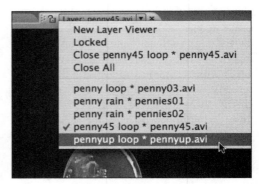

Figure 1.29 You can view another image by selecting it in the panel's viewer pull-down menu. This Layer panel's viewer lets you select another layer in the project.

Figure 1.30 However, selecting the viewer's Lock icon prevents items from opening in the panel; instead, they open in a separate panel. Here, a locked Layer panel forces subsequent layers to open in another Layer panel.

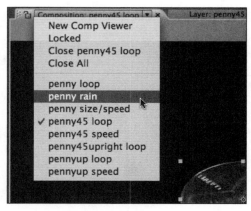

Figure 1.31 The viewer pull-down menu lists other items (note how layer names are preceded by the comp that contains them). Select the name of the item you want to view...

Figure 1.32 ...to see its image in the panel.

Figure 1.33 Click the Lock icon in the panel's tab to toggle it from unlocked...

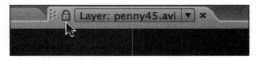

Figure 1.34 ...to locked.

To select a viewer:

◆ In a Footage, Layer, Comp, or Effect Controls panel, select the name of the item you want to see in the tab's viewer pull-down menu (**Figure 1.31**).

The image in the panel changes accordingly (**Figure 1.32**).

To lock or unlock a view:

◆ In a Footage, Layer, Comp, or Effect Controls panel's tab, select the Lock icon to toggle it on and off (**Figures 1.33** and **1.34**).

The icon indicates the panel's viewer is unlocked and will let items open in the panel. The icon indicates the panel's viewer is locked; new items must open in a separate, unlocked panel.

✔ Tips

■ Comps open as separately tabbed Timeline panels and don't utilize viewers. Typically, the frame that contains Timeline panels is wide and easily accommodates numerous tabs.

■ The Comp panel also has a View Layout pull-down menu, which allows the panel to display multiple images simultaneously. Seeing the adjustments you make to a comp from several perspectives at once is particularly useful when you're working with 3D layers. Using multiple comp views is discussed in detail in Chapter 4, "Compositions," and Chapter 15, "3D Layers."

USING VIEWERS

IMPORTING FOOTAGE INTO A PROJECT

2

Think of an After Effects project as a musical score. Just as a score refers to instruments and indicates how they should be played, your project lists the files you want to use and how you want to use them. When you've finished creating your project, you can output an animation as a movie file or an image sequence. The important thing to remember is that the project contains only references to the source files, not the files themselves. The project contains neither the sources nor the end result, any more than a sheet of music contains a tuba or a recording of the concert. For this reason, a project file takes up little drive space.

Source files, on the other hand, consume considerably more storage. You need both the project and the source files to preview or output your animation, just as a composer needs the orchestra to hear a work in progress or, ultimately, to perform it in concert. Non-linear editing systems (such as Adobe Premiere Pro and Apple Final Cut Pro) also work by referring to source files. Thus, if you're familiar with those programs, you have a head start on the concept of using file references in a project.

In this chapter, you'll learn how to create a project and import various types of footage. The chapter covers the specifics of importing still images, motion footage, audio, and even other projects. In fact, After Effects ships with a number of astonishingly useful preset project templates. And that's not all: After Effects arrives accompanied by a full-fledged asset management program, Adobe Bridge.

Don't be intimidated by the length or depth of the chapter. Importing different types of footage into your project is a simple and straightforward process. As you go through the chapter, take just what you need. As you begin to incorporate a wider range of formats in your work, revisit sections to learn the idiosyncrasies of those particular formats. To revisit the musical metaphor, if a project is like a score, start by composing for an ensemble, and then build up to an orchestra.

Creating and Saving Projects

Creating a project is especially simple in After Effects, which doesn't prompt you to select project settings. As you'll see in the next chapter, most settings you specify are associated with compositions within the project.

You save After Effects projects as you would save a file in just about any program. But to more easily track changes to your work, you can instruct After Effects to save each successive version of a project using an incremental naming scheme.

Although you don't have to actively specify project settings when you start a project, you can change the default values at any time by choosing File > Project Settings. In the Project Settings dialog box, you can change the project's time display style, the sample rate at which audio is processed, and color settings—which includes a color depth setting as well as new color management options. You can find out more about these settings in the After Effects Help system.

To create a new project:

◆ *Do one of the following:*

▲ Launch After Effects.

▲ With After Effects running, choose File > New > New Project (**Figure 2.1**).

If a project is open, After Effects prompts you to save it. Otherwise, a new Project panel appears (**Figure 2.2**).

To save using incremental project names automatically:

◆ After the project has been saved, choose File > Increment and Save, or press Command-Opt-Shift-S (Mac) or Ctrl-Alt-Shift-S (Windows).

After Effects saves a copy of the project, appending a number to the filename that increases incrementally with each successive Increment and Save command.

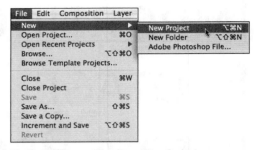

Figure 2.1 Choose File > New > New Project.

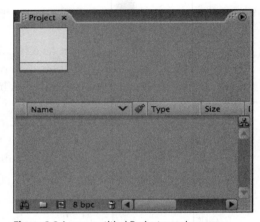

Figure 2.2 A new, untitled Project panel appears.

✔ Tips

■ A project's name appears at the top of the main application window, not the Project panel. When a project has unsaved changes, an asterisk (*) appears next to the project's name.

■ You can instruct After Effects to save the current project at an interval you specify by choosing After Effects > Preferences > Auto-Save (Mac) or Edit > Preferences > Auto-Save (Windows) and specifying how frequently After Effects saves.

■ As you might expect, the File menu also includes Save, Copy, and Revert to Last Saved commands.

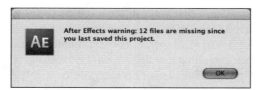

Figure 2.3 After Effects alerts you if it can't locate source files.

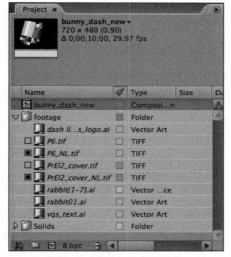

Figure 2.4 The names of missing footage items appear in italics, and the source footage is temporarily replaced by a color bar placeholder.

Opening and Closing Projects

In After Effects, you can have only one project open at a time. Opening another project closes the current project. However, closing the Project panel doesn't close the project; it merely removes the Project panel from the workspace.

As you learned in this chapter's introduction, an After Effects project contains footage items that refer to files on your system. When you reopen a project, After Effects must locate the source files to which each footage item refers. If After Effects can't locate a source file, the project considers it missing (**Figure 2.3**). (In Premiere Pro and other non-linear editing programs, missing footage is called *offline*.) The names of missing footage items appear in italics in the Project panel (**Figure 2.4**), and a placeholder consisting of colored bars temporarily replaces the source footage. You can continue working with the project, or you can locate the source footage. For more about missing source footage, see Chapter 3, "Managing Footage."

✔ Tips

- To open a project you worked on recently, choose File > Open Recent Projects and choose the name of the project in the submenu.

- With After Effects running, press Shift-Command-Opt-P (Mac) or Shift-Ctrl-Alt-P (Windows) to open the most recently opened project (think *p* for *previous project*).

- After Effects ships with a number of incredibly useful and inspiring preset project templates. See the section "Importing with Adobe Bridge," later in this chapter, for details.

Importing Files

After Effects allows you to import a wide variety of still images, motion footage, and audio, as well as projects from After Effects and Premiere Pro. The procedures for importing footage are essentially variations on a theme, so you should get the hang of them quickly.

Although you may be tempted to speed through some sections in this part of the chapter, make sure you understand how the methods differ for each file type. Depending on the file, you may need to invoke the Interpret Footage command, which contains special handling options such as how to set the duration of stills or the frame rate of motion footage. The Interpret Footage command also lets you properly handle other aspects of footage, such as the alpha channel, field order, and pixel aspect ratio. If you're already familiar with these concepts, go directly to the numbered tasks; if not, check out the sidebars in this chapter for some technical grounding.

You'll find that you can often use several methods to import footage: menu bar, keyboard shortcuts, or context menu. You can even drag and drop from the desktop. Once you know your options, you can choose the method that best fits your needs or preferences.

The maximum resolution for import and export is 30,000 × 30,000 pixels. However, the PICT format is limited to 4,000 × 4,000 pixels and BMP to 16,000 × 30,000 pixels.

As you've already learned, After Effects Professional lets you import images with 16 bits per channel (bpc) and 32 bpc—an indispensable capability if you're doing high-end work.

The maximum image size and bit depth are limited by the amount of RAM available to After Effects (see the sidebar "Wham, Bam—Thank You, RAM").

After Effects supports an extensive and growing list of file formats, depending on your platform. Photoshop and other third-party plug-ins can also expand the possibilities.

Choosing the Color Bit-Depth Mode

If you're using After Effects Professional, the Project Settings dialog box also allows you to set the color bit-depth mode. In addition to supporting standard 8 bits-per-channel (bpc) images, After Effects Pro lets you process images using 16 and even 32 bpc.

This means your images not only can have higher color fidelity from the start, but they also retain that quality even after repeated color processing (for example, from transfer modes and effects).

But naturally, greater precision comes at a cost. For example, processing color in 16 bpc is twice as demanding as processing it in 8 bpc—that is, doing so requires twice the RAM and processing time. To save time, you may want to work in 8 bpc initially and then switch to 16 bpc when you're ready for critical color processing.

Although you can set the bit depth from the Project Settings dialog box, it's more convenient to toggle the bit-depth mode by Option/Alt-clicking the bit depth display in the Project panel.

IMPORTING FILES

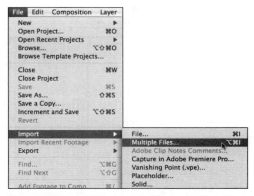

Figure 2.5 Choose File > Import > File or > Multiple Files.

Figure 2.6 The Import File or Import Multiple Files dialog box appears.

To import a file or files:

1. *Do one of the following:*
   - ▲ Choose File > Import > File to import one item.
   - ▲ Choose File > Import > Multiple Files to import several items (**Figure 2.5**).

   The Import File or Import Multiple Files dialog box appears (**Figure 2.6**).

   continues on next page

Wham, Bam—Thank You, RAM

Here's the formula for calculating how much RAM an image requires:

Width in pixels × height in pixels × 4 bytes = RAM needed to display image

So, the largest file allowed would require 3.35 GB of RAM (30,000 × 30,000 × 4 bytes)—ouch!

A tall image used as an end credit roll for video output provides a less extreme example, as you can see:

720 × 30,000 × 4 bytes = 82.4 MB of RAM

---

2. To expand or reduce the list of files, choose an option for Enable (**Figure 2.7**):

All Files—Enables all files in the list, including files of an unrecognized file type

All Acceptable Files—Enables only file types supported by After Effects

All Footage Files—Enables only files that can be imported as footage items and excludes otherwise acceptable file types (such as After Effects or Premiere Pro project files)

AAF, AE Project, and so on—Enables only files of the same file type you select

Enabled files can be selected for import, whereas other files are unavailable and appear grayed out.

3. In the Import File or Import Multiple Files dialog box, choose Footage from the Import As pull-down menu.

To import files as compositions or to import projects, see the corresponding sections later in this chapter.

4. Select the file you want to import, and then click Open (**Figure 2.8**).

To select a range of files in the same folder, click the file at the beginning of the range to select it, Shift-click the end of the range, and then click Open.

To select multiple noncontiguous files in the same folder, Command/Ctrl-click multiple files, and then click Open.

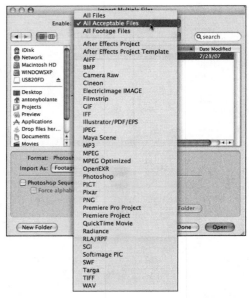

Figure 2.7 To sift the list of files, specify an option in the Enable pull-down menu.

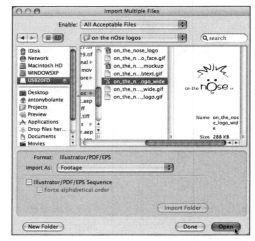

Figure 2.8 Select the file or files you want to import and click Open.

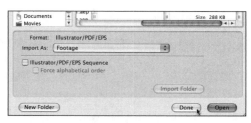

Figure 2.9 If you chose to import multiple files, click Done to close the dialog box.

Figure 2.10 Imported items appear in the Project panel as footage files.

5. If prompted, specify other options for each file you import (such as its alpha channel type or how to import a layered file).

The options for particular file types are discussed later in this chapter.

6. If you chose to import multiple files in step 1, repeat the subsequent steps until you've imported all the files you want to use; then, click Done to close the Import Multiple Files dialog box (**Figure 2.9**).

The file(s) appear as item(s) in the Project panel (**Figure 2.10**).

✔ Tips

■ Double-clicking in an empty area of the Project panel is a great shortcut for opening the Import File dialog box.

■ You can also import files by dragging them directly from the operating system to the Project panel. But because After Effects' interface usually covers the entire screen, it may discourage this technique. The integration of Adobe Bridge (covered later in this chapter) provides yet another convenient way to browse for files to import.

Setting Still-Image Durations

When you import a still image as a footage file and make it a layer in a composition, you can set its duration to any length. By default, the duration of a still image matches the duration of the composition. However, you can also manually set the default duration for still images. Doing so comes in handy when you plan to use several stills for the same duration, such as a series of title cards for a credit sequence. Of course, you can always change the duration (or trim) of the layer later. See Chapter 4, "Compositions," for more about adding footage to a composition as layers; see Chapter 6, "Layer Editing," for more about editing layers.

To change the default duration of still images:

1. Choose After Effects > Preferences > Import (Mac) or Edit > Preferences > Import (Windows) (**Figure 2.11**).

   The Import panel of the Preferences dialog box appears (**Figure 2.12**).

2. In the Still Footage section, *do one of the following* (**Figure 2.13**):

   ▲ Select Length of Composition to make the still-images' duration the same as that of the composition you're adding them to.

   ▲ Select the radio button next to the Time field and enter a default duration for imported still images.

3. Click OK to set the changes and exit the Preferences dialog box.

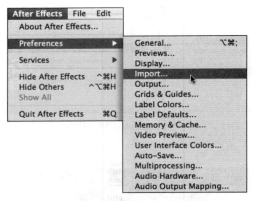

Figure 2.11 Choose After Effects > Preferences > Import (Mac) or Edit > Preferences > Import (Windows).

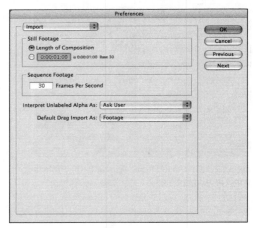

Figure 2.12 The Import panel of the Preferences dialog box appears.

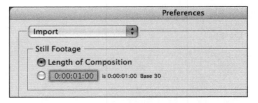

Figure 2.13 Set the default duration of still images to the duration of the composition or enter a custom duration.

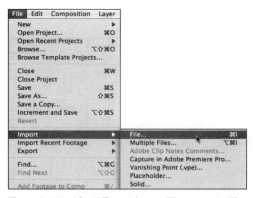

Figure 2.14 In After Effects, choose File > Import > File.

Figure 2.15 In the Import dialog box, select the first image in the sequence, and select the Sequence option.

Figure 2.16 The image sequence appears in the Project panel as a single item.

Importing Still-Image Sequences

Many programs (including After Effects) can export motion footage not as a single movie file, but as a series of still images, or a *still-image sequence*. You can import all or part of a still-image sequence as a single motion footage item.

To import a still-image sequence:

1. Make sure all the still-image files in the sequence follow a consistent numeric or alphabetical filename pattern and are contained in the same folder.

2. In After Effects, choose File > Import > File (**Figure 2.14**).

   The Import File dialog box appears.

3. *Do either of the following*:

   ▲ To import the entire sequence as a single motion footage item, select the first file in the sequence.

   ▲ To import part of the sequence as a single motion footage item, select the first file in the range, and then Shift-click the last file in the range.

4. Select the box for the Sequence option (**Figure 2.15**).

   The Import File dialog box automatically indicates the file format for the Sequence check box (for example, TIFF Sequence). If you specified a limited range of sequence to import, the dialog box also displays the range next to the Sequence check box.

5. Click Open to import the file sequence and close the dialog box.

   The image file sequence appears as a single footage item in the Project panel (**Figure 2.16**).

To set the default frame rate for still-image sequences:

1. Choose After Effects > Preferences > Import (Mac) or Edit > Preferences > Import (Windows) (**Figure 2.17**).

   The Import panel of the Preferences dialog box appears.

2. In the Sequence Footage section of the Preferences dialog box, enter a frame rate (**Figure 2.18**). See Chapter 4 for more about frame rates.

3. Click OK to set the default frame rate and close the Preferences dialog box.

✔ Tip

■ Dragging a folder of stills from the operating system is another way to import the folder's contents as an image sequence. (To import separate footage items within a folder, Option/Alt-drag the folder to the Project panel.)

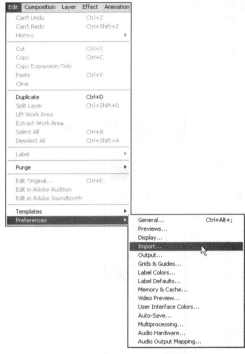

Figure 2.17 Choose After Effects > Preferences > Import (Mac) or Edit > Preferences > Import (Windows).

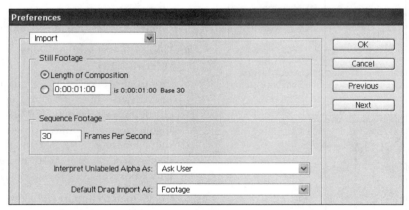

Figure 2.18 Enter a frame rate for imported still-image sequences.

IMPORTING STILL-IMAGE SEQUENCES

Figure 2.19 Misinterpreting the type of alpha results in an unwanted halo or fringe around objects. Note the dark fringe around the letters and the darkness in the transparency.

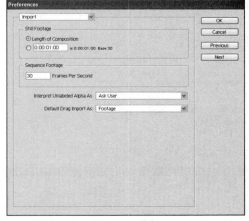

Figure 2.20 The Import panel of the Preferences dialog box appears.

Importing Files with Alpha Channels

A file's transparency information can be saved in two ways: as straight alpha or as premultiplied alpha. Both types store transparency information in an alpha channel. But in a file with a premultiplied alpha channel, the visible channels also take transparency into account. In semitransparent areas (including smooth edges), the RGB channels are mixed—or *multiplied*—with the background color (usually black or white).

When you import a file containing an alpha channel, After Effects tries to detect a label (encoded in the file) that indicates whether the alpha is straight or premultiplied and processes, or interprets, it accordingly. But if the alpha is unlabeled, After Effects interprets it according to a default you set in the Preferences dialog box. Alternatively, you can have After Effects prompt you with an Interpret Footage dialog box where you select how to interpret the alpha manually.

If the alpha channel is interpreted incorrectly, the footage may appear with an unwanted black or white halo or fringe around the edges of objects (**Figure 2.19**). Don't worry, you can reinterpret the footage item afterwards.

To set the default alpha interpretation:

1. Choose After Effects > Preferences > Import (Mac) or Edit > Preferences > Import (Windows).

   The Import panel of the Preferences dialog box appears (**Figure 2.20**).

continues on next page

2. *Choose one of the following* default interpretation methods from the Interpret Unlabeled Alpha As pull-down menu (**Figure 2.21**):

Ask User—You're prompted to choose an interpretation method each time you import footage with an unlabeled alpha channel.

Guess—After Effects attempts to automatically detect the file's alpha channel type. If After Effects can't make a confident guess, it beeps at you.

Ignore Alpha—After Effects disregards the alpha channel of imported images.

Straight (Unmatted)—After Effects interprets the alpha channel as straight alpha. Choose this option for a single Photoshop layer with an alpha or layer mask.

Premultiplied (Matted With Black)— After Effects interprets the alpha channel as premultiplied with black.

Premultiplied (Matted With White)— After Effects interprets the alpha channel as premultiplied with white. Choose this option to import merged Photoshop layers that use transparency.

3. Click OK to close the Preferences dialog box.

To set the alpha channel interpretation for a file in a project:

1. In the Project panel, select a file containing an alpha channel.

2. Choose File > Interpret Footage > Main (**Figure 2.22**).

The Interpret Footage dialog box appears (**Figure 2.23**).

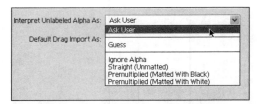

Figure 2.21 Choose a default interpretation method from the pull-down menu.

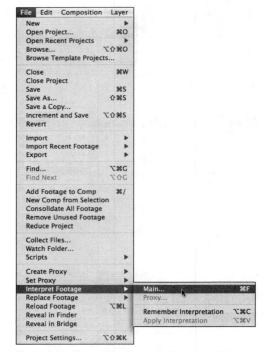

Figure 2.22 Choose File > Interpret Footage > Main.

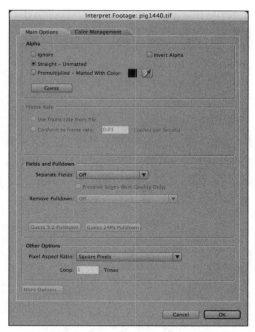

Figure 2.23 The Interpret Footage dialog box appears.

Figure 2.24 Choose an alpha channel interpretation method from the Interpret Footage dialog box.

3. In the Alpha section of the Interpret Footage dialog box, choose an interpretation method (**Figure 2.24**).

If the options are grayed out, the footage doesn't contain an alpha channel.

4. Click OK to close the Interpret Footage dialog box.

✔ Tips

- If an unexpected fringe or halo appears around the edges of a composited image, you should change the alpha interpretation.

- Internally, After Effects works in 32-bit depth (when a project is set to 8-bpc mode; see "Choosing the Color Bit-Depth Mode" earlier in this chapter). If a footage item's color space is less than this—as with a grayscale image—After Effects converts it to 32-bit depth when it displays. Similarly, if the footage doesn't contain an alpha channel, After Effects automatically supplies a full white alpha channel (which defines the image as fully opaque and visible).

IMPORTING STILL-IMAGE SEQUENCES

Importing a Layered File as a Single Footage Item

When you import a layered Photoshop or Illustrator file as a footage item, you can either import all the layers as a single merged item or import layers individually. Importing the merged file results in a footage item with the same dimensions of the source file (**Figure 2.25**).

However, when you import individual layers, you have a choice. You can import the layer at the document's dimensions so that the layer appears as it did in the context of the other layers (**Figure 2.26**). On the other hand, you can choose to use the layer's dimensions—that is, the size of the layer only regardless of the document's size (**Figure 2.27**).

When importing a Photoshop layer that has layer styles, you can specify whether to merge the layer styles into the footage or to ignore them.

After Effects can also import all the layers assembled just as they were in Photoshop or Illustrator; you'll learn that technique in the following section.

Figure 2.25 You can import a layered file so that the layers are merged into a single footage item that uses the source document's dimensions.

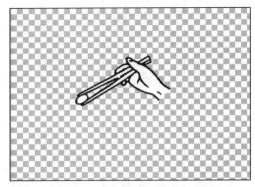

Figure 2.26 You can also import an individual layer using either the dimensions of the document (in this case, 720 × 486)...

Figure 2.27 ...or the minimum dimensions to contain the layer's image (this layer is 228 x 142).

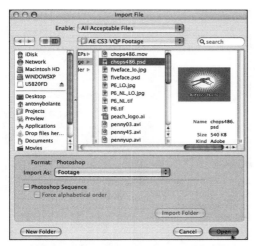

Figure 2.28 In the Import File dialog box, locate a Photoshop or Illustrator file and be sure Footage is selected in the Import As pull-down menu.

Figure 2.29 You can choose to import a single layer of a Photoshop or Illustrator file or to import merged layers.

To import a Photoshop or Illustrator file or layer as a single footage item:

1. Choose File > Import > File.

   The Import File dialog box appears.

2. Locate and select a Photoshop or Illustrator file.

3. Make sure Footage is selected in the Import As pull-down menu, and then click Open (**Figure 2.28**).

   The Import Photoshop/Illustrator dialog box appears. The dialog box has the same name as the file you're importing.

4. In the dialog box's Import Kind pull-down menu, make sure Footage is selected.

5. In the Layer Options area, *do either of the following* (**Figure 2.29**):

   ▲ Choose Merged Layers to import all layers in the file as a single footage item in After Effects.

   ▲ Select Choose Layer. Then, in the pull-down menu, choose a layer to import.

   continues on next page

IMPORTING A LAYERED FILE

6. If you chose a single layer in step 5, specify the following options (**Figure 2.30**):

Merge Layer Styles—Includes a Photoshop file's layer styles in the imported footage item under the property heading "Layer Styles."

Ignore Layer Styles—Excludes a Photoshop file's layer styles from the imported footage item.

Layer Size—Choosing this option in the pull-down menu imports the layer at its native size. Choose this option when you plan to use the layer outside the context of the other layers in the file.

Document Size—Choosing this option in the pull-down menu imports the layer using the frame size of the document that contains the layer. Choose this option to maintain the layer's size and position relative to the document as a whole.

7. Click OK to close the dialog box.

A footage item appears in the Project panel. When you import a single layer, the name of the footage item is the name of the layer followed by the name of the Photoshop or Illustrator file. When you import merged layers, the name of the footage item is the name of the Photoshop or Illustrator file (**Figure 2.31**).

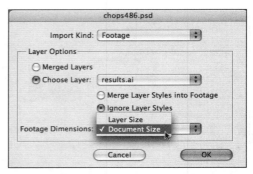

Figure 2.30 If you chose to import a single layer, specify whether to merge or ignore a Photoshop layer's layer style, and choose an option in the Footage Dimensions pull-down menu.

Figure 2.31 In the Project panel, single and merged Photoshop or Illustrator layers are clearly named.

Photoshop Styles and Text

After Effects retains practically every aspect of Photoshop files, including text and layer styles (such as drop shadow, inner glow, and so on). Initially, text and layer styles aren't fully editable—but you can remedy that with a simple menu command. Once you make Photoshop text a full-fledged After Effects text layer, you can employ all of After Effects' typesetting and text animation capabilities (covered in Chapter 12). By making layer styles After Effects-native, you can modify and animate layer styles as you would any other layer property (covered in Chapter 7).

In After Effects' timeline, select the layer that contains text imported from Photoshop and choose Layer > Convert to Editable Text. Similarly, you can select a layer that uses Photoshop layer styles and choose Layer > Layer Styles > Convert to Editable Styles.

Figure 2.32 After Effects can convert a layered file into a composition containing the same layers. This way, you can manipulate each layer individually in After Effects.

Figure 2.33 When you choose Composition-Cropped Layers, the imported footage includes the image only—in this case, the footage's dimensions are 314 × 125.

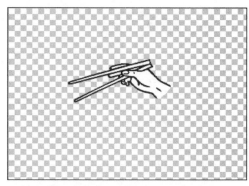

Figure 2.34 When you choose Composition, each layer uses the source document's dimensions—which, of course, match those of the imported composition. In this example, the source file's and comp's dimensions are 720 × 846.

Importing a Layered File as a Composition

One of After Effects' greatest strengths is its ability to import a layered Photoshop or Illustrator file as a ready-made composition—which, as you'll recall from Chapter 1, consists of footage items arranged in time and space. After Effects not only imports all the layers as footage items but also arranges the layers in a composition of the same dimensions. In essence, the composition replicates the layered file—suddenly transported into the world of After Effects (**Figure 2.32**).

As when you import layers separately (see "Importing a Layered File as a Single Footage Item," earlier in this chapter), you can choose whether the imported footage items (conveniently located in their own folder) use their native dimensions or share the new comp's dimensions (**Figures 2.33** and **2.34**).

To import an Adobe Photoshop or Illustrator file as a composition:

1. Choose File > Import > File (**Figure 2.35**). The Import File dialog box appears.

continues on next page

Figure 2.35 Choose File > Import > File.

2. Select an Adobe Photoshop or Illustrator file.

3. In the Import As pull-down menu, *choose either of the following* (**Figure 2.36**):

Composition - Cropped Layers— Imports each source layer at its native size.

Composition—Imports each source layer at the document's size.

4. Click Import.

In the Project panel, the imported Photoshop or Illustrator file appears both as a composition and as a folder containing the individual layers imported as separate footage items (**Figure 2.37**).

✔ Tip

■ After Effects imports Photoshop clipping groups as nested compositions within the main composition of the Photoshop file. After Effects automatically applies the Preserve Underlying Transparency option to each layer in the clipping group.

Figure 2.36 In the Import As pull-down menu of the Import File dialog box, choose the appropriate option.

Figure 2.37 The Photoshop file appears both as a composition and as a folder containing individual layers.

Importing Premiere Pro and After Effects Projects

Because After Effects can import projects from Premiere Pro, it's simple to move work from Adobe's non-linear editor for treatment in the company's advanced animation/compositing/effects program (and vice versa).

Each sequence in the Premiere Pro project appears in After Effects as a composition (in which each clip is a layer) and a folder of clips. In the composition, After Effects preserves the clip order, duration, and In and Out points, as well as marker and transition locations (**Figures 2.38** and **2.39**). Because Premiere Pro includes many After Effects filters, any effects shared by the two programs will also be transferred from Premiere Pro into After Effects—including their keyframes.

You'll learn more about compositions in Chapter 4, "Compositions"; more about keyframes in Chapter 7, "Properties and Keyframes"; and more about effects in Chapter 11, "Effects Fundamentals." For the moment, suffice it to say that you can easily integrate Premiere Pro's advantages in non-linear editing with After Effects' superior compositing and effects features.

Similarly, you can import an After Effects project into your current project—a capability that makes it possible to combine work, create complex sequences as different modules, and repeat complex effects. All the elements of an imported After Effects project are contained in a folder in the current project.

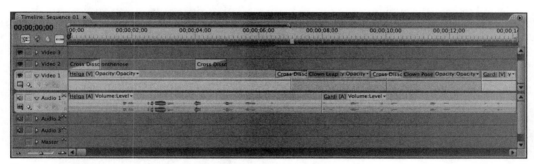

Figure 2.38 When you compare the Timeline panel of a Premiere project...

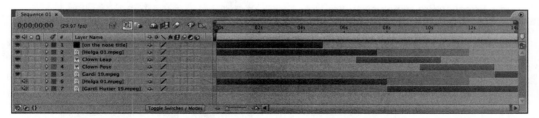

Figure 2.39 ...you can see how clips translate into layers in the Timeline panel of After Effects.

To import an Adobe Premiere Pro project:

1. Choose File > Import > File.

   The Import File dialog box appears.

2. Select a Premiere Pro project file (**Figure 2.40**).

   After Effects recognizes the file type automatically and selects Composition from the Import As pull-down menu.

3. Click Open.

   An Import Project dialog box appears.

4. Select the Premiere Pro sequences you want to import as compositions (**Figure 2.41**).

5. To import the audio clips in the selected sequences as audio footage items, select Import Audio. Leave the option unselected to omit the audio.

   The Premiere Pro project appears in the Project panel as a composition. Clips appear as footage items, and bins appear as folders (**Figure 2.42**). An After Effects project appears in the Project panel as a folder containing compositions and footage items.

✔ Tips

■ The Dynamic Link feature allows an After Effects project to appear as a clip in a Premiere Pro sequence and reflect any changes you make without an intermediate rendering step.

■ You can embed any movie exported from After Effects with a *program link*—which, as its name implies, is a link to the program that created it. This way, it's easy to reopen the project that created the movie. For more about embedding program links, see Chapter 17, "Output."

Figure 2.40 In the Import File dialog box, locate a Premiere Pro project and click Open.

Figure 2.41 Specify the Premiere Pro sequences you want to import as compositions in After Effects, and select whether you want to include audio.

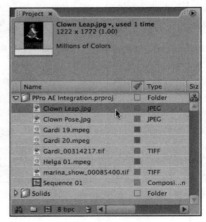

Figure 2.42 An imported Premiere Pro sequence appears in the Project panel as a composition. Clips appear as footage items, and bins appear as folders.

Importing with Adobe Bridge

Chances are, you've accumulated a seemingly countless number of assets on your hard disks. It can be a chore to find the one you need. Fortunately, After Effects and other Adobe programs ship with a companion program—a research assistant, if you will—called Adobe Bridge.

Bridge facilitates asset management by providing a convenient way to search for, sift, and preview files. Bridge also lets you see information embedded in the file, or *metadata*. You can even apply your own metadata, label, rating, and keywords to a file, adding ways to distinguish the needle from the rest of the haystack (**Figure 2.43**).

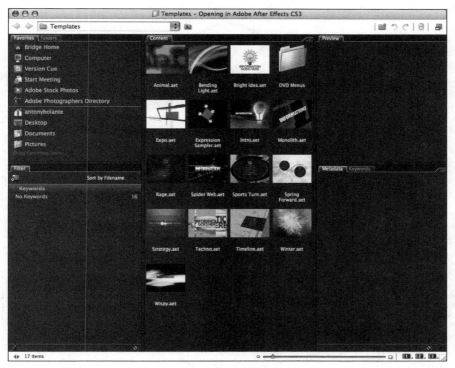

Figure 2.43 Bridge is a companion program that facilitates file management. It can help you locate and preview the file you need, including preset projects (selected here)...

Bridge also provides a great access point to numerous preset project templates. Even if you don't use these ready-made projects as templates per se, they demonstrate useful techniques and provide inspiration for your own work (**Figure 2.44**).

Naturally, this book can't cover all the features of another full-fledged program; this section focuses on browsing and importing using Bridge. Fortunately, you should get the hang of Bridge's familiar and intuitive interface with a little experimentation and a quick visit to its Help system.

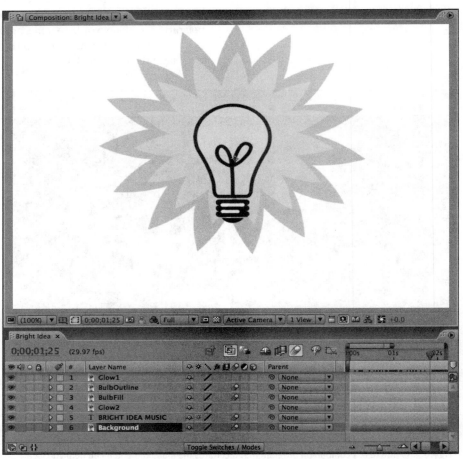

Figure 2.44 ...that you can use as a template or simply as an instructional tool or source of inspiration.

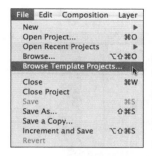

Figure 2.45 To find any file using Bridge, choose File > Browse; to go straight to project templates, choose File > Browse Template Projects (shown here).

Show Previous
Folder or Volume

Show Next Folder
or Volume

Select item
in the pull-
down menu

Go up
one level
in the
hierarchy

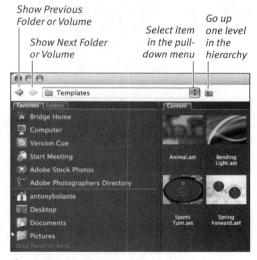

Figure 2.46 In Bridge, navigate using the browser-style navigation tools at the top of the window...

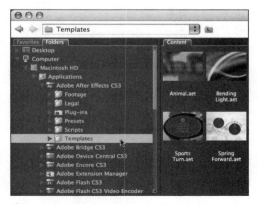

Figure 2.47 ...or select an item in the Favorites or Folders tab.

To import a file or project template using Bridge:

1. *Do either of the following:*

   ▲ To open any file, choose File > Browse.

   ▲ To navigate to project templates directly, choose File > Browse Template Projects (**Figure 2.45**).

   After Effects launches its companion program, Adobe Bridge.

2. To navigate to the file you want to view, *do either of the following:*

   ▲ Use the navigation tools at upper right of the Bridge window to select a disk volume or folder (**Figure 2.46**).

   ▲ Select an item in the Favorites or Folders tab (**Figure 2.47**).

   The selected item's content appears in Bridge's large main panel. You can also open a folder by double-clicking it in the main panel. (The appearance of items in the main panel depends on the position of the icon size and viewing mode, which you can set using controls at lower right of the window.)

continues on next page

3. To view a preview image and other information about the item, select the item.

The item's image appears in Bridge's Preview tab. Motion footage and templates include standard playback controls. The item's metadata and keywords appear in the corresponding tabbed areas (**Figure 2.48**).

4. In the Bridge's main panel, double-click the item you want to import (**Figure 2.49**).

After Effects may prompt you to specify options according to the type of item you import. (Refer to the section in this chapter pertaining to the file type.) The item appears in After Effects' Project panel (**Figure 2.50**).

Figure 2.48 The selected item appears in the Preview tab; additional information appears in the Metadata and Keywords tabs.

IMPORTING WITH ADOBE BRIDGE

Figure 2.49 Double-clicking the item in Bridge's main panel...

Figure 2.50 ...imports it into the After Effects project.

Motion Footage

The procedures for importing motion footage varies little from the procedures for importing other file types. But just as footage with alpha channels must be interpreted correctly, motion footage items possess unique attributes that must be processed properly. In the following sections, you'll use the Interpret Footage dialog box to specify how After Effects handles frame rate, field order, and pixel aspect ratio. This way, you can avoid or correct some of the most common problems that arise from misinterpreting motion footage. You'll also use the Interpret Footage dialog box to loop a footage item (without having to add it to a composition multiple times).

You can also use the Interpret Footage dialog to remove 3:2 pulldown and 24Pa pulldown from video transferred from film, expand an item's luminance levels, and specify EPS options. In After Effects CS3, the Interpret Footage dialog box includes new Color Management options. For a detailed explanation of these more advanced settings, consult the After Effects Help system or search for the topic at Peachpit.com.

✔ Tips

- You import audio-only files into an After Effects project just as you would any other file. Video footage that has audio can be imported as a single footage item.

- If your final output is destined for computer display only (not video display) or if it will be displayed at less than full screen size, you should deinterlace the video before you import it. Doing so spares you from separating fields in After Effects and from processing unnecessary information.

- In the sections to follow, you'll use the Interpret Footage dialog box to help After Effects properly interpret a footage item's attributes. You can copy the settings from one item by choosing File > Interpret Footage > Remember Interpolation, and apply it to another item by selecting it and choosing File > Interpret Footage > Apply Interpolation.

- You can customize the rules After Effects uses to interpret footage automatically by modifying the `Interpretation Rules.txt` file (contained in the After Effects folder) in a text-editing program. This way, you can determine, for example, the default pixel aspect ratio applied to footage items of certain dimensions. For more information, see the *Adobe After Effects User Guide* and Help system.

Setting the Frame Rate

Generally, you use the footage's native frame rate, which also matches the frame rate of the composition. Sometimes, however, you'll want to specify a frame rate for a footage item manually.

Because features like time stretch (see Chapter 6, "Layer Editing") and time remapping (see Chapter 14, "More Layer Techniques") provide finer control over a layer's playback speed, it's more common to set the frame rate for image sequences than for movie files.

For example, some animations are designed to play back at 10 fps. If you interpreted such a sequence to match a 30-fps composition, 30 frames would play back in one second—three times as fast as they were intended to play. Manually specifying a 10-fps frame rate for a still-image sequence of 30 frames would result in a duration of three seconds when played in a 30-fps composition.

Conversely, many programs can't render interlaced video frames. Sometimes animators choose to render 60 fps, which can be interpreted at a higher frame rate and interlaced at output.

To set the frame rate for footage:

1. In the Project panel, select a footage item.

2. Choose File > Interpret Footage > Main, or press Command/Ctrl-F.

   The Interpret Footage dialog box appears (**Figure 2.51**).

Figure 2.51 The Interpret Footage dialog box contains controls to set the frame rate of footage.

Figure 2.52 You can set movie footage to conform to a different frame rate. Note that the dialog box uses the term conform when referring to motion footage.

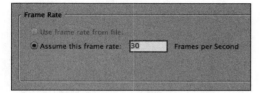

Figure 2.53 More often, you use the control to set the frame rate of still-image sequences. Note that the dialog box says "Assume this frame rate" when interpreting still-image sequences.

3. For motion footage, *choose one of the following* options in the Frame Rate section (**Figure 2.52**):

▲ **Use frame rate from file**—Uses the native frame rate of the footage item.

▲ **Conform to frame rate**—Lets you enter a custom frame rate for the footage.

Using a frame rate that differs from the original changes the playback speed of the movie.

4. For image sequences, enter a frame rate next to "Assume this frame rate" in the Frame Rate section of the Interpret Footage dialog box (**Figure 2.53**).

5. Click OK to close the Interpret Footage dialog box.

✔ Tip

■ To interpret 60-fps animation sequences for output as interlaced fields, enter 59.94 in the "Assume this frame rate" field and use the footage item in a full-frame, 29.97-fps composition. Be sure to field-render the output. See Chapter 16, "Complex Projects," for more about rendering compositions.

SETTING THE FRAME RATE

Interpreting Interlaced Video

Depending on the format, the vertically stacked lines of video are displayed using either a progressive scan or as interlaced fields. Simply put, progressive video displays each line of video in succession, from top to bottom. In contrast, interlaced video divides each frame into two fields, which contain every other line of the image. The playback device presents one field first, and then the other to complete the frame.

When you import interlaced video, After Effects must correctly interpret the field order to play back the video accurately. If the fields are presented in the wrong order, movement appears staggered.

To interpret fields in video footage:

1. In the Project panel, select an interlaced video or field-rendered footage item (**Figure 2.54**).

2. Choose File > Interpret Footage > Main (**Figure 2.55**), or press Command/Ctrl-F. The Interpret Footage dialog box opens (**Figure 2.56**).

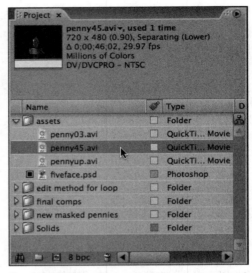

Figure 2.54 Select a footage item that uses interlaced video fields.

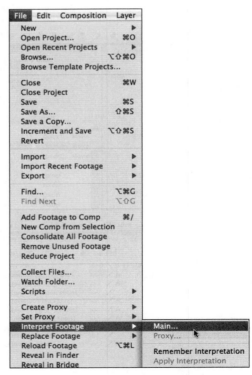

Figure 2.55 Choose File > Interpret Footage > Main.

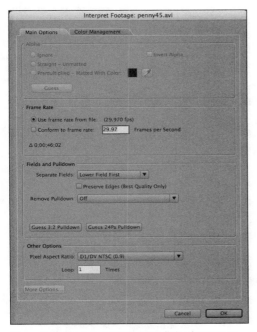

Figure 2.56 The Interpret Footage dialog box opens.

Figure 2.57 Choose the correct field dominance from the pull-down menu.

3. In the Fields and Pull-Down section, *select one of the following* options from the Separate Fields pull-down menu (**Figure 2.57**):

Off—After Effects won't separate fields. Use this option for footage that doesn't contain interlaced video fields.

Upper Field First—The fields of upper-field dominant source files will be separated correctly.

Lower Field First—The fields of lower-field dominant source files will be separated correctly.

4. Click OK to close the Interpret Footage dialog box.

Pixel Aspect Ratios

Generally, computer systems display images using square pixels (a 1:1 pixel aspect ratio, or 1.0 PAR). However, many formats, including common standards like D1 and DV, use nonsquare pixels to represent images. If you display nonsquare pixels on a square-pixel monitor, the image appears distorted. Luckily, After Effects can compensate for the difference between standards so you can use both in the same composition and output them without distortion.

After Effects automatically interprets D1 (720 × 486) and DV (720 × 480) footage to compensate correctly for their pixel aspect ratios. Nevertheless, you should check to see that your footage is interpreted correctly, and you should understand how to set the PAR for other standards. (You can even manually customize how the program automatically interprets footage; see the Help system for more about editing the interpretation rules file.)

To interpret the pixel aspect ratio:

1. In the Project panel, select a footage item.

2. Choose File > Interpret Footage > Main, or press Command/Ctrl-F.

   The Interpret Footage dialog box appears.

3. In the Other Options section, choose the appropriate Pixel Aspect Ratio setting for your footage (**Figure 2.58**):

   Square Pixels—1.0 PAR. Use for footage with a frame size of 640 × 480 or 648 × 486 and a 4:3 image aspect ratio.

   D1/DV NTSC—.9 PAR. Use for footage with a frame size of 720 × 486 (D1) or 720 × 480 (DV) and a 4:3 image aspect ratio.

Figure 2.58 In the Interpret Footage dialog box, choose the appropriate pixel aspect ratio. Most computer monitors use square pixels to represent an image with a 4:3 aspect ratio.

D1/DV NTSC Widescreen—1.2 PAR. Use for footage with a frame size of 720 × 486 (D1) or 720 × 480 (DV) to achieve a 16:9 image aspect ratio in standard definition.

D1/DV PAL—1.0666 PAR. Use for footage with a 720 × 576 (PAL) frame size and a 4:3 image aspect ratio.

D1/DV PAL Widescreen—1.422 PAR. Use for footage with a 720 × 576 (PAL) frame size and a 16:9 image aspect ratio in standard definition.

Anamorphic 2:1—2.0 PAR. Use for footage shot with a 2:1 anamorphic film lens.

D4/D16 Standard—.9481481 PAR. Use for footage with a 1440 × 1024 or 2880 × 2048 image size and a 4:3 image aspect ratio.

D4/D16 Anamorphic—1.8962962 PAR. Use for footage with a 1440 × 1024 or 2880 × 2048 image size and an 8:3 image aspect ratio.

✔ Tips

- If you import a square-pixel image that uses a frame size common to D1 (720 × 486) or DV (720 × 480), After Effects automatically (and incorrectly) interprets that image as using nonsquare pixels. This happens because After Effects' default interpretation rules are set to assume images that use these dimensions use a PAR of .9. Use the Interpret Footage dialog box to change the pixel aspect ratio setting.

- To preview compositions that use nonsquare pixel aspect ratios without distortion, you can choose Pixel Aspect Correction from the Composition panel's pull-down menu. See Chapter 4 for more information.

PIXEL ASPECT RATIOS

Looping Footage

Often, you need footage to loop continuously. Rather than add a footage item to a composition multiple times, you can set the footage item to loop using the Interpret Footage dialog box.

To loop footage:

1. In the Project panel, select a footage item you want to loop.

2. Choose File > Interpret Footage > Main, or press Command/Ctrl-F.

   The Interpret Footage dialog box appears (**Figure 2.59**).

3. In the Other Options section, enter the number of times you want the footage to loop (**Figure 2.60**).

   You can only enter integers for complete cycles, not decimals for partial cycles. When you add the footage item to a composition as a layer, its duration reflects the Loop setting.

✔ Tip

■ The Loop setting loops the content of the footage, not the movement of a layer—it's useful for turning an animation of two steps into a long walk, for example. You can't use this setting to repeat animated properties. For that, you'll need to use keyframes (Chapter 7) or expressions (Chapter 16).

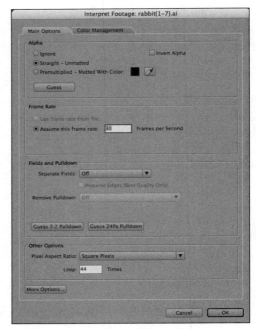

Figure 2.59 The Interpret Footage dialog box contains controls that allow you to loop a footage item (without repeating it in the composition).

Figure 2.60 Enter the number of times you want the footage item to loop.

3

MANAGING FOOTAGE

As you saw in the previous chapter, the Project panel is basically a list of all your footage and compositions. The more complex the project, the lengthier and more unwieldy this list becomes. As the receptacle of this essential information, the Project panel can resemble either a cluttered junk drawer or a neat filing cabinet, a cardboard box filled with books or the Library of Congress. In this chapter, you'll learn how to use the Project panel to organize and sort the items contained in your project. You'll also learn about other aspects of asset management—such as how to replace missing footage, and how to use placeholders and proxies to temporarily stand in for footage items. As always, taking a little time to prepare will save you a lot of time in the long run.

This chapter also introduces you to the Footage panel, which lets you not only see your footage but really scrutinize it. Most of the controls in the Footage panel are also found in the Composition and Layer panels, which means that learning these controls now will go a long way toward providing the grounding you need later.

The Footage panel also includes editing buttons; however, an in-depth explanation of those features will wait for Chapter 4, "Compositions," where you'll learn how to add footage as layers in a composition.

MANAGING FOOTAGE

Displaying Information in the Project Panel

The Project panel (**Figure 3.1**) furnishes you with several ways to manage your footage and compositions. Icons that resemble those used on the desktop (Mac) or Explorer (Windows) provide an easy means of distinguishing between footage types. You can also view more detailed information about items in the Project panel, organize items into folders, and sort items according to categories. Depending on your needs, you can rearrange, resize, hide, or reveal the categories. And if you still need help locating an item, you can find it using the Project panel's Find button. There's also a button that lets you access a flowchart view of your project—but that explanation will wait for later when it will make more sense (see Chapter 16, "Complex Projects").

To display information about a footage item or composition:

◆ In the Project panel, click a footage item to select it.

At the top of the Project panel, a thumbnail image of the footage item appears. Next to the thumbnail image, the name of the footage item appears, as well as information about the footage itself, such as frame size, color depth, codec, and so on (**Figure 3.2**).

✔ Tips

■ By default, the thumbnail image displays transparency as black. To make transparent areas appear as a checkerboard pattern, choose Thumbnail Transparency Grid in the Project panel's pull-down menu.

■ Option/Alt-clicking an item displays its file-type extension in addition to the usual information.

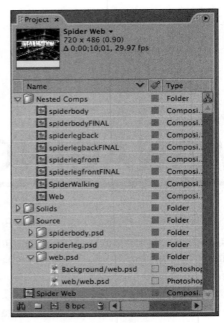

Figure 3.1 The Project panel doesn't simply list items; it helps you identify, sort, and organize them.

Figure 3.2 When you select an item in the Project panel, information about the selected item appears at the top of the panel.

Figure 3.3 In the Project panel, click the Find button.

Figure 3.4 In the Find dialog box, enter all or part of the name of the item you're looking for, and select the options you want.

Figure 3.5 The first item matching the criteria you specified appears selected in the Project panel.

Finding Items in a Project

The Project panel includes a handy Find button to help you unearth items from your project that you've lost track of. Use it, and you'll never need to search through folders again.

To find an item in the Project panel:

1. In the Project panel, click the Find button 🔍 (**Figure 3.3**).

   A Find dialog box appears.

2. Enter all or part of the name of the item you're looking for in the Find field (**Figure 3.4**).

   You can modify the search parameters by choosing the options described in the next step.

3. In the Find dialog box, select the options you want to use to modify your search:

   Match Whole Word Only—To locate only items that match the entire word you entered in the Find field.

   Match Case—To locate items that include the Find field's content, taking letter case into account. For example, a search for *Background* (with an uppercase *B*) won't locate an item called *background* (with a lowercase *b*).

   Find Missing Footage—To locate missing footage—that is, items that have lost their reference to a source file.

4. Click OK to search for the item.

   The first item that matches the criteria you specified appears selected in the Project panel (**Figure 3.5**).

✔ Tip

- Option/Alt-click the Find button to find the next item that matches the most recent Find criteria.

Sorting Footage in the Project Panel

By default, items in the Project panel are sorted by name, but you can sort the list by an assortment of other criteria, such as file type, size, duration, and so on. You can hide the column headings you don't want to use and rearrange their order. You can even assign a custom heading.

To sort footage items in the Project panel:

◆ In the Project panel, click a heading panel to sort the footage items according to the name, label, type, size, duration, file path, date, or comment (**Figure 3.6**).

To hide or display a heading panel in the Project panel:

1. In the Project panel, Control-click/right-click a heading panel.

   A context menu appears.

2. Choose an option:
   ▲ To hide the selected heading panel, choose Hide This (**Figure 3.7**). (This choice isn't available for the Name heading panel.)
   ▲ To hide any heading panel, choose Columns and a heading panel name to deselect it (**Figure 3.8**).
   ▲ To show a hidden heading panel, choose Columns and a heading panel name to select it.

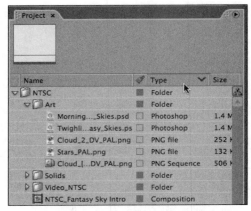

Figure 3.6 Click a heading panel to sort the items according to the information under the heading.

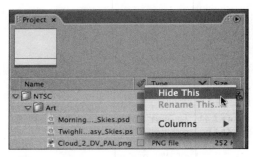

Figure 3.7 Choose Hide This to hide the selected heading panel.

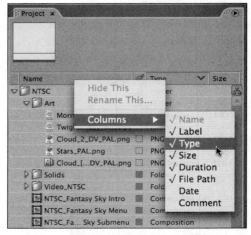

Figure 3.8 Deselect a heading name (in this case, the Type column).

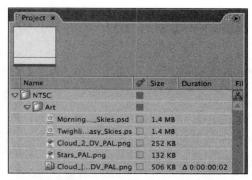

Figure 3.9 The heading and the column beneath it are hidden from view.

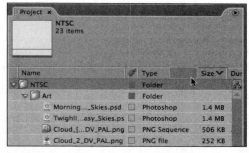

Figure 3.10 Drag the entire heading panel (in this case, the Size column) to the right or left...

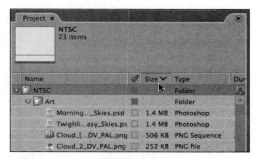

Figure 3.11 ...to change its relative position in the Project panel. Here, the Size column has been moved to the left of the Type column.

Depending on your choice, you can hide or display heading panels and the columns beneath them (**Figure 3.9**).

To reorder headings in the Project panel:

1. If necessary, resize the Project panel and make sure it displays the headings you want to rearrange.

2. Drag the heading panel(s) to the right or left to change the relative position of the heading columns (**Figures 3.10** and **3.11**).

✔ Tips

■ You can rename the Comment heading by Control-clicking/right-clicking it and choosing Rename This in the context menu.

■ By default, each type of footage is associated with a color label. You can sort items by label color, or reassign label colors in the Label Defaults panel of the Preferences dialog box. The timeline also represents layers using the color label.

Organizing Footage in Folders

As you learned in Chapter 2, "Importing Footage into a Project," footage can be imported into the Project panel as items contained in a folder. Of course, you can also create your own folders to organize items in the project. Folders look and work much like they do on your operating system (particularly on the Mac's desktop). Clicking the triangle next to the folder's icon toggles the folder open and closed. The triangle spins clockwise to reveal the folder's contents in outline fashion; the triangle spins counterclockwise to collapse the outline, hiding the folder's contents. However, the folder can't open in its own window.

To create a folder in the Project panel:

1. In the Project panel, *do one of the following:*
   - ▲ Choose File > New > New Folder.
   - ▲ Click the folder icon at the bottom (**Figure 3.12**).

   An untitled folder appears in the Project panel.

2. Press Return/Enter to highlight the name of the folder (**Figure 3.13**).

3. Type a name for the folder (**Figure 3.14**).

4. Press Return/Enter to apply the name to the folder.

   The folder is sorted with other items according to the currently selected column heading.

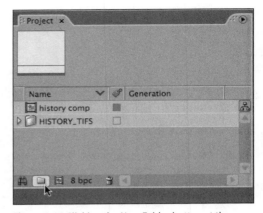

Figure 3.12 Clicking the New Folder button at the bottom of the Project panel is the easiest way to create a new folder.

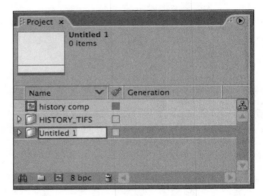

Figure 3.13 Press Return/Enter to highlight the name of the new folder...

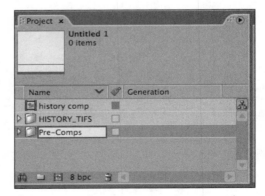

Figure 3.14 ...and type a new name. Press Return/Enter to apply the name.

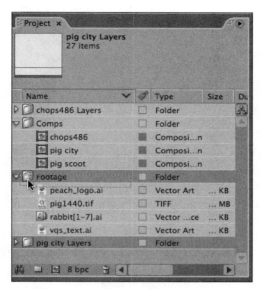

Figure 3.15 You can drag selected items directly into a folder.

Figure 3.16 To move items out of a folder, drag them from the folder to the top of the Project panel.

To organize footage items in folders:

In the Project panel, *do one of the following*:

◆ To move items into a folder, select and drag items into the folder (**Figure 3.15**).

◆ To move items out of a folder, select and drag items from the folder to the gray area at the top of the Project panel (**Figure 3.16**).

Renaming and Removing Items

You can rename any footage item in the project panel. However, you'll notice that renaming items doesn't work quite like on your operating system; you have to use the Return/Enter key.

Just as important as organizing the elements you need is disposing of the elements you don't need. You can remove individual items or have After Effects automatically discard the items that haven't been used in a composition.

To rename folders or compositions in the Project panel:

1. In the Project panel, select a folder or composition.

2. Press Return/Enter.

   The name of the item appears highlighted (**Figure 3.17**).

3. Enter a name for the folder or composition (**Figure 3.18**).

4. Press Return/Enter.

   The new name of the item is no longer highlighted and becomes the current name.

Figure 3.17 Select a folder or composition, press Return/Enter to highlight its name...

Figure 3.18 ...and then type a new name in the text box. Press Return/Enter again to apply the new name.

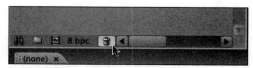

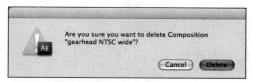

Figure 3.19 Click the Delete button at the bottom of the Project panel to delete selected items.

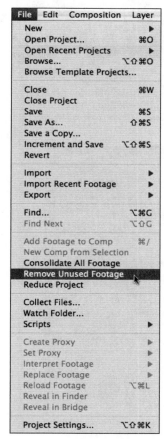

Are you sure you want to delete Composition "gearhead NTSC wide"?

Cancel   Delete

Figure 3.20 After Effects warns you if you attempt to delete an item that is in use.

File	Edit	Composition	Layer
New			▶
Open Project...			⌘O
Open Recent Projects			▶
Browse...			⌥⇧⌘O
Browse Template Projects...			
Close			⌘W
Close Project			
Save			⌘S
Save As...			⇧⌘S
Save a Copy...			
Increment and Save			⌥⇧⌘S
Revert			
Import			▶
Import Recent Footage			▶
Export			▶
Find...			⌥⌘G
Find Next			⌥⇧G
Add Footage to Comp			⌘/
New Comp from Selection			
Consolidate All Footage			
Remove Unused Footage			
Reduce Project			
Collect Files...			
Watch Folder...			
Scripts			▶
Create Proxy			▶
Set Proxy			▶
Interpret Footage			▶
Replace Footage			▶
Reload Footage			⌥⌘L
Reveal in Finder			
Reveal in Bridge			
Project Settings...			⌥⇧⌘K

Figure 3.21 Choose File > Remove Unused Footage to remove items that aren't used in a composition.

To remove items from a project:

1. In the Project panel, select one or more items.

2. *Do one of the following:*
   ▲ Press Delete.
   ▲ Click the Delete button 🗑 at the bottom of the Project panel (**Figure 3.19**).
   ▲ Drag the items to the Delete button at the bottom of the Project panel.

   If any of the items are compositions or are being used in a composition, After Effects asks you to confirm that you want to delete the items (**Figure 3.20**).

3. If After Effects prompts you to confirm your choice, click Delete to remove the footage from the project or Cancel to cancel the command and retain the footage in the project.

   The footage is removed from the project and all compositions in the project.

To remove unused footage from a project:

◆ Choose File > Remove Unused Footage (**Figure 3.21**).

   All footage items that aren't currently used in a composition are removed from the project.

✔ Tip

■ Other commands aid in project "housekeeping," especially as a project nears completion. The Consolidate All Footage removes duplicate items; Reduce Project removes unselected comps and unused footage; and Collect Files copies the project's requisite files to a single location for archiving or moving to another workstation.

RENAMING AND REMOVING ITEMS

Proxies

A *proxy* is a low-resolution version of the actual footage (**Figure 3.22**). If you're familiar with nonlinear editing applications, you might compare using proxies to using low-quality clips for offline editing (the rough cutting phase, which often utilizes relatively low-quality copies of footage). Low-quality files take less time to process, allowing you to work more quickly. Proxies may also be necessary if you have to work on a less powerful workstation—one with less RAM, for example—than you'll finish on. When you're ready, you can replace the low-quality stand-ins with the high-quality original footage.

Icons next to each item in the Project panel provide an easy way to determine whether source footage or its proxy is currently in use (**Figure 3.23**). A box containing a black square ■ indicates that the proxy is currently in use; the name of the proxy appears in bold text. An empty box □ indicates that a proxy has been assigned but that source footage is currently in use. If there is no icon, this means no proxy has been assigned to the footage item.

Proxies aren't effective for every circumstance, however. Although they can save time when you're animating motion, other effects—such as keying—can only be properly adjusted when using the footage at output quality.

Figure 3.22 Low-quality proxies (top) don't look as good as the actual footage (bottom), but they also have smaller file sizes and can be processed faster.

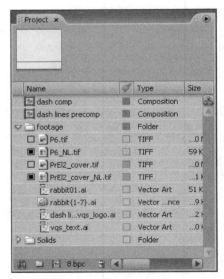

Figure 3.23 Icons indicate whether a proxy is in use or assigned to an item but not in use.

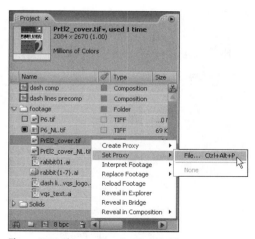

Figure 3.24 Choose File > Set Proxy > File.

Figure 3.25 In the Set Proxy File dialog box, choose a file to act as a proxy for the actual footage.

To assign a proxy to a footage item:

1. In the Project panel, select a footage item to which you want to apply a proxy.

2. *Do either of the following:*
   ▲ Choose File > Set Proxy > File.
   ▲ Control-click/right-click the item, and choose Set Proxy > File in the context menu (**Figure 3.24**).

   The Set Proxy File dialog box appears.

3. Locate the file you want to assign as the proxy (**Figure 3.25**).

4. Click Open to select the file and close the dialog box.

   In the Project panel, a proxy icon appears next to the footage item, indicating that a proxy is currently in use (**Figure 3.26**).

Figure 3.26 A black box appears next to the item, indicating that a proxy is in use.

PROXIES

To toggle between using a proxy and the original footage:

◆ In the Project panel, click the proxy icon to the left of a footage item to toggle between using the assigned proxy and using the original footage (**Figure 3.27**).

To stop using a proxy:

1. In the Project panel, select a footage item that has been assigned a proxy.

2. *Do either of the following:*

 ▲ Choose File > Set Proxy > None.

 ▲ Control-click/right-click the item, and choose Set Proxy > None in the context menu (**Figure 3.28**).

 To the left of the footage item's name in the Project panel, the proxy icon disappears.

✔ Tip

■ As pointed out in Chapter 2, After Effects automatically creates placeholders for missing footage. You can also create a placeholder manually, and then replace it with the actual footage item when it becomes available. You create placeholders by choosing File > Import > Placeholder.

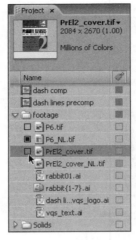

Figure 3.27 Click the proxy icon to toggle between using the proxy and using the actual footage.

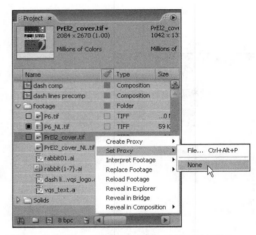

Figure 3.28 Choose File > Set Proxy > None to stop using a proxy.

Figure 3.29 Still images always open in an After Effects Footage panel.

Figure 3.30 By default, motion footage opens in a window according to the file type.

Figure 3.31 However, Option/Alt-double-clicking motion footage opens it in an After Effects Footage panel.

Viewing Footage

When you open an item in the Project panel, it appears either in an After Effects Footage panel or in the player native to its file type, depending on the file type and your preference.

Still images always open in an After Effects Footage panel. Motion footage and audio items, in contrast, open in the appropriate media player by default. For example, .mov files open in a QuickTime footage window; .avi files open in a Video for Windows footage window. However, you can opt to open them in an After Effects Footage panel instead.

Whereas a media player lets you play back motion and audio footage right away and at the full frame rate, the Footage panel relies on After Effects' frame rendering mechanism (explained fully in Chapter 8, "Playback, Previews, and RAM"). Therefore, the Footage panel won't necessarily play a movie at the full frame rate and won't play audio without rendering a preview. The Footage panel does offer a number of other viewing options (covered in the section "The Footage Panel," later in this chapter) and editing features (covered in Chapter 4).

To view a footage item:

◆ In the Project panel, double-click a footage item.

Still images open in a Footage panel (**Figure 3.29**); movie files open in the appropriate movie player (**Figures 3.30** and **3.31**).

To open a movie file in an After Effects Footage panel:

◆ In the Project panel, Option/Alt-double-click a movie footage item.

The movie file opens in an After Effects Footage panel (**Figure 3.32**).

✔ Tips

■ Some .avi files—including those using Microsoft's DirectX DV codec and files over 2 GB—will open only in an After Effects Footage panel.

■ You can open any footage item in its native application by choosing Edit > Edit Original. Any changes you make to it are updated in After Effects. If not, choose File > Reload Footage.

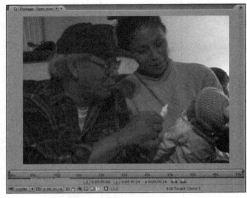

Figure 3.32 Audio files are also easier to preview in their own Footage panel.

VIEWING FOOTAGE

The Footage Panel

An After Effects Footage panel has a variety of controls for viewing footage. As you might expect, it lets you play back and cue motion footage. You can magnify or reduce your view of the image, or see its individual channels. You can also show rulers, set guides, and superimpose a grid or video-safe zones. There is also a snapshot feature that lets you save and recall a frame of footage that you can use for reference (**Figure 3.33**).

As you'll see in the chapters to follow, you can also find all of these Footage panel controls in the Composition and Layer panels. If some of the controls don't seem useful now, be patient: They'll come in handy later.

The following sections cover these shared controls. Later chapters cover only the features unique to the Composition and Layer panels. Chapter 6, "Layer Editing," discusses in detail the Footage panel's controls for editing motion footage.

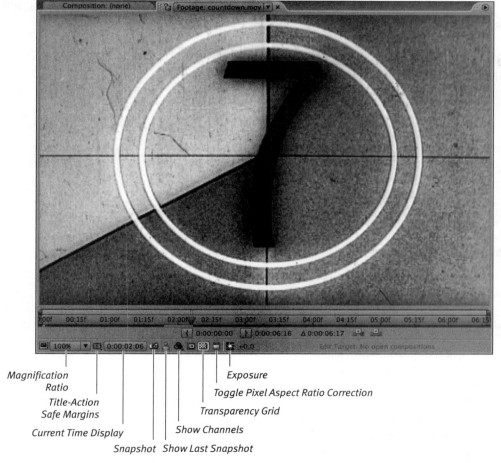

Figure 3.33 The following sections cover several features of the Footage panel that are shared by the Composition and Layer panels.

Cueing Motion Footage

Motion footage appears in the Footage, Composition, and Layer panels with a time ruler, current time indicator, and current time display. You can use the controls to view a specific frame or to play back the footage without sound.

Figure 3.34 Drag the current time indicator to cue the footage to a particular frame.

To view a frame of motion footage by dragging:

◆ In the Footage panel, drag the current time indicator to the frame you want to view (**Figure 3.34**).

The Footage panel displays the image at the current frame and the frame number.

Figure 3.35 You can click the current time display...

To cue a frame of motion footage numerically:

1. In the Footage panel, click the current time display (**Figure 3.35**).

The Go To Time dialog box opens.

2. Enter a time (**Figure 3.36**).

3. Click OK.

The current time display and the image in the Footage panel show the frame you specified.

Figure 3.36 ...and enter a frame number in the Go To Time dialog box.

To play motion footage:

◆ Make sure the Footage, Composition, or Layer panel is active. Press the spacebar to start and stop playback.

✔ Tips

■ The spacebar provides the easiest way to start and stop playback. The Time Controls panel provides more control (**Figure 3.37**).

■ In the Footage panel, the time ruler shows the length of the source file; in the Composition and Layer panels, the time ruler corresponds to the length of the composition.

Figure 3.37 The Time Controls panel provides a complete set of playback options.

Figure 3.38 Choose a magnification from the pop-up menu.

Figure 3.39 The Footage panel displays the image at the magnification you specified.

Magnifying an Image

Sometimes, you'll want to magnify your footage view so that you can closely examine a detail of the image. Other times, you'll want to reduce magnification because viewing footage at 100 percent scale takes up too much screen space. After Effects lets you change the magnification ratio to suit your needs. However, keep in mind that this is for viewing purposes only: The actual scale of the footage doesn't change. You may be surprised to discover that no matter how much you magnify the image in the Footage panel, scroll bars don't appear. To view different parts of a magnified image, use the Hand tool instead.

To change the magnification of the Footage or Composition panel:

◆ In the Footage panel, press and hold the Magnification Ratio pop-up menu to choose a magnification (**Figure 3.38**).

When you release the mouse button, the Footage panel uses the magnification ratio you selected (**Figure 3.39**).

To change the visible area of a magnified image in the Footage or Composition panel:

1. Select the Hand tool by *doing either of the following:*

   ▲ In the Tools panel, click the Hand tool (**Figure 3.40**).

   ▲ With the Selection tool active (the default tool), position the mouse pointer over the image in the Footage or Composition panel, and press the spacebar.

   The mouse changes to the hand icon 🖑 (**Figure 3.41**).

2. Drag the hand to change the visible area of the image (**Figure 3.42**).

✔ Tip

■ The Display pane of the Preferences dialog box includes the option Auto-zoom When Resolution Changes. Selecting this option makes the image's magnification change when you change the Comp panel's resolution setting. Note that the Footage and Layer panels don't include a resolution option.

Figure 3.40 In the Tools panel, select the Hand tool...

Figure 3.41 ...or position the Selection tool over the image and press the spacebar to toggle it to the Hand tool.

Figure 3.42 Drag the image with the Hand tool to move other areas into view.

Figure 3.43 Choose whether you want to view safe zones or grids in the Grids and Guides pull-down menu.

Figure 3.44 You can view Title Safe and Action Safe zones...

Viewing Safe Zones and Grids

You can superimpose a grid or video-safe zones over an image to better judge its placement. Obviously, these simple visual guides aren't included in the final output. In addition, because video-safe zones indicate the viewable area of standard video monitors, you should display safe zones for images that match television's 4:3 aspect ratio.

To show video-safe zones and grids:

◆ In the Footage panel's Grid and Guides pull-down menu, choose the options you want (**Figure 3.43**):

Title/Action Safe (**Figure 3.44**)

Proportional Grid (**Figure 3.45**)

Grid (**Figure 3.46**)

You can display any combination of zones and guides at the same time.

✔ Tip

■ You can change the safe zones from the standard setting and change the color, style, and spacing of grid lines in the Grids & Guides pane of the Preferences dialog box.

Figure 3.45 ...a proportional grid...

Figure 3.46 ...or a standard grid.

Displaying Rulers and Guides

Like Adobe Photoshop and Illustrator, After Effects lets you view rulers as well as set guides to help you arrange and align images. As usual, you can change the zero point of the rulers and toggle the rulers and guides on and off.

To toggle rulers on and off:

Do either of the following:

◆ In a Footage, Comp, or Layer panel's Grid and Guides pull-down menu, choose Rulers (**Figure 3.47**).

◆ With a Footage, Comp, or Layer panel active, press Command/Ctrl-R to toggle the rulers on and off.

To set the zero point of rulers:

1. If the rulers aren't visible, make them visible using one of the techniques described in the previous task.

2. Position the pointer at the crosshair at the intersection of the rulers in the upper-left corner of the Footage, Composition, or Layer panel.

   The pointer becomes a crosshair (**Figure 3.48**).

3. Drag the crosshair into the image area.

   Horizontal and vertical lines indicate the position of the mouse (**Figure 3.49**).

4. Release the mouse to set the zero point (**Figure 3.50**).

   The rulers use the zero point you selected.

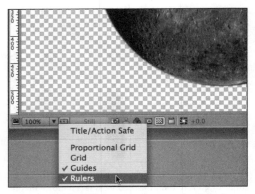

Figure 3.47 After Effects uses the same keyboard shortcut to show and hide rulers—Command/Ctrl-R—as Photoshop.

Figure 3.48 When you position the pointer at the intersection of the rulers, it becomes a crosshair icon.

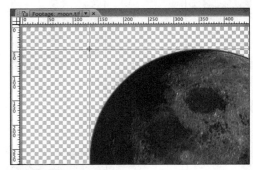

Figure 3.49 Drag the crosshair at the intersection of the rulers into the image area...

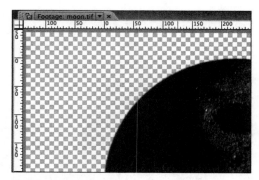

Figure 3.50 ...and release to set the zero point of the rulers.

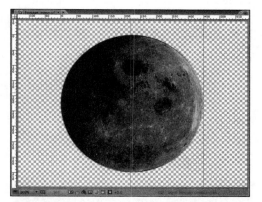

Figure 3.51 Drag from a ruler into the image area to add a guide.

To reset the zero point of the rulers:

◆ Double-click the crosshair at the intersection of the horizontal and vertical rulers.

The rulers' zero point is reset to the upper-left corner of the image.

✔ Tip

■ Need to know the exact ruler coordinates of the mouse pointer? Use the Info panel.

To set guides:

1. If the rulers aren't visible, make them visible by pressing Command/Ctrl-R.

2. Position the pointer inside the horizontal or vertical ruler.

   The pointer changes into a Move Guide icon ←→.

3. Drag into the image area (**Figure 3.51**). A line indicates the position of the new guide.

4. Release the mouse to set the guide.

To reposition or remove a guide:

Do one of the following:

◆ To reposition the guide, drag it to a new position.

◆ To remove the guide, drag it off the image area.

✔ Tips

■ You can hide, lock, clear, and have objects snap to guides by choosing the appropriate command in the View menu.

■ You can customize the default settings for safe zones, grids, and guides in the Grids & Guides pane of the Preferences dialog box.

DISPLAYING RULERS AND GUIDES

Viewing Snapshots

As you work, you'll often need to closely compare different frames. In After Effects, you can take a snapshot of a frame to store for later viewing. Then, with the click of a button, you can temporarily replace the current image in a Footage, Composition, or Layer panel with the snapshot image. The snapshot doesn't really replace anything; it's just used for quick reference—like holding a shirt up to yourself in a mirror to compare it with the one you're wearing. Toggling between the current frame and the snapshot makes it easier to see the differences.

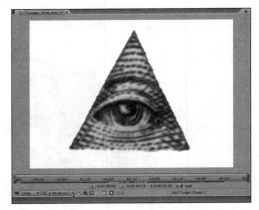

Figure 3.52 Click the Snapshot button to store the current image as a snapshot.

To take a snapshot:

1. If necessary, cue the footage to the frame you want to use as a reference snapshot.

2. Click the Snapshot button 📷 (**Figure 3.52**), or press Shift-F5.

   The current frame becomes the snapshot, and the Show Last Snapshot button becomes available.

To view the most recent snapshot:

1. If necessary, cue the footage to the frame you want to compare to the snapshot (**Figure 3.53**).

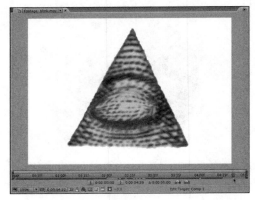

Figure 3.53 Cue to a new frame...

2. Click and hold the Show Last Snapshot button 👤, or press F5.

   As long as you hold down the mouse, the window displays the snapshot (**Figure 3.54**); when you release the mouse, the window displays the current frame.

✔ Tips

■ If a window uses a different aspect ratio than that of the snapshot, the snapshot is resized to fit into the window.

■ Snapshots are stored in memory. If After Effects requires the memory that is used by a snapshot, it will discard the snapshot.

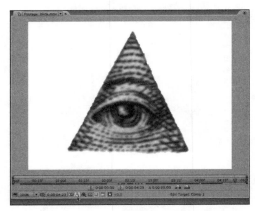

Figure 3.54 ...and then press and hold the Show Last Snapshot button to replace the current image temporarily with the snapshot. Release the Show Last Snapshot button to see the current frame again.

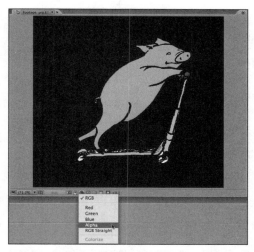

Figure 3.55 Click the Show Channel button, and then select the channel you want to view.

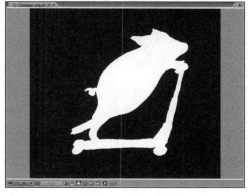

Figure 3.56 Choose Alpha to see the alpha channel.

Figure 3.57 To see the selected channel in color, select Colorize from the pull-down menu.

Viewing Channels

The Footage, Composition, and Layer panels allow you to view the individual red, green, blue, and alpha channels of an image. Color channels appear as grayscale images in which the degree of white corresponds to the color value. You can also view the color channel using its own color. The alpha channel appears as a grayscale image as well, where the degree of white corresponds to opacity. You can even view the unmultiplied color channels—that is, the color channels without the alpha taken into account.

To show individual channels:

1. In a Footage, Composition, or Layer panel, click the Show Channel button, and then choose the channel you want to view (**Figure 3.55**):

   RGB —Shows the normal image with visible channels combined.

   Red, **Green**, or **Blue** —Shows the selected channel as a grayscale.

   Alpha —Shows the alpha channel (transparency information) as a grayscale. If active, the transparency grid is disabled while Alpha is selected (**Figure 3.56**). See the next section, "Viewing Transparency."

   RGB Straight —Shows the unmultiplied RGB channels. If active, the transparency grid is disabled while RGB Straight is selected.

2. To show the selected channel depicted in color, select Colorize (**Figure 3.57**).

   The Channel pull-down menu's icon changes according to the current selection.

Viewing Transparency

In Chapter 2, you learned that the footage items you import can retain almost every aspect of their source files, including transparency. In the Footage panel, transparency always appears as black (**Figure 3.58**). However, if the black background isn't convenient, you can toggle the transparent areas to appear as a checkerboard pattern, or *transparency grid* (**Figure 3.59**).

Like many of the other buttons in the Footage panel, the Toggle Transparency Grid button is also available in the Layer and Composition panels. However, in contrast to the Footage panel, you can set the Composition panel's background to any color. The next chapter revisits viewing transparency and other unique aspects of the Composition panel.

To toggle the transparency grid:

◆ In the Footage, Composition, or Layer panel, click the Toggle Transparency Grid button 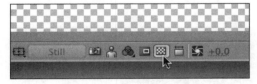 (**Figure 3.60**).

When the Toggle Transparency Grid button is selected, transparent areas appear as a checkerboard pattern; when the button isn't selected, transparent areas appear black in a Footage or Layer panel. In a Composition panel, transparent areas appear as the color you set.

✔ Tip

■ The transparency grid is disabled whenever you select the Alpha or RGB Straight viewing option in the Show Channel pull-down menu (covered in the section "Viewing Channels," earlier in this chapter).

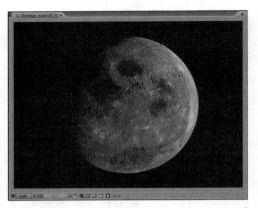

Figure 3.58 In the Footage panel, transparent areas of the image appear as black.

Figure 3.59 You can also make transparent areas appear as a checkerboard pattern, or transparency grid. This also works in the Composition and Layer panels.

Figure 3.60 Click the Toggle Transparency Grid button to toggle between showing transparent areas as black (in the Footage panel, or as the specified background color in the Composition panel) and showing them as a checkerboard pattern.

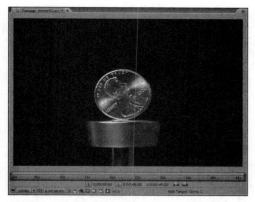

Figure 3.61 This footage uses a PAR of .9, so it appears slightly vertically squashed (or horizontally stretched) when displayed using square pixels.

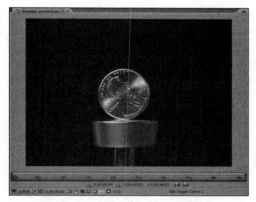

Figure 3.62 You can correct the distortion in the Layer, Composition, and Footage panels.

Figure 3.63 Click the Toggle Pixel Aspect Ratio Correction button.

Correcting for Pixel Aspect Ratios

In Chapter 2, you learned the importance of correctly interpreting an image's pixel aspect ratio (PAR) to prevent the image from appearing distorted. But even properly interpreted footage and comps that use a nonsquare PAR result in an image that looks distorted on a typical computer display (**Figure 3.61**). Fortunately, After Effects can compensate for the distortion due to PAR (**Figure 3.62**). As After Effects warns you when you use the Toggle Pixel Aspect Ratio Correction button, correcting the image this way is for viewing purposes only; it doesn't affect the image's actual scale. And because correcting an image requires some processing, it will take slightly longer to render frames.

To toggle pixel aspect correction:

1. In a Footage, Composition, or Layer panel, click the Toggle Pixel Aspect Ratio Correction button 🔲 to select it (**Figure 3.63**).

   If this is the first time you've used the button during this session, After Effects reminds you how PAR correction works and prompts you to specify whether you want to see the warning once per session or never again.

2. Select an option in the dialog box, and click OK.

   If the image's PAR doesn't match your computer monitor's PAR, After Effects scales the image so that it no longer appears distorted.

Adjusting Exposure

Starting with After Effects CS3, Footage, Comp and Layer panels have controls for the view's exposure. Just as increasing the exposure in a camera results in a brighter photograph, increasing the view's exposure value makes its image appear brighter. The exposure setting affects the view only. Even if you adjust it in a Layer or Comp panel, it won't affect the output image (to alter the output image, add effects). However, the exposure setting does help you evaluate an image's brightness and is particularly useful in identifying an image's brightest and darkest areas.

To adjust a view's exposure:

◆ In a Footage, Composition, or Layer panel, set the Adjust Exposure value next to the Reset Exposure button ![icon].

Decreasing the value makes the image darker; increasing the value makes the image brighter (**Figure 3.64**). Setting the value to anything but 0 makes the Reset Exposure button's icon appear yellow.

To toggle exposure between a custom value and zero:

◆ In a Footage, Composition, or Layer panel, click the Reset Exposure button.

Clicking the button when its icon is yellow makes the icon black and resets the exposure value to zero (**Figure 3.65**). Clicking the button again sets the exposure value to the most recent custom setting and makes the icon yellow.

Figure 3.64 Changing a view's Exposure value doesn't alter the source or output image; it helps you evaluate its brightness. Here, increasing the Exposure identifies the darkest spots in the image. The Exposure icon turns yellow when you set a custom exposure.

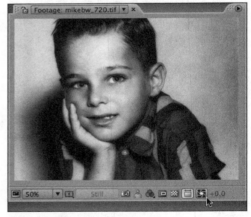

Figure 3.65 Clicking the Reset Exposure button toggles the image back to an exposure value of 0. Click it again to show the last custom setting.

COMPOSITIONS

Without compositions, a project is nothing more than a list of footage items—a grocery list without a recipe; an ensemble without choreography; finely tuned instruments without, well, a composition. This is because compositions perform the essential function of describing how footage items are arranged in space and time. This chapter shows you how to create a composition and define its spatial and temporal boundaries by setting frame size, frame rate, duration, and so on.

This chapter also describes the fundamental process of layering footage in compositions (and in so doing lays the groundwork for the rest of the book, which focuses largely on how to manipulate those layers). The footage items you add to a composition become layers, which are manipulated in the defined space and time of the composition, as represented by Composition and Timeline panels. The following pages give you an overview of these panels as well as the Time Controls panel. This chapter also introduces you to the technique of nesting, using comps as layers in other comps—a concept you'll appreciate more fully as your projects grow more complex.

Creating Compositions

A composition contains layers of footage and describes how you arrange those layers in space and time. This section explains how to create a composition; the following section describes how to choose specific settings to define a composition's spatial and temporal attributes.

To create a new composition:

1. *Do one of the following:*
   - ▲ Choose Composition > New Composition.
   - ▲ Press Command/Ctrl-N.
   - ▲ At the bottom of the Project panel, click the Create Composition button (**Figure 4.1**).

   A Composition Settings dialog box appears (**Figure 4.2**).

2. Choose a name for the composition and specify preset or custom composition settings (such as frame size, pixel aspect ratio, frame rate, display resolution, and duration) for the composition. (See "Choosing Composition Settings" later in this chapter for details.)

3. Click OK to close the Composition Settings dialog box.

   A new composition appears in the Project panel, and related Composition and Timeline panels open (**Figure 4.3**).

✔ Tip

- ■ You can create a composition that contains a footage item by dragging the item's icon to the Create Composition icon in the Project panel. The new composition will use the same image dimensions as the footage item it contains.

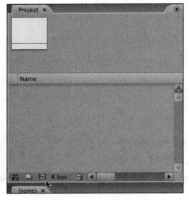

Figure 4.1 Click the Create Composition button at the bottom of the Project panel.

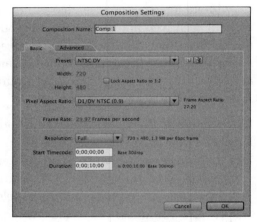

Figure 4.2 In the Composition Settings dialog box, enter the appropriate settings for the composition.

Figure 4.3 A composition appears in a Composition panel and a Timeline panel, and as an icon in the Project panel (shown here).

Choosing Composition Settings

Because compositions describe how layers are arranged in space and time, you must define a composition's spatial attributes (such as its frame size and pixel aspect ratio) as well as its temporal aspects (such as its duration and frame rate). Composition settings allow you to specify these characteristics. You can also use the composition settings to specify attributes that aren't as fundamental, such as the resolution or quality of the Composition panel's display. You can change composition settings at any time.

A project usually contains several compositions, most of which are contained as layers (or *nested*) in a final composition. Although you can set the final composition's settings according to your output format (NTSC DV, for example), you may want to employ different settings (particularly for frame size and duration) for intermediate compositions.

The Composition Settings dialog box is divided into Basic and Advanced panels. The following sections focus on the Basic settings. Although setting a Comp's anchor point is discussed here, other advanced settings are addressed in later chapters, when they'll make more sense to you. And rest assured, you'll be reminded of the appropriate Comp setting whenever a task or technique calls for it.

✔ Tips

- It's easy to forget to name your composition or to settle for the default name, *Comp 1*. Do yourself a favor and give the composition a descriptive name. This will help you remain organized as your project becomes more complex.

- You can open the Composition Settings dialog box for the current composition by pressing Command/Ctrl-K.

- You can also access the Composition Settings dialog box from the Timeline panel's pop-up menu; however, using the keyboard shortcut—Command/Ctrl-K— is the quickest way.

Specifying Composition Presets

With After Effects, you don't need to manually enter all the composition settings (frame size, pixel aspect ratio, and so on); instead, you can select the most common settings from a pull-down menu of presets. If the list doesn't include a preset for *your* most commonly used settings, you can save your custom settings to the list. You can even delete the presets you don't want. For a brief explanation of some common presets, see **Table 4.1**.

To select a composition preset:

1. In the Composition Settings dialog box, choose an option from the Preset menu (**Figure 4.4**).

    Choose the preset that matches your needs. Presets include common settings for film, video broadcast, and multimedia projects. Individual settings are set automatically. However, you may want to enter a starting frame number and duration for the comp (see "Setting a comp's start-frame number" and "Setting a comp's duration," later in this chapter).

2. Click OK to close the Composition Settings dialog box.

    The composition appears in the Project panel.

✔ Tip

■ You can restore the presets that ship with After Effects by Option/Alt-clicking the Delete button.

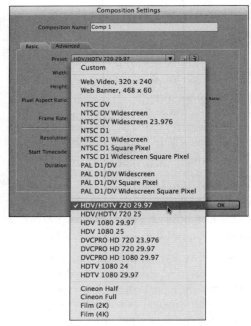

Figure 4.4 Choose an option from the Preset pull-down menu.

Table 4.1

Common composition presets				
PRESET	**FRAME SIZE**	**PAR**	**FRAME RATE**	**USE**
NTSC	640 × 480	1	29.97	Full-screen, full-motion video, used by low-end cards
NTSC DV	720 × 480	.9	29.97	DV standard for North America
NTSC D1	720 × 486	.9	29.97	Broadcast standard for North America
HDTV	1920 × 1080	1	24	High-definition standard using 16:9 image aspect ratio
Film (2k)	2048 × 1536	1	24	Film transfers
Cineon Full	3656 × 2664	1	24	Film transferred using the Cineon file format

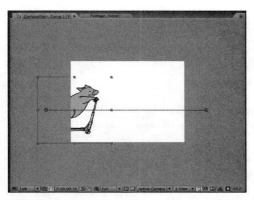

Figure 4.5 The frame size defines the dimensions of the viewable area of the composition. Over time, an element may move from the offscreen work area...

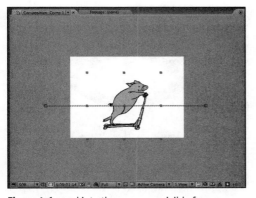

Figure 4.6 ...and into the onscreen visible frame...

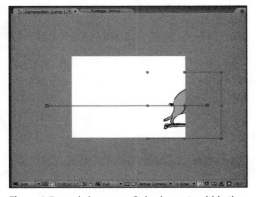

Figure 4.7 ...and vice versa. Only elements within the visible frame appear in the final output.

Setting a comp's frame size

The frame size determines the viewing area of the Composition panel. Although you may position images in the workspace outside of this viewing area (what some call the *pasteboard*), only the elements within the visible frame will be rendered for previews and output (**Figures 4.5**, **4.6**, and **4.7**).

Often, the frame dimensions of the final output determine the frame size of a composition. However, if the composition is to be nested in another composition, the frame size may be larger or smaller than the pixel dimensions of the final output. (See "Nesting Compositions," later in this chapter, or see Chapter 16, "Complex Projects.")

The Composition Settings dialog box provides a list of preset frame sizes, or you may enter a custom frame size. The frame size you choose is centered in a workspace that's limited to the same maximum dimensions as imported image files. As with imported footage files, chances are you'll run out of available RAM before you exceed the maximum image size (up to 30,000 × 30,000 pixels, depending on the output option).

For more about the maximum frame size of images, see the sidebar "Wham, Bam— Thank You, RAM" in Chapter 2, "Importing Footage into a Project." If you change the frame size of an existing composition, the Anchor setting determines where the existing layers are placed in the new comp (see "To set the anchor of a resized composition," later in this chapter).

To set the frame size:

1. In the Composition Settings dialog box, *do one of the following:*

    ▲ Enter the width and height of the frame in pixels.

    ▲ Choose a preset frame size from the pull-down menu (**Figure 4.8**).

2. If you're changing the frame size of an existing composition, choose an anchor point from the Anchor section of the Composition Settings dialog box (visible when you select the Advanced tab).

Resizing a comp

When you resize a composition, you use the Anchor control to determine how the composition and its layers are placed in the new frame—that is, whether they're anchored in the center, corner, or side of the new frame.

To set the anchor of a resized composition:

1. Select a composition, and press Command/Ctrl-K (**Figure 4.9**).

    The Composition Settings dialog box appears.

2. To change the frame size of the composition, enter new values in the Width and Height fields.

3. Click the Advanced tab.

    The Advanced settings pane of the Composition Settings dialog box appears.

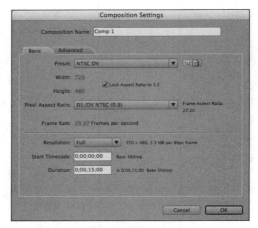

Figure 4.8 Enter the frame dimensions, or choose a preset size from the pull-down menu.

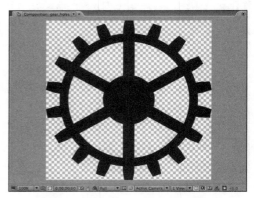

Figure 4.9 Before the composition is resized, it looks like this.

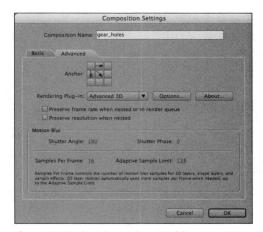

Figure 4.10 In the Advanced panel of the Composition Settings dialog box, click one of the nine anchor positions.

4. In the Anchor control, click one of the nine anchor point positions (**Figure 4.10**).

5. Click OK to close the Composition Settings dialog box.

The layers contained in the composition align to the position you specified (**Figure 4.11**).

✔ Tip

■ Don't confuse the composition's anchor with a layer's anchor point, which is something else altogether. To find out about the layer Anchor Point property, see Chapter 7, "Properties and Keyframes."

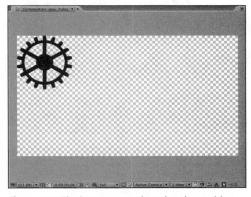

Figure 4.11 The layers are anchored to the position you specified in the resized comp.

Setting a comp's pixel aspect ratio

A typical computer monitor uses square pixels to display an image. Professional video, in contrast, uses nonsquare pixels to display images. As a result, an image created on a computer can appear distorted when transferred to video, and vice versa.

One of After Effects' great advantages is that it can compensate for differences in pixel aspect ratios. In fact, when you choose a preset frame size, After Effects automatically selects the corresponding pixel aspect ratio (PAR). If you want to override this setting, or if you enter a custom frame size, you can choose the correct PAR manually.

After Effects compensates for any difference between the PAR of the composition and that of individual footage items. For example, if you add a square-pixel footage item into a D1 composition, After Effects automatically resizes the image to prevent image distortion in the final output (**Figures 4.12** and **4.13**).

To set the pixel aspect ratio of a composition:

◆ From the Pixel Aspect Ratio pull-down menu in the Composition Settings dialog box, choose a PAR (**Figure 4.14**).

✔ Tip

■ As suggested earlier, the most common PARs are square pixel (with a PAR of 1) and D1/DV NTSC (with a PAR of .9). Square pixels correspond to formats displayed on computer monitors or consumer-level video capture cards. D1/DV NTSC corresponds to the nonsquare pixels used by professional NTSC video formats (D1 or ITU-R 601) and the DV video standards (mini DV, DVCam, and DVCPro).

Figure 4.12 Incorrectly interpreted as having nonsquare pixels, this 640 × 480 square-pixel image seems to lose its 4:3 aspect ratio in this 720 × 486 (D1/nonsquare pixels) composition.

Figure 4.13 Correctly interpreted as having square pixels, the image is automatically resized to compensate for a composition set to the D1 standard.

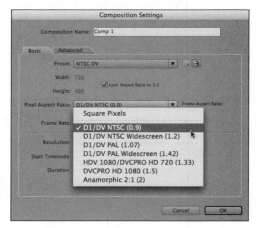

Figure 4.14 In the Pixel Aspect Ratio pull-down menu, choose the PAR that corresponds to your final output.

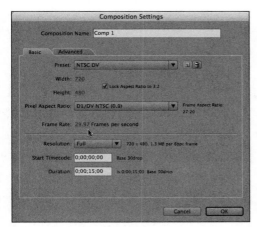

Figure 4.15 Enter the appropriate frame rate for the composition.

Frame rate

The *frame rate* is the number of frames per second (fps) used by a composition. Usually, the frame rate you choose matches the frame rate of your output format.

Individual footage items have their own frame rates, which you can interpret. (See "Setting the Frame Rate" in Chapter 2.) Ideally, the footage frame rate and the composition frame rate match. If not, After Effects makes the frame rate of the footage item conform to that of the composition.

To set the frame rate of the composition:

◆ In the Frame Rate field in the Composition Settings dialog box, enter a frame rate (**Figure 4.15**).

Usually, you'll choose a frame rate that matches the frame rate of the output format:

▲ NTSC video: 29.97 fps

▲ PAL video: 25 fps

▲ Film: 24 fps

▲ Computer presentation (often via CD-ROM or Web): 15 fps or 10 fps

Lower frame rates help reduce file size and conform to data-rate limitations.

✔ Tips

■ Film that has been transferred to video often uses video frame rates and has undergone the process of 3:2 pulldown. For more about 3:2 pulldown, see Chapter 2.

■ Use the Interpret Footage command to set the proper frame rate for a footage item; set the composition's frame rate according to your output requirements. If you're interested in changing the speed of a layer, see Chapter 6, "Layer Editing."

Setting a comp's viewing resolution

Frame size sets the actual pixel dimensions of the composition; *resolution* determines the fraction of the pixels that are displayed in the Composition panel.

By lowering the resolution, you reduce not only image quality but also the amount of memory needed to render frames. Rendering speeds increase in proportion to image quality sacrificed. Typically, you work at a lower resolution and then render the final output at full resolution.

To set a composition's resolution:

1. In the Composition Settings dialog box, choose a setting from the Resolution pull-down menu (**Figure 4.16**):

    Full—After Effects renders and displays every pixel of the composition, resulting in the highest image quality and the longest rendering time.

    Half—After Effects renders every other pixel, or one-quarter of the pixels.

    Third—After Effects renders every third pixel, or one-ninth of the pixels.

    Quarter—After Effects renders every fourth pixel, or one-sixteenth of the pixels.

    Custom—After Effects renders whatever fraction of pixels you specify.

2. If you choose Custom from the pull-down menu, enter values to determine the horizontal and vertical resolution of the image (**Figure 4.17**).

✔ Tip

- You can also change the resolution at any time by using the Resolution pull-down menu in the Composition panel (**Figure 4.18**). See "The Composition panel," later in this chapter.

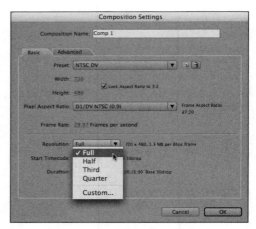

Figure 4.16 Choose a resolution from the pull-down menu.

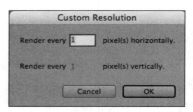

Figure 4.17 If you choose Custom, enter values to determine the resolution manually.

Figure 4.18 You can also change the resolution using the pull-down menu at the bottom of the Composition panel.

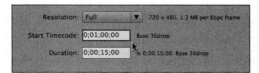

Figure 4.19 If you want to, enter a starting frame number.

Figure 4.20 Enter the duration for the composition.

Setting a comp's start-frame number

When you began your project, you set its time display—that is, the method used to count your project's frames. By default, a comp's time starts at zero, but you can set it to start at any time.

To set a composition's starting frame number:

1. In the Composition Settings dialog box, enter the starting frame number of the composition (**Figure 4.19**).

    The timebase you set for the project determines whether this number is expressed in timecode, feet and frames, or frame numbers.

2. Click OK to close the Composition Settings dialog box.

    The composition begins at the frame number you specified.

Setting a comp's duration

Duration—which sets the length of a composition—is expressed in the time display style you set in the Project Settings dialog box (timecode, frames, or feet and frames). See "Choosing Composition Settings" earlier in this chapter for more about time display options. You can change the composition's duration at any time, lengthening it to accommodate more layers or cutting it to the total duration of its layers.

To set the duration of a composition:

◆ In the Duration field in the Composition Settings dialog box, enter the duration of the composition (**Figure 4.20**).

✔ Tip

■ You can also quickly trim the comp's duration to the length of the work area by choosing Composition > Trim Comp to Work Area. For more about the work area, see Chapter 8, "Playback, Previews, and RAM."

SPECIFYING COMPOSITION PRESETS

Setting a Comp's Background Color

The default background color of compositions is black; however, you can change the background to any color you choose. Regardless of what color you make it, the background becomes the alpha channel when you output the composition as a still-image sequence or a movie with an alpha channel. Similarly, if you use the composition as a layer in another composition, the background of the nested composition becomes transparent (**Figure 4.21**) (see "Nesting Compositions," later in this chapter). And as with the Footage panel (see Chapter 3, "Managing Footage") and the Layer panel, you can also view the background as a checkerboard pattern, called a *transparency grid*.

Figure 4.21 The background of the comp (first image) becomes transparent when nested into another comp (second image). The result is the third image.

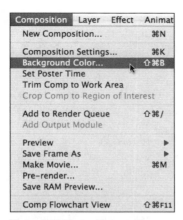

Figure 4.22 Choose Composition >
Background Color.

Figure 4.23 Click the eyedropper
to pick a screen color, or click the
swatch to open a color picker.

To choose a background color for your composition:

1. Select a composition in the Project panel, or activate a composition in a Composition or Timeline panel.

2. Choose Composition > Background Color (**Figure 4.22**), or press Shift-Command-B (Mac) or Shift-Ctrl-B (Windows).

   A Background Color dialog box appears.

3. In the Background Color dialog box, *do one of the following* (**Figure 4.23**):

   ▲ Click the color swatch to open the color picker.

   ▲ Click the eyedropper to choose a color from another window.

4. Click OK to close the Background Color dialog box.

   The selected composition uses the background color you specified.

✔ Tip

■ If you need an opaque background—in a nested composition, for example—create a solid layer as described in "To create a solid-color layer," later in this chapter.

SETTING A COMP'S BACKGROUND COLOR

The Composition and Timeline Panels

All of your compositions can be represented in the Composition and Timeline panels, which open automatically whenever you create or open a composition. These two panels furnish you with different ways of looking at a composition and manipulating its layers. This section gives you an overview of each panel, emphasizing how panels show layers along with their spatial and temporal relationships.

The Composition panel

The Composition—or Comp—panel (**Figure 4.24**) displays the layers of footage visible at the current frame of a composition. You can use the Comp panel to visually preview the way a composition's layers are rendered

within the visible frame as well as how those layers are placed outside the frame (in the *pasteboard* area). The Composition panel is where you'll find the controls for viewing composition layers (many of which are shared by the Footage and Layer panels) as well as those for setting a composition's current frame and resolution. You can move and scale layers and masks directly in the Comp panel, and you can also view information such as layer paths, keyframes, and tangents. The Comp panel also includes a few buttons that will be discussed in later chapters. A discussion of the Region of Interest (which is also available in the Footage and Layer panels) and Fast Preview buttons is reserved for Chapter 8. Chapter 15, "3D Layers," covers the Camera View pull-down menu along with other features pertaining to 3D compositing.

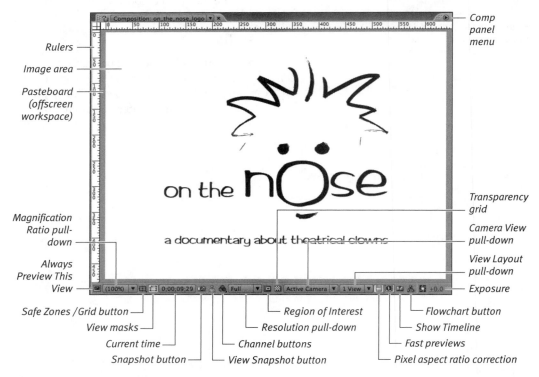

Figure 4.24 The Composition panel.

The Timeline panel

The Timeline panel (**Figure 4.25**) graphically represents a composition as layers in a timeline. A vertical line—called the *time marker*—corresponds to the current frame pictured in the Composition panel. In the Timeline panel, each layer occupies a row, and the rows are stacked vertically. (Unlike the tracks of many nonlinear editing programs, each row contains only one layer.) Layers that are higher in the Timeline panel's stacking order appear in front of lower layers when viewed in the Composition panel. The Timeline panel offers more than just an alternative view of the composition; it gives you precise control over virtually every attribute of each layer in a composition.

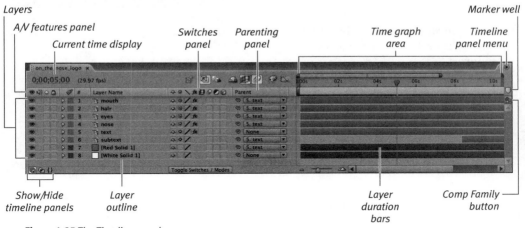

Layers

A/V features panel

Current time display

Switches panel

Parenting panel

Time graph area

Marker well

Timeline panel menu

Show/Hide timeline panels

Layer outline

Layer duration bars

Comp Family button

Figure 4.25 The Timeline panel.

Setting the Time

Before you add footage to a composition, you must specify the time at which the layer will begin in the composition. By setting the composition's current time, you can also set the starting point for an added layer. And, of course, setting the time also allows you to view a particular frame of the composition in the Comp panel. You can set the current time via the Time Controls panel, the Composition panel, or the Timeline panel; you can also use keyboard shortcuts to accomplish the task.

Using the Time Controls panel

You can control the playback of the Footage, Composition, Timeline, and Layer panels using the Time Controls panel. **Figure 4.26** shows how the panel's buttons function.

To set the current time in the Timeline panel:

◆ In the Timeline panel, drag the current time indicator to the frame you want (**Figure 4.27**).

Use the current time display to see the current time numerically.

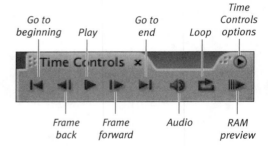

Figure 4.26 The Time Controls panel. (In this figure, the RAM preview options are hidden.)

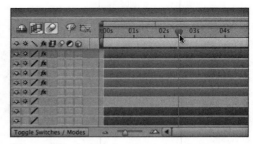

Figure 4.27 In the Timeline panel, drag the current time indicator to change the current frame (displayed in the Composition panel).

Figure 4.28 Click the time display in the Composition panel...

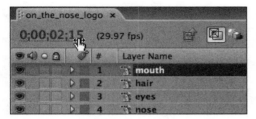

Figure 4.29 ...or in the Timeline panel...

Figure 4.30 ...or use the keyboard shortcut to open the Go to Time dialog box. Enter a specific frame number, or absolute time, to cue the current frame...

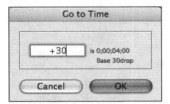

Figure 4.31 ...or enter a time relative to the current frame by entering a plus (+) or minus (-) and the number of frames.

To cue the current time of the composition numerically:

1. *Do any of the following:*
   - ▲ In the Composition panel, click the time display (**Figure 4.28**).
   - ▲ In the Timeline panel, click the time display (**Figure 4.29**).
   - ▲ Press Shift-Opt-J (Mac) or Shift-Alt-J (Windows).

   The Go to Time dialog box appears.

2. *Do one of the following:*
   - ▲ Enter an absolute time (a specific frame number) to which you want to cue the current time (**Figure 4.30**).
   - ▲ Enter a plus (+) or minus (-) and a relative time (the number of frames you want to add or subtract from the current frame) (**Figure 4.31**). Numbers greater than 99 are interpreted as seconds and frames.

3. Click OK to close the Go to Time dialog box.

✔ Tips

- ■ By clicking the arrows to the left of the Time Controls panel's name, you can cycle through different views of the window that include fewer or more controls.

- ■ Because you'll frequently need to change the current time in the Composition, Timeline, Footage, and Layer panels, you should familiarize yourself with the keyboard shortcuts that help you get around—for example (on an expanded keyboard), Page Down to advance one frame and Page Up to go back one frame. Consult the Help system for more keyboard shortcuts.

SETTING THE TIME

Adding Footage to a Composition

When you add an item to a composition, you create a layer. A layer can be a footage item in the project, a solid layer generated in After Effects, or another composition. You can add an item to a composition more than once to create multiple layers, or you can duplicate existing layers (using the Copy, Paste, and Duplicate commands). In this section, you'll learn to create layers in a composition. Later

chapters will show you how to rearrange and modify layers. (Eventually, you'll also learn about specialized layers such as adjustment layers, guide layers, and layers used in 3D compositing: 3D layers, lights, cameras, and null objects. But first things first.)

The method you use to add layers depends on how you want to set their initial position, starting point, and layer order in your composition. You can simply drag a layer to the timeline to position it at any time or level in the stacking order.

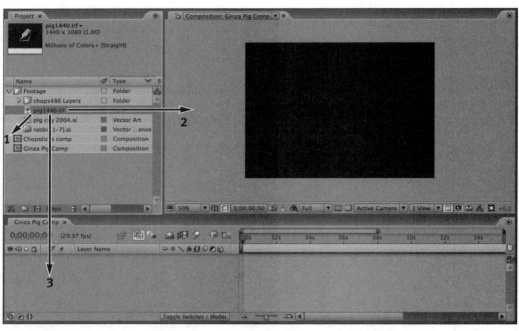

Figure 4.32 You can drag one or more items from the Project panel to a composition in the Project panel (1), its Composition panel (2), or the Timeline panel (3).

To add footage to a composition by dragging:

1. Set the current time of the composition using one of the methods described earlier in this chapter.

2. Drag one or more items from the Project panel to *any of the following* (**Figure 4.32**):

   Composition panel—To place the layers in the desired position, at the current time, and layered in the order in which the files were selected in the Project panel

   Timeline panel—To place the layers at the desired time and layer, and centered in the visible frame of the composition

   Name or icon of a composition in the Project panel—To place the layers at the current time, centered in the visible frame of the composition, and layered in the order in which you selected the items in the Project panel

   Items become layers in the composition whose position, starting time, and layer order all depend on the method you employed to add them to the composition. Layers created from still-image footage use the default duration for stills (see Chapter 2). The duration of other layers is determined by the In and Out points you set in their Footage panel (see "To set source footage edit points" later in this chapter).

✔ Tips

- Another quick way to add footage to the centered composition is to select the footage item in the Project panel and press Command/Ctrl-/.

- Option/Alt-dragging footage to a selected layer in the timeline replaces the layer with the new footage.

Adding Layers Using Insert and Overlay

You can add motion footage to your composition by using tools and techniques commonly found in non-linear editing (NLE) software. Buttons in the Footage panel, for example, allow you to perform insert and overlay edits—both of which add a layer at the current time, although each affects the timeline's existing layers differently.

When you add a layer using an *overlay* edit, the composition's layers retain their current positions in time. The new layer is added as the topmost layer at the current time (**Figures 4.33** and **4.34**).

In contrast, adding a layer via an *insert* edit causes the composition's existing layers to shift in time to accommodate the new layer. In other words, if the new layer is five seconds long, all layers after the current time move forward five seconds. If the current time occurs midway through a layer, the layer is split into two layers; the portion after the current time shifts forward (**Figure 4.35**).

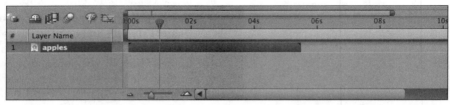

Figure 4.33 Note the arrangement of the layers before an insert or overlay edit, as well as the position of the current time indicator.

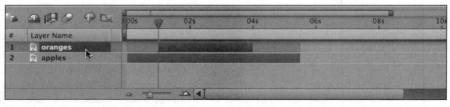

Figure 4.34 After an overlay edit, the new layer is added as the topmost layer at the current time.

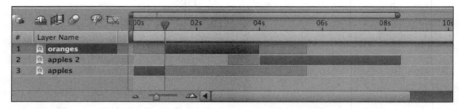

Figure 4.35 After an insert edit, layers after the current time shift forward to accommodate the new layer. One of the layers is split at the edit point, and the portion after the edit point shifts forward.

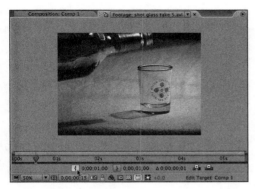

Figure 4.36 Cue the current time to the point at which you want the source footage to start, and click the Set In button to set the source In point.

Figure 4.37 Cue the current time to the point at which you want the source footage to stop, and click the Set Out button to set the source Out point.

To set source footage edit points:

1. Option/Alt-double-click a motion footage item in the Project panel.

   The motion footage item opens in an After Effects Footage panel.

2. To set an In point, cue the current time and click the Set In button.

   The In point display and the duration bar reflect the In point you set (**Figure 4.36**).

3. To set an Out point, cue the current time and click the Set Out button.

   The Out point display and the duration bar reflect the Out point you set (**Figure 4.37**).

To insert or overlay a layer:

1. Set the current time of the composition to which you want to add the layer.

   You can use the Go To Time command, the Time Controls panel, or the current time indicator in the Timeline panel (as described in the section "Setting the Time," earlier in this chapter).

2. In the Footage panel, set the source footage In and Out points (as described in the previous task).

   Make sure the Edit Target section of the Footage panel displays the name of the composition to which you want to add a layer. If the project contains more than one composition, the window displays the currently selected composition.

   continues on next page

ADDING LAYERS USING INSERT AND OVERLAY

3. In the Footage panel, *click either of the following:*

Ripple Insert—If you select this option, all other layers will be shifted forward to accommodate the new layer (**Figure 4.38**).

Overlay—If you select this option, other layers will retain their current positions in time.

The selected footage is added to the composition as the topmost layer at the current time. Other layers' positions in time will depend on whether you selected an insert or overlay edit.

✔ Tip

- In editing, the inverse of Overlay is Lift; the inverse of Insert is Extract. The menu command Lift Work Area removes a range of frames and leaves a gap in the timeline. Extract Work Area removes the frames and shifts subsequent layers back in time so there is no gap. For more about setting the Work Area, see Chapter 8. For other editing techniques, see Chapter 6.

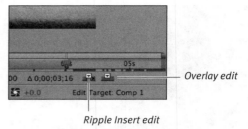

Overlay edit

Ripple Insert edit

Figure 4.38 Depending on the type of edit you want to perform, click the Ripple Insert or Overlay button.

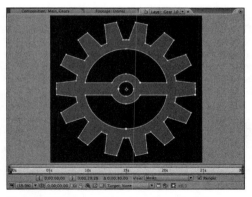

Figure 4.39 You can add text or other effects to a solid; you can mask a solid to create graphical elements (shown here); or you can use it as a solid-color background.

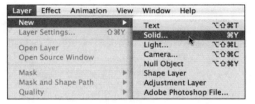

Figure 4.40 Choose Layer > New > Solid, or use the keyboard shortcut.

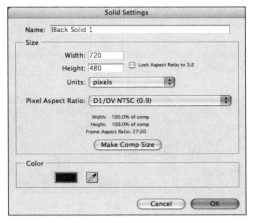

Figure 4.41 In the Solid Settings dialog box, enter a name for the solid layer. Click the Make Comp Size button to make the solid the same size as the composition, or enter a custom width and height.

Creating Solid Layers

As you might expect, a *solid* layer is a layer in the size and color of your choice. You create a solid layer when you need an opaque background for a nested composition. You can also use solids with masks to create graphic elements (**Figure 4.39**). And you can even use this type of layer to create text effects within After Effects. (For more about text effects, see Chapter 11, "Effects Fundamentals"; for more about masks, see Chapter 10, "Mask Essentials.")

Creating a solid doesn't produce an actual media file on your hard drive. But in other respects, a solid layer works like any other footage item: It has specified dimensions and PAR, as well as a color. (This is notable because older versions of After Effects didn't allow you to set a solid's PAR, forcing you to treat it a little differently than other footage items.) However, this doesn't mean the solid's settings are fixed; you can change its attributes at any time.

To create a solid-color layer:

1. Open the Composition panel or Timeline panel for the composition in which you want to add a solid layer, or make sure one is active.

2. Choose Layer > New > Solid, or press Command/Ctrl-Y (**Figure 4.40**).

   The Solid Settings dialog box appears (**Figure 4.41**).

3. Enter a name for the new solid.

   After Effects uses the solid's current color as the basis for the default name: for example, Gray Solid 1.

continues on next page

4. Set the size by *doing any of the following:*

▲ To make the solid the same size as the composition, click the Make Comp Size button.

▲ To enter a custom size, choose a unit of measure from the Units pull-down menu, and enter a width and height (**Figure 4.42**).

▲ To maintain the aspect ratio of the current width and height, click the Lock Aspect Ratio button before you change the size.

5. Choose an option from the Pixel Aspect Ratio pull-down menu (**Figure 4.43**).

6. Set the color by *doing one of the following:*

▲ Click the color swatch to open the color picker, and choose a color.

▲ Click the eyedropper to select a color from the screen.

7. Click OK to close the Solid Settings dialog box.

The solid appears as a layer in the composition. Like any layer, the solid layer starts at the current time and uses the default duration of still images. (See "To change the default duration of still images" in Chapter 2.) In the Project panel, After Effects creates a folder called Solids that contains all the solid footage items you create.

To change a solid's settings:

1. *Do either of the following:*

▲ In the Project panel, select a solid footage item.

▲ In the Composition or Timeline panel, click a solid layer to select it (**Figure 4.44**).

You may also use a variety of other methods to select a layer; for more information, see "Selecting Layers" in Chapter 5.

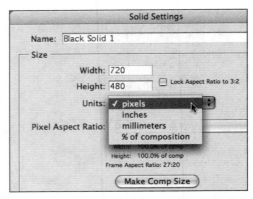

Figure 4.42 Choose a unit of measure from the pull-down menu before you enter a custom size.

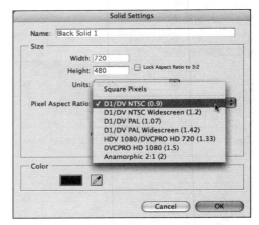

Figure 4.43 Specify an option in the Pixel Aspect Ratio pull-down menu.

Figure 4.44 Select a solid footage item in the Project panel, or a solid layer in the Comp or Timeline panel (shown here).

Figure 4.45 Choose Layer ›
Solid Settings.

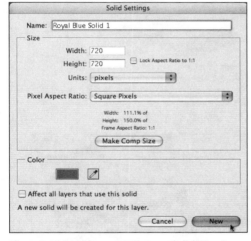

Figure 4.46 Specify new settings, and click New to
modify a selected layer only...

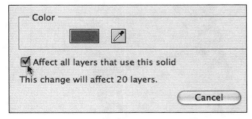

Figure 4.47 ...or select "Affect all layers that use this
solid" to modify all layers created from the solid.

2. *Do either of the following:*
- ▲ Choose Layer > Solid Settings (**Figure 4.45**).
- ▲ Press Shift-Command-Y (Mac) or Shift-Ctrl-Y (Windows).

The Solid Settings dialog box appears.

3. Specify any changes you want to make to the solid footage, such as its name, dimensions, PAR, or color (**Figure 4.46**).

4. If you selected the solid layer from the Timeline or Composition panel in step 1, specify whether you want the changes to affect layers already created from the solid footage item by selecting "Affect all layers that use this solid" (**Figure 4.47**).

Leave this option unselected if you want to change only this layer and not layers already created from it.

5. Click OK.

Depending on your choices, the changes you specified are applied to the selected solid layer, solid footage item, or both.

✔ Tips

- You can continuously rasterize a solid layer. That way, its edges (particularly when you have a mask applied to it) remain crisp and smooth when you scale it up. See Chapter 5 for more about the Continuously Rasterize switch; see Chapter 10 for more about masks.

- You can convert an ordinary visible layer to a *guide layer*, an invisible layer you can use to position and align other layers in a composition. Just select the layer and choose Layer > Guide Layer. A guide layer icon ▣ appears next to the layer's name in the Timeline panel's layer outline.

CREATING SOLID LAYERS

Nesting Compositions

To achieve many effects, you must make a composition a layer in another composition—a process called *nesting*. For example, rotating each layer in the composition in **Figure 4.48** doesn't achieve the desired effect. Each layer is rotated around its own anchor point and betrays the fact that each layer is a separate element. To make the layers appear unified, it would be extremely inconvenient to adjust each layer individually.

With a nested composition, it's possible to rotate the entire composition as a single layer, as in **Figure 4.49**. As a single layer within another composition, all the elements rotate around a single anchor point. You can use nested compositions to produce complex effects, to control rendering order, or to apply effects to continuously rasterized or collapsed layers. You can always reopen the nested composition. Any changes you make to the original are reflected in the nested layer.

The following tasks show you how to make one composition a layer in another. Chapter 16 revisits nested compositions in more detail.

Figure 4.48 Merely rotating each layer in this composition doesn't achieve the desired effect.

Figure 4.49 Nesting the composition makes it a single layer in another composition. Rotating the nested composition easily achieves the effect.

Figure 4.50 The nested composition looks and behaves much like any other layer.

Figure 4.51 Drag a composition to the composition icon at the bottom of the Project panel to nest it in a new composition with the same settings.

To make a composition a layer in another composition:

1. Display the Composition panel or Timeline panel of the composition that will contain the nested composition.

2. Drag a composition you want to nest from the Project panel to *any of the following*:
   - ▲ Composition panel of the target composition
   - ▲ Timeline panel of the target composition
   - ▲ Name or icon of the target composition in the Project panel

   The composition becomes a layer in the target composition. The composition layer starts at the current time and has the duration of the original composition (**Figure 4.50**).

To nest one composition in a new one with the same settings:

◆ Drag a composition in the Project panel to the composition icon ▦ at the bottom of the Project panel (**Figure 4.51**).

The composition becomes a layer in a new composition that uses the same composition settings as the nested one.

NESTING COMPOSITIONS

To open a comp's parent composition:

◆ In the Timeline panel, click the Open
Parent Composition button and choose
the name of the composition you want
to open (**Figure 4.52**).

If the current comp isn't nested in any
other comps, the button is grayed out
and unavailable.

✔ Tips

■ The default frame rate and resolution
of nested compositions depend on the
setting you chose in the Advanced panel
of the Composition Settings dialog box.
You can tell After Effects to preserve
the frame rate and resolution of nested
comps (see "Nesting Options," in Chapter
16, "Complex Projects").

■ After Effects' Parenting feature allows
you to create even more complex relationships between layers than nesting
allows. Make sure you use the best technique for the job at hand. See Chapter 16
for more about the Parenting feature.

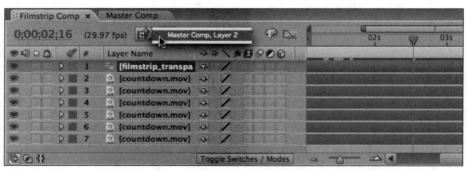

Figure 4.52 You can open a comp that contains the current comp by selecting its name in the Open
Parent Comp button's pull-down menu.

5

LAYER BASICS

Previous chapters laid the groundwork for the central activity of your After Effects work: manipulating a composition's layers. Over the next several chapters, you'll gradually increase your command over layers. This chapter focuses on the bare essentials, describing how to select, name, and label layers. You'll also learn how to control layer quality and how to choose whether to include layers in previews and renders. In addition, you'll see how to simplify working with layers by concealing ones you're not using and by locking ones you don't want to disturb. In the process, you'll become more familiar with your primary workspace, the Timeline panel.

Selecting Layers

As you would expect, you must select layers before you can adjust them. In the timeline, selected layers' names appear highlighted, as do their duration bars—the horizontal bar representing the layer under the time ruler. In the Composition panel, selected layers can appear with *transform handles* or simply, *handles*—six small boxes that demark each layer's boundaries and that you can use to transform the layer. However, you can specify whether you want these (or other layer controls) to appear in the Comp panel. See the section "Viewing Spatial Controls in the Comp Panel" in Chapter 7, "Properties and Keyframes," for more details.

Figure 5.1 You can select a layer by directly clicking it in the Composition panel. In this figure, the Comp panel is set to show selected layer handles.

To select layers in the Composition panel:

1. If you haven't already done so, cue the current frame of the composition so that the layer you want to select is visible in the Composition panel.

2. In the Composition panel, click the visible layer to select it (**Figure 5.1**).

   The selected layer's handles and anchor point appear, unless these options have been disabled (see "Viewing Spatial Controls in the Comp Panel" in Chapter 7).

3. To select more than one layer, Shift-click other visible layers in the Composition panel (**Figure 5.2**).

Figure 5.2 Shift-click to select additional layers.

Figure 5.3 You can select layers by clicking them in the Timeline panel—or by entering the layer's number on the numeric keypad.

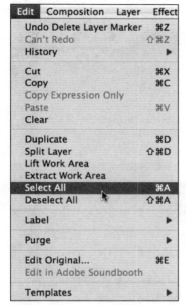

Figure 5.4 You can select all layers in the usual way—by choosing Edit > Select All (or using the keyboard shortcut).

To select layers in the Timeline panel:

In the Timeline panel, *do any of the following:*

◆ Click anywhere in the horizontal track containing the layer.

◆ To select a layer by its layer number, type the layer number on the numeric keypad (not the numbers on the main keyboard) (**Figure 5.3**).

◆ To select a range of layers, Shift-click other layers.

◆ To select a range of layers, drag a marquee around several layer names. (Take care not to drag a layer to a new position in the stacking order.)

 Selected layers appear highlighted in the Timeline panel. Selected layers are visible in the Comp panel only if the current time is cued to the layer.

To select all layers in a composition:

◆ Choose Edit > Select All, or press Command/Ctrl-A (**Figure 5.4**).

 All the layers in the composition are selected.

To deselect all layers in a composition:

Do one of the following:

◆ Click an empty area in the Timeline panel or the Composition panel.

◆ Choose Edit > Deselect All.

✔ Tips

■ Press Command/Ctrl-Up Arrow to select the next layer up in the stacking order. See the next section, "Changing the Stacking Order."

■ Press Command/Ctrl-Down Arrow to select the next layer down in the stacking order.

Changing the Stacking Order

In the Timeline panel, layers appear, well, *layered*. That is, each layer occupies a horizontal track that is stacked vertically with other layers. The horizontal position of a layer's duration bar determines its place in time; its vertical position shows its place in the *stacking order*. When layers occupy the same point in time, higher layers appear in front of lower layers when viewed in the Composition panel. You can change the relative positions of the layers in the stacking order to determine which elements appear in front and which appear behind (**Figures 5.5** and **5.6**).

A number directly to the left of a layer's name indicates a layer's position in the stacking order. The top layer is always layer 1, and the numbers increase as you go down the stack. Although layer numbers may not seem very informative, they can help you discern when layers are hidden temporarily (see "Making Layers Shy," later in this chapter) as well as provide a way for you to quickly select layers by number (see "Selecting Layers," earlier in this chapter).

✔ Tip

■ In Chapter 3, "Managing Footage," you learned that the Project panel labels each file type (motion footage, still image, and so on) using a different colored label. In the timeline, each layer's duration bar and label (the color swatch next to the layer's number) reflect the label color scheme. You can assign another color to any selected layer by choosing Edit > Label > and selecting a color.

Figure 5.5 Layers higher in the stacking order appear in front of other layers in the Composition panel (provided they're positioned at the same point in time).

Figure 5.6 When a layer is moved to a lower position in the stacking order, it appears behind the higher layers in the Composition panel.

Figure 5.7 As you drag a layer in the stacking order, a line indicates where it will appear if you release the mouse.

Figure 5.8 When you release the mouse, the layer appears in the new position.

Figure 5.9 To move the selected layer using menu commands, choose Layer > and the appropriate command.

To change the stacking order of layers in the Timeline panel:

1. In the Timeline panel, drag a layer name to a new position.

   A horizontal line appears between other layers, indicating where the layer will appear in the stacking order (**Figure 5.7**).

2. Release the mouse to place the layer in the position you want (**Figure 5.8**).

To move layers one level at a time:

1. Select a layer in the Composition or Timeline panel.

2. *Do any of the following* (**Figure 5.9**):

   ▲ Choose Layer > Bring Layer Forward, or press Command/Ctrl-].

   ▲ Choose Layer > Send Layer Backward, or press Command/Ctrl-[.

   ▲ Choose Layer > Bring Layer to Front or press Shift-Command-] (Mac) or Shift-Ctrl-] (Windows).

   ▲ Choose Layer > Send Layer to Back or press Shift-Command-[(Mac) or Shift-Ctrl-[(Windows).

   The layer is repositioned in the stacking order according to the command you specified.

✔ Tip

■ Just in case you missed it in the previous chapter, you aren't restricted to adding a layer to the top of the stacking order and then moving it down in a separate step (as in older versions of After Effects). After Effects lets you drag footage items directly to any level in the stacking order.

CHANGING THE STACKING ORDER

Naming Layers

Although you can rename comps and solids, you can't rename footage items in the Project panel (as explained in Chapter 2, "Importing Footage into a Project"). However, you can change the names of layers in a composition. (Typically, a footage item appears in the Project panel just once; however, it may make numerous appearances as layers in compositions.) In the Timeline panel, you can choose to view either the changeable layer name or the fixed source name.

To change the name of a layer:

1. In the Timeline panel, click a layer to select it.

2. Press Return/Enter.

   The layer name becomes highlighted (**Figure 5.10**).

3. Enter a new name for the layer, and press Return/Enter.

   The layer uses the name you specified; the source name can't be changed (**Figure 5.11**).

To toggle between layer name and source name:

◆ In the Timeline panel, click the Layer/Source Name button to toggle between the layer name and the source name for the layer. When the layer name and source name are the same, the layer name appears in brackets (**Figures 5.12** and **5.13**).

Figure 5.10 To change a layer's name, select the layer and press Return/Enter to edit the name.

Figure 5.11 Enter a name for the layer, and press Return/Enter.

Figure 5.12 In the Timeline panel, click the Name panel heading to toggle between the layer name (which you can change)...

Figure 5.13 ...and the source name (which is fixed).

NAMING LAYERS

A/V Features area

Figure 5.14 By default, the A/V Features panel appears to the extreme left in the Timeline panel. The panel contains three switches: Video, Audio, and Solo.

Switching Video and Audio On and Off

By default, the extreme left side of the Timeline panel displays the A/V Features panel (**Figure 5.14**). The first three columns of the A/V Features panel contain switches that control whether a layer's video and audio are included in previews or renders.

To show or hide the image for layers in the composition:

◆ Next to a layer in the Timeline panel, click the Video switch to toggle the Eye icon 👁 on and off.

When the Eye icon is visible, the layer appears in the Composition panel (**Figure 5.15**); when the icon is hidden, the layer doesn't appear (**Figure 5.16**).

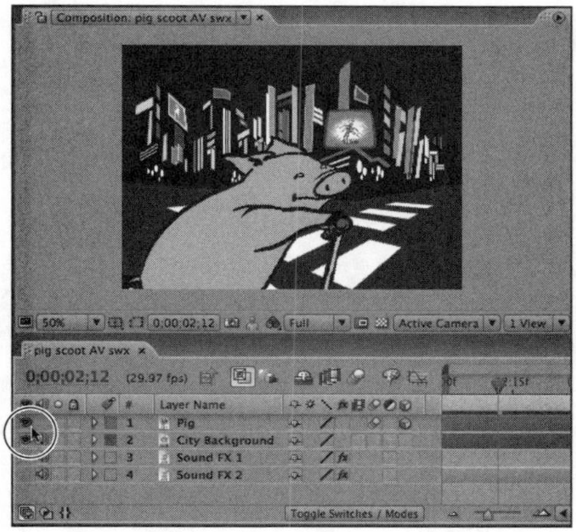

Figure 5.15 When the Video switch is on, the layer's image appears in the Composition panel.

Figure 5.16 When the Video switch is off, the layer's image doesn't appear in the Composition panel, previews, or renders.

To include a layer's audio track in the composition:

◆ Next to the layer in the Timeline panel, click the Audio switch to toggle the Speaker icon 🔊 on and off.

When the Speaker icon is visible, the audio is included when you preview or render the composition (**Figure 5.17**); when the Speaker icon is hidden, the audio is excluded (**Figure 5.18**).

Figure 5.17 When the Audio switch is on, the layer's audio track is included in previews and renders.

Figure 5.18 When the Audio switch is off, the layer's audio track isn't included in previews and renders.

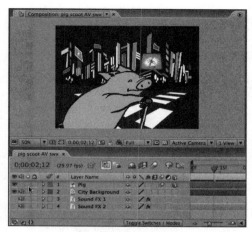

Figure 5.19 Make sure the Eye icon is visible to solo video and that the Speaker icon is visible to solo audio, and then click the Solo button.

Figure 5.20 When you solo the layer's video and audio, A/V switches for other layers are deactivated.

To solo a layer:

1. For the layer you want to solo:

   ▲ Make sure the Eye icon is visible to solo the video.

   ▲ Make sure the Speaker icon is visible to solo the audio.

   If the layer contains both video and audio, you can select either or both. If you select neither, the Solo button disappears, and you can't solo the layer.

2. Next to the layer you want to solo, click the Solo button ◯ (**Figure 5.19**).

   If you solo the video, the Video switches for all other layers are deactivated; if you solo the audio, the Audio switches for all other layers are deactivated (**Figure 5.20**).

3. To stop soloing the layer and restore other A/V settings to their original states, click the Solo button again to deactivate it.

✔ Tips

- When a transfer mode has been applied to a layer, the Eye icon 👁 looks like this: 👁. For more about transfer modes, see Chapter 14, "More Layer Techniques."

- When a track matte is applied to a layer, the video for the layer above it is automatically switched off. Switching the video back on eliminates the track matte effect. For more about track mattes, see Chapter 14.

- Not all layers are visible; adjustment layers, guide layers, lights, cameras, null objects, and, of course, layers created from audio-only footage have no video component.

SWITCHING VIDEO AND AUDIO ON AND OFF

Locking a Layer

The fourth column of the A/V Features panel contains the Lock switch, which you can use to lock layers so that they're protected against accidental changes. When you attempt to select a locked layer, its highlight blinks on and off to remind you that it's locked and thus can't be selected or altered. You must unlock the layer to make changes.

To lock or unlock a layer:

◆ Next to a layer in the Timeline panel, click the Lock switch to toggle the Lock icon 🔒 on and off.

When the Lock icon is visible, the layer can't be selected or modified (**Figure 5.21**); when the Lock icon is hidden, the layer is unlocked (**Figure 5.22**).

To unlock all layers:

◆ Choose Layer > Switches > Unlock All Layers, or press Command/Ctrl-Shift-l (**Figure 5.23**).

✔ Tip

■ Press Command/Ctrl-L to lock selected layers. You still have to click the Lock switch to unlock layers (you can't select locked layers).

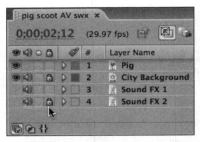

Figure 5.21 Turn on the Lock switch to protect the layer from inadvertent changes.

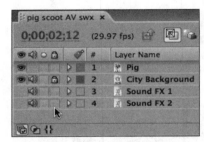

Figure 5.22 Turn off the Lock switch to unlock a layer.

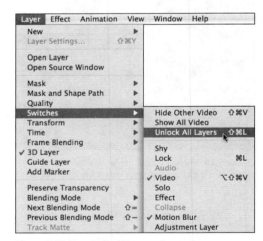

Figure 5.23 To unlock all layers, choose Layer > Switches > Unlock All Layers.

Basic Layer Switches

By default, the Layer Switches column set appears to the right of the Name column in the Timeline panel.

The Layer Switches column consists of eight switches that control various features for each layer (**Figure 5.24**). This section covers the first three layer switches: Shy, Rasterize, and Quality. Other layer switches are covered later in the book. (The Effect and Adjustment Layer switches are covered in Chapter 11,

"Effects Fundamentals"; the Frame Blending and Motion Blur switches are covered in Chapter 14; and the 3D switch is covered in Chapter 15, "3D Layers.")

Although you can control all of the layer switches via menu commands, the switches provide more direct access.

To show or hide the layer switches:

◆ In the Timeline panel, click the Expand / Collapse Layer Switches Pane button 🔲 (**Figure 5.25**).

Clicking the button hides and shows the Switches pane (**Figure 5.26**).

✔ Tip

■ You can toggle between the Switches and the Transfer Modes controls (covered in Chapter 14) by pressing the Toggle Switches / Modes button at the bottom of the Timeline panel.

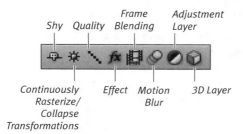

Figure 5.24 The Layer Switches panel contains eight switches.

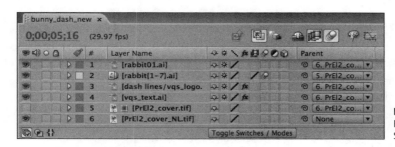

Figure 5.25 Clicking the Expand / Collapse Layer Switches Pane button...

Figure 5.26 ...toggles the switches controls open and closed (shown here).

Making Layers Shy

Because the Timeline panel contains so much information, you'll frequently find yourself scrolling through it or expanding it. Some users even use a secondary monitor just to accommodate a large Timeline panel. If you hate to scroll but are reluctant to buy another monitor, you may want to take advantage of the Shy Layers feature.

Marking layers you're not currently using as *shy* enables you to quickly conceal them in the Timeline panel. This way, you can concentrate on just the layers you're using and conserve precious screen space. Although shy layers may be hidden in the Timeline panel, they always appear in the Composition panel (provided they're visible and their corresponding video switch is on), and layer numbering remains unchanged.

To make a layer shy or not shy:

◆ Click the Shy switch for a layer in the Timeline panel to toggle the icon between Not Shy 🔲 and Shy 🔲 (**Figures 5.27** and **5.28**).

To hide or show shy layers:

◆ In the Timeline panel, click the Hide Shy Layers button 🔲 to select or deselect it.

When the button is deselected, shy layers are visible in the Timeline panel (**Figure 5.29**).

When the button is selected, shy layers are hidden from view (**Figure 5.30**).

Figure 5.27 Click the Shy switch to toggle between Not Shy...

Figure 5.28 ...and Shy.

Figure 5.29 When the Hide Shy Layers button is deselected, shy layers appear in the Timeline panel.

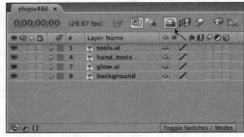

Figure 5.30 When the Hide Shy Layers button is selected, shy layers are concealed in the Timeline panel.

Figure 5.31 By default, After Effects rasterizes the image at its original size.

Figure 5.32 Enlarging an image after it has been rasterized can make the pixels apparent.

Figure 5.33 When the Continuously Rasterize switch is on, the image is scaled before it's rasterized for each frame of the composition.

Continuously Rasterizing a Layer

When you import an Illustrator or EPS file, After Effects rasterizes it, converting it from a vector-based image to a bitmapped image. Depending on how you plan to use the image, you can choose to rasterize the image once or rasterize it continuously.

If you plan to use the image at its original size (After Effects' default setting) or smaller, you only need to rasterize it once (**Figure 5.31**).

If you plan to scale the image more than 100 percent (or plan to change other geometric properties), you should choose to continuously rasterize the layer. Rasterizing the layer for each frame will ensure that image quality is maintained at any scale (**Figures 5.32** and **5.33**). Of course, these recalculations may also increase preview and rendering time. To save time, you may choose to turn off the Continuously Rasterize switch until you want to preview or render the composition at full quality.

When a composition is used as a layer, the Continuously Rasterize switch functions as the Collapse Transformations switch. Having this option selected can increase image quality while decreasing rendering time. You can find out more about the Collapse Transformations option in Chapter 16, "Complex Projects."

To change the rasterization method of a layer:

◆ In the Switches panel of the Timeline panel, click the Continuously Rasterize/Collapse Transformations switch for the layer.

When the switch is set to Off (no icon), the image is rasterized once (**Figure 5.34**); when the switch is set to On , the image is continuously rasterized (**Figure 5.35**).

✔ Tips

■ Regardless of the Continuously Rasterize setting, setting the quality switch to Full smoothes (anti-aliases) the edges of the art.

■ One way to avoid continuous rasterization and its slower rendering times is to steer clear of scaling the image beyond 100 percent. If possible, create the vector graphic at the largest dimensions it appears in the composition.

■ In older versions of After Effects, you couldn't apply an effect to a layer that had the Continuously Rasterize switch on. This is no longer the case; you're free to apply effects to a continuously rasterized layer—and free to forget the workarounds you had to use in the past.

Figure 5.34 When the switch is off, the layer is rasterized once.

Figure 5.35 When the switch is on, the layer is continuously rasterized.

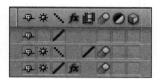

Figure 5.36 Set the switch to Draft Quality to display the layer at a lower quality in the Composition panel.

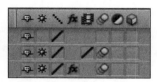

Figure 5.37 Set the switch to Full Quality to display the layer at the highest quality in the Composition panel.

Quality Setting Switches

As you'll remember from Chapter 4, "Compositions," you can set the resolution of the composition to control its image quality and thereby the speed at which frames are rendered. Just as the resolution setting controls the overall image quality of the composition, a layer's Quality switch controls the quality of an individual layer in the composition.

To change the Quality setting of a layer:

◆ In the Timeline panel, click the Quality switch to set the quality for the layer:

The Draft Quality icon indicates that the layer will preview and render at draft quality in the Composition panel (**Figure 5.36**).

The Full Quality icon indicates that the layer will preview and render at full quality in the Composition panel (**Figure 5.37**).

The Quality switch controls the quality of individual layers. To control your composition's image quality, use the Resolution controls, as described in Chapter 4.

QUALITY SETTING SWITCHES

LAYER EDITING

The term *editing*, in the sense that film and video makers use it, refers to the order and arrangement of images in time. Implicit in this definition, of course, is the term's broader meaning: to include some elements while excluding others to achieve a desired aesthetic effect. This chapter focuses on editing the layers of a composition—defining which segments to include and the order in which to present them.

You'll learn basic editing functions and terms such as *In point, Out point, duration,* and *trimming*. You'll also learn other techniques common to non-linear editing, such as setting markers and controlling the playback speed and direction of layers. In the process, you'll get acquainted with the Layer panel and take a closer look at the time graph of the Timeline panel.

Viewing Layers in the Timeline and Layer Panels

When you arrange layers in time, you work in the Layer panel and the time graph area of the Timeline panel.

As you know, the Timeline panel lets you view all of a composition's elements as vertically stacked layers. On the right side of the Timeline panel, a *time graph* represents the layers in time (**Figure 6.1**). Each layer has a duration bar, and its horizontal position in the time graph indicates when it will start and end as you play back the composition.

Time graph area of the Timeline panel

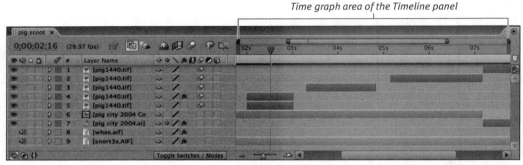

Figure 6.1 At the right side of the Timeline panel, all the layers of a composition are represented as bars in a time graph.

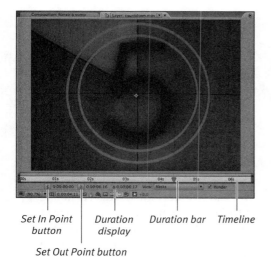

Set In Point button | Duration display | Duration bar | Timeline

Set Out Point button

Figure 6.2 You can view a single layer of the composition in a Layer panel, which includes a timeline and controls for setting the layer's starting and ending points.

Figure 6.3 Compare the view of the layer in the Layer panel and Timeline panel to the same point in time in the Composition panel. In the Composition panel, you can see how the layer has been manipulated and composited with other layers.

You can view any layer in a composition in a Layer panel. As you'll remember from Chapter 3, "Managing Footage," the Layer panel closely resembles the Footage and Composition panels. Unlike its siblings, however, the Layer panel always includes a timeline and controls for setting the starting and ending points of the layer (**Figure 6.2**).

Both the Layer and Timeline panels depict layers as duration bars. However, each panel displays layers in a different context. In the time graph, the duration bar shows a layer in the context of the entire composition. In the Layer panel, the duration bar shows you the portion of the footage item that you chose to include in the composition.

Compare the Timeline (Figure 6.1), Layer (Figure 6.2), and Composition (**Figure 6.3**) panels to see how the same layer appears in each panel. (Note that the current time always matches in all the open panels of the same composition, as explained in Chapter 4, "Compositions.") The distinctions between the time graph and the Layer panel are explained in greater detail in the sections to follow.

✔ Tip

- The Layer panel has a few other unique features not covered in detail here: the View pull-down menu and the Render check box. The section "The Layer Panel," later in this chapter, provides a brief explanation, but you'll learn more in later chapters. This chapter focuses on using the Layer panel's unique editing features— that is, on manipulating starting and ending points and on using layer markers.

VIEWING LAYERS

The Time Graph

Each layer in the composition occupies a separate horizontal track, or cell, in the time graph. The vertical arrangement of layers indicates their position in the stacking order (covered in the previous chapter). Time is displayed horizontally, from left to right, and measured by a time ruler in the increments you selected in the project preferences. Layers appear as color-coded duration bars; their length and position in the time graph indicate when the layers start and end as the composition plays back.

This chapter focuses on how to view and edit layers in the time graph. Later chapters cover how to view and manipulate additional information in the time graph (for example, keyframing attributes). Chapter 9, "Keyframe Interpolation," covers the time graph's other incarnation, the Graph Editor. **Figure 6.4** summarizes the controls covered in the following sections.

Parts of the time graph

Time ruler—Measures time horizontally (according to the time units you selected in the project preferences).

Work area start—Marks the beginning of the work area bar, which determines the portion of the composition that will be rendered during previews (see Chapter 8, "Playback, Previews, and RAM").

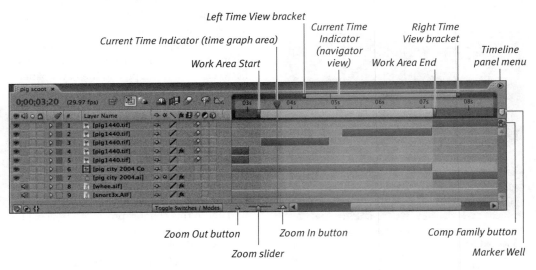

Figure 6.4 The following sections focus on the time graph area of the Timeline panel.

Work area end—Marks the end of the work area bar, which determines the portion of the composition that will be rendered during previews (see Chapter 8).

Left Time View bracket—Changes the left edge of the part of the composition visible in the main time graph. (See "The navigator view," later in this chapter.)

Right Time View bracket—Changes the right edge of the part of the composition visible in the main time graph. (See "The navigator view," later in this chapter.)

Current time indicator (CTI)—Changes the current frame of the composition in the main time graph and in the navigator view. The current time is the same in all the views of the same composition.

Timeline panel menu button—Displays a menu of functions for controlling layers and keyframes as well as accessing the Composition Settings dialog box.

Marker well—Adds markers to the time ruler. Drag a marker out of the well to add a marker or back into the well to remove it.

Comp Family button—Opens the Composition panel associated with the composition displayed in the Timeline panel.

Zoom slider—Displays the time graph in more or less detail.

Zoom In button—Displays a shorter part of the time graph in more detail.

Zoom Out button—Displays a greater part of the time graph in less detail.

THE TIME GRAPH

Navigating the Time Graph

The Timeline panel allows you to view all or part of a composition. As you arrange the layers of a composition in time, you may need to zoom into the time graph for a detailed view or zoom out for a more expansive view.

The navigator view

After Effects' Timeline panel includes a *navigator view,* located at the top of the time graph (**Figure 6.5**). The navigator view looks like a tiny version of the time graph, including a small current time indicator and small work area markers. (See Chapter 11, "Effects Fundamentals," to learn about setting the work area.) The navigator view always represents the entire duration of the composition; the white portion corresponds to the part of the composition you see in the larger main timeline. Thus, dragging the Time View brackets at either end of the white area changes the main view, and vice versa.

The navigator view helps you put the portion of the composition you see in the time graph in the context of its entire duration.

To view part of the time graph in more detail:

In the time graph area of the Timeline panel, *do any of the following* (**Figures 6.6** and **6.7**):

◆ Click the Zoom In button to view an incrementally more detailed area of the time graph.

◆ Drag the Zoom slider to the left.

◆ Drag the Left Time View bracket to the right.

◆ Drag the Right Time View bracket to the left.

◆ Press the equal sign (=) on your keyboard.

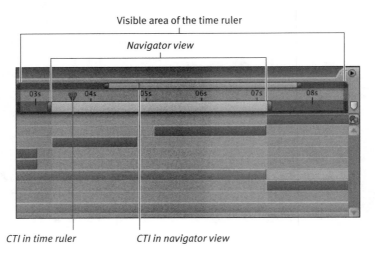

Visible area of the time ruler

Navigator view

CTI in time ruler   *CTI in navigator view*

Figure 6.5 The navigator view looks like a miniature version of the time graph. By representing the entire duration of the composition, it helps you put the area visible in the main time graph in context.

To view more of the composition in the time graph:

In the time graph area of the Timeline panel, *do any of the following:*

◆ Click the Zoom Out button to view an incrementally more detailed area of the time graph.

◆ Drag the Zoom slider to the right to view more of the time graph gradually.

◆ Drag the Left Time View bracket to the left.

◆ Drag the Right Time View bracket to the right.

◆ Press the hyphen (-) on your keyboard.

✔ Tip

■ Here's another good keyboard shortcut for zooming in and out of the time graph: Press the semicolon (;) to toggle between the frame view of the time graph and a view of the entire composition.

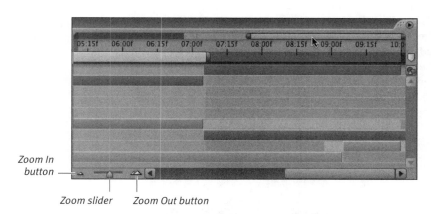

Zoom In button

Zoom slider   Zoom Out button

Figure 6.6 You can use the zoom controls at the bottom of the Timeline panel to control your view of the time graph.

Left Time View bracket   Right Time View bracket

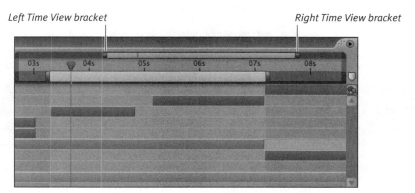

Figure 6.7 You can also drag the time brackets in the navigator view of the Timeline panel to change your view of the time graph.

129

The Layer Panel

As you learned in Chapter 3, the Layer panel resembles the Composition and Footage panels. The following sections cover the Layer panel's unique editing features, including its timeline and controls for setting In and Out points (**Figure 6.8**). Chapters 7 ("Properties and Keyframes") and 10 ("Mask Essentials") cover the Layer panel's additional features, such as its View pull-down menu and Render check box, which help you to manipulate anchor points and masks.

A Layer panel timeline corresponds to the full, unedited duration of the source footage item. As you recall, the full durations of movie and audio footage are determined by the source; the full durations of still images are determined by the preferences you set (see Chapter 2, "Importing Footage into a Project").

Note that the Layer panel has its own version of the Timeline panel's navigator view, which works in much the same way as that one. See "The navigator view," earlier in this chapter.

Using the Layer panel's controls, you can set the portion of the full duration you want to use in the composition. Time displays show the exact In point, Out point, and duration you set, which are also reflected by a duration bar.

To open a Layer panel:

◆ In the Timeline panel, double-click a layer to open a Layer panel.

Remember: Double-clicking an item in the Project panel opens a Footage panel, not a Layer panel.

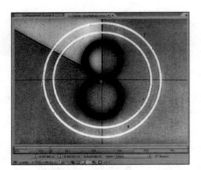

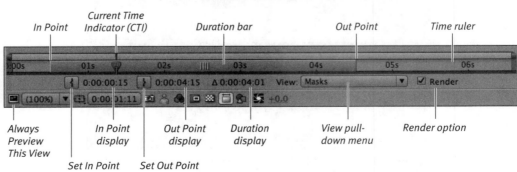

Figure 6.8 The Layer panel includes editing features not found in the Footage and Composition panels.

Parts of the Layer panel

Layer panel time ruler—Matches the full, unedited duration of the source footage.

Current time indicator (CTI)—Corresponds to the current time of the composition and the framcorree of the layer displayed in the Layer panel.

Duration bar—Corresponds to the portion of the source footage included in the composition.

Set In Point button—Marks the current frame of the layer as the first frame in the composition.

Set Out Point button—Marks the current frame of the layer as the last frame included in the composition.

Always Preview This View button—Designates the view as the default for previews (playback at or near the full frame rate) rather than whatever view is frontmost. (See Chapter 8 for more information.)

Region of Interest button—Limits the area of the image in the panel for previewing. (See Chapter 8 for more information.)

Transparency Grid button—Toggles transparent areas between a black background and a checkerboard pattern, or transparency grid. (See Chapter 4 for more information.)

Pixel Aspect Ratio Correction button—Corrects any distortion caused by differences in the layer's pixel aspect ratio (PAR) and the display's PAR. (See Chapter 4 for more information.)

View pull-down menu—Specifies whether to make additional information visible in the Layer panel, including motion-tracking points (Professional only), mask shapes, and anchor point paths. After Effects switches view options according to the task at hand. For example, selecting the Pen tool selects the layer's Mask view option automatically. (See Chapter 10 for more about masks.)

Comp Family button—Makes related composition and Timeline panels appear.

Render option—Specifies whether the window shows the layer's image only or the rendered result of any changes you make to it, such as masks and effects. (See Chapter 8 for more about previews.)

Trimming Layers

Changing a layer's In or Out point is known as *trimming*. Trimming a layer affects its duration; its timing in the composition depends on the trimming method you choose.

As you trim a layer in the Timeline panel, you also alter the time at which the layer starts or ends in the composition. This means you may have to shift the layer back to its original starting point after you trim it (**Figures 6.9** and **6.10**). Although the Timeline panel provides the most direct method of trimming, it can sometimes be difficult to use with precision.

When you trim a layer using controls in the Layer panel, the layer's duration changes accordingly but its starting point in the composition remains fixed (**Figure 6.11**). Thus, this method works best if you don't want to change the layer's start time in the composition.

Whenever you *trim in* an edit point—making the layer shorter—the unused frames of the layer appear as empty outlines extending from the duration bar's In and Out points (**Figure 6.12**). You can always restore these frames by extending the In and Out points again.

✔ Tip

- You can also remove a range of frames by specifying the Work Area (covered in Chapter 8) and choosing Edit > Lift Work Area or Edit > Extract Work Area. Both commands remove all frames under the Work Area, splitting layers if necessary. Lifting leaves a gap in time, whereas Extract shifts subsequent frames back in time to prevent a gap. Extracting is also known as ripple deleting.

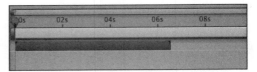

Figure 6.9 Note where the layer begins in the composition before trimming its In point.

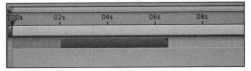

Figure 6.10 Trimming the layer's In point by dragging it in the time graph is direct and intuitive; naturally, it also moves the layer's starting point in the composition.

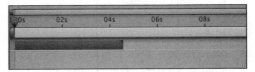

Figure 6.11 Trimming the In point using the Layer panel controls, on the other hand, doesn't affect the layer's starting point in the composition. It does, however, affect its duration.

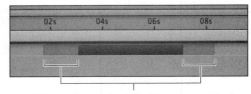

Trimmed frames (excluded from composition)

Figure 6.12 The trimmed frames of a layer appear as empty outlines extending from the layer's In and Out points. You can restore these frames at any time by extending the In or Out point again.

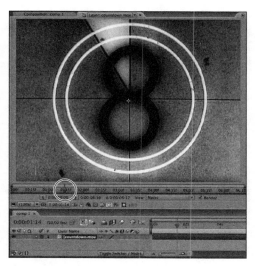

Figure 6.13 Set the current time to a frame of the layer you want to set as an edit point.

To set the In and Out points in the Layer panel:

1. Set the current time to the frame of the layer you want to trim (**Figure 6.13**).

2. To set the In point, click the Set In Point button ⬚ in the Layer panel (**Figure 6.14**).

    The current frame becomes the layer's In point, but the layer's starting time in the composition remains in place.

3. To set the Out point, click the Set Out Point button ⬚ in the Layer panel (**Figure 6.15**).

    In the Layer panel and Timeline panel, the edit points of the Layer reflect the changes you made.

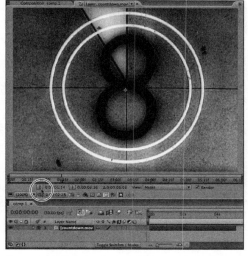

Figure 6.14 Click the Set In Point button in the Layer panel. In the Comp, the layer shifts back so the new In point starts at the same point in the comp time.

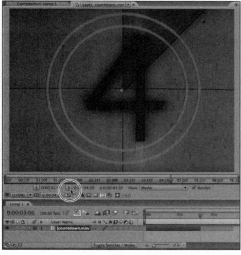

Figure 6.15 Click the Set Out Point button in the Layer panel to set the layer's Out point to the current time.

To set the In and Out points using keyboard shortcuts:

1. In the Layer panel or Timeline panel, set the current frame (**Figure 6.16**).

2. To set the In point of the layer, press Option/Alt-[.

   The In point of the layer is set to the current frame in the composition (**Figure 6.17**).

3. To set the Out point of the layer, press Option/Alt-].

   In the Layer panel and Timeline panel, the edit points reflect the changes you made. The layer's frame at the current time becomes both the layer's In point and the layer's starting point in the comp. (See **Table 6.1** for more layer editing shortcuts.)

To set the In and Out points by dragging:

In the time graph panel of the Timeline panel, *do either of the following*:

◆ To set the In point, drag the In point of a layer's duration bar (the handle at the left end of the duration bar) (**Figure 6.18**).

◆ To set the Out point, drag the Out point of a layer's duration bar (the handle at the right end of the duration bar) (**Figure 6.19**).

   Make sure you drag the ends of the layer's duration bar, not the bar itself. Otherwise, you could change the layer's position in time rather than its In or Out point.

✔ Tips

■ Pressing Shift after you begin to drag causes the In or Out point to *snap to edges*. That is, the layer's edit point behaves as though it's magnetized and aligns with the edit points of other layers, the current time indicator, and the layer and composition markers.

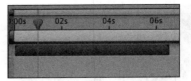

Figure 6.16 Set the current time to the frame of the layer you want to set as an edit point.

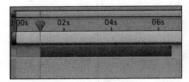

Figure 6.17 Press Option/Alt-[to set the In point of the selected layer to the current time.

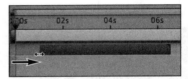

Figure 6.18 Drag the In point handle of a layer's duration bar to change both its In point and where it starts in the composition.

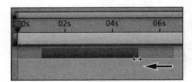

Figure 6.19 Drag the Out point handle of a layer's duration bar to change both its Out point and where it ends in the composition.

■ You can see the exact position of an edit point in time by looking at the Info panel's time display as you drag.

■ If you reach a point where you're unable to further increase a layer's duration, it means you've run out of source footage.

TRIMMING LAYERS

Figure 6.20 Drag a layer from the center portion of its duration bar...

Figure 6.21 ...to shift its position in time (without changing its duration). Press Shift after you begin dragging to activate the Snap to Edges feature.

Moving Layers in Time

When you create a layer, it begins at the current time indicator. After that, you can move its position in time either by dragging the layer's duration bar or by using the controls in the In/Out panel of the Timeline panel.

To move a layer in time by dragging:

◆ In the time graph area of the Timeline panel, drag a layer to a new position in time (**Figures 6.20** and **6.21**).

◆ Dragging a layer to the left causes the layer to begin earlier in the composition.

◆ Dragging a layer to the right causes the layer to begin later in the composition.

Make sure you drag from the middle section of the layer's duration bar; dragging either end changes the duration of the layer.

✔ Tips

■ A layer's In point can occur before the beginning of the composition, just as its Out point can occur after the end of the composition. As you would expect, any frames beyond the beginning or end of the comp won't be included in previews or output.

■ As usual, you can press Shift after you begin dragging to cause the layer to snap to edges. When you activate the Snap to Edges feature, the edges of the layer (its In and Out points) align with the edges of other layers as well as with the current time indicator as you drag them near each other. The layer also snaps to layer and composition markers.

Table 6.1

Layer Editing Shortcuts	
EDIT	SHORTCUT
Move layer's In point to CTI	[(open bracket)
Move layer's Out point to CTI	] (close bracket)
Trim layer's In point to CTI	Opt/Alt-[
Trim layer's Out point to CTI	Opt/Alt-]
Nudge layer one frame forward	Opt/Alt-Page Up
Nudge layer one frame back	Opt/Alt-Page Down

MOVING LAYERS IN TIME

Showing Numerical Editing Controls

You can view and control the timing of each layer in the timeline by revealing four columns of information:

In—The layer's starting time in the comp. Enter a value to change the layer's starting point in the comp (*not* the layer's first frame).

Out—The layer's ending time in the comp. Enter a value to set the layer's ending time in the comp (*not* the layer's last frame).

Duration—The length of the layer, expressed as a corollary of *speed*. Entering a value changes the layer's playback speed and, indirectly, its Out point.

Stretch—The layer's playback frame rate expressed as a percentage of the layer's native playback rate. Entering a value changes the layer's playback rate and, indirectly, its duration and Out point. See the next section, "Changing a Layer's Speed."

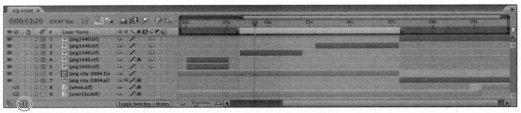

Figure 6.22 Click the In/Out/Duration/Stretch button to change the In/Out/Duration/Stretch panel from hidden...

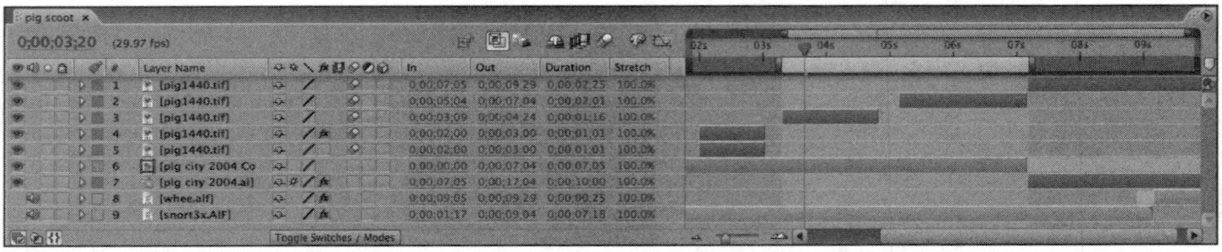

Figure 6.23 ...to visible. Click the button again to hide the panel.

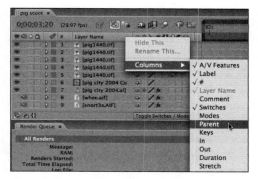

Figure 6.24 You can also Control-click/right-click any panel to access a context menu that allows you to show or hide a panel in the Timeline panel.

The timeline lets you expand all four columns as a set or each one individually.

Because this book covers several other, more convenient ways to move and trim layers, using the In and Out panels won't be covered in detail. However, turn to the next section to find out how to use the Duration and Stretch columns.

To show and hide the In, Out, Duration, and Stretch columns:

◆ *Do either of the following:*

▲ In the Timeline panel, click the In/Out/Duration/Stretch button ❬❭ to reveal the In/Out/Duration/Stretch panel; click the button again to hide the panel (**Figures 6.22** and **6.23**).

▲ Control-click/right-click any panel of the Timeline panel, and choose the panel you want to view from the context menu (**Figure 6.24**).

Changing a Layer's Speed

Changing a layer's playback speed is yet another feature After Effects shares with typical non-linear editing programs. However, you should note a crucial difference between how you set the values in those programs and in After Effects. In many non-linear editing programs, you enter a *speed*: A value greater than 100 percent *increases* the speed, and a value less than 100 percent decreases the speed. In After Effects, you can enter a *stretch factor* value: A stretch factor greater than 100 percent *decreases* the speed of a layer (stretching, or increasing, its duration), and a stretch factor less than 100 percent *increases* the speed of a layer.

Entering a negative value reverses the playback direction of the layer—and also reverses the order of its property keyframes. (For more about properties and keyframes, see Chapter 7.) To reverse a layer's speed without also reversing its keyframes, you can use the Time Remapping feature, explained in Chapter 14, "More Layer Techniques." (Time remapping also lets you adjust the playback speed of a layer over time or create a freeze-frame effect.)

✔ Tips

- You can also perform a slip edit by dragging the layer's "hidden" trimmed frames (you can see their outlines extending beyond the layer's In and Out handles).

- To review how to perform insert and overlay edits, see Chapter 4, "Compositions."

- Those who use non-linear editing software know that the counterpart to the slip edit is the *slide edit*. Because each layer in After Effects occupies a separate track, slide editing is an inherent feature: Simply drag the layer to a new position in the time ruler.

To change the playback speed of a layer:

1. *Do one of the following:*
   - ▲ In the Timeline panel, click the Duration display or Stretch display for a layer (**Figure 6.25**).
   - ▲ In the Timeline panel, select a layer and choose Layer > Time Stretch.

   The Time Stretch dialog box opens (**Figure 6.26**).

2. In the Stretch section, *do either of the following:*
   - ▲ For New Duration, enter a new duration for the layer.
   - ▲ For Stretch Factor, enter the percentage change of the layer's duration.

   To slow playback speed, enter a duration greater than that of the original or a stretch factor greater than 100 percent. To increase playback speed, enter a duration less than that of the original or a stretch factor less than 100 percent. Enter a negative value to reverse a layer's playback direction.

3. In the Hold In Place section of the Time Stretch dialog box, *select one of the following* options to determine the position of the layer when its speed and duration change:

   Layer In-point—Maintains the layer's starting point position in the composition

   Current Frame—Moves the layer's In and Out points while maintaining the frame's position at the current time indicator

   Layer Out-point—Maintains the layer's ending point position in the composition

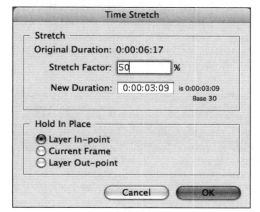

Figure 6.25 To change the speed of a layer, click its Duration or Stretch display.

Figure 6.26 In the Time Stretch dialog box, enter a new duration or stretch factor to change the speed of the layer. In the Hold In Place section, choose which frame of the layer will maintain its position in the time graph.

4. Click OK to close the Time Stretch dialog box.

The selected layer's speed, duration, and placement in time reflect your changes. However, the range of footage frames you specified to include—the layer's In and Out points—remain the same.

✔ Tips

- To quickly reverse a layer's playback (a stretch factor of –100 percent), select the layer and press Command-Option-R (Mac) or Ctrl-Alt-R (Windows).

- You can freeze-frame the current frame of the selected layer by choosing Layer > Time > Freeze Frame. This command automatically applies the appropriate time remapping settings. See Chapter 9 for more about time remapping.

CHANGING A LAYER'S SPEED

Performing a Slip Edit

After Effects includes another editing feature common to non-linear editing programs: *slip edits*.

When you're working with layers created from motion footage, you'll find that you often need to change a portion of video without altering its position or duration in the time ruler. Although you can do this by reopening the Layer panel and setting new In and Out points, you must be careful to set edit points that result in the same duration. By using a slip edit, however, you can achieve the same result in a single step.

To slip a layer:

1. In the Tools panel, select the Pan Behind tool  (**Figure 6.27**).

2. Position the mouse over a layer created from motion footage.

   The mouse pointer becomes a Slip Edit icon 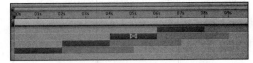 (**Figure 6.28**).

3. *Do either of the following:*
   - ▲ **Drag left** to slip the footage left, using frames that come later in the footage.
   - ▲ **Drag right** to slip the footage right, using frames that come earlier in the footage.

   The In and Out points of the source footage change by the same amount, which means the layer maintains its duration and position in the time ruler. As you drag, you can see the "hidden" footage extending from beyond the layer's In and Out points (**Figure 6.29**).

Figure 6.27 Select the Pan Behind tool.

Figure 6.28 When you position the mouse over a layer created from motion footage, the mouse pointer becomes a Slip Edit tool.

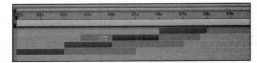

Figure 6.29 Dragging with the Slip Edit tool changes the portion of the motion footage used without changing its duration or position in the time ruler.

Sequencing and Overlapping Layers

Although you might not choose After Effects for editing, per se, you may find yourself starting many projects by creating a simple sequence. Fortunately, After Effects automates this common request with its Sequence and Overlap features.

The Sequence command quickly places selected layers one after another in the time graph, seamlessly aligning their Out and In points so that the layers play back in an uninterrupted sequence (**Figure 6.30**).

The Overlap option also places the selected layers one after another in the time graph—but in this case, they overlap by a specified amount of time (**Figure 6.31**). Using the Overlap option prepares layers for transition effects; it can even automatically create cross-fades between layers. (You'll learn more about creating transitions and other keyframed changes in Chapter 9.)

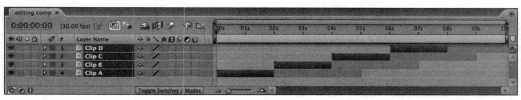

Figure 6.30 The Sequence command places selected layers one after another in the time graph in an uninterrupted sequence.

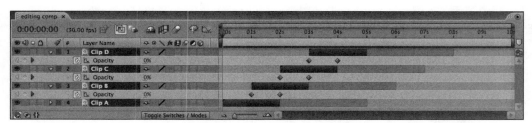

Figure 6.31 The Overlap option places the selected layers in a sequence that overlaps by a specified amount of time. It can automatically set keyframes for simple cross-fades between the layers.

To arrange layers in a sequence:

1. In the Timeline panel, select the layers you want to sequence (**Figure 6.32**).

2. Choose Animation > Keyframe Assistant > Sequence Layers (**Figure 6.33**).
   The Sequence Layers dialog box opens (**Figure 6.34**).

3. Make sure Overlap is unchecked.

4. Click OK to close the dialog box.
   The selected layers are arranged in sequence, top layer first (**Figure 6.35**).

Figure 6.32 Select the layers you want to sequence.

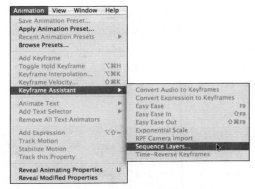

Figure 6.33 Choose Animation › Keyframe Assistant › Sequence Layers.

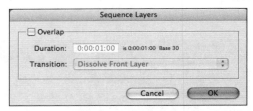

Figure 6.34 In the Sequence Layers dialog box, make sure Overlap is unchecked...

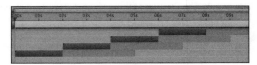

Figure 6.35 ...to arrange the selected layers into a simple sequence.

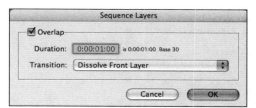

Figure 6.36 To overlap the layers of a sequence, check Overlap in the Sequence Layers dialog box. For Duration, enter the amount of time you want the layers to overlap.

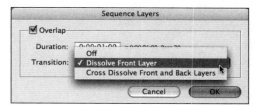

Figure 6.37 In the Transition pull-down menu, choose the appropriate option.

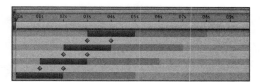

Figure 6.38 The selected layers are arranged in an overlapping sequence.

To arrange layers in an overlapping sequence:

1. In the Timeline panel, select the layers you want to arrange in an overlapping sequence.

2. Choose Animation > Keyframe Assistant > Sequence Layers.

   The Sequence Layers dialog box opens.

3. Check Overlap (**Figure 6.36**).

4. In the Duration field, enter the amount of time that the layers should overlap.

5. *Choose one of the following* cross-fade options from the Transition pull-down menu (**Figure 6.37**):

   ▲ **Off**—For no cross-fade

   ▲ **Dissolve Front Layer**—To automatically fade out the end of each preceding layer

   ▲ **Cross Dissolve Front and Back Layers**—To fade out the end of each preceding layer automatically, and to fade up the beginning of each succeeding layer

6. Click OK to close the dialog box.

   The selected layers are arranged in an overlapping sequence (top layer first) and use the cross-fade option you specified (**Figure 6.38**).

Duplicating Layers

As you learned in Chapter 4, you can add a footage item to one or more compositions as many times as you like, creating a new layer each time. However, it's often easier to duplicate a layer that's already in a composition, particularly when you want to use its edit points or other properties (such as masks, transformations, effects, and layer modes). When you create a duplicate, it appears just above the original layer in the stacking order. The duplicate uses the same name as the original, unless you specified a custom name for the original layer. When the original layer uses a custom name, duplicates have a number appended to the name; subsequent duplicates are numbered incrementally.

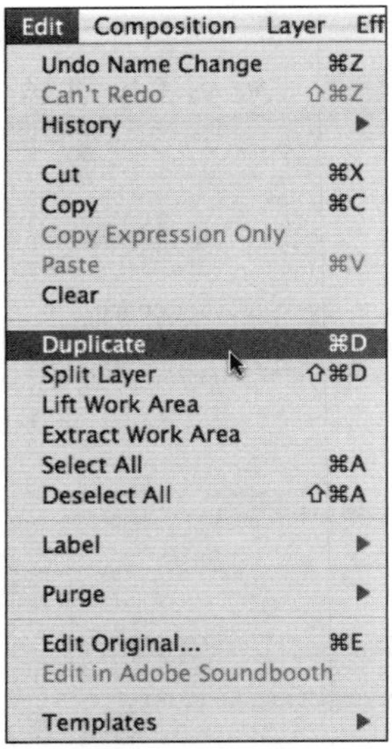

To duplicate a layer:

1. In the Timeline panel, select a layer.

2. Choose Edit > Duplicate, or press Command/Ctrl-D (**Figure 6.39**).

   A copy of the layer appears above the original layer in the stacking order (**Figure 6.40**). The copy is selected; you may want to rename the new layer (as described in "Naming Layers" in Chapter 5).

Edit	Composition	Layer	Eff
Undo Name Change			⌘Z
Can't Redo			⇧⌘Z
History			▶
Cut			⌘X
Copy			⌘C
Copy Expression Only			
Paste			⌘V
Clear			
Duplicate			⌘D
Split Layer			⇧⌘D
Lift Work Area			
Extract Work Area			
Select All			⌘A
Deselect All			⇧⌘A
Label			▶
Purge			▶
Edit Original...			⌘E
Edit in Adobe Soundbooth			
Templates			▶

Figure 6.39 To duplicate a layer, select the layer and choose Edit > Duplicate, or press Command/Ctrl-D.

Figure 6.40 A duplicate layer appears in the composition, distinguished by an incrementally higher number (in this case, "2") after its name.

Splitting Layers

You can set a preference to determine which layer—the layer before the split point or the layer after the split point—is higher in the stacking order.

To split a layer:

1. In the Timeline panel, select a layer.

2. Set the current time to the frame at which you want to split the layer (**Figure 6.41**).

3. Choose Edit > Split Layer, or press Shift-Command-D (Mac) or Shift-Ctrl-D (Windows) (**Figure 6.42**).

   The layer splits in two, creating one layer that ends at the current time indicator and another that begins at the current time indicator (**Figure 6.43**). The layer that becomes higher in the stacking order depends on the preference you specify in the General Preferences dialog box.

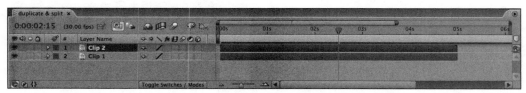

Figure 6.41 Set the current time to the frame at which you want to split the selected layer.

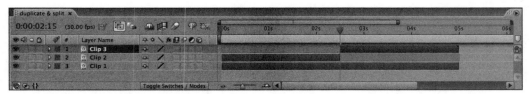

Figure 6.42 Choose Edit > Split Layer.

Figure 6.43 The selected layer splits into two layers at the current time.

Using Markers

Like most non-linear editing programs,
After Effects enables you to mark important
points in time with a visible stamp. *Markers*
allow you to identify music beats visually
and to synchronize visual effects with sound
effects. They can also help you quickly move
the current time to particular points in the
composition. You can add as many as ten
numbered markers to the time graph. And
in individual layers, you can add any number
of markers, which can include text comments to help you identify them. Because
markers are for personal reference, they only
appear in the time ruler and layer duration
bars; they don't appear in the Composition
panel or in previews or renders.

In addition to text comments, layer markers
can also contain Web or chapter links. These
links are retained when you export to certain Web- or DVD-friendly formats. When a
marker containing a link is reached during
playback, a Web link automatically opens as
a Web page in your browser; a chapter link
cues a QuickTime movie or DVD to a specified chapter. Check the After Effects Help
system for more detailed information on
these specialized features.

To add a composition marker by dragging:

◆ In the Timeline panel, drag a composition time marker from the marker well
to the desired point in the time graph
(**Figure 6.44**).

A marker appears in the time ruler of the
Timeline panel (**Figure 6.45**).

Figure 6.44 To add a composition marker, drag a
marker from the marker well...

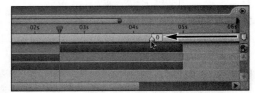

Figure 6.45 ...and drop the marker at the frame you
want to mark in the time ruler. Watch the current time
display of the Timeline panel to help accurately place
the marker.

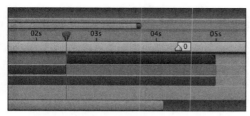

Figure 6.46 You can also place a composition marker by setting the current time...

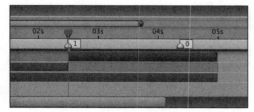

Figure 6.47 ...and then pressing Shift and a number on the main keyboard to place the numbered marker at the current time.

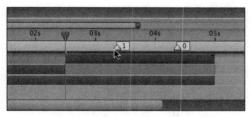

Figure 6.48 You can drag a composition marker to a new position in the time ruler.

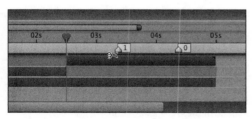

Figure 6.49 To remove a composition marker, drag it to the extreme right, until the marker well is highlighted and the marker disappears.

To add a composition marker at the current time indicator:

1. Move the current time indicator to the frame you want to mark in the composition (**Figure 6.46**).

2. Press Shift and a number on the main keyboard (not the numeric keypad).

A marker with the number you pressed appears in the time ruler of the Timeline panel (**Figure 6.47**).

To move a composition marker:

◆ Drag a composition marker to a new position in the time ruler of the Timeline panel (**Figure 6.48**).

To move the current time indicator to a composition marker:

◆ Press the number of a composition marker on the main keyboard (not the numeric keypad).

The current time indicator moves to the composition marker with the number you pressed.

To remove a composition marker:

◆ Drag a composition marker to the right until the marker well is highlighted and the marker disappears from the time ruler (**Figure 6.49**).

To add a layer marker:

1. Select the layer to which you want to add a marker.

2. Set the current time to the frame to which you want to add a marker (**Figure 6.50**).

3. *Do one of the following:*
   - ▲ Choose Layer > Add Marker (**Figure 6.51**).
   - ▲ Press the asterisk (*) on the numeric keypad (not the main keyboard).

   A marker appears on the layer's duration bar at the current time indicator (**Figure 6.52**).

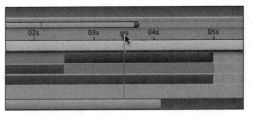

Figure 6.50 To add a layer marker, select a layer and set the current time to the frame you want to mark.

Figure 6.51 Choose Layer > Add Marker, or press the asterisk on the numeric keypad.

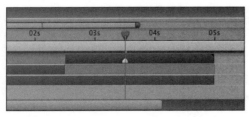

Figure 6.52 The marker appears in the duration bar of the selected layer at the current time indicator.

USING MARKERS

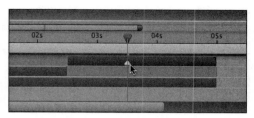

Figure 6.53 Double-click a layer marker to add a name to the marker. Make sure to double-click the marker, not the layer (or the marker name, if it already has one).

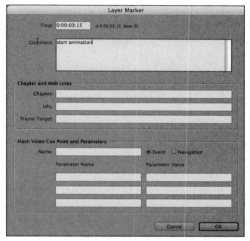

Figure 6.54 In the Marker dialog box, enter a comment for the marker.

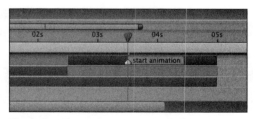

Figure 6.55 The comment you specified appears next to the marker.

To add a layer marker comment:

1. Double-click a layer marker in a layer's duration bar (**Figure 6.53**).

A Marker dialog box opens. If a Layer panel opens, you must have double-clicked the layer's duration bar or marker name rather than the marker itself.

2. In the Marker dialog box, enter a comment for the marker in the Comment field (**Figure 6.54**).

You can also add chapter links or Web links if your output format supports these features.

3. Click OK to close the dialog box.

The comment you specified appears next to the layer marker (**Figure 6.55**).

To move a layer marker:

◆ Drag a layer marker to a new position in the layer's duration bar (**Figure 6.56**).

To remove a layer marker:

◆ Command/Ctrl-click a layer marker.

The mouse pointer becomes a Scissors icon ✄ when you position it over the layer marker. The layer marker disappears from the layer's duration bar.

✔ Tips

■ When a composition is nested and becomes a layer, its composition markers appear as layer markers. However, changing its markers as a layer doesn't affect its markers as a comp. In other words, composition markers are converted into layer markers, but they don't retain a relationship thereafter. For example, if you remove a nested comp's layer marker, the corresponding marker in the original comp remains.

■ You can add layer markers on the fly as you preview audio. This makes it especially easy to mark the beats of music or other audio. Press the decimal point (.) on the numeric keypad to preview audio only. As the audio previews, press the asterisk (*) key on the numeric keypad. (Adobe Premiere Pro users should recognize this technique.)

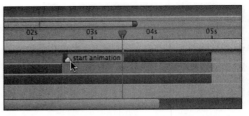

Figure 6.56 Drag a layer marker to a new frame in the layer. Make sure to grab the marker, not its name or the layer's duration bar.

USING MARKERS

PROPERTIES AND KEYFRAMES

Once they see what After Effects can do, most folks can't wait to take a closer look at the program that produces such artful results. Upon closer inspection, however, it's easy to recoil from the cryptic array of controls that look more like the tools of a scientist than those of an artist.

But don't let a few numbers and graphs intimidate you! This chapter fearlessly unveils layer properties and demystifies animation. Once you understand how to define properties, you can extend a few simple techniques to control practically any property of any layer in a composition. Having conquered that paper tiger, you'll be ready to animate those properties using something called *keyframes*.

As any scientist or artist can tell you, it's important to have full control over the variables, but some of the best innovations are arrived at randomly. By generating random variations on specified properties, After Effects' new Brainstorm feature lets you freely experiment and achieve results you might not have otherwise—in a manner not unlike a plant breeder or a Jackson Pollack. You'll find that the techniques you learn in this chapter are fundamental, and you'll be able to apply them to the features covered in subsequent chapters, from masks to effects to 3D layers. But first, you'll want to see the animation in action, using techniques covered in Chapter 8, "Playback, Previews, and RAM." And then you should build on the core keyframing techniques presented in Chapter 9, "Keyframe Interpolation." You'll realize that animating in After Effects isn't rocket science, after all. But mastering it is still an art.

Layer Property Types

A *property* refers to any of a layer's visual or audio characteristics to which you can assign different values over time. Properties fall into these main categories: masks, effects, and transform (**Figure 7.1**). In addition, layers that contain audio include an Audio property, and 3D layers include a Material Options property. (For more information on the special characteristics of 3D layers, see Chapter 15, "3D Layers.")

The order in which these categories are listed reflects the order in which After Effects renders each layer's masks, effects, transform, and audio properties. Although you don't need to concern yourself with rendering order now, it does become important as your animations grow in complexity.

Masks

Like the acetate layers used in traditional compositing, masks let you include some portions of an image and exclude others. They also make it possible for you to apply effects to selected portions of layers.

You can apply one or several masks to each layer in a composition and then define the way those masks interact. Not only can you control the shape and feather of a mask, you can also animate these attributes over time. Chapter 10, "Mask Essentials," describes using masks in more detail.

Effects

Effects include a wide range of options for modifying sound and images. You can use them to make simple adjustments—such as correcting color or filtering audio—or to make more dramatic changes, such as distorting and stylizing. *Keying effects* help to composite images, and *transition effects* blend one layer into another. You can even use effects to generate visual elements such as text, light, and particles.

You can add to your effects repertoire by using After Effects Pro or by downloading third-party plug-ins. Chapter 11, "Effects Fundamentals," provides a more detailed introduction about the use of effects.

Transform properties

Although you may not choose to apply any masks or effects to the layers of your compositions, you must still define their basic properties, including position, scale, rotation, and opacity—known as *transform properties*. This chapter focuses on these essential layer properties as they relate to 2D layers. (For a detailed discussion of the transform properties of 3D layers, see Chapter 15, "3D Layers.")

Audio properties

Layers that contain audio display an Audio property in the layer outline. Because only images can have masks or transform properties, audio-only layers contain only the Effects and Audio property categories. The Audio category includes a Levels property to control audio volume as well as a waveform display. Along with transform properties, this chapter explains how to set audio levels.

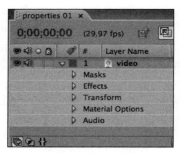

Figure 7.1 There are three major categories of visual properties: masks, effects, and transform. Layers with an audio track contain an Audio property; layers you designate as 3D have a Material Options property.

Viewing Properties

You can view any combination of layer properties in the Timeline panel in what's called a *layer outline* (**Figure 7.2**). That is, each layer works like the heading of an outline: Expanding the layer reveals property headings, which in turn can be expanded to reveal individual properties. (The property headings that are revealed depend on the layer; a layer without masks or audio won't include those headings in the outline.) Using keyboard shortcuts, you can reveal properties selectively and prevent the outline from becoming long and unwieldy.

Revealing a property also displays its current value and its *property track*, an area under the time ruler that shows the property's keyframes. Keyframes, as you'll learn, indicate points at which you define a property's values in order to make them change over time. In other words, the property track is where you can view and control animation.

To fine-tune an animation—particularly between the keyframes—you can go in for an even more detailed view using the Graph Editor (**Figure 7.3**). As its name suggests, the Graph Editor lets you see selected property values as a graph. You can manipulate the graph directly, manually changing not only the keyframes, but also how the values change between keyframes (the interpolated values).

Layer outline   Keyframes   Property track

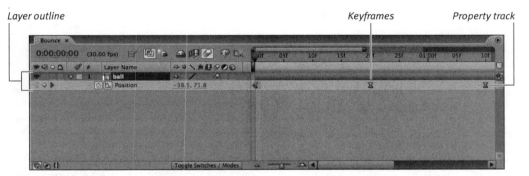

Figure 7.2 Expanding a layer reveals its properties in outline form, or layer outline. Appearing next to the property's name are its current value (under the layer switches) and keyframes (under the time ruler).

Property graph   Keyframe   Graph Editor

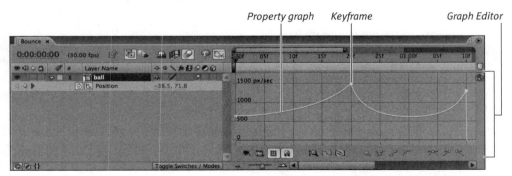

Figure 7.3 You can toggle the area under the time ruler to the Graph Editor. The Graph Editor depicts property values in graph form, allowing you to adjust both keyframed values and the manner in which After Effects calculates values between keyframes.

But don't let yourself get overwhelmed by unfamiliar terminology or seemingly complex choices. For the moment, rest assured that the Timeline panel allows you to reveal the properties you want at the level of detail you need. This chapter covers setting property values and basic keyframing. Chapter 9, "Keyframe Interpolation," covers fine-tuning animation in the Graph Editor.

To expand or collapse a layer outline by clicking:

◆ In the Timeline panel, *do any of the following:*

▲ To expand the first level of property headings, click the triangle to the left of a layer (**Figure 7.4**).

The triangle spins clockwise to point down, revealing the first level of the layer outline.

▲ To further expand the outline, click the triangle to the left of a property heading (**Figure 7.5**).

The triangle spins clockwise to point down, revealing the next level of the outline.

▲ To collapse an expanded layer outline heading, click the triangle again.

The triangle spins counterclockwise, hiding that level of the layer outline.

✔ Tips

■ You can expand the outline for multiple layers simultaneously by selecting more than one layer before expanding the outline. Expanding the outline for one selected layer expands all selected layers (**Figure 7.6**).

■ There are several ways to expand and collapse a layer outline. Although clicking the Timeline panel may be the most intuitive method, doing so often reveals more than you need. Keyboard shortcuts let you expand layer properties selectively.

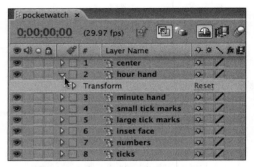

Figure 7.4 Click the triangle to the left of a layer to reveal the first level of properties.

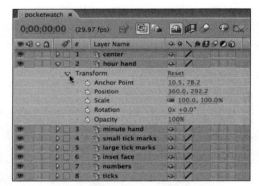

Figure 7.5 Continue to expand the outline by clicking the triangles. Click the triangles again to collapse the outline.

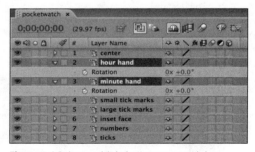

Figure 7.6 Select multiple layers to expand the outline for all of them at once.

Table 7.1

Viewing Layer Properties	
TO EXPAND/COLLAPSE TRANSFORM	PRESS THIS SHORTCUT
Anchor Point	A
Position	P
Scale	S
Rotation	R
Opacity	T
Material Options	AA (3D layers)
MASK	
Mask Shape	M
Mask Feather	F
Mask Opacity	TT
Mask Properties	MM
EFFECTS	
Effects	E
Paint Effects	EE
AUDIO	
Audio Levels	L
Audio Waveform	LL
HEADINGS	
Add/remove from outline	Shift-property shortcut
All animated	U (keyframed values)
All modified	UU

To view layer properties using keyboard shortcuts

◆ To expand the layer outline by using keyboard shortcuts, select one or more layers, and use the appropriate keyboard shortcut (see **Table 7.1**).

✔ Tip

■ Some shortcuts work differently for light and camera layers (covered in Chapter 15, "3D Layers"). Because lights aren't visible (only their effects are), pressing T reveals a light layer's Intensity property. For both lights and cameras, A reveals the Point of Interest property, and R reveals the Orientation property.

VIEWING PROPERTIES

Setting Global vs. Animated Property Values

Now that you know how to view layer properties, you can set their values. The following sections describe how to set property values globally—that is, how to set a single value for the duration of the layer. Then, you'll animate properties by setting different values at different points in time. But before we continue, it may be helpful to understand a few basic differences between global and animated properties.

As you proceed, you'll notice that a property that has a *global*, or unchanging, value has an I-beam icon at its current time in the time graph, and the Stopwatch icon next to the property's name appears deselected (**Figure 7.7**).

An animated property, in contrast, displays keyframes, which designate values at specific points in time, and an activated Stopwatch icon (**Figure 7.8**). You can set global properties without regard to the current time, but you must always specify the current frame before setting an animated property. Although global and animated properties look different in the timeline, you always reveal and use property controls the same way.

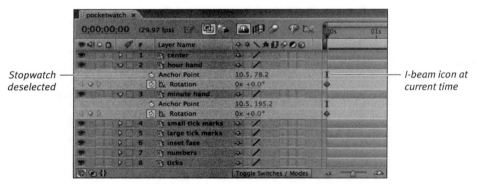

Figure 7.7 A deselected Stopwatch icon and an I-beam icon in the selected property track identify a static property.

Stopwatch deselected

I-beam icon at current time

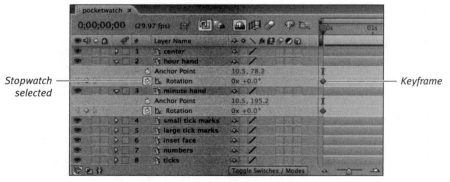

Figure 7.8 An activated Stopwatch icon and keyframe icons in the property track identify an animated property.

Stopwatch selected

Keyframe

Viewing Spatial Controls in the Comp Panel

As you know, the Composition panel lets you view how layers will appear in your final output. It also provides controls for the spatial properties of layers, including the following:

Handles appear at the perimeter of the layer, at each compass point. Dragging them affects the scale of the layer.

Masks appear as editable, color-coded mask paths. You can use them to crop out some parts of the layer while leaving other parts visible.

Effect controls show the spatial controls of many effects, such as the end points of path text.

Keyframes show the position keyframes you set as marks in the motion path. You can move and add keyframes directly in the motion path.

Motion paths show a layer's position as it changes over time as a dotted line. You can't change the path directly, but you can change the keyframes that define the ends of the line segments, as well as the tangents that define the line.

Motion path tangents control the curve of the motion path by affecting how the position values are interpreted between keyframes. They can be extended from keyframes and dragged directly to alter the motion path.

By default, the Composition panel displays layer and effect controls whenever a layer is selected (**Figure 7.9**). You can also toggle these view options on and off in the View Options dialog box or, in some instances, by using buttons in the Composition panel. You'll appreciate each control more fully as you employ corresponding techniques explained later in this and future chapters.

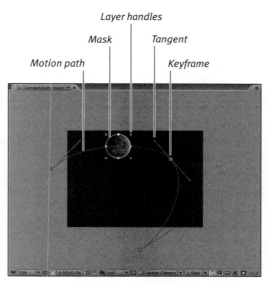

Layer handles

Mask   Tangent

Motion path   Keyframe

Figure 7.9 By default, the Composition panel displays spatial information and controls for selected layers, such as layer handles, keyframes, and the motion path.

To view layer and effect controls in the Composition panel:

1. In the Composition panel's pull-down menu, choose View Options (**Figure 7.10**). The View Options dialog box appears.

2. Select Layer Controls, and then specify the layer controls you want to make visible in the Composition panel.

   A check indicates that the controls are visible in the Composition panel when a layer is selected; no check indicates that the controls are hidden (**Figure 7.11**).

✔ Tips

- You can specify whether the motion path is visible and how many keyframes it shows at once in the Display pane of the Preferences dialog box.

- A layer's effect point controls (if present) are covered in more detail in the section "Setting an Effect Point," in Chapter 11.

- Instead of selecting Masks in the View Options dialog box, you can use the Toggle View Mask button ⬚ at the bottom of the Composition panel.

- Cameras and spotlights, are covered in Chapter 15, "3D Layers."

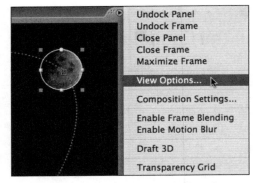

Figure 7.10 In the Composition panel menu, choose View Options.

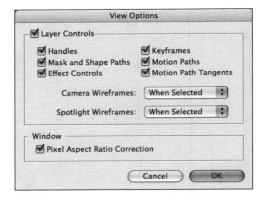

Figure 7.11 In the View Options dialog box, specify the layer controls you want to be visible in the Composition panel.

Transform Properties

Although a layer may not use masks or effects, its transform properties—the anchor point, position, scale, rotation, and opacity—are fundamental (**Figure 7.12**). When you create a layer, you actively set its position, either by dragging to the timeline or to the Composition icon to center it, or by dragging to the Composition panel to place it manually. The other transform properties all have default initial values. The following sections describe each transform property and how to change its values.

Keep in mind that even though the following sections focus on transform properties, you employ similar techniques to set values for all types of layer properties.

Anchor point

After Effects calculates the position, scale, and rotation of a layer by its anchor point. The anchor point defines the position of a layer, the point around which a layer is scaled, and the pivot point of the layer's rotation. The placement of the anchor point relative to the layer image can mean the difference between animating, say, a propeller or a pendulum.

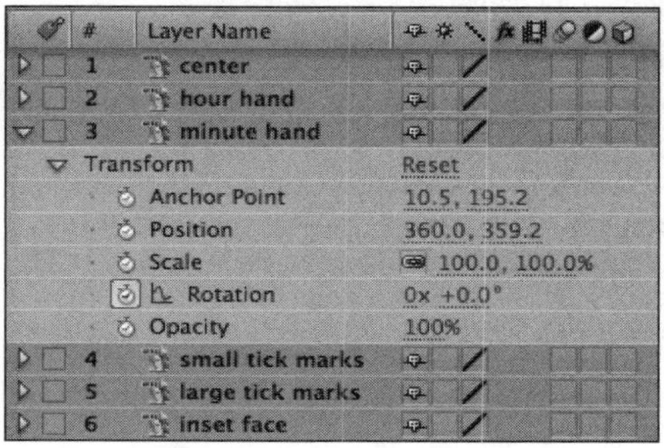

By default, a layer's anchor point is positioned in the center of the layer (**Figure 7.13**). You can move the anchor point by using controls in the Layer panel or by using the Pan Behind tool in the Composition panel.

When you change the anchor point in the Layer panel, it may appear that you've also changed the layer's position in the Composition panel. Actually, the layer's Position property remains the same; you simply changed the spot in the layer that determines its position in the composition.

Use the Layer panel to change the anchor point if you haven't already positioned the layer relative to other layers, or if you prefer to manipulate the layer in its own panel.

If you want to change a layer's anchor point without disturbing the layer's position in the composition, use the Pan Behind tool. Using the Pan Behind tool to drag the anchor point in the Composition panel recalculates the layer's position value to compensate for the new anchor point value. This way, the layer maintains its relative position in the composition.

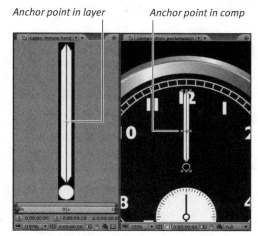

Figure 7.12 Although a layer may not use masks or effects, each of its transform properties has a value—either by default or as you choose to set them.

Figure 7.13 Typically, the anchor point is located at the center of a layer. After Effects uses the anchor point to calculate position, rotation, and scale.

To change the anchor point in the Layer panel:

1. In the Timeline panel or Composition panel, double-click a layer.

   A Layer panel appears.

2. In the Layer panel's View menu, choose Anchor Point Path (**Figure 7.14**).

   The layer's anchor point icon appears at its current position. When the anchor point's position is animated, a dotted line represents its motion path.

3. In the image area of the Layer panel, drag the anchor point to the position you want (**Figure 7.15**).

   Because the anchor point maintains its position in the Composition panel, the image in the Comp panel moves relative to the anchor point in the Layer panel (**Figure 7.16**).

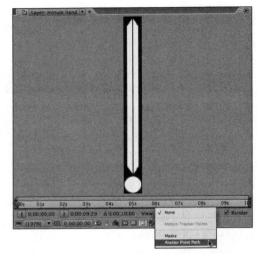

Figure 7.14 In the Layer panel's View menu, choose Anchor Point Path.

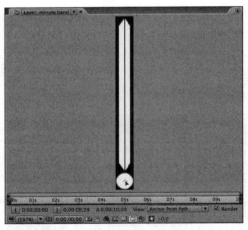

Figure 7.15 When you move an anchor point in a Layer panel...

Figure 7.16 ...the anchor point maintains its position in the comp. Here, the minute hand moves up as the anchor point is moved down to its proper point in the layer.

Figure 7.17 To move the anchor point without disturbing the arrangement of the layers, select the Pan Behind tool.

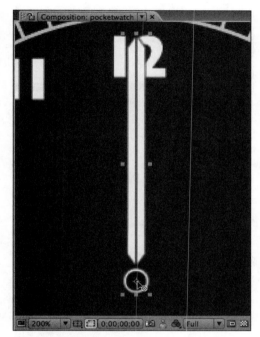

Figure 7.18 Using the Pan Behind tool recalculates the layer's position as you move the anchor point in the Composition panel. This moves the anchor point without disturbing the layer's placement.

To change the anchor point without moving the layer in the composition:

1. Select a layer in the composition.

2. If the selected layer's anchor point isn't visible in the Composition panel, choose View Options in the Composition panel menu and select Handles.

3. In the Tools panel, select the Pan Behind tool (**Figure 7.17**).

4. In the Composition panel, drag the anchor point to a new position (**Figure 7.18**). (Make sure to drag the anchor point, not the layer itself.)

   The anchor point and position values for the layer change, so the layer maintains its relative position in the Composition panel.

✔ Tips

- When importing a layered file as a composition, you can opt to import layers at each layer's size or at the document's size. The choice you make helps determine the anchor point's initial position relative to the layer's image. See Chapter 2, "Importing Footage into a Project," for more information.

- You can use the Pan Behind tool to change a layer's position relative to its mask. See Chapter 10 for more information.

TRANSFORM PROPERTIES

Position

Setting a layer's position places its anchor point in the two-dimensional space of the composition. The exact position of a layer is expressed in (X, Y) coordinates, where the top-left corner of the composition is (0, 0). (Moving the zero point of the rulers doesn't change the coordinate system.) You can position a layer inside or outside the visible area of the composition. (Position and orientation properties for 3D layers are discussed in Chapter 15.)

To change a layer's position in the Composition panel:

1. Select a layer in the Composition or Timeline panel.

2. In the Composition panel, drag the layer to the position you want (**Figure 7.19**).

   To move a layer offscreen, drag it to the pasteboard, or workspace, outside the visible area of the Composition panel.

   The layer is placed at the position you chose. If the Stopwatch icon hasn't been activated for the layer, the layer will remain at this position for its entire duration. If the Stopwatch is active, a position keyframe is created at this frame.

✔ Tips

- As you'll recall from Chapter 4, "Compositions," dragging a footage item to the Timeline panel or a Composition icon into the Project panel centers the layer automatically.

- Use the Info panel to view the exact X and Y coordinates of the layer as you move it. If you set a custom zero point for the rulers, look at the X1 and Y1 display to see the coordinates in terms of the rulers you set.

Figure 7.19 You can drag selected layers to new positions.

Subpixel Positioning

When you set a layer to Draft quality, After Effects calculates the position, rotation, and scale (or any effect that moves the pixels of an image) by using whole pixels. When layers are set to Best quality, however, these values are calculated to the thousandth of a pixel, or on a *subpixel* basis. The more you zoom in to the Composition panel, the greater the precision with which you can move a layer.

Because subpixel positioning allows layers to move with a precision greater than the resolution of the composition, movement appears much smoother than when you're not using subpixel positioning. You can see the difference by contrasting the movement of layers set to Draft quality with the same movement set to Best quality.

Subpixel positioning also requires more precise calculations, which means it takes After Effects longer to render images. Thus, you may want to do much of your work in Draft quality and then switch to Best quality when you're ready to fine-tune.

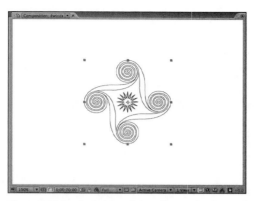

Figure 7.20 A selected layer's handles can be dragged to scale it...

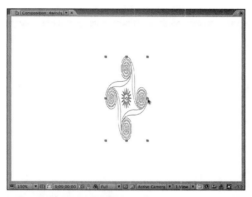

Figure 7.21 ...horizontally...

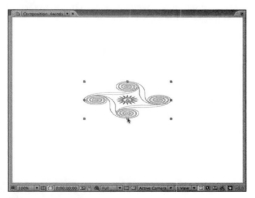

Figure 7.22 ...vertically...

Scale

By default, a layer is set to 100 percent of its original size, or scale. You scale a layer around its anchor point. In other words, the anchor point serves as the mathematical center of a change in size. When you scale a layer by dragging, you'll notice how the handles of the layer seem to stretch from the anchor point.

Remember that bitmapped images look blocky and pixelated when scaled much beyond 100 percent. When you scale path-based images beyond 100 percent, you can use the Continuously Rasterize switch to help maintain image quality. Review Chapter 2 if you need more information about image size and rasterization; see Chapter 15 for more information about how the Scale property differs for 3D layers.

To scale a layer by dragging:

1. Select a layer, and make sure its layer handles are visible in the Composition panel (see "Viewing Spatial Controls in the Comp Panel," earlier in this chapter) (**Figure 7.20**).

2. In the Composition panel, *do any of the following:*
   ▲ To scale the layer horizontally only, drag the center-left or center-right handle (**Figure 7.21**).
   ▲ To scale the layer vertically only, drag the center-bottom or the center-top handle (**Figure 7.22**).
   ▲ To scale the layer horizontally and vertically, drag a corner handle.

continues on next page

TRANSFORM PROPERTIES

▲ To scale the layer while maintaining its proportions, press Shift as you drag a corner handle (**Figure 7.23**).

▲ To flip a layer, drag one side of the layer's bounding box past the other side (**Figure 7.24**).

3. Release the mouse.

In the Composition panel, the layer appears with the scale you set. If the Stopwatch icon hasn't been activated for the layer, the layer will retain this scale for its duration. If the Stopwatch is active, a scale keyframe is created at this frame.

✔ Tip

■ You can quickly reset the scale of a layer to 100 percent by selecting the layer and double-clicking the Selection tool.

Figure 7.23 ...or by both aspects. Shift-drag a corner handle to scale the layer while maintaining its proportions.

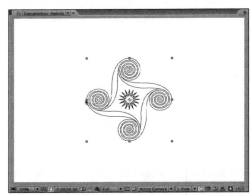

Figure 7.24 You can flip a layer by dragging one side past the other. Note how the spirals in this logo face the opposite direction.

Figure 7.25 Choose the Rotate tool.

Figure 7.26 In the Composition panel, drag the layer to rotate it around its pivot point.

Rotation

When you rotate a 2D layer, it rotates in two-dimensional space, using the anchor point as its pivot point. See Chapter 15 to learn about rotating layers in 3D space.

To rotate a layer by dragging:

1. Select a layer.

2. In the Tools panel, choose the Rotate tool (**Figure 7.25**).

3. In the Composition panel, drag a layer to rotate it around its anchor point.

   As you drag, a bounding box represents the layer's new rotation position (**Figure 7.26**).

4. Release the mouse to set the rotation.

   In the Composition panel, the layer appears with the rotation you set. If the Stopwatch icon isn't active for the layer, this is the rotation of the layer for its entire duration. If the Stopwatch icon is active, a rotation keyframe is created at this frame.

✔ Tips

- To quickly reset a selected layer's rotation to 0 degrees, double-click the Rotate tool.

- If you want an object to turn (rotate) in the direction of its motion path (animated position), you can avoid the pain of setting a lot of rotational keyframes by using the Auto-Orient Rotation command instead. See Chapter 9, "Keyframe Interpolation," for details.

Rotational Values

Rotation is expressed as an absolute, not relative, value. You might even think of it as a rotational position. A layer's default rotation is 0 degrees; setting its rotation to 0 degrees always restores it to its original upright angle. This is true when you keyframe rotational values as well (see "Viewing Spatial Controls in the Comp Panel" earlier in this chapter). For example, if you want to rotate a layer 180 degrees clockwise (upside down) and back again, the rotation values at each keyframe are 0, 180, and 0. Mistakenly setting values of 0, 180, and −180 will cause the layer to turn clockwise 180 degrees and then turn counterclockwise—past its original position—until it's upside down again.

Orienting Rotation to a Motion Path Automatically

As a layer follows a motion path, its rotation remains unaffected. The layer maintains its upright position as it follows the path: Picture, for example, someone riding up an escalator, or the cabins on a Ferris wheel; they remain upright although they follow a sloped or curved path (**Figure 7.27**). Frequently, you want the object to orient its rotation to remain perpendicular to the motion path: Now picture a roller coaster climbing a hill (**Figure 7.28**).

Fortunately, you don't have to painstakingly keyframe a layer's Rotation property to ensure that it remains oriented to the motion path; After Effects' Auto-Orient Rotation command does that for you. Technically, auto-orient rotation isn't a type of spatial interpolation; however, like an interpolation method, it dictates the behavior of a layer along a motion path—and in so doing saves you a lot of keyframing work.

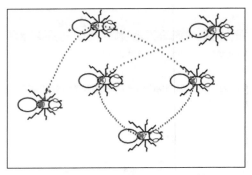

Figure 7.27 Without auto-orient rotation, objects remain upright as they follow the motion path (unless you add rotation). Notice that the ant remains horizontal regardless of the direction of motion.

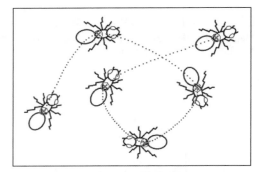

Figure 7.28 Auto-orient rotation automatically keeps a layer perpendicular to the motion path. Here, the ant faces the direction of motion.

Figure 7.29 Select a layer.

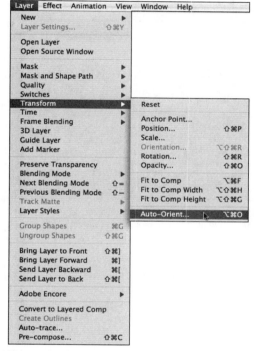

Figure 7.30 Choose Layer › Transform › Auto-Orient.

To auto-orient rotation to the motion path:

1. Select a layer (**Figure 7.29**).

2. Choose Layer > Transform > Auto-Orient, or press Option-Command-O (Mac) or Alt-Ctrl-O (Windows) (**Figure 7.30**). The Auto-Orientation dialog box appears.

3. *Choose either of the following:*
   - ▲ **Off**—Controls the layer's rotation manually
   - ▲ **Orient Along Path**—Makes the layer automatically orient its *X*-axis tangent to the motion path

4. Click OK to close the Auto-Orientation dialog box.

✔ Tips

- You can use the Path Text effect to make text follow a path while automatically remaining perpendicular to it. Text you create using the text-creation tools can also follow a path you specify.

- Chapter 15, "3D Layers," covers 3D compositing, including auto-orient options for 3D layers, cameras, and lights.

ORIENTING ROTATION TO A MOTION PATH

Opacity

At any point in time, a layer can be anywhere from 0 percent opaque (completely transparent, and thus invisible) to 100 percent opaque (with absolutely no transparency).

Bear in mind that the Opacity property merely controls the layer's overall opacity. There are plenty of other ways to define areas of transparency and opacity, including transfer modes, track mattes, keying effects, and masking techniques.

Because opacity is the only transform property you can't "grab onto" in the Comp panel, you must alter it by using numerical controls.

To change the opacity of a layer:

1. Select a layer in the Timeline panel or Composition panel.

2. Press T to display the Opacity property for the selected layer.

   The layer's Opacity property appears in the layer outline, and the current value for opacity appears across from the property under the Switches column (**Figure 7.31**).

3. Under the Switches column across from the layer's Opacity property, *do any of the following*:

   ▲ To decrease the current opacity value, drag the opacity value left (**Figure 7.32**).

   ▲ To increase the current opacity value, drag the value right.

   ▲ To set the value in a dialog box, Control-click/right-click the opacity value, and select Edit Value in the context menu.

As you change the opacity value, the layer's opacity changes in the Composition panel. If the Stopwatch icon isn't active for the layer, the layer retains this opacity for its duration. If the Stopwatch icon is active, an opacity keyframe is created at this frame.

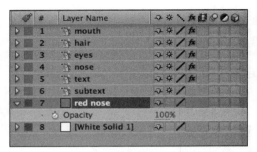

Figure 7.31 Press T to reveal the Opacity property value.

Figure 7.32 To change the value, drag right to increase the value or left to decrease it (as shown here).

✔ Tip

■ The keyboard shortcuts that display most transform properties are often the first letter of the name of the property: P for position, S for scale, and so on. However, you reveal the Opacity property by pressing T.

Table 7.2

Property Dialog Box Shortcuts

To show this dialog box	Press this
Anchor Point dialog box	Command-Option-Shift-A (Mac) or Ctrl-Alt-Shift-A (Windows)
Opacity dialog box	Command-Shift-O (Mac) or Ctrl-Shift-O (Windows)
Other dialog boxes (works with P, R, F, and M)	Command-Shift-property shortcut (Mac) or Ctrl-Shift-property shortcut (Windows)

Table 7.3

Nudging Layer Properties

To nudge this value	Do this
Nudge position one pixel	Press arrow keys (up, down, right, left)
Nudge rotation 1 degree	Press plus (+) on numeric keypad
Nudge rotation –1 degree	Press minus (-) on numeric keypad
Nudge scale 1%	Press Option-plus (+) (Mac) or Alt-plus (+) (Windows) on numeric keypad
Nudge scale –1%	Press Option-minus (-) (Mac) or Alt-minus (-) (Windows) on numeric keypad
Nudge x10	Press Shift-keyboard shortcut for nudge

Specifying Property Values

As in most other Adobe programs, numeric values in After Effects appear colored and underlined, indicating that the values are *scrubbable*. This means you can alter a property's current value by dragging, or *scrubbing*, the value display. Clicking the value highlights it so you can enter a numeric value. Pressing Return/Enter verifies the value; pressing Tab highlights the next value display. Because these controls are familiar to most users, they won't be covered here.

Alternatively, you can open a dialog box to enter property values (**Table 7.2**). Although a dialog box may not offer the convenience of scrubbing or entering the value directly, it does allow you to enter decimal values or to employ different units of measurement for the property value.

You can also use keyboard shortcuts to slightly change, or *nudge*, the position, rotation, or scale of a layer. When you nudge a layer, After Effects counts pixels at the current magnification of the Composition panel, not the layer's actual size. Therefore, nudging a layer's position moves it one pixel when viewed at 100 percent magnification, two pixels when viewed at 50 percent, four pixels at 25 percent, and so on. When layer quality is set to Best, you can nudge layers on a subpixel basis (see the sidebar "Subpixel Positioning," earlier in this chapter). Therefore, a layer set to Best quality can be nudged .5 pixel when viewed at 200 percent, .25 pixel when viewed at 400 percent, and so on. **Table 7.3** lists the keyboard shortcuts for nudging properties.

Animating Layer Properties with Keyframes

To produce animation, you change a layer's properties over time—for example, achieving motion by changing a layer's position over time. In After Effects (as with other programs), you use keyframes to define and control these changes.

A *keyframe* defines a property's value at a specific point in time. When you create at least two keyframes with different values, After Effects interpolates the value for each frame in between. After Effects calculates how to create a smooth transition from one keyframe to another—how to get from point A to point B (**Figure 7.33**).

Basic keyframing

Essentially, keyframing is nothing more than repeating a two-step process: setting the current frame, and setting the property value for that frame. The specific steps are outlined in this section.

If you're new to animating with keyframes, you may want to start with one of the transform properties such as Scale. (Chapter 9 shows how to gain even greater control over your animations by manipulating the spatial and temporal interpolation method used between keyframes.)

To set keyframes for a property:

1. In the Timeline panel, view the property of the layer (or layers) you want to keyframe.

   You may view the same property for more than one layer but not different properties.

2. Set the current time to the frame at which you want to set a keyframe.

   It's possible to set a keyframe beyond the duration of a layer.

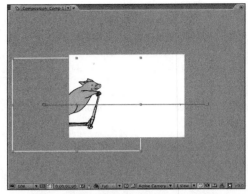

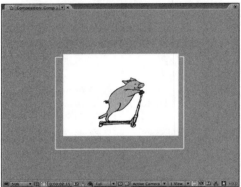

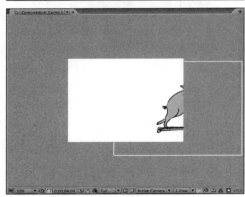

Figure 7.33 You can keyframe any property to animate it over time. In this case, After Effects calculates the position of a layer between two keyframes to create movement.

Keyframes

Keyframe is a term borrowed from traditional animation. In a traditional animation studio, a senior animator might draw only the keyframes—what the character looks like at key moments in the animation. The junior animators would then draw the rest of the frames, or *in-betweens* (a process sometimes known as *tweening*). The same principle applies to After Effects animations: If you supply the keyframes for a property, the program calculates the values in between. And you can keyframe any property, not just movement.

With After Effects, you're always the senior animator, so you should only supply the keyframes—just enough to define the animation. Setting too many keyframes defeats the purpose of this division of labor.

3. Click the Stopwatch icon next to the layer property you want to keyframe to activate the icon (and the keyframe process) (**Figure 7.34**).

The Stopwatch icon appears selected. In the property tracks of the selected layers, an initial keyframe appears; in the keyframe navigator, a check appears.

4. If the property isn't set to the value you want, set the value (as explained earlier in this chapter).

As long as the current time is set to the keyframe, any new value is applied to the keyframe.

5. Set the current time to another frame.

continues on next page

Figure 7.34 Activate the Stopwatch icon to set the first keyframe for the property at the current time indicator.

ANIMATING LAYER PROPERTIES WITH KEYFRAMES

6. To create additional keyframes, *do one of the following:*

▲ To create a keyframe with a new value, change the value of the property (**Figure 7.35**).

▲ To create a keyframe without changing the current property value, select the diamond in the keyframe navigator (**Figure 7.36**).

A new keyframe appears at the current time, and the diamond at the center of the keyframe navigator is highlighted.

7. To create additional keyframes, repeat steps 5 and 6.

8. To see your changes play in the Composition panel, use the playback controls or create a preview (see Chapter 8).

✔ Tips

■ The Motion Sketch plug-in panel provides another quick and easy way to create position keyframes: You can draw them in the Composition panel.

■ The Motion Tracker included in After Effects Pro helps you generate keyframes by detecting an object's movement within an image.

■ People often use After Effects to pan and scale large images, emulating the motion-control camera work frequently seen in documentaries. In such cases, you create pans by animating the anchor point, not the position. This technique achieves the panning you want while keeping the anchor point in the viewing area. Because the anchor point is also used to calculate scale, you'll get more predictable results when you zoom in to and out of the image.

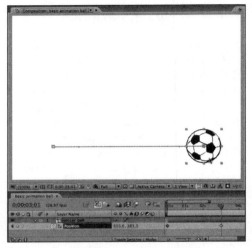

Figure 7.35 To set a keyframe with a new value, set the current time to a new frame and change the property value.

Figure 7.36 To set a keyframe without manually changing the value, select the diamond icon in the keyframe navigator.

Keyframe icons

A property's keyframes appear in its property track of the time graph. When a property heading is collapsed, the keyframes of the properties in that category appear as circles. When an individual property is visible, its keyframes appear as icons by default (**Figure 7.37**). (By checking Use Keyframe Indices in the Timeline panel's pull-down menu, you can make keyframes appear as numbered boxes instead of icons.)

Keyframe icons vary according to the interpolation method used by the keyframe. The diamond-shaped icons shown here reflect linear interpolation. (To learn about other interpolation methods, see Chapter 9, "Keyframe Interpolation.") Regardless of its interpolation method, shading indicates that the property value either before or after the keyframe hasn't been interpolated (**Figure 7.38**). This occurs for the first and last keyframes as well as for keyframes that follow hold keyframes, which are used to prevent interpolation.

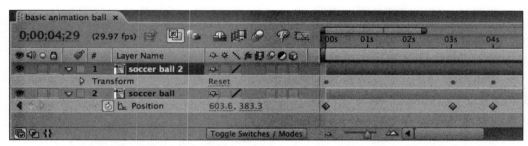

Figure 7.37 When the property heading is collapsed (as they are in the top layer), keyframes appear as small dots. When the property track is visible (as in the bottom layer) keyframes appear as icons.

No interpolation before   *No interpolation after*

Figure 7.38 Shading indicates that the property value isn't interpolated either before or after the keyframe.

Setting a New Keyframe with the Keyframe Navigator

As you learned in the section "Basic Keyframing," you can set a new keyframe by selecting the keyframe navigator's Add/Delete Keyframe button—the diamond icon ◇. Instead of using a value you actively specify, a keyframe created this way uses the value already calculated for that frame.

Usually, you use the check box to create keyframes when you want to modify an animation—or, when no animation exists yet, to repeat a value. Initially, the new keyframe doesn't alter the animation; it hasn't changed the property's value at that time. The new keyframe can serve as a good starting point for changing the animation by changing the keyframe's value or interpolation method (for more about interpolation methods, see Chapter 9).

Cueing the Current Time to Keyframes

You can only set or change a keyframe's values at the current time indicator—one reason you need a quick and convenient way to cue the time marker to keyframes. You may also want to jump to keyframes to step through your animation or to create keyframes in other layers or properties that align with existing keyframes. The *keyframe navigator* provides the solution (**Figure 7.39**).

And as you saw in the section, "Basic Keyframing," the diamond at the center of the keyframe navigator serves as the Add/Delete Keyframe button. Because it's highlighted only when the current time is cued to a keyframe, it also provides a visual confirmation, particularly if you want to confirm that keyframes in different properties are perfectly aligned.

To cue the current time to keyframes:

1. Make sure the property with the keyframes you want to see is visible in the layer outline.

2. In the Timeline panel, *do any of the following:*

   ▲ Shift-drag the current time indicator until it snaps to a visible keyframe.

   ▲ In the keyframe navigator for the property, click the left arrow to cue the current time to the previous keyframe.

   ▲ In the keyframe navigator for the property, click the right arrow to cue the current time to the next keyframe (**Figure 7.40**).

   The current time cues to the adjacent keyframe (**Figure 7.41**). If no keyframe exists beyond the current keyframe, the appropriate arrow in the keyframe navigator appears dimmed.

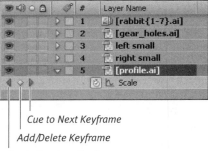

Cue to Next Keyframe
Add/Delete Keyframe
Cue to Previous Keyframe

Figure 7.39 Use the keyframe navigator to cue the current time indicator to the previous or next keyframe. The diamond icon (aka Add/Delete Keyframe button) is highlighted only when the current time is exactly on a keyframe.

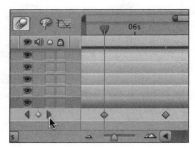

Figure 7.40 Clicking an arrow in the keyframe navigator (in this case, the right arrow)...

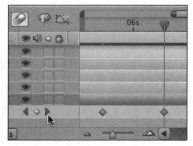

Figure 7.41 ...cues the current time indicator to the property's adjacent keyframe (here, the next keyframe). (Note that the A/V features panel has been moved closer to the time graph for the purpose of illustration.)

Selecting and Deleting Keyframes

Select keyframes when you want to move them to a different position in time, delete them, or copy and paste them to other properties or layers.

To select keyframes:

◆ *Do any of the following:*

▲ To select a keyframe, click it in the property track.

▲ To add keyframes to or subtract them from your selection, press Shift as you click additional keyframes (**Figure 7.42**).

▲ To select multiple keyframes, drag a marquee around the keyframes in the property track (**Figure 7.43**).

▲ To select all the keyframes for a property, click the name of the property in the layer outline (**Figure 7.44**).

Selected keyframes appear highlighted.

To deselect keyframes:

◆ *Do either of the following:*

▲ To deselect all keyframes, click in an empty area of the Timeline panel.

▲ To deselect certain keyframes, Shift-click an already selected keyframe.

Deselected keyframes no longer appear highlighted.

✔ Tip

■ Selecting a keyframe allows you to move it in time, delete it, or copy it. It doesn't let you edit the values of that keyframe. You can only change the value of a property at the current time.

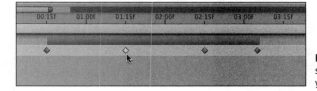

Figure 7.42 Click a keyframe to select it; Shift-click to add to your selection.

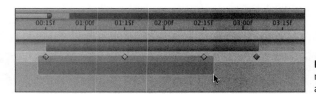

Figure 7.43 You can also select multiple keyframes by dragging a marquee around them.

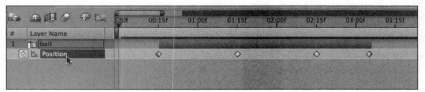

Figure 7.44 Select all the keyframes for a property by clicking the property's name in the layer outline.

To delete keyframes:

1. Select one or more keyframes, as explained in the previous section.

2. *Do any of the following:*
   ▲ Press Delete.
   ▲ Choose Edit > Clear.
   ▲ With the current time cued to the keyframe, click the keyframe navigator's Add/Delete Keyframe button.

   The keyframe disappears, and the property's interpolated values are recalculated based on the existing keyframes.

To delete all the keyframes for a property:

◆ Deactivate the Stopwatch icon for the property (**Figure 7.45**).

   All keyframes disappear. You can't restore the keyframes by reactivating the Stopwatch (doing so only starts a new keyframe process).

✔ Tip

■ If you mistakenly remove keyframes by deselecting the Stopwatch icon, choose Edit > Undo to undo previous commands, or choose File > Revert to return to the last saved version of your project.

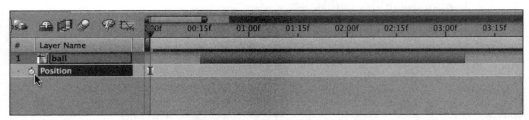

Figure 7.45 Deselecting the property's Stopwatch icon removes all keyframes. The property uses the value at the current time.

Figure 7.46 Select the keyframes you want to move...

Figure 7.47 ...and drag them to a new position in the timeline. Shift-drag to activate the Snap to Edges feature.

Figure 7.48 Although dragging a layer also moves its keyframes, trimming a layer doesn't trim off its keyframes, which still affect property values.

Moving Keyframes

You can move one or more keyframes of one or more properties to a different point in time.

To move keyframes:

1. Select one or more keyframes (as explained earlier in this chapter) (**Figure 7.46**).

2. Drag the selected keyframes to a new position in the time graph (**Figure 7.47**).

   To activate the Snap to Edges feature, press Shift after you begin dragging.

3. Release the mouse when the keyframes are at the position in time you want.

✔ Tip

- Moving a layer in time also moves its keyframes, which maintain their positions relative to the layer. Trimming a layer, on the other hand, doesn't affect the keyframes. In fact, you can set a keyframe before a layer's In point or after its Out point (**Figure 7.48**).

Copying Values and Keyframes

When you want to reuse values you set for a property, you can copy and paste them to a different point in time or even to different layers. Not only can you paste keyframes to the same property (such as from one position to another), you can also paste them to different properties that use the same kind of values (such as from a position to an anchor point).

Pasted keyframes appear in the property track of the destination in the order and spacing of the original, starting at the current time.

After Effects permits you to copy and paste keyframes one layer at a time. You can copy and paste keyframes of more than one property at a time, as long as you paste them into the same properties. If you want to copy and paste to different properties, however, you must do so one property at a time.

To copy and paste keyframes:

1. Select one or more keyframes (as explained earlier in this chapter) (**Figure 7.49**).

2. Choose Edit > Copy, or press Command/Ctrl-C (**Figure 7.50**).

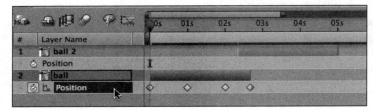

Figure 7.49 Select the keyframes you want to copy.

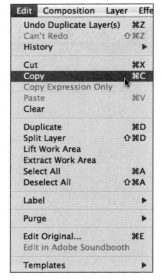

Figure 7.50 Choose Edit > Copy, or press Command/Ctrl-C.

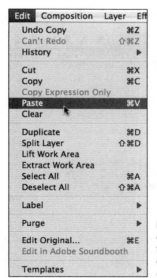

Figure 7.51 Set the current time, select the destination layer or property, and choose Edit > Paste.

3. Set the current time to the frame where you want the pasted keyframe(s) to begin.

4. To select the destination, *do one of the following:*

▲ To paste keyframes to the same property, select the destination layer.

▲ To paste keyframes to a different property, select the destination property by clicking it in the layer outline.

5. Choose Edit > Paste, or press Command/Ctrl-V (**Figure 7.51**).

The keyframes are pasted in the appropriate property in the destination layer (**Figure 7.52**).

✔ Tips

■ You can also copy and paste a global (nonkeyframed) value using the same process. Selecting the property highlights the I-beam icon in the property track rather than the keyframes.

■ To reuse an animation, you can save it as an animation preset. After Effects ships with numerous useful presets. For more about effects, see Chapter 11.

■ Certain types of animations are best accomplished by using an expression instead of numerous keyframes. See Chapter 16, "Complex Projects," for more about using expressions.

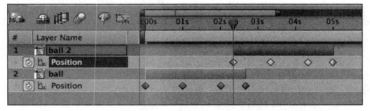

Figure 7.52 The selected keyframes appear in the destination property track, beginning at the current time.

Generating Property Values with the Brainstorm Feature

At times, having full control over a multitude of property values is more of a curse than a blessing. Trying out even a handful of the countless combinations can be a time-consuming and potentially fruitless endeavor. The aptly named Brainstorm feature generates variations of any combination of properties automatically, and lets you preview them before committing to your favorite.

To set the frames to preview for Brainstorming:

1. In the Timeline panel, set the current time to the frame you want previews to begin and press B on the keyboard.

   The beginning of the Work Area Bar aligns with the current time indicator (**Figure 7.53**).

2. In the Timeline panel, set the current time to the frame you want previews to end and press N on the keyboard.

   The ending of the Work Area Bar aligns with the current time indicator (**Figure 7.54**).

To specify the properties for Brainstorming:

1. In the Timeline panel, select any combination of global properties or keyframed property values.

2. At the top of the Timeline panel, click the Brainstorm button 🧠 (**Figure 7.55**).

   The Brainstorm panel appears. It displays nine preview images, each using a different random variant of the property values you specified in step 1 (**Figure 7.56**).

Work Area Bar

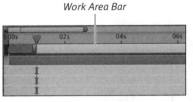

Figure 7.53 Type B to set the beginning of the Work Area Bar...

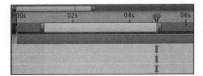

Figure 7.54 ... and type N to set the ending of the Work Area Bar. It defines the range of frames to preview—in this case, Brainstormed property values.

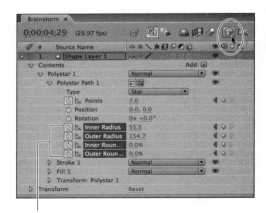

Selected Properties

Figure 7.55 Select any combination of properties and keyframes for which you want to generate values and click the Brainstorm button.

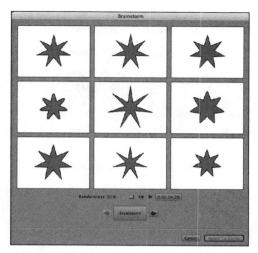

Figure 7.56 The Brainstorm panel appears, showing nine variations of the selected properties.

Figure 7.57 Specifying a value for Randomness or Spread (depending on the selected property type) and clicking the Brainstorm button...

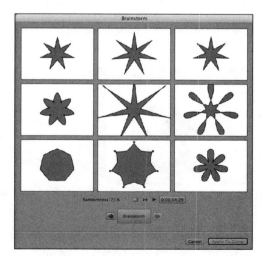

Figure 7.58 ...generates a new set of Brainstormed values.

To generate new variants:

1. To specify the magnitude of variations in the Brainstorm panel, *do either of the following:*

   ▲ For multidimensional properties, specify a value for Randomness (**Figure 7.57**).

   ▲ For single-dimensional properties, specify a value for Spread.

   Specifying a relatively high value results in greater variations of the initial selected values.

2. Click the Brainstorm button 🧠.

   The Brainstorm panel displays a new generation of variants, using the value you specified (**Figure 7.58**).

3. To keep a variant in the next Brainstorm, hover the mouse pointer over the variant and click the Include in Next Brainstorm button 🧠 (**Figure 7.59**).

4. Repeat steps 1 through 3, as needed.

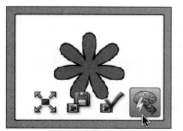

Figure 7.59 Moving the mouse pointer over a tile makes a panel of buttons appear. Click the Include in Next Brainstorm button to retain that variant when you repeat the process.

GENERATING PROPERTY VALUES

181

To preview variants in the Brainstorm panel:

1. In the Brainstorm panel, *do any of the following* (**Figure 7.60**):

   ▲ To toggle transparent areas between the background color and transparency grid, click the Toggle Transparency Grid button 🁢.

   ▲ To preview the visible variants for the Work Area you specified, click the Play button ▶.

   ▲ To rewind playback to the beginning of the Work Area you specified, click the Rewind button ◀.

   ▲ To view the previous generation of variants, press the Back button ◀.

   ▲ To view the next generation of variants, press the Forward button ▶.

To magnify a variant:

1. Move the mouse pointer over the variant you want to view so that a panel of buttons appears, and then click the Maximize Tile button ✖ (**Figure 7.61**).

2. To restore the Brainstorm panel to nine tiles, click the button again.

To apply a variant:

1. In the Brainstorm panel, move the mouse pointer over the variant you want. A panel of four buttons appears over the tile.

2. *Do any of the following* (**Figure 7.62**):

   ▲ To create a new comp containing a copy of the layer using the selected variant, click Save as New Composition 🗗.

   ▲ To apply the variant's property values to the selected layer in the current comp, click Apply to Composition ✔.

   The variant either appears in a new composition or its values are applied to the selected layer in the comp, according to your choice.

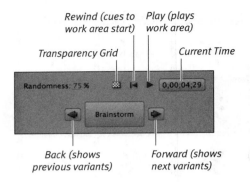

Rewind (cues to work area start)   *Play (plays work area)*

Transparency Grid   *Current Time*

Back (shows previous variants)   *Forward (shows next variants)*

Figure 7.60 The Brainstorm panel's buttons help you preview the variants it generates.

Figure 7.61 Click the Maximize Tile button to enlarge that variant. Click the button again to view all nine variants again.

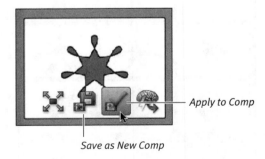

Apply to Comp

Save as New Comp

Figure 7.62 Clicking the Save as New Composition button creates a new comp containing a layer with the variant's values; clicking Apply to Composition (selected here) applies the variant's property values to the selected layer in the current comp.

PLAYBACK, PREVIEWS, AND RAM

You've already used some of the standard playback methods for each panel in After Effects. This chapter expands your repertoire and provides a more in-depth explanation of how After Effects renders frames for viewing.

You'll focus on using the Time Controls panel, which can serve as a master playback control for any selected panel. It also includes a button to render a specified range of frames (or *work area*) as a *RAM preview*. And you'll learn about other options, such as viewing your work on a video monitor, how to view changes you make to a layer interactively, and how to preview audio.

Whether you're using standard playback controls, rendering a RAM preview, or adjusting layers, After Effects utilizes RAM to store and more readily display frames. Consequently, the more RAM you have, the more rendered frames you can store (or *cache*) at once. After Effects makes the most of your RAM supply by retaining rendered frames as long as possible, a feature called *intelligent caching*. But you can also control the demand side of the rendering equation. Specifying RAM preview options to skip frames or reduce the resolution can lighten the rendering load—or eliminate the image altogether (along with the associated rendering delays) by previewing a bare-bones *wireframe* version of an animation. In addition, you can limit the area of the image to render by specifying a region of interest. After Effects can also reduce processing demands automatically, as needed, by employing *adaptive resolution*. Adaptive resolution reduces image resolution in exchange for increased rendering speed.

But rendering speed isn't necessarily attained at the expense of resolution; you can also utilize a compatible *OpenGL* graphics card. Because software-based processing usually can't match hardware dedicated to the same task, utilizing your OpenGL card's hardware-based graphics processing capabilities renders frames quickly, smoothly, and often without sacrificing resolution.

Rendering and RAM

Before proceeding to the tasks, you should familiarize yourself with how After Effects utilizes RAM. This section contrasts two basic methods used to display frames.

Cache flow

Adobe likes to describe the way After Effects uses RAM as "interactive" and "intelligent." Here's why.

Unless you specify otherwise, After Effects renders frames interactively. Whenever the current time is set to a previously unrendered frame, After Effects renders it and stores, or *caches*, it into RAM—which, as you're probably aware, is the memory your computer can access most quickly. Although it can take time to render a frame, once cached, the frame plays back more readily. The Timeline panel indicates cached frames with a green line at the corresponding point under the time ruler (**Figure 8.1**).

When a change (such as an adjustment to a layer property) makes a rendered frame obsolete, After Effects removes the frame from the cache. However, it intelligently retains the unaffected frames. In other words, After Effects doesn't stupidly discard the entire cache when you make changes that affect only some of the frames. When the cache becomes full, the oldest frames are purged from RAM as new frames are added. You can also purge the cache yourself using a menu command.

Playback and previews

Although the terms *playback* and *preview* are often used interchangeably, this book uses them to refer to two rendering methods that differ in a few important respects. Standard playback caches frames at the current time: sequentially when you click Play

Green line = Rendered frames

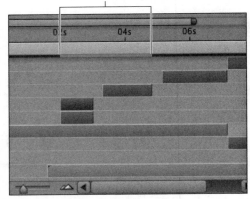

Figure 8.1 Cached frames are signified by a green line in the time ruler.

RENDERING AND RAM

Figure 8.2 Options help you balance quality and rendering speed. The Comp panel's Fast Previews button gives you access to several standard playback options...

Figure 8.3 ...whereas expanding the Time Controls panel allows you to set options for RAM previews.

✔ Tips

■ The playback performance of Footage panels doesn't benefit from the same RAM-caching mechanism as the Layer and Composition panels. Until footage becomes a layer in a composition, it depends on the movie-player software installed on your system.

■ In the Display pane of the Preferences dialog box, you can enable an option to show rendering in progress in the Info panel and the Flowchart panel.

or nonsequentially as you cue the current time. A RAM preview, in contrast, loads a specified range of frames into RAM *before* playing them back.

Both the standard playback mechanism and RAM previews utilize RAM in a similar way, caching frames and retaining them intelligently (see the previous section, "Cache flow"). But whereas standard playback respects the resolution you specified for the panel you're viewing, a RAM preview specifies resolution independent of the panel's current setting. Each method includes different options to help you balance image quality and rendering speed. In addition to the current layer quality and comp resolution settings, standard playback abides by options you set in the Comp panel's Fast Previews button (**Figure 8.2**); you set RAM preview options in the expanded Time Controls panel (**Figure 8.3**). Finally, standard playback options govern how After Effects depicts a frame while you make adjustments—or, in After Effects' parlance, during *interactions*. A RAM preview, on the other hand, only displays a range of frames at or near their full frame rate and doesn't influence the quality or speed of interactions.

No matter what method you use to view frames, processing demands are always related to the footage's native image size (and/or its audio quality) as well as any modifications you make to it as a layer in a composition: masks, transformations, effects, and so on. Note that because the Comp panel's magnification setting (not to be confused with scaling a layer) doesn't change the number or quality of pixels to be rendered, it has little influence on rendering times.

RENDERING AND RAM

Previewing to a Video Device

If your system includes a video output device (such as an IEEE-1394/FireWire/iLink connection), you can view your project on a video monitor—which is crucial for evaluating images destined for video output.

Even though you can preview full screen on your computer monitor (as explained later in this chapter), a computer monitor differs from a television monitor in several important respects. (Refer to this book's sections on interlaced video fields, pixel aspect ratio, safe zones, and NTSC video standards.)

To set video preferences:

1. Choose After Effects > Preferences > Video Preview (Mac) or Edit > Preferences > Video Preview (Windows) (**Figure 8.4**).

   The Video Preview pane of the Preferences dialog box appears (**Figure 8.5**).

2. In the Preferences dialog box, choose an option from the Output Device pull-down menu (**Figure 8.6**).

   Your choices will depend on your particular setup.

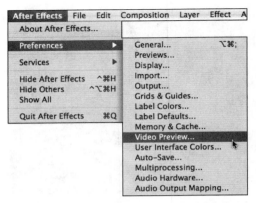

Figure 8.4 Choose Edit > Preferences > Video Preview.

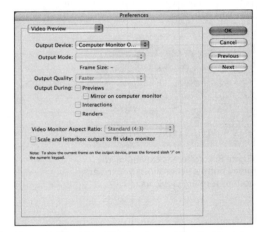

Figure 8.5 The Video Preview pane of the Preferences dialog box appears.

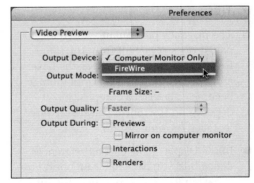

Figure 8.6 Choose an option in the Output Device pull-down menu.

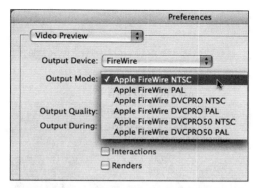

Figure 8.7 Choose an option in the Output Mode pull-down menu.

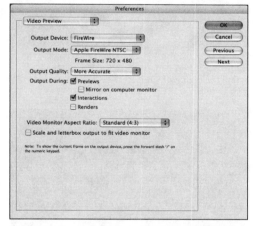

Figure 8.8 Choose an Output Quality and select other options.

3. Choose an option from the Output Mode pull-down menu (**Figure 8.7**).

   Typically, you should choose an option that's equivalent to full-screen video for your output device.

4. For Output Quality, choose whether it's more important to output the video using a Faster or More Accurate method.

5. For Output During, *choose any of the following* (**Figure 8.8**):

   ▲ **Previews**—Displays RAM previews on the NTSC monitor

   ▲ **Interactions**—Displays all window updates (such as while making adjustments to a layer's properties) on the NTSC monitor

   ▲ **Renders**—Displays rendered frames on the NTSC monitor

6. If you selected Previews in step 5, select "Mirror on computer monitor" to display previews on your computer's monitor in addition to the video device.

   To output previews to your video device only, leave this option unchecked.

7. For Video Monitor Aspect Ratio, choose the option that matches your video monitor:

   Standard (4:3)

   Widescreen (16:9)

8. If you wish, select "Scale and letterbox output to fit video monitor."

9. Click OK to close the Preferences dialog box.

   Previews appear on the connected NTSC monitor according to the preferences you set.

PREVIEWING TO A VIDEO DEVICE

Setting the Region of Interest

You can limit the portion of an image to be included in playback or previews by setting a *region of interest*. By restricting the image area to render, you decrease each frame's RAM requirements and increase both the rendering speed and the number of frames you can render.

To set the region of interest:

1. In a Comp, Layer, or Footage panel, click the Region of Interest button  (**Figure 8.9**).

2. Draw a marquee in the image area to define the region of interest (**Figure 8.10**).

    The area of the image included in playback and previews will be limited to the area within the region of interest (**Figure 8.11**).

3. To resize the region of interest, drag any of its corner handles.

To toggle between the region of interest and the full image:

◆ In the Comp, Layer, or Footage panel, click the Region of Interest button.

    When the button is selected, the panel shows the region of interest; when the button is deselected, the panel displays the full image.

✔ Tips

■ To redraw the region of interest from the full image, make sure the Region of Interest button is deselected; then, Option/Alt-click the Region of Interest button.

■ As always, you can reduce rendering times by reducing your composition's resolution or by setting layers to Draft quality.

Figure 8.9 Click the Region of Interest button.

Figure 8.10 Draw a marquee in the image area to define the region of interest.

Figure 8.11 The region of interest limits the image included in playback and previews. Click the Region of Interest button to toggle between the region you specified and the full composition image.

Using the Time Controls

Although the Footage, Layer, Composition, and Timeline panels all have their own playback controls, you can use the Time Controls panel to set the current frame in any selected panel. By default, the times of related panels are synchronized. For example, changing the current frame in a Layer panel also changes the current time in its related Timeline and Composition panels. You can change this setting in the General pane of the Preferences dialog box.

You'll recognize most of the following buttons from the Time Controls panel (**Figure 8.12**); however, a few of these aren't on your home VCR:

First Frame cues the current time to the first frame in the window.

Frame Back cues the current time one frame back.

Play/Pause plays when clicked once and stops when clicked again. Playback performance depends on After Effects' ability to render the frames for viewing. During playback, the Time Controls panel displays two frame rates side by side: the frame rate your system is currently able to achieve and the frame rate you set for the composition.

Frame Forward cues the current time one frame forward.

Last Frame cues the current time to the last frame in the panel.

Audio lets you hear audio tracks when you preview a composition. Deselect it to suppress audio playback during previews. (Standard playback doesn't include audio.)

Loop comprises three states: Loop, Play Once, and Palindrome (which plays the specified area forward and backward). The frames affected by the loop setting depend on the panel selected. In a Footage panel, the entire duration of the footage loops. In a Layer panel, the layer loops from In point to Out point. In a composition—as viewed in the Composition and Timeline panels— frames loop from the beginning to the end of the work area (see "Previewing the Work Area," later in this chapter).

RAM Preview creates a RAM preview by rendering a specified range of frames, as defined by the Timeline's work area (explained later in this chapter).

The **Time Controls panel menu** opens a menu to show or hide RAM Preview and Shift-RAM Preview settings in the Time Controls panel (see the sections on RAM previews later in this chapter).

Collapse/Expand collapses the window to hide all controls or expands it to include RAM Preview Options or show the standard controls.

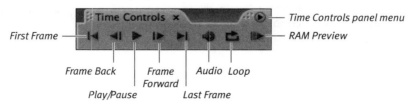

First Frame

Frame Back

Play/Pause

Frame Forward

Last Frame

Audio Loop

Time Controls panel menu

RAM Preview

Figure 8.12 The Time Controls panel can control the playback of any selected window.

Using the Live Update Option

The Live Update option lets you specify how the Comp panel depicts changes during *interactions*, or while you make changes to a layer property. With Live Update enabled, you can see the layer change dynamically *while* you adjust the property. When Live update is off, the Comp panel doesn't update until *after* you alter the property (**Figures 8.13** and **8.14**).

Live Update works with the current Fast Previews setting (explained in "Specifying a Fast Previews Option," later in this chapter). With adaptive resolution enabled (either the standard option or with OpenGL), After Effects temporarily degrades the image quality during interactions until it can process and display the layer at the specified quality and resolution (see "Using Adaptive Resolution," later in this chapter).

You should choose the combination of settings most appropriate to the task at hand, the processing demands of the frame, and your system's processing capability.

To toggle Live Update on and off:

◆ In the Timeline panel, click the Live Update button 🖳 (**Figure 8.15**).

✔ Tip

■ You specify whether to view interactions on an attached video monitor separately, as explained in the section "Previewing to a Video Device," earlier in this chapter.

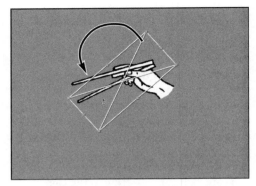

Figure 8.13 With Live Update off, the image doesn't update as you make an adjustment. Here, only the bounding box indicates the layer is being rotated...

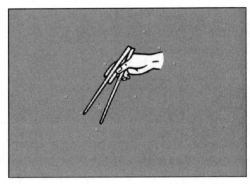

Figure 8.14 ...and the layer doesn't reflect the change until you release the mouse.

Figure 8.15 In the Timeline panel, click the Live Update button.

Specifying a Fast Previews Option

As you learned in earlier chapters, the standard playback method (pressing Play or cuing the current time) is influenced by a comp's resolution as well as the quality settings of the layers it contains. (Everything else being equal, lowering quality and resolution results in shorter rendering times.) You can specify several other options to view frames as quickly as possible by using the Comp panel's Fast Previews button ⬛.

This section covers how to specify the option you want to use and summarizes each choice. Some choices (Adaptive Resolution and OpenGL options) include additional settings, which are explained fully in later sections.

To enable a Fast Previews option:

1. In a Composition panel, choose an option from the Fast Previews button's ⬛ pull-down menu (**Figure 8.16**):

   Off deactivates the Fast Previews option. Standard playback quality is governed by the comp resolution setting and layer quality settings.

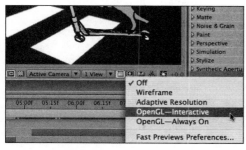

Figure 8.16 Choose an option from the Fast Previews button's pull-down menu.

Wireframe displays layer outlines only, allowing you to quickly evaluate aspects of an animation such as movement and timing by sacrificing image content.

Adaptive Resolution temporarily reduces the image resolution to a specified minimum setting in order to display changes to layers interactively or to maximize the frame rate.

OpenGL—Interactive utilizes a compatible OpenGL graphics card to process every frame requested, such as when you scrub to preview. When active, the Comp panel's Fast Previews icon appears lit.

OpenGL—Always On utilizes a compatible OpenGL graphics card for all previews. The notice *OpenGL* in the upper-left corner of the Comp panel indicates this mode is active.

OpenGL options are available only if you have a compatible OpenGL graphics card installed in your system and you've enabled OpenGL options in the Previews pane of the Preferences dialog box.

2. To use a compatible OpenGL graphics card to process the image of motion footage layers by using a still frame, choose Freeze Layer Contents in the Fast Previews pull-down menu.

   Using a still image as a proxy for motion footage reduces rendering requirements. This option is available only when you choose an OpenGL option in step 1.

✔ Tip

■ A few more options are available for controlling the rendering quality of 3D layers; these are explained in Chapter 15, "3D Layers."

SPECIFYING A FAST PREVIEWS OPTION

Using Adaptive Resolution

If your system is slow to update the Comp panel's image, After Effects can reduce the image's resolution automatically—a feature called *adaptive resolution* (**Figures 8.17** and **8.18**). This way, you can get visual feedback even when your system can't keep up at the resolution you previously specified for the panel. You set the maximum amount by which adaptive resolution degrades images in the Previews pane of the Preferences dialog box.

To set Adaptive Resolution settings:

1. In a Comp panel, click the Fast Previews button, and choose Fast Previews Preferences from the pull-down menu (**Figure 8.19**).

   The Previews pane of the Preferences dialog box appears.

2. *Select one of the following* options from the Adaptive Resolution Limit pull-down menu (**Figure 8.20**):

   ▲ **1/2**—After Effects temporarily displays the image at no less than one-half resolution while updating the comp preview.

   ▲ **1/4**—After Effects temporarily displays the image at one-quarter resolution while updating the comp preview.

   ▲ **1/8**—After Effects temporarily displays the image at one-eighth resolution while updating the comp preview.

3. Click OK to close the Preferences dialog box.

Figure 8.17 With adaptive resolution enabled, the image degrades to keep pace with your adjustments...

Figure 8.18 ...and then assumes the comp's resolution when you stop transforming the layer.

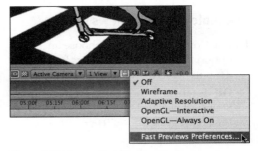

Figure 8.19 Choose Fast Previews Preferences from the Fast Previews button's pull-down menu.

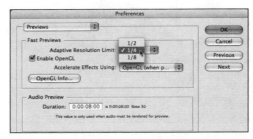

Figure 8.20 Limit the amount of degradation by choosing an option in the Adaptive Resolution Limit pull-down menu.

Using OpenGL

Generally speaking, software processing can't match hardware dedicated to the same task. After Effects takes advantage of this fact by utilizing the graphics processing power of (After Effects-certified) OpenGL graphics cards.

After Effects detects whether your system has an OpenGL graphics card automatically and, if so, activates it as the default preview option.

When OpenGL is in effect, the Fast Previews button ▣ turns green. By default, OpenGL kicks in whenever you drag layers in a comp, scrub a motion-related property, or scrub a comp's current time. However, it doesn't provide a rendering boost to nonmotion related effect properties. To view effects-intensive frames, you may opt to switch to another Fast Previews method.

Overall, OpenGL provides faster, smoother screen updates than you would get otherwise, and it does so without degrading the image. But as the following task explains, you can set OpenGL to switch to adaptive resolution as you adjust effect property values (see "Using Adaptive Resolution," earlier in this chapter). This way, you can take advantage of OpenGL for most interactions, and adaptive resolution when you're adjusting effects.

You already know how to specify your OpenGL card as the Fast Previews option (see "Specifying a Fast Previews Option" earlier in this chapter). This section explains how to set several options specific to OpenGL.

OpenGL Graphics Cards

OpenGL is a technology utilized by many advanced video graphics cards that helps to enhance graphics processing, particularly for 3D objects and subtleties like shading, lights, and shadows. When a program is designed to recognize OpenGL, the increase in graphics performance can be substantial.

Usually, a high-end graphics card isn't a standard component in an average system configuration; instead, it's an often-expensive option. However, PC gamers and graphics professionals value graphics performance and are eager to upgrade to a more advanced graphics card.

Features and processing power vary from card to card. Whether your card supports features like lights and shadows in After Effects depends on the particular card.

Before you upgrade your graphics card, check Adobe's Web site to ensure the card has been certified to work with After Effects. This is another quick way to see which features the card supports. And in addition to the card itself, make sure you install the latest software drivers, which should be available for download from the manufacturer's Web site.

To set OpenGL preferences:

1. In a Comp panel, click the Fast Previews button and choose Fast Previews Preferences from the pull-down menu (**Figure 8.21**).

   The Previews pane of the Preferences dialog box appears.

2. Select Enable OpenGL.

3. For Accelerate Effects Using, choose an option (**Figure 8.22**):

   Adaptive Resolution

   OpenGL (when possible)

4. Click OK to close the dialog box.

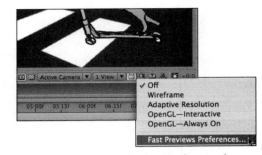

Figure 8.21 Choose Fast Previews Preferences from the Fast Previews button's pull-down menu.

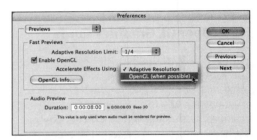

Figure 8.22 Select the OpenGL options you want.

Figure 8.23 Click OpenGL Info to access more options.

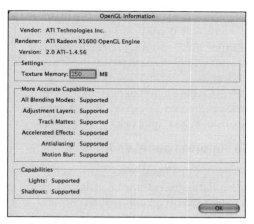

Figure 8.24 In the OpenGL Information dialog box, specify an amount for Texture Memory.

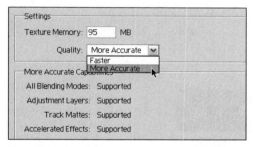

Figure 8.25 If available, choose an option from the Quality pull-down menu.

To specify other OpenGL options:

1. In the Previews pane of the Preferences dialog box, click OpenGL Info (**Figure 8.23**).

   An OpenGL Information dialog box appears.

2. Specify the amount for Texture Memory, in megabytes (MB) (**Figure 8.24**).

   Adobe recommends allocating no more than 80 percent of the video RAM (VRAM) on your display card when using Windows; on a Mac, After Effects determines the ideal value automatically.

3. Specify an option in the Quality pull-down menu (**Figure 8.25**):

   Faster—Processes more quickly, at the expense of the quality of lighting, shading, and blending, and by excluding blending modes

   More Accurate—Includes blending modes, and improves the quality of lighting, shading, and blending

4. Click OK to close the OpenGL Information dialog box, and click OK to close the Preferences dialog box.

USING OPENGL

Suppressing Panel Updates

If frames are difficult to render, it can take time to update an image. You may have already noticed how the Selection tool cycles between black and white as a particularly difficult frame renders (**Figure 8.26**). The lower-right corner of the Composition panel also includes a small activity bar (provided the window is sized wide enough for you to see it). When previewing gets in the way of your progress, you can prevent the Footage, Layer, and Composition panels from updating by activating your keyboard's Caps Lock key.

When you suppress updates, panels continue to display the current frame, even after you make changes. When you alter the image in the current frame or move to a new frame,

a red outline appears around the image in the panels that would otherwise be updated (**Figure 8.27**). Although panel controls— anchor points, motion paths, mask outlines, and so on—continue to update, the image doesn't reflect your changes. When you're ready to update, or *refresh*, the affected panels, disengage Caps Lock.

To suppress panel updates:

◆ Press Caps Lock to suppress panel updates; press Caps Lock again to turn suppression off and refresh panels.

✔ Tip

■ If slow updates are a problem, you should consider replacing particularly demanding footage items with lower-quality proxies. See Chapter 3, "Managing Footage," for more information.

Figure 8.26 The Selection tool cycles between black and white as the program pauses to render frames.

Figure 8.27 When Caps Lock is active, a red outline appears around the image in the windows that would otherwise be updated. The window also displays a friendly reminder.

Figure 8.28 Scrubbing the audio provides an alternative (or an enhancement) to expanding the Audio Waveform property to cue the current time to a particular sound.

Figure 8.29 As usual, use the VU meter of the Audio panel to see audio levels as they play.

Scrubbing Audio

In After Effects, finding a particular frame based on the image is easy. Finding a particular moment based on the sound is a different matter. An audio preview plays your audio layers, but it doesn't make it easy to cue to a particular sound. When you halt an audio preview (see the next section), the current time indicator goes back to the starting point—the current time indicator doesn't remain at the moment you stop it. Viewing the audio waveform usually doesn't help you pinpoint a sound, either; individual sounds are difficult to discern in a waveform display (**Figure 8.28**). (See Chapter 7, "Properties and Keyframes.")

Fortunately, After Effects allows you to *scrub* the audio—that is, play it back slowly as you drag the current time indicator. The term *scrubbing* refers to the back back-and-forth motion of tape over an audio head. This feature has always been taken for granted in the analog world, but it's long been considered a luxury for digital tools. (High-end equipment is still required to approximate old-fashioned tape scrubbing.)

Remember, you can always see audio levels—even while you scrub—in the Volume Units (VU) meter of the Audio panel (**Figure 8.29**).

To scrub audio:

◆ In the time ruler of the Timeline panel, Command/Ctrl-drag the current time indicator.

The audio plays back as you drag.

✔ Tip

■ To hear every syllable and beat, there's no substitute for scrubbing. Once you find the sound you're looking for, don't forget that you can mark the frame in the layer or the composition (see Chapter 6, "Layer Editing"). You can also set markers on the fly during audio previews by pressing the asterisk (*) key on the numeric keypad.

Previewing the Work Area

Until now, this chapter has focused on playback options and methods you can use to control the way the Composition panel updates when you transform layer properties. The following sections discuss previewing a specified area of the composition, a span defined by the *work area*.

The *work area bar* is an adjustable bar located above the time ruler in the Timeline menu (**Figure 8.30**). To make it easier to identify the part of the composition that's included, the entire area under the work area bar is highlighted; it appears a little brighter than the area outside the work area.

As you learned in Chapter 6, the navigator view of the Timeline panel includes a miniature version of the work area bar; however, it's for your reference only.

To set the work area by dragging:

In the Timeline panel, *do any of the following:*

- Drag the left handle of the work area bar to the time you want previews to start (**Figure 8.31**).

- Drag the right handle of the work area bar to the time you want previews to end (**Figure 8.32**).

- Drag the center of the work area bar to move the work area without changing its duration (**Figure 8.33**).

  Make sure to grab the center of the bar, where vertical lines imply a textured grip. Otherwise, you'll cue the current time indicator instead.

  Press Shift as you drag to snap the edges of the work area bar to the edges of layers, keyframes, markers, or the time indicator.

Work area bar start   Work area bar end

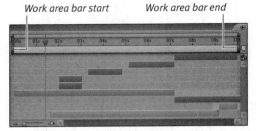

Figure 8.30 The work area bar defines the range of frames in the composition for previews.

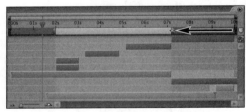

Figure 8.31 Drag the left handle of the work area bar to the time you want previews to start.

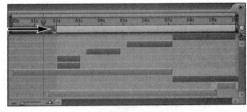

Figure 8.32 Drag the right handle of the work area bar to the time you want previews to end.

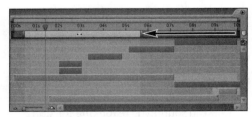

Figure 8.33 Drag the center of the work area bar to move the work area without changing its duration.

To set the work area using keyboard shortcuts:

1. In the Timeline panel, set the current time to the frame at which you want the work area to begin or end.

2. *Do one of the following:*
   ▲ Press B to set the beginning of the work area to the current time.
   ▲ Press N to set the end of the work area to the current time.

✔ Tips

■ You can't set the beginning of the work area bar after the end, or vice versa. If you can't move the end of the work area where you want, you probably have to move the other end first.

■ Using an extended keyboard, you can cue the time to the beginning of the work area by pressing Shift-Home or to the end of the work area by pressing Shift-End.

■ In principle, After Effects' work area bar is equivalent to the one in Premiere Pro. In practice, however, there are a few differences. For example, you can't use the same keyboard shortcuts for setting the work area (unless you create a custom shortcut in Premiere Pro).

PREVIEWING THE WORK AREA

Previewing Audio Only

If you only need to hear the audio tracks of your composition, you don't have to wait for a time-consuming video preview.

To preview audio only under the work area:

1. Set the work area over the range of frames you want to preview (**Figure 8.34**).

See the previous section, "Previewing the Work Area."

2. Choose Composition > Preview > Audio Preview (Work Area) (**Figure 8.35**).

The audio under the work area plays.

To preview audio only from the current time:

◆ In the Composition or Timeline panel, cue the current time to the frame at which you want to begin your audio preview and then press the decimal point (.) on the numeric keypad (not the period on the main keyboard).

The audio plays back from the current frame for the duration you set in the Preferences.

✔ Tips

■ You can set the quality of audio previews (and thereby the rendering times) in the Previews pane of the Preferences dialog box.

■ When you preview audio from the current time, it plays for the duration you set in the General pane of the Preferences dialog box.

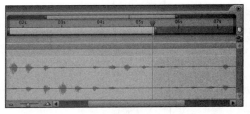

Figure 8.34 Set the work area bar over the range you want to preview.

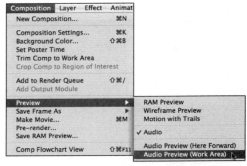

Figure 8.35 Choose Composition > Preview > Audio Preview (Work Area).

Figure 8.36 A full preview shows everything in detail but requires both more RAM and more processing time.

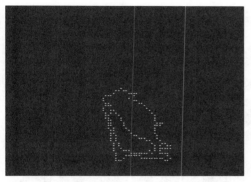

Figure 8.37 A wireframe preview represents the layer as an empty outline. It renders much faster but still shows you the motion of one or more layers.

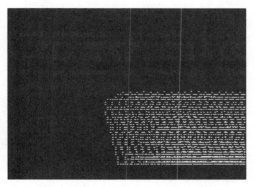

Figure 8.38 You can also preview motion with trails, in which case the wireframes at each frame remain visible as the preview progresses.

Previewing Wireframes

When you want to see just the motion of an animation—changes in position, scale, and rotation—you don't have to waste precious time by rendering a full-fledged preview of the work area. Instead, use a wireframe preview for selected layers.

A *wireframe preview* represents the motion of one or more layers as an empty outline, or wireframe. A wireframe preview gives you a clear sense of motion without consuming much of your RAM or your time (**Figures 8.36** and **8.37**). To get a sense of the sweep of the layer's complete motion, the wireframe can include a trail, which leaves the previous frames visible as the preview progresses (**Figure 8.38**). Because wireframe previews don't render frames fully, no images are stored in the cache, and no green line indicator appears below the work area bar.

To create a wireframe preview:

1. In the Timeline panel, *do one of the following:*

   ▲ Select the layers you want to preview.

   ▲ Deselect all layers to preview all of them.

2. Set the work area over the range of frames you want to preview (as explained in the section "Previewing the Work Area") (**Figure 8.39**).

3. *Do one of the following:*

   ▲ Choose Composition > Preview > Wireframe Preview (**Figure 8.40**).

   ▲ Choose Composition > Preview > Motion with Trails.

4. Press the spacebar to stop the preview.

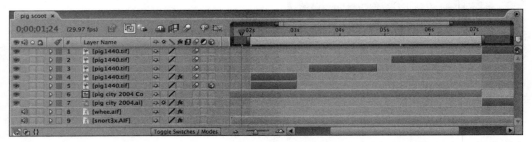

Figure 8.39 Set the work area and select the layers you want to preview. To preview all the layers, leave them deselected.

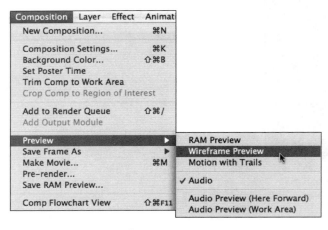

Figure 8.40 Select Composition > Preview > Wireframe Preview to view a wireframe preview, or choose Composition > Preview > Motion with Trails to view a wireframe preview with trails.

Table 8.2

Keyboard Shortcuts for Playback and Preview	
To do this	Press this
Start/pause	Spacebar
Frame advance	Page Down
Frame reverse	Page Up
First frame	Home
Last frame	End
Scrub video	Option/Alt-drag (Windows) the current time indicator
Scrub audio	Command/Ctrl-drag the current time indicator
Stop window updates	Caps Lock
Preview audio from the current time	Decimal point (.) on the numeric keypad
RAM preview	Zero on the numeric keypad
Shift+RAM preview	Shift-zero on the numeric keypad
Save RAM preview	Command/Ctrl-zero on the numeric keypad
Wireframe preview	Option/Alt-zero on the numeric keypad
Wireframe preview using a rectangular layer outline	Command-Option-zero (Mac) or Ctrl-Alt-zero (Windows) on the numeric keypad
Show layers as background during wireframe previews	Add Shift to the wireframe preview shortcut: Shift-Option-zero (Mac) or Shift-Alt-zero (Windows) on the numeric keypad

Rendering RAM Previews

To see a comp at (or near) its full frame rate, you typically render a RAM preview. In contrast to using standard playback controls, a RAM preview renders frames first and then plays them back. By default, a RAM preview renders frames in the work area only; but you can set an option to render frames beginning at the current time (similar to standard playback). RAM previews include several options to balance rendering speed with image quality and frame rate.

You can set separate options for two kinds of RAM previews: a standard RAM preview and a Shift-RAM preview. You can customize each type according to your project's demands, choosing the best RAM preview option for the task at hand. For example, you could set the standard RAM preview to render a relatively smooth, high-resolution image, and set the Shift-RAM preview to render more quickly, at the expense of smooth motion and image quality.

By default, rendering a RAM preview (including a Shift-RAM preview) renders the active panel. But you can specify a particular panel to preview, even if it isn't the currently active panel. Doing so can streamline your workflow by freeing you from finding a particular panel to preview (especially in complex projects). For example, by designating your final comp as the panel to always preview, you can work in other panels and then quickly view your changes in the final comp.

For an overview of keyboard shortcuts for rendering a RAM preview and other playback options, see **Table 8.2**.

RENDERING RAM PREVIEWS

To show and hide RAM preview options:

◆ In the Time Controls panel's menu, *select an option* (**Figure 8.41**):

▲ **RAM Preview Options**—Expands the panel to reveal the RAM preview options

▲ **Shift+RAM Preview Options**—Expands the panel to reveal the Shift-RAM preview options

The Time Controls panel expands to reveal the options you selected (**Figure 8.42**). Reselect an option to hide the RAM preview options.

✔ Tip

■ Remember, you can repeatedly click the Time Controls panel to cycle through different views: to show the panel tab only, to add the playback controls, or to add the selected RAM or Shift-RAM preview options.

To set RAM preview options:

1. In the Time Controls panel, reveal either the RAM preview or Shift-RAM preview options, as explained in the previous task.

2. In the RAM Preview Options or Shift+RAM Preview Options area of the Time Controls panel, *enter the following:*

Frame Rate—Enter the frame rate for the preview, or choose one from the pull-down menu (**Figure 8.43**).

Lower frame rates render more quickly but at the expense of smooth motion.

Skip—Enter the frequency with which frames are skipped and left unrendered.

Skipping frames speeds rendering but results in choppier motion.

Figure 8.41 In the pull-down menu, choose the RAM preview options you want to show.

Figure 8.42 The Time Controls panel expands to reveal the options you selected.

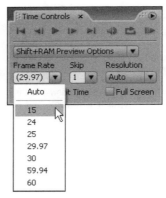

Figure 8.43 Enter a frame rate used by the preview, or choose one from the pull-down menu. Also enter the frequency at which frames are skipped.

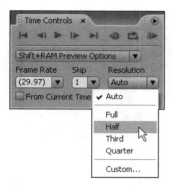

Figure 8.44 Choose an option from the Resolution pull-down menu. Select the other options you want.

Resolution—*Choose one of the following* options from the pull-down menu (**Figure 8.44**):

▲ **Auto**—Previews use the Composition panel's current resolution setting.

▲ **Full**—After Effects renders and displays every pixel of the composition, resulting in the highest image quality and the longest rendering time.

▲ **Half**—After Effects renders every other pixel, or one-quarter of the pixels of the full-resolution image in one-quarter of the time.

▲ **Third**—After Effects renders every third pixel, or one-ninth of the pixels in the full-resolution image in one-ninth of the time.

▲ **Quarter**—After Effects renders every fourth pixel, or one-sixteenth of the pixels in the full-resolution image in one-sixteenth of the time.

▲ **Custom**—After Effects renders whatever fraction of pixels you specify.

3. *Select either of the following* options:

▲ **From Current Time**—After Effects renders previews from the current time (instead of the frames defined by the work area).

▲ **Full Screen**—After Effects displays previews on a blank screen (with no windows visible).

RENDERING RAM PREVIEWS

To create a RAM preview:

1. In the Timeline panel, set the work area bar to the range of frames you want to preview (**Figure 8.45**).

2. To preview audio as well as video, click the Audio button in the Time Controls panel (**Figure 8.46**).

3. Select an option by clicking the Loop button in the Time Controls panel (**Figure 8.47**).

   Loop —loops playback beginning to end.

   Ping Pong —loops playback from beginning to end, then end to beginning.

   Play Once —plays once.

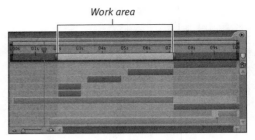

Work area

Figure 8.45 Set the work area bar over the range of frames you want to preview.

Figure 8.46 To preview audio in addition to video, click the Audio button in the Time Controls panel.

Loop

Ping Pong

Play Once

Figure 8.47 In the Time Controls panel, click the Loop button repeatedly so the icon corresponds to the option you want.

Figure 8.48 Click the RAM Preview button in the Time Controls panel, or press 0 in the numeric keypad.

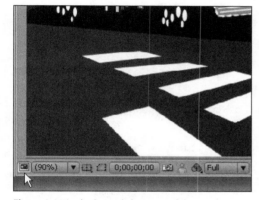

Figure 8.49 In the lower-left corner of the window you want to designate, click the Always Preview This View button.

■ The Memory & Cache pane of the Preferences dialog box allows you to specify the size and location of a disk cache. When the RAM cache is full, After Effects can move rendered frames to the location you specify. For best performance, the disk that stores source footage and the disk cache disk should use different drive controllers.

4. To use the standard RAM preview settings, *do any of the following:*

▲ Choose Composition > Preview > RAM Preview.

▲ Click the RAM Preview button in the Time Controls panel (**Figure 8.48**).

▲ Press 0 on the numeric keypad.

5. To use the Shift-RAM preview settings, *do either of the following:*

▲ Shift-click the RAM Preview button in the Time Controls panel.

▲ Hold Shift as you press 0 on the numeric keypad.

In the Timeline panel, a green line appears over the frames that are rendered to RAM. When all the frames in the work area have been rendered, or when the amount of available RAM runs out, the frames play back in the Composition panel.

To specify a panel to always preview:

◆ Click the Always Preview This View button ▤ in the panel you want to designate for previews (**Figure 8.49**).

RAM previews (including Shift-RAM previews) always render the panel you specified, which becomes active for you to view.

✔ Tips

■ Choosing Composition > Save RAM preview lets you save a RAM preview as a movie file that you can use, for example, as a draft version for your own reference or for sharing with clients. For more about exporting, see Chapter 17.

■ After Effects discards cached frames as they become obsolete or as new frames are added to a full cache. But you can empty the cache manually by choosing Edit > Purge and selecting the type of cache.

RAMming Speed: Getting the Most Out of Your RAM

In addition to using a computer with a fast processor and loads of RAM, here are some other things you can do to use RAM effectively and improve RAM playback.

Optimize Your Display

◆ Use a high-quality display card. Better yet, choose an Adobe-approved OpenGL graphics card, which can take over much of the processing.

◆ Use the latest drivers for your video display. Check with the manufacturer's Web site to make sure you're using the latest and greatest version.

Optimize Your RAM

◆ Reduce the number of undoable actions in General Preferences.

◆ Purge the image cache to free up RAM.

Reduce Memory Requirements for Compositions

◆ Set the composition to a low resolution (half, third, and so on) to achieve higher frame rates in previews.

◆ Match the composition's resolution and magnification factor. RAM previews work faster this way. For example, preview half-resolution compositions at 50 percent magnification.

◆ Use proxies when possible (see Chapter 3).

◆ Avoid footage items that use temporal compression (MPEG footage, for example). The frame differencing utilized by the compression scheme requires intensive processing.

◆ Prerender nested compositions when possible (see Chapter 16).

◆ Collapse transformations when possible (see Chapter 16).

RENDERING RAM PREVIEWS

KEYFRAME INTERPOLATION

In Chapter 7, "Properties and Keyframes," you learned to animate layer properties over time by setting keyframes. By defining only the most important, or key, frames, you assume the role of head animator. After Effects fills the role of assistant animator, providing all the in-between frames, or tweens, using what's known as an *interpolation method* to determine their values.

Fortunately, you can instruct your assistant to use a range of interpolation methods. Some methods create steady changes from one keyframe to the next; others vary the rate of change. Movement can take a direct path or a curved route; an action can glide in for a soft landing or blast off in a burst of speed.

Without a choice of interpolation methods, your loyal assistant's abilities would be severely limited. If animated values always proceeded directly and mechanically from one keyframe to another, all but the most basic animations would seem lifeless and robotic. To create a curved movement would require so many keyframes you'd begin to wonder why you had an assistant at all. Calculating acceleration or deceleration in speed would present an even thornier problem.

This chapter explains how you can assign various interpolation methods to keyframes to impart nuance and variation to your animations using the Timeline panel's Graph Editor. You'll not only learn to decipher how After Effects depicts the ineffable qualities of motion, speed, and acceleration, but you'll also see how it harnesses them. In the process, you'll begin to realize that there's a big difference between animating something and bringing it to life.

Understanding Interpolation

The beauty of keyframes is that they save you work. If you set keyframes, After Effects calculates the values for the frames in between, a process known as *interpolation*. Controlling the interpolation between keyframes allows you to set fewer keyframes than you could otherwise—without sacrificing precise control over your animation. After Effects interpolates values in terms of both space and time: in other words, spatially and temporally.

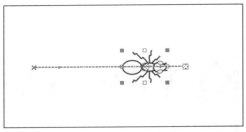

Figure 9.1 Interpolation refers to how After Effects calculates a property's values between keyframed values. Spatial interpolation determines whether movement proceeds directly from one keyframe to the next...

Spatial interpolation

Spatial interpolation refers to how After Effects calculates changes in position, how a layer or its anchor point moves in the space of the composition. Does it proceed directly from one keyframe to the next, or does it take a curved route (**Figures 9.1** and **9.2**)?

As you've seen, spatial interpolation is represented as a motion path, a dotted line connecting keyframes. Changes in a layer's position value appear as a motion path in the Composition panel; changes in a layer's anchor-point value appear in its Layer panel. Effect point paths can appear in a both panels. So far, you've learned how to set a layer's position at a keyframe by dragging in the appropriate panel; in this chapter, you'll learn how to adjust the path between keyframes, or the interpolated values.

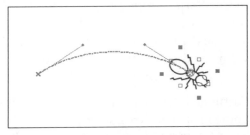

Figure 9.2 ...or takes a more curved, indirect route.

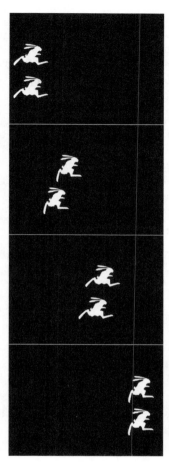

Figure 9.3
Both rabbits have the same keyframes, but they have different interpolation methods.

Temporal interpolation

Temporal interpolation refers to any property value's rate of change between keyframes. Does the value change at a constant rate from one keyframe to the next, or does it accelerate or decelerate?

For example, **Figure 9.3** shows two rabbits. They both travel the same distance in the same amount of time. However, one proceeds from the first keyframe to the last keyframe at a constant rate. The other gradually accelerates, starting slowly and then speeding up. As a result, the second rabbit falls behind at first and then gradually catches up. Both reach their destination simultaneously.

So far, you've viewed keyframes by expanding a layer's property values in the Timeline. The keyframes' relative timing and values give you some control of the overall speed of changes. But to see and manipulate the values *between* keyframes—the interpolated values—you must toggle the view under the time ruler to the Graph Editor. The *Graph Editor* represents the temporal interpolation as graphs that reflect a property's rate of change and also lets you control it (**Figure 9.4**).

Acceleration (bottom rabbit)   Constant Speed (top rabbit)

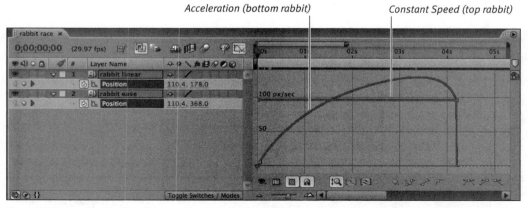

Figure 9.4 By toggling the Timeline panel to show the Graph Editor, you can see temporal interpolation represented as a graph. The straight line represents the top rabbit's speed; the curved line represents the lower rabbit's speed.

UNDERSTANDING INTERPOLATION

211

Incoming and outgoing interpolation

Although *interpolation* refers to values *between* keyframes, it's important to understand that you assign an interpolation type to keyframes themselves. The interpolation type, in turn, determines how values are calculated before the keyframe and after the keyframe—the *incoming* and *outgoing interpolation*. Therefore, the values between any two keyframes (the interpolated values) are determined by the first keyframe's outgoing interpolation type and the next keyframe's incoming interpolation type.

The concept is most easily understood in spatial terms. Just as a direction handle in a path shape influences the preceding curve, a motion keyframe's tangent affects the path preceding the keyframe. Similarly, the opposite tangent influences the motion path after the keyframe (**Figure 9.5**).

Temporal interpolation also affects a property value's rate of change before and after the keyframe. In a speed or value graph, ease handles work a lot like tangents in a motion path. But because the graph lines don't trace a spatial path, they can be a little more difficult to interpret and adjust (**Figure 9.6**).

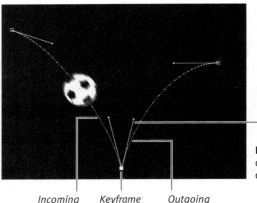

Tangent

Incoming interpolation   Keyframe   Outgoing interpolation

Figure 9.5 In a motion path, keyframe tangents define the outgoing and incoming interpolation and, hence, the curve of the motion path.

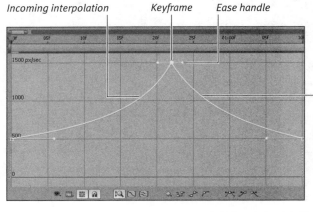

Incoming interpolation   Keyframe   Ease handle

Outgoing interpolation

Figure 9.6 A value graph's direction lines and a speed graph's ease handles (shown here) define the incoming and outgoing interpolation. Here, the rate of change gradually accelerates after the first keyframe and then decelerates into the second keyframe.

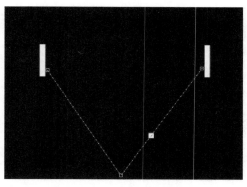

Figure 9.7 Spatially, linear interpolation defines a corner at each keyframe and a straight path between keyframes. The ball in the classic Pong game, for example, moves in perfectly straight lines and ricochets in sharp corners.

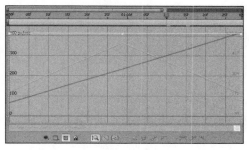

Figure 9.8 Temporally, linear interpolation results in a constant rate of change between keyframes. When speed differs between pairs of keyframes, the change is instantaneous.

Interpolation Types

With the exception of hold interpolation, After Effects uses the same methods to calculate both spatial and temporal interpolation. This section describes how each interpolation type is expressed spatially, in a motion path, and temporally, in a speed graph.

No interpolation

No interpolation is applied to properties that have no keyframes and aren't animated. Static properties display an I-beam icon (rather than keyframes) in the layer outline, and the Stopwatch icon isn't selected.

Linear

Linear interpolation dictates a constant rate of change from one keyframe to the next. Between two keyframes, linear interpolation defines a straight path; temporally, it results in a constant speed. When a keyframe's incoming and outgoing interpolation are linear, a corner is created in the motion path. Temporally, speed changes instantly at the keyframe (**Figures 9.7** and **9.8**).

Auto Bézier

Auto Bézier interpolation automatically reduces the rate of change equally on both sides of a keyframe.

Spatially, a keyframe set to auto Bézier is comparable to a smooth point, with two equal direction lines extending from it. It results in a smooth, symmetrical curve in a motion path. A satellite in an elliptical orbit, for example, takes even, round turns (**Figure 9.9**). (In addition, the satellite may auto-orient its rotation according to the direction of its movement. See "Orienting Rotation to a Motion Path Automatically," in Chapter 7.)

Temporally, auto Bézier interpolation reduces the rate of change equally before and after a keyframe, creating a gradual deceleration that eases into and out of the keyframe (**Figure 9.10**).

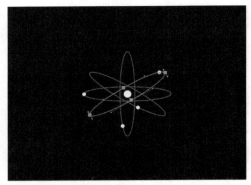

Figure 9.9 Auto Bézier interpolation creates a curved path with equal incoming and outgoing interpolation. The keyframes of an orbital path may use perfectly symmetrical curves.

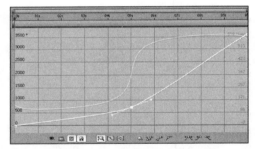

Figure 9.10 Temporally, auto Bézier interpolation yields gradual, even speed changes and a curved graph. For example, the blade of a fan goes from a lower speed to a higher speed gradually (not instantaneously).

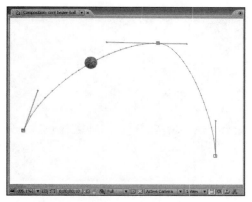

Figure 9.11 You might use continuous Bézier interpolation to trace the asymmetrically arced path of a thrown ball.

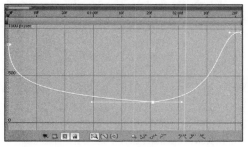

Figure 9.12 Temporally, rate of change is reduced smoothly—but unevenly—on either side of a continuous Bézier keyframe. A rolling ball may decelerate gradually as it crests a hill but accelerate more sharply on its descent.

Continuous Bézier

Like auto Bézier, continuous Bézier interpolation reduces the rate of change on both sides of a keyframe. However, continuous Bézier interpolation is set manually, so it doesn't affect the incoming and outgoing rates of change equally. In the motion path, continuous Bézier interpolation results in a smooth and continuous, but asymmetrical, curve. Typically, the path of a cannonball follows an arc that's continuous but asymmetrical (**Figure 9.11**).

Temporally, continuous Bézier interpolation reduces the rate of change before and after a keyframe unequally (**Figure 9.12**).

Bézier

Like continuous Bézier, you set Bézier interpolation manually, but the change is discontinuous. Bézier interpolation causes an abrupt decrease or increase in the rate of change on either or both sides of a keyframe.

Spatially, Bézier keyframes are comparable to a corner point in a mask path. As in a corner point, the direction lines extending from the keyframe are unequal and discontinuous. In a motion path, Bézier interpolation creates a discontinuous curve, or *cusp*, at the keyframe. Bézier interpolation can achieve the discontinuous curve of a ball's bouncing path (**Figure 9.13**).

In the value graph, Bézier interpolation can reduce or increase the rate of change before and after a keyframe (**Figure 9.14**). For example, you can use Bézier interpolation to create a sharp acceleration at a keyframe (such as when a ball falls and bounces).

✔ Tip

■ Again, the motion path and the types of spatial interpolation it uses only affect motion. For truly convincing animation, you must also adjust speed (by controlling the time between keyframes) and acceleration (via temporal interpolation). In addition, consider other physical attributes associated with motion—for example, the blurred motion of fast-moving objects, or distortion and elasticity (say, the squashing effect when a ball strikes the ground). (See Chapter 14, "More Layer Techniques," for more about motion blur.)

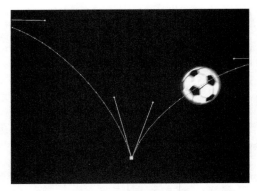

Figure 9.13 Bézier interpolation can allow the motion path to follow discontinuous curves, such as the one that describes the path of a ball's bounce.

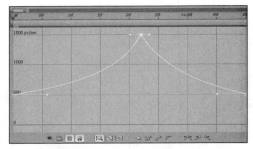

Figure 9.14 Temporally, Bézier interpolation can create sudden acceleration and deceleration. The bouncing ball accelerates until the moment of impact and then suddenly decelerates as it ascends.

Qu'est-ce Que C'est Bézier? *Qui Est* Bézier?

In case your French is rusty, *Bézier* is pronounced *bay-zee-yay*, after the late Pierre Etienne Bézier, who developed the math behind his namesake curve in the 1970s for use in computer-aided design and manufacture. This same math became the basis for Adobe PostScript fonts, path-based drawing, and—yes—the interpolation methods used in computer animation. Bézier died in 1999. *Merci*, Monsieur Bézier.

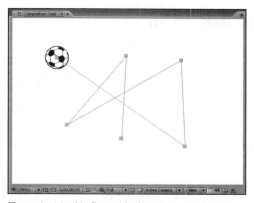

Figure 9.15 In this figure, the layer's position property uses hold keyframes. The layer remains in the position defined by a keyframe until the next keyframe is reached, at which time the layer instantly appears in its new position. A thin solid line between keyframes isn't a motion path; it indicates the order of keyframed positions.

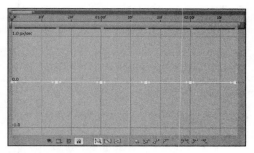

Figure 9.16 Keyframes of other properties that use hold interpolation also retain their current value until the next keyframe. The speed graph of a held property displays as disconnected keyframes at zero.

Hold

Although you can observe its effects both spatially and temporally, hold interpolation is a strictly temporal type of interpolation, halting changes in a property's value at the keyframe. The value remains fixed until the current frame of the composition reaches the next keyframe, where the property is set to a new value instantly. For example, specifying hold keyframes for a layer's Position property causes the layer to disappear suddenly and then reappear in different places. Instead of a dotted motion path, a thin solid line connects hold keyframes, indicating not the motion path but the order of keyframed positions (**Figure 9.15**). Similarly, nonspatial properties proceed instantly from one held keyframed value to another. Whereas using linearly interpolated keyframes to change a layer's opacity value from 0 to 100 is comparable to using a dimmer light, using hold keyframes is more like using a light switch. In the speed graph, hold keyframes appear as unconnected keyframes with a speed of zero (**Figure 9.16**).

Bézier Curves and the Motion Path

Motion paths consist of *Bézier curves*: the same kind of curves that define shapes in drawing programs like Photoshop and Illustrator—as well as the masks you create in After Effects. Instead of drawing a shape freehand, you can define a shape using a Bézier curve. In a Bézier curve, you define vertices (aka control points), which are connected by line segments automatically. (It already sounds a lot like keyframes and interpolation, doesn't it?)

The curves of the line segments are defined and controlled by *direction lines*. Two direction lines can extend from each vertex. The length and angle of one direction line influences the shape of the curve preceding the vertex; the other influences the curve following the vertex. (Imagine that the direction lines exert a gravitational pull on the line that enters and exits a vertex.) Dragging the end of a direction line alters the line and thus its corresponding curve (**Figure 9.17**).

Just as a Bézier curve consists of vertices connected by line segments, a *motion path* consists of position keyframes connected by line segments (albeit dotted lines). The same techniques you use to draw shapes in a drawing program can be applied to creating motion paths in After Effects (**Figure 9.18**). (In fact, you can copy a mask path into a comp as a motion path.)

Direction line/   Control point/
Tangent   Vertex   Line segment

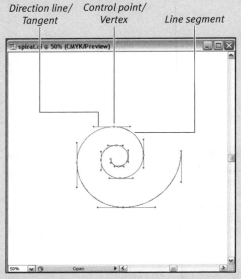

Figure 9.17 The Bézier curves you use to define a shape in a drawing program or a mask in After Effects...

Motion path   Keyframe   Tangent
(interpolated   (value you   (influences
values)   specify)   path)

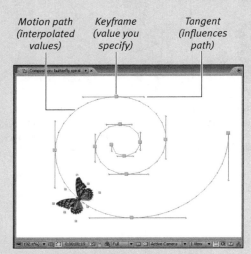

Figure 9.18 ...also define a motion path in After Effects. However, the terms used to describe the curve depend on the context.

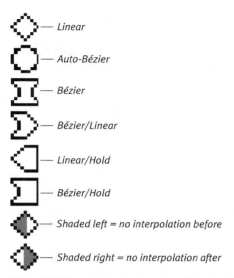

— Linear

— Auto-Bézier

— Bézier

— Bézier/Linear

— Linear/Hold

— Bézier/Hold

— Shaded left = no interpolation before

— Shaded right = no interpolation after

Figure 9.19 Though the standard view of the timeline doesn't graph interpolation, the shape of each keyframe's icons indicates the type of interpolation.

Mixed incoming and outgoing interpolation

A keyframe can use different interpolation types for its incoming and outgoing interpolation. A keyframe's incoming and outgoing spatial interpolation can be a mix of linear and Bézier. A keyframe's temporal interpolation may use any combination of linear, Bézier, and hold for its incoming and outgoing interpolation. As usual, the shape of the motion path or graph in the Graph Editor indicates mixed interpolation. In the standard view of the time graph (rather than in the Graph Editor view), keyframe icons also indicate the temporal interpolation type.

Keyframe icons and interpolation

The Graph Editor shows interpolation explicitly in the form of a value or speed graph. Regardless of the interpolation type, keyframe icons appear as small boxes, or *control points*, on the graph. Roving keyframes always appear as small dots.

But as you saw in Chapter 7, keyframe icons look different when you're not using the Graph Editor. In the standard view of the time ruler, an expanded property's keyframes appear as relatively large icons. Because no graph is visible, each icon's shape helps indicate the incoming and outgoing interpolation (**Figure 9.19**). If you expand a heading only, any individual property's keyframes appear as small dots to indicate their presence and position.

INTERPOLATION TYPES

Specifying the Default Spatial Interpolation

Ordinarily, motion-path keyframes use auto Bézier interpolation. If most of your spatial animation requires linear interpolation (or if you simply prefer it as your initial setting), you can change the default in the Preferences dialog box.

To set the default spatial interpolation:

1. Choose After Effects > Preferences > General (Mac) or Edit > Preferences > General (**Figure 9.20**).

   The General pane of the Preferences dialog box appears.

2. *Do either of the following* (**Figure 9.21**):

   ▲ Select Default Spatial Interpolation to Linear to make new motion paths use linear interpolation.

   ▲ Deselect Default Spatial Interpolation to Linear to make new motion paths use auto Bézier interpolation.

3. Click OK to close the Preferences dialog box.

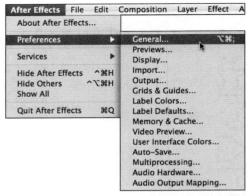

Figure 9.20 Choose After Effects > Preferences > General (Mac) or Edit > Preferences > General (Windows).

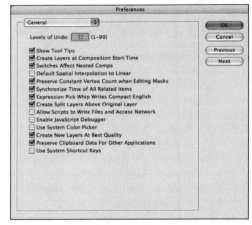

Figure 9.21 In the General pane of the Preferences dialog box, choose whether to use linear interpolation as the default.

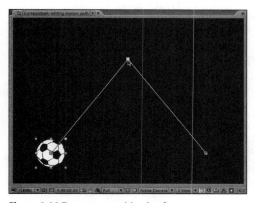

Figure 9.22 To move a position keyframe...

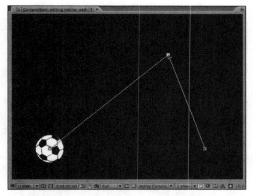

Figure 9.23 ...drag its icon to a new location in the Layer panel (for anchor point or effect point) or Comp panel (for position or effect point).

Specifying Spatial Interpolation in the Motion Path

In Chapter 7, you learned that you can change the spatial positioning of each keyframe by dragging it directly into a Composition or Layer panel. This section focuses on using spatial interpolation to change the course of the motion path from one keyframe to the next.

The following tasks assume you remember how to set a Comp or Layer panel to show motion paths. To refresh your memory, turn to "Parts of the Layer panel" in Chapter 6, and "Viewing Spatial Controls in the Comp Panel" in Chapter 7. And because you can apply your mastery of mask paths to editing motion paths, this section covers just the essentials. (See the sidebar "Bézier Curves and the Motion Path," earlier in this chapter; see Chapter 10, "Mask Essentials," for more about editing mask paths.)

To move a position keyframe:

1. Select a layer with an animated property to reveal its motion path in a Composition or Layer panel.

   Position and effect-point paths appear in the Composition panel (**Figure 9.22**); anchor-point paths appear in the Layer panel.

2. Using the selection tool, drag a keyframe (an x icon in the motion path) to a new position (**Figure 9.23**).

To toggle between auto Bézier and linear interpolation:

1. Select a layer with an animated property to reveal its motion path in a Composition or Layer panel.

   Position and effect-point paths appear in the Composition panel (**Figure 9.24**); anchor-point paths appear in the Layer panel.

2. In the Tools panel, select the Pen tool (**Figure 9.25**).

3. In the motion path, click a keyframe icon to convert it.

   The Pen tool becomes the Convert Vertex tool ⊢ when you position it over a keyframe (**Figure 9.26**). A keyframe using linear interpolation is converted to auto Bézier, with two equal control handles (motion path tangents) extending from the keyframe. Any Bézier-type keyframe is converted to linear, with no direction handles.

4. In the Tools panel, choose the Selection tool.

   Once you convert a keyframe, adjust it with the Selection tool. Clicking it without changing tools converts it back.

To convert auto Bézier to continuous Bézier:

1. Select a layer with an animated property to reveal its motion path in a Composition or Layer panel.

2. Using the Selection tool, drag one tangent of an auto Bézier keyframe so that it's shorter or longer than the other (**Figure 9.27**).

   Both of the keyframe's tangents form a continuous line, but they influence the path by different amounts.

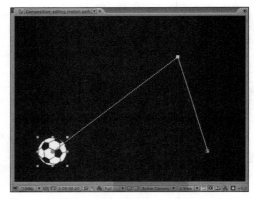

Figure 9.24 Select a layer so that its motion path is visible in the Comp panel.

Figure 9.25 In the Tools panel, select the Pen tool.

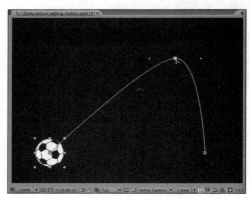

Figure 9.26 Clicking a keyframe with the Convert Vertex tool changes the keyframe from auto Bézier to linear and vice versa.

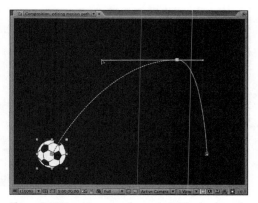

Figure 9.27 Dragging one of an auto Bézier keyframe's tangents makes it a continuous Bézier keyframe. The tangents remain continuous, but they influence the path unequally.

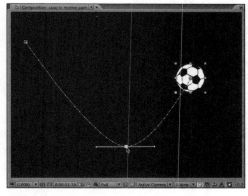

Figure 9.28 Select one or more keyframes in the motion path.

Figure 9.29 Select the Pen tool.

To convert continuous Bézier to Bézier, and vice versa:

1. Select a layer with an animated property to reveal its motion path in a Composition or Layer panel.

2. Select one or more keyframes in the motion path (**Figure 9.28**).

   The selected keyframe's motion path tangents (control handles) become visible.

3. In the Tools panel, select the Pen tool (**Figure 9.29**).

4. In the motion path, drag a direction handle (**Figure 9.30**).

   The Pen tool becomes the Convert Vertex tool ⋀ when you position it over a motion path tangent (direction handle). Dragging a direction handle of a Bézier keyframe converts it to continuous Bézier with two related tangents; dragging a tangent of a continuous Bézier keyframe splits the two tangents, converting it to Bézier.

5. In the Tools panel, choose the Selection tool ⬉.

   Once you convert a keyframe, adjust its direction handles with the Selection tool. Otherwise, you'll convert it back.

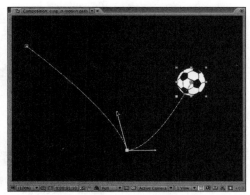

Figure 9.30 When positioned over a path tangent, the Pen becomes the Convert Vertex icon. Drag a tangent to change continuous Bézier to Bézier and vice versa.

SPECIFYING SPATIAL INTERPOLATION

To toggle between the Selection tool and a Pen tool:

1. Position the mouse over a motion path in a Comp or Layer panel, and *do either of the following*:

   ▲ To toggle the current Pen tool to the Selection tool, press and hold the Command/Ctrl key.

   ▲ To toggle the Selection tool to the Pen tool currently visible in the Tools panel, press and hold Command-Opt (Mac) or Ctrl-Alt (Windows) (**Figure 9.31**).

2. Release the keyboard modifier to continue using the currently selected tool.

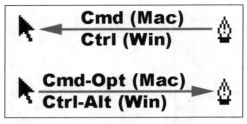

Figure 9.31 Press and hold Cmd/Ctrl to toggle between the currently selected Pen tool and the Selection tool; press Cmd-Opt/Ctrl-Alt to toggle between the Selection tool and the Pen tool.

Speed in the Motion Path

In the motion path, the spacing between dots indicates speed. Closely spaced dots indicate slower speeds; more widely spaced dots indicate faster speeds. If the dot spacing changes between keyframes, this means the speed is changing—accelerating or decelerating (**Figure 9.32**). (A solid line means hold interpolation has been applied; see the section "Interpolation Types," earlier in this chapter).

Remember that the motion path gives you direct control over the physical distance between keyframes—not their timing or the temporal interpolation. As you use controls in the timeline to alter the speed or temporal interpolation of a spatial property, watch how the motion path also changes.

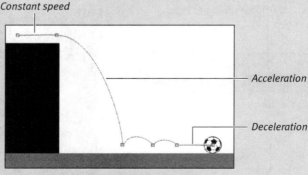

Figure 9.32 The spacing of dots in the motion path indicate speed: the more closely spaced the dots, the slower the motion. A solid line indicates hold interpolation (and no actual motion).

Using the Graph Editor: An Overview

By taking over the area under the timeline's time ruler, the Graph Editor affords a detailed view of property changes and a spacious area in which to edit them (**Figures 9.33** and **9.34**). The number of options reflects the Graph Editor's flexibility but may also make the process seem more complex than it really is. The following task provides an overview.

Later sections cover each aspect of the process in greater detail. First, you'll learn how to adjust the timing and values of keyframes using the Graph Editor instead of the methods you learned in Chapter 7. Then, you'll move on to using the graphs to adjust interpolation (the values between keyframes).

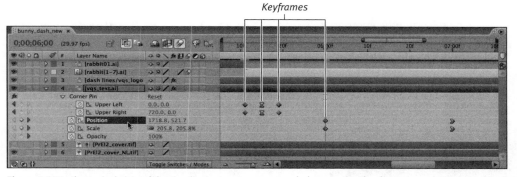

Figure 9.33 In the typical view of the timeline, you can see expanded properties' keyframe icons but no graphical representation of interpolated values.

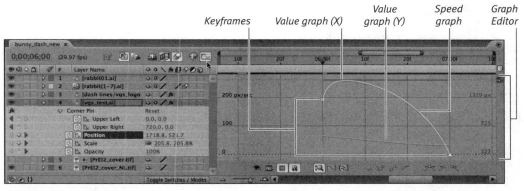

Figure 9.34 The Graph Editor depicts any combination of properties as graphs in a spacious and detailed view under the time ruler.

To adjust properties in the Graph Editor:

1. In the Timeline panel, select the Graph Editor button ![] (**Figure 9.35**).

2. Specify which properties are visible by choosing an option in the Show Properties pull-down menu (**Figure 9.36**).

3. Specify the graph types you want to edit for the visible properties in the Graph Type and Options pull-down menu.

4. Specify the other information you want to view by selecting the appropriate option in the Graph Type and Options pull-down menu (**Figure 9.37**).

   Optional information includes layer In and Out point icons, layer markers, and so on.

5. Edit the visible property graphs using techniques described later in this chapter (**Figure 9.38**).

   You can select, move, add, and delete property keyframes; you can adjust their interpolation types using either manual or automatic methods.

✔ Tip

■ Technically, you can use a keyboard shortcut to specify preset interpolation types to a keyframe without switching to the Graph Editor. Both methods are covered in the section "Setting a Keyframe's Temporal Interpolation Type," later in this chapter.

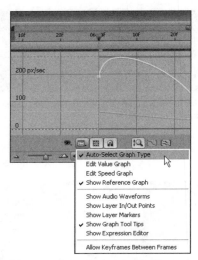

Figure 9.37 Specify the graph type you want to edit and other options.

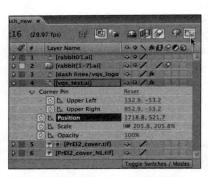

Figure 9.35 Select the Graph Editor button.

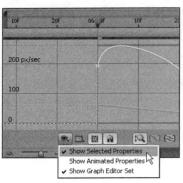

Figure 9.36 Specify the visible properties in the Show Properties pull-down menu.

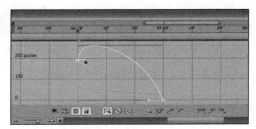

Figure 9.38 Edit a property graph by dragging its keyframe and ease handles or by using an automated method (keyframe assistant).

USING THE GRAPH EDITOR: AN OVERVIEW

Table 9.2

Recognizing Temporal Interpolation

TEMPORAL INTERPOLATION	IN THE VALUE GRAPH	IN THE SPEED/VELOCITY GRAPH
No speed change	Horizontal line	Horizontal line
Constant speed	Straight line with any slope	Horizontal line
Sudden speed change	Sharp corner	Disconnected line/ease handles
Acceleration	Curve with steep slope	Upward-sloping curve
Deceleration	Curve with shallow slope	Downward-sloping curve
Holding	Horizontal line, unconnected	Horizontal line, where current speed = zero

Understanding Value and Speed Graphs

In the following sections, you'll use the Graph Editor to (what else?) edit a graph of a property. But first, let's take a moment to examine the two types of graphs you'll encounter: the value graph and speed graph. As you proceed with the graph-editing tasks in the following sections, note how the shape of a value graph or speed graph corresponds to the animation (**Figures 9.39** and **9.40**, and **Table 9.2**).

continues on next page

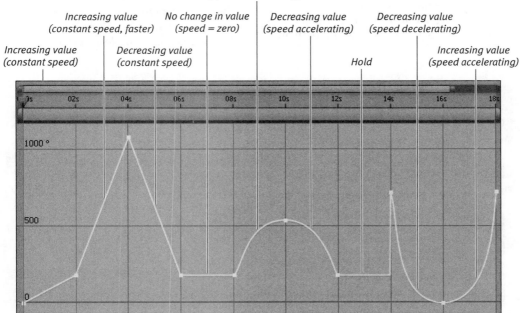

Figure 9.39 A value graph shows changes in a property's value (in this case, Rotation). Examine how each graph shape corresponds with certain types of temporal interpolation.

UNDERSTANDING VALUE AND SPEED GRAPHS

Value graph

A *value graph* measures a property's value vertically and its time horizontally. The units in which values are expressed depend on the type of property: Rotation is measured in rotations and degrees, Opacity in percentages, and so on. The slope of the line between keyframes represents the rate of change in units/second. Straight lines indicate a constant rate; curved lines indicate a changing rate, or acceleration (Figure 9.39).

A value graph is particularly well suited to properties such as Opacity and Audio Levels, because these properties correspond well with the "up and down" or "high and low" nature of the graph.

Note that some properties consist of more than one value, or *dimension*. For example, a Position property includes values for both an X and Y coordinate. Hence, a position value graph includes two, color-coded lines: one representing the X coordinate value and the other representing the Y coordinate value.

Speed graph

A speed graph measures rates of change in a property's values. The units measured by a speed graph depend on the property type: degrees of rotation/sec, percentage opacity/sec, and so on. Regardless of the specific property, the rate of change (units/sec) is measured vertically, and time (sec) is measured horizontally in both graphs. Therefore, the slope of the line represents acceleration (units/sec/sec). Compared to interpreting a value graph, interpreting a speed graph isn't as straightforward. For example, a property's value may be increasing or decreasing—but if its rate of change is constant, it results in a horizontal line in the speed graph.

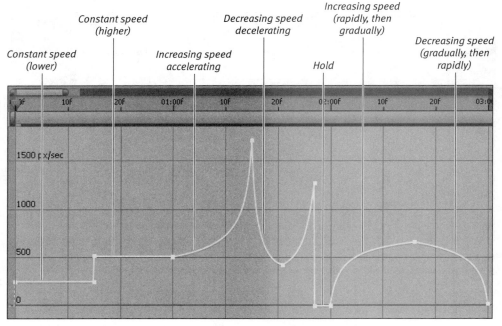

Figure 9.40 A speed graph shows changes in a property's speed (here, Position).

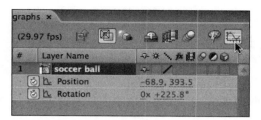

Figure 9.41 In the switches area of the Timeline panel, select the Show Graph Editor button.

Viewing Property Graphs

To view temporal interpolation and control it manually, toggle the area under the time ruler to the Graph Editor.

The Graph Editor's flexible viewing options help you view the combination of properties you want: selected properties, animated properties, or properties you specify by including them in what's known as the *graph editor set*.

To toggle the Graph Editor:

◆ In the Timeline panel, select the Show Graph Editor button [icon] (**Figure 9.41**).

The area under the time ruler changes to the Graph Editor (**Figure 9.42**). The properties visible in the Graph Editor depend on options you specify in the Show Properties pull-down menu; the types of graphs visible depends on the options you specify in the Graph Type and Options pull-down menu. (See the tasks "To specify visible properties in the Graph Editor" and "To specify the graph types displayed in the Graph Editor," later in this chapter.)

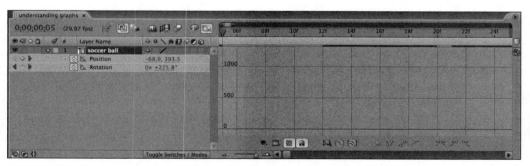

Figure 9.42 The time ruler area toggles to the Graph Editor view.

To specify visible properties in the Graph Editor:

◆ In the Graph Editor, click the Show Properties pull-down menu , and *choose any of the following* (**Figure 9.43**):

▲ **Show Selected Properties**—Includes the property you select in the layer outline

▲ **Show Animated Properties**—Includes all of the selected layer's animated properties

▲ **Show Graph Editor Set**—Includes all properties you specify as part of the graph editor set (see the next task, "To designate a graph editor set")

The properties you specify appear in the Graph Editor.

Figure 9.43 In the Graph Editor's Show Properties pull-down menu, select which properties are visible.

Figure 9.44 Expand the layer outline to reveal the properties you want to add to the graph editor set, and then select their Include in Graph Editor Set button.

To designate a graph editor set:

1. In a comp's layer outline, expand layers to reveal the properties you want to add to the graph editor set.

2. For each property you want to add to the graph editor set, select the Include in Graph Editor Set button (**Figure 9.44**).

Properties in the set appear in the Graph Editor when the Show Graph Editor Set option is selected (see the previous task, "To specify visible properties in the Graph Editor").

✔ Tips

■ Here's a reminder of something you learned in Chapter 7: Press U to reveal all the animated properties of all the selected layers.

■ Keyboard shortcuts make it easy to reveal just the properties you want. See Chapter 7 for a table of some of the most common keyboard shortcuts.

Specifying the Graph Type

The Graph Editor can represent any property as a value graph or speed graph. Turn back to the section "Understanding Value and Speed Graphs," earlier in this chapter, to review how the graphs work. Later sections explain how to manipulate the graphs.

To specify the graph types displayed in the Graph Editor:

1. In the Graph Editor, click the Graph Type and Options pull-down menu, and then *choose any of the following options* (**Figure 9.45**):

   ▲ **Auto-Select Graph Type**—After Effects determines the most appropriate type of graph to display for editing.

   ▲ **Edit Value Graph**—Displays the visible properties' value graph for editing.

   ▲ **Edit Speed Graph**—Displays the visible properties' speed graph for editing.

   In the Graph Editor, the type of graph you choose appears for the visible properties (**Figure 9.46**).

2. To display the type of graph you *did not* specify in step 1 for reference, select Show Reference Graph (**Figure 9.47**).

   For example, if you chose Edit Speed Graph in step 1, then selecting Show Reference Graph makes the value graph visible. However, you can't edit the reference graph (**Figure 9.48**).

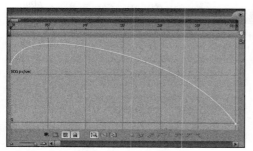

Figure 9.45 Selecting an option in the Graph Editor's Graph Type and Options pull-down menu...

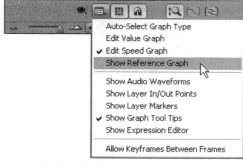

Figure 9.47 Selecting Show Reference Graph...

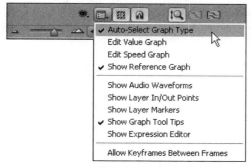

Figure 9.46 ...displays that type of graph for the visible property. Here, the property's speed graph is visible for editing.

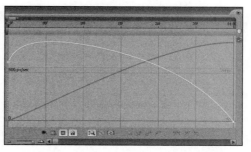

Figure 9.48 ...makes the other graph visible (in this case, the value graph). The reference graph can't be edited, but it reflects the changes you make to the other graph.

Viewing Optional Information in the Graph Editor

The Graph Editor not only lets you select which property and type of graph you want to view but also lets you reveal other helpful information, such as audio waveforms, In point and Out point icons, markers, tool tips, and expressions (**Figure 9.49**).

Other options help you home in on the graph you want to work with and scale the graph when adjustments make it exceed the available space.

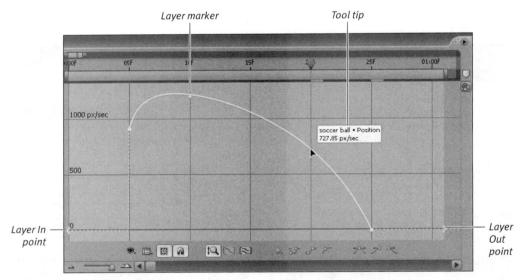

Layer marker

Tool tip

soccer ball • Position
727.85 px/sec

Layer In point

Layer Out point

Figure 9.49 The Graph Editor can display optional information. Hovering the mouse over a graph reveals a tool tip, which in this case shows the property value's speed at that point.

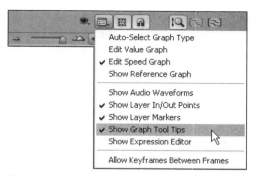

Figure 9.50 Select the options you want in the Graph Editor's Graph Type and Options pull-down menu.

To specify Graph Editor options:

◆ In the Graph Editor, click the Graph Type and Options pull-down menu, and then *choose any of the following options* (**Figure 9.50**):

▲ **Show Audio Waveforms**—When you're viewing an audio layer's Audio Levels property, this option displays a waveform, or graphical representation of audio power.

▲ **Show Layer In/Out Points**—Shows In point and Out point icons for the layer containing properties visible in the Graph Editor.

▲ **Show Layer Markers**—Shows marker icons for the layer containing properties visible in the Graph Editor.

▲ **Show Graph Tool Tips**—Displays a tool tip containing the current speed or value at the point where you position the mouse over a graph.

▲ **Show Expression Editor**—Shows an area to add and edit an *expression*, or script-based formula for determining the property's value (see Chapter 16, "Complex Projects," for more about expressions).

▲ **Allow Keyframes Between Frames**—Permits you to set keyframes between timebase divisions, which can be especially useful when you're timing keyframes with audio.

The Graph Editor activates the options you specify.

To scale the graph automatically:

◆ In the Graph Editor, *select any of the following options*:

▲ **Auto-zoom Graph Height** ▨

▲ **Fit Selection to View** ▨

▲ **Fit All Graphs to View** ▨

The view adjusts according to your selection.

Moving Keyframes in the Graph Editor

You select keyframes in the Graph Editor using the same methods you use to select keyframes in a motion path (covered earlier in this chapter) or, for that matter, to select keyframes in the standard view of the time ruler (covered in Chapter 7). The keyframe icons differ, but the procedures are the same, and we won't review them here. However, the Graph Editor includes a couple of unique features when it comes to keyframes.

First, the Graph Editor has its own *snap* feature. As you know from other chapters (and other programs), snapping gives objects a magnetic quality, so they tend to align with one another. In the Graph Editor, enabling snapping helps you align keyframes with In points, Out points, markers, the current time indicator (CTI), and other keyframes.

The Graph Editor also includes a more unexpected feature, a *keyframe transform box*. With this option active, selecting multiple keyframes includes them in a transform box—just like the bounding box that lets you scale a layer. Ordinarily, selecting multiple keyframes lets you move all of them by the same amount. In contrast, a transform box lets you adjust keyframes *proportionally*. In other words, keyframes included in the transform box maintain their relative positions on the box.

To enable keyframe snapping in the Graph Editor:

◆ In the Graph Editor, select the Snap button ▣ (**Figure 9.51**).

When the Snap button is selected, keyframes align with other keyframes, markers, the CTI, and other elements more easily.

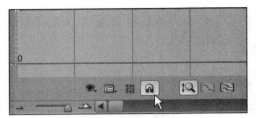

Figure 9.51 Select the Graph Editor's Snap button to assist in aligning keyframes with In points, Out points, the CTI, or other keyframes.

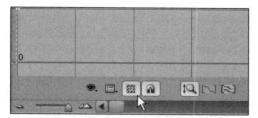

Figure 9.52 Selecting the Graph Editor's Show Bounding Box button...

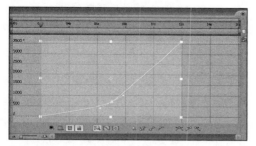

Figure 9.53 ...creates a bounding box around selected keyframes.

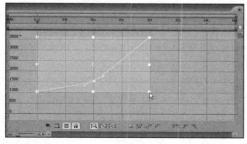

Figure 9.54 Dragging the bounding box scales the box and moves the keyframes accordingly.

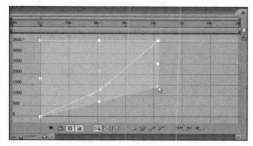

Figure 9.55 Press Option/Alt to drag a bounding box's handle independently of other handles.

To move keyframes using a transform box:

◆ In the Graph Editor, select the Show Bounding Box button ▦ (**Figure 9.52**).

When you select multiple keyframes, a bounding box appears around the keyframes (**Figure 9.53**).

To move multiple keyframes using a transform box:

1. With the Show Bounding Box option selected, *do either of the following:*

   ▲ Shift-click multiple keyframes.

   ▲ Drag a marquee around consecutive keyframes.

   A bounding box appears around the selected keyframes.

2. *Do any of the following:*

   ▲ Drag any of the bounding box's handles to scale the box (**Figure 9.54**).

   ▲ Press Option/Alt to move a handle on the bounding box independently of the other handles (**Figure 9.55**).

   The keyframes contained in the bounding box move according to your adjustments, maintaining their relative positions on the box.

Adding and Removing Keyframes in the Graph Editor

You can add keyframes to and remove keyframes from a property graph as you would a motion or mask path. Even so, it's worth reviewing the techniques in the context of keyframing properties in the Graph Editor. Don't forget that you can still add and remove keyframes using the methods you learned in Chapter 7.

To add or remove keyframes in the graph:

1. *Do either of the following:*
   - ▲ In the Tools panel, select the Pen tool ![pen] (**Figure 9.56**).
   - ▲ With the Selection tool selected, press Command/Ctrl.

2. In the Graph Editor, *do any of the following:*
   - ▲ To add a keyframe, position the Pen tool over the line in a graph so that the Pen tool appears as an Add Vertex icon ![addvertex] (**Figure 9.57**) and then click.

     A keyframe is added on the graph where you click (**Figure 9.58**).
   - ▲ To remove a keyframe, position the Pen tool over a keyframe in a graph so that the Pen tool appears as a Delete Vertex icon ![deletevertex] and then click (**Figure 9.59**).

     The keyframe is removed and the line (interpolation) reshapes accordingly (**Figure 9.60**).

3. Make sure to choose the Selection tool when you're finished.

✔ Tip

- ■ If you use the Pen tool to add a keyframe to the graph, dragging extends a direction line, or ease handle.

Figure 9.56 In the Tools panel, choose the Pen tool (shown here) or press Command/Ctrl with the Selection tool.

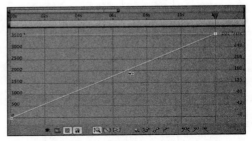

Figure 9.57 The Pen tool becomes the Add Vertex tool.

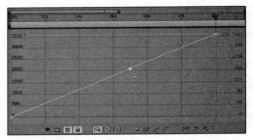

Figure 9.58 Click the value graph to create a new keyframe.

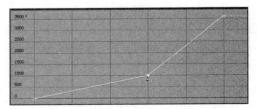

Figure 9.59 Position the Pen tool over a keyframe so that the mouse becomes a Delete Vertex icon, and then click...

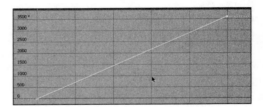

Figure 9.60 ...to remove the keyframe. The graph adjusts accordingly.

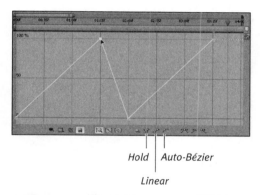

Hold | *Auto-Bézier*

Linear

Figure 9.61 Select a keyframe, and select the button that corresponds with the interpolation type you want to use. Here, a keyframe that uses linear interpolation...

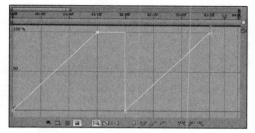

Figure 9.62 ...is converted to one that uses hold interpolation.

Setting a Keyframe's Temporal Interpolation Type

The Graph Editor includes buttons that apply hold, linear, or auto Bézier interpolation to selected keyframes.

If the automatic method doesn't yield the result you want, you can adjust the interpolation manually or apply a keyframe assistant to achieve other common effects (see the following sections for details).

To set a keyframe's interpolation using a button:

1. In the Graph Editor, select the keyframes you want to adjust.

2. At the bottom of the Graph Editor, click the button that corresponds with the type of temporal interpolation you want the keyframe to use (**Figure 9.61**):

   Hold
   Linear
   Auto-Bézier

   The selected keyframes use the interpolation method you specify (**Figure 9.62**).

✔ Tips

- You can toggle a keyframe between using linear and auto Bézier interpolation by Command/Ctrl-clicking the keyframe.

- You can specify selected keyframes' interpolation by choosing Animation > Keyframe Interpolation in the main menu or Keyframe Interpolation in the Graph Editor's Edit Keyframe pull-down menu. In the dialog box, specify the type of interpolation you want.

Adjusting Temporal Interpolation Manually

As you've seen, many of the principles of adjusting a motion path apply to adjusting a property graph. Both are described by Bézier curves, although the terminology can differ. And whereas a motion path traces a literal course through space, the line of a graph corresponds to a property's value or speed. But although the techniques you use to edit Bézier curves resemble one another in principle, they differ in practice. The main difference lies in how you adjust the curves manually: dragging direction lines in a value graph, or ease handles in a speed graph.

In a value graph, you can drag direction lines 180 degrees to influence the graph's curve—and, hence, its incoming and outgoing interpolation. Bézier curves closely resemble their counterparts in a motion path.

In a speed graph, ease handles influence the shape of the curve and, thereby, the interpolation. However, ease handles always extend horizontally from a keyframe; their length but not their angle helps shape the curve. Whereas a sudden change in a value plots a cusp in a value graph, a sudden change in speed splits the keyframe so that it occupies two different vertical positions on the speed graph.

To adjust a value graph manually:

1. Expand the layer outline to view the value graph for an animated layer property.

2. Select the keyframes you want to adjust.

3. *Do any of the following* to the incoming or outgoing direction lines:
   - ▲ Drag a keyframe up to increase the value or down to decrease the value (**Figures 9.63** and **9.64**).

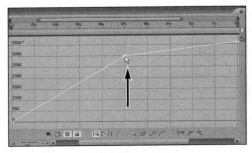

Figure 9.63 Drag a keyframe up to increase...

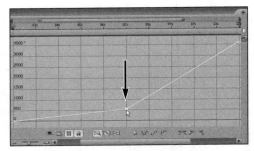

Figure 9.64 ...or down to decrease the value (shown here) or speed.

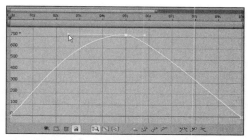

Figure 9.65 In the value graph, extend a direction line manually to use continuous Bézier interpolation.

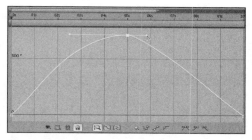

Figure 9.66 In the value graph, Option/Alt-drag a direction handle.

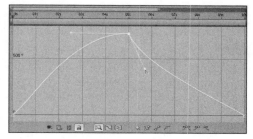

Figure 9.67 Dragging a direction handle of a continuous Bézier keyframe splits the direction handles, converting it to Bézier.

▲ To convert auto Bézier to continuous Bézier, drag one direction line so that the direction lines are unequal but retain their continuous relationship (**Figure 9.65**).

▲ To toggle between continuous Bézier and Bézier, Option/Alt-drag a direction handle (**Figure 9.66**).

The Selection tool becomes the Convert Vertex tool when you position it over a direction handle. Dragging a direction handle of a Bézier keyframe converts it to continuous Bézier with two related direction handles; dragging a direction handle of a continuous Bézier keyframe splits the direction handles, converting it to Bézier (**Figure 9.67**).

✔ Tip

■ As usual, avoid converting a keyframe unintentionally: Invoke the Convert Vertex tool only when you want to convert a keyframe; otherwise, use the Selection tool.

To adjust a speed graph manually:

1. Expand the layer outline to view the speed graph for an animated layer property.

2. Select the keyframes you want to adjust (**Figure 9.68**).

continues on next page

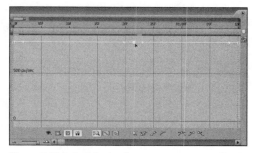

Figure 9.68 Select the keyframes you want to adjust.

3. *Do any of the following* to the incoming or outgoing ease handles:

▲ Drag an ease handle up to increase the incoming or outgoing speed at a keyframe (**Figure 9.69**).

▲ Drag an ease handle down to decrease the incoming or outgoing speed at a keyframe.

▲ Drag the left ease handle to change its length and influence on the preceding curve (**Figure 9.70**).

▲ Drag the right ease handle to adjust its length and influence on the following curve.

▲ Option/Alt-click a keyframe to toggle it between linear and auto Bézier.

The shape of the graph and the corresponding property's speed change according to your adjustments (**Figures 9.71** and **9.72**). When the incoming and outgoing speeds differ, a keyframe's icon splits, occupying two different vertical positions on the graph.

✔ Tip

■ You can adjust a graph with numerical precision by selecting the keyframe and choosing Keyframe Velocity from the Edit Keyframe button's pull-down menu.

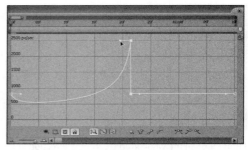

Figure 9.69 Drag an ease handle up to increase the incoming or outgoing speed at a keyframe.

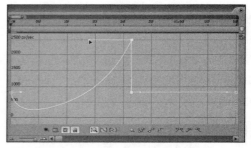

Figure 9.70 Drag an incoming ease handle to the left to increase the influence of the previous keyframe's value.

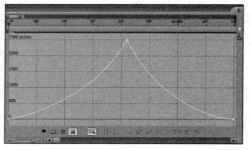

Figure 9.71 An abrupt shift from acceleration to deceleration, or bounce, looks like this in a speed graph.

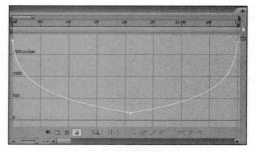

Figure 9.72 A gradual deceleration followed by a gradual acceleration (as when a rising object slows at its apex) looks like this in a speed graph.

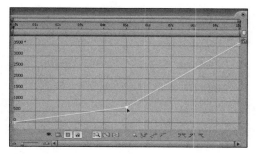

Figure 9.73 Select the keyframes you want to ease with a keyframe assistant. This keyframe uses linear interpolation.

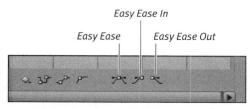

Figure 9.74 In the Graph Editor, select the icon that corresponds to the keyframe assistant you want to apply.

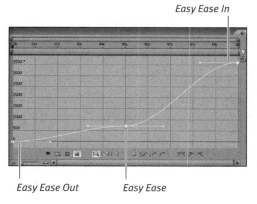

Figure 9.75 The selected keyframe's interpolation is adjusted according to your choice. The linear interpolation pictured in Figure 9.73 looks like this after you apply keyframe assistants.

Applying Keyframe Assistants

Adding slight deceleration to soften or ease the speed into and out of keyframes is such a commonly used technique that After Effects has provided the following *keyframe assistants* to automate the task:

Easy Ease smoothes both the keyframe's incoming and outgoing interpolation.

Easy Ease In smoothes the keyframe's incoming interpolation.

Easy Ease Out smoothes the keyframe's outgoing interpolation.

Try employing a keyframe assistant and observing its effects on a layer's property graph and animation.

To apply a keyframe assistant in the Graph Editor:

1. In the Graph Editor, select the keyframes to which you want to apply a keyframe assistant (**Figure 9.73**).

2. At the bottom of the Graph Editor, click the icon that corresponds to the keyframe assistant you want to use (**Figure 9.74**):

   Easy Ease ![icon] to ease both incoming and outgoing speed

   Easy Ease In ![icon] to ease incoming speed

   Easy Ease Out ![icon] to ease outgoing speed

   The icons and graphs associated with the selected keyframes reflect your choice, and the animation plays accordingly (**Figure 9.75**).

Smoothing Motion with Roving Keyframes

Frequently, adjusting a motion path causes drastic and unwanted fluctuations in timing. The layer goes where you want in terms of space, but its movement lags and lurches from one keyframe to the next. In the speed graph, these abrupt changes look like steep hills and chasms. You can adjust the speed and timing of the problem keyframes manually, or you can convert them into *roving keyframes*.

Roving keyframes retain their values; but their position in time is adjusted automatically so that the property's speed becomes more consistent, and the property's speed graph flattens out. The adjustments are derived from the values of the standard, time-bound keyframes before and after the roving keyframes. Moving the first or last keyframe automatically readjusts the roving keyframes in between. This way, you can change the duration of the animation without having to carefully adjust the speed between each part.

If you don't want a keyframe to rove, you can convert it back to a standard keyframe, which is *locked to time.*

To smooth motion with roving keyframes:

1. Reveal a property's speed graph in the Graph Editor.

2. Select a range of keyframes other than the first or last keyframe for the property (**Figure 9.76**).

   The keyframes preceding and after the range must be locked to time. That is, they must be standard, nonroving keyframes.

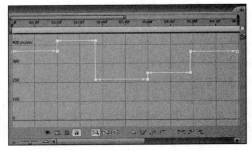

Figure 9.76 Select a range of keyframes between two keyframes. This uneven speed graph indicates sudden changes in speed between keyframed positions.

Figure 9.77 Selecting Rove Across Time in the Graph Editor's Edit Keyframe pull-down menu...

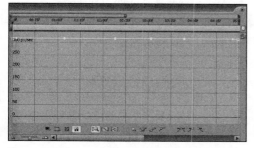

Figure 9.78 ...converts the selected keyframes to roving keyframes, which shift in time to create constant speed between the standard keyframes. Contrast this speed graph with the one in Figure 9.76.

3. In the Graph Editor, click the Edit Keyframe button, and then choose Rove Across Time from the pull-down menu (**Figure 9.77**).

The selected keyframes become roving keyframes, moving in time so that the speed is constant (as evidenced by the speed graph). The roving keyframe icons appear as small dots (**Figure 9.78**).

To convert a roving keyframe to a standard keyframe:

1. Reveal a property's speed graph in the Graph Editor, and select one or more of its roving keyframes (**Figure 9.79**).

2. Click the Graph Editor's Edit Keyframe button, and deselect Rove Across Time in the pull-down menu (**Figure 9.80**).

   The keyframe is converted from a roving keyframe to a standard keyframe that is locked to time. Its keyframe icon changes from a small dot to its standard icon (a small box in the Graph Editor, or a diamond icon in the standard view of the time ruler).

✔ Tip

■ You don't have to view Graph Editor to toggle between standard and roving keyframes. After selecting keyframes in the standard view of the time ruler, choose Animation > Keyframe Interpolation, and then specify whether the keyframes Rove Across Time or are Locked to Time.

Figure 9.79 Reveal the speed graph of a property, and select one or more of its roving keyframes...

Figure 9.80 ...and deselect Rove Across Time to convert the selection to standard keyframes, which are locked to time.

10

MASK ESSENTIALS

A *mask* is a shape, or path, that you create in a layer. You can draw a mask manually with a tool, define it numerically using the Mask Shape dialog box, or copy it from Adobe Illustrator or Photoshop. A mask can be a closed shape (such as a circle) or an open path (such as a curved line). Masks are essential to compositing images and to creating a number of other effects.

A *closed mask* modifies or creates an alpha channel—which, as you recall, defines the opaque and transparent areas of an image. The image within the masked area remains visible; the area outside the mask reveals the layers below. An open path, in contrast, consists of a curve, or path, with two endpoints. By itself, an open path can't define areas of opacity, but it can be used to achieve a variety of other effects. For example, you can use the Stroke effect to trace a mask with a color. Or, you can paste a mask path into the Comp panel to use it as a motion path. A mask can also define a curved baseline for path text. You can apply these techniques to both open and closed masks, but you can imagine how an open mask is sometimes the more appropriate choice.

This chapter is devoted to the fundamentals of mask making. You can apply what you learn in other chapters to animate mask properties, apply effects to masks, and combine masks with other techniques, such as layer modes. Later, you'll discover that the same tools that apply masks to layers can also be used to define a new type of layer, graphical objects called *shape layers*.

Understanding Masks

Masks are shapes you can apply to a layer to define areas of opacity or to specify a path on which to base other effects. For example, you can have text follow a mask path (as explained in Chapter 12, "Creating and Animating Text") or apply effects to masks to generate graphical elements.

After Effects includes a number of tools for creating masks, which can be closed shapes or open paths. You can control the contour of mask paths manually using Bézier curves or allow After Effects to calculate curves automatically with RotoBézier curves.

Remember that you always apply a mask to a layer. You can use many of the same tools and techniques to create a new layer, called a shape layer. For creating certain graphical elements, shape layers have some advantages over using masks. To learn more, see Chapter 14.

Mask creation tools

The Tools panel contains several tools for creating and modifying masks, but they fall into two main categories: Shape tools and Pen tools.

Shape tools allow you to draw some common geometric shapes with just a single drag of the mouse (**Figure 10.1**). Pressing certain keyboard modifiers as you drag lets you customize the shape. For example, you can constrain an ellipse's dimensions to a perfect circle or specify the number of points in a star.

Pen tools let you create custom shapes defined by Bézier curves used by many drawing programs, such as Illustrator. To create custom shapes using a simpler procedure, you can enable the RotoBézier option (**Figure 10.2**). You can also use the Pen tools to modify the shape of any mask.

Figure 10.1 Press and hold on the current Shape tool to reveal an extended panel of Shape tools...

Figure 10.2 ...or the current Pen tool to show various Pen tools.

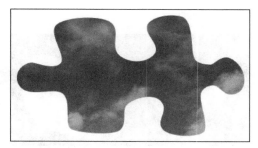

Figure 10.3 A closed path creates a typical mask, which defines the opaque areas of the layer image.

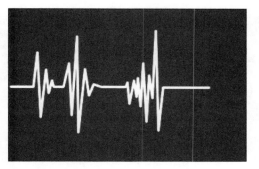

Figure 10.4 An open path doesn't create a mask per se, but it can be used for other effects, such as creating stroked lines. Open paths can also be used to create motion paths.

Open and closed paths

Masks can be closed shapes or open paths.

Closed masks—Strictly speaking, the term *mask* refers to a closed shape that defines areas of opacity. You can draw closed paths with any of the drawing tools (**Figure 10.3**). By default, the interior of a closed mask shape defines the opaque area of a layer; the exterior defines transparency. However, you can manipulate the transparency numerous ways.

Open masks—You can create open paths with the Pen tool, or you can open a closed path by using a menu command. Open paths aren't used as masks per se, but they can serve as the basis for path text and path-based effects (**Figure 10.4**). For example, they can serve as the baseline for text or be pasted into a motion path.

Bezier and RotoBézier curves

It can be useful to describe the contour of a mask as a path. When creating a path, you specify the position of control points (aka vertices), which are connected by line segments automatically. You can always control the position of each vertex, but the amount of control you have over the connecting segments depends on whether you're using Bézier or RotoBézier curves (**Figure 10.5**).

Bézier curves—In a standard mask, each line segment is a Bézier curve that you control manually. In a Bézier curve, each vertex can have direction lines, or tangents. The length and angle of the direction line at each end of a segment determines the shape of the curve.

RotoBézier curves—When you create a mask using the RotoBézier option, you set vertices only, not direction lines. After Effects calculates the curves automatically; however, you can change the relative amount of each curve by adjusting each point's *tension*. It's often easier to create masks using the RotoBézier option, but you can't create certain types of shapes, such as cusps.

✔ Tips

- Bézier curves should be a familiar concept by now; the same math used to calculate curves also applies to keyframe interpolation, covered in Chapter 9, "Keyframe Interpolation." When you think about it, control points on a mask path are analogous to keyframes, and line segments on a mask are comparable to interpolated values.

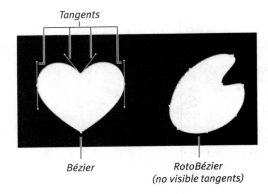

Tangents

Bézier RotoBézier
(no visible tangents)

Figure 10.5 It's easier to create shapes like the palette using the RotoBézier option, but manually adjusting tangents in a Bézier shape lets you create cusps like the ones at the top and bottom of the heart.

- Option/Alt-clicking a control point in a Bézier curve converts it from a smooth point to a corner point and vice versa; the same shortcut changes the tension of selected RotoBezier control points from an automatically calculated value to 100 percent and vice versa. Although the result is equivalent, this action doesn't convert the mask from one type to another.

UNDERSTANDING MASKS

Figure 10.6 The Layer panel shows masks in the context of the layer; it also lets you see the image outside the mask.

Figure 10.7 The Comp panel shows the layer after masks and other property changes have taken effect.

Viewing Masks in the Layer and Comp Panels

Although you mask a layer, you can create and work with masks not only in the Layer panel but in the Composition panel as well. The panel you use will depend on the task at hand as well as your personal preference. A Layer panel shows masks in the context of a single layer, letting you view the image outside the masked areas (**Figure 10.6**). In addition, the Layer panel shows you the layer before any property changes (Scale, Rotation, and so on) are applied. In contrast, the Composition panel shows only the masked portions of a layer and places them in the context of all the layers that are visible at the current time (**Figure 10.7**). By the time you're able to view a layer in the Comp panel, Mask, Effect, Transform, and 3D properties have all been applied.

When you want to create or modify a mask in the Comp panel, you must select the layer that contains the mask. Tasks throughout this chapter assume you have done so.

Viewing Masks in the Layer Outline

Each mask you create appears in the layer outline of the Timeline panel under the Mask property heading. The Target pull-down menu of the Layer panel also lists the layer's masks. The most recent mask appears at the top of the stacking order (**Figure 10.8**).

When you expand the Mask property heading, it reveals four properties: Mask Shape, Mask Feather, Mask Opacity, and Mask Expansion. The following sections deal with these properties as well as other ways to control layer masks.

Because you can rename, reorder, and lock masks just like layers, that information won't be covered here (**Figure 10.9**). (See Chapter 5, "Layer Basics," to learn the analogous procedures for layers).

You can also hide and apply motion blur to masks much as you can with a layer as a whole. But instead of clicking a button in the Timeline panel, you access these commands in the Layer > Mask menu (**Figure 10.10**). For example, masks don't have a video switch, but you can hide locked masks via the Layer > Mask > Hide Locked Masks command. Again, these commands won't be covered in detail here.

✔ Tip

■ Although locked and hidden masks are invisible in the Layer panel, their masking effect can still be seen in the Comp panel's image.

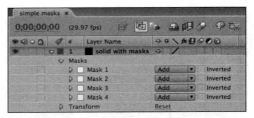

Figure 10.8 Masks appear in the layer outline in the order they were created. Expanding a mask reveals several properties: Shape, Feather, Opacity, and Expansion.

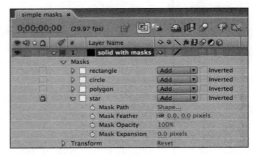

Figure 10.9 You can rename, reorder, and lock masks just like layers. Here, the default names have been replaced with more descriptive names, and the "star" mask has been locked.

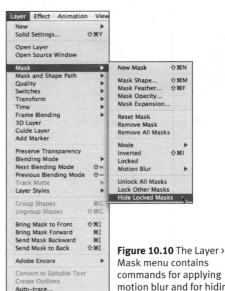

Figure 10.10 The Layer › Mask menu contains commands for applying motion blur and for hiding locked masks (shown here).

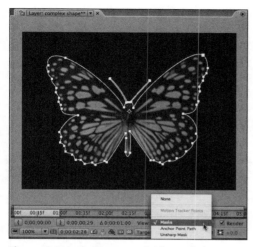

Figure 10.11 In the Layer panel's View pull-down menu, select Masks to make mask paths visible.

Figure 10.12 In the Comp panel, click the View Masks button...

Figure 10.13 ...to reveal the selected layer's masks.

Hiding and Showing Mask Paths

Because the Layer and Comp panels serve several purposes, sometimes you'll want to hide the mask paths from view. When you want to work with the layer masks, you can make them visible again. Creating a new mask reveals the masks for the selected layer automatically.

To view and hide masks in the Layer panel:

1. View a layer in a Layer panel.

2. In the Layer panel's View pull-down menu, select Masks to make mask paths visible (**Figure 10.11**).

   Selecting another option deselects the Masks option.

To view and hide masks in the Composition panel:

◆ In the Comp panel, click the View Masks button (**Figure 10.12**).

   Mask paths for selected layers can be viewed and edited in the Composition panel (**Figure 10.13**). Deselect the View Masks button to hide mask paths.

✔ Tips

■ You can hide locked masks only by choosing Layer > Mask > Hide Locked Masks. Although invisible in the Layer panel, locked and hidden masks still function in the Comp panel.

■ By default, mask paths appear yellow. By double-clicking a mask's color swatch in the timeline, you can assign a unique color to help distinguish one mask from another.

■ You can even have After Effects assign each subsequent mask a different color automatically by selecting the Cycle Mask Colors option in the User Interface Colors pane of the Preferences dialog box.

HIDING AND SHOWING MASK PATHS

Targeting Masks

You can create as many as 127 masks for each layer. The Target pull-down menu at the bottom of the Layer panel provides one way to select the mask you want to use. Note that the Target pull-down menu appears only when the layer contains one or more masks.

To choose the target mask:

1. View a layer containing one or more masks in a Layer panel.

2. At the bottom of the Layer panel, choose a mask from the Target pull-down menu (**Figure 10.14**):

   ▲ Choose None to create a new mask without changing an existing mask.

   ▲ Choose the name of an existing mask to target that mask for changes.

   The mask you choose appears selected (**Figure 10.15**).

✔ Tip

■ Don't forget: To create an additional mask in the same Layer panel, make sure the Target pull-down menu is set to None. Otherwise, the new mask *replaces* the target mask.

Figure 10.14 In the Target menu, choose a mask you want to select, or target, for changes.

Figure 10.15 The targeted mask appears selected, with solid square vertices. If you create a new mask shape, it replaces the targeted mask.

Figure 10.16 In the Tools panel, choose a Shape tool.

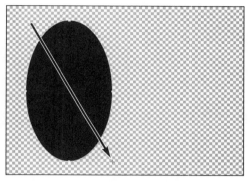

Figure 10.17 In the Layer or Comp panel, drag to define the shape from one corner of the shape to its opposite corner.

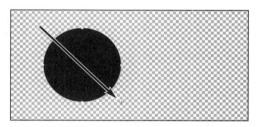

Figure 10.18 Shift-drag to constrain the shape to equal proportions so that you can create a square or circle.

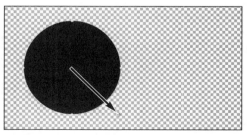

Figure 10.19 Command-drag (Mac) or Ctrl-drag (Windows) to create a mask shape that extends from the center instead of the corner.

Creating Masks Using Shape Tools

You can create simple mask shapes quickly with the Shape tools. On the other hand, a simple rectangle or ellipse can serve as the starting point of a more complex shape. As you'll see in later sections, you can easily alter any mask's shape. In addition, you can effectively combine masks using mask modes.

To draw a shape mask:

1. View the layer you want to mask in a Layer panel, or select it in the Composition panel.

   Dragging a Shape tool in the Comp panel when a layer is not selected results in a new shape layer, not a mask. Shape layers are covered in Chapter 14.

2. In the Tools panel, select a Shape tool (**Figure 10.16**).

3. In the Layer or Comp panel, drag to define the position and size of the mask on the layer.

4. To modify the shape as you drag, press the appropriate keyboard modifier (**Figures 10.17–10.19**).

continues on next page

For a list of modifiers and their results, see **Table 10.1**.

5. Release the mouse when you've finished creating the mask.

In the Layer and Comp panels, the mask appears as a path with selected control points (as long as you set the window to display masks; see "Hiding and Showing Mask Paths," earlier in this chapter). In the Composition panel, the areas of the layer outside the mask are concealed, whereas the areas inside the mask are visible. In the timeline, the layer's outline includes a Mask property.

✔ Tip

■ To create a mask that fills the layer, double-click the Shape tool.

Table 10.1

Keyboard Modifiers for Creating Masks			
MODIFIER	ELLIPSES/RECTANGLES	ROUNDED RECTANGLE	POLYGON/STAR
Shift	Constrain Proportions	Constrain Proportions	Constrain Rotation
Command (Mac)			
Ctrl (Win)	Create from Center	Create from Center	Maintain Inner Radius
Opt (Mac)			
Alt (Win)	Render Mask After Releasing Mouse		
Up Arrow	N/A	Increase Corner Roundness	Increase Sides/Points
Down Arrow	N/A	Decrease Corner Roundness	Decrease Sides/Points
Right Arrow	N/A	Minimum Corner Roundness	Increase Star Outer Roundness
Left Arrow	N/A	Maximum Corner Roundness	Decrease Star Outer Roundness
Page Up	N/A	N/A	Increase Star Inner Roundness
Page Down	N/A	N/A	Decrease Star Inner Roundness

Table 10.2

Keyboard Modifiers for Mask Paths	
TO DO THIS	PRESS THIS
Constrain new segment to 45 degrees	Shift
Temporarily switch to the Vertex tool	Option (Mac) Convert or Alt (Windows)
Temporarily switch to the Selection tool	Command (Mac) or Ctrl (Windows)

Figure 10.20 In the Tools panel, select the Pen tool.

Figure 10.21 Click to create an anchor point with no direction lines.

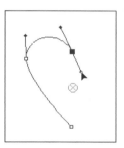

Figure 10.22 Click and drag to create a smooth point with two continuous direction lines.

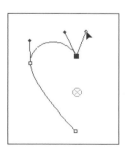

Figure 10.23 Drag a direction handle to break the relationship between the two handles, converting the point into a corner point.

Building a Standard Mask with the Pen

The following steps explain how to create a path using the Pen tool and Bézier curves. You'll probably want to start by creating simple straight segments. Then, as you become comfortable, you can try using smooth points to create curves and then corner points to create even more complex shapes. Once you're fluent in using the keyboard modifiers listed in **Table 10.2**, you've mastered making mask paths.

In later sections, you'll use the RotoBezier option to create curved segments without using direction lines.

To build a path:

1. *Do either of the following:*
   ▲ Open a Layer panel for the layer for which you want to create a mask.
   ▲ Select a layer in the Composition panel.

2. In the Tools panel, select the Pen tool 🖋 (**Figure 10.20**).

3. In the Layer or Comp panel, *do one of the following:*
   ▲ To create an anchor point, click (**Figure 10.21**).
   ▲ To create a smooth point, drag (**Figure 10.22**).
   ▲ To create a corner point, drag to create a smooth point, select one of the smooth point's direction handles, and then drag again (**Figure 10.23**).

continues on next page

4. Repeat step 3 to create straight and curved segments between points.

Don't click an existing segment unless you want to add a control point to the path. Don't click an existing direction handle unless you want to convert it.

5. To leave the path open, stop clicking in the Layer panel (**Figure 10.24**).

6. To close the path, *do one of the following*:

▲ Double-click in the Layer panel to create the final control point and connect it to the first control point.

▲ Position the Pen tool over the first control point until a circle icon appears, and then click (**Figure 10.25**).

▲ Choose Layer > Mask > Closed.

If the first control point is smooth, the path is closed with a smooth point.

When you are finished, remember to choose the Selection tool, which is required for most other tasks.

✔ Tips

■ In most cases, you'll achieve the smoothest-looking curve if you make each direction line about one-third the length of the curve it influences.

■ Typically, using the minimum possible number of control points results in a curve that's both smoother and easier to control.

■ Combining several simple masks can be faster and more effective than drawing a single complex path. Similarly, you can start with a simple shape and then modify it using techniques explained in the section "Changing the Shape of a Mask," later in this chapter.

■ The Pen tool ✎ changes into the Add Vertex tool ✎⁺ when positioned over a path; it changes into the Convert Vertex tool ⋀ when positioned over a direction handle.

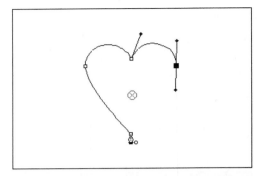

Figure 10.24 Continue clicking to create control points that define straight and curved segments. You can leave the path open, or position the tool over the first point so that a circle icon appears next to the Pen tool...

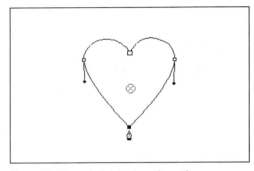

Figure 10.25 ...and click to close the path.

Figure 10.26 Select the Pen tool, and select the RotoBezier option.

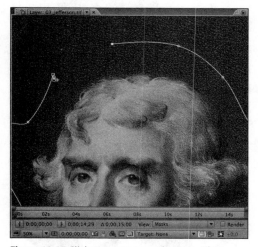

Figure 10.27 Click to create control points. After Effects calculates the curved segments automatically.

Creating a RotoBezier Mask

Even if you're a master of Bézier curves, you can often create a mask more quickly and easily using a *RotoBezier mask*. The Pen tool's RotoBezier option lets you define a curved path by clicking to create control points; After Effects calculates curved segments automatically. You avoid using direction lines, which can take time to adjust properly.

To create a RotoBezier mask:

1. In the Tools panel, select the Pen tool and then select the RotoBezier option (**Figure 10.26**).

2. In the Layer or Composition panel, click with the Pen tool to create the vertices of the mask shape.

3. Repeat step 2 to create additional control points connected by curved segments (**Figure 10.27**).

   Don't click an existing segment unless you want to add a control point to the path.

continues on next page

4. To close the path, *do one of the following*:

▲ Double-click in the Layer panel to create the final control point and connect it to the first control point.

▲ Position the Pen tool over the first control point until a circle icon appears 🖊o, and then click.

▲ Choose Layer > Mask > Closed.

The mask path closes (**Figure 10.28**).

5. To leave the path open, stop clicking in the Layer panel.

You may want to choose a new tool, such as the Selection tool.

✔ Tips

■ You can convert a RotoBézier to a Bézier mask and vice versa by selecting the mask and choosing Layer > Mask > RotoBézier.

■ Although RotoBézier curves are calculated automatically, you can adjust the relative amount of curves, or *tension*. Select the points you want to affect and then drag one with the Convert Vertex tool ◥. Dragging right increases the tension until adjacent segments are flat, making sharp corners. Dragging left makes adjacent segments more curved (**Figure 10.29**).

Figure 10.28 Position the Pen tool over the first control point so that a small circle appears next to the tool and click to close the shape. Otherwise, you can leave the mask open and choose another tool.

Figure 10.29 The two figures started as identical RotoBezier masks. However, selecting control points and then dragging with the Convert Vertex tool changes *tension* at the selected vertices.

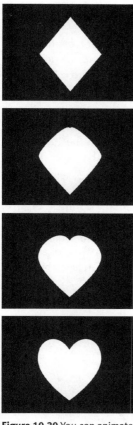

Figure 10.30 You can animate mask properties—including a mask's shape (shown here)—using the same keyframing techniques covered in Chapter 9.

Changing the Shape of a Mask

You can modify the shape of a mask at any time by applying the same Pen tool techniques covered in the task, "Building a Standard Mask with the Pen," earlier in this chapter. Because you use essentially the same techniques to add, remove, and convert vertices on masks as you do in a motion path (or for that matter in other graphics programs, like Photoshop and Illustrator) those techniques aren't repeated here.

Later sections cover techniques that affect the entire mask (such as using the Free Transform command), mask properties (mask feather, opacity, and expansion), and mask modes. These tasks don't vary according to the type of mask, and the results are identical.

As with nearly every other layer property, you can animate mask properties over time—including its Shape property—using the same keyframe animation techniques you learned in Chapter 9. There's no need to reiterate those methods in this chapter, but it's worth remembering that an animated mask can serve many uses—from adapting a garbage mask in conjunction with a keying effect, to transforming graphical elements (**Figure 10.30**).

✔ Tips

- The way curves adjust to changes depends on whether the mask consists of Bézier or RotoBezier curves. As you learned in the earlier section, "Understanding Masks," Bézier curves use direction lines you specify manually, whereas RotoBezier curves are calculated automatically. Each mask type's characteristic behavior continues to operate when you edit it.

- This chapter covers the essentials of After Effects' powerful mask and path making features. When you're ready, you can explore the Create Outlines and Auto-Trace commands, and how Smart Mask Interpolation can aid in animating mask shape.

Selecting Masks and Points

To alter all or part of a mask, you must first select its control points—usually accomplished via (what else?) the Selection tool. Select one or more control points to change the shape of a mask. Select all the points to move the mask. You can use the same methods to select masks and control points in both standard and RotoBezier masks. As usual, selected vertices appear as solid squares; deselected vertices appear as hollow squares.

To move, scale, or rotate the entire mask, use the transform technique described in the section "Scaling and Rotating Masks," later in this chapter.

To select masks or points in a Layer or Comp panel:

1. In the Tools panel, choose the Selection tool (if you haven't done so already) (**Figure 10.31**).

2. Make sure the Layer or Comp panel is set to show masks.

   See the sections on viewing masks, earlier in this chapter.

3. To select mask points in the Comp panel, select the layer containing the mask.

4. To select mask points in either the Layer panel or the Comp panel, *do any of the following*:

   ▲ To select a control point, click the control point on a mask.

   ▲ To add to or subtract from your selection, press Shift as you click or drag a marquee around control points.

   ▲ To select points at both ends of a segment, click the segment.

   ▲ To select an entire mask with the mouse, Option/Alt-click the mask.

5. To select mask points in the Layer panel only, *do any of the following*:

   ▲ To select any or all control points, drag a marquee around the points you want to select (**Figure 10.32**).

   ▲ To select all mask points, press Command/Ctrl-A.

   ▲ To select an entire mask by name, choose the mask from the Target pull-down menu in the Layer panel.

In the Layer or Comp panel, selected control points appear solid; other control points appear as hollow outlines (**Figure 10.33**). Segments associated with the selected points also display direction lines. When no control points of a mask are selected, only the path is visible in the Layer or Comp panel.

Figure 10.31 In the Tools panel, choose the Selection tool.

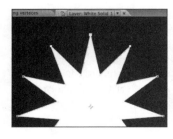

Figure 10.32 In the Layer panel, you can select several mask vertices simultaneously by dragging a marquee around them.

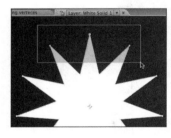

Figure 10.33 Selected points appear as solid squares; deselected points appear as hollow squares.

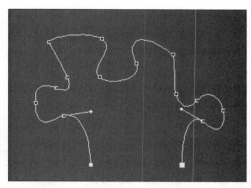

Figure 10.34 Choose the control points at each end of an open path.

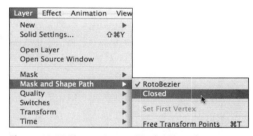

Figure 10.35 Choose Layer › Mask › Closed.

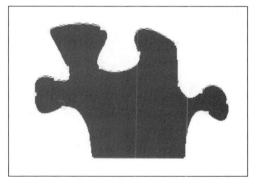

Figure 10.36 The open path becomes closed. You can use the same method to open a closed path.

Opening and Closing Paths

You can use menu commands to close an open path or open a closed one.

To close an open path:

1. In a Layer panel, choose the control points at each end of an open path (**Figure 10.34**).

2. Choose Layer > Mask > Closed (**Figure 10.35**).

   The control points are connected to close the path (**Figure 10.36**).

To open a closed path:

1. In a Layer panel, choose two adjacent control points in a closed path.

2. Choose Layer > Mask > Closed.

   The Closed option is deselected, and the segment between the control points disappears.

Scaling and Rotating Masks

Using the Free Transform Points command, you can scale and rotate all or part of one or more masks. Masks are rotated and scaled around their own anchor points, separate from the anchor point of the layer that contains them. As the word *free* suggests, these adjustments are controlled manually, not numerically, and they can't be keyframed to animate over time. Of course, you can still keyframe the rotation and scale of the layer containing the masks.

To move, scale, or rotate all or part of a mask:

1. Open a Layer panel for the layer that contains the mask you want to transform, or select the layer in the Comp panel.

2. *Do one of the following:*

   ▲ Select the mask or mask points you want to transform, and Choose Layer > Mask > Free Transform Points.

   ▲ Double-click a mask to transform it completely.

   A bounding box and mask anchor point appear (**Figure 10.37**).

3. To reposition the anchor point for the mask's bounding box, drag the anchor.

   The Selection tool turns into a Move Anchor Point icon when you position it over the anchor point (**Figure 10.38**).

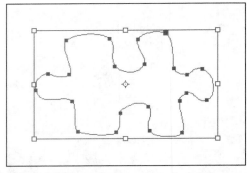

Figure 10.37 A bounding box and mask anchor point appear.

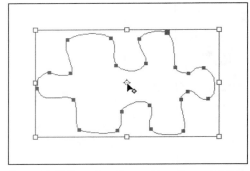

Figure 10.38 If you drag the mask's anchor point, the Selection tool becomes a Move Anchor Point icon.

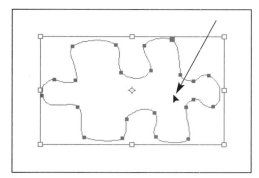

Figure 10.39 To move the mask or selected points, place the cursor inside the bounding box and drag to a new position.

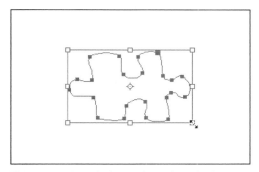

Figure 10.40 To scale the mask or selected points, place the cursor on one of the handles of the bounding box until it becomes a Scale icon, and then drag.

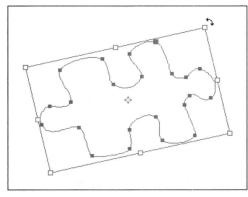

Figure 10.41 To rotate the mask or selected points, place the pointer slightly outside the bounding box until it becomes a Rotation icon, and then drag.

4. *Do any of the following*:

   ▲ To move the mask or selected points, place the cursor inside the bounding box and drag to a new position (**Figure 10.39**).

   ▲ To scale the mask or selected points, place the cursor on one of the handles of the bounding box until it becomes a Scale icon ⬉, and then drag (**Figure 10.40**).

   ▲ To rotate the mask or selected points, place the pointer slightly outside the bounding box until it becomes a Rotation icon ↻, and then drag (**Figure 10.41**).

5. To exit Free Transform Points mode, double-click anywhere in the Layer or Comp panel, or press Return/Enter.

✔ Tips

■ As you can see, using the Free Transform Points command to scale and rotate a mask or mask points works much the same way as transforming a layer. You'll be happy to know that all the keyboard modifications—Shift, Command/Ctrl, Option/Alt—also work the same.

■ You can copy paths from Adobe Photoshop or Illustrator and paste them as a layer mask in After Effects. By pasting a path as a layer mask, you can take advantage of After Effects' ability to animate its Shape, Feather, Opacity, and Expansion properties.

SCALING AND ROTATING MASKS

Converting Mask Paths into Motion Paths

Not only is an open mask path analogous to a motion path, but it can also be converted into one. Just make sure you paste the path into a compatible layer property, such as its Position property. If you paste into a Layer panel, the path is pasted as a mask (as you saw in the previous section).

To paste a mask path as a motion path:

1. *Do either of the following:*

   ▲ Select an open mask path in a layer in After Effects.

   ▲ Select an open mask path in Photoshop or Illustrator.

2. Choose Edit > Copy, or press Command/Ctrl-C (**Figure 10.42**).

3. In the Timeline panel, expand the layer outline to reveal the spatial property you want to paste the path into.

   You can use the Position, Effect Point, or Anchor Point property.

4. Select the property name.

   The property's keyframes are highlighted. If the property has no keyframes, the I-beam icon is highlighted.

5. Set the current time to the frame where you want the pasted keyframes to start (**Figure 10.43**).

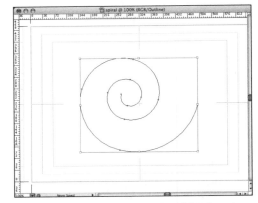

Figure 10.42 Select an open mask path in a layer in After Effects, or in Photoshop or Illustrator (shown here). Press Command/Ctrl-C.

Figure 10.43 In After Effects, select a layer property, and set the current time to the frame you want the pasted motion to start.

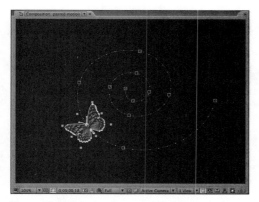

Figure 10.44 Pressing Command/Ctrl-V pastes the path in the composition as a motion path...

6. Choose Edit > Paste, or press Command/Ctrl-V.

The path appears in the Comp panel as a motion path (**Figure 10.44**). In the property's track, keyframes begin at the current time and end two seconds later (**Figure 10.45**). The first and last keyframes are standard keyframes; the rest are roving keyframes (see Chapter 7).

7. Edit the motion path as you would any other.

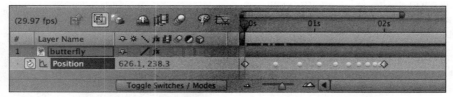

Figure 10.45 ...and in the property's track as keyframes starting at the current time.

Moving Masks Relative to the Layer Image

You can move a mask to reveal a different part of a layer in two ways: in a Layer panel or in a Composition panel.

When you move a mask in a Layer panel, its relative position in the Composition panel also changes (**Figures 10.46** and **10.47**). This approach works well if you want to change both the part of the image revealed by the mask and the mask's position in the composition. The mask moves, but the layer's position remains the same. Think of an iris effect at the end of a cartoon, in which the circular mask closes in on the character for a final good-bye.

Alternatively, you can use the Pan Behind tool in the Composition panel. Panning the layer behind the mask reveals a different part of the image without moving the mask's relative position in the composition. When you look back at the Layer panel, you can see that the mask has moved. However, After Effects recalculates the layer's position to compensate for this movement, maintaining the layer's position in the composition (**Figures 10.48** and **10.49**). Imagine a scene from a pirate movie, in which a spyglass scans the horizon. The circle doesn't move, but the horizon pans through the viewfinder to reveal an island.

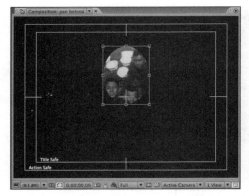

Figure 10.46 When you move a mask in a Layer or Comp panel...

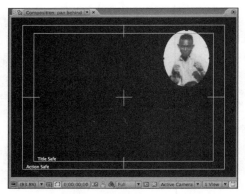

Figure 10.47 ...the mask's position changes in both the Layer and the Comp panel. The position value of the layer containing the mask doesn't change.

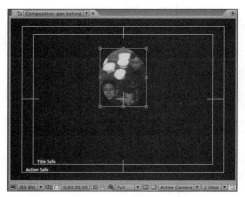

Figure 10.48 When you use the Pan Behind tool in the Composition panel...

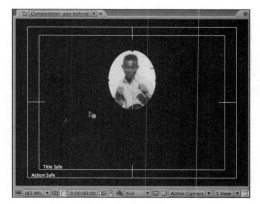

Figure 10.49 ...the mask changes its position in the layer while maintaining its position in the composition. After Effects recalculates the layer's position value automatically. You can see the anchor point's new position in the Comp panel.

Figure 10.50 In the Tools panel, choose the Pan Behind tool.

Figure 10.51 In the Comp panel, place the Pan Behind tool inside the masked area and drag.

To move a mask in the Layer panel:

1. Select an entire mask in the Layer panel.

2. Drag one of the control points to move the entire mask to a new position.

   Make sure to drag a control point, not a path segment. The mask changes position in both the Layer panel and the composition.

To pan a layer behind its mask:

1. In the Tools panel, select the Pan Behind tool (**Figure 10.50**).

2. In the Composition panel, position the Pan Behind tool inside the masked area of the layer, and then drag (**Figure 10.51**).

   In the Composition panel, the mouse pointer becomes the Pan Behind icon , and the layer pans behind the masked area. After Effects calculates the layer's position in the composition and the mask's placement in the Layer panel.

MOVING MASKS RELATIVE TO THE LAYER IMAGE

267

Inverting a Mask

Ordinarily, the area within a closed layer mask defines the opaque parts of the layer's image; the area outside the mask is transparent, revealing the layers beneath it. However, just as you can invert a layer's alpha channel, you can invert a layer mask to reverse the opaque and transparent areas.

To invert a mask created in After Effects:

1. In the Layer, Comp, or Timeline panel, select the mask you want to invert.

2. *Do one of the following:*

   ▲ In the Timeline panel, click Inverted for the selected mask (**Figure 10.52**).

   ▲ Choose Layer > Mask > Invert.

   ▲ Press Shift-Command-I (Mac) or Shift-Ctrl-I (Windows).

   Viewed in the Composition panel, the mask is inverted (**Figures 10.53** and **10.54**).

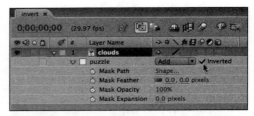

Figure 10.52 Click Inverted for the mask in the layer outline of the Timeline panel, or use the equivalent menu command or keyboard shortcut.

Figure 10.53 Ordinarily, the area within the mask defines the opaque parts of the layer's image.

Figure 10.54 Inverting the mask reverses the opaque and transparent areas of the layer.

Mask Modes

When you add multiple masks to the same layer, you can determine how the masks interact by selecting a mask *mode*. Although modes don't create true compound paths (as do the Boolean functions in Illustrator), you can use them to achieve similar effects (**Figures 10.55**).

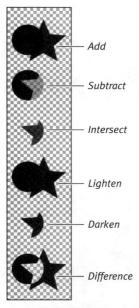

Add

Subtract

Intersect

Lighten

Darken

Difference

Figure 10.55 Here, both masks are applied to a black solid and are set to 75 percent opacity. The upper mask (left) is set to Add. Changing the lower mask's mode changes how it interacts with the one above it.

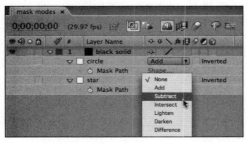

Figure 10.56 To the right of the mask in the Timeline panel, choose a mask mode from the pull-down menu.

None eliminates the effects of the mask on the layer's alpha channel. However, you can still apply effects (such as strokes or fills) to the mask.

Add includes the mask with the masks above it to display all masked areas. Areas where the mask overlaps with the masks above it use their combined opacity values.

Subtract cuts, or subtracts, areas where the mask overlaps with the mask above it.

Intersect adds the mask to all the masks above it so that only the areas where the mask overlaps with higher masks display in the composition.

Lighten adds the mask to the masks above it to display all masked areas. Areas where the mask overlaps with the masks above it use the highest opacity value, not the combined values.

Darken adds the mask to the masks above it to display only the areas where the masks overlap. Areas where multiple masks overlap use the highest opacity value, not the combined values.

Difference adds the mask to the masks above it to display only the areas where the masks don't overlap.

To set the mask mode:

1. Select the mask for which you want to set the mode.

2. *Do one of the following:*
   ▲ In the Timeline panel, choose a mode from the pull-down menu across from the mask (in the Switches/Modes panel) (**Figure 10.56**).
   ▲ Choose Layer > Mask > Mode > and select a mode from the submenu.

   The mode you choose affects how the mask interacts with the masks above it in the layer outline (for that layer only).

Adjusting Other Mask Properties

In addition to Mask Shape, mask properties include Feather, Opacity, and Expansion (**Figure 10.57**). Along with Mask Shape, you can view, adjust, and animate them as you would any layer property (as you learned about in Chapters 7 and 9).

Feather controls the softness of a mask's edge; the Mask Feather value determines the width of the edge's transition from opacity to transparency. The feathered width always extends equally from each side of the mask edge—that is, a Feather value of 30 extends 15 pixels both outside and inside the mask edge (**Figure 10.58**).

Opacity controls the mask's overall opacity—that is, how solid the masked area of the layer appears. Mask opacity works in conjunction with the layer's Opacity setting. If the layer is 100 percent opaque and a mask is 50 percent opaque, the masked area of the layer appears 50 percent opaque. Each mask's opacity also influences the net effect of mask modes, which are explained in the previous section, "Mask Modes." (**Figure 10.59**).

Expansion lets you expand or contract a mask's edges and is particularly useful for fine-tuning the feathered edge of a mask (**Figure 10.60**).

✔ Tip

- If you set the feather to extend beyond the perimeter of the layer containing the mask, the feather will appear cut off and the edges of the layer will be apparent. Make the mask or feather small enough to fit within the confines of the layer. If the layer is a solid or nested composition, you can also increase the size of the layer.

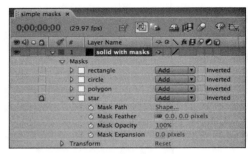

Figure 10.57 In addition to Mask Shape, mask properties include Feather, Opacity, and Expansion.

Figure 10.58 These masks are identical except for their Mask Feather values.

Figure 10.59 In this figure, several masks in the same layer use different opacity values.

Figure 10.60 This figure shows three masks with identical shapes and feather values. However, each mask's Expansion value is different.

EFFECTS
FUNDAMENTALS

At last, you come to the program's namesake: effects. As if you didn't already know, effects are used to alter the audio and visual characteristics of layers in almost countless ways. You can employ them to enhance, combine, or distort layers. You can simulate audio-visual phenomena from light to lightning. You can make changes that are subtle or spectacular. And, most important, you can animate these effects over time.

Effects are stored in the Plug-Ins folder, which is contained in the After Effects folder. The number and type of effects at your disposal depends on whether you have the standard version of After Effects or After Effects Pro. You can also add to your repertoire by using effects created by third-party developers.

This chapter explains the process you use to apply effects to layers. It also describes how to use the Effect Controls panel as a complement or alternative to the property controls in the layer outline.

Using the Effects & Presets Panel

Although you can find and apply any effect using the Effects menu, it can be more convenient to use the Effects & Presets panel. As its name implies, the Effects & Presets panel lists not only effects, but also animation presets (**Figure 11.1**). In Chapter 7, "Properties and Keyframes," you learned how to save animations as a preset that can be easily applied to other layers. Animation presets also include a number of built-in text animations, as explained in Chapter 12, "Creating and Animating Text."

By default, the effects are listed by category. As usual, you can click the triangle next to the item to expand it, revealing its contents in outline form. By expanding items, you can view effects contained in a category or see the components of a saved preset (when those viewing options are selected).

Icons indicate the type of item listed (**Figure 11.2**).

To find an item in the Effects & Presets panel:

◆ In the Effects & Presets panel, type all or part of the name of the item you want in the Contains field (**Figure 11.3**).

As you type, the items on the list that don't match are hidden from view, leaving only the matching items (**Figure 11.4**).

Figure 11.1 The Effects & Presets panel makes it easy to find and apply effects to layers.

Figure 11.2 In the Effects & Presets panel, icons indicate the type of item listed.

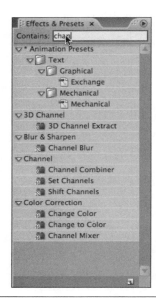

Figure 11.3 As you type the name of the item you want in the Contains field…

Figure 11.4 ...the list sifts to show only the matching items.

To show all the items in the Effects & Presets panel:

◆ Highlight the search criteria in the Effects & Presets panel's Contains field, and press Delete (Mac) or Backspace (Windows).

The panel lists all items (**Figure 11.5**) according to other sorting options you specify (explained in the following tasks).

✔ Tip

■ Options in the Effects panel's pull-down menu includes other options for sorting and sifting effects. Instead of listing effects by category, you can list them alphabetically or according to how they're organized on your hard disk. And you can include or exclude certain types of effects (such as presets) from the list.

Figure 11.5 Clear the Contains field to make the panel list all items.

Applying Effects

Although effects are numerous and varied, you apply all of them in essentially the same way.

You can also save any combination of effects (as well as animation keyframes) as a preset. To learn how to save and apply a preset, see the section "Saving and Applying Effect Presets" later in this chapter.

To apply an effect:

1. Select a layer in a composition (**Figure 11.6**).

2. *Do any of the following*:
   ▲ Double-click the effect or preset you want to apply in the Effects & Presets panel (**Figure 11.7**).
   ▲ Choose Effect, and then choose an effect category and an individual effect from the submenu.
   ▲ Control-click (Mac) or right-click (Windows), and hold the mouse button to access an Effects menu.

3. If an options dialog box appears, select options for the effect and then click OK to close the dialog box.

   An Effect Controls panel appears with the effect selected (**Figure 11.8**).

Figure 11.6 Select a layer.

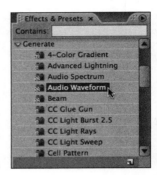

Figure 11.7 In the Effects & Presets panel, double-click the effect or preset you want.

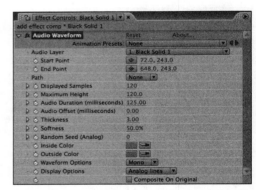

Figure 11.8 The effect appears selected in the Effect Controls panel. You can adjust the settings here...

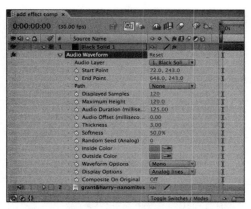

Figure 11.9 ...or in the layer outline of the Timeline panel.

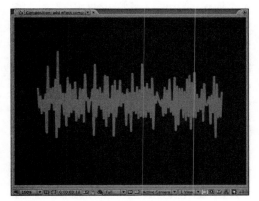

Figure 11.10 You can view and preview the effect in the Composition panel.

Figure 11.11 Choose Effect, and select the most recently applied effect from the menu.

4. Using controls in the Effect Controls panel or in the expanded layer outline of the Timeline panel, adjust the property values for the effect, and animate them if you want (**Figure 11.9**).

The applied effect appears in the composition (**Figure 11.10**). The quality and aspects (such as shading or shadows) of the effect depend on the preview options you specify; see Chapter 8, "Playback, Previews, and RAM," for more information.

To apply the most recent effect:

1. Select a layer in a composition.

2. *Do one of the following:*

▲ Choose Effect, and select the most recently used effect from the top of the menu (**Figure 11.11**).

▲ Press Shift-Command-Option-E (Mac) or Shift-Ctrl-Alt-E (Windows).

The effect is applied to the selected layer.

✔ Tips

■ After Effects includes a preset workspace for Effects. Where the Standard workspace has a Project panel, the Effects workspace places the Effect Controls panel.

■ Many effects are best applied to solid-black layers—particularly those that don't rely on a layer's underlying pixels, such as effects in the Generate category. This permits you to manipulate the layer containing the effect independently from other layers, which can give you more flexibility. Other times, you may want to use the effect to interact with a solid color to create graphical elements.

APPLYING EFFECTS

Viewing Effect Property Controls

Once you add effects to a layer, you can view their property controls in both the Timeline panel and the Effect Controls panel.

As you saw in Chapter 7, you can view any layer property—including effects—by expanding the layer outline. Chances are, you even recall the keyboard shortcut: E for *effects*. However, you'll soon find that many effects include a long list of parameters—often too long to view in the layer outline conveniently (**Figure 11.12**).

For this reason, the Effect Controls panel is indispensable. Selecting a layer makes all of its effects appear in the Effect Controls panel (**Figure 11.13**). Or, if it's not open already, you can invoke the Effect Controls panel by double-clicking the effect in the layer outline. As in the Comp and Layer panels, a viewer pull-down menu in the Effect Controls panel's tab lets you open a new viewer; selecting the tab's lock icon prevents it from toggling to a different layer's effects (**Figure 11.14**).

VIEWING EFFECT PROPERTY CONTROLS

Figure 11.12 Pressing E reveals a selected layer's effect properties in the Timeline panel's layer outline...

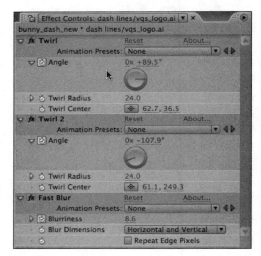

Figure 11.13 ...and selecting a layer containing effects reveals its effect properties in the Effect Controls panel. Typically, you use the two views in tandem to adjust and animate effects.

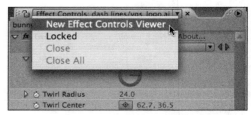

Figure 11.14 Much like the Comp and Layer panels, the Effect Controls panel's tab lets you open a new tabbed viewer; select the tab's lock icon to prevent that viewer from toggling another layer's effects.

Figure 11.15 Some effects let you set a spatially based property (an effect point) by clicking directly in the Comp panel. Here, the center point of a lens flare effect is being placed using the mouse.

Generally, you use a Layer or Comp panel to view the result of your adjustments. However, some effects include a spatial property that you can set directly in the Layer or Comp panels by clicking where you want the *effect point* (**Figure 11.15**). See "Setting an Effect Point," later in this chapter.

As you can see, the Timeline panel's property controls are ideally suited for viewing the properties in time, whereas the Effect Controls panel provides a dedicated space for viewing and adjusting numerous effect properties at once. Naturally, you'll use both views in tandem. Don't forget that After Effects already includes a preset workspace called Effects that places an emphasis on both areas (see Chapter 1 to review workspaces).

VIEWING EFFECT PROPERTY CONTROLS

Removing and Resetting Effects

If you don't like an effect, remove it. If you need to restore the default settings, reset them.

To remove an effect:

1. In the Effect Controls panel, select the name of an effect.

2. Press Delete (Mac) or Backspace (Windows).

   The effect is removed.

To remove all effects for a layer:

1. Select a layer containing one or more effects (**Figure 11.16**).

2. Choose Effect > Remove All, or press Shift-Command-E (Mac) or Shift-Ctrl-E (Windows) (**Figure 11.17**).

   All effects are removed from the layer.

To reset an effect to its default settings:

◆ *Do either of the following:*

   ▲ In the Switches panel of the expanded Layer panel, click Reset for the effect.

   ▲ For the effect in the Effect Controls panel, click Reset (**Figure 11.18**).

   All the values for the effect are restored to the defaults.

✔ Tip

■ In addition to a Reset button, each effect includes an About button that displays the name and version number of each effect. A handful of effects also include a button to access additional options not listed in the Effect Controls panel. Depending on the effect, the button is labeled Options, Edit Text, or the like.

Figure 11.16 To remove all of a layer's effects, select the layer...

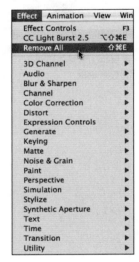

Figure 11.17 ...and choose Effect > Remove All, or use the keyboard shortcut.

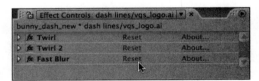

Figure 11.18 In the Effect Controls panel, clicking Reset returns all of the effects' properties to their defaults.

Disabling Effects Temporarily

You can turn off effects temporarily without removing them from the layer. Doing so is helpful when you want to see a single effect without other effects obscuring your view. Once you're satisfied with an effect's settings, you may want to disable it to speed up frame rendering.

To disable and enable individual effects:

◆ In the Timeline panel or the Effect Controls panel, click the Effect icon next to the effect's name.

When the icon is visible, the effect is enabled; when the icon is hidden, the effect is disabled (**Figures 11.19** and **11.20**).

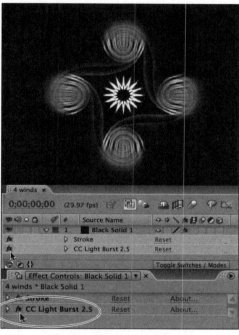

Figure 11.19 In the Effect Controls panel, clicking the Effect icon next to the effect name...

Figure 11.20 ...toggles the icon off and disables the effect.

To disable and enable all effects in a layer:

◆ In the Switches/Modes panel of the Timeline panel, click the Effect icon next to a layer.

When the icon is visible, all effects for the layer are enabled; when the icon is hidden, all effects are disabled (**Figures 11.21** and **11.22**).

Figure 11.21 Clicking the Effect switch for a layer in the Switches/Modes panel of the Timeline panel...

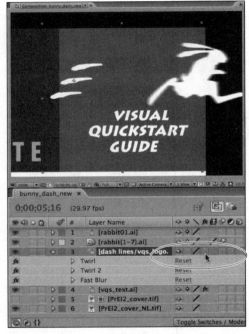

Figure 11.22 ...toggles the icon off and disables all effects contained by the layer.

Adjusting Effects in the Effect Controls Panel

Although you can adjust effect properties in the layer outline just as you would any other layer property (using techniques covered in Chapter 7), the roomier Effect Controls panel can accommodate larger, more graphical controls for several effect properties. Most are intuitive or should already be familiar to you (**Figure 11.23**), so they won't be covered here. However, this chapter does discuss the slightly less intuitive effect point control (see the following section, "Setting an Effect Point").

Covering every possible graphical control is beyond the scope of this chapter. Other effects may offer a color range control (Hue/Saturation); a grid of control points (Mesh Warp); a histogram (Levels); or other graphs, such as those that represent an image's input/output levels (Curves) or an audio layer's frequency response (Parametric EQ). Some effects include an Options button to open a separate dialog box, and third-party plug-ins may offer other exotic controls. Consult the documentation for each effect for detailed information on its individual controls.

✔ Tips

- By default, After Effects uses its own color picker for selecting colors. However, you can have After Effects use your system's color picker by selecting the appropriate option in the General pane of the Preferences dialog box.

- Once you start dragging an angle control knob, you can drag the cursor outside the angle controller to move it with greater precision.

- You can set some property values using a slider control. However, the slider's range (say, 0 to 20) doesn't always represent the possible range of values (let's say 0 to 1000). Control-click/right-click the property name and choose Edit Value to open a dialog box and set the range of the slider.

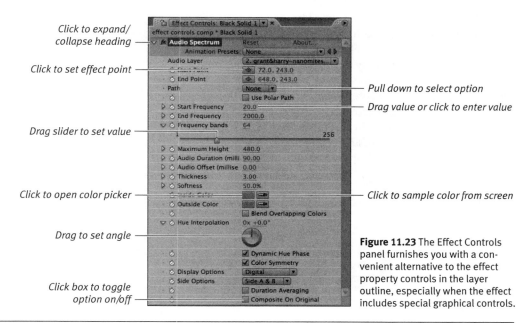

Figure 11.23 The Effect Controls panel furnishes you with a convenient alternative to the effect property controls in the layer outline, especially when the effect includes special graphical controls.

Labels (left, top to bottom): Click to expand/collapse heading · Click to set effect point · Drag slider to set value · Click to open color picker · Drag to set angle · Click box to toggle option on/off

Labels (right, top to bottom): Pull down to select option · Drag value or click to enter value · Click to sample color from screen

Setting an Effect Point

An *effect point* represents the position of an effect on a layer: It can be the focus of a Lens Flare effect, the center point of a Reflection effect, or the starting point for Path Text. Some effects require more than one effect point, such as the start and end of a Stroke effect or the four corners of the Corner Pin effect.

You can set the effect point with the Effect Controls panel's Effect Point button or by manipulating it in the Composition or Layer panel. For an effect point to be visible in the Comp panel, Effect Controls must be selected in the Comp panel's View Options dialog box (accessed from the Comp panel's pull-down menu). In the Layer panel, the effect's name must be selected in the Layer panel's View pull-down menu.

When you animate the effect point over time, you can view and manipulate its path in the Layer panel just as you would adjust an anchor point path or motion path in the Composition panel (**Figure 11.24**). In most ways, the effect point path works just like any other kind of motion path. Unlike a layer's position, however, the effect point's coordinates are unaffected by the layer's anchor point. (See "Animating Effects," at the end of this chapter; Chapter 7 about basic animation; and Chapter 9 about adjusting a motion path.) And because effects are applied to a layer, the coordinates of an effect point refer to the layer, not the composition.

The following task explains how to set an effect point; you can animate it as you would any property.

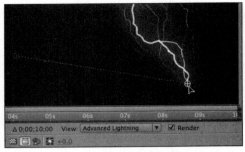

Figure 11.24 You can view and manipulate an effect point and its motion path in the Layer panel. Here, you can see the path of an Advanced Lightning effect's endpoint. See Chapter 9 for more about using motion paths.

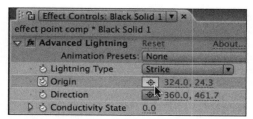

Figure 11.25 Click the Effect Point button for an effect property.

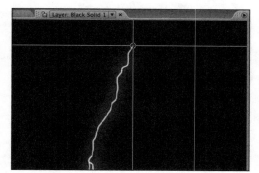

Figure 11.26 Position the cursor in a Layer or Comp panel (shown here), and click to set the effect point.

To set an effect point with the Effect Point button:

1. In the Effect Controls panel, click the Effect Point button for an effect property (**Figure 11.25**).

   Any effect property that uses layer coordinate values has an Effect Point button. When the button is active, the cursor becomes the Effect Point icon -⊹- when positioned in a Composition or Layer panel.

2. Position the cursor in a Composition or Layer panel, and click to set the effect point (**Figure 11.26**).

   The coordinate values reflect the effect point you chose. Even if you clicked the Effect Point icon in the Composition panel, the coordinate values correspond to the coordinate system of the layer that contains the effect.

SETTING AN EFFECT POINT

Saving and Applying Effect Presets

Occasionally, you'll create a complex effect that you're particularly proud of or that you need to reuse. You can save a combination of effect settings—including keyframes—as a *preset*.

You save preset effects as independent, cross-platform files, which use an .ffx extension. Because preset effects are independent files, you can store them separately from your project so that you can easily access them for other projects or share them with other After Effects artists. To further facilitate your work, After Effects makes it possible for you to access your saved presets via the Animation > Recent Animation Presets menu command.

To view presets in the Effect Controls panel:

◆ In the Effect Controls panel's menu, select Show Animation Presets (**Figure 11.27**).

When the option is selected, a layer's effects listed in the Effect Controls panel include an Animation Presets pull-down menu (**Figure 11.28**); otherwise, the pull-down menu is hidden.

Figure 11.27 In the Effect Controls panel's menu, choose Show Animation Presets.

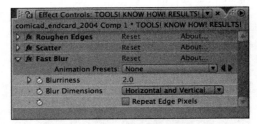

Figure 11.28 An Animation Presets pull-down menu appears.

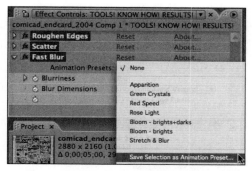

Figure 11.29 In the Effect Controls panel, select one or more of the effects you applied to the layer, and choose Save Selection as Animation Preset in the Animation Presets pull-down menu...

Figure 11.30 ...or choose Animation ﹥ Save Animation Preset.

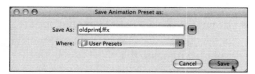

Figure 11.31 Specify the name and destination of the preset file in the "Save Animation Preset as" dialog box.

To save effects as a preset:

1. Apply one or more effects to a layer in the composition.

   If you want, animate them over time (using techniques explained in Chapter 7).

2. In the Effect Controls panel, select one or more of the effects you applied to the layer.

3. *Do either of the following:*

   ▲ In any effect's Animation Presets pull-down menu, choose Save Selection as Animation Preset (**Figure 11.29**).

   ▲ Choose Animation > Save Animation Preset (**Figure 11.30**).

   A "Save Animation Preset as" dialog box appears.

4. Specify the name and destination of the preset file (**Figure 11.31**).

   The file uses the .ffx extension.

5. Click Save to save the settings and close the dialog box.

   The preset is added to the appropriate categories in the Effects & Presets panel.

To apply a preset effect:

1. Select the layers to which you want to apply a preset, and set the current time to where you want keyframes (if included in the preset) to begin.

2. *Do one of the following:*

   ▲ In the Effects & Presets panel, double-click the name of the preset you want to apply to the selected layers (**Figure 11.32**).

   ▲ Choose Animation > Apply Animation Preset.

   ▲ Choose Animation > Apply Recent Preset, and select the name of a recently used preset.

   The preset is applied to the selected layers. Any animated properties' keyframes begin at the current time.

To apply an effect or preset by dragging:

1. In the Effects & Presets panel, locate and select the effect or preset you want to apply.

2. Drag the selected effect or preset to *any of the following places:*

   ▲ The target layer's name in the Timeline panel

   ▲ The target layer's effect list heading in the Timeline panel

   ▲ Any position in the target layer's list of effects in the Timeline panel (**Figure 11.33**)

   ▲ The target layer's list of effects in the Effect Controls panel

   ▲ The target layer in the Comp panel; the Info panel displays the name of the currently targeted layer as you drag over it

   When you release the mouse, the effect is added to the layer.

Figure 11.32
Select a layer, and apply a preset by using an option in the Animation menu or by double-clicking the preset in the Effects & Presets panel (shown here).

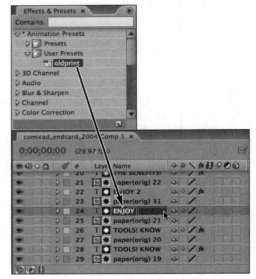

Figure 11.33 You can also drag an effect or preset icon to the target layer in the timeline, dropping it on the layer's name, on the layer's effect property heading, or at any position in the layer's effect list.

✔ Tip

■ When the Show Preset Contents option is selected in the Effects & Presets panel's pull-down menu, the panel lists both the preset's name and the individual effects the preset contains. You can click the triangle to expand a preset and show its constituent effects. Moreover, you can apply any individual effect the preset contains to a layer.

Figure 11.34 In the Effect Controls panel, select one or more effects, and press Command/Ctrl-C.

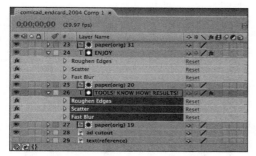

Figure 11.35 Selecting a target layer, and pressing Command/Ctrl-V pastes the effects, but it doesn't contain the same keyframes. (You can press E to view the selected layer's effects in the layer outline.)

Copying and Pasting Effects

To save time and labor, you can copy effects from one layer into another.

To copy a layer's effects into another layer:

1. In the Effect Controls panel, select one or more effects (**Figure 11.34**).

2. Select Edit > Copy, or press Command/Ctrl-C.

3. In the Timeline panel, select one or more layers.

4. Choose Edit > Paste, or press Command/Ctrl-V.

   The selected layer contains the pasted effects; however, it doesn't contain the same keyframes (**Figure 11.35**).

✔ Tip

■ You can also copy and paste keyframes from one property to another property that uses compatible values. For example, you can copy position keyframes to an Effect Point property. See Chapter 7 to review this technique.

Applying Multiple Effects

The Effect Controls panel lists effects in the order you add them, from top to bottom. Because each effect is applied to the result of the one above it, changing the order of effects can change the final appearance (or sound) of the layer (**Figures 11.36** and **11.37**). You can reorder effects in the Effect Controls panel as well as directly in the layer outline of the Timeline panel.

To reorder effects:

1. In the Effect Controls panel or in the layer outline of the Timeline panel, drag the name of an effect up or down to a new position in the effect stacking order.

   A dark horizontal line indicates the effect's new position when you release the mouse (**Figure 11.38**).

2. Release the mouse button to place the effect in its new position in the list (**Figure 11.39**).

   Changing the order of effects in the list changes the order in which they're applied to the layer.

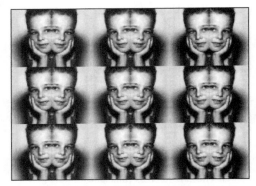

Figure 11.36 The Mirror effect followed by the Motion Tile effect results in this image...

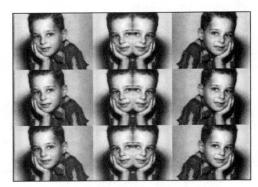

Figure 11.37 ...whereas reversing the order of the effects results in this image.

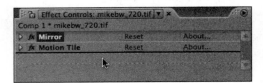

Figure 11.38 Drag the name of an effect up or down to a new position in the stacking order. A dark line indicates the effect's new position.

Figure 11.39 Release the mouse to place the effect in its new position in the list.

Figure 11.40 Masking an adjustment layer restricts its effects. Here, the Blur and Brightness & Contrast filters affect only masked areas (defined by an elliptical mask that's inverted).

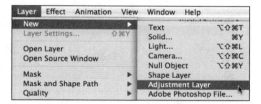

Figure 11.41 Choose Layer > New > Adjustment Layer.

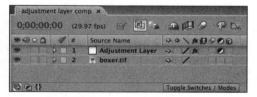

Figure 11.42 The adjustment layer appears as the topmost layer in the comp and uses the default still image duration.

Applying Effects to an Adjustment Layer

An *adjustment layer* contains effects, not footage. The effects contained in an adjustment layer are applied to all the layers below it. Adjustment layers save time and effort by letting you apply effects to a single layer rather than multiple layers.

You can also limit the areas affected by an adjustment layer by using a mask or by employing a layer's existing alpha channel.

Ordinarily, a mask modifies a layer's alpha channel to define opaque and transparent areas of a layer's image. Applying a mask to an adjustment layer—which by definition can't contain an image—allows the masked area of the effect to influence the lower layers; the areas outside the mask remain unaffected (**Figure 11.40**).

You can also use the alpha channel of another layer in a similar manner by converting the layer to an adjustment layer. As an adjustment layer, its image is ignored. However, any effects you add to the layer are restricted to the areas defined by its alpha channel.

To create an adjustment layer:

1. Open the Composition panel or Timeline panel for the composition in which you want to add an adjustment layer, or make sure one of these panels is active.

2. Choose Layer > New > Adjustment Layer (**Figure 11.41**).

    An adjustment layer appears in the composition. The adjustment layer starts at the current time and uses the default duration for still images (**Figure 11.42**).

To convert a layer to an adjustment layer, and vice versa:

◆ In the Switches area of the Timeline panel, click the Adjustment Layer switch for the layer you want to convert to make the icon appear or disappear.

When the Adjustment Layer icon is visible, the layer functions as an adjustment layer—its image disappears from the Composition panel, and its effects are applied to lower layers (**Figures 11.43** and **11.44**).

When the Adjustment Layer icon isn't visible, the layer functions as a standard layer, and its image appears in the composition. If the adjustment layer was created in After Effects, it becomes a solid layer. Any effects contained by the layer are applied only to that layer.

Figure 11.43 Alternatively, you can convert a layer into an adjustment layer by selecting its Adjustment Layer switch in the Timeline panel.

Figure 11.44 Here a solid containing the Invert effect has been converted into an adjustment layer. The solid isn't visible, but its effect alters the underlying layers, making the left side of the image look like a negative.

APPLYING EFFECTS TO AN ADJUSTMENT LAYER

Understanding Compound Effects

Effects that require two layers to operate are called *compound effects*. Rather than appear in a separate category, compound effects are distributed among effects in various categories. Although some compound effects use the word *compound* in their names, you can identify others only by knowing their controls.

As with other effects, you apply compound effects to the layers you want to alter. Unlike other effects, however, compound effects rely on a second layer—an effect source or modifying layer—that acts as a kind of map for the effect. Typically, this takes the form of a grayscale image because many compound effects are based on the modifying layer's brightness levels. In a Compound Blur effect, for example, the brightness levels of the modifying layer determine the placement and intensity of the blurry areas of the target layer. The modifying layer can be a still image, movie, or nested composition (**Figure 11.45**).

✔ Tip

- You don't need ready-made footage to serve as an effect source; you can create your own within After Effects. You can use a combination of solids, masks, and effects to create a dynamic effect source. The effect source in Figure 11.45 was created by applying the Fractal Noise effect to a solid.

Figure 11.45 Compound effects rely on a second layer as a kind of map for the effect.

Using Compound Effects

Due to their peculiar nature, compound effects have certain unique features. This section summarizes those attributes. Other implications are addressed in Chapter 16.

Specifying an effect source

In compound effects, you must use a pull-down menu to specify the modifying layer (**Figure 11.46**). Although the modifying layer must be included in the composition to appear in the list, you usually switch off its video in the Timeline panel. This is necessary because the modifying layer appears in the composition only as an effect source, not a visible layer.

Resolving size differences between source and target layers

Because compound effects use the pixels of the modifying layer as a map, that layer's dimensions should match those of the layer it affects (**Figure 11.47**). This way, your results will be more predictable and easier to control. If the dimensions of the two layers don't match, compound effects offer several ways to compensate (**Figure 11.48**). Keep in mind that although the following options can work to your advantage, they can also produce unwanted results:

Tile repeats the modifying layer to map the entire target layer. In some cases, the modifying layer won't tile evenly, cutting off some tiles. If images don't tile seamlessly, the edges may be evident in the effect.

Center positions the modifying layer in the center of the target layer. If the modifying layer is smaller, the effect may appear to be cut off; if it's larger, the extraneous portions aren't used in the effect.

Stretch to Fit scales the modifying layer to match the dimensions of the target layer. Sometimes, this can distort the modifying layer or make it difficult to position.

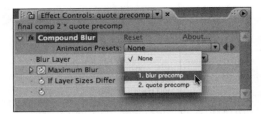

Figure 11.46 Compound effects contain a pull-down menu to specify the modifying layer, or effect source.

Figure 11.47 When the dimensions of the modifying layer match those of the layer it affects, the final result is more predictable. This example shows the effect source, target image, background image, and result of the Gradient Wipe effect.

Figure 11.48 If the dimensions of the two layers don't match, compound effects offer ways to compensate for the difference.

Figure 11.49 Compound effects refer directly to the effect source—before any mask, effect, or transform property changes have occurred. Apply the Displacement Map effect to this layer...

Using a nested composition as the effect source

It's important to understand that the three placement options described previously don't alter the modifying layer, only the way its pixels are mapped to the target layer. Conversely, scaling or positioning the modifying layer in the composition doesn't influence the compound effect. This is the case because the compound effect refers directly to the effect source, before any mask, effect, or transform property changes occur (**Figures 11.49**, **11.50**, and **11.51**).

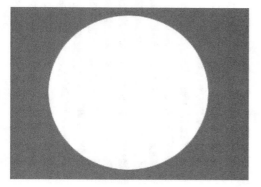

Figure 11.50 ...and use this layer as the effect source (the displacement map)...

Figure 11.51 ...and this is the result.

If a layer needs to be scaled (or otherwise treated) before it becomes an effect source, place it into another composition first. The nested composition, in turn, can serve as the modifying layer for the compound effect. This way, you can make any necessary changes to the layer within a composition—before it becomes the effect source. And unlike the layer it contains, the dimensions of the composition can be set to match the compound effect's target layer. As a result, the nested composition—and the layer it contains—maps perfectly to the target layer of the compound effect (**Figures 11.52** and **11.53**).

If all this talk of nesting sounds complicated, don't worry: Chapter 16 explains such topics as nesting and precomposing in greater detail.

Figure 11.52 If a layer requires treatment before becoming an effect source, place it into another comp first. Here, the effect source is scaled and repositioned.

Figure 11.53 You must use the nested comp as the effect source to achieve the desired result.

Animating Effects

Apart from the fact that you can use the Effect Controls panel to adjust values, animating effect properties is no different than animating any other properties. As you learned back in Chapter 7, once you activate the Stopwatch for a property, the procedure for creating keyframes is simple: Set the current time, set a property value, repeat.

Unlike transform and mask properties, however, each effect can contain numerous animated properties—a fact that can lead to an extremely long (and sometimes unwieldy) expanded layer outline or Effect Controls panel. For this reason, you may want to take advantage of property features you overlooked in the past. Remember to use pop-up slider controls to avoid expanding the layer outline ad infinitum. You may also want to reacquaint yourself with the keyboard shortcuts for hiding properties from the layer outline (showing just the animated properties).

Better yet, learn how you can use the Effect Controls panel to control the keyframing process. Now that the panel includes a Stopwatch icon, you can initiate the keyframing process right from the Effect Controls panel. You can also use a context menu to set, remove, and navigate property keyframes.

To set keyframes from the Effect Controls panel:

1. Select the layer containing the effect you want to keyframe, and reveal the effect in the Effect Controls panel.

2. Set the current time to the frame at which you want to set an effect property keyframe (**Figure 11.54**).

continues on next page

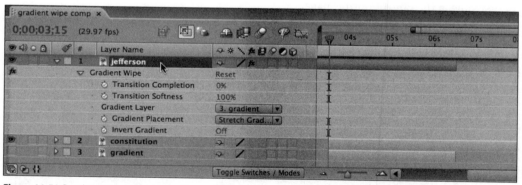

Figure 11.54 Set the current time to the frame at which you want to set an effect property keyframe.

3. In the Effect Controls panel, select the Stopwatch icon next to the name of the property you want to animate (**Figure 11.55**).

Doing so activates the keyframing process. In the Timeline panel, a keyframe appears at the current time (**Figure 11.56**).

4. Adjust the value of the property in the Effect Controls panel.

5. Set the current time to the point at which you want to set another keyframe.

6. Using the controls in the Effect Controls panel, alter the property's values.

In the Timeline, a new keyframe appears for the property at the current time.

7. Repeat steps 5 and 6 as needed.

✔ Tip

■ Control-clicking/right-clicking a property's name in the Effect Controls panel invokes a context menu you can use to set and cue to keyframes.

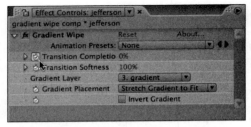

Figure 11.55 In the Effect Controls panel or in the Timeline's layer outline (shown here), select the Stopwatch icon next to the effect property you want to keyframe.

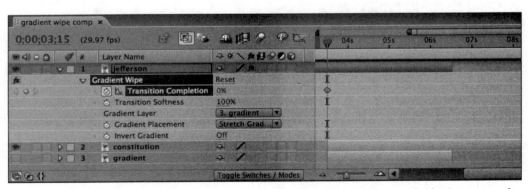

Figure 11.56 A keyframe appears at the current time. The layer outline shown here is expanded for the purpose of illustration; using the Effect Controls panel lets you avoid using the layer outline.

ANIMATING EFFECTS

CREATING AND ANIMATING TEXT

12

With all its strengths in animation and compositing motion footage, you might expect After Effects to possess more limited text-creation tools, leaving serious type-setting to Photoshop or Illustrator. Not so. After Effects lets you create text with the same ease and flexibility as its software siblings.

In After Effects CS3, you can create a text layer by typing with a Type tool directly in a Comp panel. Moreover, you can adjust the text using full-featured Character and Paragraph panels. You can even convert a text layer imported from Photoshop into a text layer you can edit in After Effects. And as in Illustrator, you can convert text into outlines you can manipulate as mask paths.

You can animate text layers as you would any other layer in a comp. But you can also animate *the text itself.* Text layers include unique properties that allow you to change the content of the text over time and, yes, animate the text along a mask path you specify. But more amazing, you can animate individual components of the text—a line, a word, a character—as though it were its own layer. It's like having a text-based animation system within the layer-based animation system. And although the text-animation paradigm employs a unique feature called *animator groups*—each consisting of the properties and parts of the text you want to affect—it also uses the familiar keyframing process you learned about in Chapter 7, "Properties and Keyframes." Animator groups let you create intricate animations using relatively simple controls. Or, if you prefer, you can apply a canned text animation. After Effects includes an astonishingly varied, useful, and generous collection of preset animations you can apply to text with a click of the mouse. OK, *double-click.*

Setting the Workspace for Text

Text creation starts with selecting a Type tool. The Tools panel includes both Horizontal and Vertical Type tools, although one is always hidden; press and hold the visible tool to reveal an extended palette.

To format the text you create, you employ the Character and Paragraph panels. Switching to the Text workspace invokes these panels and rearranges the workspace to accommodate them. When you're using another workspace, you can use the Tools panel's Toggle Panels button to quickly open the panels related to the current tool—in this case, those related to the Text tool. If you prefer, you can activate Auto-Open Panels so that the panels related to the selected tool open automatically.

To specify the Text workspace:

◆ In the Tools panel's Workspace pull-down menu, choose Text (**Figure 12.1**).

The panels rearrange according to the preset and include the Character and Paragraph panels.

To toggle the Character and Paragraph panels:

1. In the Tools panel, select either the Vertical Type or Horizontal Type tool.

2. In the Tools panel, click the Toggle Panels button ▤ (**Figure 12.2**).

Clicking the button toggles the Character and Paragraph panels open and closed.

To open tool-related panels automatically:

1. In the Tools panel, select a tool that has panels associated with it.

The Type tools, Brush, Clone, and Eraser tools, have related panels.

2. In the Tools panel, select Auto-Open Panels (**Figure 12.3**).

Whenever the tool is selected, related panels open automatically.

✔ Tip

■ The Toggle Panels and Auto-Open Panels options also work with the Paint and Clone tools.

Figure 12.1 Choosing the Text workspace rearranges the interface so it includes the Character and Paragraph panels.

Figure 12.2 With a Type tool selected, clicking the Toggle Panels button opens and closes the Character and Paragraph panels.

Figure 12.3 Select Auto-Open Panels to make related panels appear whenever you select the tool.

Figure 12.4 Click and hold either Type tool to expand the panel and reveal the other.

Standard Vertical Roman Alignment

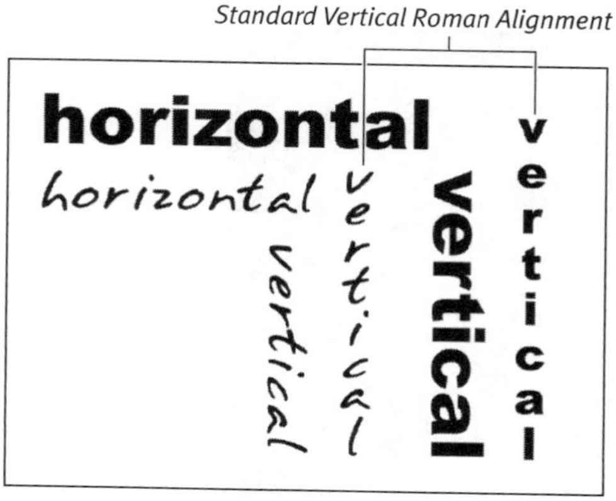

Figure 12.5 The Horizontal Type tool created the horizontal text; the Vertical Type tool created the vertical text. The way characters appear in a vertical line depends on whether you specify Standard Vertical Roman Alignment.

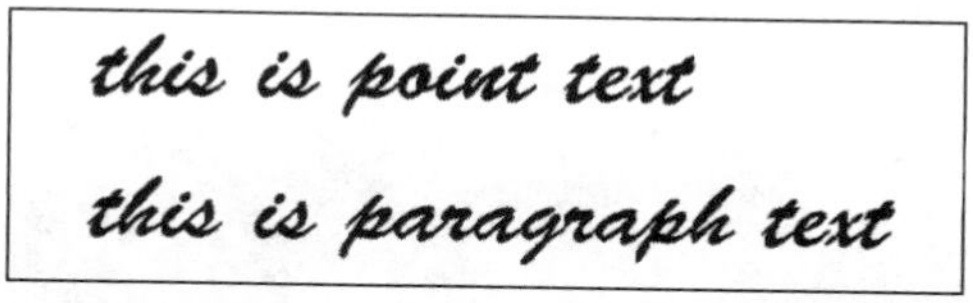

Figure 12.6 Although the point text on top doesn't look any different from the paragraph text on the bottom...

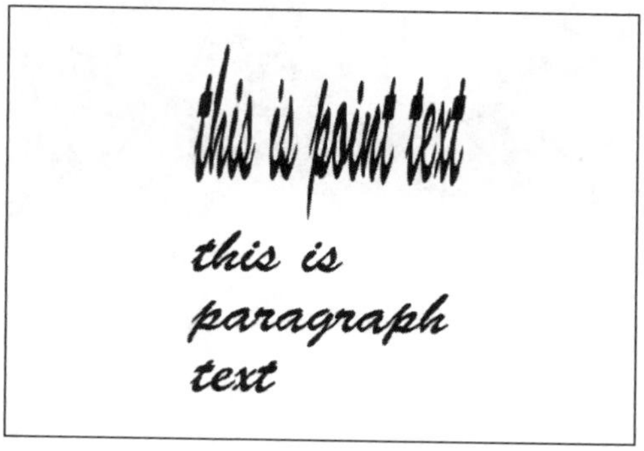

Figure 12.7 ...resizing the point text's bounding box (its normal layer handles) scales the type, whereas resizing the paragraph text's text box reflows the type.

Creating Type

After Effects' Tools panel includes two tools for creating type: the Horizontal Type and Vertical Type tools. Both tools occupy the same location in the panel, but you can access them by clicking and holding one tool to expand the panel and reveal the other (**Figure 12.4**). As you've guessed, the tool you choose depends on whether you want the type to be oriented horizontally or vertically (**Figure 12.5**).

Point text and paragraph text

Both tools let you create two kinds of text objects: *point text* and *paragraph text*. When you create point text, you use a Type tool to set the insertion point and start typing. When you create paragraph text, on the other hand, you first define a *text box* that contains the text.

Initially, there seems to be little difference between the two methods (**Figure 12.6**). But a practical distinction emerges when it's time to edit the text. With both kinds of text, changing the size of the text layer's bounding box *transforms* the text (scales or stretches it). That happens because the bounding box consists of layer handles that work like any other layer's handles. But in contrast to point text, paragraph text also lets you resize its *text box*. Paragraph text *reflows* to fit in its text box, creating line breaks if necessary (**Figure 12.7**). This behavior is also known as *word wrap*.

As its name suggests, paragraph text is better suited for lengthier messages that may need to be reflowed to better fit the comp or that require paragraph-style layout adjustments, such as margins.

✔ Tips

- The four corner handles of a layer's bounding box appear as solid boxes, whereas all the corner handles of a text box appear hollow.

- The vertical orientation is particularly useful for Chinese, Japanese, and Korean text.

CREATING TYPE

To create point text:

1. In the Tools panel, *choose either of the following tools:*

   ▲ **Horizontal Type** —Creates horizontally oriented text (**Figure 12.8**)

   ▲ **Vertical Type** —Creates vertically oriented text

   Both tools occupy the same location in the panel. To choose the hidden tool, click and hold the tool button to expand the panel, or use the keyboard shortcut Command/Ctrl-T.

2. Specify character and paragraph options using controls in the appropriate panel (**Figure 12.9**).

   You can select and modify the text at any time. See sections later in this chapter for more information.

3. In the Composition panel, position the mouse where you want the text to begin.

   As you position the mouse pointer, it appears as an I-beam icon ⌶. The short horizontal line in the I-beam icon indicates the location of the text's baseline.

4. When the I-beam icon is where you want, click the mouse.

   A vertical line appears where you clicked, indicating the text's insertion point.

5. Type the text you want (**Figure 12.10**).

   Text appears at the insertion point, using the current character settings (font, size, fill color, and so on) and paragraph settings. The direction in which characters proceed from the insertion point depends on the current alignment or justification setting (see "Alignment and Justification," later in this chapter).

Figure 12.8 Choose the Vertical Type or Horizontal Type tool (shown here).

Figure 12.9 Specify how you want the text to look by choosing options in the Character and Paragraph panels.

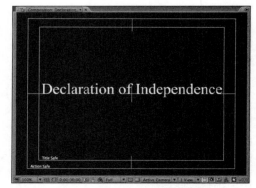

Figure 12.10 Click to set the text's insertion point (indicated by a vertical line), and type the message you want.

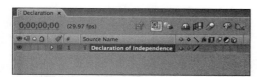

Figure 12.11 When you choose the Selection tool, the new text layer is selected in the Comp panel. In the Timeline panel, its layer name matches what you typed.

Figure 12.12 Choose the Vertical Type or Horizontal Type tool (shown here).

Figure 12.13 Specify character and paragraph options before you enter the text. You can reformat the text later if you want.

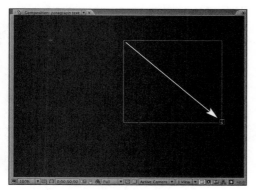

Figure 12.14 In the Comp panel, drag the mouse diagonally to define the size of the text box.

6. When you're finished typing, choose the Selection tool ▶.

In the Comp panel, bounding box handles indicate that the new text object is selected. In the Timeline panel, a text layer appears, and its name matches what you typed (**Figure 12.11**).

To create paragraph text:

1. In the Tools panel, *choose either of the following tools:*

▲ **Horizontal Type** —Creates horizontally oriented text (**Figure 12.12**)

▲ **Vertical Type** —Creates vertically oriented text

Both tools occupy the same location in the panel. To choose the hidden tool, click and hold the tool button to expand the panel, or use the keyboard shortcut Command/Ctrl-T.

2. Specify character and paragraph options using controls in the appropriate panel (**Figure 12.13**).

You can select and modify the text at any time. See sections later in this chapter for more information.

3. In the Composition panel, drag the mouse diagonally to define a text box (**Figure 12.14**).

When you release the mouse, a text box appears with a vertical insertion point icon in the upper-left corner.

continues on next page

CREATING TYPE

4. Type the text you want.

When the text box you defined can't contain the text horizontally, the text continues on the next line (by means of a *soft return*). Text that exceeds the vertical limit of its text box remains hidden until you resize the text box. When text is hidden this way, the bottom-right handle of the text box includes a plus sign, or crosshairs (**Figure 12.15**).

5. To resize the text box to include hidden text or reflow visible text, drag any of its eight handles.

The text reflows to fit within the text box. When the text box is large enough to hold all the text, the bottom-right handle no longer displays a plus sign (**Figure 12.16**).

6. When you're finished creating the message and resizing the text box, click the Selection tool .

In the Timeline panel, a text layer appears; its name matches what you typed (**Figure 12.17**). In the Comp panel, bounding box handles indicate that the new text object is selected. Note that resizing the text layer's bounding box scales the text object. To change the size of the text box and reflow the text, you must enter text-editing mode (as explained in the following task, "To resize a text bounding box").

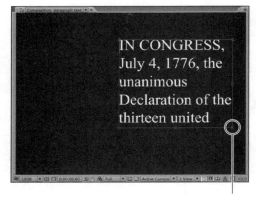

Indicates hidden type

Figure 12.15 When text reaches the side border of the text box, it flows to the next line automatically. If you type more than the text box can contain vertically, the text box's bottom-right handle displays a plus sign (+).

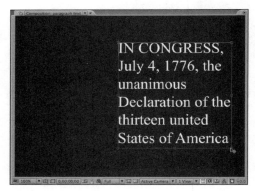

Figure 12.16 While in editing mode, you can drag the text box's handles to resize it and reveal hidden text.

Figure 12.17 Choosing the Selection tool exits editing mode, and the text layer appears selected in the Comp panel. In the Timeline panel, the layer's name matches the text.

CREATING TYPE

Figure 12.18 Clicking text with a Type tool or double-clicking text with the Selection tool (shown here) activates text-editing mode. Layer handles are replaced by text box handles.

Figure 12.19 In text-editing mode, drag any of the text box handles to resize the box...

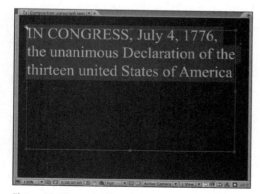

Figure 12.20 ...and reflow the text.

To resize a text bounding box:

1. *Do either of the following:*

▲ Select the Horizontal Type tool ![T] or Vertical Type tool , and click paragraph text.

▲ Using the Selection tool ![arrow], double-click paragraph text (**Figure 12.18**).

An insertion point cursor appears, indicating that you can edit the text. Text box handles also appear. Note that all the handles in a text box are hollow, whereas the four corners of regular layer handles (bounding box handles) are solid (**Figure 12.19**).

2. Drag any of the text box handles to resize the text box.

The text contained in the box reflows to fit in the box horizontally (**Figure 12.20**). Text that doesn't fit in the text box vertically is hidden, and the text box's lower-right handle appears with a crosshair ⊞.

3. When you're finished editing the text box or text, be sure to choose the Selection tool ![arrow] to exit text-editing mode and select the text layer.

✔ Tips

■ You can convert point text to paragraph text and horizontal text to vertical text and vice versa by Control-clicking/right-clicking the text object and choosing the appropriate option in the context menu.

■ By default, vertical text is aligned to a vertical baseline, so that it appears sideways. You can make each letter in vertically oriented text appear upright by selecting the text and choosing Standard Vertical Roman Alignment from the Character panel's pull-down menu.

■ If you import a layered Photoshop file, you can convert its text layers to editable text in After Effects by choosing Layer > Convert to Editable Text.

Editing and Formatting Type

Chances are you're already familiar with the procedures for selecting text for modifying its content or format from using other programs. This chapter won't cover those techniques, so you can spend more time learning text features unique to After Effects.

As in other Adobe programs, you format text with controls in the Character panel and Paragraph panel. Both panels let you choose settings by using buttons, specifying numerical values, or by choosing a preset option in a pull-down menu. (The following sections assume you know how to use these common controls.)

Font, style, fill, and stroke

Near the top of the Character panel you can specify the text's font, style, fill, and stroke using controls common with other programs, such as Photoshop and Illustrator (**Figure 12.21**). Controls for setting the stroke's width and how it's applied are located a bit farther down the panel.

Font contains a set of *typefaces*, or type designs; it determines the overall look of the text characters.

Font style specifies a variation on the font, such as bold, italic, condensed, light, and so on.

Fill specifies the color within a character's contours.

Stroke specifies the color of the character's contours: its outlines. You can detect the stroke color only if the stroke has a thickness greater than zero.

Stroke width sets the thickness of a stroke in pixels (**Figure 12.22**).

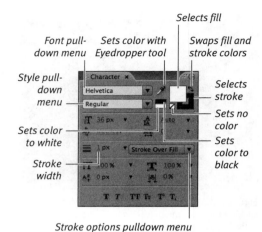

Selects fill

Font pull-down menu · Sets color with Eyedropper tool · Swaps fill and stroke colors

Style pull-down menu · Selects stroke

Sets color to white · Sets no color · Sets color to black

Stroke width · Stroke options pulldown menu

Figure 12.21 The Character panel includes standard controls for font, fill, and stroke.

Figure 12.22 Here, each line of text uses a different stroke width.

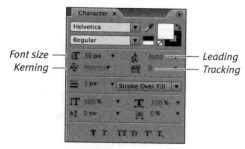

Font size
Kerning
Leading
Tracking

Figure 12.23 Specify values for font size and other options.

Figure 12.24 You can adjust tracking to tight (so tight that characters overlap) or loose.

✔ Tips

■ When kerning characters, you can choose between two options in the Character panel. **Metrics** uses the kern pair values built into the font's design. **Optical** sets the value according to the shape of adjacent characters.

■ Options in the Character panel's pull-down menu let you specify how leading is calculated, whether to use "smart quotes" instead of standard quotation marks, and foreign language features. For more about these options, consult the Help system.

Stroke options let you specify whether the stroke is applied over the fill or vice versa for the selected characters or for all characters in the text object.

✔ Tips

■ By reducing kerning or tracking values, it's possible to make characters in the same text layer overlap. You can specify how overlapping letters interact by setting their Inter-Character Blending mode, found in the text layer's property outline under the heading More Options. Chapter 14 explains how Blending modes work.

■ For video output, avoid light text or text with fine features like *serifs* (the little tapering corners of letters in so-called old-style typefaces, like this one). Interlacing causes fine horizontal lines to flicker, making some text difficult to read. See Chapter 2 for more about video interlacing.

■ In the Character panel's pull-down menu, select Show Font Names in English to list foreign language fonts in English; deselect the option to list them in their native language.

Font size, leading, kerning, and tracking

Going down the Character panel, the second section contains controls for setting the font's size and for specifying the space between lines, letters, and pairs of characters (**Figure 12.23**).

Font size specifies the size of the font, expressed in pixels.

Leading defines the space between lines of text.

Kerning describes the process of adjusting the value of *kern pairs*, spacing that the typeface's designer built into particular pairs of characters.

Tracking refers to adjusting the overall space between letters in a range of text (**Figure 12.24**).

Scale, baseline shift, and tsume

The next set of controls lets you modify the text's horizontal and vertical scale, its baseline, and the spacing of text in languages that are typically vertically aligned (**Figure 12.25**).

Vertical Scale sets the vertical aspect of selected characters, making them relatively shorter or taller than the font size dictates (**Figure 12.26**).

Horizontal Scale sets the vertical aspect of selected characters, making them relatively shorter or taller than the font size dictates.

Baseline Shift shifts or offsets the selected character's baseline, the invisible "floor" on which the text rests. Adjusting the baseline can help you create mathematical notation or fractions (**Figure 12.27**).

Tsume determines the amount of space around each character in Chinese, Japanese, and Korean (CJK) vertically aligned text.

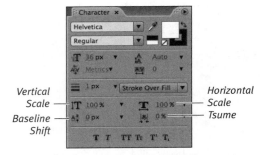

Figure 12.25 Specify scaling, baseline shift, or spacing for CJK fonts.

Figure 12.26 In this example, you can contrast the original text with the same text scaled vertically and horizontally.

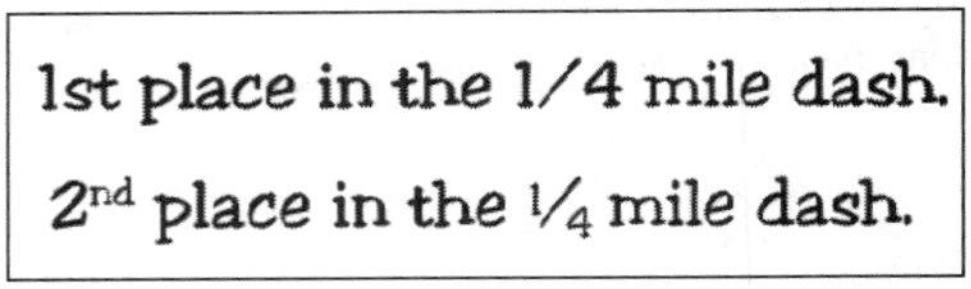

1st place in the 1/4 mile dash.

2nd place in the 1/4 mile dash.

Figure 12.27 Here, the baselines of characters have been shifted to create the fraction within the text. (The font size of the numerals has also been reduced.)

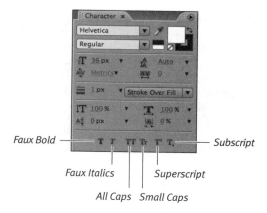

Faux Bold — | — Subscript

Faux Italics   Superscript

All Caps   Small Caps

Figure 12.28 Specify options for simulating typeface styles.

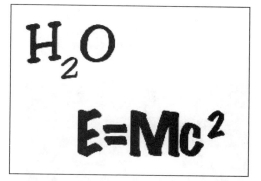

Figure 12.29 Here, the 2 in $E=Mc^2$ is superscripted, the 2 in H_2O is subscripted.

Faux bold, faux italics, all caps, small caps, superscript, and subscript

The bottom section of the Character panel contains controls for simulating typeface styles the selected font doesn't include by design (**Figure 12.28**).

Faux Bold simulates boldface for fonts that don't include a bold typeface by design.

Faux Italics simulates italics for fonts that don't include a bold typeface by design.

All Caps changes lowercase letters to uppercase, or capital, letters. For example, it would change a lowercase "a" to an uppercase "A."

Small Caps changes lowercase characters to a miniature version of uppercase characters.

Superscript makes characters appear higher than other characters on the text line. For example, the 2 in the familiar equation $E=Mc^2$ is superscript (**Figure 12.29**).

Subscript makes characters appear lower than other characters on the text line. For example, the 2 in the chemical notation for water, H_2O, is subscript.

Formatting Paragraph Text

Whenever paragraph text reaches the edge of the text box, it flows into another line automatically—something often referred to as a *soft return*. A new *paragraph* occurs when you press Return/Enter, also known as a *hard return*. You can format paragraph text using the Paragraph panel.

Alignment and Justification

The topmost section of the Paragraph panel contains a number of buttons with icons that correspond to different alignment and justification options (**Figure 12.30**).

Alignment determines how the lines in a paragraph are positioned relative to the margins (the left and right sides of the text box) (**Figure 12.31**).

Justification alters the spacing in each line of text so that all the lines are flush with both the right and left margins. You can specify how After Effects aligns the last line, which is usually shorter than the others and doesn't lend itself to justification (**Figure 12.32**).

Justify Last Left
Align Right
Justify Last Center
Align Center
Justify Last Right
Align Left
Justify All
0 px
0 px
0 px
0 px
0 px

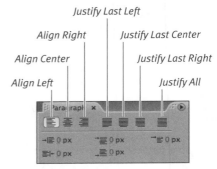

Figure 12.30 The Paragraph panel includes standard buttons for aligning and justifying paragraphs in a text box.

When in the course of human events it becomes necessary for one people to dissolve the political bonds which have connected them with another, and to assume among the powers of the earth, the separate and equal station to which the Laws of Nature and of Nature's God entitle them, a decent respect to
When in the course of human events it becomes necessary for one people to dissolve the political bonds which have connected them with another, and to assume among the powers of the earth, the separate and equal station to which the Laws of Nature and of Nature's God entitle them, a decent respect to

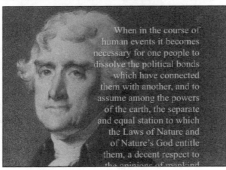

Figure 12.31 Compare the effect of different alignment options.

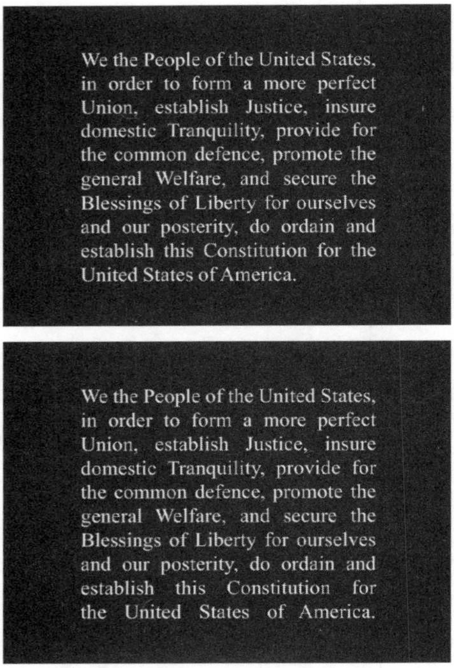

We the People of the United States, in order to form a more perfect Union, establish Justice, insure domestic Tranquility, provide for the common defence, promote the general Welfare, and secure the Blessings of Liberty for ourselves and our posterity, do ordain and establish this Constitution for the United States of America.
We the People of the United States, in order to form a more perfect Union, establish Justice, insure domestic Tranquility, provide for the common defence, promote the general Welfare, and secure the Blessings of Liberty for ourselves and our posterity, do ordain and establish this Constitution for the United States of America.

Figure 12.32 Choosing Justify Last Left (top) leaves the last line ragged. However, choosing Justify All (bottom) can result in awkward spacing.

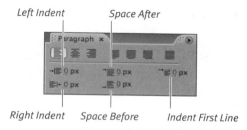

Left Indent   Space After

Right Indent   Space Before   Indent First Line

Figure 12.33 In the Paragraph panel, specify the amount you want to indent the text from the sides of the text box, and the space between paragraphs.

Adobe CS3 Production Premium

After Effects Pro
Premiere Pro
Encore
Soundbooth
Photoshop Extended
Illustrator
Flash Pro
OnLocation
Ultra

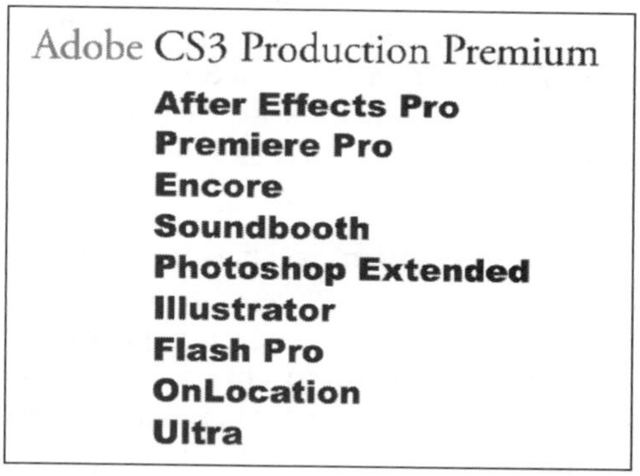

Figure 12.34 This example shows a single text layer, but the list is indented.

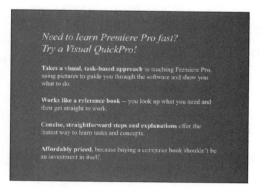

Figure 12.35 Here, a single text layer contains several paragraphs. Increasing the default Space After Value creates extra space between paragraphs.

Indent and Spacing

The controls located in the bottom section of the Paragraph panel let you specify how to indent a paragraph's first line, and the spacing between paragraphs (**Figure 12.33**).

Indent increases one or both of its margins, shifting it away from the margins defined by the sides of the text box (**Figure 12.34**).

Spacing specifies the space before or after new paragraphs (hard returns), independent of the line spacing (or leading) within each paragraph (**Figure 12.35**).

✔ Tips

- Hanging punctuation allows punctuation marks to appear outside the text box. To enable hanging punctuation, select the paragraph text and choose Roman Hanging Punctuation from the Paragraph panel's pull-down menu.

- After Effects determines line breaks in paragraph text using either of two methods you specify in the Paragraph panel's pull-down menu: Adobe Single-Line or Every-Line Composer. For more about these methods, consult the Help system.

Animating Text

In most respects, text layers are just like other layers, and they include the same layer properties you learned about in Chapter 7. But text layers have a number of unique text properties, as well. You can animate the layer and the text within the layer. But, unlike other layers, you can't open a text layer in a Layer panel.

Standard layer properties

Text layers include the same transform properties—Anchor Point, Position, Scale, Rotation, and Opacity—that you find in any layer (and learned about in Chapter 7). Text layers accept masks and effects; and, like other layers, you can make a text layer 3D. But the standard layer property controls affect the *layer as a whole*; they can't alter the content of the text (what it says) or apply to characters individually (not without using masks, anyway).

Text properties

A special set of text properties makes it possible to animate words or individual characters without complex keyframing, elaborate masking techniques, or resorting to using numerous text layers:

Source text lets you change the content of a text message over time. This way, a single text layer can convey a series of messages. Used in combination with animator groups and selectors (described in a moment), you can change the content more gradually. For example, you can make the letters in a word appear to encode themselves, cycling through other letters, and gradually decode themselves into another word.

Path text lets you make a line of text follow a path that you specify. You can animate the border to make the text appear to glide over the path. You can also specify other options, such as whether the type is perpendicular to the path.

Animator groups let you animate properties of any range of characters within the text. Each animator group you create can include any number or combination of properties, including both familiar transform properties and properties unique to text. You can specify the range of text affected by the animator properties with one or more *range selectors*. Numerous other options let you fine-tune the animation.

Figure 12.36 Create a text layer, and format and arrange it into its initial state (before animating it).

Animating Source Text

You can animate a text layer's *source text* (the content of the text message). Source text keyframes always use Hold interpolation. As you'll see in Chapter 16, "Complex Projects," *Hold interpolation* retains a keyframe value until the next keyframe value is reached. The message instantly changes to the text you specify at each keyframe. This way, a single layer can contain multiple text messages; you don't have to create multiple layers.

Note that you can change the source text while animating other properties. For example, by creating an animator group and animating the Character Offset property, you can change the characters in a word—encoding or decoding it. Changing an encoded word's source text during the animation lets you make one word change into another.

To animate source text:

1. Create and format a text layer, and arrange the layer in the comp (**Figure 12.36**).

   To create the text layer, use techniques described earlier in this chapter. To arrange the layer in the comp, use techniques covered in Chapter 5, "Layer Basics," and Chapter 6, "Layer Editing."

2. Set the current time to the frame where you want the message you created in step 1 to begin.

continues on next page

3. In the Timeline panel, expand the text layer's property outline, and click the Stopwatch icon for the layer's Source Text property.

An initial keyframe is created for the Source Text property (**Figure 12.37**). Source text keyframes always use the Hold interpolation method (see Chapter 9, "Keyframe Interpolation").

4. Set the current time to the frame where you want a new message to appear.

5. Select the text, and type a new message (**Figure 12.38**).

A new Hold keyframe appears at the current time for the layer's Source Text property (**Figure 12.39**).

6. Repeat steps 4 and 5 as needed.

When you preview the animation, each message appears until the current time reaches the next source text keyframe.

Figure 12.37 In the text layer's property outline, click the Source Text property's Stopwatch icon to create an initial keyframe.

Figure 12.38 Set the current time to the frame where you want the message to change, and edit the text...

Figure 12.39 ...to create a new Hold keyframe for the Source Text property (seen here in the layer outline).

Figure 12.40 Create a text layer and, with the layer selected, create a mask path.

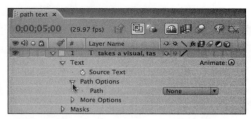

Figure 12.41 In the Timeline panel, expand the text layer's property outline to reveal its Path Options property heading.

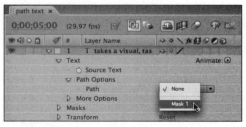

Figure 12.42 Choose the path you want the text to follow in the Path pull-down menu.

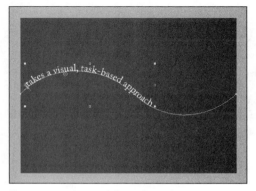

Figure 12.43 The text follows the path.

Making Text Follow a Path

You can make the type in any text layer follow a path you specify, without sacrificing any of the formatting or text animation options available to the text layer.

To create path text:

1. Create and format a text layer.

   You can use any of the techniques discussed earlier in this chapter.

2. With the text layer selected, create a mask path to serve as the baseline of the text (**Figure 12.40**).

   Use any of the techniques described in Chapter 10, "Mask Essentials." In the Timeline panel, the mask you create appears in the text layer's property outline.

3. In the Timeline panel, expand the text layer's property outline; then, expand its Text property heading and Path Options property heading (**Figure 12.41**).

4. In the Path pull-down menu, choose the path you created in step 2 (**Figure 12.42**).

   The text uses the specified path as its baseline (**Figure 12.43**).

To animate path text:

1. Create path text as described in the previous task, "To create path text."

2. Set the current time to the frame where you want the animation to begin.

3. In the path text layer's property outline, set the First Margin value to specify the text's starting point on the path, and click the Stopwatch icon to set the initial keyframe (**Figure 12.44**).

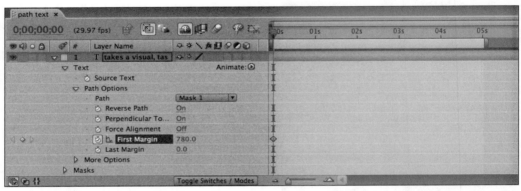

Figure 12.44 Set the current time to the frame where you want the animation to begin, and set a keyframe for the First Margin property value.

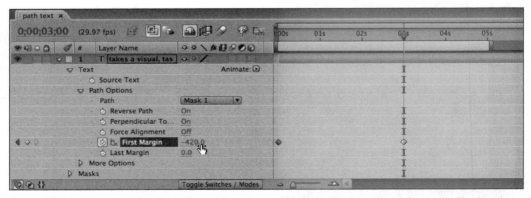

Figure 12.45 Set the current time to the frame where you want the animation to end, and change the First Margin property value to its final position along the path.

MAKING TEXT FOLLOW A PATH

Figure 12.46 Animating the First Margin property moves the text along the path.

4. Set the current time to the frame where you want the animation to end, and set the First Margin value to set the text's starting point on the path when the animation ends (**Figure 12.45**).

When you preview the animation, the text moves along the path (**Figure 12.46**). Use the techniques covered in Chapter 7, "Properties and Keyframes," and Chapter 9, "Keyframe Interpolation," to refine the animation.

Using Text Animation Presets

After Effects includes a generous and varied collection of text animation presets, conveniently sorted by category in the Effects & Presets panel (**Figure 12.47**). You're just as likely to modify one of these excellent presets as you are to build a text animation from scratch.

As you learn about text animation, start by examining some of the presets. Once you see what text animation can do, dig into the sections on animator groups to find out what makes them tick and, ultimately, how to create your own.

To view a gallery of text animation presets:

1. Choose Animation > Browse Presets (**Figure 12.48**).

   Bridge opens and displays the contents of the Presets folder within the After Effects CS3 folder.

2. To view text animation samples by category, click the appropriate link (**Figure 12.49**).

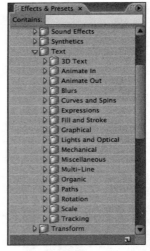

Figure 12.47 The Effects & Presets panel contains numerous preset text animations.

Figure 12.48 Choose Animation > Browse Presets.

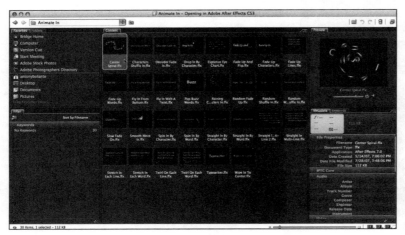

Figure 12.49 Click the category of text animations for which you want to see examples.

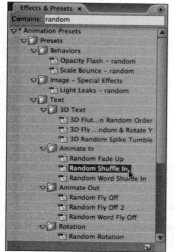

Figure 12.50 Create and format a text layer.

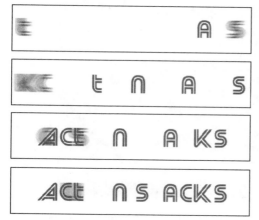

Figure 12.51 With the text layer selected, double-click the text preset you want in the Effects & Presets panel.

To apply a text animation preset:

1. Create and format a text layer, and select the layer (**Figure 12.50**).

   Make sure to select the entire text layer, not a range of characters. To animate part of a text layer, you can use range selectors (as explained later in this chapter).

2. In the Effects & Presets panel, double-click the text animation preset you want to apply to the selected text (**Figure 12.51**).

   The preset you specify is applied to the selected text (**Figure 12.52**). For more about using the Effects & Presets panel, see Chapter 11.

3. If you want, modify the effect by changing the position or value of its keyframed text animation properties (as explained in Chapter 7). You can also add, delete, or modify the preset effect's animator properties or range selector values (as explained later in this chapter).

Figure 12.52 The preset is applied to the selected text layer.

Understanding Animator Groups

You animate type by adding one or more *animator groups* to a text layer. Animator groups appear in the layer outline under a text layer's Text property heading (**Figure 12.53**). You create an animator group by choosing a property you want to affect in the layer's Animator pull-down menu. You can add as many groups as you need to achieve the animation you want.

Each animator group consists of at least one *animator property* and one *selector*. You can add properties and selectors to a group by using its Add pull-down menu.

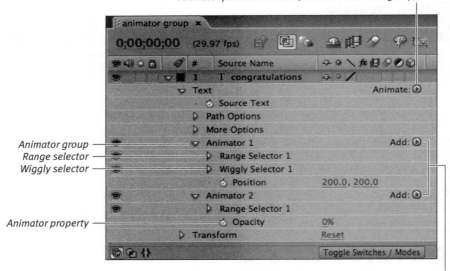

Animator pull-down menu (to add an animator group)

Animator group
Range selector
Wiggly selector

Animator property

Add pull-down menu (to add properties and selectors to a group)

Figure 12.53 Animator groups appear in the layer outline.

Animator properties

Animator properties include familiar transform properties (such as position, rotation, and so on). With type, however, each character, word, or line can possess its own anchor point. You can also animate properties unique to text (fill, stroke, tracking, and so on), as well as per-character blur. You can even set each character's value—the numerical code that determines which character is displayed. And starting with After Effects CS3, you can enable Per-Character 3D, which endows text with the same 3D properties you can give layers (as explained in Chapter 15).

Each animator group can have any number and combination of properties, which can be set to any value. But unlike when you're animating layers, you probably won't animate the property values to create the animation. Instead, you'll animate the range of characters affected by the properties by keyframing a selector.

Range selectors

A *selector* lets you specify a *range*, or the part of the type that's affected by an animator group's properties. Most animations are achieved by animating the range, not the properties. Selectors are comparable to layer masks in that they limit the areas affected by your adjustments. Just as you can add multiple masks to a layer, you can add multiple selectors to an animator group. Multiple selectors let you specify ranges that you

couldn't define with a single selector (such as a noncontinuous range of characters). And like masks, you can specify how multiple ranges interact by choosing a mode. You can fine-tune the rate and manner in which the range includes units by specifying a number of options listed under the range selector's Advanced category in the expanded property outline.

In addition to a standard range selector, you can apply a *wiggly selector* to vary the selection, giving it a more random or organic feel. You can also specify an *expression selector*, which can link the selection to another property or base it on a mathematical function.

As you might guess, the scope of this chapter prevents a detailed discussion of every animator group property and range selector option and their possible combinations. The following sections start with an overview of the text animation process and then go on to describe how to specify animator group properties and ranges. For a detailed explanation of the numerous options, see the After Effects Help system.

✔ Tip

■ In After Effects, an "expression" is a JavaScript-based formula that can generate property values without keyframes. An expression selector controls an animator group's Amount property in a text layer. Standard expressions can be applied to any property in any layer, as explained in Chapter 16.

Animating Type with Animator Groups

As you gleaned from the previous section, "Understanding Animator Groups," animator groups grant you a great deal of control over text animation and can include numerous components.

The following task provides an overview of the steps required to create a simple text animation. The basic steps include creating an animator group, specifying its property value and range, and then animating the range. For the sake of clarity, the task doesn't mention particular property and selector options. It also doesn't include steps to add animator groups or to add properties or selectors to existing groups. Follow this task to create a simple animation, and then explore later sections to add complexity to your text animations.

To animate type with animator groups:

1. Create and format a text layer.

   Use the techniques explained earlier in this chapter.

2. In the Timeline panel, expand the text layer to reveal its Text property heading.

3. In the Timeline panel, choose the Text property you want to animate from the Animate pull-down menu (**Figure 12.54**).

   An Animator property heading appears under the layer's Text property heading. The Animator property contains a Range Selector property heading and the property you specified (**Figure 12.55**).

4. Set the values for the property you specified in step 3.

   The values are applied to the entire text (**Figure 12.56**). You can limit the range of affected characters in step 5. Typically, you'll animate the range, not the property values (as explained in the next step).

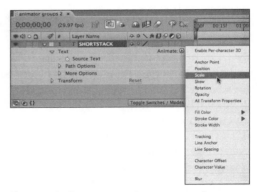

Figure 12.54 To create an animator group, choose a property in the Animate pull-down menu.

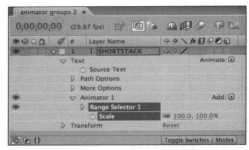

Figure 12.55 The new animator group includes the property you selected and a range selector.

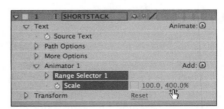

Figure 12.56 Set the property values. Here, the type's vertical scale has been increased. Until you limit the range, the property value affects all of the text.

Figure 12.57 Set the current time, and specify values for the range. In this example, the range's end has been moved next to its start, so the property doesn't affect any of the characters at the beginning of the animation.

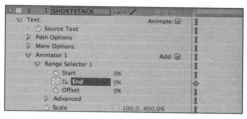

Figure 12.58 Click the Stopwatch icon to set the initial keyframe. Here, an initial keyframe is set for the end of the range.

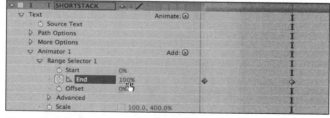

Figure 12.59 Set the current time to another frame and change the range. Here, the current time is set 2 seconds later, and the end of the range has been moved from its original position (shown in Figure 12.57) so that all the characters are affected.

5. Set the current time, and specify values for the range selector.

You can set the range by dragging the Range Start and Range End icons in the Comp panel (**Figure 12.57**) or by setting Start and End values in the property outline. For details, see "Specifying a Range," later in this chapter.

6. For the range properties you want to animate, click the Stopwatch icon to set the initial keyframe at the current time.

You can set keyframes for any combination of the selector's Start, End, and Offset values (**Figure 12.58**).

7. Set the current time to another frame, and change the animated range property values to set another keyframe (**Figure 12.59**).

For example, you can increase the range over time by animating the range's End property, or make the range travel through the characters by animating the Offset property.

continues on next page

ANIMATING TYPE WITH ANIMATOR GROUPS

8. If necessary, repeat step 7 to create additional keyframes.

9. Preview the type animation using any of the techniques covered in Chapter 8, "Playback, Previews, and RAM."

As the range animates, different parts of the text are affected by the properties in the animator group (**Figure 12.60**).

✔ Tip

- As with other elements in a project (comps, duplicate layers, expressions, and so on), it's a good idea to give animator groups and range selectors unique names. Doing so makes it easier to distinguish them and to ascertain their purpose at a glance. Select the animator or range selector, press Return/Enter, edit the name, and press Return/Enter when you're finished.

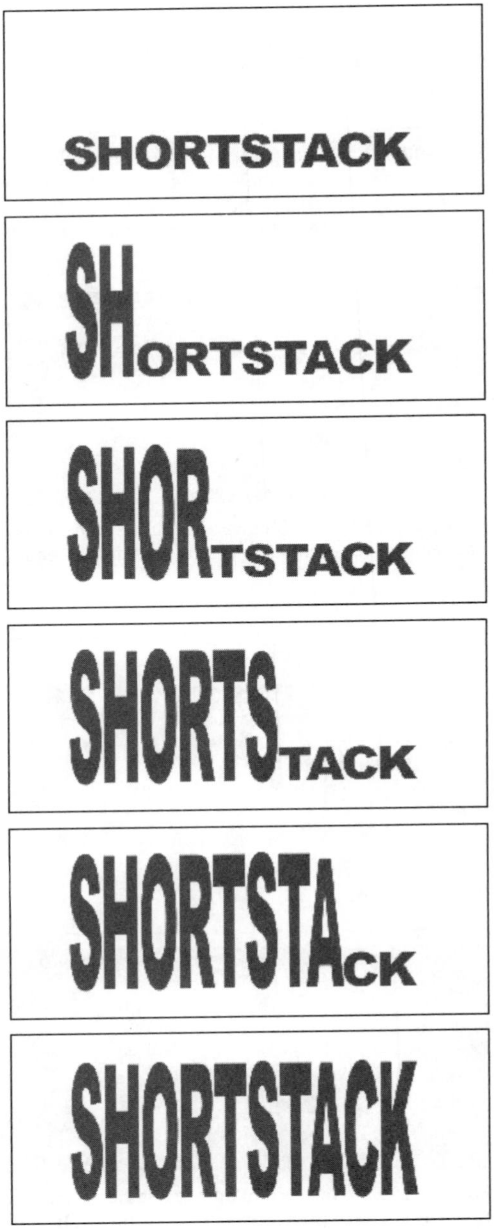

Figure 12.60 Previewing the animation shows how animating the range changes which parts of the text are affected by the animator property you set.

ANIMATING TYPE WITH ANIMATOR GROUPS

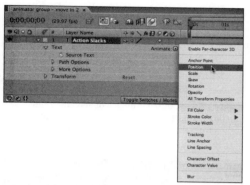

Figure 12.61 To create an animator group, choose a property from the Animate pull-down menu.

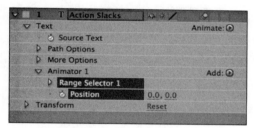

Figure 12.62 The animator group appears in the text layer's property outline; it contains the property and a default range selector.

Creating Animator Groups

You can add any number of animator groups to a text layer, and each animator group can contain any combination of properties and range selectors. However, each group must contain at least one property and one selector.

To create an animator group:

1. If necessary, expand the text layer's property outline in the Timeline panel.

2. In the Switches/Modes panel of the Timeline, choose a property from the text layer's Animate pull-down menu (across from the layer's Text property) (**Figure 12.61**).

   An Animator property heading appears under the layer's Text property heading. The Animator property (called Animator 1 by default) contains a Range Selector property heading (called Range Selector 1 by default) and the property you specified (**Figure 12.62**).

To add to an animator group:

1. If necessary, expand the layer outline of a text layer containing at least one animator.

2. In the Switches/Modes panel of the Timeline, choose an option from the animator's Add pull-down menu (**Figure 12.63**):

   Property adds a property to the specified animator.

   Selector adds a selector to the specified animator.

   The property or selector is added to the animator (**Figure 12.64**).

To remove a group, property, or selector:

◆ In a text layer's property outline, select an animator group, animator property, or selector, and press Delete.

   The selected item is removed from the layer.

✔ Tips

■ As with other items in a project, it's a good idea to give animator groups unique, descriptive names. You can rename animator groups just like layers and other items: Select the name, press Return/Enter, type the new name, and press Return/Enter again.

■ Animator properties and selectors include a video switch just like layers. Turn off a switch to exclude the effects of the item.

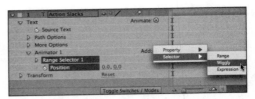

Figure 12.63 To add a property or selector to an existing animator group, select the appropriate option from the group's Add pull-down menu.

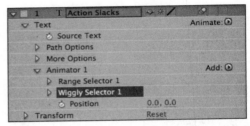

Figure 12.64 The group includes the added item. In this example, an additional selector has been added to the group.

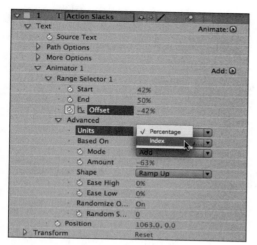

Figure 12.65 In the Units pull-down menu, choose whether range values are expressed as a percentage of the entire type or are expressed by indexing, or numbering, each unit.

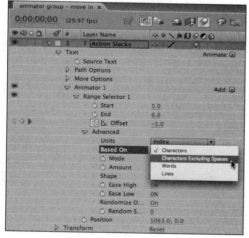

Figure 12.66 For Based On, choose the units on which the range is based.

Specifying a Range

You can set a range either by dragging its left and right borders in the Comp panel or by using controls in the text layer's property outline. A range can be applied to different units of type: each character, word, or line. When you're specifying a range, these units are measured either in terms of a percentage of total units, or by the unit (1, 2, 3, and so on).

To specify how a range is measured:

1. In the layer outline of the Timeline panel, expand the range selector you want to adjust, and expand its Advanced property heading.

2. To specify how Start, End, and Offset range values are expressed, choose an option in the Units pull-down menu (**Figure 12.65**):

   Percentage expresses values in percentages.

   Index expresses values according to a numerical indexing scheme in which the first unit of text is assigned a value of 1, the next unit 2, and so on.

3. To specify the units on which a range is based (how the range is counted), choose an option in the Based On pull-down menu (**Figure 12.66**):

   Characters counts each character, including spaces, as a unit in the range.

   Characters Excluding Spaces counts each character as a unit in the range but excludes spaces.

   Words counts each word as a unit in the range.

   Lines counts each line (of a multiline text layer) as a unit in the range.

   The values for Start, End, and Offset are based on the option you specify.

To specify a range:

1. Expand the text layer animator group you want to adjust, and then expand the range selector you want to set.

2. To set the start of the range, *do either of the following:*
   ▲ In the text layer's expanded outline, specify a value for Start.
   ▲ With the text layer's Animator group heading selected in the expanded outline, drag the Range Start icon ⊩ in the Composition panel (**Figure 12.67**).

3. To set the end of the range, *do either of the following:*
   ▲ In the text layer's expanded outline, specify a value for End.
   ▲ With the text layer's Animator property selected, drag the Range End icon ⊩ in the Composition panel (**Figure 12.68**).

4. To change both the Start and End values by the same amount, specify an Offset value in the text layer's expanded outline (**Figure 12.69**).

Figure 12.67 With the range selected in the property outline, you can drag the start of the range in the Comp panel...

Figure 12.68 ...or drag the Range End icon to set the end of the range.

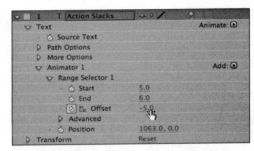

Figure 12.69 To change both the Start and End values by the same amount, change the Offset value in the property outline.

SPECIFYING A RANGE

PAINTING
ON A LAYER

Although it appears as a single effect in the layer's property outline, the Paint effect feels like an entirely separate set of features meriting a chapter of its own. The Tools panel includes several tools devoted to painting: the Brush tool, Eraser tool, and Clone Stamp tool. And the Paint feature's numerous options require two specialized panels: the Paint panel and Brush Tips panel. With the Brush and Eraser tools, you can simulate handwriting, create hand-drawn graphics, or alter a layer's alpha channel to create (or fix) a track matte. Or you can make more subtle adjustments to an image with each stroke by using Blending modes. You can also use a Clone Stamp tool to retouch an image or to aid in tasks like wire removal.

Using your mouse—or, better yet, a tablet and stylus—you can record strokes directly onto a layer in real time, change their characteristics, and play them back in a number of ways. The Brush Tips panel includes a varied set of preset brushes and allows you to create and save your own variations—small or large, hard or soft-edged, round or elliptical. Because strokes are vector-based, you can scale them without adversely affecting resolution. And like all effects, brush strokes are nondestructive, which means they don't alter your source files. Even strokes you make with the Eraser tool are nondestructive.

Paint also deserves special attention because of its unique animation paradigm. Each stroke appears as its own layer within a layer—that is, each stroke appears as a duration bar within the paint effect. This way, you can toggle strokes on and off, control how they're layered and how they interact with strokes lower in the stacking order, and precisely adjust when and how quickly they appear.

In this chapter, you'll learn this single effect's numerous options so you can explore its unlimited possibilities.

Using the Paint and Brush Tips Panels

After Effects includes two panels for controlling Paint: the Paint panel and Brush Tips panel. Both panels are nearly identical to their counterparts in other Adobe programs.

The panels are part of the Paint preset workspace. You can also summon the panels by clicking the Tools panel's Toggle Panels button 📇 whenever the Brush ✐, Clone 🖋, or Eraser ⬛ tool is selected (**Figure 13.1**).

To specify the Paint workspace:

◆ In the Tools panel's Workspace pull-down menu, select Paint (**Figure 13.2**).

After Effects arranges the workspace automatically and includes the Paint and Brush Tips panels (**Figures 13.3** and **13.4**).

Figure 13.1 Clicking the Toggle Panels button when the Brush, Clone, or Eraser tool is selected...

Figure 13.2 ...or selecting Paint from the Workspace pull-down menu...

Figure 13.3 ...opens the Paint panel...

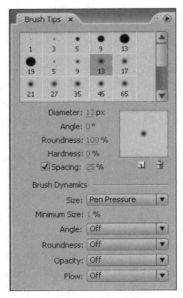

Figure 13.4 ...and the Brush Tips panel.

Figure 13.5 Opacity determines the paint's coverage strength; Flow determines the speed of coverage. Here, the words Opacity and flow are repeated, each time using a lower Opacity or Flow setting, respectively.

Specifying Paint Stroke Options

Before you start using the Brush and Eraser tools, take a moment to get a more detailed understanding of each option, starting with the options at the top of the Paint panel. These options not only allow you to control the character and color of each stroke, but also let you specify which of the layer's channels are affected by each stroke and how long strokes appear.

Depending on the options you choose, you can make visible strokes, resembling those made by a loaded paintbrush or by an airbrush lightly applying each coat; or you can make strokes that affect the layer's alpha channel, effectively creating or modifying a matte. The strokes can appear for any length of time or reenact the painting process. Later, you'll specify many of the same options to determine the effects of the Clone Stamp tool.

Generally, you set these options before you paint a stroke. However, you can change these and most other options by selecting the stroke under the Paint effect and adjusting its values in the property outline.

Opacity and Flow

Opacity and Flow settings determine the paint's coverage strength and the speed of coverage, respectively. Together, they can make paint seem opaque or semitransparent (**Figure 13.5**). When you're using the Eraser, the same options determine how effectively and quickly pixels are removed:

Opacity sets the maximum opacity of each stroke, from 0% to 100%; opacity is analogous to how well a real-world paint covers a surface. (A brush's Hardness setting also contributes to a stroke's opacity near its edges.)

Flow determines how quickly paint is applied with each stroke, from 0% to 100%. Lower Flow settings apply less of the paint color in a stroke, making the paint appear more transparent; low Flow values also result in greater spaces between brush tip marks when the brush's Spacing option is active (see "Customizing Brush Tips," later in this chapter).

Brush tip

As you'd expect, the brush tip simulates the camel hair on the end of a brush (or the point of a pen, or the spray pattern of an airbrush). Brush tip settings define the character of strokes. The Paint panel displays the currently selected brush tip as an icon that represents its roundness, angle, and hardness settings; a number indicates the brush's size, in pixels (**Figure 13.6**). Clicking the current brush tip icon activates (or if necessary, opens) the Brush Tip panel, from which you can select a preset brush tip or create your own (see "Using Brush Tips," later in this chapter) (**Figure 13.7**).

Color

Like a real panel of paint, the Paint panel lets you choose the color you want to use. The upper-left swatch sets the *foreground color*, which specifies the paint applied by the brush; the lower-right swatch sets the *background color*, or secondary color. Clicking a swatch lets you choose a color from a color picker, or you can sample a color from the screen using a standard Eyedropper tool ![eyedropper]. Click the smaller icon to reset the foreground and background colors to black and white, respectively; click the Swap icon ![swap] to switch the colors (**Figure 13.8**).

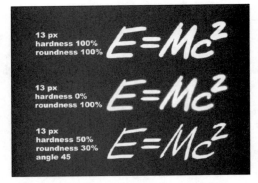

Figure 13.6 This figure shows strokes created by various brush tips.

Figure 13.7 In the Paint panel, click the arrow next to the current brush tip icon to reveal the Brush Tips Selector.

Foreground Color   Swap

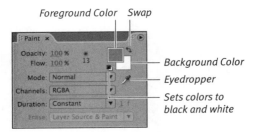

Background Color

Eyedropper

Sets colors to black and white

Figure 13.8 In the Paint panel, the upper-left swatch sets the foreground color; the lower-right swatch sets the background, or secondary color.

Figure 13.9 You can set how brushes interact with lower strokes or the underlying image with Blending modes. Here, a soft, transparent brush uses a Dodge mode to lighten shadows in this photo.

Figure 13.10 In this example, strokes are painted on the layer's alpha channel to reveal the parts of the layer's image (a tangerine) just as a mask or matte would do. The Paint effect's Paint on Transparent option is on.

Mode

The Mode pull-down menu lets you specify how each stroke interacts with underlying pixels (**Figure 13.9**). The menu's Blending mode options are explained in Chapter 14, "More Layer Techniques." However, the stroke Blending mode menu doesn't include the Dissolve or Dancing Dissolve Blending modes. Note that each stroke can use a Blending mode, and the layer containing the paint effect (and all its strokes) can use a Blending mode also.

Channels

The Channels pull-down menu specifies which of the layer's channels are affected by a stroke. You can affect the visible red, green, and blue channels (RGB), the alpha channel (which defines transparency), or all channels (RGBA). Painting on a layer's RGB channels creates visible strokes, whereas painting on its alpha channel affects its transparent areas. For example, you can animate strokes applied to a layer's alpha channel to reveal portions of the layer's image (**Figure 13.10**).

Duration

The Duration pull-down menu specifies how strokes are displayed over time. Duration options facilitate animating strokes the way you want—or if you prefer, keeping them static:

Constant displays all strokes from the current time to the end of the layer containing the stroke.

Write On reveals the stroke over time, from beginning to end, depending on the speed at which you paint it. You can change the speed of the effect by adjusting each stroke's End property; you can reverse or create a write off effect by adjusting the strokes' Start property (**Figure 13.11**).

Single Frame displays the stroke at the current frame only.

Custom displays the stroke for the number of frames you specify. Set the duration by adjusting the value that appears next to the Duration pull-down menu (**Figure 13.12**).

These options set each stroke's initial duration—and, in the case of Write On, the stroke's initial End property's keyframes. After a stroke is created, you can't change the Duration setting in the property outline, per se; instead, you control when strokes are displayed by manipulating their duration bars and by keyframing properties such as Start and End.

✔ Tips

- Remember, paint doesn't always have to act like paint. For example, by applying certain modes, you can subtly retouch an image. Use a lightening mode (like Dodge) to brighten unwanted shadows. If necessary, animate the layer to follow the area you want to affect.

- By painting on the layer's alpha channel, you can use the advantages of various brush tips and duration options to affect the layer's transparency in ways that might be more difficult to do using masks or other methods.

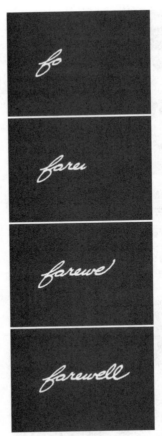

Figure 13.11 Strokes always start at the current time, but you can set how long they appear by setting a duration option. Here, the Write On option makes the strokes appear over time, to simulate handwriting.

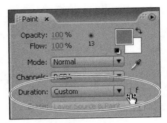

Figure 13.12 When you choose a Custom duration, specify the number of frames you want the stroke to appear.

Figure 13.13 Select the Brush tool.

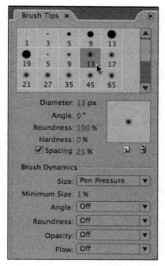

Figure 13.14 To change the current brush tip, choose a brush in the Brush Tips panel.

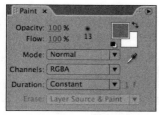

Figure 13.15 In the Paint panel, specify the brush's Opacity, Flow, and Color.

Painting with the Brush Tool

Generally speaking, painting in After Effects is as easy as grabbing a brush and painting on the layer. But at the same time, this straightforward task includes numerous options. Not only can you change the characteristics of the brush, but you can also specify which channels the strokes modify and how long they appear on screen. (See the previous section, "Specifying Paint Stroke Options," for detailed descriptions of each menu option.)

To paint on a layer:

1. Open the layer you want to paint on in a Layer panel.

2. In the Tools panel, select the Brush tool ✎ (**Figure 13.13**).

   If the Auto Open Panels option is selected, the Paint and Brush Tips panels open.

3. In the Brush Tips panel, specify a brush (**Figure 13.14**).

   The selected brush becomes the current brush in the Paint panel.

4. In the Paint panel, specify options for the brush attributes (**Figure 13.15**):

   Opacity sets the relative opacity of pixels in a stroke.

   Flow sets the speed, or relative number of pixels applied with each stroke.

   Foreground Color sets the brush's color.

   Background Color sets a secondary color.

   When you're using the Eraser tool, Opacity sets the strength of the eraser, and Foreground Color has no effect.

   continues on next page

5. To specify how brush strokes in the layer interact with the underlying image, choose a Blending mode from the Mode pull-down menu (**Figure 13.16**).

6. To specify the layer channels affected by the strokes, choose an option from the Channels pull-down menu (**Figure 13.17**).

7. To specify how strokes appear over time, choose an option from the Duration pull-down menu (**Figure 13.18**).

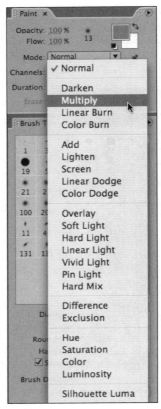

Figure 13.16 Choose a Blending mode from the Mode pull-down menu.

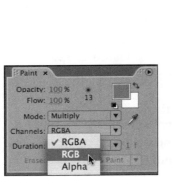

Figure 13.17 Specify the channels you want to paint on in the Channels pull-down menu. In this example, strokes are applied to the layer's RGB channels.

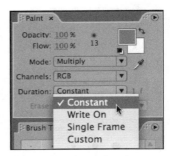

Figure 13.18 Choose how long you want the stroke to appear in the Duration pull-down menu. In this example, the strokes are set to appear from the current frame onward.

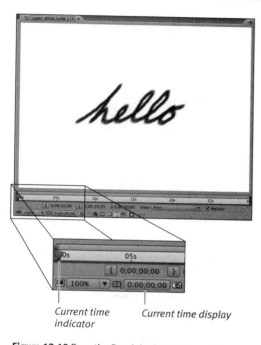

Current time indicator   *Current time display*

Figure 13.19 Drag the Brush in the Layer panel to create a stroke that starts at the current time. You can't paint in the Comp panel, but you can open a separate Comp panel to see the results.

Figure 13.20 In the Timeline panel, each stroke appears as an individual item.

Figure 13.21 Under the Paint effect's property heading, set the Paint on Transparent option to On.

8. Set the current time to the frame where you want the first stroke to begin.

9. Using the Brush tool, drag in the Layer panel to paint strokes on the layer (**Figure 13.19**).

The mouse pointer appears as a circle that corresponds with the brush's size, angle, and roundness. Strokes use the options you specified. In the layer's property outline, the Paint effect appears. Expanding the Paint effect reveals that each stroke is listed separately and has a corresponding layer bar under the time ruler (**Figure 13.20**).

To make the painted layer transparent:

1. Select the layer containing the Paint effect.

2. In the layer's expanded property outline, expand the layer's Paint effect property heading.

or

Open the Effect Controls panel to view the layer's Paint effect.

3. Under the Paint effect's property heading, set the Paint on Transparent option to On (**Figure 13.21**).

The selected layer becomes transparent, leaving only the Paint effect visible.

✔ Tip

■ The Paint effect discussed in this chapter must be applied to a layer in its Layer panel. After Effects Professional also includes a Vector Paint effect that you can use to paint in the Comp panel. However, it uses a different toolset and procedures.

Erasing Strokes

In practice, the Eraser tool does just what you'd expect: It removes pixels from a layer. You can specify whether it affects the target layer's pixels and paint strokes, paint only, or just the most recent paint stroke.

It might be more accurate to say that the Eraser *negates* pixels rather than removes them. A look in the Paint effect's property outline reveals that Eraser strokes appear in the stacking order along with Brush strokes. Like the other paint options, Eraser strokes are nondestructive; they don't permanently affect either the layer or paint strokes. Turn off an Eraser stroke's video (by clicking its Eye icon 👁 in the timeline), and its effects disappear.

In most respects, the Eraser works like a brush—except it's an "anti-brush." The Eraser tool uses the same brush tips as the Brush tool, but you can't apply a color to an eraser. And whereas a brush's Opacity and Flow settings control the strength of the brush—how thick you lay on the painted pixels—the same settings control how thoroughly the eraser removes pixels. Otherwise, the Eraser's settings are analogous to those of the Brush tool.

To use the Eraser tool:

1. In the Tools panel, select the Eraser tool 🩹 (**Figure 13.22**).

2. In the Paint panel, specify values for Opacity and Flow (**Figure 13.23**).

   When you're using the Eraser tool, Opacity and Flow refer to the Eraser's strength.

3. To specify the layer channels affected by the strokes, choose an option from the Channels pull-down menu (**Figure 13.24**).

   RGBA erases pixels in the layer's red, green, blue, and alpha channels.

Figure 13.22 Select the Eraser tool.

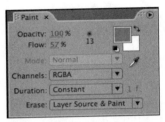

Figure 13.23 In the Paint panel, set the Opacity and Flow. These options help determine how completely pixels are removed with each stroke.

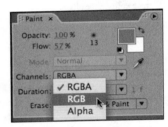

Figure 13.24 Choose which of the layer's channels are affected by the Eraser strokes in the Channels pull-down menu.

ERASING STROKES

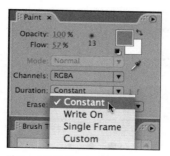

Figure 13.25 Choose how long pixels remain erased in the Duration pull-down menu.

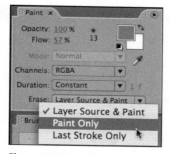

Figure 13.26 Specify the pixels affected by the eraser by choosing an option in the Erase pull-down menu.

Figure 13.27 Drag the eraser in the Layer panel to remove pixels.

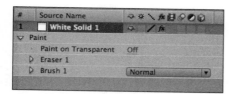

Figure 13.28 Like paint strokes, eraser strokes appear as individual items (including a layer bar) in the Paint effect's property outline.

RGB erases pixels in the layer's red, green, and blue channels; alpha is unaffected.

Alpha erases pixels in the layer's alpha channel (transparency information).

4. To specify how strokes appear over time, choose an option from the Duration pull-down menu (**Figure 13.25**):

   Constant displays all strokes from the current time to the end of the layer containing the stroke.

   Write On reveals the stroke over time, from beginning to end, depending on the speed at which you paint it.

   Single Frame displays the stroke at the current frame only.

   Custom displays the stroke for the number of frames you specify.

5. To specify the pixels affected by the eraser, choose an option from the Erase pull-down menu (**Figure 13.26**):

   Layer Source & Paint erases pixels in the source layer and any paint strokes at the same time.

   Paint Only erases pixels created by paint strokes.

   Last Stroke Only erases pixels created by the most recently painted paint stroke.

6. Using the Eraser tool, drag in the Layer panel to remove pixels from the layer (**Figure 13.27**).

   Pixels are erased according to the options you specified. Expanding the Paint effect in the layer's property outline reveals that each eraser stroke is listed separately and has a corresponding layer bar under the time ruler (**Figure 13.28**).

Using Brush Tips

The brush tip you use determines the character of the strokes you paint with any of the paint tools (Brush, Eraser, or Clone Stamp). You can select from a number of preset brush tips that appear in the Brush Tips panel. If the preset brushes aren't to your liking, you can create a brush tip that uses specific characteristics (such as size, roundness, angle, and hardness). The following tasks explain how to choose, save, remove, and restore preset brush tips. The section "Customizing Brush Tips," later in this chapter, covers each brush tip characteristic in detail.

Toggling the Brush Tips panel from the Paint panel:

1. In the Paint panel, click the current brush tip icon (**Figure 13.29**).

   If it's not part of the current workspace, the Brush Tips panel appears. If it's visible, it becomes the active panel.

2. In the Brush Tips panel, click the preset brush you want to use (**Figure 13.30**).

✔ Tips

- If the presets don't include a brush with the attributes you want, you can create one, as explained in the task "To create a brush tip," later in this chapter.

- Options in the Brush Tips panel's pull-down menu let you customize the panel, such as the size of brush icons.

Figure 13.29 In the Paint panel, click the current brush tip icon...

Figure 13.30 ...to activate or open the Brush Tips panel, where you can specify a different preset brush, modify the current brush, or save a custom brush.

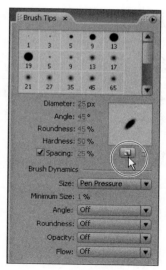

Figure 13.31 In the Brush Tips panel, set the brush's attributes and click the Save icon.

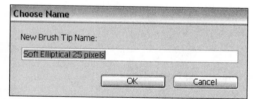

Figure 13.32 Name the new brush tip in the Choose Name dialog box.

Figure 13.33 Your custom brush tip appears in the preset brush tips area (shown here) and in Brush Tips Selector of the Paint panel.

To create a brush tip:

1. In the Brush Tips panel, specify the brush's attributes, including Diameter, Angle, Roundness, and so on.

   In the preview area of the Brush Tips panel, the brush's icon reflects your choices.

   See the section "Customizing Brush Tips," later in this chapter, for a detailed explanation of brush tip options.

2. Click the Save icon ▣ (**Figure 13.31**).

   A Choose Name dialog box appears with a descriptive name for the brush already entered.

3. Leave the suggested name or enter a custom name for the new brush, and click OK (**Figure 13.32**).

   The brush tip appears selected among the other preset brush tips (**Figure 13.33**). The new brush tip uses the attributes of the brush that was selected most recently. How presets appear in the panel depends on the option you choose in the Brush Tips panel's pull-down menu.

USING BRUSH TIPS

To rename a preset brush tip:

1. In the Brush Tips panel, double-click the brush tip you want to rename (**Figure 13.34**).

   A Choose Name dialog box appears.

2. In the Choose Name dialog box, type a new name for the brush tip, and click OK (**Figure 13.35**).

To remove a preset brush tip:

1. In the Brush Tips panel, click the preset brush tip you want to remove, and click the Delete icon 🗑 (**Figure 13.36**).

   After Effects prompts you to confirm your choice (**Figure 13.37**).

2. In the warning dialog box, click OK.

   The brush you selected is removed from the list of presets (**Figure 13.38**).

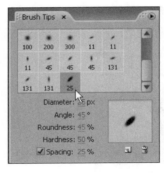

Figure 13.34 Double-click the brush tip you want to rename in the Brush Tips panel.

Figure 13.35 Enter a new name in the Choose Name dialog box, and click OK.

Figure 13.36 In the Brush Tips panel, click the brush tip you want to remove, and click the Delete (trash) icon.

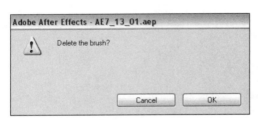

Figure 13.37 Confirm your choice by clicking OK.

Figure 13.38 The selected brush is removed from the panel.

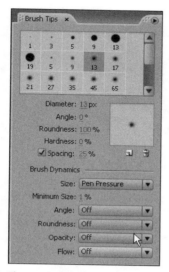

Figure 13.39 The Brush Tips panel includes several options that let you create custom brushes.

Figure 13.40 The strokes in this figure use different diameters.

Customizing Brush Tips

Even though the Brush Tips panel includes a useful assortment of preset brush tips, chances are you'll want to create your own brush tips to suit a particular task. As you learned in the previous section, "Using Brush Tips," you can save each of your special brush tips as a preset that appears in the Brush Tips panel. Controlling a brush's attributes gives you a great deal of control over the character of the strokes it produces. This section covers the brush tip options; the next section, "Using Brush Dynamics," explains how to vary these qualities with a pen and tablet.

In the Brush Tips panel, you can specify the following attributes for each brush (**Figure 13.39**):

Diameter determines the size, measured in pixels, across the diameter of the brush's widest axis (for elliptical brushes) (**Figure 13.40**).

Angle specifies the amount, measured in degrees, from which the widest axis of an elliptical brush deviates from the horizontal.

continues on next page

Roundness refers to the width of a brush's shortest diameter, expressed as a percentage of its widest diameter (determined by the Diameter value): 100% creates a circular brush; 0% creates a linear brush; intermediate values create an elliptical brush (**Figure 13.41**).

Hardness sets the relative opacity of the brush's stroke from its center to the edges, analogous to feathering the edge of the brush. At 100%, the brush is opaque from its center to its edges (although the edge is anti-aliased); at 0%, the brush's edge has the maximum feather (although its center is opaque). Don't confuse hardness with the brush's overall opacity, which you can set in the Paint panel (**Figure 13.42**).

Spacing indicates the distance between brush marks within a stroke, expressed as a percentage of the brush's diameter. Setting Spacing to a relatively low value allows the brush to create continuous stroke marks; setting Spacing to a higher value causes the brush tip to make contact with the layer intermittently, creating a stroke with gaps between brush marks. The speed with which you paint the stroke also affects the spacing. Moving the brush more quickly as you paint results in greater spacing between marks (**Figure 13.43**). You can set the Spacing to values over 100%.

✔ Tip

■ To restore the brush tip presets to their defaults, choose Reset Brush Tips in the Brush Tip panel's pull-down menu.

Figure 13.41 The stroke on top was created using a perfectly round brush; lower strokes used smaller Roundness settings and an Angle of 45 degrees. Otherwise, the strokes are identical.

Figure 13.42 These strokes are identical, except for their hardness settings.

Figure 13.43 The three words, spacing, are identical, except for their spacing values.

Using Brush Dynamics

You don't have to be a traditionalist to know that painting with a computer program isn't as tactile as using actual brushes and canvas. But swapping your mouse for a tablet and stylus (such as those available from the computer peripheral manufacturer Wacom) can make you feel a lot more like a painter. Just as important, using a stylus makes your strokes look more painterly. That's because you can set the attributes of each stroke—its size, angle, roundness, opacity, and flow—to vary with the pressure you apply to the tablet or the tilt of the pen. If your *stylus* (sometimes referred to as a *pen*) has a wheel control, you can also use it to vary the brush.

To set Brush Dynamics options:

1. In the Brush Tips panel, make sure the Brush Dynamics options are visible.

   If necessary, resize the bottom of the panel to reveal the options.

2. For each of the attributes listed in the Brush Dynamics area, choose an option from the pull-down menu (**Figure 13.44**).

   Off disables the dynamic option and uses the static setting you specified elsewhere in the Brush Tips and Paint panels.

   Pen Pressure varies the attribute according to the pressure of the pen on the tablet; pressing harder increases the value.

   Pen Tilt varies the attribute according to the angle of the pen in relation to the tablet. For example, tilting the pen away from the angle perpendicular to the tablet can decrease the brush's roundness.

   Stylus Wheel varies the attribute when you scroll the pen's wheel control (a small roller on the side of the pen).

3. If you enabled Size, specify a Minimum Size (**Figure 13.45**).

   The brush's smallest possible diameter is limited by the value (1%–100%) you specify.

Figure 13.44 Specify which of the pen's characteristics affect each of the brush's attributes in the corresponding pull-down menu.

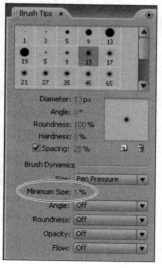

Figure 13.45 If you enabled Size, specify a Minimum Size.

Adjusting Strokes

As you learned in the chapter's introduction, Paint is an effect. It appears in the layer's property outline under its Effects category. But in contrast to other effects, the Effect Controls panel provides almost no controls for Paint. And whereas most effects include a single set of properties (however extensive they may be), the Paint effect lists each stroke individually, and each stroke contains its own set of properties.

Strokes are really layers within the layer containing the effect. Each stroke has its own duration bar, its own video switch, and its own set of properties that can be keyframed (**Figure 13.46**). You can precisely control when each stroke appears and for how long. In the case of animated strokes, this paradigm lets you specify how quickly a stroke draws onto the screen.

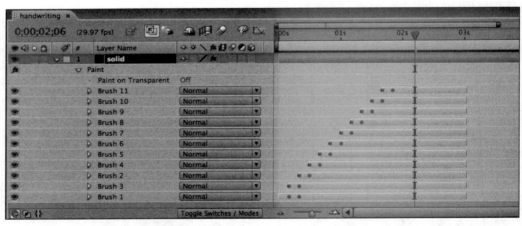

Figure 13.46 Each stroke has its own duration bar, its own video switch, and its own set of properties that you can animate with keyframes.

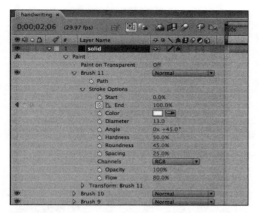

Figure 13.47 Each stroke includes Stroke Options and Transform properties.

Figure 13.48 A selected stroke (here, the "g") appears as a line in the center of the paint. An anchor point icon also appears at the beginning of each selected stroke.

Strokes in the timeline

Setting the current frame determines a stroke's initial In point. Its duration depends on the Duration option you specified in the Paint panel: Constant, Write On, Single Frame, or Custom (see the section "Specifying Paint Stroke Options" earlier in this chapter). As with layers, the strokes' stacking order in the property outline determines the order in which strokes are applied, and their Blending mode determines how they interact with strokes lower in the stack.

In general, you can manipulate strokes just as you would adjust layers: switch them on and off; change their stacking order; set their In and Out points and duration; and view, adjust, and keyframe their properties. However, the keyboard shortcuts you use with layers (cuing to or setting In and Out points, for example) don't work with strokes' duration bars.

In addition to all the properties that are unique to strokes, each stroke also includes its own set of Transform properties. You can use these to set each stroke's anchor point, position, scale, and rotation. Remember, for strokes, Opacity is listed in the other Stroke Options property category (**Figure 13.47**).

Selecting strokes

Selecting a stroke in the layer's property outline makes it visible in the Layer panel. A stroke appears as a thin line running through the center of the painted line, much like a selected mask path is visible in the center of a stroked path. An anchor point icon appears at the beginning of the stroke (**Figure 13.48**). When a stroke is selected, you can use the Selection tool to drag it to a new position within the layer. (You can always move the layer within the comp, but doing so moves the entire layer—its image, its paint, and any other effects it contains.)

However, strokes appear in a Layer panel only when the Paint effect is selected in the Layer panel's View pull-down menu. This occurs automatically when you apply paint, but it can get confusing if you work on other tasks and return to the Layer panel to find the Paint effect is no longer selected—and no longer visible. The same holds true if the layer contains more than one Paint effect; make sure the Layer panel's View pull-down menu is set to the Paint effect you want.

Multiple Paint effects

Painting multiple strokes adds to the current Paint effect, and a single layer can contain more than one Paint effect. This can be useful when you want to treat sets of strokes as separate groups. For example, you can disable all of one Paint effect's strokes by clicking its effect icon. However, the Layer panel can only show the Paint effect you specify in the View pull-down menu. The strokes of any Paint effects higher in the stacking order are *visible*, but you can't tell whether they're selected; Paint effects lower in the stacking order than the selected effect aren't visible in the Layer panel (**Figures 13.49** and **13.50**). You must choose a Paint effect in the View pull-down menu in order to view and drag its selected strokes in the Layer panel.

You can duplicate or add a Paint effect as you would any other effect. When you add strokes to a Paint effect, be sure to select the effect you want to modify in the layer's View pull-down menu.

✔ Tip

■ It can be useful to view the layer you're painting in a Layer panel and the composition that contains the layer in a separate Comp panel.

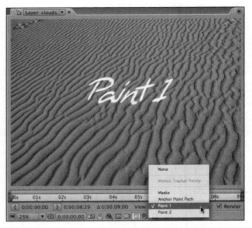

Figure 13.49 To see and manipulate strokes in the Layer panel, choose the Paint effect in the Layer panel's View pull-down menu.

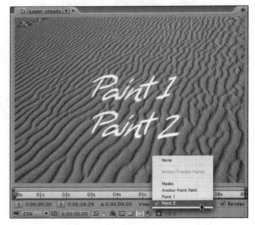

Figure 13.50 When the Layer contains more than one Paint effect, choose the one you want. Strokes of Paint effects higher in the stacking order are visible, but you can only manipulate strokes in the selected effect.

Figure 13.51 Select a paint tool: the Brush (shown here), Clone, or Eraser.

Figure 13.52 Choose Write On from the Paint panel's Duration pull-down menu.

Figure 13.53 Set the current time to the frame where you want the first stroke to begin.

Animating Strokes

The following tasks apply what you learned in this chapter to achieve a few common Paint effects. The first employs the Duration option, Write On, to simulate natural writing. The next task explains how to adjust the timing of the strokes in the Timeline panel. The last task shows how to animate a stroke by keyframing its Shape property, making it appear as though one stroke is transforming into another.

These tasks focus on employing different animation techniques and don't cover other options (such as brush tips, channels, and modes) in any detail. To find out about those options, refer back to the appropriate sections earlier in the chapter.

To animate strokes using the Write On option:

1. In the Tools panel, select a paint tool (**Figure 13.51**).

2. In the Paint panel, specify paint options, including Opacity, Flow, Color, Mode, and Channels.

   For a detailed explanation, see "Specifying Paint Stroke Options," earlier in this chapter.

3. In the Paint panel's Duration pull-down menu, choose Write On (**Figure 13.52**).

4. Set the current time to the frame where you want the first stroke to begin (**Figure 13.53**).

continues on next page

5. Using the Brush tool, drag in the Layer panel to paint strokes on the layer (**Figure 13.54**).

The speed at which you paint determines the duration and speed of the stroke animation. Lifting the mouse or pen to start a new stroke creates a separate brush layer in the Paint effect's property outline (**Figure 13.55**).

6. Preview the stroke animation in the Layer or Comp panel.

Strokes appear gradually, as you painted them (**Figure 13.56**).

✔ Tips

■ You can adjust the speed of the animation as you would any layer property by changing the timing of the keyframes—in this case, the End property keyframe. See Chapter 7 for more about keyframes.

■ Essentially, the Write On option animates the End property automatically. You can animate any stroke to create the same effect manually by animating the End property and duration of any stroke.

■ The Write On option works effortlessly when animating a single stroke. However, lifting the mouse or pen creates multiple strokes that all begin at the current time. Therefore, multiple strokes will animate simultaneously, which doesn't simulate natural handwriting. To make each stroke animate sequentially, you must change the In points (and, possibly, the durations).

Figure 13.54 Drag in the layer's Layer panel to draw or write in the layer. Lifting the mouse or pen ends the stroke, and because Write On is selected, the stroke disappears.

Figure 13.55 Each stroke appears in the layer's property outline under its Paint effect. The Write On option animates the stroke's End property automatically.

Figure 13.56 When you preview the animation, strokes appear in the same manner in which they were painted.

Figure 13.57 Set the current time and paint the stroke's initial shape.

Figure 13.58 In the layer's property outline, expand the Paint effect and click the Shape property's Stopwatch icon to set the initial keyframe.

Figure 13.59 With the previous stroke selected, set the current time to the frame where you want the stroke to assume a new shape, and paint that shape.

To animate a stroke by keyframing its shape:

1. Set the time you want the stroke to begin and, using a paint tool and the techniques described earlier in this chapter, create a stroke in a layer (**Figure 13.57**).

2. In the Timeline panel, expand the layer's property outline to reveal the stroke you want to animate.

3. Set the current time to the frame where you want the stroke's shape to begin changing, and select the Shape property's Stopwatch icon.

   A Shape keyframe appears at the current time for the stroke (**Figure 13.58**).

4. Set the current time to the frame where you want to paint a new stroke.

5. With the first stroke selected, paint a new stroke (**Figure 13.59**).

   Instead of creating a new stroke layer, a new Shape keyframe appears in the selected stroke's property outline (**Figure 13.60**).

continues on next page

Figure 13.60 Instead of creating a new stroke, the same stroke gets a new Shape keyframe at the current time.

ANIMATING STROKES

6. Repeat step 5, as needed.

7. Preview the stroke animation.

The stroke transforms from the shape defined by one keyframe to the shape defined by the next keyframe (**Figure 13.61**).

✔ Tip

- You can keyframe any stroke or paint option that includes a Stopwatch icon in the Paint effect's property outline or Effect Controls panel.

Figure 13.61 When you preview the animation, the stroke transforms from one shape into another. In this example, the line that crosses the t was created as a separate stroke using the Write On option.

Cloning

Like the Brush tool, the Clone Stamp tool adds pixels to a layer using the paint brush options you specify (Duration, Brush Tip, and the like). But as the name implies, the Clone Stamp doesn't add pixels according to a specified color; instead, it copies, or *clones*, pixels from a layer's image. Photoshop veterans will instantly recognize the Clone Stamp tool and appreciate its value in retouching an image. They'll also have a big head start on using the tool; it works nearly the same in After Effects—except nondestructively, and over time.

As when you use the other paint tools, you must first specify brush options for the Clone Stamp tool. But instead of specifying a color, you specify the layer, frame, and location of the pixels you want to copy to the target layer. Once you've set these options, you paint pixels from the source to the target.

For the sake of clarity, the following sections break the cloning process into smaller tasks: setting the sample point, and then cloning. After that, you'll learn how to make cloning easier by superimposing the source image over the target image and saving clone options as convenient presets.

Setting the sample point for cloning

When cloning, pixels are copied, or *sampled*, from a particular layer, frame, and physical location in a source image. You can specify these three aspects of the clone source by using the Paint panel or by sampling manually. You can change the sample point at any time using either method, as needed.

You also need to understand the difference between setting a fixed sample point and one that maintains a consistent relationship with strokes in the target layer. In terms of space, you specify your choice with the Paint panel's Aligned option; in terms of time, you specify your choice with the Lock Source Time option.

The Aligned option

The starting point for a clone stroke in the target layer always corresponds to the sample point you set in the source image. The Paint panel displays the distance between the stroke's starting point in the target and the sample point in the source as the Offset value. (When the target and source are different images, the distance is the difference in the corresponding points in each image's own coordinate system.)

However, the Aligned option determines which pixels are copied in subsequent strokes (**Figure 13.62**). By default, the Aligned option is selected, and pixels are always copied from a point in the source that is a consistent distance (the Offset value) from the corresponding location of the Clone Stamp in the target image (**Figure 13.63**). In contrast, unchecking Aligned copies pixels using the initial sample as a fixed starting point (**Figure 13.64**).

Figure 13.62 The Aligned option determines whether pixels are copied from a fixed point or offset from a corresponding location of the Clone Stamp.

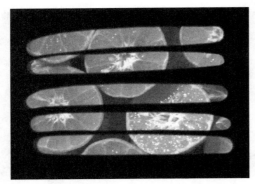

Figure 13.63 With Aligned checked, pixels are copied from a consistent distance from the corresponding location of the Clone Stamp.

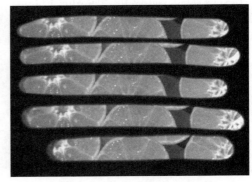

Figure 13.64 With Aligned unchecked, all strokes copy pixels from a fixed sample point in the source.

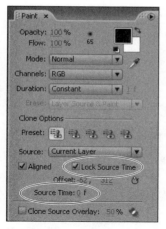

Figure 13.65 Checking Lock Source Time lets you specify a Source Time—a fixed frame from which to copy pixels.

Figure 13.66 Unchecking Lock Source Time lets you specify a Source Time Shift—a consistent time difference between the target layer frame and source layer frame.

Figure 13.67 Select the Clone Stamp tool.

The Lock Source Time option

The Lock Source Time option sets whether the Clone Stamp tool copies pixels from a fixed frame or maintains a time difference between the target frame and source frame (**Figure 13.65**). When Lock Source Time is selected, pixels are copied from a fixed frame that the Paint panel displays as the Source Time. If you change the target frame, the Source Time remains the same (unless you change it manually or sample from a different source frame). When Lock Source Time is unchecked, the Paint panel displays a Source Time Shift value. This way, After Effects maintains a time difference between the target frame and source frame (**Figure 13.66**).

To set a clone source in the Paint panel:

1. If necessary, arrange the source and target layers in a composition.

2. Select the Clone Stamp tool (**Figure 13.67**).

   Clone Stamp options appear in the Paint panel.

   continues on next page

3. In the Paint panel's Source pull-down menu, select the source layer from which the Clone Stamp tool will sample pixels (**Figure 13.68**).

4. *Do either of the following:*
   ▲ To clone from a point offset from the corresponding point in the target layer, check Aligned (**Figure 13.69**).
   ▲ To clone from the same starting point in the source layer with each new stroke, uncheck Aligned.

5. Specify the difference, or *offset*, between the starting point of the sample (in the source layer) and the stroke (in the target layer) by setting X and Y values for the Offset value.

   Offset values are expressed as the distance from the sample point to the stroke point in pixels, measured along the X and Y axes (**Figure 13.70**).

Figure 13.68 From the Paint panel's Source pull-down menu, specify the layer from which you want to clone.

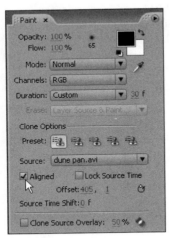

Figure 13.69 In the Paint panel, check Aligned if you want the sample point in the source to maintain a consistent relationship with each stroke in the target; uncheck Aligned to sample from the same point in the source layer with each stroke.

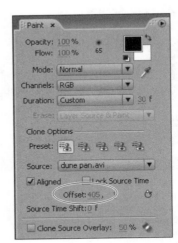

Figure 13.70 To specify an offset between the sample point in the source layer and the beginning of the stroke in the target layer, set X and Y values for Offset.

Figure 13.71
To sample from the same source frame regardless of the target frame, check Lock Source Time.

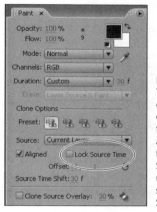

Figure 13.72
To maintain a consistent time difference between the source frame and the target frame, leave Lock Source Time unchecked and specify a value for Source Time Shift.

Figure 13.73 Option/Alt-click to set the sample point in the source image. Here, the sample is taken from a future frame in order to eliminate an obtrusive string of dust on the lens.

6. *Do either of the following:*

   ▲ To specify a specific source frame from which to sample, check Lock Source Time and specify a value for Source Time (**Figure 13.71**).

   ▲ To specify a consistent time difference between the target frame and source frame, uncheck Lock Source Time and specify a value for Source Time Shift (**Figure 13.72**).

   Checking or unchecking Lock Source Time makes the corresponding time value appear in the Paint panel.

To set a clone source by clicking:

1. Follow steps 1–2 in the previous task, "To set a clone source in the Paint panel."

2. Specify options for the Aligned and Lock Source Time check boxes, as described in the previous task.

3. Set the current time to the frame from which you want to sample in the source layer, and Option/Alt-click the sample point in the source layer's Layer panel (**Figure 13.73**).

   In the Paint panel, the source layer's name appears in the Source pull-down menu, and values appear for Offset. Values also appear for Source Time or Source Time Shift, depending on the options you chose earlier.

CLONING

Using the Clone Stamp Tool

Now that you understand how setting a sample point works, you can integrate that knowledge into the overall cloning process. Once you master this task, turn to later sections to learn about additional features, including overlaying the clone source's image over the target and saving Clone Stamp settings.

Figure 13.74 This example uses the same layer for the target and source.

To clone pixels:

1. Arrange the clone source and target layers in a Comp panel, and open the target layer in a separate Layer panel (**Figure 13.74**).

   The Comp panel must be selected for the source layer to appear in the pull-down menu in step 4.

Figure 13.75 Choose the Clone Stamp tool.

2. In the Tools panel, choose the Clone Stamp tool (**Figure 13.75**).

3. In the Paint and Brush Tips panels, specify a brush tip and paint options, such as Opacity, Flow, Mode, and Duration (**Figure 13.76**).

   See the "Specifying Paint Stroke Options" and "Using Brush Tips" sections, earlier in this chapter.

Figure 13.76 Specify paint options, such as Opacity, Flow, Mode, and Duration.

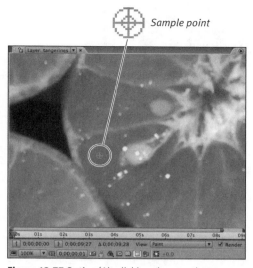

Sample point

Figure 13.77 Option/Alt-clicking changes the cursor into a crosshairs icon and sets the sample point (the layer, frame, and location of the source pixels).

4. Specify the sample source by *doing either of the following*:

▲ Using the Clone Stamp tool, Option/Alt-click in the source Layer panel at the frame and location you want to sample (**Figure 13.77**).

▲ In the Paint panel, specify the settings you want for the Source, Aligned, Lock Source Time (including the Source Time or Source Time Shift), and Offset options. (See the section "Setting the sample point for cloning," earlier in this chapter.)

5. Set the current time to the frame from which you want to clone pixels onto the target layer.

6. Click or drag in the target layer's Layer panel.

Pixels from the source layer are painted onto the target layer according to the options you specified (**Figure 13.78**). In the target layer's property outline, the Paint effect appears and includes each clone stroke you make (**Figure 13.79**).

✔ Tip

■ You can create a perfectly straight cloned stroke by clicking the stroke's starting point and Shift-clicking its ending point. This technique is great for cloning out linear elements such as wires or power lines.

Figure 13.78 Click or drag in the target layer with the Clone Stamp tool to copy pixels from the source layer. Here, cloning eliminates a distracting seed from the tangerine image.

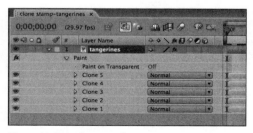

Figure 13.79 In the target layer's property outline, the Paint effect appears and includes each clone stroke you make.

Overlaying the Clone Source

Although cloning can be painstaking, the most recent version of After Effects makes the process easier by letting you superimpose the source image over the target layer as you clone.

To superimpose the source over the target layer as you clone:

1. Prepare layers for cloning and set options for the Clone Stamp tool, as explained in the previous task, "To clone pixels."

2. In the Paint panel, check Clone Source Overlay and specify the source layer's opacity (**Figure 13.80**).

   The overlay appears when the Clone Stamp tool is positioned over the target layer's image (**Figure 13.81**).

3. To apply the Difference Blending mode to the superimposed source layer image, click the Difference Mode button (**Figure 13.82**).

   The Difference blending mode can help you identify differences between similar source and target frames. See Chapter 14 for more about blending modes.

✔ Tip

- You can also toggle the overlay by pressing Option/Alt-Shift as you use the Clone Stamp tool.

Figure 13.80 In the Paint panel, check Clone Source Overlay and specify the source layer's opacity.

Figure 13.81 The overlay appears when the Clone Stamp tool is positioned over the target layer's image.

Figure 13.82 To see differences in the source and target layers more easily, click the Difference Mode button in the Paint panel.

Figure 13.83 Select the Clone Stamp tool.

Figure 13.84 In the Paint panel, click a Clone Stamp Preset button and specify the settings you want associated with the button.

Saving Clone Stamp Settings

Meticulous retouching can require that you switch Clone Stamp tool settings often. Luckily, the Paint panel includes five Clone Stamp Preset buttons that you can use to store and quickly recall settings.

To save Clone Stamp settings:

1. In the Tools panel, select the Clone Stamp tool (**Figure 13.83**).

   The Clone Options become available.

2. In the Clone Options area of the Paint panel, click a Clone Stamp Preset button.

3. Specify the options you want (as described in the previous sections) to associate with the selected preset button (**Figure 13.84**).

   The options you specify are associated with the selected preset button.

To use a Clone Stamp preset:

1. In the Tools panel, select the Clone Stamp tool.

2. In the Clone Options area of the Paint panel, *do either of the following:*
   ▲ Click the Clone Stamp Preset button that corresponds to the preset you want to use.
   ▲ Press the number keyboard shortcut that corresponds to the preset you want: 3=first preset; 4=second preset; 5=third preset; 6=fourth preset; 7=fifth preset.

3. Use the Clone Stamp tool as explained in the previous tasks.

MORE LAYER TECHNIQUES

This chapter tackles several techniques that encompass a wide range of topics: motion footage, playback time, blending layers together, a new way to create graphical objects, and an exciting new distortion effect.

Specifically, you'll start by learning about a pair of layer switches—Frame Blending and Motion Blur—that influence how After Effects deals with motion between frames. Then, you'll play with the comp's frame rate using time remapping. From there, you'll take a closer look at the Transfer Controls panel, where you'll find a long list of Modes you can use to blend a layer with underlying layers, expanding your repertoire of compositing tools. You'll also find out what the mysterious T option stands for and, more important, how to use it. You'll complete your tour of the Transfer Controls by learning about yet another compositing option, Track Mattes. As you near the end of the chapter, you'll learn about two powerful new features in After Effects CS3. The first is a new kind of layer, called a shape layer. Shape layers let you create and animate graphical elements in countless variation. (What text layers did for creating and animating type, shape layers do for creating and animating graphical objects.) Finally, you'll animate layers using a powerful distortion effect that you control with a set of tools called, appropriately enough, Puppet tools.

Using Frame Blending

When the frame rate of motion footage is lower than that of the composition, movement within the frame can appear jerky—either because the footage's native frame rate is lower than that of the composition, or because you time-stretched the footage. Whatever the case, After Effects reconciles this difference by repeating frames of the source footage. For example, each frame of a 15-fps movie is displayed twice in a composition with a frame rate of 30 fps. However, because there aren't enough unique frames to represent full motion, the result can sometimes resemble a crude flip-book animation.

In these instances, you can smooth the motion by activating the Frame Blending switch. When frame blending is on, After Effects interpolates between original frames, blending them rather than simply repeating them (**Figures 14.1** and **14.2**). Motion footage that has been sped up can also benefit from frame blending.

You can specify either of two types of frame blending: Frame Mix and Pixel Motion. Comparing the two methods, Frame Mix renders faster but is lower quality; hence, the layer's Frame Blending switch ▚ resembles a jagged backslash (which looks like the draft quality switch). Pixel Motion renders more slowly but can produce better results; it's indicated by a smooth slash ╱ (similar to the full quality switch).

Figure 14.1 Ordinarily, After Effects interpolates frames by repeating the original frames. Because this simple animation is interpreted as 15 frames per second, frames are repeated to compensate for a 30-fps composition.

Figure 14.2 When frame blending is applied and enabled, it blends the original frames to create interpolated frames.

Pixel Motion frame blending

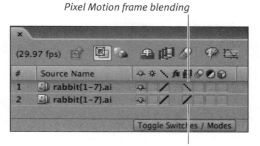

Frame Mix frame blending

Figure 14.3 Clicking a motion footage layer's Frame Blending switch repeatedly changes its state from no frame blending to frame mix to pixel motion.

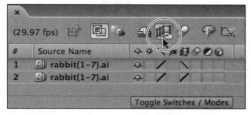

Figure 14.4 Click the Enable Frame Blending button at the top of the Timeline panel.

To apply or remove frame blending in a layer:

1. If necessary, click the Timeline panel's Switches button to make the layer switches appear.

2. For a layer created from motion footage, click the Frame Blending switch to toggle its icon to the option you want:

   No Icon—no frame blending applied

   Frame Mix—blends frames using a faster but lower-quality method

   Pixel Motion—blends frames using a slower but higher quality method

   The layer uses the frame blending method associated with the icon you specify (**Figure 14.3**). Frame blending must be enabled for its effect to be rendered in the Comp panel (see the next task).

To enable or disable frame blending for all layers in a composition:

Do either of the following:

◆ Click the Enable Frame Blending button 🔳 at the top of the Timeline panel (**Figure 14.4**).

◆ Select Enable Frame Blending in the Timeline panel's pull-down menu.

   When the Enable Frame Blending button is clicked, frame blending is enabled for all layers with frame blending applied.

✔ Tip

■ Because frame blending can significantly slow previewing and rendering, you may want to apply it to layers but refrain from enabling it until you're ready to render the final animation.

USING FRAME BLENDING

Using Motion Blur

Ordinarily, an animated layer appears sharp and distinct as it moves through the frame of a composition (**Figure 14.5**). This can appear unnatural, however, because you're accustomed to seeing objects blur as they move. In the time it takes to perceive the object at a single position (or, in the case of a camera, to record it to a frame), that object has occupied a continuous range of positions, causing it to appear blurred.

To simulate this effect, you can activate the Motion Blur switch for an animated layer (**Figure 14.6**). To reduce the time it takes to preview your animation, you may want to apply motion blur to layers but wait to enable it until you're ready to render.

Because motion blur simulates the blur captured by a camera, it uses similar controls. As with a film camera, a Shutter Angle control works with the frame rate to simulate exposure time and thus the amount of blur. The optional Shutter Phase setting determines the shutter's starting position at the frame start.

To apply or remove motion blur:

1. If necessary, click the Timeline panel's Switches button to make the layer switches appear.

2. Select the Motion Blur switch for a layer with animated motion (**Figure 14.7**). When the Motion Blur switch is selected, motion blur is applied to the layer. The Motion Blur button determines whether motion blur is enabled (see the next task for details).

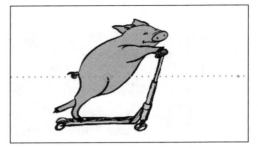

Figure 14.5 Ordinarily, an animated layer appears sharp and distinct as it moves through the frame of the composition.

Figure 14.6 To simulate a more natural-looking, blurred motion, activate the Motion Blur switch for an animated layer.

Figure 14.7 Select the Motion Blur switch for a layer with animated motion to apply motion blur.

Figure 14.8 Click the Enable Motion Blur button at the top of the Timeline panel to enable motion blur for the layers with motion blur applied to them.

Figure 14.9
Choose Composition ›
Composition Settings.

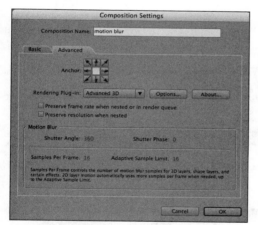

Figure 14.10 In the Composition Settings dialog box, enter a value for the Shutter Angle, in degrees.

- The Render Queue panel also lets you reset the shutter angle for motion blur before you render a movie.

- You can apply motion blur to a mask by selecting the mask, choosing Layer > Mask > Motion Blur, and choosing an option in the submenu.

To enable or disable motion blur for all layers in a composition:

Do either of the following:

◆ Click the Enable Motion Blur button at the top of the Timeline panel (**Figure 14.8**).

◆ Select Enable Motion Blur in the Timeline panel's pull-down menu.

When the Enable Motion Blur button is clicked or the Enable Motion Blur item is selected, motion blur is enabled for all layers with motion blur applied.

To set the amount of motion blur for previews:

1. Choose Composition > Composition Settings (**Figure 14.9**).

The Composition Settings dialog box appears.

2. In the Advanced panel of the Composition Settings dialog box, enter a value for the Shutter Angle, in degrees (**Figure 14.10**).

You can enter a value between 0 and 360 degrees. The higher the value, the greater the amount of blur.

3. To set the position of the shutter relative to the start frame, enter a value for Shutter Phase.

You can enter an angle between 0 and 360 degrees.

4. Click OK to close the Composition Settings dialog box.

✔ Tips

■ When you render the final output, you can choose whether to enable motion blur and frame blending in the Render Queue panel. This way, you don't have to return to your composition to check the setting. See Chapter 17, "Output."

Understanding Time Remapping

Back in Chapter 6, "Layer Editing," you learned how to change the speed of a layer using the Time Stretch command (or by changing the layer's Stretch value in the In/Out panel in the Timeline panel). Although it's useful, the Time Stretch command is limited to changing the layer's overall playback speed. To make the playback speed up, slow down, reverse, or come to a halt (or *freeze frame*), you need to use *time remapping*.

In a normal layer, a direct relationship exists between the layer's time and the frame you see and hear. In a time-remapped layer, the normal time controls show the layer's elapsed time but no longer dictate which frame is displayed (or heard) at that time. Instead, the Time Remap values determine the visible (or audible) frame at that time.

For example, when you first apply time remapping, keyframes appear at the layer's In and Out points, and the Time Remap values at those keyframes match the layer's original time values. Initially, there's no change in the layer's playback (**Figure 14.11**). However, changing the Time Remap value of the keyframe at the end of the clip (say, at 4 seconds) to a frame in the middle of the clip (2 seconds) redistributes, or *remaps*, the first 2 seconds of the layer over 4 seconds—slowing down the frame rate between keyframes (**Figure 14.12**).

This example achieves a result similar to that of the Time Stretch command. But consider that you can set additional time-remapped keyframes in the same layer and apply the temporal interpolation methods covered in Chapter 9, "Keyframe Interpolation."

Figure 14.11 Here, the Time Remap property values match the layer's original time values. The layer time is the top number; the remapped time is the lower number.

Figure 14.12 Here, the last Time Remap keyframe is still positioned at 04;00 into the clip, but its value has been changed to the frame at 02;00. The layer's frame rate slows between the keyframes.

Using the same layer as in the previous example, suppose you set a time-remap keyframe at 2 seconds into the clip and leave its value set to 2 seconds. The layer plays normally between the first and second keyframes (the first 2 seconds). But if you change the Time Remap value of the last keyframe—positioned 4 seconds into the clip—to 0 seconds (not the keyframe's position in time, just its value), then playback reverses between the second and third keyframes (**Figure 14.13**).

Although time remapping can sound confusing, it works just like keyframing other properties. But whereas most keyframes define a visible characteristic (like position) at a given frame, a time-remap keyframe specifies the *frame* you see (or hear) at a given point in the layer's time.

Figure 14.13 Here, the layer plays back normally between the first keyframe and a second keyframe, set halfway through the layer's duration. The Time Remap value of the last keyframe—positioned at 04;00—has been changed to 00;00, which reverses the playback.

Controlling Time Remap Values in the Layer Panel

When you enable time remapping on a layer, the Layer panel displays additional controls for changing the frame rate. In addition to the layer's ordinary time ruler, current time indicator (CTI), and current time display, a corresponding remap-time ruler, marker, and display also appear (**Figure 14.14**). The lower CTI shows the (normal) time; the upper CTI shows the frame you specify to play at that time.

Remap-time marker   *Remap-time display*   *Remap-time ruler*

Figure 14.14 Enabling time remapping makes additional controls appear in the Layer panel.

As is the case for any property value, you can set keyframes for the Time Remap property using controls in the Timeline panel (**Figure 14.15**). As usual, use the Add/Remove Keyframe button in the property's keyframe navigator to set keyframes that use previously interpolated values. You can also view the property's value graph in the Graph Editor and drag control points on the graph to change the value of the corresponding keyframe. This technique lets you accelerate, decelerate, or reverse playback speed (see the task "To change playback speed over time," later in this chapter). For more about viewing and using a value graph and using interpolation methods (how After Effects calculates property values between keyframes), see Chapter 9.

Value graph

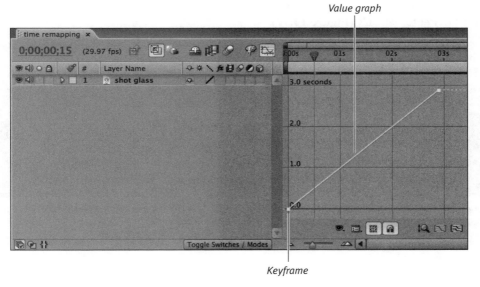

Keyframe

Figure 14.15 You also use controls in the Timeline panel to set Time Remap values and keyframes. Here, the time remapping values are seen in the graph editor view.

Using Time Remapping

The tasks in this section explain how to enable time remapping for a layer and how to set keyframes to pause, reverse, or change the speed of playback. Once you get the hang of these techniques, you can explore other ways to control playback using time remapping. Turn to Chapter 9 for more about keyframe interpolation and how you can specify the way After Effects calculates property changes from one keyframe to the next.

To enable time remapping:

1. Select a layer, and choose Layer > Time > Enable Time Remapping (**Figure 14.16**).

   In the Timeline panel, the Time Remap property appears in the layer outline for the selected layer. After Effects creates keyframes at the beginning and end of the layer automatically (**Figure 14.17**).

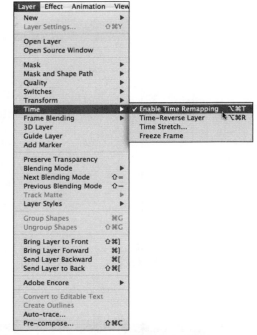

Figure 14.16 Select a layer, and choose Layer > Time > Enable Time Remapping.

Figure 14.17 After Effects sets a time-remap keyframe at the layer's In and Out points automatically. However, the values match the layer's original values, and the layer's frame rate remains unchanged.

Figure 14.18 Double-click the layer in the Timeline panel to view it in a Layer panel and use the time-remapping controls.

Figure 14.19 Set the current time to the frame where you want playback to stop. There's no need to change the remap time; it should match the current time.

2. In the Timeline panel, double-click the layer to view it in a Layer panel.

In addition to the standard controls, the Layer panel includes time-remapping controls (**Figure 14.18**).

To create a freeze frame with time remapping:

1. Select a layer and enable time remapping as explained in the previous task, "To enable time remapping."

After Effects sets beginning and ending keyframes automatically.

2. Set the current time to the frame where you want the layer's playback to stop (**Figure 14.19**).

3. In the Timeline panel, select the keyframe navigator's Add/Remove Keyframe button for the layer's Time Remap property.

A keyframe appears at the current time, using the previously interpolated value. In this case, the Time Remap value matches the frame's original value (**Figure 14.20**).

continues on next page

continues on next page

USING TIME REMAPPING

Figure 14.20 In the Timeline panel, click the diamond icon in the Time Remap property's keyframe navigator to create a keyframe at the current frame.

4. With the new keyframe selected, choose Animation > Toggle Hold Keyframe (**Figure 14.21**).

The new keyframe uses Hold interpolation, evidenced by its Hold keyframe icon (**Figure 14.22**). This holds the Time Remap value until the next keyframe is reached.

5. Select the last keyframe, and press Delete (Mac) or Backspace (Windows).

The last keyframe is removed (**Figure 14.23**). The layer's frames play back at normal speed; then, the layer freezes when it reaches the Hold keyframe.

6. View the remapped layer in the Layer or Comp panel by dragging the CTI.

You can't use RAM previews to see the layer play back using the remapped frame rate.

✔ Tip

■ The Layer > Time > Freeze Frame command applies Time Remap and sets a Hold keyframe so that the current frame plays for the layer's entire duration.

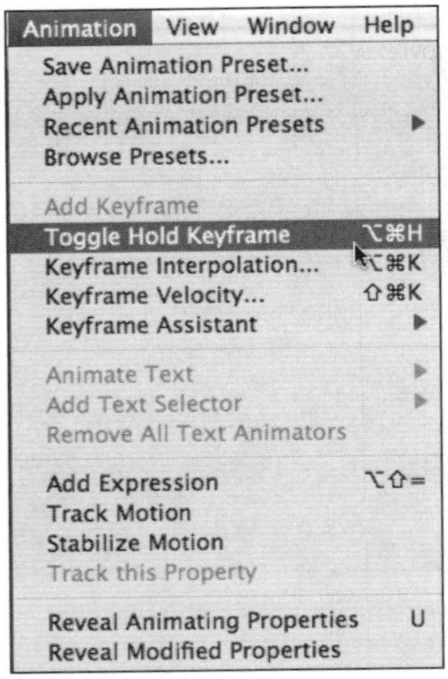

Figure 14.21 With the new keyframe selected, choose Animation › Toggle Hold Keyframe.

Figure 14.22 The keyframe icon changes to a Hold keyframe icon, indicating that the property value will remain at that value until the next keyframe is reached.

Figure 14.23 Select the last keyframe, and press Delete (Mac) or Backspace (Windows). The layer's playback now freezes at the Hold keyframe you created in steps 3 and 4.

To reverse playback:

1. Select a layer, and enable time remapping as explained in the task "To enable time remapping" earlier in this section.

2. Set the current time to the frame where you want the layer's playback direction to reverse, and select the Add/Remove Keyframe button in the Time Remap property's keyframe navigator.

   A keyframe appears at the current time, using the previously interpolated value. In this case, the keyframe's value matches the frame's original value (**Figure 14.24**).

3. Set the current frame later in time, to the point where you want the reversed playback to end (**Figure 14.25**).

continues on next page

Figure 14.24 Set the current time to the point where you want the layer's playback to reverse, and click the box in the Time Remap property's keyframe navigator to set a keyframe.

Figure 14.25 Set the current time to the point where you want the reversed playback to end. Here, the current time is set to the Out point (which changes the keyframe value that was set automatically when remapping was applied).

USING TIME REMAPPING

373

4. In the Layer panel, drag the remap-time indicator to an earlier frame (**Figure 14.26**).

The layer's original frame value is mapped to the frame you specified with the remap-time indicator.

5. View the time-remapped layer in the Layer or Comp panel by dragging the CTI.

You can't use RAM previews to see the layer play back using the remapped frame rate. The layer's frames play back normally until the keyframe you set in step 2; the layer then plays in reverse until the keyframe you set in step 3. The remap frame you set in step 4 determines the actual frame played by the time the last keyframe is reached (**Figure 14.27**).

Figure 14.26 In the Layer panel, drag the remap-time marker to a time earlier than the one you chose in step 3.

Figure 14.27 The layer plays forward between the first and second keyframes and then plays in reverse between the second and last keyframes.

Figure 14.28 In the Timeline panel, expand the layer's Time Remap property to reveal its value graph.

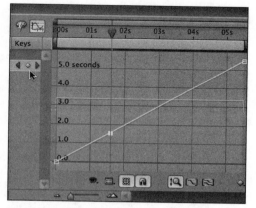

Figure 14.29 Set the current time when you want the speed to change to begin, and click the diamond icon in the keyframe navigator. (For illustration purposes, the Keys column—containing the keyframe navigator—is set to appear near the Graph Editor.)

To change playback speed over time:

1. Select a layer and enable time remapping as explained in the task "To enable time remapping" earlier in this section.

2. In the Timeline panel, *do either of the following:*

   ▲ Expand the selected layer's Time Remap property to reveal its keyframes in standard view.

   ▲ Enable the Graph Editor and set the layer's Time Remap property to appear as a value graph (**Figure 14.28**).

   See Chapter 9 for more about using the Graph Editor.

3. Set the current time to the frame where you want the speed change to begin, and click the Add/Remove Keyframe button in the Time Remap property's keyframe navigator (**Figure 14.29**).

   A keyframe appears at the current time; its value matches the frame's original time value.

continues on next page

USING TIME REMAPPING

4. In the Time Remap property's value graph, drag the control point that corresponds to the keyframe you set in step 3 *in either of the following ways:*

▲ To slow playback speed, drag the control point down (**Figure 14.30**).

▲ To increase playback speed, drag the control point up (**Figure 14.31**).

When the value is higher than the previous keyframe's value, the layer plays forward; when the value is lower, the layer plays in reverse. If the layer is already playing in reverse, drag the value graph's control point in the opposite direction.

5. Repeat steps 3 and 4 as needed.

The layer's playback speed and direction change according to your choices.

6. View the remapped layer in the Layer or Comp panel by dragging the CTI.

You can't use RAM previews to see the layer play back using the remapped frame rate.

✔ Tip

■ You can use Hold keyframes to make a layer's playback "jump" from one frame to another instantaneously. For more about Hold keyframes, see Chapter 9.

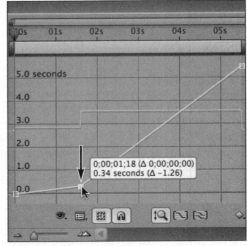

Figure 14.30 In the value graph, drag the control point corresponding to the keyframe. Decreasing the slope decreases speed; here, motion slows between the first and second keyframes. (In this figure, a reference speed graph is visible to better illustrate the result of the change.)

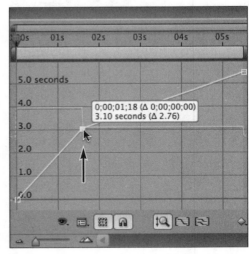

Figure 14.31 Increasing the slope of the line increases speed; here, motion between the first and second keyframe speeds up.

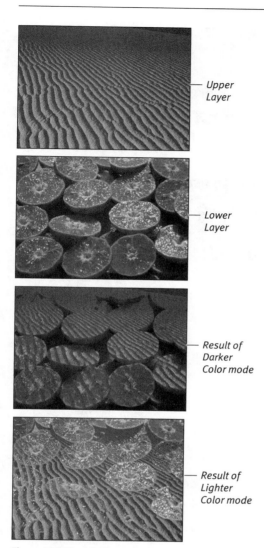

Upper Layer

Lower Layer

Result of Darker Color mode

Result of Lighter Color mode

Figure 14.32 In this figure, the first image is the upper layer; the second image the lower layer. Subsequent images show the result of just a few Blending modes.

Using Blending Modes

In previous chapters, you learned that higher layers in the stacking order are superimposed on lower layers according to their alpha channel (which can also be modified with masks) or their Opacity property value. If you want to combine layers in more varied and subtle ways, you can use a variety of Blending modes (formerly known as layer modes).

A *Blending mode* changes the value of a layer's pixels according to the values of the corresponding pixels in the underlying image. Depending on how the values interact, the result often appears as a blend of the two (**Figure 14.32**). You may recognize most of the Blending modes from Photoshop; you'll find they work the same way here.

By default, a layer's mode is set to Normal. You can change the mode by selecting an option from a pull-down menu in the Transfer Controls panel of the timeline. When you do, the Video switch for the layer changes from a normal Eye icon 🐱 to a darkened Eye icon 🐱. Although most layer modes only blend color values (RGB channels), some—such as the Stencil and Silhouette modes—affect transparency (alpha channel) information.

This section describes how to set any Blending mode, but doesn't describe all 33 modes or illustrate their results. (That would require a lot of pages, including ones in color.) The After Effects Help system provides a full-color gallery.

To apply a Blending mode:

1. If necessary, click the Transfer Modes button to make the Modes menu appear (**Figure 14.33**).

2. Choose a mode from a layer's Modes menu (**Figure 14.34**).

   The Video switch for the layer becomes a darkened eye ![eye icon]. The mode you select affects how the layer combines with underlying layers.

✔ Tip

■ As you apply Blending modes, bear in mind that After Effects renders the bottommost layer first and works its way up the stacking order. Because a Blending mode determines how a layer interacts with the image beneath it, the resulting image becomes the underlying image for layer modes applied to the next higher layer in the stacking order, and so on. For more about render order, see Chapter 16, "Complex Projects."

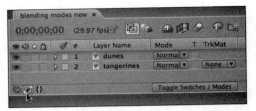

Figure 14.33 If necessary, click the Transfer Modes button to make the Modes menu appear.

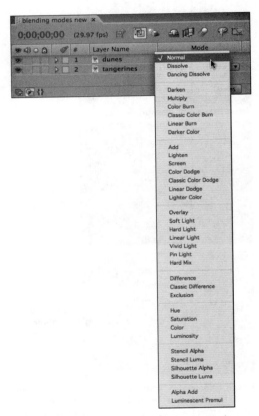

Figure 14.34 Choose a mode from a layer's Modes menu.

Figure 14.35 When composited without Preserve Underlying Transparency selected, the entire highlight is superimposed over the underlying image.

Figure 14.36 When Preserve Underlying Transparency is selected, the opaque areas of the highlight layer appear only in the opaque areas of the underlying image.

Figure 14.37 Click the box under the T heading to select Preserve Underlying Transparency.

Preserving Underlying Transparency

To the right of the Mode menu is a layer switch in a column marked *T*. This innocuous looking T switch performs an important function: It preserves the underlying transparency. When you select this option, the opaque areas of a layer display only where they overlap with opaque areas in the underlying image (**Figures 14.35** and **14.36**).

The Preserve Underlying Transparency option is commonly used to make it appear as though light is being reflected from the surface of the underlying solid. You can use Preserve Underlying Transparency in conjunction with any layer mode or track matte. When you activate it, the Video switch becomes a darkened Eye icon 🔘.

To preserve underlying transparency:

1. Make sure the Modes column is visible in the Timeline panel.

2. For a layer you want to composite with the underlying image, click the box under the T heading (**Figure 14.37**).

   A transparency grid icon ▦ indicates that Preserve Underlying Transparency is active; no icon indicates that it's inactive. When you activate the option, the Video switch becomes a darkened Eye icon 🔘.

Track Mattes

So far, you've learned to define transparent areas in a layer by using the Opacity property, alpha channels, masks, and certain layer modes and effects—all options that are part of the layer. Sometimes, however, you won't want to use the transparency provided by the image, or you may find that creating a mask is impractical. This is especially true if you want to use a moving image or one that lacks an alpha channel to define transparency. Whatever the case, you may want to use a separate image to define transparency. Any image used to define transparency in another image is called a *matte*. Because mattes use alpha-channel or luminance information to create transparency, they're usually grayscale images (or images converted into grayscale).

In After Effects, *track matte* refers to a method of defining transparency using an image layer, called the *fill*, and a separate matte layer. In the Timeline panel, the matte must be directly above the fill in the stacking order. Because the matte is included only to define transparency, not to appear in the output, its Video switch is turned off. The track matte is assigned to the fill layer using the Track Matte pull-down menu in the Switches panel. Transparent areas reveal the underlying image, which consists of lower layers in the stacking order (**Figures 14.38** and **14.39**).

Figure 14.38 Arrange the matte, the fill, and the background layers in the timeline. Note the settings in the A/V panel and the Modes panel.

Figure 14.39 The matte, the fill, the background, and the final composite.

Traveling Mattes

The term *track matte* often refers to a matte that's in motion, although in After Effects a track matte doesn't have to move. Animated mattes are also called *traveling mattes*, a term used when the same techniques were accomplished with film.

Figure 14.40 The Track Matte pull-down menu lists several track matte options.

Figure 14.41 In the following example, the matte layer is an image of the moon...

Figure 14.42 ...which also contains an alpha channel.

Types of track mattes

The Track Matte pull-down menu lists several track matte options (**Figure 14.40**). Each option specifies whether the matte's alpha or luminance information is used to define transparency in the fill layer. Ordinarily, white defines opaque areas, and black defines transparent areas. Inverted options reverse the opaque and transparent areas.

In the following example, a grayscale image of the moon serves as the matte layer (**Figure 14.41**). It also contains a corresponding circular alpha channel (**Figure 14.42**). A water image serves as the fill (**Figure 14.43**), and the background image is black.

No Track Matte, the default, specifies no track matte.

continues on next page

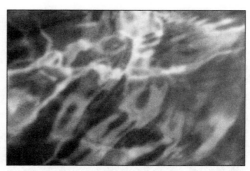

Figure 14.43 The water image serves as the fill layer, and black serves as the background.

TRACK MATTES

Alpha Matte specifies the alpha channel of the matte and defines the transparency in the fill. White defines opaque areas; black defines transparent areas. Grays are semitransparent (**Figure 14.44**).

Alpha Inverted Matte specifies the inverted alpha channel of the matte and defines the transparency in the fill. Black defines opaque areas; white defines transparent areas. Grays are semitransparent (**Figure 14.45**).

Luma Matte specifies the luminance values of the matte and defines transparency in the fill. White defines opaque areas; black defines transparent areas. Grays are semitransparent (**Figure 14.46**).

Luma Inverted Matte specifies the inverted luminance values of the matte and defines transparency in the fill. Black defines opaque areas; white defines transparent areas. Grays are semitransparent (**Figure 14.47**).

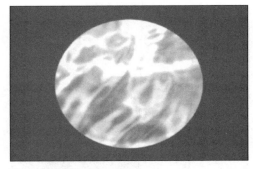

Figure 14.44 An alpha matte.

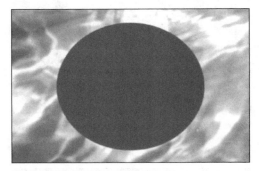

Figure 14.45 An alpha inverted matte.

Figure 14.46 A luma matte.

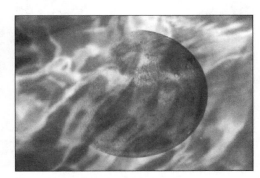

Figure 14.47 A luma inverted matte.

Figure 14.48 Arrange the fill and matte in the Timeline panel.

Figure 14.49 Choose an option in the Track Matte pull-down menu.

Figure 14.50 The layer directly above the fill layer in the stacking order becomes the track matte, and its Video switch is turned off automatically.

To create a track matte:

1. If necessary, click the Switches/Modes button in the Timeline panel to display the Modes panel.

2. Arrange two layers in the Timeline panel so that the matte layer is directly above the fill layer in the stacking order (**Figure 14.48**).

3. In the Modes panel for the fill layer, *choose one of the following* options from the Track Matte pull-down menu (**Figure 14.49**):
   ▲ No Track Matte
   ▲ Alpha Matte
   ▲ Alpha Inverted Matte
   ▲ Luma Matte
   ▲ Luma Inverted Matte

   The layer directly above the fill layer in the stacking order becomes the track matte, and its Video switch is turned off automatically. In the Timeline panel, the thin border that usually appears between layers no longer appears between the fill and the matte layers (**Figure 14.50**).

4. If you want, place a layer lower in the stacking order to serve as the background.

✔ Tip

■ Any grayscale image—still or moving— can make a good matte layer. Use techniques you've learned throughout this book to create grayscale images, or treat images to convert them into usable mattes. For example, use effects such as Text, Waveform, Block Dissolve, and Fractal Noise to create animated mattes. Or use the Hue/Saturation and Levels effects to turn a movie layer into a high-contrast matte layer.

TRACK MATTES

383

Using Shape Layers

In addition to video images and audio, After Effects animations often require purely graphical objects. At times, these elements are inconspicuous, serving as track mattes, effect sources, and the like. At other times, they take center stage. To help you create these elements, After Effects CS3 introduces a new type of layer, called *shape layers*.

Shape layers consist of one or more shapes you draw using the same drawing tools you use to create masks. But whereas masks are always defined by Bézier curves, shapes can be either Bézier shapes defined by vertices or parametric shapes defined by a set of numerical parameters.

Either way, shapes are vector-based and possess a unique set of attributes you can modify and animate. In addition to the path that defines their, well, shape, shapes also possess fill and stroke properties. You can also add properties to modify each shape's path, fill, and stroke. These include some of the path and paint operations you found in Adobe Illustrator.

A shape layer can contain multiple shapes that you can manipulate individually or in groups. And best of all, you can animate nearly every aspect of the shapes to create countless variations. With shape layers, you can achieve some effects easier than ever before and create other imagery never before possible (**Figures 14.51** and **14.52**).

As you might guess, the following sections won't attempt to explain every attribute or their countless combinations. But after you complete them, you'll know more than enough to start creating shape layers and explore the possibilities on your own.

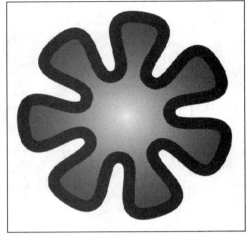

Figure 14.51 With shape layers, you don't have to turn to effects or a program like Illustrator to create graphical elements like this one.

Figure 14.52 Moreover, you can animate numerous shape properties to create more elaborate effects. This Brainstorm panel shows just a handful of variations on a shape layer's properties.

Figure 14.53 Bézier shapes work just like masks or motion paths. Because you can control each vertex in a Bézier shape, it's easy to create asymmetrical shapes.

Figure 14.54 Parametric shapes are defined by parameters you specify, such as the number of points in a star, and so on. This makes them well suited for creating and animating symmetrical, geometric shapes.

Bézier and parametric shapes

In shape layers, you can create two kinds of shapes: Bézier and parametric shapes.

Bézier shapes are defined by vertices (aka control points) connected by line segments. Invisible direction lines (or tangents) extending from each vertex influence the curve before and after the vertex. You modify a Bézier shape just as you would a mask or motion path, by adjusting control points and direction lines, or by using a transform box to scale or rotate it. When creating a shape with the Pen tool, you can have After Effects calculate continuous curves automatically by selecting the RotoBézier option. Typically, you would use Bézier shapes to create asymmetrical, organic looking shapes (**Figure 14.53**).

Parametric shapes are defined by a set of parameters (parametric, parameter, get it?) instead of Bézier curves. In After Effects, these parameters—for example, the number of points in a star—are listed in the shape layer's property outline. With parametric shapes, you can't manipulate individual points as you would in a Bézier shape, but you can more easily create and modify symmetrical, geometric shapes (**Figure 14.54**).

You can also see the difference between Bézier and parametric shapes in the layer's property outline; Bézier objects are defined by a Path property, whereas parametric objects list their parameters, depending on the type of shape (**Figure 14.55**).

Shapes you create with the Pen tool are always Bézier objects. Because you already learned about Bézier curves in Chapter 10, the following sections focus on creating parametric objects using the shape tools.

✔ Tip

■ Because the shapes they create are similar in nature, both the Polygon and Star shape tools create a path identified in the shape layer's property outline as a *Polystar Path*.

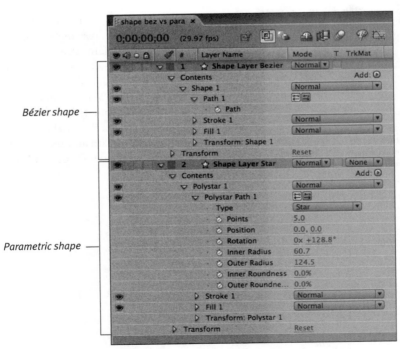

Figure 14.55 In a shape layer's property outline, a Bézier has a Path property, and a parametric object is defined by properties according to its type. Here, you can see the properties for a Polystar shape (created by using the Star).

Figure 14.56 Make sure no layers are selected, and choose a shape tool. In this example, the Star tool is selected.

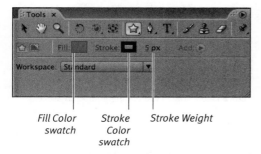

Fill Color   Stroke   Stroke Weight
swatch   Color
swatch

Figure 14.57 You can specify the shape's fill and stroke beforehand using controls in the Tools panel. You can change (and animate) these and other properties at any time.

Creating Shape Layers

You create shape layers in much the same way as you would create a mask. In fact, you can use the same tools and many of the same techniques you learned in Chapter 10, "Mask Essentials."

However, note the important differences between shapes and masks. By default, drawing with a shape tool creates a para-metric object, not Bézier objects. (Drawing with the Pen always creates Bézier objects.) To create a shape layer, no other type of layer can be selected. Otherwise, drawing creates a mask path. If a shape layer is selected, you must specify whether you want to add a shape to the shape layer or mask the shape layer.

To create a new shape layer using a shape tool:

1. Make sure no layers are selected.

   If a layer is selected, you will create a mask instead of a shape layer. If a shape layer is selected, you can decide whether to add the new shape to the shape layer or mask it.

2. In the Tools panel, select one of the shape tools (**Figure 14.56**).

   As long as no layer is selected, the Create Shape button 🟊 and Create Mask button ▨ in the Tools panel are grayed out.

3. In the Tools panel, *do any of the following*:

   ▲ To specify the shape's fill or stroke color, click the corresponding color swatch icon to open a color picker (**Figure 14.57**).

   ▲ To specify the shape's stroke weight, specify a value, in pixels.

   You can add fills and strokes (including gradients) and other attributes after you create the shape.

continues on next page

CREATING SHAPE LAYERS

4. In the Comp panel, *do either of the following:*

▲ To create a parametric shape, drag with the tool (**Figure 14.58**).

▲ To create a Bézier shape, Option/Alt-drag with the shape tool.

Whether you create a parametric or Bézier shape, you can use other keyboard modifiers to determine the shape while you draw.

5. To complete the shape, release the mouse.

The shape layer appears in the Comp and in the Timeline panel's layer outline (**Figure 14.59**). By default, the shape layer contains a path, fill, and stroke property. It also possesses the usual transform properties that all image layers possess.

To add a shape or mask to a shape layer:

1. Select a shape layer (**Figure 14.60**).

2. In the Tools panel, select a drawing tool. You can select a shape tool or Pen tool.

Figure 14.58 Drag in the Comp panel to create a parametric shape (shown here). Pressing Option/Alt creates a Bézier shape.

Figure 14.59 The shape layer appears in the layer outline and uses the default still image duration.

Figure 14.60 Select the shape layer to which you want to add a shape or mask.

Create Mask

Create Shape

Figure 14.61 Select a drawing tool, and then specify whether you want to draw a shape or mask.

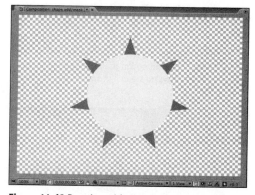

Figure 14.62 Drawing with Create Shape selected adds a shape to the shape layer. Here, an ellipse path has been added to the shape layer containing a star.

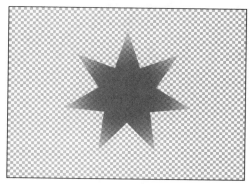

Figure 14.63 Drawing with Create Mask selected masks the shape layer. Here, an ellipse masks part of the star. The mask edge is feathered (shapes don't have a feather property).

3. In the Tools panel, *do either of the following* (**Figure 14.61**):

▲ To add a shape to the shape layer, select the Create Shape button

▲ To mask the shape layer, select the Create Mask button

4. In the Comp panel, draw the shape.

If you chose the Create Shape button, a new shape is added to the shape layer and is listed in the layer's property outline (**Figure 14.62**). If you chose the Create Mask button, the new shape masks the shape layer (**Figure 14.63**).

✔ Tips

■ You can deselect all layers by pressing F2 on the keyboard. This way, you'll be sure to create a shape layer and not a mask.

■ You can also create a shape layer using the Pen tool. As usual, you can check the RotoBézier option to have After Effects calculate curves automatically; leave RotoBézier unchecked to draw Bézier curves manually.

■ Shape creation tools retain the most recent settings. For example, drawing with the Star tool creates a polystar with the same number of points as the last time the tool was used.

CREATING SHAPE LAYERS

Working with shape layer properties

When you first create a shape layer, it contains three shape property categories: a path (such as a polystar), a fill, and a stroke. But these properties are more comprehensive than you may expect. For example, you can specify the number of points in a star and its inner and outer radius and roundness. You can determine which part of a complex shape is filled; you can make strokes dashed and set the appearance of caps and joins (**Figure 14.64**).

The shape layer also possesses all the usual layer transform properties, such as position, anchor point, and so on.

Adding properties

What's more, you can add properties to a shape layer (**Figure 14.65**). (The process may remind you of adding properties to a text animator.) These properties can include additional paths, strokes, and fills. They can also specify other modifications, or operations. *Path operations* affect the path. For example, you can combine paths or add a random wiggle to a shape. *Paint operations* affect fill and stroke. For example, you can add gradients.

Stacking order

Each shape and attribute behaves a lot like a layer within a layer. You can rename shapes and properties, and each one has a Blending mode pull-down menu and a video switch that lets you exclude or include it in output. Because the attributes listed in the shape layer's property outline are applied from the bottom of the list to the top, their relative order affects the final result. You can change the order by dragging in the shape's property outline (in much the same way as you would change the order of effects in the Effect Controls panel).

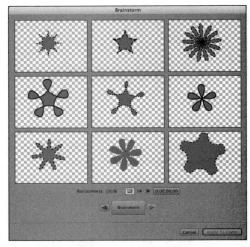

Figure 14.64 This Brainstorm panel shows several variations on a polygon's basic properties.

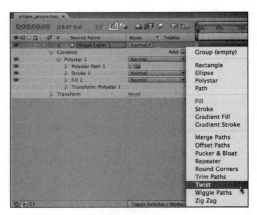

Figure 14.65 An Add pull-down menu lets you add attributes to the shape layer.

Figure 14.66 A single shape layer can contain multiple paths that you can arrange into groups. Selecting this shape layer depicting a gear...

Groups

For an even greater degree of control, you can group shapes and properties. You can create an empty group using the Add pull-down menu, or simply drag items into a property heading. This way, each group is affected by its own set of attributes, yet coexist in the same shape layer (**Figures 14.66** and **14.67**).

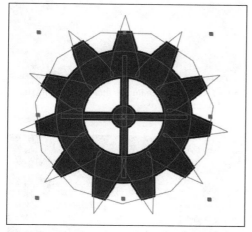

Figure 14.67 ...reveals that it consists of several paths: a star, polygon, rectangles, and circles.

Paint and path operations

The bottom two sections of a shape layer's Add pull-down menu (also available in the Tools panel when the shape layer is selected) lists paint and path operations.

Paint operations are very useful and relatively straightforward: They let you apply additional fills, strokes, or gradients.

Path operations are more exciting; they include vector-based effects like the ones found in Illustrator. Path operations help you form more complex shapes (as you saw in Figure 14.67). Effects like pucker and bloat can transform a star into a flower or curvy ornamentation (**Figures 14.68** and **14.69**). Wiggle or Zig Zag turns smooth contours into a vibrating squiggle (**Figure 14.70**).

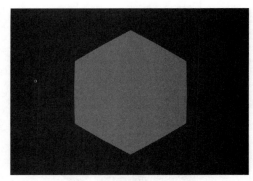

Figure 14.68 Start with a simple shape like this star...

Figure 14.69 ...and use Pucker and Bloat to warp it into a flowerlike figure.

Figure 14.70 Adding Zig Zag turns it into this complex pattern.

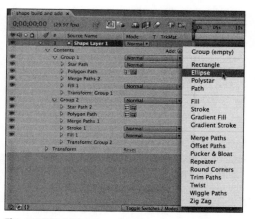

Figure 14.71 In the shape layer's property outline, click the Add button and select an option in the pull-down menu.

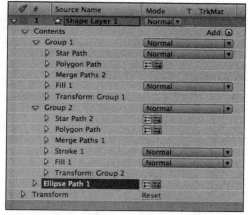

Figure 14.72 The property you specified appears in the selected category heading of the shape layer's property outline.

To add a group or property to a shape layer:

1. In the Timeline panel, expand a shape layer's property outline and select the property heading to which you want to add a property.

2. In the shape layer's property outline, click the Add button and select an item from the pull-down menu (**Figure 14.71**).

   The attribute appears as the bottommost property in the layer's property outline (**Figure 14.72**). If you add a group, a group heading appears but doesn't contain anything until you add items to the group, as explained in the following task, "To reorder or group shape properties."

To reorder or group shape properties:

1. In the Timeline panel, expand the shape layer's property outline.

2. In the shape layer's property outline, *do any of the following:*

   ▲ To group a property, drag it to highlight a property heading (**Figure 14.73**).

   The property is moved to the position you specified, or becomes listed within the group heading (**Figure 14.74**).

   ▲ To change the stacking order of shape layer properties, drag the property to the position you want (**Figures 14.75** and **14.76**).

✔ Tip

■ The procedures for adding shape attributes may remind you of adding text properties and ranges to text animator groups; the concept of applying shape attributes up the stacking order reflects After Effect's overall process for rendering comps.

Figure 14.73 To group a shape or property, drag it to highlight another property heading and release the mouse...

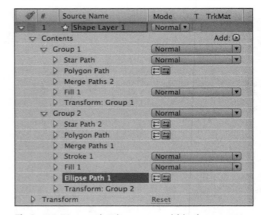

Figure 14.74 ... so that it appears within the property category.

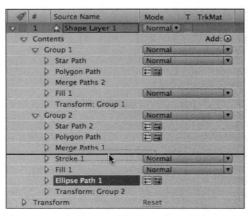

Figure 14.75 To change a shape attribute's place in the stacking order, drag it so that a black line indicates its new position...

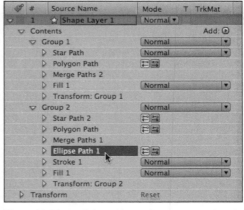

Figure 14.76 ...and then release the mouse to place it in that position.

CREATING SHAPE LAYERS

Figure 14.77 The Tools panel includes a new set of tools, Puppet tools.

Figure 14.78 A Puppet effect uses a mesh that interconnects points within the layer...

Figure 14.79 ...so that distortions seem organic and natural.

Using the Puppet Effect

Not every new effect merits a section devoted to it. But the new Puppet effect, introduced in After Effects CS3, is so useful it deserves special treatment. In fact, alongside the other tools that have become mainstays—camera tools, path creation tools, and paint—you'll find a new set of tools: Puppet tools (**Figure 14.77**).

Like Paint, you can apply the Puppet effect by just using its tools. However, you can still find the Puppet effect listed in the Effects & Presets panel under the Distort category. That's because the Puppet effect is essentially a kind of mesh warp effect. That is, it moves the pixels in a layer based on a *mesh*, an overlay of interconnected points that resembles a web, or a net (albeit one with a triangular weave) (**Figure 14.78**). Instead of moving a layer's pixels independent of one another, the mesh connects any given point on the layer to nearby points. This way, when you move a point on the layer, the rest of the layer responds in an organic, natural-looking way (**Figure 14.79**).

With the Puppet effect, you specify the points you want to manipulate with the Puppet Pin tool . "Pinned" points don't move unless you move them and act as the layer's pivot points. In this way, they articulate the layer—your puppet, if you will. To control the malleability or stiffness of the mesh between pinned points, you can use the Puppet Starch tool . And to specify whether part of the puppet appears in front of or behind an overlapping part, use the Puppet Overlap tool .

By animating the position of the Pins (as well as the Starch and Overlap) you can move a puppet as though the layer were a bendable, poseable toy. You can even record your mouse movements as keyframes for even more natural movement.

When working with the Puppet effect, bear in mind that the mesh is based on the layer's alpha channel at its native size. And remember that as an effect, a Puppet effect renders after masks but before transformations. This means that in order to transform (scale, rotate, etc.) a puppet layer, you may have to use nesting or the Transform effect.

✔ Tip

■ For more about using nesting and the Transform effect to subvert the rendering order, see Chapter 16.

To animate with Puppet tools:

1. Set the current time to the point you want to begin animating a layer with the Puppet effect.

2. In the Tools panel, select the Puppet Pin tool.

3. In the Tools panel, specify *any of the following* options (**Figure 14.80**):

   View Mesh—to display the puppet mesh as you work

   Expansion—shrinks or expands the mesh area

   Triangles—sets the relative density of the mesh

   You can change these settings at any time. See the section, "Refining Puppet Animations," later in this chapter.

4. Using the Puppet Pin tool, click the points on the layer you want to pin.

   A yellow dot or circle indicates a Puppet Pin (**Figure 14.81**). In the Timeline panel, the Puppet effect appears in the layer's property outline. A keyframe for each Puppet Pin's position is set at the current time automatically.

Figure 14.80 Set the current time to the point you want to start animating, and then choose the Puppet Pin tool and specify mesh options.

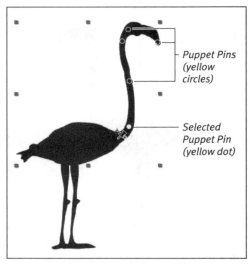

Puppet Pins (yellow circles)

Selected Puppet Pin (yellow dot)

Figure 14.81 Clicking the layer sets Puppet Pins, indicated by yellow dots.

Figure 14.82 In the layer's property outline, you can see that a keyframe is set for each Puppet Pin's position automatically.

Figure 14.83 Set the current time to the frame you want to set a new Puppet Pin keyframe and move a Puppet Pin to a new position. The puppet distorts according to the pins.

Figure 14.84 In the layer's property outline, a new keyframe is created.

5. To view the Puppet Pin points in the layer's property outline, expand the Puppet effect until you reveal the Puppet Pin properties (**Figure 14.82**).

6. Set the current time to the frame you want to set a Puppet Pin position keyframe.

7. *Do either of the following:*

▲ In the layer's property outline, click the Add Keyframe button to create a keyframe that uses the previously interpolated values for that frame.

▲ In the Comp panel, drag the Puppet Pin to a new position (**Figure 14.83**).

In the layer's property outline, you can see a new keyframe for the selected Puppet Pin (**Figure 14.84**).

8. Repeat steps 6 and 7 as needed and preview the animation.

✔ Tip

■ Once you set a Puppet Pin, you can't move it without also distorting the puppet layer. If you don't like the Puppet Pin's position relative to the mesh, select the Puppet Pin (so that the dot is solid) and then delete it.

USING THE PUPPET EFFECT

Refining Puppet Animations

The previous section explained the overall procedure for animating a layer with the Puppet effect; the following sections explain how to fine-tune the animation. First, you'll learn to refine the mesh. Then, you'll learn how the Puppet Starch and Puppet Overlap tools can make movement more convincing. Finally, you'll animate Pin points by recording the movements of the mouse.

Mesh triangles and expansion

Puppet distortions are influenced by the mesh's fundamental properties: its triangles and expansion. The Triangles property refers to the number of triangular areas described by the intersecting lines of the mesh. The more triangles a mesh has, the more points on which to base distortions. The result is greater precision, but also longer processing time. The Expansion property affects the mesh's coverage of the puppet layer. Although the mesh is based on the layer's alpha channel, you can expand or contract the mesh (just as you might change the effective edges of a mask). You might, for example, expand the mesh so that you can place Puppet Pin points outside the visible part of the layer. In some cases, this could prevent the Pin from causing unwanted distortions. Unlike other Puppet effect properties, you can't animate Triangles or Expansion.

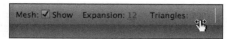

Figure 14.85 You can customize the mesh according to your needs by setting a value for Triangles and for Expansion.

Figure 14.86 This mesh's Triangle and Expansion values are set to the defaults.

Figure 14.87 Here, the mesh's expansion is increased to 12; its density is increased to 700.

To set the mesh triangles and expansion:

1. To view the mesh options, *do either of the following*:

   ▲ Select the layer containing the Puppet effect and select the Puppet Pin tool ![icon].

   ▲ In the Timeline panel, expand the layer's property outline to reveal the Puppet effect and the properties it contains.

   The Comp panel shows Puppet Pin points.

2. To make the mesh visible, select View Mesh in the Tools panel.

3. In either the property outline or the Tools panel, specify the following options (**Figure 14.85**):

   Triangles—specifies the density of the mesh; higher values create more intersections in the mesh, thereby increasing precision and rendering times.

   Expansion—specifies the mesh's size; lower values shrink the mesh, whereas higher values expand the mesh beyond the sides of the layer (determined by the layer's alpha channel).

   The mesh uses the values you specify (**Figures 14.86** and **14.87**).

REFINING PUPPET ANIMATIONS

Using Puppet Starch

Like its namesake, the Starch tool ▣ makes areas on the mesh more stiff—or put another way, it makes parts of the mesh less responsive to distortions caused by the Puppet Pin points. By making some parts of the puppet less flexible than others, the puppet's movements can seem more natural (**Figure 14.88** and **14.89**).

Clicking on the mesh with the Starch tool sets Starch points, which appear as red dots on the puppet layer in the Comp panel. In the layer's property outline, Starch points appear under a category called Stiffness. You can control the size of the area affected by each starch point (the Extent), and the degree of stiffness (its Amount).

Whereas Pin points remain attached to a particular point on the mesh, Starch points can be moved relative to the mesh. You can animate a Starch point's Position, Amount, and Extent properties.

Figure 14.88 In this figure, the flamingo has no starch.

Figure 14.89 Here, the same puppet has starch in one part of its neck.

Figure 14.90 Select the Puppet Starch tool and specify values for Amount and Extent.

To make the mesh more or less flexible:

1. In the Tools panel, select the Puppet Starch tool ![icon].

2. In the Tools panel, specify the following options (**Figure 14.90**):

   View Mesh—select to view the puppet effect's mesh as you work

   Amount—specifies the relative stiffness of the mesh surrounding the Starch point; high values make the mesh more inflexible.

   Extent—specifies the area surrounding the Starch point affected by the Starch Amount setting; higher Extent values affect a larger area of the mesh.

3. In the Comp panel, click the puppet layer where you want to affect the mesh's flexibility.

   Starch points appear as red dots; the Extent appears as a shaded area around the dot; the opacity of the shaded area correlates with the specified Amount value (**Figure 14.91**), so that 0% appears transparent and higher values appear gray.

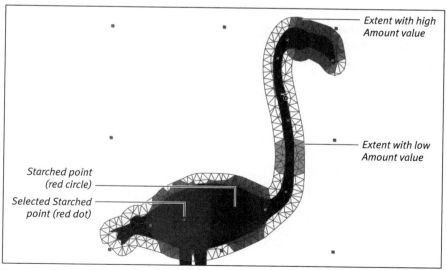

Figure 14.91 Clicking sets Starch points, indicated by red dots. The size and opacity of shaded areas correspond to the Extent and Amount values, respectively.

USING PUPPET STARCH

Using Puppet Overlap

It's possible to distort a puppet layer so that one area overlaps with another. When areas overlap, viewers expect one part to be in front, and the other behind—despite the fact all parts of the layer occupy the same plane and have no real depth (**Figure 14.92**).

Fortunately, you can specify layering with the Puppet Overlap tool. Clicking with the tool creates Overlap points, which appear as blue dots on the mesh. An Extent property determines the area surrounding the point affected by the In Front value. When a layer with a higher In Front value overlaps one with a lower value, it appears (predictably) in front—hence, creating the illusion of depth.

To specify how areas of the puppet overlap:

1. In the Tool panel, select the Puppet Overlap tool .

2. In the Tools panel, specify the following options (**Figure 14.93**):

   View Mesh—select to view the puppet effect's mesh as you work.

   In front—specifies the area's apparent depth relative to other areas.

   Extent—specifies the area surrounding the Overlap point affected by the In Front setting; higher Extent values affect a larger area of the mesh.

Figure 14.92 In this example, points of the star with higher overlap values appear above points with lower values.

Figure 14.93 Select the Puppet Overlap tool and specify values for In Front and Extent.

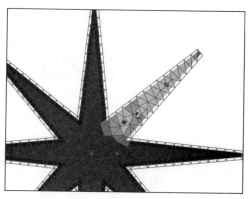

Figure 14.94 Clicking sets Overlap points, indicated by blue dots. The size and brightness of highlighted areas correspond to the Extent and In Front values, respectively.

3. In the Comp panel, click the puppet layer where you want areas to control.

   Overlap points appear as blue dots; the Extent appears as a shaded area around the dot; the brightness of the shaded area correlates with the specified In Front value, so that higher values appear whiter (**Figure 14.94**). In the property outline, each Overlap point is listed under the Overlap category.

Selecting and Modifying Puppet Properties

You can change the mesh's density and expansion at any time, but you can't keyframe those values. In contrast, you can change the position and properties of Starch and Overlap points at any time, and keyframe their values.

To make Starch and Overlap points appear in the Comp panel, you must select a layer's Puppet effect and the corresponding tool. For example, select the Puppet effect and the Puppet starch tool to make Starch points appear in the Comp panel. Whatever kind of point you're viewing (Pin, Starch, or Overlap), selected points appear as solid dots; deselected points appear as hollow dots. When setting Starch or Overlap points, Puppet Pin points appear as small yellow "x"s. And remember that you can always toggle the mesh visibility by clicking the View Mesh option in the Tools panel.

Animating Puppets by Sketching with the Mouse

A real-world puppet seems to come to life by the deft string-pulling of its puppet master. Puppet layers in After Effects don't have strings, but they do have the digital equivalent. Each tug—I mean drag—of the mouse on a Puppet Pin point can be recorded in real-time as keyframes. So instead of painstakingly and mechanically setting keyframes in the usual fashion, the puppet simply reenacts your puppeteering performance.

To animate puppets by sketching:

1. Set Puppet Pins points, Starch points, and Overlap points, as described in the previous sections.

2. In the Tools panel, select the Puppet Pin tool 📌.

3. In the Tools panel, click Record Options (**Figure 14.95**).

4. In the Puppet Record Options dialog box, specify the following options (**Figure 14.96**):

    Speed—specifies the recording speed relative to the playback speed of the motion; a value of 100% plays back motion at the same speed at which it was recorded; higher values play back the motion more slowly.

    Smoothing—specifies how much to smooth the recorded motion by removing extraneous keyframes; higher values result in fewer recorded keyframes and smoother motion.

Figure 14.95 Select the Puppet Pin tool and then click Record Options.

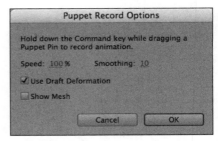

Figure 14.96 In the Puppet Record Options dialog box, specify the settings you want and then click OK.

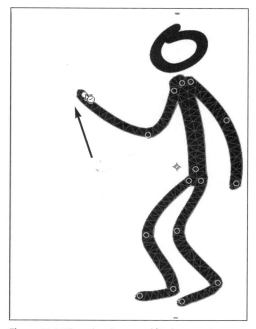

Figure 14.97 Pressing Command/Ctrl as you drag a Puppet Pin...

Use Draft Deformation—when selected, the outline that indicates the distortion doesn't reflect Starch points; the preview outline can be less accurate, but the recording performance can be improved.

Show Mesh—selecting this option makes the puppet mesh visible while you record mouse movements.

5. Click OK to close the Puppet Record Options dialog box.

6. In the Comp panel, press Command/Ctrl as you position the mouse pointer over a Puppet Pin.

   The Puppet Pin tool appears with a clock icon ⏱.

7. Pressing Command/Ctrl, drag the Pin in the manner you want the puppet to move (**Figure 14.97**).

   After Effects records the mouse's movements as keyframes for the selected Pin (**Figure 14.98**).

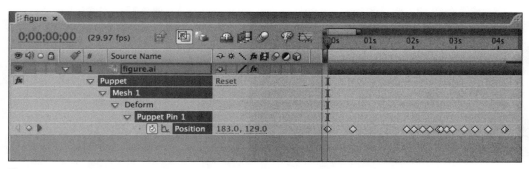

Figure 14.98 ...records the movement as keyframes, according to the options you specified.

3D LAYERS

Up to now, you've dealt strictly with layers in two dimensions: horizontal and vertical, as measured on the X and Y axes. However, After Effects includes depth as well, measured along the Z axis. As in other 3D programs, you can create one or more cameras from which to view and render your 3D composition. You can also create lights to illuminate 3D layers that cast realistic shadows and have adjustable reflective properties. And despite their unique properties, you can adjust and animate 3D layers, cameras, and lights just as you would any 2D layer.

True, After Effects' 3D layers are just 2D panels in 3D space, and the program doesn't incorporate any of the modeling tools or other features you're likely to find in a dedicated 3D application. Even so, bringing the program into the 3D space *does* open a new frontier of creative exploration. For example, the sole ability to view the composition from custom camera views fundamentally alters how you would have approached a similar animation in the past. Similarly, 3D lighting features let you manipulate light and shadows in ways that were once difficult or impossible to achieve.

3D LAYERS

Using 3D

With the exception of adjustment layers, any layer can be designated as a 3D layer. When a layer becomes three-dimensional, it acquires additional transform properties as well as "material" properties exclusive to 3D layers (**Figure 15.1**). (See "Using 3D Orientation and Rotation," "Using 3D Position," and "Using 3D Material Options," later in this chapter.) By default, 3D layers are positioned at a Z coordinate of 0.

With After Effects, you can use 2D and 3D layers in the same compositions, although doing so can add complexity to the rendering order. (See "Combining 2D and 3D," later in this chapter for more about rendering order.) Note that cameras and lights are inherently 3D objects and can't be transformed to 2D objects.

To designate a layer as 3D:

◆ On the Switches panel of the Timeline panel, click the 3D switch that corresponds to the layer you want to designate (**Figure 15.2**).

The Cube icon appears 🔳. The layer becomes a 3D layer and acquires 3D transform and material properties.

To convert a 3D layer back to 2D:

◆ On the Switches panel of the Timeline panel, click the Cube icon 🔳 to make it disappear and convert the layer back into a 2D layer.

The layer becomes a 2D layer and loses its 3D transform and material properties.

✔ Tip

■ Most effects that simulate three-dimensional distortions (like the Bulge effect) are really 2D effects. Thus, when you make a layer 3D, these effects remain 2D and won't distort the layer along the Z axis.

Figure 15.1 When you make a layer three-dimensional, it acquires new transform properties that take Z-depth and rotation into account. 3D layers also have a Material Options property category.

Figure 15.2 In the Switches panel of the Timeline panel, click the 3D switch for a layer to make a Cube icon appear.

Viewing 3D Layers in the Comp Panel

Figure 15.3 Orthogonal views (Front, Left, Right, Back, Top, and Bottom) accurately represent lengths and distances at the expense of perspective. (Compare this Front view with Figure 15.5.)

Figure 15.4 By default, Custom View 1 shows the composition from above and to the left. Although Custom views aren't associated with an actual camera layer, you can adjust them using Camera tools.

Figure 15.5 Select a camera's name in the 3D View pull-down menu to see the composition through the lens of that camera.

The presence of 3D objects in a composition activates additional viewing options in a 3D View pull-down menu in the Composition panel. By selecting different views, you can see and manipulate 3D layers, cameras, and lights from different angles. The views in this list fall into three categories: Orthogonal views, Custom views, and Camera views.

Orthogonal views show the composition from the six sides of its 3D space: front, left, right, back, top, and bottom. In an Orthogonal view, lengths and distances are displayed accurately at the expense of perspective (**Figure 15.3**).

Custom views show the composition from three predefined viewpoints, which you can adjust by using Camera tools (see "Adjusting Views with Camera Tools," later in this chapter). However, these views aren't associated with an actual camera layer in the composition (**Figure 15.4**).

Camera views show the composition from a camera layer you create or—if there's no camera—from a default Camera view (**Figure 15.5**).

Unlike Orthogonal views, both Custom views and Camera views represent the composition from a three-dimensional perspective. Distant objects look smaller; closer objects appear larger. Objects viewed at an angle are foreshortened so that right angles appear acute or obtuse, and lengths and distances appear compressed. The type of lens emulated by a camera also affects perspective. (See "Using Cameras," later in this chapter.)

To specify a 3D view:

◆ In the Composition panel, select a view from the pull-down menu (**Figure 15.6**):

Active Camera—Activates the Camera view listed at the top of the Timeline panel's layer outline. If no cameras are present, Active Camera uses a default view.

Front—Shows the composition from the front, without perspective.

Left—Shows the composition from the left side, without perspective.

Top—Shows the composition from above, without perspective.

Back—Shows the composition from behind, without perspective.

Right—Shows the composition from the right side, without perspective.

Bottom—Shows the composition from below, without perspective.

Custom View 1–3—Show the composition from a point of view you can adjust using the Camera tools. These views aren't associated with a camera layer.

[Custom Camera Name]—Shows the composition from the view of the camera you create. Camera views appear in the 3D View pull-down menu when you create a camera layer.

The Composition panel shows the composition from the perspective of the selected view.

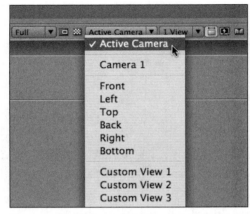

Figure 15.6 In the Composition panel, select a view from the pull-down menu.

✔ Tips

■ You can assign a 3D view to keyboard shortcuts F10, F11, and F12. To assign the shortcut, set the current 3D view and press Shift and F10, F11, or F12. From then on, pressing the function key alone invokes the assigned view.

■ As you progress through this chapter, view your 3D layers from different angles. After you grow accustomed to adjusting 3D layer properties, you'll learn how to adjust the views themselves using Camera tools. Finally, you'll create your own cameras and move them around the 3D composition. In other words, take it one step at a time.

Figure 15.7 Select a Camera tool.

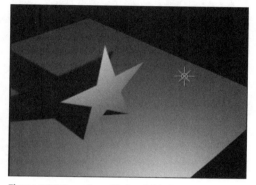

Figure 15.8 Dragging with the Orbit Camera tool...

Figure 15.9 ...rotates the view.

Adjusting Views with Camera Tools

Camera tools move the perspective of a 3D view much as you would move a real camera left, right, toward, or around a subject. When the 3D view is set to a Custom view, a camera tool changes its perspective for viewing purposes. When the 3D view is set to a camera layer you create, a camera tool moves the camera's position.

In this section, you'll use Camera tools to change the perspective of a 3D view, particularly a Custom view. By definition, the Orthogonal views prohibit camera angles other than their namesake (Front, Back, Left, Right, Top, or Bottom) and thereby prevent the use of the Orbit Camera tool. Orthogonal views do permit the Track XY and Track Z Camera tools, however.

Once you learn how to create and use camera layers, you can use Camera tools to move the camera (see the section "Moving Cameras with Camera Tools" later in this chapter).

To adjust a camera or view using Camera tools:

1. In the 3D View pull-down menu of the Composition panel, select a Custom or Orthogonal view.

   Note that you can't use the Orbit Camera tool in an Orthogonal view (Front, Back, Left, Right, Top, or Bottom).

2. In the Tools panel, select a Camera tool (**Figure 15.7**):

   Orbit Camera 💿—Dragging the tool in a 3D view rotates the perspective around its center in any direction (**Figures 15.8** and **15.9**). This tool can't be used in an orthogonal view.

continues on next page

Track XY Camera ✛—Dragging the tool in a 3D view shifts the perspective along the view's *X* or *Y* axis (side-to-side or up and down) (**Figure 15.10**).

Track Z Camera —Dragging the tool in a 3D view moves the perspective along the view's *Z* axis (similar to a camera dollying in or out) (**Figure 15.11**).

In an Orthogonal view, the 3D layers limit how far you can track in along the *Z* axis.

3. In the Composition panel, drag the selected Camera tool.

The camera position or view changes according to the Camera tool you use.

To focus a 3D view on selected layers:

1. Set the Comp panel to the 3D view you want to adjust.

2. In a Comp panel or Timeline panel, select one or more 3D layers (**Figure 15.12**).

Figure 15.10 Dragging with the Track XY Camera tool lets you move the view or camera along its *X* and *Y* axes. Here, the camera has tracked left (from its position in Figure 15.9).

Figure 15.11 Dragging with the Track Z Camera tool lets you move the view or camera along its *Z* axis. Here, the view has dollied in from its position in Figure 15.10, closer to the star layer.

Figure 15.12 Select the 3D view you want to adjust, and select one or more 3D layers.

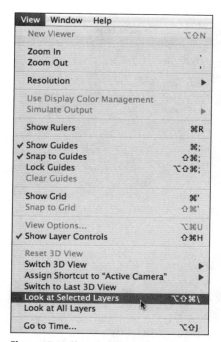

Figure 15.13 Choosing View > Look at Selected Layers...

Figure 15.14 ...adjusts the view to frame-up that layer automatically.

3. Choose View > Look at Selected Layers (**Figure 15.13**).

The 3D view adjusts so that the selected layers appear large and centered in the 3D view (**Figure 15.14**).

To reset a 3D view:

1. Set the Comp panel to the 3D view you want to reset.

2. Choose View > Reset 3D View (**Figure 15.15**).

The view's perspective adjusts to its default setting.

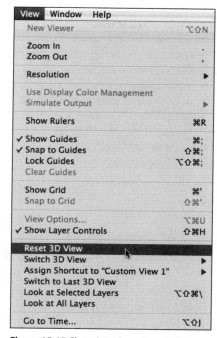

Figure 15.15 Choosing View > Reset 3D View resets the current view to its default state.

Using Comp Panel Layouts

As you've seen, it would be practically impossible to work in 3D without being able to view layers from various perspectives. But the usefulness of 3D views would be severely limited if you could see only one at a time; having to switch from one view to another would make your progress awkward and slow (**Figure 15.16**). Fortunately, you can show several views in a single Comp panel by selecting a Comp panel layout (**Figure 15.17**).

You can make changes in the view best suited to the task. And by seeing the changes you make from different perspectives at once, it's easier to get them right the first time.

You can specify whether the views share Comp View Options and other settings (such as grids and guides, channels, and so on) or use individual settings. However, all views use the same Resolution setting. You can set each view's magnification setting and 3D view (Orthogonal, Custom, or Camera view) individually, and at any time.

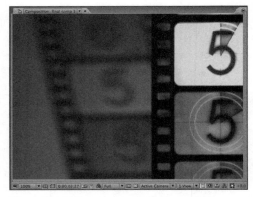

Figure 15.16 Although you can change a single 3D view...

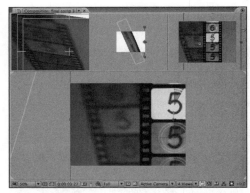

Figure 15.17 ...it's better to set the Comp panel's view layout to show several views at once.

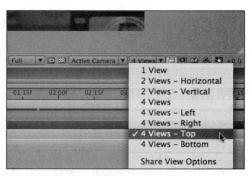

Figure 15.18 Choose a layout in the Comp panel's View Format pull-down menu.

Figure 15.19 Clicking a view activates it, as evidenced by highlights in the view's corners. Comp panel buttons affect the active view.

To specify a view layout in the Comp panel:

1. In the Comp panel's View Layout pull-down menu (located next to the 3D View pull-down menu), choose an option (**Figure 15.18**):

   1 View

   2 Views – Horizontal

   2 Views – Vertical

   4 Views

   4 Views – Left

   4 Views – Right

   4 Views – Top

   4 Views – Bottom

   The Comp panel reflects your choice.

2. To make all views use the same view options, select Share View Options in the View Layout pull-down menu.

   Options include those in the View Options dialog box (accessed via the Comp panel's pull-down menu) and other Comp view settings, except for Magnification and Resolution.

To specify the active view:

◆ In the Comp panel, click the view you want to use.

   Triangular highlights appear in the corners of the active view (**Figure 15.19**). Comp panel buttons affect the active view.

✔ Tip

■ If your mouse has a scroll wheel, you can hover the mouse over the view and use the scroll wheel to change the view's magnification setting, even if it's not the active view.

Using Axis Modes

In the layer outline, the spatial transform properties (Position and Rotation) are expressed in terms of *X, Y,* and *Z* axes, which intersect at the center of your composition's 3D "world." When you transform a layer by dragging in the Composition panel, however, you won't always want changes to occur according to these world axes.

Axis modes let you specify whether transformations you make in the Comp panel are expressed in terms of the 3D object (Local Axis mode), the 3D world (World Axis mode), or the current view (View Axis mode). Choosing how the axes are aligned makes moving and rotating 3D objects in the Comp panel a more flexible and intuitive process. The axis mode you employ doesn't affect transformations you make using the property controls in the layer outline; instead, these are expressed in terms of the world axis coordinate system.

To change axis modes:

1. Select a 3D layer, camera, or light.

2. In the Tools panel, select an axis mode (**Figure 15.20**):

Local Axis mode 🔛—Aligns the axes used for transformations to the selected 3D object (**Figure 15.21**)

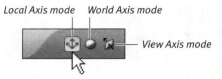

Local Axis mode   World Axis mode

View Axis mode

Figure 15.20 In the Tools panel, select an axis mode.

Figure 15.21 Here, the Local Axis mode aligns the axes to the selected object (a light). *X* is red, *Y* is green, and *Z* is blue. In Figures 15.22–15.24, the axes are highlighted and labeled to make them identifiable in a black-and-white image.

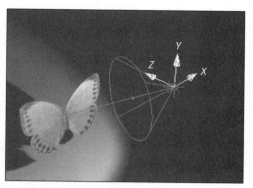

Figure 15.22 World Axis mode aligns the axes to the 3D world of the composition.

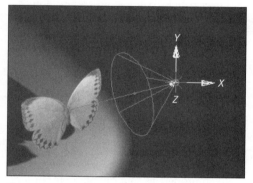

Figure 15.23 View Axis mode aligns the axes to the current 3D view.

World Axis mode ⊙—Aligns the axes used for transformations to the 3D space of the composition **(Figure 15.22)**

View Axis mode ⊡—Aligns the axes used for transformations to the current view **(Figure 15.23)**

The set of axes you select appears in the Composition panel.

3. Transform the selected object in the Composition panel by dragging it or by altering its transform properties in the layer outline.

Transformations occur according to the axes you selected. However, the transformation property values in the layer outline continue to be expressed in absolute terms, according to the world axis coordinate system.

Using 3D Position

For 3D layers, position is expressed as a three-dimensional property with values for *X, Y,* and *Z* coordinates along the world axes. As with 2D position, 3D position corresponds to a layer's anchor point.

To move a 3D layer in the Comp panel:

1. In the 3D View pull-down menu, select a view.

2. In Tools, select an axis mode.

3. Select a 3D layer, camera, or light.

   The selected layer's axes appear. The *X* axis is red; the *Y* axis is green; the *Z* axis is blue. The axes align according to the axis mode you specified.

4. In the Composition panel, position the Selection tool over the axis along which you want to move the layer (**Figure 15.24**).

   The Selection tool icon includes the letter corresponding to the axis: ▸x to move the layer along the *X* axis, ▸Y to move the layer along the *Y* axis, or ▸z to move the layer along the *Z* axis.

5. Drag the layer along the selected axis (**Figure 15.25**).

   In the layer outline of the Timeline panel, the layer's Position property reflects the changes in terms of the world axis coordinate system.

✔ Tips

■ You can change the anchor point of a 3D layer just as you would a 2D layer—except that the anchor point for 3D layers includes a value for its *Z*-axis coordinate. You will only be able to adjust the *X* and *Y* values of an anchor point in a Layer panel. To adjust an anchor point's position along the *Z* axis, use the property controls in the layer outline, or drag the anchor point in the Composition panel using the Pan Behind tool ▦. As you'll recall from Chapter 7, "Properties and Keyframes," the Pan Behind tool recalculates position as it transforms the anchor point, leaving the layer's relative position in the composition undisturbed.

■ Lights and cameras can also have transform properties that define their point of interest. See "Using the Point of Interest," later in this chapter.

Figure 15.24 In the Composition panel, position the Selection tool over the axis along which you want to move the layer. The Selection tool icon should include the axis letter.

Figure 15.25 Drag the layer along the selected axis.

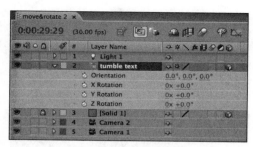

Figure 15.26 Three-dimensional layers, cameras, and lights can be rotated using a single Orientation property, or X, Y, and Z Rotation properties.

Figure 15.27 In the Tools panel, select the Rotation tool.

Figure 15.28 In the pull-down menu, choose Orientation.

Using 3D Orientation and Rotation

Making a layer three-dimensional adds a Z-axis dimension not only to its Position property but also to its Rotation property. However, the properties that control the way a layer rotates along its axes fall into two categories: Orientation and Rotation (**Figure 15.26**). The property you choose to adjust depends on the task at hand.

The Orientation property is expressed as a three-dimensional value: x, y, and z angles. In the Comp panel, you adjust orientation with the standard Rotation tool.

You adjust rotation using three separate property values: X Rotation, Y Rotation, and Z Rotation. Unlike orientation, Rotation properties allow you to adjust the number of rotations in addition to the angle along each axis. You can adjust Rotation values in the Composition panel by using a Rotation tool option.

To adjust the orientation in the Comp panel:

1. In the 3D View pull-down menu, select a view.

2. In the Tools panel, select an axis mode.

3. Select a 3D layer, camera, or light.
   The selected layer's axes appear. The X axis is red; the Y axis is green; the Z axis is blue. The axes align according to the axis mode you specified.

4. In the Tools panel, select the Rotation tool ⟳ (**Figure 15.27**).
   A pull-down menu containing rotation options appears in the Tools panel.

5. In the pull-down menu, choose Orientation (**Figure 15.28**).

continues on next page

USING 3D ORIENTATION AND ROTATION

6. In the Composition panel, *do one of the following:*

▲ To adjust the orientation along all axes, drag the Rotation tool in any direction (**Figures 15.29** and **15.30**).

▲ To adjust the orientation along a single axis, position the Rotation tool over the axis you want to adjust so that the Rotation icon displays the letter corresponding to the axis, and then drag (**Figures 15.31** and **15.32**).

If the Orientation property's Stopwatch icon isn't activated, this will remain the Orientation value of the layer for the layer's duration. If the Stopwatch is activated, an orientation keyframe is created at this frame.

Figure 15.29 Drag the Rotation tool in any direction...

Figure 15.30 ...to adjust the orientation along all axes.

Figure 15.31 Position the Rotation tool over the axis you want to adjust so that the Rotation tool icon displays the axis letter...

Figure 15.32 ...and drag to rotate the object around that axis.

Figure 15.33 In the Tools panel, select the Rotation tool.

Figure 15.34 In the pull-down menu, choose Rotation.

Figure 15.35 Position the 3D Rotation tool over the axis around which you want to rotate the 3D object, and then drag.

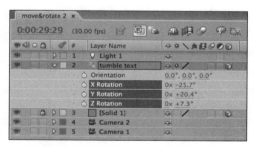

Figure 15.36 Dragging with the 3D Rotation tool adjusts the layer's 3D Rotation properties, not its Orientation properties.

To adjust 3D rotation in the Composition panel:

1. In the 3D View pull-down menu, select a view.

2. In the Tools panel, select an axis mode.

3. Select a 3D layer, camera, or light.

   The selected layer's axes appear. The X axis is red; the Y axis is green; the Z axis is blue. The axes align according to the axis mode you specified.

4. In the Tools panel, select the Rotation tool ⟳ (**Figure 15.33**).

   A pull-down menu containing rotation options appears in the Tools panel.

5. In the pull-down menu, choose Rotation (**Figure 15.34**).

6. In the Composition panel, position the 3D Rotation tool over the axis around which you want to rotate the 3D object (**Figure 15.35**).

   The 3D Rotation tool displays the letter corresponding to the axis.

7. Drag to rotate the 3D layer, camera, or light around the selected axis.

   If the Stopwatch icons for the Rotation properties aren't activated, the Rotation values are set for the layer's duration (**Figure 15.36**). If the Stopwatch icons are activated, rotation keyframes are created at this frame.

✔ Tip

- As usual, don't forget to switch back to the Selection tool after you've finished using the Rotation tool (or any other tool). Otherwise, you could easily make accidental changes to layers.

USING 3D ORIENTATION AND ROTATION

Auto-Orienting 3D Layers

Using the Auto-Orientation command, you can make a 3D layer automatically rotate along its motion path or toward the top camera layer (see "Using Cameras," later in this chapter)—which saves you the trouble of keyframing the Orientation property manually. Alternatively, you can leave Auto-Orientation off and adjust the layer's rotation independently of other factors.

To specify an Auto-Orientation setting:

1. Select a 3D layer.

2. Choose Layer > Transform > Auto-Orient, or press Command-Option-O (Mac) or Ctrl-Alt-O (Windows) (**Figure 15.37**).

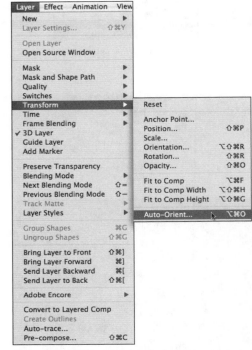

Figure 15.37 Choose Layer > Transform > Auto-Orient.

Orientation vs. Rotation

When you're animating a layer's rotation in 3D, the Orientation property and the Rotation properties offer unique advantages and disadvantages. Choose the method best suited for the task at hand—and to avoid confusion, try not to use both methods simultaneously.

You may find that it's easier to achieve predictable results by animating the Orientation property rather than the Rotation properties, because interpolated Orientation values take the shortest path between one keyframe and the next. You can also smooth orientation using Bézier curves (just as you'd smooth a motion path for position). However, Orientation doesn't allow for multiple rotations along an axis. And although Orientation's speed graph allows you to ease motion, it doesn't display rates of change in rotations per second. Because of these limitations, some animators prefer to use Orientation to set rotational position—its angle or tilt in 3D space—and animate using the Rotation property.

Separate Rotation property values permit more keyframing options than Orientation does, but the results can be more difficult to control. Each Rotation property permits multiple rotations and can display a velocity graph that accurately measures the rotations per second at any frame.

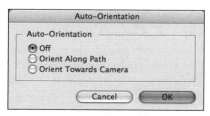

Figure 15.38 The Auto-Orientation dialog box appears.

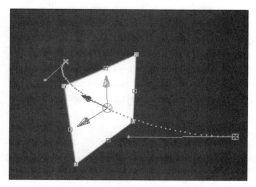

Figure 15.39 Orient Along Path makes the layer rotate so that its local *Z* axis points in the direction of the layer's motion.

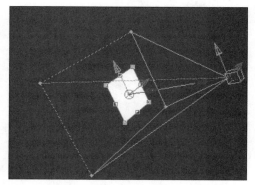

Figure 15.40 Orient Towards Camera makes the layer rotate so that its local *Z* axis points in the direction of the active camera.

The Auto-Orientation dialog box appears (**Figure 15.38**).

3. *Select one of the following* options:

Off—Turns off Auto-Orient and adjusts rotation independently

Orient Along Path—Makes the layer rotate so that its local *Z* axis points in the direction of the layer's motion path (**Figure 15.39**)

Orient Towards Camera—Makes the layer rotate so that its local *Z* axis points in the direction of the top camera layer (**Figure 15.40**)

For more information, see "Using Cameras," later in this chapter.

4. Click OK to close the dialog box.

✔ Tip

■ You can also apply special Auto-Orientation options to cameras and lights. See "Using the Point of Interest," later in this chapter.

AUTO-ORIENTING 3D LAYERS

Using 3D Material Options

Three-dimensional layers add a property category called Material Options that defines how 3D layers respond to lights in a comp. For more about lights, see "Using Lights," later in this chapter.

To set a 3D layer's Material Options:

1. Select a 3D layer.

2. Expand the layer outline to reveal the Material Options properties, or press AA (**Figure 15.41**).

   The layer's Material Options properties are revealed in the layer outline.

3. Set each Material Options property:

   Casts Shadows—Turn on this option to enable the layer to cast shadows on other layers within the range of the shadow. This property can't be keyframed.

   Light Transmission—Adjust this value to set the percentage of light that shines through a layer. A value of zero causes the layer to act as an opaque object and cast a black shadow. Increasing the value allows light to pass through the object and cast a colored shadow, much like a transparency or stained glass does.

   Accepts Shadows—Turn on this option to enable shadows cast from other layers to appear on the layer. This property can't be keyframed.

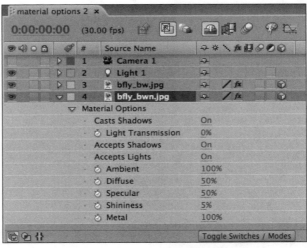

Figure 15.41 Expand the layer outline to reveal the Material Options properties, or press AA.

Figure 15.42 In this example, both 3D layers use the default material options, with Casts Shadows turned on.

Figure 15.43 Here, the Casts Shadows and Accepts Shadows settings are off on the left layer, and the Diffuse property on the right layer has been increased from 50 percent to 100 percent.

Accepts Lights—Turn on this option to enable the layer to be illuminated by lights in the composition. This property can't be keyframed.

Ambient—Adjust this value to set the amount of *ambient*, or nondirectional, reflectivity of the layer.

Diffuse—Adjust this value to set the amount of *diffuse*, or omnidirectional, reflectivity of the layer.

Specular—Adjust this value to set the amount of *specular*, or directional, reflectivity of the layer.

Shininess—Adjust this value to set the size of the layer's *specular highlight*, or shininess. This property is available only when the Specular property value is greater than 0 percent.

Metal—Adjust this value to specify the color of the specular highlight (as defined by the Specular and Shininess values). A value of 100 percent sets the color to match the layer, whereas a value of 0 percent sets the color to match the light source.

The layer in the Composition panel reflects your choices (**Figures 15.42 and 15.43**).

Using Cameras

You can view a composition from any angle by creating one or more 3D cameras. Cameras emulate the optical characteristics of real cameras. However, unlike real cameras, you can move these cameras through space unrestrained by tripods, gravity, or even union rules. This task summarizes how to create a new camera; the following sections explain each camera setting in detail.

To create a camera:

1. *Do either of the following:*
   ▲ Choose Layer > New > Camera (**Figure 15.44**).
   ▲ Press Shift-Option-Command-C (Mac) or Shift-Alt-Ctrl-C (Windows).
   A Camera Settings dialog box appears (**Figure 15.45**).

2. *Do one of the following:*
   ▲ Select a preset camera from the Preset pull-down menu (**Figure 15.46**).
   Presets are designed to emulate a 35mm camera of the specified focal length. Although presets are named for particular focal lengths, they set various camera settings automatically.
   ▲ Choose the custom camera options you want.
   See the next section, "Choosing Camera Settings," for a detailed description of each camera setting option.

3. To give the camera a custom name, enter one in the Name field of the Camera Settings dialog box.
   If you don't enter a name, After Effects uses the default naming scheme.

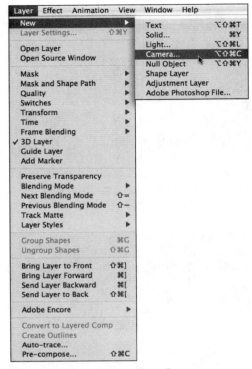

Figure 15.44 Choose Layer > New > Camera.

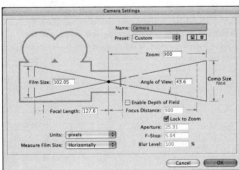

Figure 15.45 A Camera Settings dialog box appears.

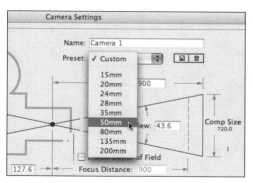

Figure 15.46 Select a preset camera from the Preset pull-down menu.

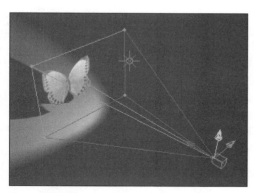

Figure 15.47 The new camera appears as the top layer in the composition, starting at the current time and using the default duration for still footage.

4. Click OK to close the Camera Settings dialog box.

The new camera appears as the top layer in the composition, starting at the current time and using the default duration for still footage (**Figure 15.47**). The camera's default position depends on the camera settings you chose. Its default point of interest is at the center of the composition (see "Using the Point of Interest," later in this chapter). You can also switch the 3D view to see the camera's positioning in the Composition panel (**Figure 15.48**). (See "Viewing 3D Layers in the Comp Panel," earlier in this chapter.)

✔ Tips

- If you don't name cameras, After Effects applies default names—Camera 1, Camera 2, and so on. When you delete a camera, After Effects assigns the lowest available number to the next camera you create. To avoid confusion, always give your cameras custom names. Note that always naming cameras will help you avoid problems when using expressions.

- To revisit a camera's settings, double-click the camera's name in the Timeline panel's layer outline.

Figure 15.48 Changing the 3D view allows you to see the camera as a selectable object in the Composition panel.

Choosing Camera Settings

When you create a camera, the Camera Settings dialog box prompts you to set various attributes for it—such as focal length and film size—that emulate physical cameras.

You can choose from a list of presets, designed to mimic a number of typical real-world cameras. Or, if you prefer, you can customize the settings. The dialog box provides a helpful illustration of the camera attributes (although it's not to scale, of course).

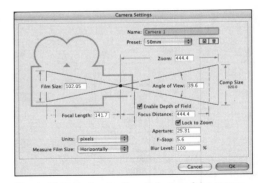

Figure 15.49 Customize the attributes of the camera in the Camera Settings dialog box.

The following tasks divide an explanation of camera settings into two parts. The first explains the basic settings, which govern film size and most of the camera's optical attributes. The next task explains the Depth of Field settings, which can be activated to mimic the limited focus range of real-world cameras.

To choose basic camera settings:

1. *Do one of the following:*
   - ▲ To create a new camera, press Shift-Option-Command-C (Mac) or Shift-Alt-Ctrl-C (Windows).
   - ▲ To modify a camera in the composition, double-click the name of the camera you want to modify in the layer outline of the Timeline panel.

   The Camera Settings dialog box appears (**Figure 15.49**).

2. Enter a name in the Name field.

   If you don't enter a name, After Effects will use the default naming scheme in which the first camera is called Camera 1 and additional cameras are numbered in ascending order. If you delete a camera that uses this naming scheme, however, new cameras are named using the lowest available number.

CHOOSING CAMERA SETTINGS

3. If you want to use predefined camera settings, select a preset from the Preset pulldown menu.

Presets are designed to emulate a 35mm camera of the specified focal length. Although Presets are named for particular focal lengths, they set various camera settings automatically. You can also create a Custom camera by modifying individual settings manually.

4. In the same dialog box, choose the units by which measurements are expressed:

Units—Sets whether the variables in the Camera Settings dialog box are expressed in pixels, inches, or millimeters (**Figure 15.50**)

Measure Film Size—Measures film size horizontally, vertically, or diagonally (**Figure 15.51**).

Typically, film size is measured horizontally. In other words, 35mm motion picture film measures 35mm across the image area. Measured vertically, the image is about 26.25mm.

5. Enter the following variables:

Zoom—Sets the distance between the camera's focal point and the image plane.

Angle of View—Sets the width of the scene included in the image. Angle of View is directly related to Focal Length, Film Size, and Zoom. Adjusting this setting changes those variables, and vice versa.

Film Size—Controls the size of the exposed area of the film being simulated. When you change Film Size, Zoom and Angle are adjusted automatically to maintain the width of the scene in the camera's view.

Focal Length—Controls the distance between the focal point and the film plane of the camera. When you change Focal Length, the Zoom value changes automatically to maintain the scene's width in the camera's view.

6. Click OK to close the Camera Settings dialog box.

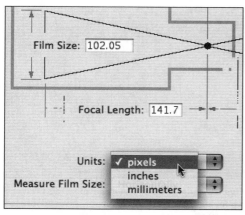

Figure 15.50 Select a unit of measure for the Camera Settings dialog box in the Units pull-down menu.

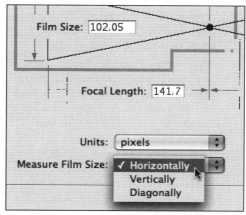

Figure 15.51 Select a unit of measure from the Measure Film Size pull-down menu.

To select Depth of Field options:

1. In the Camera Settings dialog box, select Enable Depth of Field (**Figure 15.52**).

   Selecting this option activates variables that affect the range of distance when the image is in focus, including Focus Distance, Aperture, F-Stop, and Blur Level.

2. To keep Focus Distance and Zoom the same, select Lock to Zoom.

   Deselect this option to allow Focus Distance and Zoom to be adjusted independently.

3. In the same dialog box, set the following options:

   Focus Distance—Sets the distance from the camera's focal point to the focal plane (the plane of space that is in perfect focus) (**Figure 15.53**).

   If Lock to Zoom is selected, adjusting Focus Distance also adjusts Zoom.

   Aperture—Sets the size of the lens opening. Because the Aperture and F-Stop settings measure the same thing in different ways, adjusting one results in a corresponding change in the other. Aperture (or F-Stop) is directly related to depth of field.

   F-Stop—Sets the aperture in terms of *f/stop*, a measurement system commonly used in photography. An f/stop is expressed as the ratio of the focal length to the aperture. On a real camera, increasing the f/stop by one full stop decreases the aperture to allow half the amount of light to expose the film; decreasing it by one stop doubles the amount of light. The term *stopping down* the lens refers to reducing aperture size.

   Blur Level—Controls the amount of blur that results when a layer is outside the camera's depth of field. A value of 100 percent creates the amount of blur appropriate to the other camera settings. Lower values reduce the blur.

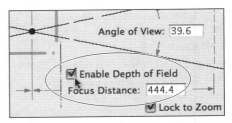

Figure 15.52 In the Camera Settings dialog box, select Enable Depth of Field.

Focal plane

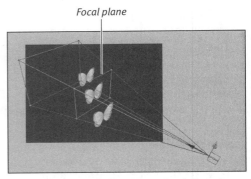

Figure 15.53 The Focus Distance value defines the distance from the camera to the focal plane. When Lock to Zoom isn't selected, you can see the focal plane represented in a selected camera's icon.

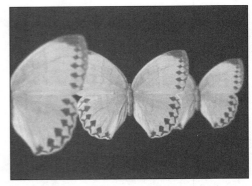

Figure 15.54 Here, the focal plane intersects the center butterfly, and objects outside the depth of field appear blurry.

4. Click OK to close the Camera Settings dialog box.

When viewed through the camera, objects outside the depth of field appear blurred (**Figure 15.54**).

✔ Tips

■ After Effects uses the term *position,* which is synonymous with the camera's Position property. In the physical world, the camera's position is synonymous with its focal point. In a real camera, the focal point defines where the light in the lens converges into a single point before it goes on to expose the film at the film plane (**Figure 15.55**). Distances associated with a camera are measured from its focal point.

■ The Camera Settings dialog box includes buttons to save 🖫 and delete 🗑 camera presets. They look like the buttons you use to save and delete composition presets.

■ Photographers may wonder why the cameras in After Effects seem to have controls for everything but shutter speed and shutter angle. You'll find these controls in the Advanced panel of the Composition Settings dialog box. See Chapter 4, "Compositions," for more information.

■ You can switch focus from one object in the scene to another, a technique cinematographers call *rack focus* or *pulling focus.* Make sure the Lock to Zoom camera setting is deselected, and animate the Focus Distance property.

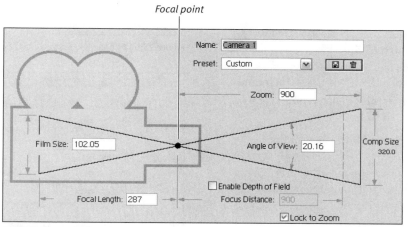

Focal point

Figure 15.55 The camera's position corresponds to the focal point, which is illustrated in the Camera Settings dialog box but not labeled.

Using Lights

You can create any number of lights to illuminate a 3D scene, and you can select and control these lights much as you would in the real world. In After Effects, however, lights are evident only when they illuminate 3D layers that are set to accept lights. You can select a light to place it in the scene and then point it at a subject, but you'll never see a lighting instrument in the scene. Pointing a light into a camera won't cause a lens flare or overexposed image—you won't see anything at all. And you'll never blow a lamp or overload a circuit breaker.

As in the "Using Cameras" section, this section contains two tasks: The first summarizes how to create a light; the second describes light settings in more detail.

To create a light:

1. *Do either of the following:*
   ▲ Choose Layer > New > Light (**Figure 15.56**).
   ▲ Press Shift-Option-Command-L (Mac) or Shift-Alt-Ctrl-L (Windows).

   A Light Settings dialog box appears (**Figure 15.57**).

2. Enter a name for the light in the Name field.

   If you don't enter a name, After Effects uses the default naming scheme.

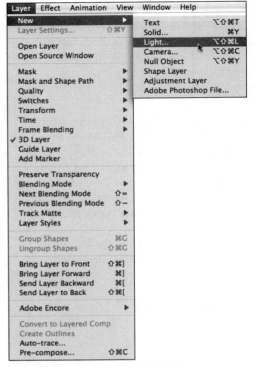

Figure 15.56 Choose Layer > New > Light.

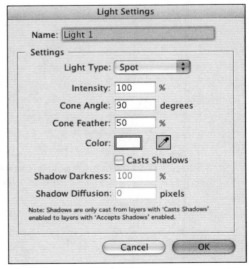

Figure 15.57 A Light Settings dialog box appears.

USING LIGHTS

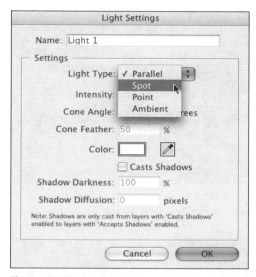

Figure 15.58 In the Light Settings dialog box, select the type of light you want from the pull-down menu.

3. In the same dialog box, select the type of light you want from the pull-down menu (**Figure 15.58**):

Parallel—Radiates directional light from an infinite distance. In this respect, a parallel light simulates sunlight (**Figure 15.59**).

Spot—Radiates from a source positioned within an opaque cone, allowing the light to emit only through its open end. Adjusting the cone's angle changes the spread of the light. This type of light emulates those commonly used in film and stage productions (**Figure 15.60**).

continues on next page

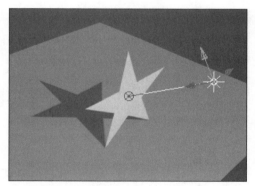

Figure 15.59 A parallel light radiates directional light from a source infinitely far away, much like sunlight.

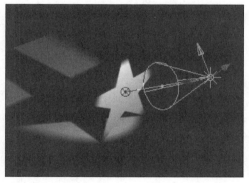

Figure 15.60 A spot light is constrained by a cone and appears much like the lights used in film and stage productions.

USING LIGHTS

Point—Emits omnidirectional light from its point of origin, comparable to a bare bulb or an unflickering signal flare (**Figure 15.61**).

Ambient—Doesn't emanate from a specific source but rather contributes to the overall illumination of the scene. Ambient light settings only include those for intensity and color (**Figure 15.62**).

The type of light you select determines which options are available in the Light Settings dialog box.

4. Specify the light settings available for the type of light you selected.

   See the next section, "Choosing Light Settings," for more information.

5. Click OK to close the Light Settings dialog box.

   The new light appears as the top layer in the composition, starting at the current time and using the default duration for still footage (**Figure 15.63**). The light's default position depends on the type of light you select.

✔ Tips

- You can revisit the Light Settings dialog box at any time by double-clicking the name of a light in the layer outline of the Timeline panel.

- If you need a lens flare or visible light beams, try an effect. After Effects includes a lens flare, and many third-party plug-in packages create light beams and other lighting effects.

Figure 15.61 A point light emits an omnidirectional light, much like a bare bulb.

Figure 15.62 An ambient light contributes to the overall illumination of the 3D space. Here, an ambient light is set to 30 percent intensity.

Figure 15.63 The new light appears as the top layer in the composition, starting at the current time and using the default duration for still footage.

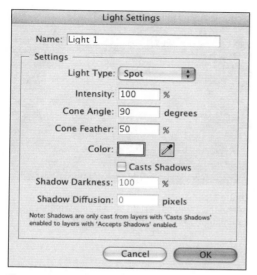

Figure 15.64 In the Light Settings dialog box, specify the settings available for the type of light you're using.

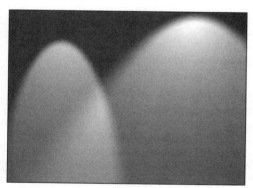

Figure 15.65 Both spot lights are the same intensity and distance from the layer. The light on the left uses a 45-degree cone angle; the light on the right uses a 90-degree cone angle.

Choosing Light Settings

The options available in the Light Settings dialog box depend on the type of light you're using. They control the character of the light and the shadows it casts.

To select light settings:

1. *Do one of the following:*

   ▲ To create a new light, press Shift-Option-Command-L (Mac) or Shift-Alt-Ctrl-L (Windows).

   ▲ To modify a light in the composition, double-click the name of the light you want to modify in the layer outline of the Timeline panel.

   The Light Settings dialog box appears (**Figure 15.64**).

2. In the Light Settings dialog box, specify the following options:

   Intensity—Sets the brightness of light. Negative values create *nonlight*—they subtract color from an already illuminated layer, in effect shining darkness onto a layer.

   Cone Angle—Sets the angle of the cone used to restrict a spot type of light. Wider cone angles emit a broader span of light; smaller angles restrict the light to a narrower area (**Figure 15.65**).

   continues on next page

Cone Feather—Sets the softness of the edges of a spot type of light. Larger values create a softer light edge (**Figure 15.66**).

Color—Selects the light's color; comparable to placing a colored gel over a light. You can use the color swatch or eyedropper control.

Casts Shadows—When selected, makes the light cast shadows onto layers with the Accepts Shadows property selected. See "Using 3D Material Options," earlier in this chapter, for more information.

Shadow Darkness—Sets the darkness level of shadows cast by the light. This option is available only when the light's Casts Shadows option is enabled.

Shadow Diffusion—Sets the softness of shadows, based on the apparent distance between the light and the layers casting shadows made by the light. Larger values create softer shadows. This option is available only when the light's Casts Shadows option is enabled.

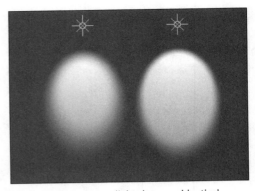

Figure 15.66 Both spot lights here are identical, except the light on the right uses a Cone Feather setting of 25, whereas the light on the left uses a Cone Feather setting of 50.

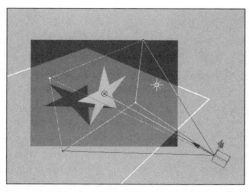

Figure 15.67 In the Composition panel, the point of interest appears as a crosshair at the end of a line extending from a camera or light.

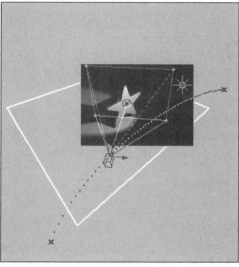

Figure 15.68 You can set a camera or light to automatically orient toward its point of interest as it moves.

Using the Point of Interest

Point of Interest is a transform property unique to cameras and lights. It defines the point in space at which the camera or light is pointed. By default, a new camera's or light's point of interest is at the center of the composition (at the coordinates (0,0,0) in terms of the world axes). In the Composition panel, the point of interest appears as a crosshair at the end of a line extending from a camera or light (**Figure 15.67**).

As you can see, a camera's or light's Point of Interest value is closely related to its other transform property values: A change in position or rotation can affect the point of interest, and vice versa.

Because of its relationship to other transform properties, the Point of Interest property is available only when you activate a 3D object's Auto-Orient option. When you animate the position of a light or camera, auto-orienting a layer saves you the effort of setting rotation keyframes manually.

By default, cameras and lights are set to orient toward the point of interest automatically. That is, moving a camera or light causes it to rotate so that it always points toward its point of interest. When applied to a camera, this setting may create a point of view similar to that of careless drivers who turn their head to see an accident as they drive by (**Figure 15.68**).

You can also set each light or camera to auto-orient along its motion path. When applied to a camera, this setting may mimic the view from a roller coaster, automatically rotating the camera to point in a 3D tangent to the motion path (**Figure 15.69**).

Finally, you can turn off the Auto-Orient setting so that the light's or camera's orientation isn't automatically adjusted to maintain a relationship with its motion path or point of interest. When you set Auto-Orient to off, the light or camera loses its Point of Interest property.

To choose the Auto-Orient setting for cameras and lights:

1. Select the camera or light you want to adjust.

2. Choose Layer > Transform > Auto-Orient (**Figure 15.70**).
   An Auto-Orientation dialog box appears (**Figure 15.71**).

3. *Choose an option:*
   Off—Turns off Auto-Orient, so that the camera or light rotates independently of its motion path or point of interest. Selecting this option eliminates the camera's or light's Point of Interest property.

   Orient Along Path—Makes the camera or light rotate automatically so that it remains oriented to its motion path.

   Orient Towards Point of Interest— Makes the camera or light rotate automatically as you move it so that it remains oriented toward the point of interest.

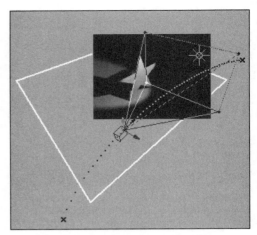

Figure 15.69 Or you can set a camera or light to automatically orient along its motion path.

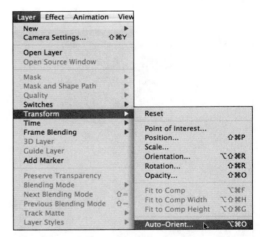

Figure 15.70 Choose Layer > Transform > Auto-Orient.

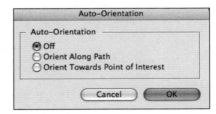

Figure 15.71 An Auto-Orientation dialog box appears.

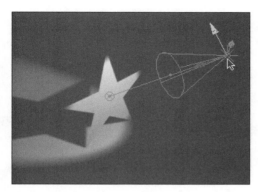

Figure 15.72 If Orient Towards Point of Interest is active...

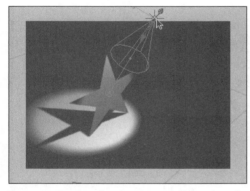

Figure 15.73 ...dragging the camera or light orients it automatically.

To move a light or camera without changing the point of interest:

1. Select a camera or light.

2. In the 3D View pull-down menu, select a view.

   You may also want to choose a different magnification setting in the Composition pull-down menu so that you can see the light or camera in the Composition panel.

3. In the Tools panel, select an axis mode. The selected layer's axes appear. The X axis is red; the Y axis is green; the Z axis is blue. The axes align according to the axis mode you specified.

4. If necessary, make sure Auto-Orient is set to Orient Towards Point of Interest. This is the default setting.

5. *Do any of the following:*
   ▲ In the Composition panel, drag the camera or light (**Figure 15.72**).

   Make sure the Selection tool icon doesn't include an axis letter. If it does, you'll move the camera or light by an axis, and the point of interest will move in tandem with the camera or light.

   ▲ In the Composition panel, position the Selection tool over an axis (so that the cursor displays the letter corresponding to the axis), and Command/Ctrl-drag (**Figure 15.73**).

   ▲ In the layer outline, adjust the light's or camera's Position property.

   The selected camera's or light's position changes, but the camera rotates so that its point of interest remains stationary.

To move a camera or light and the point of interest:

1. Select a camera or light.

2. In the 3D View pull-down menu, select a view.

   You may also want to choose a different magnification setting in the Composition pull-down menu so that you can see the light or camera in the Composition panel.

3. In the Tools panel, select an axis mode.

   The selected layer's axes appear. The X axis is red; the Y axis is green; the Z axis is blue. The axes align according to the axis mode you specified.

4. If necessary, make sure Auto-Orient is set to Orient Towards Point of Interest. This is the default setting.

5. In the Composition panel, position the Selection tool over a camera's or light's axes.

   The Selection tool icon appears with a letter that corresponds to the axis (**Figure 15.74**).

6. Drag the camera or light along the selected axis (**Figure 15.75**).

   As you move the camera or light, its point of interest moves accordingly.

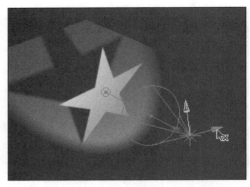

Figure 15.74 Command/Ctrl-dragging the camera or light by one of its axes also activates the Orient Towards Point of Interest command...

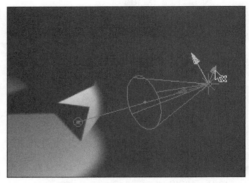

Figure 15.75 ...but dragging the camera or light by one of its axes doesn't allow it to auto-orient. Here, moving the light also moves its point of interest away from the star layer.

Figure 15.76 Select the Camera tool you want to use.

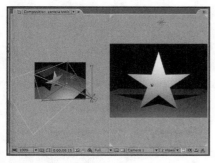

Figure 15.77 When Auto-Orient is set to Orient Towards Point of Interest, dragging with the Orbit Camera tool...

Figure 15.78 ...rotates the camera around its point of interest.

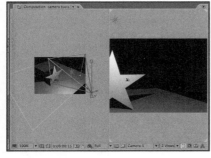

Figure 15.79 Otherwise, the camera rotates around its position.

Moving Cameras with Camera Tools

Camera tools provide you with another way to easily adjust Camera views. In contrast to dragging the camera from a separate Camera view, Camera tools let you change a camera's Position property while viewing the composition from the camera's point of view. Although it's harder to see the camera's motion path, you get to see the movement from the camera's perspective. You can also use Camera tools to adjust one of the Custom 3D views (see "Viewing 3D Layers in the Comp Panel," earlier in this chapter). By definition, the Orthogonal views (Front, Back, Left, Right, Top, and Bottom) prohibit other camera angles and, hence, the Orbit Camera tool 🔆. Orthogonal views do permit the Track XY and Track Z Camera tools.

To adjust a camera using Camera tools:

1. In the Composition panel's 3D View pull-down menu, select a Camera view.

   Selecting another 3D view adjusts that view, not a camera layer's Position property. See "Adjusting Views with Camera Tools," earlier in this chapter.

2. If necessary, set the camera's Auto-Orient option to determine how the Orbit Camera tool functions.

   See the next step to learn how Auto-Orient options affect the Orbit Camera tool.

3. In the Tools panel, select a Camera tool (**Figure 15.76**):

   Orbit Camera 🔆—Rotates the camera around its point of interest when Auto-Orient is set to Orient Towards Point of Interest. Otherwise, the camera rotates around its position (much like a camera panning on a tripod) (**Figures 15.77, 15.78,** and **15.79**).

continues on next page

Track XY Camera ✥—Moves the camera along its *X* and *Y* axes (similar to a real-world camera tracking right or left, or craning up or down). Regardless of the Auto-Orient setting, the camera's rotation is unaffected (**Figure 15.80**).

Track Z Camera ⬍—Moves the camera along its *Z* axis (similar to a camera dollying in or out). Regardless of the Auto-Orient setting, the camera's rotation remains unaffected (**Figure 15.81**).

4. In the Composition panel, drag the selected Camera tool.

   The camera position or view changes according to the Camera tool you use.

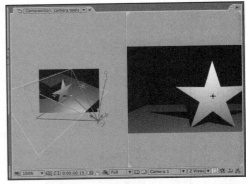

Figure 15.80 Dragging with the Track XY Camera tool lets you move the camera along its *X* and *Y* axes. Here, the camera is tracking left (from its position in Figure 15.79).

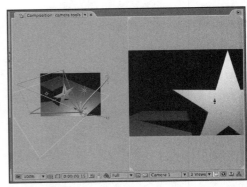

Figure 15.81 Dragging with the Track Z Camera tool lets you move the camera along its *Z* axis. Here, the camera is dollying back from its position in Figure 15.80.

Figure 15.82 In the Timeline panel, click the Draft 3D mode button.

Figure 15.83 When Draft 3D mode is off, the Composition panel displays lights, shadows, and depth-of-field blur.

Figure 15.84 With Draft 3D mode on, the Composition panel doesn't preview lights, shadows, or depth-of-field blur.

Previewing 3D

Draft 3D disables lights and shadows as well as blur caused by camera Depth of Field settings. As you've made your way through this book, you've encountered several ways of reducing a composition's preview quality so that you can increase rendering speed. The increased processing demands of 3D compositing will make you appreciate this trade-off even more.

To enable or disable Draft 3D mode:

◆ In the Timeline panel, click the Draft 3D mode button (**Figure 15.82**).

The image in the Composition panel no longer previews 3D lights, shadows, or depth-of-field blur. Click the button again to deselect it and turn off Draft 3D (**Figures 15.83** and **15.84**).

✔ Tip

■ In the Advanced panel of the Composition Settings dialog box, you can specify the Rendering Plug-In used to composite layers in 3D. The standard package comes with the standard 3D rendering plug-in; After Effects Pro includes an advanced 3D plug-in, which supports more sophisticated 3D features such as the intersection of 3D layers, diffuse shadows, and the like. If your computer is equipped with an After Effects–compatible OpenGL graphics card, you can designate it for 3D rendering.

PREVIEWING 3D

Understanding 3D Layer Order

As you learned in Chapter 5, "Layer Basics," layers listed higher in the Timeline panel's layer outline appear in front of other layers in the Composition panel. After Effects always renders 2D layers in order, from the bottom of the layer stacking order to the top. (See "Rendering Order" in Chapter 16, "Complex Projects.")

However, the simple 2D stacking order becomes irrelevant in 3D compositing, where object layering is determined by objects' relative positions in 3D space according to the current 3D view.

For 3D layers, After Effects renders from the most distant layer (with the highest Z-coordinate value) to the closest (with the lowest Z-coordinate value).

Combining 2D and 3D

When a composition contains both 2D and 3D layers, the rendering order becomes even more complex, combining aspects of both 2D and 3D rendering. Once again, layers are rendered from the bottom of the stacking order to the top. However, 3D layers are rendered in independent sets, separated by 2D layers.

In other words, placing a 2D layer so that it doesn't separate the 3D layers in the Timeline's stacking order allows the 3D layers to interact geometrically. 3D layers appear in front of one another and interact with lights and shadows according to their position in 3D space (as well as according to light settings and material options). The 2D layers neither share the same space as 3D layers nor interact with lights or cameras (**Figure 15.85**).

In contrast, positioning a 2D layer between 3D layers in the stacking order splits the 3D layers into separate groups. Although the 3D layers share the same lights and cameras, they exist in identical but separate 3D "worlds" and are rendered independently of one another (**Figure 15.86**).

✔ Tip

- For more on working effectively with the rendering order, see "Rendering Order" in Chapter 16.

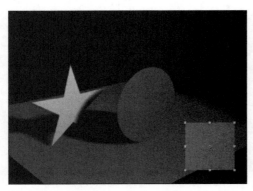

Figure 15.85 In this example, the 2D layer is higher in the stacking order than the 3D layers, allowing the 3D layers to be rendered together.

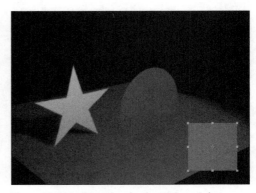

Figure 15.86 In this example, the 2D layer is between the circle and star in the stacking order, causing the 3D layers to be rendered separately. Notice how the circle no longer casts shadows.

UNDERSTANDING 3D LAYER ORDER

16

COMPLEX PROJECTS

As your projects become more ambitious, their structures will grow increasingly complex as well. A typical project contains not only layers created from individual footage items but also layers created from other compositions—called *nested compositions*. In this chapter, you'll find out how to employ nesting to group layers into a single element as well as to manipulate a project's hierarchy to create effects you couldn't otherwise achieve.

After Effects includes several other features that help you create complex projects without resorting to complicated procedures. The Parenting feature, for example, makes it possible to create a hierarchical relationship between a parent layer and any number of child layers, thus allowing you to link or group layers so that they behave as a single system.

Using another powerful feature—Expressions—you can create relationships between layer properties (in the same layer, in different layers, even in layers contained within different compositions). Rather than keyframing multiple properties independently, you can link one property's values to another property's values using a JavaScript-based instruction, or *expression*. (Don't worry: you'll be able to work with expressions without being a JavaScript programmer.)

Finally, this chapter provides the lowdown on *render order*, After Effects' hierarchical scheme for rendering frames. You'll learn how render order influences your results as well as how *you* can influence render order. You'll also find out how to inspect your work using the Flowchart view, as well as how to reduce render and preview time via a process called *prerendering*.

Nesting

A composition used as a layer in another composition is called a *nested composition*. Such compositions can serve various inter-connected purposes.

Nesting enables you to treat several layers as a group. When you're working with a nested composition, you can manipulate several layers as a unit rather than keyframe each individually (**Figures 16.1** and **16.2**).

Similarly, you can use a nested composition as often as you would any single layer—which means you need to build a multilayered animation only once to use it several times in a composition (**Figure 16.3**).

Whether a nested composition is used multiple times in one composition or several, you can revise every instance in a single step; each nested composition reflects any changes you make to its source. Therefore, it makes sense to use nested compositions for components you plan to reuse.

Nested compositions can also help you circumvent After Effects' default rendering order. The sequence in which properties are rendered often makes it difficult or impossible to achieve the desired effect. Although you can't break the rules, you can use nesting to work the system. To learn more about rendering order, move on to the next section, "Rendering Order." To see how rendering order and nesting apply to compound effects, see the section "Understanding Compound Effects," in Chapter 11.

Figure 16.1 Doing something as simple as adjusting the rotation can be difficult if you need to apply it to a number of separate layers.

Figure 16.2 Nesting the composition containing those layers lets you treat them as a single element.

Figure 16.3 It's easier to repeat a sequence of layers as a nested composition. You can revise multiple copies in a single step by altering layers in the source composition.

To nest a composition:

1. Display the Composition panel or Timeline panel of the composition that will contain the nested composition.

2. Drag a composition you want to nest from the Project panel *to any of the following* (**Figure 16.4**):

   ▲ Composition panel of the target composition

   ▲ Timeline panel of the target composition

   ▲ Name or icon of the target composition in the Project panel

   The composition becomes a layer in the target composition, beginning at the current time and having the same duration as the original composition.

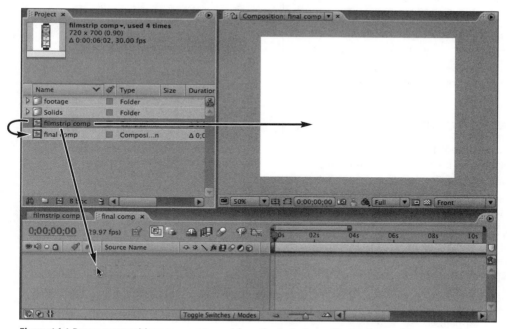

Figure 16.4 Drag a composition you want to nest from the Project panel to the Composition panel, the Timeline panel, or the icon of the target composition.

To nest one composition in a new composition with the same settings:

◆ Drag a composition in the Project panel to the Composition icon at the bottom of the Project panel (**Figure 16.5**).

The composition becomes a layer in a new composition that uses the same composition settings as the nested one.

✔ Tips

■ Nesting will help you get around some of the compound-effect restrictions that you learned about in Chapter 11, "Effects Fundamentals."

■ To find out how to turn selected layers into a nested composition retroactively, see "Precomposing," later in this chapter.

■ Like nesting, the Parenting feature can also link layers as a group or system. See "Parenting Layers" later in this chapter.

■ By creating relationships between layer properties, the Expressions feature provides another method of working around After Effects' rendering order.

Nesting options

In the composition's settings, nesting options dictate whether nested compositions retain their own frame rate and resolution settings or assume those of the composition in which they're nested.

To set nesting options:

1. With a comp selected, choose Composition > Composition Settings or press Control/Cmd-K (**Figure 16.6**). The Composition Settings dialog box appears.

2. In the Composition Settings dialog box, click the Advanced tab.

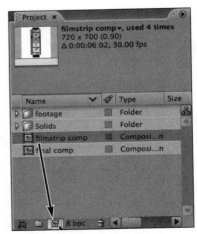

Figure 16.5 Dragging a composition to the Composition icon nests the composition in another composition that has the same settings.

Figure 16.6 Choose Composition > Composition Settings.

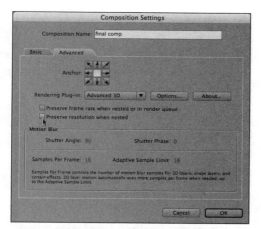

Figure 16.7 In the Advanced Panel of the Composition Settings dialog box, select the nesting options you want.

3. In the Advanced panel of the Composition Settings dialog box, *select one or both of the following* options (**Figure 16.7**):

   Preserve frame rate when nested or in render queue—Choosing this option allows nested compositions to retain their frame rates regardless of the frame rate of the composition that contains them.

   Preserve resolution when nested— If this option is selected, nested compositions retain their resolution settings regardless of the resolution of the composition that contains them.

   If you select neither option, nested compositions will take on the frame rate and resolution of the composition in which they're nested.

4. Click OK to close the Composition Settings dialog box.

✔ Tips

- The Render Queue dialog box allows you to use the current resolution settings or to reset them for all nested comps. See Chapter 17 for more about the render queue.

- By preserving the frame rate of a nested composition, you can achieve results similar to those produced by the Posterize Time effect.

Nesting Preferences

When working with nested comps, you should consider a few options you can find by choosing File > Preferences > General (Windows) or After Effects > Preferences > General (Mac).

When viewing a comp alongside a comp nested within it, you can specify whether the time in their respective panels are synchronized by selecting, "Synchronize Time of All Related Items."

When the "Switches Affect Nested Comps," is selected, switches operate *recursively*. That is, setting a switch for a composition also sets the switch for the comps nested within it. These switches include Collapse Transformations, Continuously Rasterize, and Quality. The composition's Resolution, Enable Motion Blur, and Enable Frame Blending settings also operate recursively.

In general, recursive switches can save you time and effort. Sometimes, however, recursive switches can produce undesired results. For example, recursive switches could prevent you from enabling Motion Blur selectively in a series of nested compositions. As a rule, use recursive switches. If using a switch has unintended consequences, disable recursive switches.

NESTING

Rendering Order

When After Effects renders frames for play-back or output, it calculates each attribute in a particular sequence referred to as the *rendering order*.

Having interpreted the source footage according to your specifications, After Effects processes each frame layer by layer. Starting with a composition's bottom layer, After Effects renders layer properties in the order they're listed in the layer outline: masks, effects, and transform. Then the program processes layer modes and track mattes before combining the layer with the underly-ing layers. Rendering proceeds in this fashion for successively higher layers in the stacking order until the frame is complete (**Figures 16.8, 16.9, 16.10, 16.11,** and **16.12**).

Figure 16.8 Starting with the bottom layer...

Figure 16.9 ...After Effects renders the masks first...

Figure 16.10 ...then applies effects in the order they appear in the Effect Controls panel...

Figure 16.11 ...then calculates transform properties...

Figure 16.12 ...and finally calculates track mattes and modes before combining the layer with the underlying image.

For audio layers, rendering proceeds in the same sequence: effects followed by levels. If you were to change the audio speed, time remapping would be calculated first and time stretch would be calculated last.

When compositing 3D layers, rendering order is determined by each layer's relative Z-coordinate value as well as by whether the composition contains a mix of 2D and 3D layers. See "Understanding 3D Layer Order" in Chapter 15, "3D Layers," for more information.

To identify most problems you're likely to encounter with an animation, you need to understand its render order and how to circumvent it.

RENDERING ORDER

Subverting the Render Order

If you were to strictly adhere to the render order, certain effects would be impossible to achieve. For example, you might want to use the Motion Tile effect to replicate a rotating object. However, rendering order dictates that the Motion Tile effect be rendered before the rotation, a transform property. Unfortunately, this causes the layer to rotate after tiling—*not* the effect you desire (**Figure 16.13**). To solve the problem, you must defy the rendering order so that the effects are calculated after transformations (**Figure 16.14**).

Although you can't alter the rendering order directly, you can do so indirectly. For example, you can subvert render order by using the Transform effect or an adjustment layer, or by nesting or precomposing. In some cases, you can use an expression to make continual adjustments to a property automatically, effectively defeating limitations imposed by the rendering order.

Figure 16.13 Because After Effects calculates effects before transform properties, a mosaic effect is applied to the butterfly image before it's rotated. The squares produced by the mosaic are tilted so they become diamonds—which, in this case, isn't the result we want.

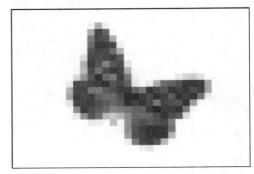

Figure 16.14 To create the desired effect, the effect must be calculated before the rotation. Note how the mosaic squares remain level, parallel to the sides of the comp.

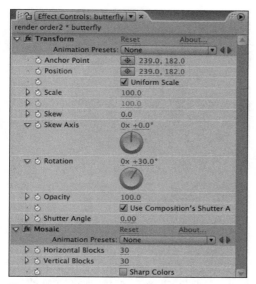

Figure 16.15 The Transform effect emulates the transform properties. To render it before other effects, you can place it higher in the list in the Effect Controls panel.

Figure 16.16 You can postpone the rendering of an effect by placing it in an adjustment layer higher in the layer stack.

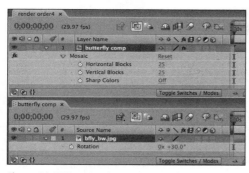

Figure 16.17 You can also use a nested composition to effectively change the render order. Before After Effects renders the nested composition (top) as a layer, it must complete the rendering sequence within the nested composition (bottom).

Transform effect

In many instances, you'll need a transform property to render before an effect property. Fortunately, all the transform properties (as well as the Skew and Shutter Angle properties) are also available in the form of an effect, the Transform effect. By placing the Transform effect higher on the list in the Effect Controls panel, you can render it before subsequent effects on the list (**Figure 16.15**).

Adjustment layer

Because the render order proceeds from the bottom of the layer stack, you can postpone rendering an effect by placing it in an adjustment layer. After Effects then calculates the properties in the lower layers before the adjustment layer affects them (**Figure 16.16**).

As you'll recall from Chapter 11, the effects contained in an adjustment layer are applied to all the underlying layers. To limit an adjustment layer's effects to just some of those lower layers, you must nest or precompose them with the adjustment layer.

Nesting or precomposing

Another way to effectively change the rendering order is to place layers in a nested composition. (*Precomposing* refers to another method of creating a nested composition—you might think of it as nesting retroactively—so it works the same way.)

As you'll recall, *nesting* describes the process of using a composition as a layer in another composition. Before After Effects can render the nested composition as a layer, however, it must complete the rendering sequence within the nested composition. In other words, the properties of the layers contained by the nested composition are calculated first. Then the nested composition is treated like the other layers, and its properties are processed according to the render order (**Figure 16.17**).

Expressions

In some cases, an expression can compensate for the unwanted effects of the rendering order. For example, an expression can link an effect property to a transform property, so that the effect adjusts dynamically to compensate for the fact that it's calculated before the transformations (**Figures 16.18** and **16.19**). (In contrast to putting the effect in an adjustment layer, this approach also lets you scale or reposition the layer and maintain the effect.)

Figure 16.18 Here, the Mirror effect is applied to a rotating layer to achieve a kind of kaleidoscopic effect. Because the effect is calculated first, the angle of reflection rotates with the layer.

Figure 16.19 Using an expression, the angle of reflection changes opposite of the layer's rotation. The angle of reflection remains vertical even as the image is rotated.

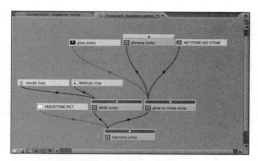

Figure 16.20 The Flowchart view displays the structure of a project or composition as a flowchart.

Figure 16.21 Click the Flowchart View button in the Composition panel to view a flowchart of the composition...

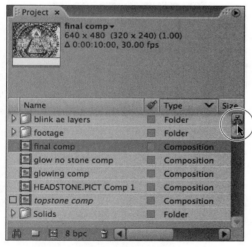

Figure 16.22 ...or click the Flowchart View button in the Project panel to view a flowchart of the entire project.

Using the Flowchart View

The Flowchart view enables you to see the structure and hierarchy of the current composition or the entire project. In the Flowchart view, you can see the relationship between project and/or composition elements in flowchart fashion (**Figure 16.20**). This view can be particularly useful for evaluating your final composition, which typically contains nested compositions. It also provides a good way to familiarize yourself with an old project or one that someone else produced.

You can customize the layout and level of detail of the flowchart. You can even open a composition directly from the Flowchart view. However, you can't use the Flowchart view to change the way your project is organized.

To display the Flowchart view:

Do one of the following:

◆ To view a flowchart for the current composition, click the Flowchart View button ![icon] in the Composition panel (**Figure 16.21**).

◆ To view a flowchart for the entire project, click the Flowchart View button in the Project panel (**Figure 16.22**).

A Flowchart window appears.

Precomposing

As you've probably figured out by now, it can take a fair amount of planning to nest compositions and create hierarchies of elements. However, you can't always anticipate the need to nest. Often, you realize that layers should be contained in a nested composition only after they're part of the current composition. Fortunately, you can repackage layers of an existing composition into a nested composition by using a method called *precomposing*.

The Pre-compose command places one or more selected layers in a nested composition (or, if you prefer, a *precomp*), thus accomplishing in a single step what could otherwise be a tedious reorganization process (**Figures 16.23** and **16.24**).

When you precompose more than one layer, the layers' properties (masks, effects, transform) and associated keyframes are retained and moved into the nested composition. When you precompose a single layer, on the other hand, you may choose whether its properties and keyframes move with it or remain in the current composition (becoming properties of the nested composition). After Effects prompts you with a dialog box that lists your choices (**Figure 16.25**):

Leave all attributes in [current composition] moves a single layer into a nested composition. The nested composition has the size and duration of the layer, and it acquires the layer's properties and keyframes.

Move all attributes into the new composition moves one or more layers into a nested composition, which has the size and duration of the current composition. All properties and keyframes are retained by the layers and move with them into the nested composition.

Open New Composition opens the newly created nested composition automatically. Leaving this option unselected creates a nested composition but leaves the current composition open.

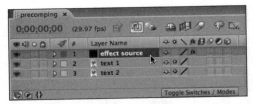

Figure 16.23 Precomposing allows you to select one or more layers...

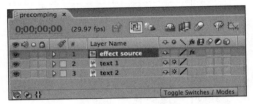

Figure 16.24 ...and place them into a nested composition.

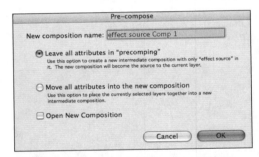

Figure 16.25 When you precompose one or more layers, After Effects prompts you with a dialog box of options.

Figure 16.26 Select one or more layers in the Timeline panel.

Figure 16.27 Choose Layer > Pre-compose.

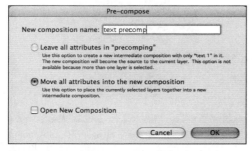

Figure 16.28 In the Pre-compose dialog box, select an option.

To precompose one or more layers:

1. Select one or more layers in the Timeline panel (**Figure 16.26**).

2. *Do either of the following*:
   ▲ Choose Layer > Pre-compose (**Figure 16.27**).
   ▲ Press Shift-Command-C (Mac) or Shift-Ctrl-C (Windows).
   A Pre-compose dialog box appears (**Figure 16.28**).

3. *Select an option*:
   ▲ Leave all attributes in [current composition]
   ▲ Move all attributes into the new composition
   If you're precomposing more than one layer, only the second option is available.

4. To have After Effects open the nested composition automatically, select Open New Composition.

5. Click OK to close the Pre-compose dialog box.
   The selected layers are moved into another composition, which is nested in the current composition (**Figure 16.29**). The nested composition is also listed in the Project panel.

Figure 16.29 The selected layers are moved into another composition, which replaces them in the current composition.

PRECOMPOSING

Collapsing Transformations

Sometimes the render order in nested compositions can cause image resolution to degrade. This happens because transform properties, such as Scale, are calculated at every tier in the project hierarchy: first in the most deeply nested composition, then in the next, and so on. At each level, the image is *rasterized*—its resolution is defined and then redefined in successive compositions.

Scaling down an image in a nested composition rasterizes the image at the smaller size and, consequently, at a lower resolution (**Figures 16.30** and **16.31**). Because the smaller image becomes the source for successive compositions, scaling it up again makes the reduced resolution more apparent (**Figure 16.32**).

This rescaling process is sometimes unavoidable, especially when a boss or client dictates revisions. In such circumstances, you can maintain image quality by *collapsing transformations.*

Figure 16.30 When an image at one resolution...

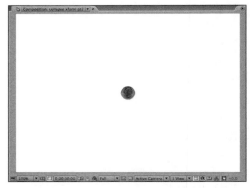

Figure 16.31 ...is scaled down, it's rasterized at the new size.

Figure 16.32 Scaling the image up again in a subsequent composition doesn't restore the original resolution.

Figure 16.33 By collapsing transformations, you can postpone rasterization until rendering reaches the nested composition in which the switch is selected.

By collapsing transformations, you prevent After Effects from rasterizing the image in every successive composition, instead forcing it to calculate all the transform property changes and rasterize the image only once—in the composition with the Collapse Transformations switch selected. This way, the composition uses the resolution of the source image rather than that of intermediate versions (**Figure 16.33**).

To collapse transformations:

1. If necessary, click the Switches/Modes button in the Timeline panel to display the Switches panel.

2. For a nested composition, select the Collapse Transformations switch ![switch icon] (**Figure 16.34**).

   The same switch is used to continuously rasterize a layer created from path-based artwork.

✔ Tips

■ When applied to a layer created from a path-based illustration (such as an Illustrator file), the Collapse Transformations switch functions as the Continuously Rasterize switch. See Chapter 2, "Importing Footage into a Project," for more information.

■ The Opacity settings for the nested compositions are retained and combine with the opacity of the layer that uses collapsed transformations.

Figure 16.34 Click the Collapse Transformations switch for a nested composition.

Prerendering

It seems that if you're not occupied with making the project better, you're preoccupied with making it render faster. A process known as *prerendering* is one strategy you can use to reduce rendering times.

Typically, you'll complete work on nested compositions long before the final composition is ready—which makes it all the more frustrating to wait for the nested comps to render (not to mention unnecessary).

With prerendering, you can render nested compositions and use the movie file as a proxy. Thereafter, render times are reduced because After Effects refers to the movie instead of calculating every element in the nested composition (**Figures 16.35** and **16.36**). If you decide you need to make changes, you can stop using the proxy and switch back to the source composition (**Figure 16.37**). Prerender the composition again to save the changes in the proxy. When exporting, the Render Queue lets you prerender a comp and set the rendered file as a proxy in a single step, using something called a *post-render action*.

To reduce render times for the final output, make sure that the Pre-render settings are compatible with the settings of your final file and that you've set the Render settings to Use Proxies.

To use prerendering, consult Chapter 17 as well as the "Proxies" section in Chapter 3, "Managing Footage."

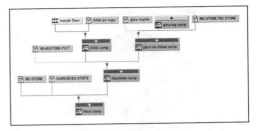

Figure 16.35 By prerendering, you avoid rendering every element of a nested composition (here, the layers contained in the nested "Topstone" comp)...

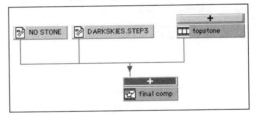

Figure 16.36 ...and replace the nested comp with a rendered version. (This flowchart illustrates the process; the actual Flowchart view continues to show the nested composition.)

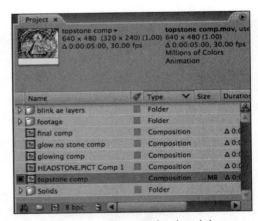

Figure 16.37 Because the prerendered movie is a proxy, you can always switch back to the nested composition.

Parenting Layers

Often, you need layers to act as a group or an integrated system. For example, you may want to connect the parts of a machine or simulate the orbits of a planetary system. You can do either of these things by estab-

lishing a relationship between one layer's transformation properties and the transformation properties of one or more other layers—a technique fittingly known as *parenting* (**Figures 16.38**).

Changing a parent layer's transformation properties (with the exception of its Opacity property) provokes a corresponding change in its related child layers. For example, if you were to change a parent layer's position, the child layers' positions would change accordingly. Although you can animate child layers independently, the transformations occur relative to the parent, not the composition. In the layer outline of the timeline, note that child layers' property values don't reflect the layer's actual appearance, which is a product of the parent's property values. For example, scaling the parent layer also scales the child layer—even though the child layer's Scale property continues to display the same value (**Figures 16.39** and **16.40**).

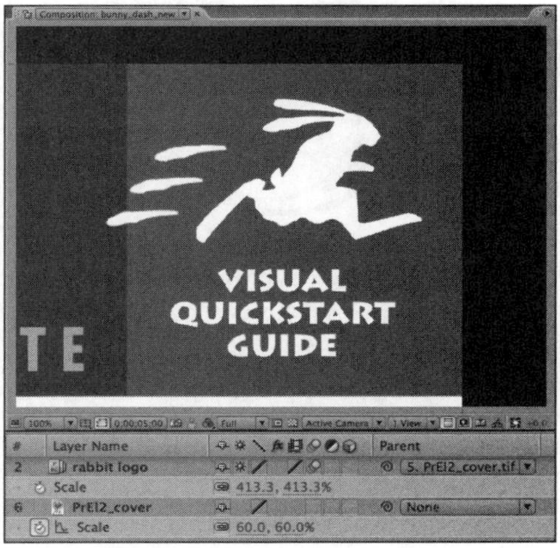

Figure 16.38 In this example, the logo and book cover are separate layers, but parenting links them so they move as one.

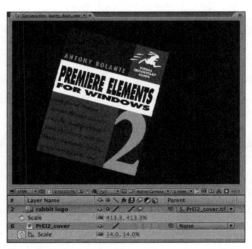

Figure 16.39 When the child layer's (the rabbit logo's) and parent layer's (the book cover's) transform properties are linked...

Figure 16.40 ...changing the parent's property value isn't reflected in the child layer's property value display.

461

It may be helpful to compare parenting to traveling in a vehicle, such as an airplane. In this analogy the plane is like the parent layer. Relative to the earth, a plane moves hundreds of miles per hour. And as a passenger on the plane, so do you. However, sitting in your cramped coach seat, you think of yourself as motionless. You're like the child layer; relative to the plane, you're not going anywhere. Just as the child layer can move relative to the parent layer, you can get up and move about the cabin and stretch your legs. But as long as you're on the plane, you'll measure movements relative to say, your seat on the plane—and not the ground far below.

Jumping

When you assign (or remove) a parent-child relationship, you can specify whether the child layer *jumps*—changes its transform properties relative to its parent layer. Ordinarily, assigning a parent-child relationship leaves the child layer's transform properties unchanged until you make subsequent alterations to either the parent or child layers (**Figure 16.41**). In contrast, when you set the child layer to jump, its transformation properties are immediately altered relative to the parent layer (**Figure 16.42**). Conversely, you can make a child layer jump when you remove the parent-child relationship, so that its transform properties immediately shift relative to the composition.

Figure 16.41 Ordinarily, assigning a parent-child relationship leaves the child layer's relative transform properties unchanged in the Comp panel, by changing its values.

Figure 16.42 In contrast, when you have the child layer jump, its transformation properties are altered relative to the parent layer immediately.

To assign a parent-child relationship:

1. If necessary, reveal the Parenting panel in the Timeline panel by choosing Panels > Parent in the Timeline pull-down menu.

2. For the child layer, *do either of the following:*

   ▲ Choose the layer you want to assign as the parent in the Parent pull-down menu (**Figure 16.43**).

   ▲ Drag the Pickwhip to the layer you want to designate as the parent (**Figure 16.44**).

   You can drag the Pickwhip anywhere in the layer's horizontal track in the layer

outline to select it. The name of the parent layer appears in the Parenting pull-down menu for the child layer.

To remove a parent from a layer:

◆ In the Parent pull-down menu for the child layer, choose None (**Figure 16.45**).

   The parent-child relationship is removed, and you can now transform the layer.

To make a child jump when assigning or removing a parent:

◆ Press Option/Alt when you select a layer name in the Parent pull-down menu, or select a layer with the Parent Pickwhip.

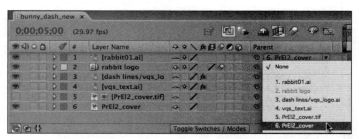

Figure 16.43 Choose the layer you want to assign as the parent in the Parent pull-down menu...

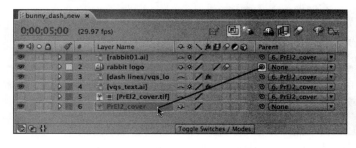

Figure 16.44 ...or drag the Pickwhip to anywhere in the parent layer's horizontal track in the Timeline panel.

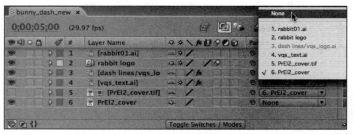

Figure 16.45 In the Parent pull-down menu for the child layer, choose None to cut the apron strings.

PARENTING LAYERS

Using Null Objects

You can add invisible layers, called *null objects,* to a composition to create sophisticated animations that don't rely on the movement of visible layers. For example, a null object can serve as a parent layer, exerting an invisible influence over several child layers. Because these layers aren't visible in previews or output, you can't apply effects to them. When selected, a null object appears in the Composition panel as a framed outline. A null object's anchor point is positioned in its upper-left corner (**Figure 16.46**). Otherwise, null objects behave like other layers.

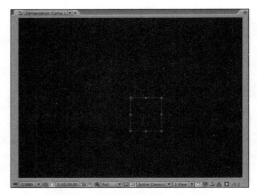

Figure 16.46 When selected, a null object appears in the Composition panel as a framed outline. A null object's anchor point is positioned in its upper-left corner.

To create a null object:

◆ Choose Layer > New > Null Object (**Figure 16.47**).

A Null Object layer appears as the top layer in the timeline, beginning at the current time and using the specified default duration for still images (**Figure 16.48**).

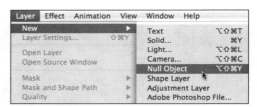

Figure 16.47 Choose Layer > New > Null Object.

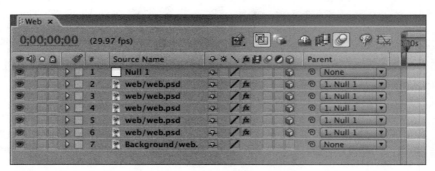

Figure 16.48 A Null Object layer appears as the top layer, beginning at the current time and using the specified default duration for still images. Here, the null layer has been assigned as the parent to other layers.

Figure 16.49 Expressions are especially useful in depicting the parts of a machine. Here, the smaller gear's rotation is linked to the larger gear's rotation via an expression.

Using Expressions

Expressions are a set of instructions that can generate and animate property values without necessarily using keyframes. Frequently, an expression generates a property's values based on another property (in the same layer, in a different layer, or even in a layer that resides in different compositions). This way, expressions allow you to create sophisticated relationships between properties that you could otherwise produce only through painstaking keyframing. Alternatively, an expression can generate values independently, via a set of instructions akin to a mathematical formula.

Expressions are especially useful for depicting the parts of a machine: wheels turning as a car moves, a small gear turning in response to a larger gear, or a meter increasing in height as a dial is turned (**Figure 16.49**). Because you can link all kinds of properties using simple or complex formulas, expressions afford endless possibilities. And because you can change the timing of the whole system by modifying a single element, you save time and effort as well.

Because expressions are based on JavaScript, experience with that language or a similar scripting language gives you a definite head start. However, even with no knowledge of JavaScript and only basic math skills, you can create useful expressions. Using the Pickwhip tool, you can generate a basic expression automatically. You can then modify your basic expression by appending a little arithmetic. When you're ready to write your own scripts, After Effects supplies the terms you need in a convenient pull-down menu.

To create an expression using the Expression Pickwhip:

1. Expand the layer outline to reveal the properties you want to link via an expression (**Figure 16.50**).

2. With the property selected, *do either of the following:*

   ▲ Choose Animation > Add Expression (**Figure 16.51**).

   ▲ Press Shift-Option-Equal sign (Mac) or Shift-Alt-Equal sign (Windows).

   An Equal Sign icon **▤** appears next to the property to indicate an expression is enabled. The property also expands to reveal buttons in the Switches panel of the timeline. Under the time ruler, the expression script appears selected (**Figure 16.52**).

3. In the Switches panel, click the Expression Pickwhip button **◎**, and drag the Pickwhip to the name of the property value to which you want to link the expression (**Figure 16.53**).

Figure 16.50 Expand the layer outline to reveal the properties you want to link using an expression.

Figure 16.51 Choose Animation › Add Expression, or press Shift-Option-Equal sign (Mac) or Shift-Alt-Equal sign (Windows).

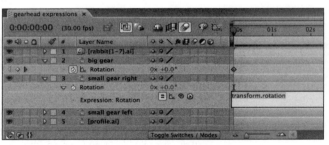

Figure 16.52 An Equal Sign icon appears next to the property, and the property expands to reveal buttons in the Switches panel. In the time ruler area, the expression script appears selected.

Figure 16.53 In the Switches panel, drag the Expression Pickwhip to the name of the property value to which you want to link the expression.

The property's name becomes highlighted when the Pickwhip touches it. When you release the mouse, the expression script is entered in the script area under the time ruler (**Figure 16.54**).

4. Modify the script by doing *either of the following* (**Figure 16.55**):

▲ Enter changes or additions to the script using standard JavaScript syntax.

▲ Use the Expressions pull-down menu to select from a list of common scripting terms.

If you make a mistake, After Effects prompts you with a warning dialog box and advises you to correct the script.

5. Keyframe the linked property (the one without the expression) using the methods you learned in Chapter 7, "Properties and Keyframes."

The property using the expression changes automatically according to the relationship defined by the expression (**Figure 16.56**).

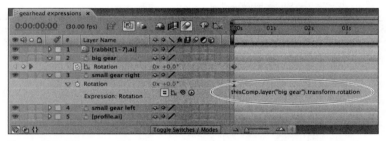

Figure 16.54 When you release the mouse, the expression script is entered in the script area under the time ruler.

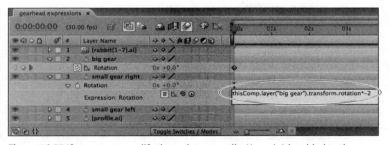

Figure 16.55 If necessary, modify the script manually. Here, *-2 is added to the script to multiply the rotation value by negative two.

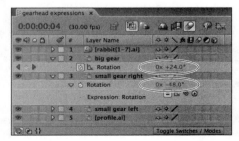

Figure 16.56 The property using the expression changes automatically, according to the relationship defined by the expression.

To disable and enable expressions:

◆ In the layer outline, click the Expression icon next to the property containing the expression to toggle it on and off.

An Equal Sign icon ▣ indicates the expression is enabled; a crossed-out equal sign ▣ indicates the expression has been temporarily disabled (**Figure 16.57**).

✔ Tips

■ Despite their similar names, JavaScript isn't related to Java.

■ After Effects includes a project template called Expression Sampler. See Chapter 2 for more about importing project templates.

Expression disabled

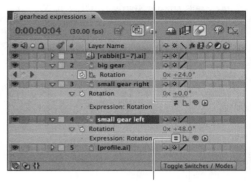

Expression enabled

Figure 16.57 An Equal Sign icon indicates that the expression is enabled; a crossed-out equal sign indicates that the expression is temporarily disabled.

Expression Errors

If you exit expression editing mode before the expression is complete, or if the expression uses incorrect syntax, an error dialog box appears containing a description of the problem (**Figure 16.58**). When you close the dialog box, a Warning icon appears in the Switches panel, and the expression is disabled automatically (**Figure 16.59**). You must correct the expression language to enable it. Click the Warning icon to reopen the warning dialog box.

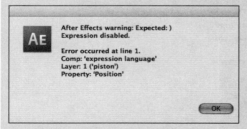

Figure 16.58 If you exit editing mode before the expression is complete or if the expression uses incorrect syntax, an error dialog box appears.

Figure 16.59 When you close the dialog box, a Warning icon appears in the Switches panel, and the expression is disabled automatically. Click the Warning icon to reopen the Warning dialog box.

Viewing Expressions

Although expressions don't create keyframes, you can still see how an expression modifies the property in a property graph.

In contrast to the Graph Editor Set button, which appears to the left of a property, the button that reveals how an expression affects a property appears to the right of the property in the Switches panel's column. Otherwise, the button looks and works just like the Graph Editor Set button. (See Chapter 9, "Keyframe Interpolation," for more about reading property graphs.) This book always refers to the icon as a Graph Editor Set button, even though a tool tip identifies the one next to an expression as the Show Post-Expression Graph button.

To view an expression graph:

1. Expand the layer outline to reveal the layer property containing the expression.

2. In the Switches panel, click the Graph Editor Set icon ![icon] (**Figure 16.60**).

3. In the Timeline panel, select the Show Graph Editor button ![icon].

   In the Graph Editor, a graph shows the property's value or speed/velocity after the expression has been applied (**Figure 16.61**).

✔ Tips

- To view expressions for all layers in the composition, select the layers and press EE.

- You can convert property values calculated by an expression into keyframed values by choosing Animation > Keyframe Assistant > Convert Expression to Keyframes.

Figure 16.60
In the Switches panel, click the Expression's Graph Editor Set icon...

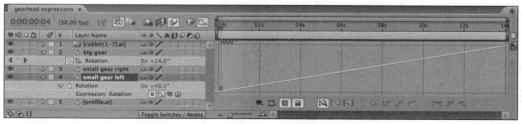

Figure 16.61 ...and then click the Timeline panel's Show Graph Editor button to view how the expression affects the property.

Using the Expression Language Menu

When you start writing your own expressions, you'll discover that the language's vocabulary is extensive. Fortunately, you can plug in most of the terms you'll need automatically by selecting them from a categorized list contained in a convenient pull-down menu.

To use the Expression pull-down menu:

1. Expand the layer outline to reveal the property you want to adjust with an expression.

2. With the property selected, *do either of the following:*

   ▲ Choose Animation > Add Expression.

   ▲ Press Shift-Option-Equal sign (Mac) or Shift-Alt-Equal sign (Windows).

   An Equal Sign icon ▤ appears next to the property, and a default expression appears under the time ruler. The default expression won't modify the property values. The property also expands to reveal buttons in the Switches panel of the timeline.

3. In the Switches panel of the timeline, click the Expressions pull-down menu.

   A categorized menu of expression-language terms appears (**Figure 16.62**).

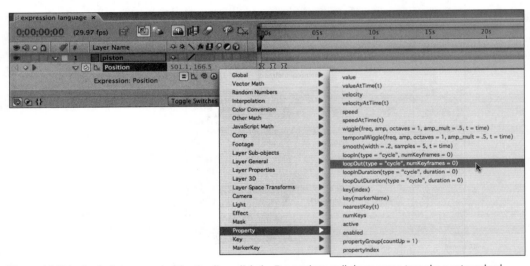

Figure 16.62 In the Switches panel of the timeline, click the Expressions pull-down menu to make a categorized menu of expression-language terms appear.

4. In the pull-down menu, select the term you need.

In the time ruler area of the timeline, the term appears in the expression text. A cursor appears at the end of the text, indicating the insertion point for additional expression terms (**Figure 16.63**).

5. If necessary, enter expression language manually (**Figure 16.64**).

6. Repeat steps 3–5 as needed.

7. Click anywhere outside the expression text field to get out of edit mode.

Figure 16.63 The term appears in the expression text. A cursor appears at the end of the text, indicating the insertion point for additional expression terms.

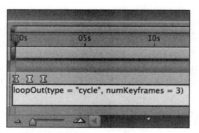

Figure 16.64 If necessary, enter expression language manually.

Writing Expressions

Once you've created a few simple expressions with the Pickwhip, you'll probably want to try writing some of your own—a process that can appear daunting if you don't have experience with JavaScript or scripting in general (especially because After Effects discourages your early attempts with warning dialog boxes about syntax errors, bad arguments, and the like).

Once you understand a few basic concepts, however, you should feel confident enough to experiment a bit. You'll also find it easier to decipher Adobe's Expressions guide (or an entire book on the subject of JavaScript) and to analyze other expressions.

Translating a simple expression

Consider the following example, which was created by dragging the Expression Pickwhip ⊚ to a Rotation property:

```
this_comp.layer("panel1").rotation
```

This simple expression links a layer's property (in this case, Rotation) to the Rotation property of a layer called panel1. A plain-English translation would read something like the following: "To set Rotation values for this property, look in this composition, find the layer called panel1, and take its Rotation value." Adjusting panel1's Rotation property results in a corresponding change in the layer containing the expression.

Typically, you would modify the expression:

```
this_comp.layer("panel1").rotation+60
```

The +60 adds 60 to the rotational value, which is measured in degrees. Setting panel1's Rotation value to 30 degrees would cause the layer containing the expression to rotate 90 degrees (30+60=90).

✔ Tips

- You may be familiar with JavaScript as it applies to Web design. Expressions are based on the same core JavaScript language but not particular JavaScript interpreters, which are browser-specific.

- Throughout this book, you've been advised to give your layers and comps descriptive names (rather than use the default names) and to refrain from changing them. The former habit helps you make clear expressions; the latter keeps your expressions from losing their links and becoming disabled.

- Although the term *property* is used in JavaScript, After Effects' Expressions reference substitutes the term *attribute* to avoid confusion with layer properties (which can be attributes in an expression).

OUTPUT

Finally.

The beginning of this book likened your project and compositions to a musical score. Now that you've written and rehearsed that score, it's time to put on the show!

In your case, that show is a comp rendered and exported to a particular format. You can export all or part of a comp to a multitude of formats—each one containing an extensive number of variable settings. The number of choices can be daunting.

But with few exceptions, the procedures to export any format are essentially the same: add the comp to the Render Queue and specify the Render Settings and one or more Output Modules.

The typical export option is a movie file, saved in a format tailored for a particular playback device or medium: videotape, DVD, Blu-Ray disc, the Web, or a mobile device (such as a video-capable phone). Some workflows require exporting a still-image sequence for transferring (usually high-resolution) images from After Effects to an editing system or even to film. On the other hand, you may need to export just a single image or audio-only file.

Your particular output goals (and, unfortunately, your equipment's limitations) will help determine a wide range of output settings; this chapter will guide you through those myriad options. You'll start by familiarizing yourself with the panel dedicated to rendering and output: the Render Queue. You'll learn the overall process to export a movie and still image frame, as well as how to tailor the render and output options to any goal. To deal with the thornier formats, you'll employ the Adobe Media Encoder, which lets you start from a list of presets designed for particular scenarios. Although this chapter can't cover every output specification, it can provide you with enough information so that you know which questions to ask to derive your own answers.

The Render Queue Panel

You control the rendering process from the Render Queue panel, listing the items you want to render and assigning their rendering settings (**Figure 17.1**). This section provides an overview of the Render Queue panel; following sections explain each feature in more detail.

Rendering progress

The top of the panel contains buttons to start, stop, or pause the render. It also displays information about rendering progress. Clicking the triangle next to Current Render Details reveals detailed information about the current render (**Figure 17.2**). This information not only indicates the remaining rendering time and disk space, but it also helps you identify the areas of the composition that render more slowly than others.

Rendering settings

The lower portion of the Render Queue panel is the "queue" portion of the panel: This is where you list items in the order you want to render them. You can assign rendering settings to each item as well as render the same item with different settings.

By default, the triangle next to each item's name is set to reveal four types of information (**Figure 17.3**).

On the left side, the settings you assign each item in the queue are grouped into two categories: Render Settings and Output Module. The first step, Render Settings, calculates each frame for output. Once the attributes of the frames have been rendered, the Output Module determines how they're saved to disk. Clicking the triangle next to each setting category reveals a summary of the setting (**Figure 17.4**). These settings are explained in detail later in this chapter.

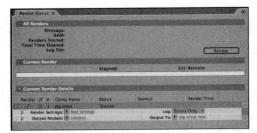

Figure 17.1 You control and monitor the rendering process from the Render Queue panel.

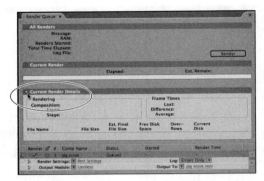

Figure 17.2 Clicking the triangle next to Current Render Details reveals detailed information about the current render.

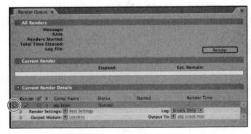

Figure 17.3 By default, the triangle next to the name of each item points down to reveal four categories of information.

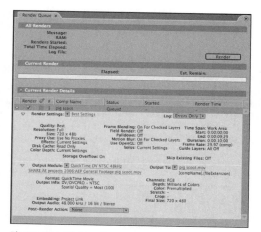

Figure 17.4 Clicking the arrow next to the Render Settings and Output Module options reveals a summary of each group of settings.

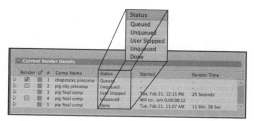

Figure 17.5 When the view of the items in the queue is collapsed, it's easier to see customizable columns of information, including the Render Status.

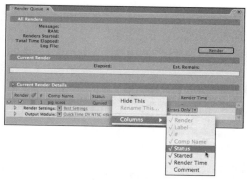

Figure 17.6 Control-click/right-click to use a context menu to customize the panel headings.

On the right side, you can specify the type of record After Effects generates in the Log pull-down menu; you can also specify a name and destination for Output To.

Panel headings and Render Status

In the Render Queue panel, clicking the triangle next to each item collapses the queue information, making several columns of information more apparent (**Figure 17.5**). Although most panel headings are self-explanatory, Render Status merits special attention because it indicates the current state of each item in the queue:

Queued indicates that the item is ready to be rendered.

Unqueued indicates that the item is listed but not ready for rendering, meaning you need to assign a name and destination to it, or you need to check the Render option.

Failed indicates that the render was unsuccessful. Check the render log generated by After Effects to determine the error.

User Stopped indicates that you stopped the rendering process.

Done indicates that the item has been rendered successfully.

After an item is rendered or stopped, it remains in the Render Queue panel until you remove it. Although you can't change the status of rendered items, you can duplicate them as other items in the queue. You can then assign new settings to the new item and render it.

✔ Tip

■ You can customize the panel headings of the Render Queue panel just as you would the Project panel headings. Control-click/right-click to invoke a context menu (**Figure 17.6**).

Making a Movie

This section explains how to add a composition to the Render Queue panel using the Make Movie command. Later sections focus on the Render Queue panel and choosing specific settings.

To make a movie from a composition:

1. Be sure to save your project.

2. Select a composition.

   Projects frequently contain several compositions; make sure you select the one you want to output.

3. Choose Composition > Make Movie, or press Command/Ctrl-M (**Figure 17.7**).

   An Output Movie To dialog box appears (**Figure 17.8**).

4. Specify a name and destination for the final movie.

   If you want to save the movie as a single file, make sure your chosen destination has sufficient storage space to contain it.

5. Click Save to close the Output Movie To dialog box.

   The composition appears as an item in the Render Queue panel (**Figure 17.9**).

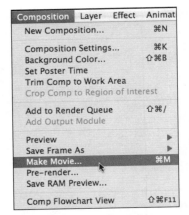

Figure 17.7 Choose Composition › Make Movie.

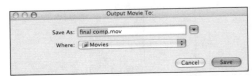

Figure 17.8 An Output Movie To dialog box appears. Specify the name and destination for the rendered composition.

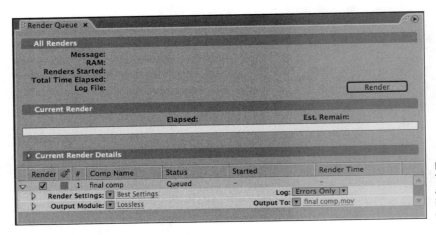

Figure 17.9 The composition appears as an item in the Render Queue panel.

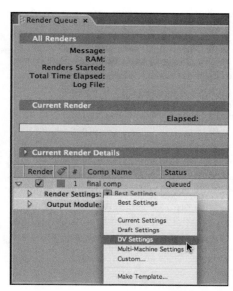

Figure 17.10 Choose a template from the Render Settings pull-down menu, or click the underlined name of the current settings to open a dialog box.

6. In the Render Queue panel, choose render settings by doing *one of the following:*
   ▲ Choose a template from the Render Settings pull-down menu (**Figure 17.10**).
   ▲ Click the name of the current render settings to open the Render Settings dialog box.

7. In the Render Queue panel, choose output options by doing *one of the following:*
   ▲ Choose a template from the Output Module pull-down menu (**Figure 17.11**).
   ▲ Click the name of the current output options to open the Output Options dialog box.

8. In the Render Queue panel, choose an option from the Log pull-down menu (**Figure 17.12**):
   ▲ Errors Only
   ▲ Plus Settings
   ▲ Plus Per Frame Info

continues on next page

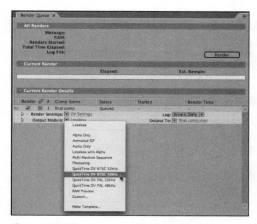

Figure 17.11 Choose a template from the Output Module pull-down menu, or click the underlined name of the current settings to open a dialog box.

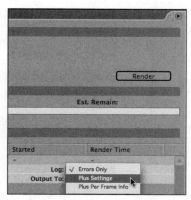

Figure 17.12 Select the type of log After Effects will generate in the Log pull-down menu.

9. Click the Render button near the top of the Render Queue panel (**Figure 17.13**).

   After Effects begins to render the composition. A progress bar and rendering-time data indicate the elapsed render time as well as the estimated time remaining in the rendering process. After Effects sounds a chime when rendering is complete.

✔ Tips

■ To reopen the Output Movie To dialog box so that you can change the name or destination of the saved movie, click the name of the movie next to Output To (**Figure 17.14**).

■ Whereas exporting to a movie file format is generally an all-or-nothing affair, exporting a still-image sequence allows you to stop rendering and resume where you left off. Better yet, you can make changes to the comp and then render the changes only (numbering them accordingly). This can spare you hours of rerendering entire movie files.

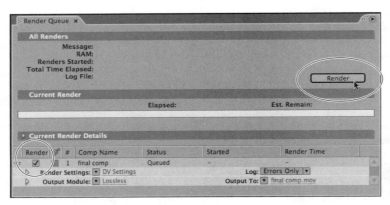

Figure 17.13 Make sure the Render column is checked for the item, and click Render.

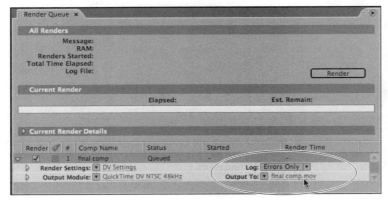

Figure 17.14 To change the name or destination of the saved movie, click the name of the movie next to Output To.

MAKING A MOVIE

Using the Render Queue Panel

Among other things, the Render Queue panel is just that: a queue, or line, of compositions waiting to be rendered.

To manage items in the render queue:

◆ In the Render Queue panel, *do any of the following:*

▲ To add a composition to the queue, drag a Composition icon from the Project panel to the Render Queue panel (**Figure 17.15**).

▲ To remove a composition from the queue, select a composition in the queue and press Delete.

▲ To change the order of the compositions in the queue, drag a composition up or down (**Figure 17.16**).

A dark horizontal line indicates where the composition's new position in the queue will be when you release the mouse.

▲ To prevent a composition in the queue from rendering, click the Render option box to deselect it (**Figure 17.17**).

The composition remains in the list, but its status changes to Unqueued; it won't render until you select the Render option box.

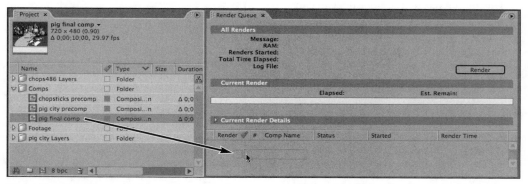

Figure 17.15 To add a composition to the queue, drag a Composition icon from the Project panel to the Render Queue panel.

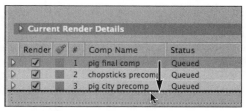

Figure 17.16 To change the order of the compositions in the queue, drag an item up or down.

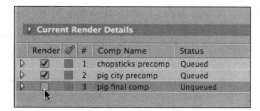

Figure 17.17 To unqueue a composition, click the Render option box to deselect it.

USING THE RENDER QUEUE PANEL

Pausing and Stopping Rendering

After you click the Render button, Pause and Stop buttons appear in its place. Pausing a render comes in handy if you need to access other programs, or if you didn't plan ahead and find you need to clear some drive space for the render. Stopping a render won't adversely affect a frame sequence—you can pick up where you left off—but it will disturb the integrity of a movie file, creating two movies instead of one.

To pause rendering:

1. After the composition has begun to render, click the Pause button in the Render Queue panel (**Figure 17.18**).

   During the pause in rendering, you can use other applications or manage files on the desktop. However, you can't do anything in After Effects (not even close a window) except restart the render.

2. To resume rendering, click Continue.

   After Effects continues to render to the same file from where it left off.

To stop rendering:

◆ After the composition has begun rendering, click the Stop button in the Render Queue panel (**Figure 17.19**).

   When rendering stops, the composition's status changes to User Stopped. A new item—with an Unqueued status—is added to the queue. If you render this item, it will render a new movie, starting with the next unrendered frame of the interrupted movie (**Figure 17.20**).

✔ Tip

■ Pausing allows you to use other programs or the desktop but not After Effects. If you want to collapse the Composition panel, do so before you start rendering.

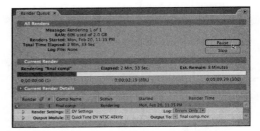

Figure 17.18 Click the Pause button in the Render Queue panel to pause rendering and use the desktop or other programs.

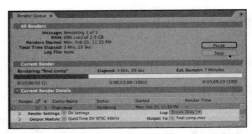

Figure 17.19 Click Stop to halt rendering completely.

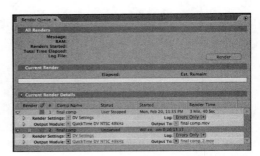

Figure 17.20 When you stop the rendering, the item's status changes to User Stopped, and a new item is added with the status Unqueued. This item will start rendering at the next unrendered frame.

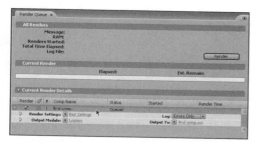

Figure 17.21 Select an item in the Render Queue panel.

Figure 17.22 Choose Composition > Add Output Module.

Assigning Multiple Output Modules

You can assign more than one output module to a single item in the queue—a capability that allows you to easily create multiple versions of the same composition.

To assign additional output modules:

1. Select an item in the Render Queue panel (**Figure 17.21**).

2. Choose Composition > Add Output Module (**Figure 17.22**).

   Another output module appears for the item in the queue (**Figure 17.23**).

3. Specify settings or a template for the output module, and render the items in the queue (as explained earlier in this chapter in the section "Making a Movie").

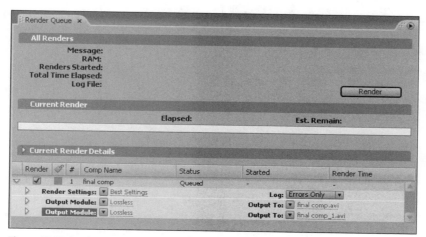

Figure 17.23 Another output module appears for the item in the queue.

Choosing Render Settings

Determining render settings is the first step in the rendering process. These settings dictate how each frame of a composition is calculated for the final output, in much the same way that composition settings calculate frames for playback in the Composition panel.

Initially, the render settings are set to match the composition's current settings. Although in some cases these settings may meet your output goals, it's best to take a more active role in choosing render settings. By selecting each render setting (or by using a template of settings), you can ensure that each layer of your composition (including those in nested compositions) uses the settings you want before it's saved to disk.

To choose render settings manually:

1. In the render queue, click the under-lined name of the render settings (**Figure 17.24**).

   A Render Settings dialog box appears (**Figure 17.25**).

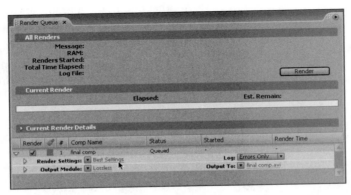

Figure 17.24 In the render queue, click the underlined name of the render settings.

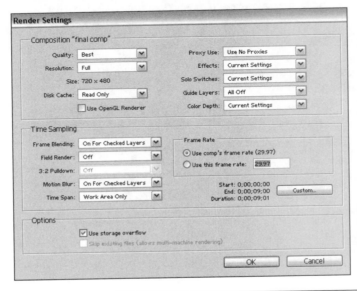

Figure 17.25 In the Render Settings dialog box, specify various settings for rendering the frames of the composition.

CHOOSING RENDER SETTINGS

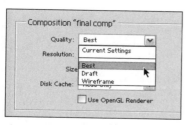

Figure 17.26 Set the Quality setting for all layers from the Quality pull-down menu.

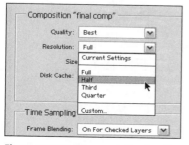

Figure 17.27 Set the resolution for all layers in the composition in the Resolution pull-down menu.

Figure 17.28 Specify an option for Disk Cache.

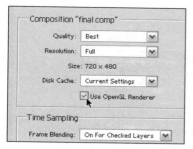

Figure 17.29 To employ OpenGL hardware, select Use OpenGL Renderer.

2. Make a selection *for each of the following options:*

Quality sets the quality for all layers (**Figure 17.26**). (See "Quality Setting Switches" in Chapter 5, "Layer Basics.")

Resolution sets the resolution for all layers in a composition. (See "Setting a Comp's Viewing Resolution" in Chapter 4, "Compositions.") Setting the resolution to Half, for example, renders every other pixel, resulting in an image with half the dimensions of the full-sized composition (**Figure 17.27**).

Disk Cache specifies whether After Effects uses the current cache settings—the ones you specified in the Memory & Cache pane of the Preferences dialog box. Setting this option to Read Only specifies that no new frames are written to the cache during rendering (**Figure 17.28**).

Use OpenGL Renderer, when selected, utilizes an OpenGL graphics card to render (see "Using OpenGL" in Chapter 8, "Playback, Previews, and RAM," for more information) (**Figure 17.29**).

Proxy Use specifies whether proxies or source footage are used for output (**Figure 17.30**). (See "Proxies" in Chapter 3, "Managing Footage.")

continues on next page

Figure 17.30 Specify whether proxies or source footage are used for output in the Proxy Use pull-down menu.

Effects specifies whether effects appear in the output. (See "Disabling Effects Temporarily" in Chapter 11, "Effects Fundamentals.") Set Effects to All On to enable all effects, including ones you had disabled temporarily; set it to Current Settings to exclude effects you disabled deliberately (**Figure 17.31**).

Solo Switches specifies whether After Effects renders only layers with their Solo switch on (see "Switching Video and Audio On and Off" in Chapter 5) or turns off all Solo switches and renders all the layers in the comp (**Figure 17.32**).

Guide Layers specifies whether After Effects renders guide layers or deactivates all guide layers (**Figure 17.33**).

Color Depth specifies color bit depth, if you're using After Effects Pro, which supports 16 bpc and 32 bpc processing (see the sidebar "Choosing the Color Bit-Depth Mode" in Chapter 2, "Importing Footage into a Project," for more information) (**Figure 17.34**).

Frame Blending specifies whether frame blending is applied to layers with the Frame Blending switch enabled (regardless of a composition's Frame Blending setting) (**Figure 17.35**). (See "Using Frame Blending" in Chapter 14, "More Layer Techniques.")

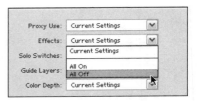

Figure 17.31 In the Effects menu, specify whether effects appear in the output.

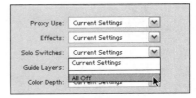

Figure 17.32 In the Solo Switches pull-down menu, specify whether to render layers with the Solo switch activated or to render layers without regard to their Solo switch.

Figure 17.33 In the Guide Layers pull-down menu, specify whether to render guide layers or to turn off guide layers.

Figure 17.34 In the Color Depth pull-down menu, specify the color depth of the exported file.

Figure 17.35 In the Frame Blending pull-down menu, specify whether frame blending is applied to layers with the Frame Blending switch enabled.

Field Render specifies whether to field-render the output movie and, if so, which field is dominant. (See the sidebar "Interpreting Interlaced Video" in Chapter 2.") Set this option to Off unless the output is destined for video (**Figure 17.36**).

3:2 Pulldown specifies whether to reintroduce pulldown to the footage and determines the phase of the pulldown. (See the sidebar "The Lowdown on Pulldown" in Chapter 2.) You need to set the proper phase only if the movie will be cut back into the original footage (**Figure 17.37**).

Motion Blur specifies whether motion blur is applied to layers with the Motion Blur switch enabled regardless of a composition's Motion Blur setting. Or, you can set this option to respect the composition's current Motion Blur setting. When you enable motion blur, it uses the settings you specified in the Composition settings (see "Using Motion Blur," in Chapter 14). Alternatively, you can select "Override shutter angle" and enter the shutter angle to be used instead. A setting of 360 degrees results in the maximum motion blur (**Figure 17.38**).

Time Span defines the part of the composition for output (**Figure 17.39**). Choosing Custom from the Time Span pull-down menu or clicking the Set button opens a Custom Time Span dialog box. (See "Previewing the Work Area" in Chapter 8, "Playback, Previews, and RAM.")

continues on next page

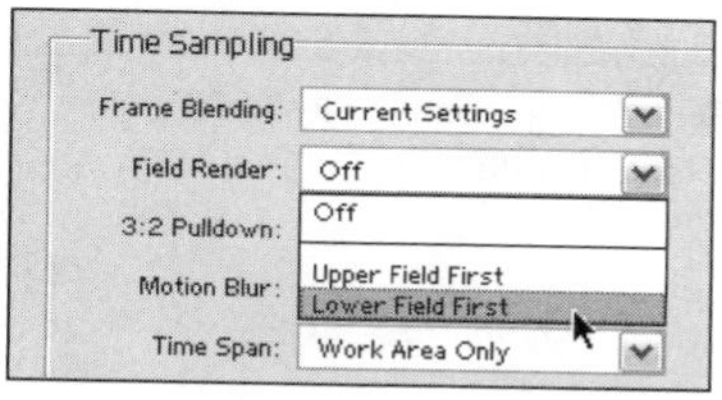

Figure 17.36 In the Field Render pull-down menu, choose whether to field-render the output.

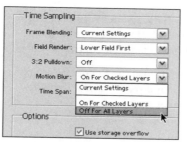

Figure 17.38 In the Motion Blur pull-down menu, specify whether motion blur is applied to layers with the Motion Blur switch enabled.

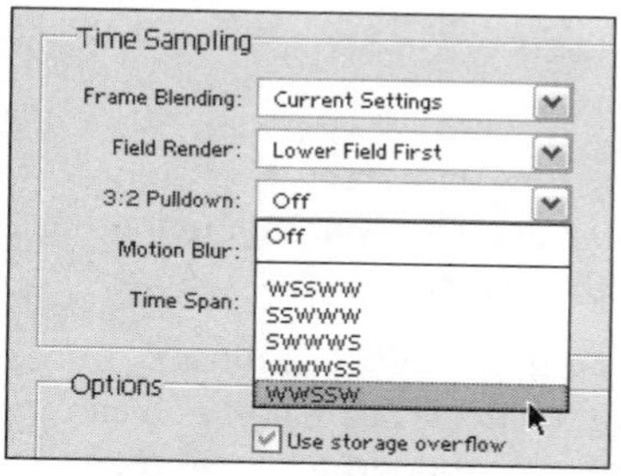

Figure 17.37 To reintroduce pulldown to the footage, choose an option from the 3:2 Pulldown menu.

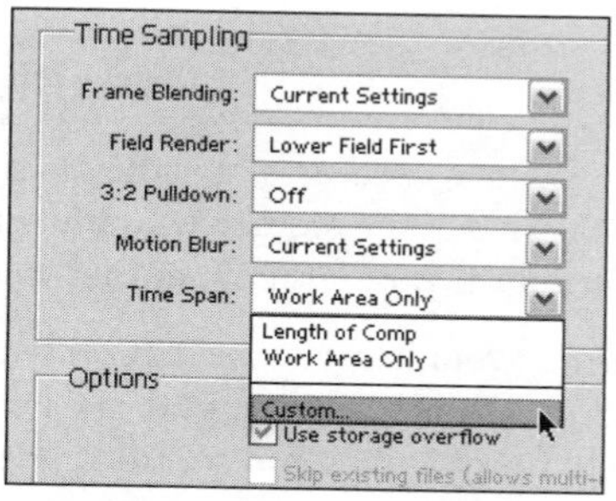

Figure 17.39 Define the part of the composition for output in the Time Span pull-down menu. Choosing Custom lets you specify a custom time span in a dialog box.

Frame Rate sets the frame rate used to render the composition. You can select the composition's frame rate or enter a custom frame rate. (See "Frame Rate," in Chapter 4.) As you'll recall from Chapter 4, the Frame Rate setting doesn't affect playback speed, just smoothness (**Figure 17.40**).

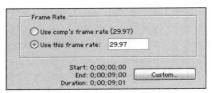

Figure 17.40 Select the frame rate of the composition, or enter a custom frame rate.

Use storage overflow determines whether rendering continues to an overflow volume when the output file exceeds the capacity of the first storage volume (**Figure 17.41**). You can set the Overflow Volumes in the Output pane of the Preferences dialog box. See the sidebar "Overflow Volumes."

Figure 17.41 Select "Use storage overflow" to ensure that rendering continues to an overflow volume when the output file exceeds the capacity of the first storage volume.

Skip existing files enables After Effects to render or rerender frames of an existing frame sequence. This option also allows multiple computers to render parts of the same image sequence to a Watch folder (**Figure 17.42**). (Consult your After Effects documentation for more about network rendering features.)

Figure 17.42 Select "Skip existing files" to enable After Effects to render or rerender frames of an existing frame sequence.

3. Click OK to close the Render Settings dialog box and return to the Render Queue panel.

Overflow Volumes

If a file or sequence exceeds either the file size limit imposed by the computer's operating system or the size of the storage volume, you can instruct After Effects to continue rendering into a folder on the root level of another volume on a hard disk, called an *overflow volume*.

To set overflow volumes, choose After Effects > Preferences > Output (Mac) or Edit > Preferences > Output (Windows). In the Output pane of the Preferences dialog box, you can specify up to five volumes and set the disk space that remains before rendering to the subsequent volume. For sequences, you can set the maximum number of files each volume contains; for movie files, you can set the maximum size before segmenting the file. Finally, you can set a movie file's audio block size and whether to use the default filename and folder.

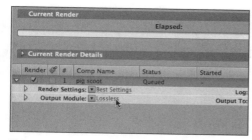

Figure 17.43 In the render queue, click the underlined name of the output module.

Choosing Output-Module Settings

Choosing output-module settings is the second step in the movie-making process. These settings determine how processed frames are saved.

To choose an output module manually:

1. In the render queue, click the underlined name of the output module (**Figure 17.43**).

   An Output Module Settings dialog box appears (**Figure 17.44**).

2. Make a selection *for each of the following options:*

   Format determines the output's file format and includes a variety of movie and still-image-sequence formats (**Figure 17.45**). Although your particular project

   continues on next page

Figure 17.44 An Output Module Settings dialog box appears.

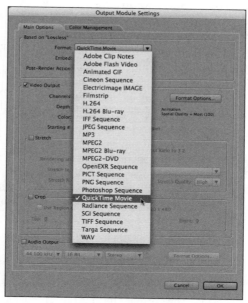

Figure 17.45 Choose the format of the saved file in the Format pull-down menu.

and/or equipment will dictate your choice, QuickTime Movie and Video For Windows are common choices for motion files, and TIFF Sequence and PICT Sequence are common choices for still-image formats.

Embed determines whether After Effects embeds a project link into the output movie. When opening the output file in a program that supports project links—such as Adobe Premiere Pro—you can use the Edit Original command to reopen the source project and make any necessary changes to it. Select Project Link from the pull-down menu to create a link between the output file and the source project. Select Project Link and Copy to embed both a link to the original project and a copy of the project into the output file. If the original project isn't available when you use the Edit Original command, After Effects allows you to open the embedded copy of the project (**Figure 17.46**).

Post-Render Action specifies whether After Effects utilizes the rendered movie in the project. You can instruct After Effects to import the movie, replace the source composition (including its nested instances) with the movie, or use the movie as a proxy in place of its source (**Figure 17.47**). This way, you can replace complex, processing-intensive elements with a single, easy-to-render footage item—thereby reducing render times. Using a post-render action is part of a strategy called *prerendering*; see "Prerendering" in Chapter 16, "Complex Projects."

Format Options opens a dialog box that includes options associated with particular formats (**Figure 17.48**). For example, if you choose QuickTime Movie as the format, the Format Options button opens a Compression Settings dialog box for QuickTime movies.

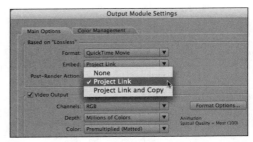

Figure 17.46 Embed determines whether After Effects embeds a project link into the output movie.

Figure 17.47 In the Post-Render Action pull-down menu, choose whether you want to use the rendered movie in the project. You can import the rendered movie, use it in place of its source footage, or set it as a proxy for its source footage.

Figure 17.48 Click Format Options to open a dialog box containing format-specific settings.

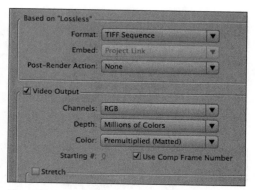

Figure 17.49 When you're exporting a still image sequence, specify the starting number, or select Use Comp Frame Number.

Figure 17.50 Specify the channels present in the output in the Channels pull-down menu.

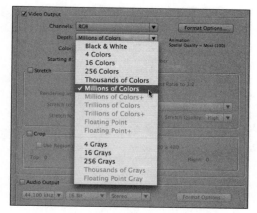

Figure 17.51 The options available in the Depth menu depend on the format and channels you selected.

Starting # lets you specify the starting frame number in the filenames when you're exporting an image sequence. Alternatively, you can select Use Comp Frame Number to match exported frame numbers to the frame numbering in the comp (the option is checked by default) (**Figure 17.49**).

Channels specifies the channels present in the output (**Figure 17.50**). Depending on the format, you can choose to export the RGB channels, the alpha channel, or RGB + Alpha.

Depth specifies the color depth of the output. The available options depend on the format and channels you selected (**Figure 17.51**).

Color specifies how color channels factor in the alpha channel (if one is present), determining whether the output uses a straight alpha or is premultiplied with black (**Figure 17.52**).

Stretch lets you specify the frame size of your output. By selecting this option, you can choose common frame sizes from a pull-down menu or enter custom dimensions.

continues on next page

Figure 17.52 If you chose to output an alpha channel, use the Color pull-down menu to choose between straight alpha or premultiplied with black.

You may also choose between a low- and high-quality resizing method in the Stretch Quality pull-down menu. Stretch resizes the image after it's been rendered (**Figure 17.53**).

Crop lets you add pixels to or, more likely, remove pixels from the edges of the image frame (**Figure 17.54**). Cropping is useful for removing black edges from video footage.

Audio Output specifies the audio-track attributes (if any) of your output. Settings include sample rate, bit depth, and format (mono or stereo). Note that the Format Options button remains grayed out and doesn't permit you to apply audio compression (**Figure 17.55**). To compress the audio, you can use an option available under the Export command, or you can compress the final movie using a program such as QuickTime Pro or Media Cleaner Pro.

Color Management contains options that can modify color values of the comp's images according to the presentation medium's color space (**Figure 17.56**). Color management options are available only when you enable Color Management in the Project Settings dialog box. For more about color management, see the After Effects Help system.

3. Click OK to close the Output Module dialog box and return to the Render Queue panel.

Figure 17.53 Select Stretch options to resize the image after it's been rendered. Several common options are available in a Preset pull-down menu.

Figure 17.54 Select Crop options to add pixels to or remove pixels from the edges of the frame.

Figure 17.55 Specify the sample rate, the bit depth, and whether the audio track is stereo or mono.

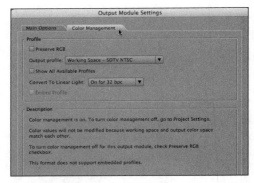

Figure 17.56 If you enabled Color Management in the Project Settings, the Color Management tab contains options for modifying the color values on export.

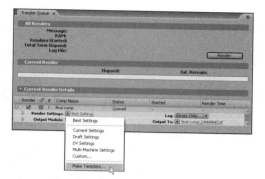

Figure 17.57 Choose Make Template in the Render Settings pull-down menu.

Figure 17.58 In the Render Settings Template dialog box, click Edit to specify settings for the untitled template.

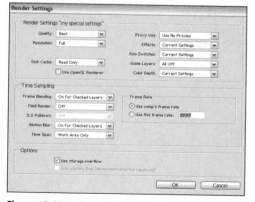

Figure 17.59 In the Render Settings dialog box, choose the options you want to save as a template, and click OK to return to the Render Settings Templates dialog box.

Creating Templates

You should save your most commonly used settings as templates so that you can apply them by selecting templates in the Render Settings and Output Module pull-down menus in the Render Queue panel. You can also make your most useful render settings and output-module templates your default settings. You can even save templates as stand-alone files that you can then move to other systems or share with other users.

To create a template:

1. *Do one of the following:*

   ▲ To create a render settings template, choose Make Template in the Render Settings pull-down menu (**Figure 17.57**).

   ▲ To create an output-module template, choose Make Template in the Output Module pull-down menu.

   Depending on your choice, a Render Settings Templates or Output Module Templates dialog box appears. An untitled template appears in the Settings Name field.

2. Click Edit in the Render Settings Templates or Output Module Templates dialog box (**Figure 17.58**).

   Depending on the type of template you're creating, the Render Settings dialog box or the Output Module dialog box appears (**Figure 17.59**).

   continues on next page

3. Choose the render-settings or output-module options you want to save as a template.

4. When you've finished selecting settings, click OK to close the Render Settings or Output Module dialog box and return to the Render Settings Templates or Output Module Templates dialog box.

5. In the Render Settings Templates or Output Module Templates dialog box, enter a settings name for the new template (**Figure 17.60**).

6. Click OK to close the dialog box and save the template.

From now on, the template will appear in the appropriate pull-down menu in the Render Queue panel (**Figure 17.61**).

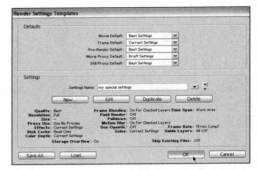

Figure 17.60 In the Render Settings Templates dialog box, enter a name for the new template, and click OK to close the dialog box.

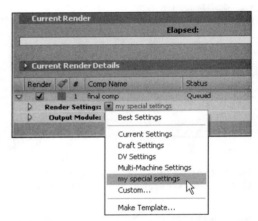

Figure 17.61 From now on, the template will appear in the Render Settings Templates pull-down menu in the Render Queue panel.

CREATING TEMPLATES

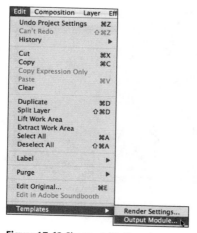

Figure 17.62 Choose Edit > Templates.

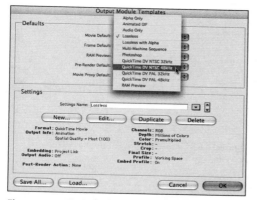

Figure 17.63 In the Render Settings Templates or Output Module Templates (shown here) dialog box, specify a template in each output type's pull-down menu. Here, a template is assigned as the new Movie Default.

To set a default template:

1. *Do one of the following*:
   ▲ To set the default render settings template, choose Edit > Templates > Render Settings
   ▲ To set the default output module template, choose Edit > Templates > Output Module (**Figure 17.62**).

   Depending on your choice, the Output Module Templates dialog box or the Render Settings Templates dialog box appears.

2. In the Defaults area of the dialog box, specify a template for each output type in the corresponding pull-down menu.

   For example, choose the template you want to be the default settings for rendering or exporting movies in the Movie Default pull-down menu (**Figure 17.63**).

3. Repeat step 2 to set templates for other defaults.

   Pre-Render and Movie Proxy defaults affect movies created using post-render actions, explained in "Choosing Output-Module Settings," earlier in this chapter.

4. Click OK to close the dialog box.

   The selected templates become the default templates for the corresponding output types.

CREATING TEMPLATES

493

Saving Single Frames of a Composition

Frequently, you'll want to render a single frame of a composition. For example, when an animation halts its motion, substituting a single still image for multiple static layers can lighten the rendering load. Or you may need a still for a storyboard or client review. After Effects lets you save a single frame using the default frame settings or as a layered Photoshop file.

Figure 17.64 Set the current time of the composition to the frame you want to export.

To save a composition frame as a still-image file:

1. Set the current time of the composition to the frame you want to export (**Figure 17.64**).

2. Choose Composition > Save Frame As > File (**Figure 17.65**).

   The composition appears selected in the Render Queue panel (**Figure 17.66**).

3. To change the destination of the saved image, click the name of the file next to Output To.

   An Output Frame To dialog box opens.

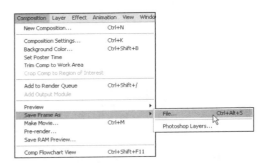

Figure 17.65 Choose Composition › Save Frame As › File.

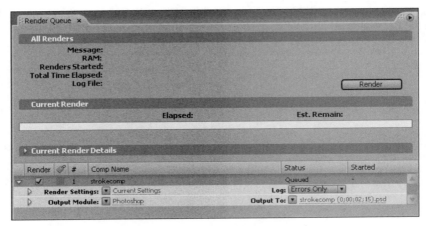

Figure 17.66 The item appears selected in the Render Queue panel.

4. Specify the destination and name of the saved frame (**Figure 17.67**).

5. Click Save to close the Output Frame To dialog box.

6. To change the default settings for frames, select render settings and output module settings, or choose templates.

7. In the Render Queue panel, click Render.

✔ Tips

■ If you want to use the still frame in the project, be sure to specify a post-render action in the Output Module Settings dialog box. See "Choosing Output-Module Settings," earlier in this chapter, and "Prerendering" in Chapter 16.

■ You can export the current frame as a layered Photoshop file in a similar manner by choosing Composition > Save Frame As > Photoshop Layers.

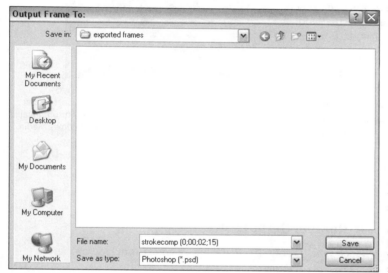

Figure 17.67 To change the destination of the saved file, click its name next to Output To; in the Output Frame To dialog box, specify the destination and name of the saved frame.

Clip Notes

Exporting to the Clip Notes format isn't essentially different than exporting to any other movie format—but what you can do with a Clip Notes file is unique.

Exporting to Clip Notes creates a draft-quality movie that is embedded into (or linked to) a PDF file (Adobe's Portable Document Format). Using the free Adobe Reader software, colleagues can enter comments into the PDF that are linked to specific points in the movie. When imported into the originating project, reviewers' comments appear as markers at corresponding points in the comp's timeline. Just double-click the markers to see the comments and make adjustments accordingly. The Clip Notes feature (also found in Premiere Pro) facilitates a collaborative process—though coming to an agreement is still up to you.

Using the Adobe Media Encoder

Several movie formats—particularly those designed for encoding video to DVD or Web delivery—include numerous settings that merit a specialized export dialog box, generally referred to as the *Adobe Media Encoder*.

Strictly speaking, *Adobe Media Encoder* refers to the output mechanism, not the name of the dialog box. In After Effects, choosing certain formats in the Output Module Settings invokes the appropriate variation of the Adobe Media Encoder, which bears the name of the specified format and contains options particular to that format.

But despite differences in the particular options, the overall appearance of the dialog box is consistent. General settings appear in the upper part of the dialog box; the lower part of the dialog box consists of tabbed panels that organize settings by category (**Figure 17.68**).

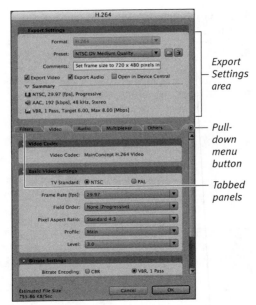

Export Settings area

Pull-down menu button

Tabbed panels

Figure 17.68 Choosing MPEG2, MPEG2-DVD, RealMedia, or Windows Media as the export format invokes a specialized export dialog box automatically. This figure shows the dialog box for Windows Media.

Notable Output Formats

In addition to the standard Video for Windows (.avi) and QuickTime (.mov) file formats, other common Output formats include the following:

Adobe Flash (SWF) and Flash Video (FLV)—formats chiefly intended for delivering media over the Web using Flash Player (or compatible player software). Flash Player is available as free stand-alone software but is even more widespread as a Web browser plug-in.

MPEG-2—variations on this format are commonly used to encode video for burning to DVD media or the newer Blu-Ray disc format. Note that MPEG-2 formats are supported on Windows and Intel-based Macs only (not PowerPC-based Macs).

H.264—is a relatively new and versatile standard capable of encoding video for a wide range of applications—from highly compressed video for playback on mobile devices to HD video on Blu-Ray disc. H.264 is also known as MPEG-4 Part 10, and AVC (Advanced Video Coding).

Windows Media—Microsoft's standard for low-data rate applications, particularly downloading and streaming audio and video over the Web.

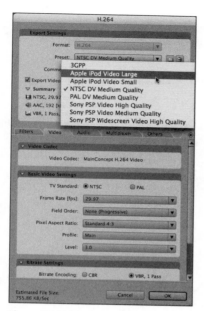

Figure 17.69 A Preset pull-down menu automatically optimizes extensive settings for a particular goal.

Settings for these formats are extensive and can require an in-depth understanding of file compression. Fortunately, you can select from a list of presets designed for particular delivery media (**Figure 17.69**). (You can also save custom presets or delete ones you don't need.) For a detailed explanation of each setting, consult the After Effects User Guide/Help and the documentation provided by the format's developer.

✔ Tips

- When you export to a format designed for playback on mobile devices, you can test for compatibility using Adobe Device Central, which is part of the Adobe Production Premium.

- Premiere Pro and Encore also employ the Adobe Media Encoder, although the corresponding dialog boxes differ in appearance and in the way you access them.

USING THE ADOBE MEDIA ENCODER

INDEX

INDEX

UNITED STATES BANKRUPTCY CODE
TITLE 11
UNITED STATES CODE
2018 Edition

Updated through January 1, 2018

Michigan Legal Publishing Ltd.
QUICK DESK REFERENCE SERIES™

Academic and bulk discounts available at
www.michlp.com

WE WELCOME YOUR FEEDBACK: info@michlp.com

ISBN-13: 978-1-64002-025-2
ISBN-10: 1-64002-025-X

TABLE OF CONTENTS

PLEASE NOTE: Relevant dollar amounts have been adjusted for inflation according to the figures published by the Judicial Conference of the United States pursuant to 11 USC 104(a). The adjusted figures in this publication are effective from April 1, 2016 to March 31, 2019.

TITLE 11— BANKRUPTCY

CHAPTER 1—GENERAL PROVISIONS

§101. Definitions

In this title the following definitions shall apply:

(1) The term "accountant" means accountant authorized under applicable law to practice public accounting, and includes professional accounting association, corporation, or partnership, if so authorized.

(2) The term "affiliate" means—

   (A) entity that directly or indirectly owns, controls, or holds with power to vote, 20 percent or more of the outstanding voting securities of the debtor, other than an entity that holds such securities—

      (i) in a fiduciary or agency capacity without sole discretionary power to vote such securities; or

      (ii) solely to secure a debt, if such entity has not in fact exercised such power to vote;

   (B) corporation 20 percent or more of whose outstanding voting securities are directly or indirectly owned, controlled, or held with power to vote, by the debtor, or by an entity that directly or indirectly owns, controls, or holds with power to vote, 20 percent or more of the outstanding voting securities of the debtor, other than an entity that holds such securities—

      (i) in a fiduciary or agency capacity without sole discretionary power to vote such securities; or

      (ii) solely to secure a debt, if such entity has not in fact exercised such power to vote;

   (C) person whose business is operated under a lease or operating agreement by a debtor, or person substantially all of whose property is operated under an operating agreement with the debtor; or

   (D) entity that operates the business or substantially all of the property of the debtor under a lease or operating agreement.

(3) The term "assisted person" means any person whose debts consist primarily of consumer debts and the value of whose nonexempt property is less than $192,450.

(4) The term "attorney" means attorney, professional law association, corporation, or partnership, authorized under applicable law to practice law.

(4A) The term "bankruptcy assistance" means any goods or services sold or otherwise provided to an assisted person with the express or implied purpose of providing information, advice, counsel, document preparation, or filing, or attendance at a creditors' meeting or appearing in a case or proceeding on behalf of another or providing legal representation with respect to a case or proceeding under this title.

(5) The term "claim" means—

   (A) right to payment, whether or not such right is reduced to judgment, liquidated, unliquidated, fixed, contingent, matured, unmatured, disputed, undisputed, legal, equitable, secured, or unsecured; or

   (B) right to an equitable remedy for breach of performance if such breach gives rise to a right to payment, whether or not such right to an equitable remedy is reduced to judgment, fixed, contingent, matured, unmatured, disputed, undisputed, secured, or unsecured.

(6) The term "commodity broker" means futures commission merchant, foreign futures commission merchant, clearing organization, leverage transaction merchant, or commodity options dealer, as defined in section 761 of this title, with respect to which there is a customer, as defined in section 761 of this title.

(7) The term "community claim" means claim that arose before the commencement of the case concerning the debtor for which property of the kind specified in section 541(a)(2) of this title is liable, whether or not there is any such property at the time of the commencement of the case.

(7A) The term "commercial fishing operation" means—

   (A) the catching or harvesting of fish, shrimp, lobsters, urchins, seaweed, shellfish, or other aquatic species or products of such species; or

   (B) for purposes of section 109 and chapter 12, aquaculture activities consisting of raising for market any species or product described in subparagraph (A).

(7B) The term "commercial fishing vessel" means a vessel used by a family fisherman to carry out a commercial fishing operation.

(8) The term "consumer debt" means debt incurred by an individual primarily for a personal, family, or household purpose.

(9) The term "corporation"—

   (A) includes—

(i) association having a power or privilege that a private corporation, but not an individual or a partnership, possesses;

(ii) partnership association organized under a law that makes only the capital subscribed responsible for the debts of such association;

(iii) joint-stock company;

(iv) unincorporated company or association; or

(v) business trust; but

(B) does not include limited partnership.

(10) The term "creditor" means—

(A) entity that has a claim against the debtor that arose at the time of or before the order for relief concerning the debtor;

(B) entity that has a claim against the estate of a kind specified in section 348(d), 502(f), 502(g), 502(h) or 502(i) of this title; or

(C) entity that has a community claim.

(10A) The term "current monthly income"—

(A) means the average monthly income from all sources that the debtor receives (or in a joint case the debtor and the debtor's spouse receive) without regard to whether such income is taxable income, derived during the 6-month period ending on—

(i) the last day of the calendar month immediately preceding the date of the commencement of the case if the debtor files the schedule of current income required by section 521(a)(1)(B)(ii); or

(ii) the date on which current income is determined by the court for purposes of this title if the debtor does not file the schedule of current income required by section 521(a)(1)(B)(ii); and

(B) includes any amount paid by any entity other than the debtor (or in a joint case the debtor and the debtor's spouse), on a regular basis for the household expenses of the debtor or the debtor's dependents (and in a joint case the debtor's spouse if not otherwise a dependent), but excludes benefits received under the Social Security Act, payments to victims of war crimes or crimes against humanity on account of their status as victims of such crimes, and payments to victims of international terrorism (as defined in section 2331 of title 18) or domestic terrorism (as defined in section 2331 of title 18) on account of their status as victims of such terrorism.

(11) The term "custodian" means—

(A) receiver or trustee of any of the property of the debtor, appointed in a case or proceeding not under this title;

(B) assignee under a general assignment for the benefit of the debtor's creditors; or

(C) trustee, receiver, or agent under applicable law, or under a contract, that is appointed or authorized to take charge of property of the debtor for the purpose of enforcing a lien against such property, or for the purpose of general administration of such property for the benefit of the debtor's creditors.

(12) The term "debt" means liability on a claim.

(12A) The term "debt relief agency" means any person who provides any bankruptcy assistance to an assisted person in return for the payment of money or other valuable consideration, or who is a bankruptcy petition preparer under section 110, but does not include—

(A) any person who is an officer, director, employee, or agent of a person who provides such assistance or of the bankruptcy petition preparer;

(B) a nonprofit organization that is exempt from taxation under section 501(c)(3) of the Internal Revenue Code of 1986;

(C) a creditor of such assisted person, to the extent that the creditor is assisting such assisted person to restructure any debt owed by such assisted person to the creditor;

(D) a depository institution (as defined in section 3 of the Federal Deposit Insurance Act) or any Federal credit union or State credit union (as those terms are defined in section 101 of the Federal Credit Union Act), or any affiliate or subsidiary of such depository institution or credit union; or

(E) an author, publisher, distributor, or seller of works subject to copyright protection under title 17, when acting in such capacity.

(13) The term "debtor" means person or municipality concerning which a case under this title has been commenced.

(13A) The term "debtor's principal residence"—

(A) means a residential structure if used as the principal residence by the debtor, including incidental property, without regard to whether that structure is attached to real property; and

(B) includes an individual condominium or cooperative unit, a mobile or manufactured home, or trailer if used as the principal residence by the debtor.

(14) The term "disinterested person" means a person that—

(A) is not a creditor, an equity security holder, or an insider;

(B) is not and was not, within 2 years before the date of the filing of the petition, a director, officer, or employee of the debtor; and

(C) does not have an interest materially adverse to the interest of the estate or of any class of creditors or equity security holders, by reason of any direct or indirect relationship to, connection with, or interest in, the debtor, or for any other reason.

(14A) The term "domestic support obligation" means a debt that accrues before, on, or after the date of the order for relief in a case under this title, including interest that accrues on that debt as provided under applicable nonbankruptcy law notwithstanding any other provision of this title, that is—

  (A) owed to or recoverable by—

    (i) a spouse, former spouse, or child of the debtor or such child's parent, legal guardian, or responsible relative; or

    (ii) a governmental unit;

  (B) in the nature of alimony, maintenance, or support (including assistance provided by a governmental unit) of such spouse, former spouse, or child of the debtor or such child's parent, without regard to whether such debt is expressly so designated;

  (C) established or subject to establishment before, on, or after the date of the order for relief in a case under this title, by reason of applicable provisions of—

    (i) a separation agreement, divorce decree, or property settlement agreement;

    (ii) an order of a court of record; or

    (iii) a determination made in accordance with applicable nonbankruptcy law by a governmental unit; and

  (D) not assigned to a nongovernmental entity, unless that obligation is assigned voluntarily by the spouse, former spouse, child of the debtor, or such child's parent, legal guardian, or responsible relative for the purpose of collecting the debt.

(15) The term "entity" includes person, estate, trust, governmental unit, and United States trustee.

(16) The term "equity security" means—

  (A) share in a corporation, whether or not transferable or denominated "stock", or similar security;

  (B) interest of a limited partner in a limited partnership; or

  (C) warrant or right, other than a right to convert, to purchase, sell, or subscribe to a share, security, or interest of a kind specified in subparagraph (A) or (B) of this paragraph.

(17) The term "equity security holder" means holder of an equity security of the debtor.

(18) The term "family farmer" means—

  (A) individual or individual and spouse engaged in a farming operation whose aggregate debts do not exceed $4,153,150 and not less than 50 percent of whose aggregate noncontingent, liquidated debts (excluding a debt for the principal residence of such individual or such individual and spouse unless such debt arises out of a farming operation), on the date the case is filed, arise out of a farming operation owned or operated by such individual or such individual and spouse, and such individual or such individual and spouse receive from such farming operation more than 50 percent of such individual's or such individual and spouse's gross income for—

    (i) the taxable year preceding; or

    (ii) each of the 2d and 3d taxable years preceding;

the taxable year in which the case concerning such individual or such individual and spouse was filed; or

  (B) corporation or partnership in which more than 50 percent of the outstanding stock or equity is held by one family, or by one family and the relatives of the members of such family, and such family or such relatives conduct the farming operation, and

    (i) more than 80 percent of the value of its assets consists of assets related to the farming operation;

    (ii) its aggregate debts do not exceed $4,153,150 and not less than 50 percent of its aggregate noncontingent, liquidated debts (excluding a debt for one dwelling which is owned by such corporation or partnership and which a shareholder or partner maintains as a principal residence, unless such debt arises out of a farming operation), on the date the case is filed, arise out of the farming operation owned or operated by such corporation or such partnership; and

    (iii) if such corporation issues stock, such stock is not publicly traded.

(19) The term "family farmer with regular annual income" means family farmer whose annual income is sufficiently stable and regular to enable such family farmer to make payments under a plan under chapter 12 of this title.

(19A) The term "family fisherman" means—

  (A) an individual or individual and spouse engaged in a commercial fishing operation—

    (i) whose aggregate debts do not exceed $1,924,550 and not less than 80 percent of whose aggregate noncontingent, liquidated debts (excluding a debt for the principal residence of such individual or such individual and spouse, unless such debt arises out of a commercial fishing operation), on the date the case is filed, arise out of a commercial fishing operation owned or operated by such individual or such individual and spouse; and

(ii) who receive from such commercial fishing operation more than 50 percent of such individual's or such individual's and spouse's gross income for the taxable year preceding the taxable year in which the case concerning such individual or such individual and spouse was filed; or

(B) a corporation or partnership—

(i) in which more than 50 percent of the outstanding stock or equity is held by—

(I) 1 family that conducts the commercial fishing operation; or

(II) 1 family and the relatives of the members of such family, and such family or such relatives conduct the commercial fishing operation; and

(ii)

(I) more than 80 percent of the value of its assets consists of assets related to the commercial fishing operation;

(II) its aggregate debts do not exceed $1,924,550 and not less than 80 percent of its aggregate noncontingent, liquidated debts (excluding a debt for 1 dwelling which is owned by such corporation or partnership and which a shareholder or partner maintains as a principal residence, unless such debt arises out of a commercial fishing operation), on the date the case is filed, arise out of a commercial fishing operation owned or operated by such corporation or such partnership; and

(III) if such corporation issues stock, such stock is not publicly traded.

(19B) The term "family fisherman with regular annual income" means a family fisherman whose annual income is sufficiently stable and regular to enable such family fisherman to make payments under a plan under chapter 12 of this title.

(20) The term "farmer" means (except when such term appears in the term "family farmer") person that received more than 80 percent of such person's gross income during the taxable year of such person immediately preceding the taxable year of such person during which the case under this title concerning such person was commenced from a farming operation owned or operated by such person.

(21) The term "farming operation" includes farming, tillage of the soil, dairy farming, ranching, production or raising of crops, poultry, or livestock, and production of poultry or livestock products in an unmanufactured state.

(21A) The term "farmout agreement" means a written agreement in which—

(A) the owner of a right to drill, produce, or operate liquid or gaseous hydrocarbons on property agrees or has agreed to transfer or assign all or a part of such right to another entity; and

(B) such other entity (either directly or through its agents or its assigns), as consideration, agrees to perform drilling, reworking, recompleting, testing, or similar or related operations, to develop or produce liquid or gaseous hydrocarbons on the property.

(21B) The term "Federal depository institutions regulatory agency" means—

(A) with respect to an insured depository institution (as defined in section 3(c)(2) of the Federal Deposit Insurance Act) for which no conservator or receiver has been appointed, the appropriate Federal banking agency (as defined in section 3(q) of such Act);

(B) with respect to an insured credit union (including an insured credit union for which the National Credit Union Administration has been appointed conservator or liquidating agent), the National Credit Union Administration;

(C) with respect to any insured depository institution for which the Resolution Trust Corporation has been appointed conservator or receiver, the Resolution Trust Corporation; and

(D) with respect to any insured depository institution for which the Federal Deposit Insurance Corporation has been appointed conservator or receiver, the Federal Deposit Insurance Corporation.

(22) The term "financial institution" means—

(A) a Federal reserve bank, or an entity that is a commercial or savings bank, industrial savings bank, savings and loan association, trust company, federally-insured credit union, or receiver, liquidating agent, or conservator for such entity and, when any such Federal reserve bank, receiver, liquidating agent, conservator or entity is acting as agent or custodian for a customer (whether or not a "customer", as defined in section 741) in connection with a securities contract (as defined in section 741) such customer; or

(B) in connection with a securities contract (as defined in section 741) an investment company registered under the Investment Company Act of 1940.

(22A) The term "financial participant" means—

(A) an entity that, at the time it enters into a securities contract, commodity contract, swap agreement, repurchase agreement, or forward contract, or at the time of the date of the filing of the petition, has one or more agreements or transactions described in paragraph (1), (2), (3), (4), (5), or (6) of section 561(a) with the debtor or any other entity (other than an affiliate) of a total gross dollar value of not less than $1,000,000,000 in notional or actual principal amount outstanding (aggregated across counterparties) at such time or on any day during the 15-month period preceding the date of the filing of the petition, or has gross mark-to-market positions of not less than $100,000,000 (aggregated across counterparties) in one or more such agreements or transactions with the debtor or any other entity (other than an affiliate) at such time or on any day during the 15-month period preceding the date of the filing of the petition; or

(B) a clearing organization (as defined in section 402 of the Federal Deposit Insurance Corporation Improvement Act of 1991).

(23) The term "foreign proceeding" means a collective judicial or administrative proceeding in a foreign country, including an interim proceeding, under a law relating to insolvency or adjustment of debt in which proceeding the assets and affairs of the debtor are subject to control or supervision by a foreign court, for the purpose of reorganization or liquidation.

(24) The term "foreign representative" means a person or body, including a person or body appointed on an interim basis, authorized in a foreign proceeding to administer the reorganization or the liquidation of the debtor's assets or affairs or to act as a representative of such foreign proceeding.

(25) The term "forward contract" means—

(A) a contract (other than a commodity contract, as defined in section 761) for the purchase, sale, or transfer of a commodity, as defined in section 761(8) of this title, or any similar good, article, service, right, or interest which is presently or in the future becomes the subject of dealing in the forward contract trade, or product or byproduct thereof, with a maturity date more than two days after the date the contract is entered into, including, but not limited to, a repurchase or reverse repurchase transaction (whether or not such repurchase or reverse repurchase transaction is a "repurchase agreement", as defined in this section) [1] consignment, lease, swap, hedge transaction, deposit, loan, option, allocated transaction, unallocated transaction, or any other similar agreement;

(B) any combination of agreements or transactions referred to in subparagraphs (A) and (C);

(C) any option to enter into an agreement or transaction referred to in subparagraph (A) or (B);

(D) a master agreement that provides for an agreement or transaction referred to in subparagraph (A), (B), or (C), together with all supplements to any such master agreement, without regard to whether such master agreement provides for an agreement or transaction that is not a forward contract under this paragraph, except that such master agreement shall be considered to be a forward contract under this paragraph only with respect to each agreement or transaction under such master agreement that is referred to in subparagraph (A), (B), or (C); or

(E) any security agreement or arrangement, or other credit enhancement related to any agreement or transaction referred to in subparagraph (A), (B), (C), or (D), including any guarantee or reimbursement obligation by or to a forward contract merchant or financial participant in connection with any agreement or transaction referred to in any such subparagraph, but not to exceed the damages in connection with any such agreement or transaction, measured in accordance with section 562.

(26) The term "forward contract merchant" means a Federal reserve bank, or an entity the business of which consists in whole or in part of entering into forward contracts as or with merchants in a commodity (as defined in section 761) or any similar good, article, service, right, or interest which is presently or in the future becomes the subject of dealing in the forward contract trade.

(27) The term "governmental unit" means United States; State; Commonwealth; District; Territory; municipality; foreign state; department, agency, or instrumentality of the United States (but not a United States trustee while serving as a trustee in a case under this title), a State, a Commonwealth, a District, a Territory, a municipality, or a foreign state; or other foreign or domestic government.

(27A) The term "health care business"—

(A) means any public or private entity (without regard to whether that entity is organized for profit or not for profit) that is primarily engaged in offering to the general public facilities and services for—

    (i) the diagnosis or treatment of injury, deformity, or disease; and

    (ii) surgical, drug treatment, psychiatric, or obstetric care; and

(B) includes—

    (i) any—

      (I) general or specialized hospital;

      (II) ancillary ambulatory, emergency, or surgical treatment facility;

      (III) hospice;

      (IV) home health agency; and

      (V) other health care institution that is similar to an entity referred to in subclause (I), (II), (III), or (IV); and

    (ii) any long-term care facility, including any—

      (I) skilled nursing facility;

      (II) intermediate care facility;

      (III) assisted living facility;

      (IV) home for the aged;

      (V) domiciliary care facility; and

      (VI) health care institution that is related to a facility referred to in subclause (I), (II), (III), (IV), or (V), if that institution is primarily engaged in offering room, board, laundry, or personal assistance with activities of daily living and incidentals to activities of daily living.

(27B) The term "incidental property" means, with respect to a debtor's principal residence—

(A) property commonly conveyed with a principal residence in the area where the real property is located;

(B) all easements, rights, appurtenances, fixtures, rents, royalties, mineral rights, oil or gas rights or profits, water rights, escrow funds, or insurance proceeds; and

(C) all replacements or additions.

(28) The term "indenture" means mortgage, deed of trust, or indenture, under which there is outstanding a security, other than a voting-trust certificate, constituting a claim against the debtor, a claim secured by a lien on any of the debtor's property, or an equity security of the debtor.

(29) The term "indenture trustee" means trustee under an indenture.

(30) The term "individual with regular income" means individual whose income is sufficiently stable and regular to enable such individual to make payments under a plan under chapter 13 of this title, other than a stockbroker or a commodity broker.

(31) The term "insider" includes—

(A) if the debtor is an individual—

    (i) relative of the debtor or of a general partner of the debtor;

    (ii) partnership in which the debtor is a general partner;

    (iii) general partner of the debtor; or

    (iv) corporation of which the debtor is a director, officer, or person in control;

(B) if the debtor is a corporation—

    (i) director of the debtor;

    (ii) officer of the debtor;

    (iii) person in control of the debtor;

    (iv) partnership in which the debtor is a general partner;

    (v) general partner of the debtor; or

    (vi) relative of a general partner, director, officer, or person in control of the debtor;

(C) if the debtor is a partnership—

    (i) general partner in the debtor;

    (ii) relative of a general partner in, general partner of, or person in control of the debtor;

    (iii) partnership in which the debtor is a general partner;

    (iv) general partner of the debtor; or

    (v) person in control of the debtor;

(D) if the debtor is a municipality, elected official of the debtor or relative of an elected official of the debtor;

(E) affiliate, or insider of an affiliate as if such affiliate were the debtor; and

(F) managing agent of the debtor.

(32) The term "insolvent" means—

(A) with reference to an entity other than a partnership and a municipality, financial condition such that the sum of such entity's debts is greater than all of such entity's property, at a fair valuation, exclusive of—

    (i) property transferred, concealed, or removed with intent to hinder, delay, or defraud such entity's creditors; and

    (ii) property that may be exempted from property of the estate under section 522 of this title;

(B) with reference to a partnership, financial condition such that the sum of such partnership's debts is greater than the aggregate of, at a fair valuation—

    (i) all of such partnership's property, exclusive of property of the kind specified in subparagraph (A)(i) of this paragraph; and

    (ii) the sum of the excess of the value of each general partner's nonpartnership property, exclusive of property of the kind specified in subparagraph (A) of this paragraph, over such partner's nonpartnership debts; and

(C) with reference to a municipality, financial condition such that the municipality is—

(i) generally not paying its debts as they become due unless such debts are the subject of a bona fide dispute; or

(ii) unable to pay its debts as they become due.

(33) The term "institution-affiliated party"—

(A) with respect to an insured depository institution (as defined in section 3(c)(2) of the Federal Deposit Insurance Act), has the meaning given it in section 3(u) of the Federal Deposit Insurance Act; and

(B) with respect to an insured credit union, has the meaning given it in section 206(r) of the Federal Credit Union Act.

(34) The term "insured credit union" has the meaning given it in section 101(7) of the Federal Credit Union Act.

(35) The term "insured depository institution"—

(A) has the meaning given it in section 3(c)(2) of the Federal Deposit Insurance Act; and

(B) includes an insured credit union (except in the case of paragraphs (21B) and (33)(A) of this subsection).

(35A) The term "intellectual property" means—

(A) trade secret;

(B) invention, process, design, or plant protected under title 35;

(C) patent application;

(D) plant variety;

(E) work of authorship protected under title 17; or

(F) mask work protected under chapter 9 of title 17;

to the extent protected by applicable nonbankruptcy law.

(36) The term "judicial lien" means lien obtained by judgment, levy, sequestration, or other legal or equitable process or proceeding.

(37) The term "lien" means charge against or interest in property to secure payment of a debt or performance of an obligation.

(38) The term "margin payment" means, for purposes of the forward contract provisions of this title, payment or deposit of cash, a security or other property, that is commonly known in the forward contract trade as original margin, initial margin, maintenance margin, or variation margin, including mark-to-market payments, or variation payments.

(38A) The term "master netting agreement"—

(A) means an agreement providing for the exercise of rights, including rights of netting,

setoff, liquidation, termination, acceleration, or close out, under or in connection with one or more contracts that are described in any one or more of paragraphs (1) through (5) of section 561(a), or any security agreement or arrangement or other credit enhancement related to one or more of the foregoing, including any guarantee or reimbursement obligation related to 1 or more of the foregoing; and

(B) if the agreement contains provisions relating to agreements or transactions that are not contracts described in paragraphs (1) through (5) of section 561(a), shall be deemed to be a master netting agreement only with respect to those agreements or transactions that are described in any one or more of paragraphs (1) through (5) of section 561(a).

(38B) The term "master netting agreement participant" means an entity that, at any time before the date of the filing of the petition, is a party to an outstanding master netting agreement with the debtor.

(39) The term "mask work" has the meaning given it in section 901(a)(2) of title 17.

(39A) The term "median family income" means for any year—

(A) the median family income both calculated and reported by the Bureau of the Census in the then most recent year; and

(B) if not so calculated and reported in the then current year, adjusted annually after such most recent year until the next year in which median family income is both calculated and reported by the Bureau of the Census, to reflect the percentage change in the Consumer Price Index for All Urban Consumers during the period of years occurring after such most recent year and before such current year.

(40) The term "municipality" means political subdivision or public agency or instrumentality of a State.

(40A) The term "patient" means any individual who obtains or receives services from a health care business.

(40B) The term "patient records" means any record relating to a patient, including a written document or a record recorded in a magnetic, optical, or other form of electronic medium.

(41) The term "person" includes individual, partnership, and corporation, but does not include governmental unit, except that a governmental unit that—

(A) acquires an asset from a person—

(i) as a result of the operation of a loan guarantee agreement; or

(ii) as receiver or liquidating agent of a person;

(B) is a guarantor of a pension benefit payable by or on behalf of the debtor or an affiliate of the debtor; or

(C) is the legal or beneficial owner of an asset of—

(i) an employee pension benefit plan that is a governmental plan, as defined in section 414(d) of the Internal Revenue Code of 1986; or

(ii) an eligible deferred compensation plan, as defined in section 457(b) of the Internal Revenue Code of 1986;

shall be considered, for purposes of section 1102 of this title, to be a person with respect to such asset or such benefit.

(41A) The term "personally identifiable information" means—

(A) if provided by an individual to the debtor in connection with obtaining a product or a service from the debtor primarily for personal, family, or household purposes—

(i) the first name (or initial) and last name of such individual, whether given at birth or time of adoption, or resulting from a lawful change of name;

(ii) the geographical address of a physical place of residence of such individual;

(iii) an electronic address (including an e-mail address) of such individual;

(iv) a telephone number dedicated to contacting such individual at such physical place of residence;

(v) a social security account number issued to such individual; or

(vi) the account number of a credit card issued to such individual; or

(B) if identified in connection with 1 or more of the items of information specified in subparagraph (A)—

(i) a birth date, the number of a certificate of birth or adoption, or a place of birth; or

(ii) any other information concerning an identified individual that, if disclosed, will result in contacting or identifying such individual physically or electronically.

(42) The term "petition" means petition filed under section 301, 302, 303 and ² 1504 of this title, as the case may be, commencing a case under this title.

(42A) The term "production payment" means a term overriding royalty satisfiable in cash or in kind—

(A) contingent on the production of a liquid or gaseous hydrocarbon from particular real property; and

(B) from a specified volume, or a specified value, from the liquid or gaseous hydrocarbon produced from such property, and determined without regard to production costs.

(43) The term "purchaser" means transferee of a voluntary transfer, and includes immediate or mediate transferee of such a transferee.

(44) The term "railroad" means common carrier by railroad engaged in the transportation of individuals or property or owner of trackage facilities leased by such a common carrier.

(45) The term "relative" means individual related by affinity or consanguinity within the third degree as determined by the common law, or individual in a step or adoptive relationship within such third degree.

(46) The term "repo participant" means an entity that, at any time before the filing of the petition, has an outstanding repurchase agreement with the debtor.

(47) The term "repurchase agreement" (which definition also applies to a reverse repurchase agreement)—

(A) means—

(i) an agreement, including related terms, which provides for the transfer of one or more certificates of deposit, mortgage related securities (as defined in section 3 of the Securities Exchange Act of 1934), mortgage loans, interests in mortgage related securities or mortgage loans, eligible bankers' acceptances, qualified foreign government securities (defined as a security that is a direct obligation of, or that is fully guaranteed by, the central government of a member of the Organization for Economic Cooperation and Development), or securities that are direct obligations of, or that are fully guaranteed by, the United States or any agency of the United States against the transfer of funds by the transferee of such certificates of deposit, eligible bankers' acceptances, securities, mortgage loans, or interests, with a simultaneous agreement by such transferee to transfer to the transferor thereof certificates of deposit, eligible bankers' acceptance, securities, mortgage loans, or interests of the kind described in this clause, at a date certain not later than 1 year after such transfer or on demand, against the transfer of funds;

(ii) any combination of agreements or transactions referred to in clauses (i) and (iii);

(iii) an option to enter into an agreement or transaction referred to in clause (i) or (ii);

(iv) a master agreement that provides for an agreement or transaction referred to in clause (i), (ii), or (iii), together with all supplements to any such master agreement, without regard to whether such master agreement provides for an agreement or transaction that is not a repurchase agreement under this paragraph, except that such master agreement shall be considered to be a repurchase agreement under this paragraph only with respect to each agreement or transaction under the master agreement that is referred to in clause (i), (ii), or (iii); or

(v) any security agreement or arrangement or other credit enhancement related to any agreement or transaction referred to in clause (i), (ii), (iii), or (iv), including any guarantee or reimbursement obligation by or to a repo participant or financial participant in connection with any agreement or transaction referred to in any such clause, but not to exceed the damages in connection with any such agreement or transaction, measured in accordance with section 562 of this title; and

(B) does not include a repurchase obligation under a participation in a commercial mortgage loan.

(48) The term "securities clearing agency" means person that is registered as a clearing agency under section 17A of the Securities Exchange Act of 1934, or exempt from such registration under such section pursuant to an order of the Securities and Exchange Commission, or whose business is confined to the performance of functions of a clearing agency with respect to exempted securities, as defined in section 3(a)(12) of such Act for the purposes of such section 17A.

(48A) The term "securities self regulatory organization" means either a securities association registered with the Securities and Exchange Commission under section 15A of the Securities Exchange Act of 1934 or a national securities exchange registered with the Securities and Exchange Commission under section 6 of the Securities Exchange Act of 1934.

(49) The term "security"—

  (A) includes—

    (i) note;

    (ii) stock;

    (iii) treasury stock;

    (iv) bond;

    (v) debenture;

    (vi) collateral trust certificate;

    (vii) pre-organization certificate or subscription;

    (viii) transferable share;

    (ix) voting-trust certificate;

    (x) certificate of deposit;

    (xi) certificate of deposit for security;

    (xii) investment contract or certificate of interest or participation in a profit-sharing agreement or in an oil, gas, or mineral royalty or lease, if such contract or interest is required to be the subject of a registration statement filed with the Securities and Exchange Commission under the provisions of the Securities Act of 1933, or is exempt under section 3(b) of such Act from the requirement to file such a statement;

    (xiii) interest of a limited partner in a limited partnership;

    (xiv) other claim or interest commonly known as "security"; and

    (xv) certificate of interest or participation in, temporary or interim certificate for, receipt for, or warrant or right to subscribe to or purchase or sell, a security; but

  (B) does not include—

    (i) currency, check, draft, bill of exchange, or bank letter of credit;

    (ii) leverage transaction, as defined in section 761 of this title;

    (iii) commodity futures contract or forward contract;

    (iv) option, warrant, or right to subscribe to or purchase or sell a commodity futures contract;

    (v) option to purchase or sell a commodity;

    (vi) contract or certificate of a kind specified in subparagraph (A)(xii) of this paragraph that is not required to be the subject of a registration statement filed with the Securities and Exchange Commission and is not exempt under section 3(b) of the Securities Act of 1933 from the requirement to file such a statement; or

    (vii) debt or evidence of indebtedness for goods sold and delivered or services rendered.

(50) The term "security agreement" means agreement that creates or provides for a security interest.

(51) The term "security interest" means lien created by an agreement.

(51A) The term "settlement payment" means, for purposes of the forward contract provisions of this title, a preliminary settlement payment, a partial settlement payment, an interim settlement payment, a settlement payment on account, a final settlement payment, a net settlement payment, or any other similar payment commonly used in the forward contract trade.

(51B) The term "single asset real estate" means real property constituting a single property or project, other than residential real property with fewer than 4 residential units, which generates substantially all of the gross income of a debtor who is not a family farmer and on which no substantial business is being conducted by a debtor other than the business of operating the real property and activities incidental thereto.

(51C) The term "small business case" means a case filed under chapter 11 of this title in which the debtor is a small business debtor.

(51D) The term "small business debtor"—

  (A) subject to subparagraph (B), means a person engaged in commercial or business activities (including any affiliate of such person that is also a debtor under this title and excluding a person whose primary activity is the business of owning or operating real property or activities incidental thereto) that has aggregate noncontingent liquidated secured and unsecured debts as of the date of the filing of the petition or the date of the order for relief in an amount not more than $2,566,050 (excluding debts owed to 1 or more affiliates or insiders) for a case in which the United States trustee has not appointed under section 1102(a)(1) a committee of unsecured creditors or where the court has determined that the committee of unsecured creditors is not sufficiently active and representative to provide effective oversight of the debtor; and

  (B) does not include any member of a group of affiliated debtors that has aggregate noncontingent liquidated secured and unsecured debts in an amount greater than $2,566,050 (excluding debt owed to 1 or more affiliates or insiders).

(52) The term "State" includes the District of Columbia and Puerto Rico, except for the purpose of defining who may be a debtor under chapter 9 of this title.

(53) The term "statutory lien" means lien arising solely by force of a statute on specified circumstances or conditions, or lien of distress for rent, whether or not statutory, but does not include security interest or judicial lien, whether or not such interest or lien is provided by or is dependent on a statute and whether or not such interest or lien is made fully effective by statute.

(53A) The term "stockbroker" means person—

  (A) with respect to which there is a customer, as defined in section 741 of this title; and

  (B) that is engaged in the business of effecting transactions in securities—

    (i) for the account of others; or

    (ii) with members of the general public, from or for such person's own account.

(53B) The term "swap agreement"—

  (A) means—

    (i) any agreement, including the terms and conditions incorporated by reference in such agreement, which is—

      (I) an interest rate swap, option, future, or forward agreement, including a rate floor, rate cap, rate collar, cross-currency rate swap, and basis swap;

      (II) a spot, same day-tomorrow, tomorrow-next, forward, or other foreign exchange, precious metals, or other commodity agreement;

      (III) a currency swap, option, future, or forward agreement;

      (IV) an equity index or equity swap, option, future, or forward agreement;

      (V) a debt index or debt swap, option, future, or forward agreement;

      (VI) a total return, credit spread or credit swap, option, future, or forward agreement;

      (VII) a commodity index or a commodity swap, option, future, or forward agreement;

      (VIII) a weather swap, option, future, or forward agreement;

      (IX) an emissions swap, option, future, or forward agreement; or

      (X) an inflation swap, option, future, or forward agreement;

    (ii) any agreement or transaction that is similar to any other agreement or transaction referred to in this paragraph and that—

      (I) is of a type that has been, is presently, or in the future becomes, the subject of recurrent dealings in the swap or other derivatives markets (including terms and conditions incorporated by reference therein); and

      (II) is a forward, swap, future, option, or spot transaction on one or more rates, currencies, commodities, equity securities, or other equity instruments, debt securities or other debt instruments, quantitative measures associated with an occurrence, extent of an occurrence, or contingency associated with a financial, commercial, or economic consequence, or economic or financial indices or measures of economic or financial risk or value;

(iii) any combination of agreements or transactions referred to in this subparagraph;

(iv) any option to enter into an agreement or transaction referred to in this subparagraph;

(v) a master agreement that provides for an agreement or transaction referred to in clause (i), (ii), (iii), or (iv), together with all supplements to any such master agreement, and without regard to whether the master agreement contains an agreement or transaction that is not a swap agreement under this paragraph, except that the master agreement shall be considered to be a swap agreement under this paragraph only with respect to each agreement or transaction under the master agreement that is referred to in clause (i), (ii), (iii), or (iv); or

(vi) any security agreement or arrangement or other credit enhancement related to any agreements or transactions referred to in clause (i) through (v), including any guarantee or reimbursement obligation by or to a swap participant or financial participant in connection with any agreement or transaction referred to in any such clause, but not to exceed the damages in connection with any such agreement or transaction, measured in accordance with section 562; and

(B) is applicable for purposes of this title only, and shall not be construed or applied so as to challenge or affect the characterization, definition, or treatment of any swap agreement under any other statute, regulation, or rule, including the Gramm-Leach-Bliley Act, the Legal Certainty for Bank Products Act of 2000, the securities laws (as such term is defined in section 3(a)(47) of the Securities Exchange Act of 1934) and the Commodity Exchange Act.

(53C) The term "swap participant" means an entity that, at any time before the filing of the petition, has an outstanding swap agreement with the debtor.

(56A) [3] The term "term overriding royalty" means an interest in liquid or gaseous hydrocarbons in place or to be produced from particular real property that entitles the owner thereof to a share of production, or the value thereof, for a term limited by time, quantity, or value realized.

(53D) The term "timeshare plan" means and shall include that interest purchased in any arrangement,

plan, scheme, or similar device, but not including exchange programs, whether by membership, agreement, tenancy in common, sale, lease, deed, rental agreement, license, right to use agreement, or by any other means, whereby a purchaser, in exchange for consideration, receives a right to use accommodations, facilities, or recreational sites, whether improved or unimproved, for a specific period of time less than a full year during any given year, but not necessarily for consecutive years, and which extends for a period of more than three years. A "timeshare interest" is that interest purchased in a timeshare plan which grants the purchaser the right to use and occupy accommodations, facilities, or recreational sites, whether improved or unimproved, pursuant to a timeshare plan.

(54) The term "transfer" means—

(A) the creation of a lien;

(B) the retention of title as a security interest;

(C) the foreclosure of a debtor's equity of redemption; or

(D) each mode, direct or indirect, absolute or conditional, voluntary or involuntary, of disposing of or parting with—

(i) property; or

(ii) an interest in property.

(54A) The term "uninsured State member bank" means a State member bank (as defined in section 3 of the Federal Deposit Insurance Act) the deposits of which are not insured by the Federal Deposit Insurance Corporation.

(55) The term "United States", when used in a geographical sense, includes all locations where the judicial jurisdiction of the United States extends, including territories and possessions of the United States.

---

[1] So in original. Probably should be followed by a comma.

[2] So in original. Probably should be "or".

[3] So in original.

§102. Rules of construction

In this title—

(1) "after notice and a hearing", or a similar phrase—

(A) means after such notice as is appropriate in the particular circumstances, and such opportunity for a hearing as is appropriate in the particular circumstances; but

(B) authorizes an act without an actual hearing if such notice is given properly and if—

(i) such a hearing is not requested timely by a party in interest; or

(ii) there is insufficient time for a hearing to be commenced before such act must be done, and the court authorizes such act;

(2) "claim against the debtor" includes claim against property of the debtor;

(3) "includes" and "including" are not limiting;

(4) "may not" is prohibitive, and not permissive;

(5) "or" is not exclusive;

(6) "order for relief" means entry of an order for relief;

(7) the singular includes the plural;

(8) a definition, contained in a section of this title that refers to another section of this title, does not, for the purpose of such reference, affect the meaning of a term used in such other section; and

(9) "United States trustee" includes a designee of the United States trustee.

§103. Applicability of chapters

(a) Except as provided in section 1161 of this title, chapters 1, 3, and 5 of this title apply in a case under chapter 7, 11, 12, or 13 of this title, and this chapter, sections 307, 362(o), 555 through 557, and 559 through 562 apply in a case under chapter 15.

(b) Subchapters I and II of chapter 7 of this title apply only in a case under such chapter.

(c) Subchapter III of chapter 7 of this title applies only in a case under such chapter concerning a stockbroker.

(d) Subchapter IV of chapter 7 of this title applies only in a case under such chapter concerning a commodity broker.

(e) Scope of Application.—Subchapter V of chapter 7 of this title shall apply only in a case under such chapter concerning the liquidation of an uninsured State member bank, or a corporation organized under section 25A of the Federal Reserve Act, which operates, or operates as, a multilateral clearing organization pursuant to section 409 of the Federal Deposit Insurance Corporation Improvement Act of 1991.

(f) Except as provided in section 901 of this title, only chapters 1 and 9 of this title apply in a case under such chapter 9.

(g) Except as provided in section 901 of this title, subchapters I, II, and III of chapter 11 of this title apply only in a case under such chapter.

(h) Subchapter IV of chapter 11 of this title applies only in a case under such chapter concerning a railroad.

(i) Chapter 13 of this title applies only in a case under such chapter.

(j) Chapter 12 of this title applies only in a case under such chapter.

(k) Chapter 15 applies only in a case under such chapter, except that—

(1) sections 1505, 1513, and 1514 apply in all cases under this title; and

(2) section 1509 applies whether or not a case under this title is pending.

§104. Adjustment of dollar amounts

(a) On April 1, 1998, and at each 3-year interval ending on April 1 thereafter, each dollar amount in effect under sections 101(3), 101(18), 101(19A), 101(51D), 109(e), 303(b), 507(a), 522(d), 522(f)(3) and 522(f)(4), 522(n), 522(p), 522(q), 523(a)(2)(C), 541(b), 547(c)(9), 707(b), 1322(d), 1325(b), and 1326(b)(3) of this title and section 1409(b) of title 28 immediately before such April 1 shall be adjusted—

(1) to reflect the change in the Consumer Price Index for All Urban Consumers, published by the Department of Labor, for the most recent 3-year period ending immediately before January 1 preceding such April 1, and

(2) to round to the nearest $25 the dollar amount that represents such change.

(b) Not later than March 1, 1998, and at each 3-year interval ending on March 1 thereafter, the Judicial Conference of the United States shall publish in the Federal Register the dollar amounts that will become effective on such April 1 under sections 101(3), 101(18), 101(19A), 101(51D), 109(e), 303(b), 507(a), 522(d), 522(f)(3) and 522(f)(4), 522(n), 522(p), 522(q), 523(a)(2)(C), 541(b), 547(c)(9), 707(b), 1322(d), 1325(b), and 1326(b)(3) of this title and section 1409(b) of title 28.

(c) Adjustments made in accordance with subsection (a) shall not apply with respect to cases commenced before the date of such adjustments.

§105. Power of court

(a) The court may issue any order, process, or judgment that is necessary or appropriate to carry out the provisions of this title. No provision of this title providing for the raising of an issue by a party in interest shall be construed to preclude the court from, sua sponte, taking any action or making any determination necessary or appropriate to enforce or implement court orders or rules, or to prevent an abuse of process.

(b) Notwithstanding subsection (a) of this section, a court may not appoint a receiver in a case under this title.

(c) The ability of any district judge or other officer or employee of a district court to exercise any of the authority or responsibilities conferred upon the court under this title shall be determined by reference to the provisions relating to such judge, officer, or employee set forth in title 28. This subsection shall not be interpreted to exclude bankruptcy judges and other officers or employees appointed pursuant to chapter 6 of title 28 from its operation.

(d) The court, on its own motion or on the request of a party in interest—

(1) shall hold such status conferences as are necessary to further the expeditious and economical resolution of the case; and

(2) unless inconsistent with another provision of this title or with applicable Federal Rules of Bankruptcy Procedure, may issue an order at any such conference prescribing such limitations and conditions as the court deems appropriate to ensure that the case is handled expeditiously and economically, including an order that—

(A) sets the date by which the trustee must assume or reject an executory contract or unexpired lease; or

(B) in a case under chapter 11 of this title—

(i) sets a date by which the debtor, or trustee if one has been appointed, shall file a disclosure statement and plan;

(ii) sets a date by which the debtor, or trustee if one has been appointed, shall solicit acceptances of a plan;

(iii) sets the date by which a party in interest other than a debtor may file a plan;

(iv) sets a date by which a proponent of a plan, other than the debtor, shall solicit acceptances of such plan;

(v) fixes the scope and format of the notice to be provided regarding the hearing on approval of the disclosure statement; or

(vi) provides that the hearing on approval of the disclosure statement may be combined with the hearing on confirmation of the plan.

§106. Waiver of sovereign immunity

(a) Notwithstanding an assertion of sovereign immunity, sovereign immunity is abrogated as to a governmental unit to the extent set forth in this section with respect to the following:

(1) Sections 105, 106, 107, 108, 303, 346, 362, 363, 364, 365, 366, 502, 503, 505, 506, 510, 522, 523, 524, 525, 542, 543, 544, 545, 546, 547, 548, 549, 550, 551, 552, 553, 722, 724, 726, 744, 749, 764, 901, 922, 926, 928, 929, 944, 1107, 1141, 1142, 1143, 1146, 1201, 1203, 1205, 1206, 1227, 1231, 1301, 1303, 1305, and 1327 of this title.

(2) The court may hear and determine any issue arising with respect to the application of such sections to governmental units.

(3) The court may issue against a governmental unit an order, process, or judgment under such sections or the Federal Rules of Bankruptcy Procedure, including an order or judgment awarding a money recovery, but not including an award of punitive damages. Such order or judgment for costs or fees under this title or the Federal Rules of Bankruptcy Procedure against any governmental unit shall be consistent with the provisions and limitations of section 2412(d)(2)(A) of title 28.

(4) The enforcement of any such order, process, or judgment against any governmental unit shall be consistent with appropriate nonbankruptcy law applicable to such governmental unit and, in the case of a money judgment against the United States, shall be paid as if it is a judgment rendered by a district court of the United States.

(5) Nothing in this section shall create any substantive claim for relief or cause of action not otherwise existing under this title, the Federal Rules of Bankruptcy Procedure, or nonbankruptcy law.

(b) A governmental unit that has filed a proof of claim in the case is deemed to have waived sovereign immunity with respect to a claim against such governmental unit that is property of the estate and that arose out of the same transaction or occurrence out of which the claim of such governmental unit arose.

(c) Notwithstanding any assertion of sovereign immunity by a governmental unit, there shall be offset against a claim or interest of a governmental unit any claim against such governmental unit that is property of the estate.

§107. Public access to papers

(a) Except as provided in subsections (b) and (c) and subject to section 112, a paper filed in a case under this title and the dockets of a bankruptcy court are public records and open to examination by an entity at reasonable times without charge.

(b) On request of a party in interest, the bankruptcy court shall, and on the bankruptcy court's own motion, the bankruptcy court may—

(1) protect an entity with respect to a trade secret or confidential research, development, or commercial information; or

(2) protect a person with respect to scandalous or defamatory matter contained in a paper filed in a case under this title.

(c)

(1) The bankruptcy court, for cause, may protect an individual, with respect to the following types of information to the extent the court finds that disclosure of such information would create undue risk of identity theft or other unlawful injury to the individual or the individual's property:

(A) Any means of identification (as defined in section 1028(d) of title 18) contained in a paper filed, or to be filed, in a case under this title.

(B) Other information contained in a paper described in subparagraph (A).

(2) Upon ex parte application demonstrating cause, the court shall provide access to information protected pursuant to paragraph (1) to an entity acting pursuant to the police or regulatory power of a domestic governmental unit.

(3) The United States trustee, bankruptcy administrator, trustee, and any auditor serving under section 586(f) of title 28—

(A) shall have full access to all information contained in any paper filed or submitted in a case under this title; and

(B) shall not disclose information specifically protected by the court under this title.

§108. Extension of time

(a) If applicable nonbankruptcy law, an order entered in a nonbankruptcy proceeding, or an agreement fixes a period within which the debtor may commence an action, and such period has not expired before the date of the filing of the petition, the trustee may commence such action only before the later of—

(1) the end of such period, including any suspension of such period occurring on or after the commencement of the case; or

(2) two years after the order for relief.

(b) Except as provided in subsection (a) of this section, if applicable nonbankruptcy law, an order entered in a nonbankruptcy proceeding, or an agreement fixes a period within which the debtor or an individual protected under section 1201 or 1301 of this title may file any pleading, demand, notice, or proof of claim or loss, cure a default, or perform any other similar act, and such period has not expired before the date of the filing of the petition, the trustee may only file, cure, or perform, as the case may be, before the later of—

(1) the end of such period, including any suspension of such period occurring on or after the commencement of the case; or

(2) 60 days after the order for relief.

(c) Except as provided in section 524 of this title, if applicable nonbankruptcy law, an order entered in a nonbankruptcy proceeding, or an agreement fixes a period for commencing or continuing a civil action in a court other than a bankruptcy court on a claim against the debtor, or against an individual with respect to which such individual is protected under section 1201 or 1301 of this title, and such period has not expired before the date of the filing of the petition, then such period does not expire until the later of—

(1) the end of such period, including any suspension of such period occurring on or after the commencement of the case; or

(2) 30 days after notice of the termination or expiration of the stay under section 362, 922, 1201, or 1301 of this title, as the case may be, with respect to such claim.

§109. Who may be a debtor

(a) Notwithstanding any other provision of this section, only a person that resides or has a domicile, a place of business, or property in the United States, or a municipality, may be a debtor under this title.

(b) A person may be a debtor under chapter 7 of this title only if such person is not—

(1) a railroad;

(2) a domestic insurance company, bank, savings bank, cooperative bank, savings and loan association, building and loan association, homestead association, a New Markets Venture Capital company as defined in section 351 of the Small Business Investment Act of 1958, a small business investment company licensed by the Small Business Administration under section 301 of the Small Business Investment Act of 1958, credit union, or industrial bank or similar institution which is an insured bank as defined in section 3(h) of the Federal Deposit Insurance Act, except that an uninsured State member bank, or a corporation organized under section 25A of the Federal Reserve Act, which operates, or operates as, a multilateral clearing organization pursuant to section 409 of the Federal Deposit Insurance Corporation Improvement Act of 1991 may be a debtor if a petition is filed at the direction of the Board of Governors of the Federal Reserve System; or

(3)

(A) a foreign insurance company, engaged in such business in the United States; or

(B) a foreign bank, savings bank, cooperative bank, savings and loan association, building and loan association, or credit union, that has a branch or agency (as defined in section 1(b) of the International Banking Act of 1978) in the United States.

(c) An entity may be a debtor under chapter 9 of this title if and only if such entity—

(1) is a municipality;

(2) is specifically authorized, in its capacity as a municipality or by name, to be a debtor under such chapter by State law, or by a governmental officer or organization empowered by State law to authorize such entity to be a debtor under such chapter;

(3) is insolvent;

(4) desires to effect a plan to adjust such debts; and

(5)

(A) has obtained the agreement of creditors holding at least a majority in amount of the claims of each class that such entity intends to impair under a plan in a case under such chapter;

(B) has negotiated in good faith with creditors and has failed to obtain the agreement of creditors holding at least a majority in amount of the claims of each class that such entity intends to impair under a plan in a case under such chapter;

(C) is unable to negotiate with creditors because such negotiation is impracticable; or

(D) reasonably believes that a creditor may attempt to obtain a transfer that is avoidable under section 547 of this title.

(d) Only a railroad, a person that may be a debtor under chapter 7 of this title (except a stockbroker or a commodity broker), and an uninsured State member bank, or a corporation organized under section 25A of the Federal Reserve Act, which operates, or operates as, a multilateral clearing organization pursuant to section 409 of the Federal Deposit Insurance Corporation Improvement Act of 1991 may be a debtor under chapter 11 of this title.

(e) Only an individual with regular income that owes, on the date of the filing of the petition, noncontingent, liquidated, unsecured debts of less than $394,725 and noncontingent, liquidated, secured debts of less than $1,184,200, or an individual with regular income and such individual's spouse, except a stockbroker or a commodity broker, that owe, on the date of the filing of the petition, noncontingent, liquidated,

unsecured debts that aggregate less than $394,725 and noncontingent, liquidated, secured debts of less than $1,184,200 may be a debtor under chapter 13 of this title.

(f) Only a family farmer or family fisherman with regular annual income may be a debtor under chapter 12 of this title.

(g) Notwithstanding any other provision of this section, no individual or family farmer may be a debtor under this title who has been a debtor in a case pending under this title at any time in the preceding 180 days if—

(1) the case was dismissed by the court for willful failure of the debtor to abide by orders of the court, or to appear before the court in proper prosecution of the case; or

(2) the debtor requested and obtained the voluntary dismissal of the case following the filing of a request for relief from the automatic stay provided by section 362 of this title.

(h)

(1) Subject to paragraphs (2) and (3), and notwithstanding any other provision of this section other than paragraph (4) of this subsection, an individual may not be a debtor under this title unless such individual has, during the 180-day period ending on the date of filing of the petition by such individual, received from an approved nonprofit budget and credit counseling agency described in section 111(a) an individual or group briefing (including a briefing conducted by telephone or on the Internet) that outlined the opportunities for available credit counseling and assisted such individual in performing a related budget analysis.

(2)

(A) Paragraph (1) shall not apply with respect to a debtor who resides in a district for which the United States trustee (or the bankruptcy administrator, if any) determines that the approved nonprofit budget and credit counseling agencies for such district are not reasonably able to provide adequate services to the additional individuals who would otherwise seek credit counseling from such agencies by reason of the requirements of paragraph (1).

(B) The United States trustee (or the bankruptcy administrator, if any) who makes a determination described in subparagraph (A) shall review such determination not later than 1 year after the date of such determination, and not less frequently than annually thereafter. Notwithstanding the preceding sentence, a nonprofit budget and credit counseling agency may be disapproved by the United States trustee (or the bankruptcy administrator, if any) at any time.

(3)

   (A) Subject to subparagraph (B), the requirements of paragraph (1) shall not apply with respect to a debtor who submits to the court a certification that—
      (i) describes exigent circumstances that merit a waiver of the requirements of paragraph (1);
      (ii) states that the debtor requested credit counseling services from an approved nonprofit budget and credit counseling agency, but was unable to obtain the services referred to in paragraph (1) during the 7-day period beginning on the date on which the debtor made that request; and
      (iii) is satisfactory to the court.
   (B) With respect to a debtor, an exemption under subparagraph (A) shall cease to apply to that debtor on the date on which the debtor meets the requirements of paragraph (1), but in no case may the exemption apply to that debtor after the date that is 30 days after the debtor files a petition, except that the court, for cause, may order an additional 15 days.

(4) The requirements of paragraph (1) shall not apply with respect to a debtor whom the court determines, after notice and hearing, is unable to complete those requirements because of incapacity, disability, or active military duty in a military combat zone. For the purposes of this paragraph, incapacity means that the debtor is impaired by reason of mental illness or mental deficiency so that he is incapable of realizing and making rational decisions with respect to his financial responsibilities; and "disability" means that the debtor is so physically impaired as to be unable, after reasonable effort, to participate in an in person, telephone, or Internet briefing required under paragraph (1).

§110. Penalty for persons who negligently or fraudulently prepare bankruptcy petitions

(a) In this section—
   (1) "bankruptcy petition preparer" means a person, other than an attorney for the debtor or an employee of such attorney under the direct supervision of such attorney, who prepares for compensation a document for filing; and
   (2) "document for filing" means a petition or any other document prepared for filing by a debtor in a United States bankruptcy court or a United States district court in connection with a case under this title.

(b)

   (1) A bankruptcy petition preparer who prepares a document for filing shall sign the document and print on the document the preparer's name and address. If a bankruptcy petition preparer is not an individual, then an officer, principal, responsible person, or partner of the bankruptcy petition preparer shall be required to—
      (A) sign the document for filing; and
      (B) print on the document the name and address of that officer, principal, responsible person, or partner.

   (2)
      (A) Before preparing any document for filing or accepting any fees from or on behalf of a debtor, the bankruptcy petition preparer shall provide to the debtor a written notice which shall be on an official form prescribed by the Judicial Conference of the United States in accordance with rule 9009 of the Federal Rules of Bankruptcy Procedure.
      (B) The notice under subparagraph (A)—
         (i) shall inform the debtor in simple language that a bankruptcy petition preparer is not an attorney and may not practice law or give legal advice;
         (ii) may contain a description of examples of legal advice that a bankruptcy petition preparer is not authorized to give, in addition to any advice that the preparer may not give by reason of subsection (e)(2); and
         (iii) shall—
            (I) be signed by the debtor and, under penalty of perjury, by the bankruptcy petition preparer; and
            (II) be filed with any document for filing.

(c)

   (1) A bankruptcy petition preparer who prepares a document for filing shall place on the document, after the preparer's signature, an identifying number that identifies individuals who prepared the document.
   (2)
      (A) Subject to subparagraph (B), for purposes of this section, the identifying

number of a bankruptcy petition preparer shall be the Social Security account number of each individual who prepared the document or assisted in its preparation.

(B) If a bankruptcy petition preparer is not an individual, the identifying number of the bankruptcy petition preparer shall be the Social Security account number of the officer, principal, responsible person, or partner of the bankruptcy petition preparer.

(d) A bankruptcy petition preparer shall, not later than the time at which a document for filing is presented for the debtor's signature, furnish to the debtor a copy of the document.

(e)

(1) A bankruptcy petition preparer shall not execute any document on behalf of a debtor.

(2)

(A) A bankruptcy petition preparer may not offer a potential bankruptcy debtor any legal advice, including any legal advice described in subparagraph (B).

(B) The legal advice referred to in subparagraph (A) includes advising the debtor—

(i) whether—

(I) to file a petition under this title; or

(II) commencing a case under chapter 7, 11, 12, or 13 is appropriate;

(ii) whether the debtor's debts will be discharged in a case under this title;

(iii) whether the debtor will be able to retain the debtor's home, car, or other property after commencing a case under this title;

(iv) concerning—

(I) the tax consequences of a case brought under this title; or

(II) the dischargeability of tax claims;

(v) whether the debtor may or should promise to repay debts to a creditor or enter into a reaffirmation agreement with a creditor to reaffirm a debt;

(vi) concerning how to characterize the nature of the debtor's interests in property or the debtor's debts; or

(vii) concerning bankruptcy procedures and rights.

(f) A bankruptcy petition preparer shall not use the word "legal" or any similar term in any advertisements, or advertise under any category that includes the word "legal" or any similar term.

(g) A bankruptcy petition preparer shall not collect or receive any payment from the debtor or on behalf of the debtor for the court fees in connection with filing the petition.

(h)

(1) The Supreme Court may promulgate rules under section 2075 of title 28, or the Judicial Conference of the United States may prescribe guidelines, for setting a maximum allowable fee chargeable by a bankruptcy petition preparer. A bankruptcy petition preparer shall notify the debtor of any such maximum amount before preparing any document for filing for the debtor or accepting any fee from or on behalf of the debtor.

(2) A declaration under penalty of perjury by the bankruptcy petition preparer shall be filed together with the petition, disclosing any fee received from or on behalf of the debtor within 12 months immediately prior to the filing of the case, and any unpaid fee charged to the debtor. If rules or guidelines setting a maximum fee for services have been promulgated or prescribed under paragraph (1), the declaration under this paragraph shall include a certification that the bankruptcy petition preparer complied with the notification requirement under paragraph (1).

(3)

(A) The court shall disallow and order the immediate turnover to the bankruptcy trustee any fee referred to in paragraph (2)—

(i) found to be in excess of the value of any services rendered by the bankruptcy petition preparer during the 12-month period immediately preceding the date of the filing of the petition; or

(ii) found to be in violation of any rule or guideline promulgated or prescribed under paragraph (1).

(B) All fees charged by a bankruptcy petition preparer may be forfeited in any case in which the bankruptcy petition preparer fails to comply with this subsection or subsection (b), (c), (d), (e), (f), or (g).

(C) An individual may exempt any funds recovered under this paragraph under section 522(b).

(4) The debtor, the trustee, a creditor, the United States trustee (or the bankruptcy administrator, if any) or the court, on the initiative of the court, may file a motion for an order under paragraph (3).

(5) A bankruptcy petition preparer shall be fined not more than $500 for each failure to comply with a court order to turn over funds within 30 days of service of such order.

(i)

(1) If a bankruptcy petition preparer violates this section or commits any act that the court finds to be fraudulent, unfair, or deceptive, on the motion of the debtor, trustee, United States trustee (or the bankruptcy administrator, if any), and after notice and a hearing, the court shall order the bankruptcy petition preparer to pay to the debtor—

    (A) the debtor's actual damages;

    (B) the greater of—

      (i) $2,000; or

      (ii) twice the amount paid by the debtor to the bankruptcy petition preparer for the preparer's services; and

    (C) reasonable attorneys' fees and costs in moving for damages under this subsection.

(2) If the trustee or creditor moves for damages on behalf of the debtor under this subsection, the bankruptcy petition preparer shall be ordered to pay the movant the additional amount of $1,000 plus reasonable attorneys' fees and costs incurred.

(j)

(1) A debtor for whom a bankruptcy petition preparer has prepared a document for filing, the trustee, a creditor, or the United States trustee in the district in which the bankruptcy petition preparer resides, has conducted business, or the United States trustee in any other district in which the debtor resides may bring a civil action to enjoin a bankruptcy petition preparer from engaging in any conduct in violation of this section or from further acting as a bankruptcy petition preparer.

(2)

    (A) In an action under paragraph (1), if the court finds that—

      (i) a bankruptcy petition preparer has—

      (I) engaged in conduct in violation of this section or of any provision of this title;

      (II) misrepresented the preparer's experience or education as a bankruptcy petition preparer; or

      (III) engaged in any other fraudulent, unfair, or deceptive conduct; and

      (ii) injunctive relief is appropriate to prevent the recurrence of such conduct, the court may enjoin the bankruptcy petition preparer from engaging in such conduct.

    (B) If the court finds that a bankruptcy petition preparer has continually engaged in conduct described in subclause (I), (II), or (III) of clause (i) and that an injunction

prohibiting such conduct would not be sufficient to prevent such person's interference with the proper administration of this title, has not paid a penalty imposed under this section, or failed to disgorge all fees ordered by the court the court may enjoin the person from acting as a bankruptcy petition preparer.

(3) The court, as part of its contempt power, may enjoin a bankruptcy petition preparer that has failed to comply with a previous order issued under this section. The injunction under this paragraph may be issued on the motion of the court, the trustee, or the United States trustee (or the bankruptcy administrator, if any).

(4) The court shall award to a debtor, trustee, or creditor that brings a successful action under this subsection reasonable attorneys' fees and costs of the action, to be paid by the bankruptcy petition preparer.

(k) Nothing in this section shall be construed to permit activities that are otherwise prohibited by law, including rules and laws that prohibit the unauthorized practice of law.

(l)

(1) A bankruptcy petition preparer who fails to comply with any provision of subsection (b), (c), (d), (e), (f), (g), or (h) may be fined not more than $500 for each such failure.

(2) The court shall triple the amount of a fine assessed under paragraph (1) in any case in which the court finds that a bankruptcy petition preparer—

    (A) advised the debtor to exclude assets or income that should have been included on applicable schedules;

    (B) advised the debtor to use a false Social Security account number;

    (C) failed to inform the debtor that the debtor was filing for relief under this title; or

    (D) prepared a document for filing in a manner that failed to disclose the identity of the bankruptcy petition preparer.

(3) A debtor, trustee, creditor, or United States trustee (or the bankruptcy administrator, if any) may file a motion for an order imposing a fine on the bankruptcy petition preparer for any violation of this section.

(4)

    (A) Fines imposed under this subsection in judicial districts served by United States trustees shall be paid to the United States trustees, who shall deposit an amount equal to such fines in the United States Trustee Fund.

(B) Fines imposed under this subsection in judicial districts served by bankruptcy administrators shall be deposited as offsetting receipts to the fund established under section 1931 of title 28, and shall remain available until expended to reimburse any appropriation for the amount paid out of such appropriation for expenses of the operation and maintenance of the courts of the United States.

§111. Nonprofit budget and credit counseling agencies; financial management instructional courses

(a) The clerk shall maintain a publicly available list of—

(1) nonprofit budget and credit counseling agencies that provide 1 or more services described in section 109(h) currently approved by the United States trustee (or the bankruptcy administrator, if any); and

(2) instructional courses concerning personal financial management currently approved by the United States trustee (or the bankruptcy administrator, if any), as applicable.

(b) The United States trustee (or bankruptcy administrator, if any) shall only approve a nonprofit budget and credit counseling agency or an instructional course concerning personal financial management as follows:

(1) The United States trustee (or bankruptcy administrator, if any) shall have thoroughly reviewed the qualifications of the nonprofit budget and credit counseling agency or of the provider of the instructional course under the standards set forth in this section, and the services or instructional courses that will be offered by such agency or such provider, and may require such agency or such provider that has sought approval to provide information with respect to such review.

(2) The United States trustee (or bankruptcy administrator, if any) shall have determined that such agency or such instructional course fully satisfies the applicable standards set forth in this section.

(3) If a nonprofit budget and credit counseling agency or instructional course did not appear on the approved list for the district under subsection (a) immediately before approval under this section, approval under this subsection of such agency or such instructional course shall be for a probationary period not to exceed 6 months.

(4) At the conclusion of the applicable probationary period under paragraph (3), the United States trustee (or bankruptcy administrator, if any) may only approve for an additional 1-year period, and for successive 1-year periods thereafter, an agency or instructional course that has demonstrated during the probationary or applicable subsequent period of approval that such agency or instructional course—

(A) has met the standards set forth under this section during such period; and

(B) can satisfy such standards in the future.

(5) Not later than 30 days after any final decision under paragraph (4), an interested person may seek judicial review of such decision in the appropriate district court of the United States.

(c)

(1) The United States trustee (or the bankruptcy administrator, if any) shall only approve a nonprofit budget and credit counseling agency that demonstrates that it will provide qualified counselors, maintain adequate provision for safekeeping and payment of client funds, provide adequate counseling with respect to client credit problems, and deal responsibly and effectively with other matters relating to the quality, effectiveness, and financial security of the services it provides.

(2) To be approved by the United States trustee (or the bankruptcy administrator, if any), a nonprofit budget and credit counseling agency shall, at a minimum—

(A) have a board of directors the majority of which—

(i) are not employed by such agency; and

(ii) will not directly or indirectly benefit financially from the outcome of the counseling services provided by such agency;

(B) if a fee is charged for counseling services, charge a reasonable fee, and provide services without regard to ability to pay the fee;

(C) provide for safekeeping and payment of client funds, including an annual audit of the trust accounts and appropriate employee bonding;

(D) provide full disclosures to a client, including funding sources, counselor qualifications, possible impact on credit reports, and any costs of such program that will be paid by such client and how such costs will be paid;

(E) provide adequate counseling with respect to a client's credit problems that includes an analysis of such client's current financial condition, factors that caused such financial condition, and how such client can develop a plan to respond to the problems without incurring negative amortization of debt;

(F) provide trained counselors who receive no commissions or bonuses based on the outcome of the counseling services provided by such agency, and who have adequate experience, and have been adequately trained to provide counseling services to individuals in financial difficulty, including the matters described in subparagraph (E);

(G) demonstrate adequate experience and background in providing credit counseling; and

(H) have adequate financial resources to provide continuing support services for budgeting plans over the life of any repayment plan.

(d) The United States trustee (or the bankruptcy administrator, if any) shall only approve an instructional course concerning personal financial management—

(1) for an initial probationary period under subsection (b)(3) if the course will provide at a minimum—

(A) trained personnel with adequate experience and training in providing effective instruction and services;

(B) learning materials and teaching methodologies designed to assist debtors in understanding personal financial management and that are consistent with stated objectives directly related to the goals of such instructional course;

(C) adequate facilities situated in reasonably convenient locations at which such instructional course is offered, except that such facilities may include the provision of such instructional course by telephone or through the Internet, if such instructional course is effective;

(D) the preparation and retention of reasonable records (which shall include the debtor's bankruptcy case number) to permit evaluation of the effectiveness of such instructional course, including any evaluation of satisfaction of instructional course requirements for each debtor attending such instructional course, which shall be available for inspection and evaluation by the Executive Office for United States Trustees, the United States trustee (or the bankruptcy administrator, if any), or the chief bankruptcy judge for the district in which such instructional course is offered; and

(E) if a fee is charged for the instructional course, charge a reasonable fee, and provide services without regard to ability to pay the fee; and

(2) for any 1-year period if the provider thereof has demonstrated that the course meets the standards of paragraph (1) and, in addition—

(A) has been effective in assisting a substantial number of debtors to understand personal financial management; and

(B) is otherwise likely to increase substantially the debtor's understanding of personal financial management.

(e) The district court may, at any time, investigate the qualifications of a nonprofit budget and credit counseling agency referred to in subsection (a), and request production of documents to ensure the integrity and effectiveness of such agency. The district court may, at any time, remove from the approved list under subsection (a) a nonprofit budget and credit counseling agency upon finding such agency does not meet the qualifications of subsection (b).

(f) The United States trustee (or the bankruptcy administrator, if any) shall notify the clerk that a nonprofit budget and credit counseling agency or an instructional course is no longer approved, in which case the clerk shall remove it from the list maintained under subsection (a).

(g)

(1) No nonprofit budget and credit counseling agency may provide to a credit reporting agency information concerning whether a debtor has received or sought instruction concerning personal financial management from such agency.

(2) A nonprofit budget and credit counseling agency that willfully or negligently fails to comply with any requirement under this title with respect to a debtor shall be liable for damages in an amount equal to the sum of—

(A) any actual damages sustained by the debtor as a result of the violation; and

(B) any court costs or reasonable attorneys'; fees (as determined by the court) incurred in an action to recover those damages.

§112. Prohibition on disclosure of name of minor children

The debtor may be required to provide information regarding a minor child involved in matters under this title but may not be required to disclose in the public records in the case the name of such minor child. The debtor may be required to disclose the name of such minor child in a nonpublic record that is maintained by the court and made available by the court for examination by the United States trustee, the trustee, and the auditor (if any) serving under section 586(f) of title 28, in the case. The court, the United States trustee, the trustee, and such auditor shall not disclose the name of such minor child maintained in such nonpublic record.

CHAPTER 3—CASE ADMINISTRATION

SUBCHAPTER I— COMMENCEMENT OF A CASE

§301. Voluntary cases

(a) A voluntary case under a chapter of this title is commenced by the filing with the bankruptcy court of a petition under such chapter by an entity that may be a debtor under such chapter.

(b) The commencement of a voluntary case under a chapter of this title constitutes an order for relief under such chapter.

§302. Joint cases

(a) A joint case under a chapter of this title is commenced by the filing with the bankruptcy court of a single petition under such chapter by an individual that may be a debtor under such chapter and such individual's spouse. The commencement of a joint case under a chapter of this title constitutes an order for relief under such chapter.

(b) After the commencement of a joint case, the court shall determine the extent, if any, to which the debtors' estates shall be consolidated.

§303. Involuntary cases

(a) An involuntary case may be commenced only under chapter 7 or 11 of this title, and only against a person, except a farmer, family farmer, or a corporation that is not a moneyed, business, or commercial corporation, that may be a debtor under the chapter under which such case is commenced.

(b) An involuntary case against a person is commenced by the filing with the bankruptcy court of a petition under chapter 7 or 11 of this title—

    (1) by three or more entities, each of which is either a holder of a claim against such person that is not contingent as to liability or the subject of a bona fide dispute as to liability or amount, or an indenture trustee representing such a holder, if such noncontingent, undisputed claims aggregate at least $15,775 more than the value of any lien on property of the debtor securing such claims held by the holders of such claims;

    (2) if there are fewer than 12 such holders, excluding any employee or insider of such person and any transferee of a transfer that is voidable under section 544, 545, 547, 548, 549, or 724(a) of this title, by one or more of such holders that hold in the aggregate at least $15,775 of such claims;

    (3) if such person is a partnership—

        (A) by fewer than all of the general partners in such partnership; or

        (B) if relief has been ordered under this title with respect to all of the general partners in such partnership, by a general partner in such partnership, the trustee of such a general partner, or a holder of a claim against such partnership; or

    (4) by a foreign representative of the estate in a foreign proceeding concerning such person.

(c) After the filing of a petition under this section but before the case is dismissed or relief is ordered, a creditor holding an unsecured claim that is not contingent, other than a creditor filing under subsection (b) of this section, may join in the petition with the same effect as if such joining creditor were a petitioning creditor under subsection (b) of this section.

(d) The debtor, or a general partner in a partnership debtor that did not join in the petition, may file an answer to a petition under this section.

(e) After notice and a hearing, and for cause, the court may require the petitioners under this section to file a bond to indemnify the debtor for such amounts as the court may later allow under subsection (i) of this section.

(f) Notwithstanding section 363 of this title, except to the extent that the court orders otherwise, and until an order for relief in the case, any business of the debtor may continue to operate, and the debtor may continue to use, acquire, or dispose of property as if an involuntary case concerning the debtor had not been commenced.

(g) At any time after the commencement of an involuntary case under chapter 7 of this title but before an order for relief in the case, the court, on request of a party in interest, after notice to the debtor and a hearing, and if necessary to preserve the property of the estate or to prevent loss to the estate, may order the United States trustee to appoint an interim trustee under section 701 of this title to take possession of the property of the estate and to operate any business of the debtor. Before an order for relief, the debtor may regain possession of property in the possession of a trustee ordered appointed under this subsection if the debtor files such bond as the court requires, conditioned on the debtor's accounting for and delivering to the trustee, if there is an order for relief in the case, such property, or the value, as of the date the debtor regains possession, of such property.

(h) If the petition is not timely controverted, the court shall order relief against the debtor in an involuntary case under the chapter under which the petition was filed. Otherwise, after trial, the court shall order relief against the debtor in an involuntary case under the chapter under which the petition was filed, only if—

(1) the debtor is generally not paying such debtor's debts as such debts become due unless such debts are the subject of a bona fide dispute as to liability or amount; or

(2) within 120 days before the date of the filing of the petition, a custodian, other than a trustee, receiver, or agent appointed or authorized to take charge of less than substantially all of the property of the debtor for the purpose of enforcing a lien against such property, was appointed or took possession.

(i) If the court dismisses a petition under this section other than on consent of all petitioners and the debtor, and if the debtor does not waive the right to judgment under this subsection, the court may grant judgment—

(1) against the petitioners and in favor of the debtor for—

(A) costs; or

(B) a reasonable attorney's fee; or

(2) against any petitioner that filed the petition in bad faith, for—

(A) any damages proximately caused by such filing; or

(B) punitive damages.

(j) Only after notice to all creditors and a hearing may the court dismiss a petition filed under this section—

(1) on the motion of a petitioner;

(2) on consent of all petitioners and the debtor; or

(3) for want of prosecution.

(k)

(1) If—

(A) the petition under this section is false or contains any materially false, fictitious, or fraudulent statement;

(B) the debtor is an individual; and

(C) the court dismisses such petition,

the court, upon the motion of the debtor, shall seal all the records of the court relating to such petition, and all references to such petition.

(2) If the debtor is an individual and the court dismisses a petition under this section, the court may enter an order prohibiting all consumer reporting agencies (as defined in section 603(f) of the Fair Credit Reporting Act (15 U.S.C. 1681a(f))) from making any consumer report (as defined in section 603(d) of that Act) that contains any information relating to such petition or to the case commenced by the filing of such petition.

(3) Upon the expiration of the statute of limitations described in section 3282 of title 18, for a violation of section 152 or 157 of such title, the court, upon the motion of the debtor and for good cause, may expunge any records relating to a petition filed under this section.

§305. Abstention

(a) The court, after notice and a hearing, may dismiss a case under this title, or may suspend all proceedings in a case under this title, at any time if—

(1) the interests of creditors and the debtor would be better served by such dismissal or suspension; or

(2)

(A) a petition under section 1515 for recognition of a foreign proceeding has been granted; and

(B) the purposes of chapter 15 of this title would be best served by such dismissal or suspension.

(b) A foreign representative may seek dismissal or suspension under subsection (a)(2) of this section.

(c) An order under subsection (a) of this section dismissing a case or suspending all proceedings in a case, or a decision not so to dismiss or suspend, is not reviewable by appeal or otherwise by the court of appeals under section 158(d), 1291, or 1292 of title 28 or by the Supreme Court of the United States under section 1254 of title 28.

§306. Limited appearance

An appearance in a bankruptcy court by a foreign representative in connection with a petition or request under section 303 or 305 of this title does not submit such foreign representative to the jurisdiction of any court in the United States for any other purpose, but the bankruptcy court may condition any order under section 303 or 305 of this title on compliance by such foreign representative with the orders of such bankruptcy court.

§307. United States trustee

The United States trustee may raise and may appear and be heard on any issue in any case or proceeding under this title but may not file a plan pursuant to section 1121(c) of this title.

§308. Debtor reporting requirements

(a) For purposes of this section, the term "profitability" means, with respect to a debtor, the amount of money that the debtor has earned or lost during current and recent fiscal periods.

(b) A debtor in a small business case shall file periodic financial and other reports containing information including—

    (1) the debtor's profitability;

    (2) reasonable approximations of the debtor's projected cash receipts and cash disbursements over a reasonable period;

    (3) comparisons of actual cash receipts and disbursements with projections in prior reports;

    (4) whether the debtor is—

        (A) in compliance in all material respects with postpetition requirements imposed by this title and the Federal Rules of Bankruptcy Procedure; and

        (B) timely filing tax returns and other required government filings and paying taxes and other administrative expenses when due;

    (5) if the debtor is not in compliance with the requirements referred to in paragraph (4)(A) or filing tax returns and other required government filings and making the payments referred to in paragraph (4)(B), what the failures are and how, at what cost, and when the debtor intends to remedy such failures; and

    (6) such other matters as are in the best interests of the debtor and creditors, and in the public interest in fair and efficient procedures under chapter 11 of this title.

SUBCHAPTER II—OFFICERS

§321. Eligibility to serve as trustee

(a) A person may serve as trustee in a case under this title only if such person is—

    (1) an individual that is competent to perform the duties of trustee and, in a case under chapter 7, 12, or 13 of this title, resides or has an office in the judicial district within which the case is pending, or in any judicial district adjacent to such district; or

    (2) a corporation authorized by such corporation's charter or bylaws to act as trustee, and, in a case under chapter 7, 12, or 13 of this title, having an office in at least one of such districts.

(b) A person that has served as an examiner in the case may not serve as trustee in the case.

(c) The United States trustee for the judicial district in which the case is pending is eligible to serve as trustee in the case if necessary.

§322. Qualification of trustee

(a) Except as provided in subsection (b)(1), a person selected under section 701, 702, 703, 1104, 1163, 1202, or 1302 of this title to serve as trustee in a case under this title qualifies if before seven days after such selection, and before beginning official duties, such person has filed with the court a bond in favor of the United States conditioned on the faithful performance of such official duties.

(b)

    (1) The United States trustee qualifies wherever such trustee serves as trustee in a case under this title.

    (2) The United States trustee shall determine—

        (A) the amount of a bond required to be filed under subsection (a) of this section; and

        (B) the sufficiency of the surety on such bond.

(c) A trustee is not liable personally or on such trustee's bond in favor of the United States for any penalty or forfeiture incurred by the debtor.

(d) A proceeding on a trustee's bond may not be commenced after two years after the date on which such trustee was discharged.

§323. Role and capacity of trustee

(a) The trustee in a case under this title is the representative of the estate.

(b) The trustee in a case under this title has capacity to sue and be sued.

§324. Removal of trustee or examiner

(a) The court, after notice and a hearing, may remove a trustee, other than the United States trustee, or an examiner, for cause.

(b) Whenever the court removes a trustee or examiner under subsection (a) in a case under this title, such trustee or examiner shall thereby be removed in all other cases under this title in which such trustee or examiner is then serving unless the court orders otherwise.

§325. Effect of vacancy

A vacancy in the office of trustee during a case does not abate any pending action or proceeding, and the successor trustee shall be substituted as a party in such action or proceeding.

§326. Limitation on compensation of trustee

(a) In a case under chapter 7 or 11, the court may allow reasonable compensation under section 330 of this title of the trustee for the trustee's services, payable after the trustee renders such services, not to exceed 25 percent on the first $5,000 or less, 10 percent on any amount in excess of $5,000 but not in excess of $50,000, 5 percent on any amount in excess of $50,000 but not in excess of $1,000,000, and reasonable compensation not to exceed 3 percent of such moneys in excess of $1,000,000, upon all moneys disbursed or turned over in the case by the trustee to parties in interest, excluding the debtor, but including holders of secured claims.

(b) In a case under chapter 12 or 13 of this title, the court may not allow compensation for services or reimbursement of expenses of the United States trustee or of a standing trustee appointed under section 586(b) of title 28, but may allow reasonable compensation under section 330 of this title of a trustee appointed under section 1202(a) or 1302(a) of this title for the trustee's services, payable after the trustee renders such services, not to exceed five percent upon all payments under the plan.

(c) If more than one person serves as trustee in the case, the aggregate compensation of such persons for such service may not exceed the maximum compensation prescribed for a single trustee by subsection (a) or (b) of this section, as the case may be.

(d) The court may deny allowance of compensation for services or reimbursement of expenses of the trustee if the trustee failed to make diligent inquiry into facts that would permit denial of allowance under section 328(c) of this title or, with knowledge of such facts, employed a professional person under section 327 of this title.

§327. Employment of professional persons

(a) Except as otherwise provided in this section, the trustee, with the court's approval, may employ one or more attorneys, accountants, appraisers, auctioneers, or other professional persons, that do not hold or represent an interest adverse to the estate, and that are disinterested persons, to represent or assist the trustee in carrying out the trustee's duties under this title.

(b) If the trustee is authorized to operate the business of the debtor under section 721, 1202, or 1108 of this title, and if the debtor has regularly employed attorneys, accountants, or other professional persons on salary, the trustee may retain or replace such professional persons if necessary in the operation of such business.

(c) In a case under chapter 7, 12, or 11 of this title, a person is not disqualified for employment under this section solely because of such person's employment by or representation of a creditor, unless there is objection by another creditor or the United States trustee, in which case the court shall disapprove such employment if there is an actual conflict of interest.

(d) The court may authorize the trustee to act as attorney or accountant for the estate if such authorization is in the best interest of the estate.

(e) The trustee, with the court's approval, may employ, for a specified special purpose, other than to represent the trustee in conducting the case, an attorney that has represented the debtor, if in the best interest of the estate, and if such attorney does not represent or hold any interest adverse to the debtor or to the estate with respect to the matter on which such attorney is to be employed.

(f) The trustee may not employ a person that has served as an examiner in the case.

§328. Limitation on compensation of professional persons

(a) The trustee, or a committee appointed under section 1102 of this title, with the court's approval, may employ or authorize the employment of a professional person under section 327 or 1103 of this title, as the case may be, on any reasonable terms and conditions of employment, including on a retainer, on an hourly basis, on a fixed or percentage fee basis, or on a contingent fee basis. Notwithstanding such terms and conditions, the court may allow compensation different from the compensation provided under such terms and conditions after the conclusion of such employment, if such terms and conditions prove to have been improvident in light of developments not capable of being anticipated at the time of the fixing of such terms and conditions.

(b) If the court has authorized a trustee to serve as an attorney or accountant for the estate under section 327(d) of this title, the court may allow compensation for the trustee's services as such attorney or accountant only to the extent that the trustee performed services as attorney or accountant for the estate and not for performance of any of the trustee's duties that are generally performed by a trustee without the assistance of an attorney or accountant for the estate.

(c) Except as provided in section 327(c), 327(e), or 1107(b) of this title, the court may deny allowance of compensation for services and reimbursement of expenses of a professional person employed under section 327 or 1103 of this title if, at any time during such professional person's employment under section 327 or 1103 of this title, such professional person is not a disinterested person, or represents or holds an interest adverse to the interest of the estate with respect to the matter on which such professional person is employed.

§329. Debtor's transactions with attorneys

(a) Any attorney representing a debtor in a case under this title, or in connection with such a case, whether or not such attorney applies for compensation under this title, shall file with the court a statement of the compensation paid or agreed to be paid, if such payment or agreement was made after one year before the date of the filing of the petition, for services rendered or to be rendered in contemplation of or in connection with the case by such attorney, and the source of such compensation.

(b) If such compensation exceeds the reasonable value of any such services, the court may cancel any such agreement, or order the return of any such payment, to the extent excessive, to—
> **(1)** the estate, if the property transferred—
>> **(A)** would have been property of the estate; or
>> **(B)** was to be paid by or on behalf of the debtor under a plan under chapter 11, 12, or 13 of this title; or
> **(2)** the entity that made such payment.

§330. Compensation of officers

(a)
> **(1)** After notice to the parties in interest and the United States Trustee and a hearing, and subject to sections 326, 328, and 329, the court may award to a trustee, a consumer privacy ombudsman appointed under section 332, an examiner, an ombudsman appointed under section 333, or a professional person employed under section 327 or 1103—
>> **(A)** reasonable compensation for actual, necessary services rendered by the trustee, examiner, ombudsman, professional person, or attorney and by any paraprofessional person employed by any such person; and
>> **(B)** reimbursement for actual, necessary expenses.
> **(2)** The court may, on its own motion or on the motion of the United States Trustee, the United States Trustee for the District or Region, the trustee for the estate, or any other party in interest, award compensation that is less than the amount of compensation that is requested.
> **(3)** In determining the amount of reasonable compensation to be awarded to an examiner, trustee under chapter 11, or professional person, the court shall consider the nature, the extent, and the value of such services, taking into account all relevant factors, including—
>> **(A)** the time spent on such services;
>> **(B)** the rates charged for such services;
>> **(C)** whether the services were necessary to the administration of, or beneficial at the time at which the service was rendered toward the completion of, a case under this title;
>> **(D)** whether the services were performed within a reasonable amount of time commensurate with the complexity, importance, and nature of the problem, issue, or task addressed;
>> **(E)** with respect to a professional person, whether the person is board certified or otherwise has demonstrated skill and experience in the bankruptcy field; and
>> **(F)** whether the compensation is reasonable based on the customary compensation charged by comparably skilled practitioners in cases other than cases under this title.
> **(4)**
>> **(A)** Except as provided in subparagraph (B), the court shall not allow compensation for—
>>> **(i)** unnecessary duplication of services; or
>>> **(ii)** services that were not—

(I) reasonably likely to benefit the debtor's estate; or

(II) necessary to the administration of the case.

(B) In a chapter 12 or chapter 13 case in which the debtor is an individual, the court may allow reasonable compensation to the debtor's attorney for representing the interests of the debtor in connection with the bankruptcy case based on a consideration of the benefit and necessity of such services to the debtor and the other factors set forth in this section.

(5) The court shall reduce the amount of compensation awarded under this section by the amount of any interim compensation awarded under section 331, and, if the amount of such interim compensation exceeds the amount of compensation awarded under this section, may order the return of the excess to the estate.

(6) Any compensation awarded for the preparation of a fee application shall be based on the level and skill reasonably required to prepare the application.

(7) In determining the amount of reasonable compensation to be awarded to a trustee, the court shall treat such compensation as a commission, based on section 326.

(b)

(1) There shall be paid from the filing fee in a case under chapter 7 of this title $45 to the trustee serving in such case, after such trustee's services are rendered.

(2) The Judicial Conference of the United States—

(A) shall prescribe additional fees of the same kind as prescribed under section 1914(b) of title 28; and

(B) may prescribe notice of appearance fees and fees charged against distributions in cases under this title;

to pay $15 to trustees serving in cases after such trustees' services are rendered. Beginning 1 year after the date of the enactment of the Bankruptcy Reform Act of 1994, such $15 shall be paid in addition to the amount paid under paragraph (1).

(c) Unless the court orders otherwise, in a case under chapter 12 or 13 of this title the compensation paid to the trustee serving in the case shall not be less than $5 per month from any distribution under the plan during the administration of the plan.

(d) In a case in which the United States trustee serves as trustee, the compensation of the trustee

under this section shall be paid to the clerk of the bankruptcy court and deposited by the clerk into the United States Trustee System Fund established by section 589a of title 28.

§331. Interim compensation

A trustee, an examiner, a debtor's attorney, or any professional person employed under section 327 or 1103 of this title may apply to the court not more than once every 120 days after an order for relief in a case under this title, or more often if the court permits, for such compensation for services rendered before the date of such an application or reimbursement for expenses incurred before such date as is provided under section 330 of this title. After notice and a hearing, the court may allow and disburse to such applicant such compensation or reimbursement.

§332. Consumer privacy ombudsman

(a) If a hearing is required under section 363(b)(1)(B), the court shall order the United States trustee to appoint, not later than 7 days before the commencement of the hearing, 1 disinterested person (other than the United States trustee) to serve as the consumer privacy ombudsman in the case and shall require that notice of such hearing be timely given to such ombudsman.

(b) The consumer privacy ombudsman may appear and be heard at such hearing and shall provide to the court information to assist the court in its consideration of the facts, circumstances, and conditions of the proposed sale or lease of personally identifiable information under section 363(b)(1)(B). Such information may include presentation of—

(1) the debtor's privacy policy;

(2) the potential losses or gains of privacy to consumers if such sale or such lease is approved by the court;

(3) the potential costs or benefits to consumers if such sale or such lease is approved by the court; and

(4) the potential alternatives that would mitigate potential privacy losses or potential costs to consumers.

(c) A consumer privacy ombudsman shall not disclose any personally identifiable information obtained by the ombudsman under this title.

§333. Appointment of patient care ombudsman

(a)

(1) If the debtor in a case under chapter 7, 9, or 11 is a health care business, the court shall order, not later than 30 days after the commencement of the case, the appointment of an ombudsman to monitor the quality of patient care and to represent the interests of the patients of the health care business unless the court finds that the appointment of such ombudsman is not necessary for the protection of patients under the specific facts of the case.

(2)

(A) If the court orders the appointment of an ombudsman under paragraph (1), the United States trustee shall appoint 1 disinterested person (other than the United States trustee) to serve as such ombudsman.

(B) If the debtor is a health care business that provides long-term care, then the United States trustee may appoint the State Long-Term Care Ombudsman appointed under the Older Americans Act of 1965 for the State in which the case is pending to serve as the ombudsman required by paragraph (1).

(C) If the United States trustee does not appoint a State Long-Term Care Ombudsman under subparagraph (B), the court shall notify the State Long-Term Care Ombudsman appointed under the Older Americans Act of 1965 for the State in which the case is pending, of the name and address of the person who is appointed under subparagraph (A).

(b) An ombudsman appointed under subsection (a) shall—

(1) monitor the quality of patient care provided to patients of the debtor, to the extent necessary under the circumstances, including interviewing patients and physicians;

(2) not later than 60 days after the date of appointment, and not less frequently than at 60-day intervals thereafter, report to the court after notice to the parties in interest, at a hearing or in writing, regarding the quality of patient care provided to patients of the debtor; and

(3) if such ombudsman determines that the quality of patient care provided to patients of the debtor is declining significantly or is otherwise being materially compromised, file with the court a motion or a written report, with notice to the parties in interest immediately upon making such determination.

(c)

(1) An ombudsman appointed under subsection (a) shall maintain any information obtained by such ombudsman under this section that relates to patients (including information relating to patient records) as confidential information. Such ombudsman may not review confidential patient records unless the court approves such review in advance and imposes restrictions on such ombudsman to protect the confidentiality of such records.

(2) An ombudsman appointed under subsection (a)(2)(B) shall have access to patient records consistent with authority of such ombudsman under the Older Americans Act of 1965 and under non-Federal laws governing the State Long-Term Care Ombudsman program.

SUBCHAPTER III— ADMINISTRATION

§341. Meetings of creditors and equity security holders

(a) Within a reasonable time after the order for relief in a case under this title, the United States trustee shall convene and preside at a meeting of creditors.

(b) The United States trustee may convene a meeting of any equity security holders.

(c) The court may not preside at, and may not attend, any meeting under this section including any final meeting of creditors. Notwithstanding any local court rule, provision of a State constitution, any otherwise applicable nonbankruptcy law, or any other requirement that representation at the meeting of creditors under subsection (a) be by an attorney, a creditor holding a consumer debt or any representative of the creditor (which may include an entity or an employee of an entity and may be a representative for more than 1 creditor) shall be permitted to appear at and participate in the meeting of creditors in a case under chapter 7 or 13, either alone or in conjunction with an attorney for the creditor. Nothing in this subsection shall be construed to require any creditor to be represented by an attorney at any meeting of creditors.

(d) Prior to the conclusion of the meeting of creditors or equity security holders, the trustee shall orally examine the debtor to ensure that the debtor in a case under chapter 7 of this title is aware of—

(1) the potential consequences of seeking a discharge in bankruptcy, including the effects on credit history;

(2) the debtor's ability to file a petition under a different chapter of this title;

(3) the effect of receiving a discharge of debts under this title; and

(4) the effect of reaffirming a debt, including the debtor's knowledge of the provisions of section 524(d) of this title.

(e) Notwithstanding subsections (a) and (b), the court, on the request of a party in interest and after notice and a hearing, for cause may order that the United States trustee not convene a meeting of creditors or equity security holders if the debtor has filed a plan as to which the debtor solicited acceptances prior to the commencement of the case.

§342. Notice

(a) There shall be given such notice as is appropriate, including notice to any holder of a community claim, of an order for relief in a case under this title.

(b) Before the commencement of a case under this title by an individual whose debts are primarily consumer debts, the clerk shall give to such individual written notice containing—

    (1) a brief description of—

        (A) chapters 7, 11, 12, and 13 and the general purpose, benefits, and costs of proceeding under each of those chapters; and

        (B) the types of services available from credit counseling agencies; and

    (2) statements specifying that—

        (A) a person who knowingly and fraudulently conceals assets or makes a false oath or statement under penalty of perjury in connection with a case under this title shall be subject to fine, imprisonment, or both; and

        (B) all information supplied by a debtor in connection with a case under this title is subject to examination by the Attorney General.

(c)

    (1) If notice is required to be given by the debtor to a creditor under this title, any rule, any applicable law, or any order of the court, such notice shall contain the name, address, and last 4 digits of the taxpayer identification number of the debtor. If the notice concerns an amendment that adds a creditor to the schedules of assets and liabilities, the debtor shall include the full taxpayer identification number in the notice sent to that creditor, but the debtor shall include only the last 4 digits of the taxpayer identification number in the copy of the notice filed with the court.

    (2)

        (A) If, within the 90 days before the commencement of a voluntary case, a creditor supplies the debtor in at least 2 communications sent to the debtor with the current account number of the debtor and the address at which such creditor requests to receive correspondence, then any notice required by this title to be sent by the debtor to such creditor shall be sent to such address and shall include such account number.

        (B) If a creditor would be in violation of applicable nonbankruptcy law by sending any such communication within such 90-day period and if such creditor supplies the debtor in the last 2 communications with the current account number of the debtor and the address at which such creditor requests to receive correspondence, then any notice required by this title to be sent by the debtor to such creditor shall be sent to such address and shall include such account number.

(d) In a case under chapter 7 of this title in which the debtor is an individual and in which the presumption of abuse arises under section 707(b), the clerk shall give written notice to all creditors not later than 10 days after the date of the filing of the petition that the presumption of abuse has arisen.

(e)

    (1) In a case under chapter 7 or 13 of this title of a debtor who is an individual, a creditor at any time may both file with the court and serve on the debtor a notice of address to be used to provide notice in such case to such creditor.

    (2) Any notice in such case required to be provided to such creditor by the debtor or the court later than 7 days after the court and the debtor receive such creditor's notice of address, shall be provided to such address.

(f)

    (1) An entity may file with any bankruptcy court a notice of address to be used by all the bankruptcy courts or by particular bankruptcy courts, as so specified by such entity at the time such notice is filed, to provide notice to such entity in all cases under chapters 7 and 13 pending in the courts with respect to which such notice is filed, in which such entity is a creditor.

    (2) In any case filed under chapter 7 or 13, any notice required to be provided by a court with respect to which a notice is filed under paragraph (1), to such entity later than 30 days after the filing of such notice under paragraph (1) shall be provided to such address unless with respect to a particular case a different address is specified in a notice filed and served in accordance with subsection (e).

(3) A notice filed under paragraph (1) may be withdrawn by such entity.

(g)

(1) Notice provided to a creditor by the debtor or the court other than in accordance with this section (excluding this subsection) shall not be effective notice until such notice is brought to the attention of such creditor. If such creditor designates a person or an organizational subdivision of such creditor to be responsible for receiving notices under this title and establishes reasonable procedures so that such notices receivable by such creditor are to be delivered to such person or such subdivision, then a notice provided to such creditor other than in accordance with this section (excluding this subsection) shall not be considered to have been brought to the attention of such creditor until such notice is received by such person or such subdivision.

(2) A monetary penalty may not be imposed on a creditor for a violation of a stay in effect under section 362(a) (including a monetary penalty imposed under section 362(k)) or for failure to comply with section 542 or 543 unless the conduct that is the basis of such violation or of such failure occurs after such creditor receives notice effective under this section of the order for relief.

§343. Examination of the debtor

The debtor shall appear and submit to examination under oath at the meeting of creditors under section 341(a) of this title. Creditors, any indenture trustee, any trustee or examiner in the case, or the United States trustee may examine the debtor. The United States trustee may administer the oath required under this section.

§344. Self-incrimination; immunity

Immunity for persons required to submit to examination, to testify, or to provide information in a case under this title may be granted under part V of title 18.

§345. Money of estates

(a) A trustee in a case under this title may make such deposit or investment of the money of the estate for which such trustee serves as will yield the maximum reasonable net return on such money, taking into account the safety of such deposit or investment.

(b) Except with respect to a deposit or investment that is insured or guaranteed by the United States or by a department, agency, or instrumentality of the United States or backed by the full faith and credit of the United States, the trustee shall require from an entity with which such money is deposited or invested—

(1) a bond—

(A) in favor of the United States;

(B) secured by the undertaking of a corporate surety approved by the United States trustee for the district in which the case is pending; and

(C) conditioned on—

(i) a proper accounting for all money so deposited or invested and for any return on such money;

(ii) prompt repayment of such money and return; and

(iii) faithful performance of duties as a depository; or

(2) the deposit of securities of the kind specified in section 9303 of title 31;

unless the court for cause orders otherwise.

(c) An entity with which such moneys are deposited or invested is authorized to deposit or invest such moneys as may be required under this section.

§346. Special provisions related to the treatment of State and local taxes

(a) Whenever the Internal Revenue Code of 1986 provides that a separate taxable estate or entity is created in a case concerning a debtor under this title, and the income, gain, loss, deductions, and credits of such estate shall be taxed to or claimed by the estate, a separate taxable estate is also created for purposes of any State and local law imposing a tax on or measured by income and such income, gain, loss, deductions, and credits shall be taxed to or claimed by the estate and may not be taxed to or claimed by the debtor. The preceding sentence shall not apply if the case is dismissed. The trustee shall make tax returns of income required under any such State or local law.

(b) Whenever the Internal Revenue Code of 1986 provides that no separate taxable estate shall be created in a case concerning a debtor under this title, and the income, gain, loss, deductions, and credits of an estate shall be taxed to or claimed by the debtor, such income, gain, loss, deductions, and credits shall be taxed to or claimed by the debtor under a State or local law imposing a tax on or measured by income and may not be taxed to or claimed by the estate. The trustee shall make such tax returns of income of corporations and of partnerships as are required under any State or local law, but with respect to partnerships, shall make such returns only to the extent such returns are also required to be made under such Code. The estate shall be liable for any tax imposed on such corporation or partnership, but not for any tax imposed on partners or members.

(c) With respect to a partnership or any entity treated as a partnership under a State or local law imposing a tax on or measured by income that is a debtor in a case under this title, any gain or loss resulting from a distribution of property from such partnership, or any distributive share of any income, gain, loss, deduction, or credit of a partner or member that is distributed, or considered distributed, from such partnership, after the commencement of the case, is gain, loss, income, deduction, or credit, as the case may be, of the partner or member, and if such partner or member is a debtor in a case under this title, shall be subject to tax in accordance with subsection (a) or (b).

(d) For purposes of any State or local law imposing a tax on or measured by income, the taxable period of a debtor in a case under this title shall terminate only if and to the extent that the taxable period of such debtor terminates under the Internal Revenue Code of 1986.

(e) The estate in any case described in subsection (a) shall use the same accounting method as the debtor used immediately before the commencement of the case, if such method of accounting complies with applicable nonbankruptcy tax law.

(f) For purposes of any State or local law imposing a tax on or measured by income, a transfer of property from the debtor to the estate or from the estate to the debtor shall not be treated as a disposition for purposes of any provision assigning tax consequences to a disposition, except to the extent that such transfer is treated as a disposition under the Internal Revenue Code of 1986.

(g) Whenever a tax is imposed pursuant to a State or local law imposing a tax on or measured by income pursuant to subsection (a) or (b), such tax shall be imposed at rates generally applicable to the same types of entities under such State or local law.

(h) The trustee shall withhold from any payment of claims for wages, salaries, commissions, dividends, interest, or other payments, or collect, any amount required to be withheld or collected under applicable State or local tax law, and shall pay such withheld or collected amount to the appropriate governmental unit at the time and in the manner required by such tax law, and with the same priority as the claim from which such amount was withheld or collected was paid.

(i)

(1) To the extent that any State or local law imposing a tax on or measured by income provides for the carryover of any tax attribute from one taxable period to a subsequent taxable period, the estate shall succeed to such tax attribute in any case in which such estate is subject to tax under subsection (a).

(2) After such a case is closed or dismissed, the debtor shall succeed to any tax attribute to which the estate succeeded under paragraph (1) to the extent consistent with the Internal Revenue Code of 1986.

(3) The estate may carry back any loss or tax attribute to a taxable period of the debtor that ended before the date of the order for relief under this title to the extent that—

(A) applicable State or local tax law provides for a carryback in the case of the debtor; and

(B) the same or a similar tax attribute may be carried back by the estate to such a taxable period of the debtor under the Internal Revenue Code of 1986.

(j)

(1) For purposes of any State or local law imposing a tax on or measured by income, income is not realized by the estate, the debtor, or a successor to the debtor by reason of discharge of indebtedness in a case under this title, except to the extent, if any, that such income is subject to tax under the Internal Revenue Code of 1986.

(2) Whenever the Internal Revenue Code of 1986 provides that the amount excluded from gross income in respect of the discharge of indebtedness in a case under this title shall be applied to reduce the tax attributes of the debtor or the estate, a similar reduction shall be made under any State or local law imposing a tax on or measured by income to the extent such State or local law recognizes such attributes. Such State or local law may also provide for the reduction of other attributes to the extent that the full amount of income from

the discharge of indebtedness has not been applied.

(k)

(1) Except as provided in this section and section 505, the time and manner of filing tax returns and the items of income, gain, loss, deduction, and credit of any taxpayer shall be determined under applicable nonbankruptcy law.

(2) For Federal tax purposes, the provisions of this section are subject to the Internal Revenue Code of 1986 and other applicable Federal nonbankruptcy law.

§347. Unclaimed property

(a) Ninety days after the final distribution under section 726, 1226, or 1326 of this title in a case under chapter 7, 12, or 13 of this title, as the case may be, the trustee shall stop payment on any check remaining unpaid, and any remaining property of the estate shall be paid into the court and disposed of under chapter 129 of title 28.

(b) Any security, money, or other property remaining unclaimed at the expiration of the time allowed in a case under chapter 9, 11, or 12 of this title for the presentation of a security or the performance of any other act as a condition to participation in the distribution under any plan confirmed under section 943(b), 1129, 1173, or 1225 of this title, as the case may be, becomes the property of the debtor or of the entity acquiring the assets of the debtor under the plan, as the case may be.

§348. Effect of conversion

(a) Conversion of a case from a case under one chapter of this title to a case under another chapter of this title constitutes an order for relief under the chapter to which the case is converted, but, except as provided in subsections (b) and (c) of this section, does not effect a change in the date of the filing of the petition, the commencement of the case, or the order for relief.

(b) Unless the court for cause orders otherwise, in sections 701(a), 727(a)(10), 727(b), 1102(a), 1110(a)(1), 1121(b), 1121(c), 1141(d)(4), 1201(a), 1221, 1228(a), 1301(a), and 1305(a) of this title, "the order for relief under this chapter" in a chapter to which a case has been converted under section 706, 1112, 1208, or 1307 of this title means the conversion of such case to such chapter.

(c) Sections 342 and 365(d) of this title apply in a case that has been converted under section 706, 1112, 1208, or 1307 of this title, as if the conversion order were the order for relief.

(d) A claim against the estate or the debtor that arises after the order for relief but before conversion in a case that is converted under section 1112, 1208, or 1307 of this title, other than a claim specified in section 503(b) of this title, shall be treated for all purposes as if such claim had arisen immediately before the date of the filing of the petition.

(e) Conversion of a case under section 706, 1112, 1208, or 1307 of this title terminates the service of any trustee or examiner that is serving in the case before such conversion.

(f)

(1) Except as provided in paragraph (2), when a case under chapter 13 of this title is converted to a case under another chapter under this title—

(A) property of the estate in the converted case shall consist of property of the estate, as of the date of filing of the petition, that remains in the possession of or is under the control of the debtor on the date of conversion;

(B) valuations of property and of allowed secured claims in the chapter 13 case shall apply only in a case converted to a case under chapter 11 or 12, but not in a case converted to a case under chapter 7, with allowed secured claims in cases under chapters 11 and 12 reduced to the extent that they have been paid in accordance with the chapter 13 plan; and

(C) with respect to cases converted from chapter 13—

(i) the claim of any creditor holding security as of the date of the filing of the petition shall continue to be secured by that security unless the full amount of such claim determined under applicable nonbankruptcy law has been paid in full as of the date of conversion, notwithstanding any valuation or determination of the amount of an allowed secured claim made for the purposes of the case under chapter 13; and

(ii) unless a prebankruptcy default has been fully cured under the plan at the time of conversion, in any proceeding under this title or otherwise, the default shall have the effect given under applicable nonbankruptcy law.

(2) If the debtor converts a case under chapter 13 of this title to a case under another chapter under this title in bad faith, the property of the estate in the converted case shall consist of the property of the estate as of the date of conversion.

§349. Effect of dismissal

(a) Unless the court, for cause, orders otherwise, the dismissal of a case under this title does not bar the discharge, in a later case under this title, of debts that were dischargeable in the case dismissed; nor does the dismissal of a case under this title prejudice the debtor with regard to the filing of a subsequent petition under this title, except as provided in section 109(g) of this title.

(b) Unless the court, for cause, orders otherwise, a dismissal of a case other than under section 742 of this title—

  (1) reinstates—

   (A) any proceeding or custodianship superseded under section 543 of this title;

   (B) any transfer avoided under section 522, 544, 545, 547, 548, 549, or 724(a) of this title, or preserved under section 510(c)(2), 522(i)(2), or 551 of this title; and

   (C) any lien voided under section 506(d) of this title;

  (2) vacates any order, judgment, or transfer ordered, under section 522(i)(1), 542, 550, or 553 of this title; and

  (3) revests the property of the estate in the entity in which such property was vested immediately before the commencement of the case under this title.

§350. Closing and reopening cases

(a) After an estate is fully administered and the court has discharged the trustee, the court shall close the case.

(b) A case may be reopened in the court in which such case was closed to administer assets, to accord relief to the debtor, or for other cause.

§351. Disposal of patient records

If a health care business commences a case under chapter 7, 9, or 11, and the trustee does not have a sufficient amount of funds to pay for the storage of patient records in the manner required under applicable Federal or State law, the following requirements shall apply:

(1) The trustee shall—

   (A) promptly publish notice, in 1 or more appropriate newspapers, that if patient records are not claimed by the patient or an insurance provider (if applicable law permits the insurance provider to make that claim) by the date that is 365 days after the date of that notification, the trustee will destroy the patient records; and

   (B) during the first 180 days of the 365-day period described in subparagraph (A), promptly attempt to notify directly each patient that is the subject of the patient records and appropriate insurance carrier concerning the patient records by mailing to the most recent known address of that patient, or a family member or contact person for that patient, and to the appropriate insurance carrier an appropriate notice regarding the claiming or disposing of patient records.

(2) If, after providing the notification under paragraph (1), patient records are not claimed during the 365-day period described under that paragraph, the trustee shall mail, by certified mail, at the end of such 365-day period a written request to each appropriate Federal agency to request permission from that agency to deposit the patient records with that agency, except that no Federal agency is required to accept patient records under this paragraph.

(3) If, following the 365-day period described in paragraph (2) and after providing the notification under paragraph (1), patient records are not claimed by a patient or insurance provider, or request is not granted by a Federal agency to deposit such records with that agency, the trustee shall destroy those records by—

   (A) if the records are written, shredding or burning the records; or

   (B) if the records are magnetic, optical, or other electronic records, by otherwise destroying those records so that those records cannot be retrieved.

SUBCHAPTER IV— ADMINISTRATIVE POWERS

§361. Adequate protection

When adequate protection is required under section 362, 363, or 364 of this title of an interest of an entity in property, such adequate protection may be provided by—

   (1) requiring the trustee to make a cash payment or periodic cash payments to such entity, to the extent that the stay under section 362 of this title, use, sale, or lease under section 363 of this title, or any grant of a lien under section 364 of this title results in a decrease in the value of such entity's interest in such property;

   (2) providing to such entity an additional or replacement lien to the extent that such stay,

use, sale, lease, or grant results in a decrease in the value of such entity's interest in such property; or

(3) granting such other relief, other than entitling such entity to compensation allowable under section 503(b)(1) of this title as an administrative expense, as will result in the realization by such entity of the indubitable equivalent of such entity's interest in such property.

§362. Automatic stay

(a) Except as provided in subsection (b) of this section, a petition filed under section 301, 302, or 303 of this title, or an application filed under section 5(a)(3) of the Securities Investor Protection Act of 1970, operates as a stay, applicable to all entities, of—

(1) the commencement or continuation, including the issuance or employment of process, of a judicial, administrative, or other action or proceeding against the debtor that was or could have been commenced before the commencement of the case under this title, or to recover a claim against the debtor that arose before the commencement of the case under this title;

(2) the enforcement, against the debtor or against property of the estate, of a judgment obtained before the commencement of the case under this title;

(3) any act to obtain possession of property of the estate or of property from the estate or to exercise control over property of the estate;

(4) any act to create, perfect, or enforce any lien against property of the estate;

(5) any act to create, perfect, or enforce against property of the debtor any lien to the extent that such lien secures a claim that arose before the commencement of the case under this title;

(6) any act to collect, assess, or recover a claim against the debtor that arose before the commencement of the case under this title;

(7) the setoff of any debt owing to the debtor that arose before the commencement of the case under this title against any claim against the debtor; and

(8) the commencement or continuation of a proceeding before the United States Tax Court concerning a tax liability of a debtor that is a corporation for a taxable period the bankruptcy court may determine or concerning the tax liability of a debtor who is an individual for a taxable period ending before the date of the order for relief under this title.

(b) The filing of a petition under section 301, 302, or 303 of this title, or of an application under section 5(a)(3) of the Securities Investor Protection Act of 1970, does not operate as a stay—

(1) under subsection (a) of this section, of the commencement or continuation of a criminal action or proceeding against the debtor;

(2) under subsection (a)—

(A) of the commencement or continuation of a civil action or proceeding—

(i) for the establishment of paternity;

(ii) for the establishment or modification of an order for domestic support obligations;

(iii) concerning child custody or visitation;

(iv) for the dissolution of a marriage, except to the extent that such proceeding seeks to determine the division of property that is property of the estate; or

(v) regarding domestic violence;

(B) of the collection of a domestic support obligation from property that is not property of the estate;

(C) with respect to the withholding of income that is property of the estate or property of the debtor for payment of a domestic support obligation under a judicial or administrative order or a statute;

(D) of the withholding, suspension, or restriction of a driver's license, a professional or occupational license, or a recreational license, under State law, as specified in section 466(a)(16) of the Social Security Act;

(E) of the reporting of overdue support owed by a parent to any consumer reporting agency as specified in section 466(a)(7) of the Social Security Act;

(F) of the interception of a tax refund, as specified in sections 464 and 466(a)(3) of the Social Security Act or under an analogous State law; or

(G) of the enforcement of a medical obligation, as specified under title IV of the Social Security Act;

(3) under subsection (a) of this section, of any act to perfect, or to maintain or continue the perfection of, an interest in property to the extent that the trustee's rights and powers are subject to such perfection under section 546(b) of this title or to the extent that such act is accomplished within the period provided under section 547(e)(2)(A) of this title;

(4) under paragraph (1), (2), (3), or (6) of subsection (a) of this section, of the commencement or continuation of an action or proceeding by a governmental unit or any organization exercising authority under the Convention on the Prohibition of the Development, Production, Stockpiling and Use of Chemical Weapons and on Their Destruction, opened for signature on January 13, 1993, to enforce such governmental unit's or organization's police and regulatory power, including the enforcement of a judgment other than a money judgment, obtained in an action or proceeding by the governmental unit to enforce such governmental unit's or organization's police or regulatory power;

[(5) Repealed. Pub. L. 105–277, div. I, title VI, §603(1), Oct. 21, 1998, 112 Stat. 2681–866;]

(6) under subsection (a) of this section, of the exercise by a commodity broker, forward contract merchant, stockbroker, financial institution, financial participant, or securities clearing agency of any contractual right (as defined in section 555 or 556) under any security agreement or arrangement or other credit enhancement forming a part of or related to any commodity contract, forward contract or securities contract, or of any contractual right (as defined in section 555 or 556) to offset or net out any termination value, payment amount, or other transfer obligation arising under or in connection with 1 or more such contracts, including any master agreement for such contracts;

(7) under subsection (a) of this section, of the exercise by a repo participant or financial participant of any contractual right (as defined in section 559) under any security agreement or arrangement or other credit enhancement forming a part of or related to any repurchase agreement, or of any contractual right (as defined in section 559) to offset or net out any termination value, payment amount, or other transfer obligation arising under or in connection with 1 or more such agreements, including any master agreement for such agreements;

(8) under subsection (a) of this section, of the commencement of any action by the Secretary of Housing and Urban Development to foreclose a mortgage or deed of trust in any case in which the mortgage or deed of trust held by the Secretary is insured or was formerly insured under the National Housing Act and covers property, or combinations of property, consisting of five or more living units;

(9) under subsection (a), of—

(A) an audit by a governmental unit to determine tax liability;

(B) the issuance to the debtor by a governmental unit of a notice of tax deficiency;

(C) a demand for tax returns; or

(D) the making of an assessment for any tax and issuance of a notice and demand for payment of such an assessment (but any tax lien that would otherwise attach to property of the estate by reason of such an assessment shall not take effect unless such tax is a debt of the debtor that will not be discharged in the case and such property or its proceeds are transferred out of the estate to, or otherwise revested in, the debtor).

(10) under subsection (a) of this section, of any act by a lessor to the debtor under a lease of nonresidential real property that has terminated by the expiration of the stated term of the lease before the commencement of or during a case under this title to obtain possession of such property;

(11) under subsection (a) of this section, of the presentment of a negotiable instrument and the giving of notice of and protesting dishonor of such an instrument;

(12) under subsection (a) of this section, after the date which is 90 days after the filing of such petition, of the commencement or continuation, and conclusion to the entry of final judgment, of an action which involves a debtor subject to reorganization pursuant to chapter 11 of this title and which was brought by the Secretary of Transportation under section 31325 of title 46 (including distribution of any proceeds of sale) to foreclose a preferred ship or fleet mortgage, or a security interest in or relating to a vessel or vessel under construction, held by the Secretary of Transportation under chapter 537 of title 46 or section 109(h) of title 49, or under applicable State law;

(13) under subsection (a) of this section, after the date which is 90 days after the filing of such petition, of the commencement or continuation, and conclusion to the entry of final judgment, of an action which involves a debtor subject to reorganization pursuant to chapter 11 of this title and which was brought by the Secretary of Commerce under section 31325 of title 46 (including distribution of any proceeds of sale) to foreclose a preferred ship or fleet mortgage in a vessel or a mortgage, deed of trust, or other security interest in a fishing facility held by the Secretary of Commerce under chapter 537 of title 46;

(14) under subsection (a) of this section, of any action by an accrediting agency regarding the accreditation status of the debtor as an educational institution;

(15) under subsection (a) of this section, of any action by a State licensing body regarding the licensure of the debtor as an educational institution;

(16) under subsection (a) of this section, of any action by a guaranty agency, as defined in section 435(j) of the Higher Education Act of 1965 or the Secretary of Education regarding the eligibility of the debtor to participate in programs authorized under such Act;

(17) under subsection (a) of this section, of the exercise by a swap participant or financial participant of any contractual right (as defined in section 560) under any security agreement or arrangement or other credit enhancement forming a part of or related to any swap agreement, or of any contractual right (as defined in section 560) to offset or net out any termination value, payment amount, or other transfer obligation arising under or in connection with 1 or more such agreements, including any master agreement for such agreements;

(18) under subsection (a) of the creation or perfection of a statutory lien for an ad valorem property tax, or a special tax or special assessment on real property whether or not ad valorem, imposed by a governmental unit, if such tax or assessment comes due after the date of the filing of the petition;

(19) under subsection (a), of withholding of income from a debtor's wages and collection of amounts withheld, under the debtor's agreement authorizing that withholding and collection for the benefit of a pension, profit-sharing, stock bonus, or other plan established under section 401, 403, 408, 408A, 414, 457, or 501(c) of the Internal Revenue Code of 1986, that is sponsored by the employer of the debtor, or an affiliate, successor, or predecessor of such employer—

    (A) to the extent that the amounts withheld and collected are used solely for payments relating to a loan from a plan under section 408(b)(1) of the Employee Retirement Income Security Act of 1974 or is subject to section 72(p) of the Internal Revenue Code of 1986; or

    (B) a loan from a thrift savings plan permitted under subchapter III of chapter

84 of title 5, that satisfies the requirements of section 8433(g) of such title;

but nothing in this paragraph may be construed to provide that any loan made under a governmental plan under section 414(d), or a contract or account under section 403(b), of the Internal Revenue Code of 1986 constitutes a claim or a debt under this title;

(20) under subsection (a), of any act to enforce any lien against or security interest in real property following entry of the order under subsection (d)(4) as to such real property in any prior case under this title, for a period of 2 years after the date of the entry of such an order, except that the debtor, in a subsequent case under this title, may move for relief from such order based upon changed circumstances or for other good cause shown, after notice and a hearing;

(21) under subsection (a), of any act to enforce any lien against or security interest in real property—

    (A) if the debtor is ineligible under section 109(g) to be a debtor in a case under this title; or

    (B) if the case under this title was filed in violation of a bankruptcy court order in a prior case under this title prohibiting the debtor from being a debtor in another case under this title;

(22) subject to subsection (l), under subsection (a)(3), of the continuation of any eviction, unlawful detainer action, or similar proceeding by a lessor against a debtor involving residential property in which the debtor resides as a tenant under a lease or rental agreement and with respect to which the lessor has obtained before the date of the filing of the bankruptcy petition, a judgment for possession of such property against the debtor;

(23) subject to subsection (m), under subsection (a)(3), of an eviction action that seeks possession of the residential property in which the debtor resides as a tenant under a lease or rental agreement based on endangerment of such property or the illegal use of controlled substances on such property, but only if the lessor files with the court, and serves upon the debtor, a certification under penalty of perjury that such an eviction action has been filed, or that the debtor, during the 30-day period preceding the date of the filing of the certification, has endangered property or illegally used or allowed to be used a controlled substance on the property;

(24) under subsection (a), of any transfer that is not avoidable under section 544 and that is not avoidable under section 549;

(25) under subsection (a), of—

    (A) the commencement or continuation of an investigation or action by a securities self regulatory organization to enforce such organization's regulatory power;

    (B) the enforcement of an order or decision, other than for monetary sanctions, obtained in an action by such securities self regulatory organization to enforce such organization's regulatory power; or

    (C) any act taken by such securities self regulatory organization to delist, delete, or refuse to permit quotation of any stock that does not meet applicable regulatory requirements;

(26) under subsection (a), of the setoff under applicable nonbankruptcy law of an income tax refund, by a governmental unit, with respect to a taxable period that ended before the date of the order for relief against an income tax liability for a taxable period that also ended before the date of the order for relief, except that in any case in which the setoff of an income tax refund is not permitted under applicable nonbankruptcy law because of a pending action to determine the amount or legality of a tax liability, the governmental unit may hold the refund pending the resolution of the action, unless the court, on the motion of the trustee and after notice and a hearing, grants the taxing authority adequate protection (within the meaning of section 361) for the secured claim of such authority in the setoff under section 506(a);

(27) under subsection (a) of this section, of the exercise by a master netting agreement participant of any contractual right (as defined in section 555, 556, 559, or 560) under any security agreement or arrangement or other credit enhancement forming a part of or related to any master netting agreement, or of any contractual right (as defined in section 555, 556, 559, or 560) to offset or net out any termination value, payment amount, or other transfer obligation arising under or in connection with 1 or more such master netting agreements to the extent that such participant is eligible to exercise such rights under paragraph (6), (7), or (17) for each individual contract covered by the master netting agreement in issue; and

(28) under subsection (a), of the exclusion by the Secretary of Health and Human Services of the debtor from participation in the medicare program or any other Federal health care program (as defined in section 1128B(f) of the Social Security Act pursuant to title XI or XVIII of such Act).

The provisions of paragraphs (12) and (13) of this subsection shall apply with respect to any such petition filed on or before December 31, 1989.

(c) Except as provided in subsections (d), (e), (f), and (h) of this section—

(1) the stay of an act against property of the estate under subsection (a) of this section continues until such property is no longer property of the estate;

(2) the stay of any other act under subsection (a) of this section continues until the earliest of—

    (A) the time the case is closed;

    (B) the time the case is dismissed; or

    (C) if the case is a case under chapter 7 of this title concerning an individual or a case under chapter 9, 11, 12, or 13 of this title, the time a discharge is granted or denied;

(3) if a single or joint case is filed by or against a debtor who is an individual in a case under chapter 7, 11, or 13, and if a single or joint case of the debtor was pending within the preceding 1-year period but was dismissed, other than a case refiled under a chapter other than chapter 7 after dismissal under section 707(b)—

    (A) the stay under subsection (a) with respect to any action taken with respect to a debt or property securing such debt or with respect to any lease shall terminate with respect to the debtor on the 30th day after the filing of the later case;

    (B) on the motion of a party in interest for continuation of the automatic stay and upon notice and a hearing, the court may extend the stay in particular cases as to any or all creditors (subject to such conditions or limitations as the court may then impose) after notice and a hearing completed before the expiration of the 30-day period only if the party in interest demonstrates that the filing of the later case is in good faith as to the creditors to be stayed; and

    (C) for purposes of subparagraph (B), a case is presumptively filed not in good faith (but such presumption may be rebutted by clear and convincing evidence to the contrary)—

        (i) as to all creditors, if—

            (I) more than 1 previous case under any of chapters 7, 11, and 13 in which the individual was a debtor was pending within the preceding 1-year period;

(II) a previous case under any of chapters 7, 11, and 13 in which the individual was a debtor was dismissed within such 1-year period, after the debtor failed to—

(aa) file or amend the petition or other documents as required by this title or the court without substantial excuse (but mere inadvertence or negligence shall not be a substantial excuse unless the dismissal was caused by the negligence of the debtor's attorney);

(bb) provide adequate protection as ordered by the court; or

(cc) perform the terms of a plan confirmed by the court; or

(III) there has not been a substantial change in the financial or personal affairs of the debtor since the dismissal of the next most previous case under chapter 7, 11, or 13 or any other reason to conclude that the later case will be concluded—

(aa) if a case under chapter 7, with a discharge; or

(bb) if a case under chapter 11 or 13, with a confirmed plan that will be fully performed; and

(ii) as to any creditor that commenced an action under subsection (d) in a previous case in which the individual was a debtor if, as of the date of dismissal of such case, that action was still pending or had been resolved by terminating, conditioning, or limiting the stay as to actions of such creditor; and

(4)

(A)

(i) if a single or joint case is filed by or against a debtor who is an individual under this title, and if 2 or more single or joint cases of the debtor were pending within the previous year but were dismissed, other than a case refiled under a chapter other than chapter 7 after dismissal under section 707(b), the stay under subsection (a) shall not go into effect upon the filing of the later case; and

(ii) on request of a party in interest, the court shall promptly enter an order confirming that no stay is in effect;

(B) if, within 30 days after the filing of the later case, a party in interest requests the court may order the stay to take effect in the case as to any or all creditors (subject to such conditions or limitations as the court may impose), after notice and a hearing, only if the party in interest demonstrates that the filing of the later case is in good faith as to the creditors to be stayed;

(C) a stay imposed under subparagraph (B) shall be effective on the date of the entry of the order allowing the stay to go into effect; and

(D) for purposes of subparagraph (B), a case is presumptively filed not in good faith (but such presumption may be rebutted by clear and convincing evidence to the contrary)—

(i) as to all creditors if—

(I) 2 or more previous cases under this title in which the individual was a debtor were pending within the 1-year period;

(II) a previous case under this title in which the individual was a debtor was dismissed within the time period stated in this paragraph after the debtor failed to file or amend the petition or other documents as required by this title or the court without substantial excuse (but mere inadvertence or negligence shall not be substantial excuse unless the dismissal was caused by the negligence of the debtor's attorney), failed to provide adequate protection as ordered by the court, or failed to perform the terms of a plan confirmed by the court; or

(III) there has not been a substantial change in the financial or personal affairs of the debtor since the dismissal of the next most previous case under this title, or any other reason to conclude that the later case will not be concluded, if a case under chapter 7, with a discharge, and if a case under chapter 11 or 13, with a confirmed plan that will be fully performed; or

(ii) as to any creditor that commenced an action under subsection (d) in a previous case in which the individual was a debtor if, as of the date of dismissal of such case, such action was still pending or had been resolved by terminating, conditioning, or limiting the stay as to such action of such creditor.

(d) On request of a party in interest and after notice and a hearing, the court shall grant relief from the stay provided under subsection (a) of this section, such as by terminating, annulling, modifying, or conditioning such stay—

(1) for cause, including the lack of adequate protection of an interest in property of such party in interest;

(2) with respect to a stay of an act against property under subsection (a) of this section, if—

(A) the debtor does not have an equity in such property; and

(B) such property is not necessary to an effective reorganization;

(3) with respect to a stay of an act against single asset real estate under subsection (a), by a creditor whose claim is secured by an interest in such real estate, unless, not later than the date that is 90 days after the entry of the order for relief (or such later date as the court may determine for cause by order entered within that 90-day period) or 30 days after the court determines that the debtor is subject to this paragraph, whichever is later—

(A) the debtor has filed a plan of reorganization that has a reasonable possibility of being confirmed within a reasonable time; or

(B) the debtor has commenced monthly payments that—

(i) may, in the debtor's sole discretion, notwithstanding section 363(c)(2), be made from rents or other income generated before, on, or after the date of the commencement of the case by or from the property to each creditor whose claim is secured by such real estate (other than a claim secured by a judgment lien or by an unmatured statutory lien); and

(ii) are in an amount equal to interest at the then applicable nondefault contract rate of interest on the value of the creditor's interest in the real estate; or

(4) with respect to a stay of an act against real property under subsection (a), by a creditor whose claim is secured by an interest in such real property, if the court finds that the filing of the petition was part of a scheme to delay, hinder, or defraud creditors that involved either—

(A) transfer of all or part ownership of, or other interest in, such real property without the consent of the secured creditor or court approval; or

(B) multiple bankruptcy filings affecting such real property.

If recorded in compliance with applicable State laws governing notices of interests or liens in real property, an order entered under paragraph (4) shall be binding in any other case under this title purporting to affect such real property filed not later than 2 years after the date of the entry of such order by the court, except that a debtor in a subsequent case under this title may move for relief from such order based upon changed circumstances or for good cause shown, after notice and a hearing. Any Federal, State, or local governmental unit that accepts notices of interests or liens in real property shall accept any certified copy of an order described in this subsection for indexing and recording.

(e)

(1) Thirty days after a request under subsection (d) of this section for relief from the stay of any act against property of the estate under subsection (a) of this section, such stay is terminated with respect to the party in interest making such request, unless the court, after notice and a hearing, orders such stay continued in effect pending the conclusion of, or as a result of, a final hearing and determination under subsection (d) of this section. A hearing under this subsection may be a preliminary hearing, or may be consolidated with the final hearing under subsection (d) of this section. The court shall order such stay continued in effect pending the conclusion of the final hearing under subsection (d) of this section if there is a reasonable likelihood that the party opposing relief from such stay will prevail at the conclusion of such final hearing. If the hearing under this subsection is a preliminary hearing, then such final hearing shall be concluded not later than thirty days after the conclusion of such preliminary hearing, unless the 30-day period is extended with the consent of the parties in interest or for a specific time which the court finds is required by compelling circumstances.

(2) Notwithstanding paragraph (1), in a case under chapter 7, 11, or 13 in which the debtor is an individual, the stay under subsection (a) shall terminate on the date that is 60 days after a request is made by a party in interest under subsection (d), unless—

(A) a final decision is rendered by the court during the 60-day period beginning on the date of the request; or

(B) such 60-day period is extended—
    (i) by agreement of all parties in interest; or
    (ii) by the court for such specific period of time as the court finds is required for good cause, as described in findings made by the court.

(f) Upon request of a party in interest, the court, with or without a hearing, shall grant such relief from the stay provided under subsection (a) of this section as is necessary to prevent irreparable damage to the interest of an entity in property, if such interest will suffer such damage before there is an opportunity for notice and a hearing under subsection (d) or (e) of this section.

(g) In any hearing under subsection (d) or (e) of this section concerning relief from the stay of any act under subsection (a) of this section—
    (1) the party requesting such relief has the burden of proof on the issue of the debtor's equity in property; and
    (2) the party opposing such relief has the burden of proof on all other issues.

(h)
    (1) In a case in which the debtor is an individual, the stay provided by subsection (a) is terminated with respect to personal property of the estate or of the debtor securing in whole or in part a claim, or subject to an unexpired lease, and such personal property shall no longer be property of the estate if the debtor fails within the applicable time set by section 521(a)(2)—
        (A) to file timely any statement of intention required under section 521(a)(2) with respect to such personal property or to indicate in such statement that the debtor will either surrender such personal property or retain it and, if retaining such personal property, either redeem such personal property pursuant to section 722, enter into an agreement of the kind specified in section 524(c) applicable to the debt secured by such personal property, or assume such unexpired lease pursuant to section 365(p) if the trustee does not do so, as applicable; and
        (B) to take timely the action specified in such statement, as it may be amended before expiration of the period for taking action, unless such statement specifies the debtor's intention to reaffirm such debt on the original contract terms and the creditor refuses to agree to the reaffirmation on such terms.

(2) Paragraph (1) does not apply if the court determines, on the motion of the trustee filed before the expiration of the applicable time set by section 521(a)(2), after notice and a hearing, that such personal property is of consequential value or benefit to the estate, and orders appropriate adequate protection of the creditor's interest, and orders the debtor to deliver any collateral in the debtor's possession to the trustee. If the court does not so determine, the stay provided by subsection (a) shall terminate upon the conclusion of the hearing on the motion.

(i) If a case commenced under chapter 7, 11, or 13 is dismissed due to the creation of a debt repayment plan, for purposes of subsection (c)(3), any subsequent case commenced by the debtor under any such chapter shall not be presumed to be filed not in good faith.

(j) On request of a party in interest, the court shall issue an order under subsection (c) confirming that the automatic stay has been terminated.

(k)
    (1) Except as provided in paragraph (2), an individual injured by any willful violation of a stay provided by this section shall recover actual damages, including costs and attorneys' fees, and, in appropriate circumstances, may recover punitive damages.
    (2) If such violation is based on an action taken by an entity in the good faith belief that subsection (h) applies to the debtor, the recovery under paragraph (1) of this subsection against such entity shall be limited to actual damages.

(l)
    (1) Except as otherwise provided in this subsection, subsection (b)(22) shall apply on the date that is 30 days after the date on which the bankruptcy petition is filed, if the debtor files with the petition and serves upon the lessor a certification under penalty of perjury that—
        (A) under nonbankruptcy law applicable in the jurisdiction, there are circumstances under which the debtor would be permitted to cure the entire monetary default that gave rise to the judgment for possession, after that judgment for possession was entered; and
        (B) the debtor (or an adult dependent of the debtor) has deposited with the clerk of the court, any rent that would become due during the 30-day period after the filing of the bankruptcy petition.

(2) If, within the 30-day period after the filing of the bankruptcy petition, the debtor (or an adult dependent of the debtor) complies with paragraph (1) and files with the court and serves upon the lessor a further certification under penalty of perjury that the debtor (or an adult dependent of the debtor) has cured, under nonbankruptcy law applicable in the jurisdiction, the entire monetary default that gave rise to the judgment under which possession is sought by the lessor, subsection (b)(22) shall not apply, unless ordered to apply by the court under paragraph (3).

(3)

(A) If the lessor files an objection to any certification filed by the debtor under paragraph (1) or (2), and serves such objection upon the debtor, the court shall hold a hearing within 10 days after the filing and service of such objection to determine if the certification filed by the debtor under paragraph (1) or (2) is true.

(B) If the court upholds the objection of the lessor filed under subparagraph (A)—

(i) subsection (b)(22) shall apply immediately and relief from the stay provided under subsection (a)(3) shall not be required to enable the lessor to complete the process to recover full possession of the property; and

(ii) the clerk of the court shall immediately serve upon the lessor and the debtor a certified copy of the court's order upholding the lessor's objection.

(4) If a debtor, in accordance with paragraph (5), indicates on the petition that there was a judgment for possession of the residential rental property in which the debtor resides and does not file a certification under paragraph (1) or (2)—

(A) subsection (b)(22) shall apply immediately upon failure to file such certification, and relief from the stay provided under subsection (a)(3) shall not be required to enable the lessor to complete the process to recover full possession of the property; and

(B) the clerk of the court shall immediately serve upon the lessor and the debtor a certified copy of the docket indicating the absence of a filed certification and the applicability of the exception to the stay under subsection (b)(22).

(5)

(A) Where a judgment for possession of residential property in which the debtor resides as a tenant under a lease or rental agreement has been obtained by the lessor, the debtor shall so indicate on the bankruptcy petition and shall provide the name and address of the lessor that obtained that pre-petition judgment on the petition and on any certification filed under this subsection.

(B) The form of certification filed with the petition, as specified in this subsection, shall provide for the debtor to certify, and the debtor shall certify—

(i) whether a judgment for possession of residential rental housing in which the debtor resides has been obtained against the debtor before the date of the filing of the petition; and

(ii) whether the debtor is claiming under paragraph (1) that under nonbankruptcy law applicable in the jurisdiction, there are circumstances under which the debtor would be permitted to cure the entire monetary default that gave rise to the judgment for possession, after that judgment of possession was entered, and has made the appropriate deposit with the court.

(C) The standard forms (electronic and otherwise) used in a bankruptcy proceeding shall be amended to reflect the requirements of this subsection.

(D) The clerk of the court shall arrange for the prompt transmittal of the rent deposited in accordance with paragraph (1)(B) to the lessor.

(m)

(1) Except as otherwise provided in this subsection, subsection (b)(23) shall apply on the date that is 15 days after the date on which the lessor files and serves a certification described in subsection (b)(23).

(2)

(A) If the debtor files with the court an objection to the truth or legal sufficiency of the certification described in subsection (b)(23) and serves such objection upon the lessor, subsection (b)(23) shall not apply, unless ordered to apply by the court under this subsection.

(B) If the debtor files and serves the objection under subparagraph (A), the court shall hold a hearing within 10 days after the filing and service of such objection to determine if the situation giving rise to the lessor's certification under paragraph (1) existed or has been remedied.

(C) If the debtor can demonstrate to the satisfaction of the court that the situation giving rise to the lessor's certification under paragraph (1) did not exist or has been remedied, the stay provided under subsection (a)(3) shall remain in effect until the termination of the stay under this section.

(D) If the debtor cannot demonstrate to the satisfaction of the court that the situation giving rise to the lessor's certification under paragraph (1) did not exist or has been remedied—

(i) relief from the stay provided under subsection (a)(3) shall not be required to enable the lessor to proceed with the eviction; and

(ii) the clerk of the court shall immediately serve upon the lessor and the debtor a certified copy of the court's order upholding the lessor's certification.

(3) If the debtor fails to file, within 15 days, an objection under paragraph (2)(A)—

(A) subsection (b)(23) shall apply immediately upon such failure and relief from the stay provided under subsection (a)(3) shall not be required to enable the lessor to complete the process to recover full possession of the property; and

(B) the clerk of the court shall immediately serve upon the lessor and the debtor a certified copy of the docket indicating such failure.

(n)

(1) Except as provided in paragraph (2), subsection (a) does not apply in a case in which the debtor—

(A) is a debtor in a small business case pending at the time the petition is filed;

(B) was a debtor in a small business case that was dismissed for any reason by an order that became final in the 2-year period ending on the date of the order for relief entered with respect to the petition;

(C) was a debtor in a small business case in which a plan was confirmed in the 2-year period ending on the date of the order for relief entered with respect to the petition; or

(D) is an entity that has acquired substantially all of the assets or business of a small business debtor described in subparagraph (A), (B), or (C), unless such entity establishes by a preponderance of the evidence that such entity acquired substantially all of the assets or business of such small business debtor in good faith

and not for the purpose of evading this paragraph.

(2) Paragraph (1) does not apply—

(A) to an involuntary case involving no collusion by the debtor with creditors; or

(B) to the filing of a petition if—

(i) the debtor proves by a preponderance of the evidence that the filing of the petition resulted from circumstances beyond the control of the debtor not foreseeable at the time the case then pending was filed; and

(ii) it is more likely than not that the court will confirm a feasible plan, but not a liquidating plan, within a reasonable period of time.

(o) The exercise of rights not subject to the stay arising under subsection (a) pursuant to paragraph (6), (7), (17), or (27) of subsection (b) shall not be stayed by any order of a court or administrative agency in any proceeding under this title.

§363. Use, sale, or lease of property

(a) In this section, "cash collateral" means cash, negotiable instruments, documents of title, securities, deposit accounts, or other cash equivalents whenever acquired in which the estate and an entity other than the estate have an interest and includes the proceeds, products, offspring, rents, or profits of property and the fees, charges, accounts or other payments for the use or occupancy of rooms and other public facilities in hotels, motels, or other lodging properties subject to a security interest as provided in section 552(b) of this title, whether existing before or after the commencement of a case under this title.

(b)

(1) The trustee, after notice and a hearing, may use, sell, or lease, other than in the ordinary course of business, property of the estate, except that if the debtor in connection with offering a product or a service discloses to an individual a policy prohibiting the transfer of personally identifiable information about individuals to persons that are not affiliated with the debtor and if such policy is in effect on the date of the commencement of the case, then the trustee may not sell or lease personally identifiable information to any person unless—

(A) such sale or such lease is consistent with such policy; or

(B) after appointment of a consumer privacy ombudsman in accordance with section 332, and after notice and a hearing, the court approves such sale or such lease—

(i) giving due consideration to the facts, circumstances, and conditions of such sale or such lease; and

(ii) finding that no showing was made that such sale or such lease would violate applicable nonbankruptcy law.

(2) If notification is required under subsection (a) of section 7A of the Clayton Act in the case of a transaction under this subsection, then—

(A) notwithstanding subsection (a) of such section, the notification required by such subsection to be given by the debtor shall be given by the trustee; and

(B) notwithstanding subsection (b) of such section, the required waiting period shall end on the 15th day after the date of the receipt, by the Federal Trade Commission and the Assistant Attorney General in charge of the Antitrust Division of the Department of Justice, of the notification required under such subsection (a), unless such waiting period is extended—

(i) pursuant to subsection (e)(2) of such section, in the same manner as such subsection (e)(2) applies to a cash tender offer;

(ii) pursuant to subsection (g)(2) of such section; or

(iii) by the court after notice and a hearing.

(c)

(1) If the business of the debtor is authorized to be operated under section 721, 1108, 1203, 1204, or 1304 of this title and unless the court orders otherwise, the trustee may enter into transactions, including the sale or lease of property of the estate, in the ordinary course of business, without notice or a hearing, and may use property of the estate in the ordinary course of business without notice or a hearing.

(2) The trustee may not use, sell, or lease cash collateral under paragraph (1) of this subsection unless—

(A) each entity that has an interest in such cash collateral consents; or

(B) the court, after notice and a hearing, authorizes such use, sale, or lease in accordance with the provisions of this section.

(3) Any hearing under paragraph (2)(B) of this subsection may be a preliminary hearing or may be consolidated with a hearing under subsection (e) of this section, but shall be scheduled in accordance with the needs of the debtor. If the hearing under paragraph (2)(B) of this subsection is a preliminary hearing, the court may authorize such use, sale, or lease only if there is a reasonable likelihood that the trustee will prevail at the final hearing under subsection (e) of this section. The court shall act promptly on any request for authorization under paragraph (2)(B) of this subsection.

(4) Except as provided in paragraph (2) of this subsection, the trustee shall segregate and account for any cash collateral in the trustee's possession, custody, or control.

(d) The trustee may use, sell, or lease property under subsection (b) or (c) of this section—

(1) in the case of a debtor that is a corporation or trust that is not a moneyed business, commercial corporation, or trust, only in accordance with nonbankruptcy law applicable to the transfer of property by a debtor that is such a corporation or trust; and

(2) only to the extent not inconsistent with any relief granted under subsection (c), (d), (e), or (f) of section 362.

(e) Notwithstanding any other provision of this section, at any time, on request of an entity that has an interest in property used, sold, or leased, or proposed to be used, sold, or leased, by the trustee, the court, with or without a hearing, shall prohibit or condition such use, sale, or lease as is necessary to provide adequate protection of such interest. This subsection also applies to property that is subject to any unexpired lease of personal property (to the exclusion of such property being subject to an order to grant relief from the stay under section 362).

(f) The trustee may sell property under subsection (b) or (c) of this section free and clear of any interest in such property of an entity other than the estate, only if—

(1) applicable nonbankruptcy law permits sale of such property free and clear of such interest;

(2) such entity consents;

(3) such interest is a lien and the price at which such property is to be sold is greater than the aggregate value of all liens on such property;

(4) such interest is in bona fide dispute; or

(5) such entity could be compelled, in a legal or equitable proceeding, to accept a money satisfaction of such interest.

(g) Notwithstanding subsection (f) of this section, the trustee may sell property under subsection (b) or (c) of this section free and clear of any vested or contingent right in the nature of dower or curtesy.

(h) Notwithstanding subsection (f) of this section, the trustee may sell both the estate's interest, under subsection (b) or (c) of this section, and the interest of any co-owner in property in which the debtor had, at the time of the commencement of the case, an undivided interest as a tenant in common, joint tenant, or tenant by the entirety, only if—

(1) partition in kind of such property among the estate and such co-owners is impracticable;

(2) sale of the estate's undivided interest in such property would realize significantly less for the estate than sale of such property free of the interests of such co-owners;

(3) the benefit to the estate of a sale of such property free of the interests of co-owners outweighs the detriment, if any, to such co-owners; and

(4) such property is not used in the production, transmission, or distribution, for sale, of electric energy or of natural or synthetic gas for heat, light, or power.

(i) Before the consummation of a sale of property to which subsection (g) or (h) of this section applies, or of property of the estate that was community property of the debtor and the debtor's spouse immediately before the commencement of the case, the debtor's spouse, or a co-owner of such property, as the case may be, may purchase such property at the price at which such sale is to be consummated.

(j) After a sale of property to which subsection (g) or (h) of this section applies, the trustee shall distribute to the debtor's spouse or the co-owners of such property, as the case may be, and to the estate, the proceeds of such sale, less the costs and expenses, not including any compensation of the trustee, of such sale, according to the interests of such spouse or co-owners, and of the estate.

(k) At a sale under subsection (b) of this section of property that is subject to a lien that secures an allowed claim, unless the court for cause orders otherwise the holder of such claim may bid at such sale, and, if the holder of such claim purchases such property, such holder may offset such claim against the purchase price of such property.

(l) Subject to the provisions of section 365, the trustee may use, sell, or lease property under subsection (b) or (c) of this section, or a plan under chapter 11, 12, or 13 of this title may provide for the use, sale, or lease of property, notwithstanding any provision in a contract, a lease, or applicable law that is conditioned on the insolvency or financial condition of the debtor, on the commencement of a case under this title concerning the debtor, or on the appointment of or the taking possession by a trustee in a case under this title or a custodian, and that effects, or gives an option to effect, a forfeiture, modification, or termination of the debtor's interest in such property.

(m) The reversal or modification on appeal of an authorization under subsection (b) or (c) of this section of a sale or lease of property does not affect the validity of a sale or lease under such authorization to an entity that purchased or leased such property in good faith, whether or not such entity knew of the pendency of the appeal, unless such authorization and such sale or lease were stayed pending appeal.

(n) The trustee may avoid a sale under this section if the sale price was controlled by an agreement among potential bidders at such sale, or may recover from a party to such agreement any amount by which the value of the property sold exceeds the price at which such sale was consummated, and may recover any costs, attorneys' fees, or expenses incurred in avoiding such sale or recovering such amount. In addition to any recovery under the preceding sentence, the court may grant judgment for punitive damages in favor of the estate and against any such party that entered into such an agreement in willful disregard of this subsection.

(o) Notwithstanding subsection (f), if a person purchases any interest in a consumer credit transaction that is subject to the Truth in Lending Act or any interest in a consumer credit contract (as defined in section 433.1 of title 16 of the Code of Federal Regulations (January 1, 2004), as amended from time to time), and if such interest is purchased through a sale under this section, then such person shall remain subject to all claims and defenses that are related to such consumer credit transaction or such consumer credit contract, to the same extent as such person would be subject to such claims and defenses of the consumer had such interest been purchased at a sale not under this section.

(p) In any hearing under this section—

(1) the trustee has the burden of proof on the issue of adequate protection; and

(2) the entity asserting an interest in property has the burden of proof on the issue of the validity, priority, or extent of such interest.

§364. Obtaining credit

(a) If the trustee is authorized to operate the business of the debtor under section 721, 1108, 1203, 1204, or 1304 of this title, unless the court orders otherwise, the trustee may obtain unsecured credit and incur unsecured debt in the ordinary course of business allowable under section 503(b)(1) of this title as an administrative expense.

(b) The court, after notice and a hearing, may authorize the trustee to obtain unsecured credit or to incur unsecured debt other than under subsection (a) of this section, allowable under section 503(b)(1) of this title as an administrative expense.

(c) If the trustee is unable to obtain unsecured credit allowable under section 503(b)(1) of this title as an administrative expense, the court, after notice and a hearing, may authorize the obtaining of credit or the incurring of debt—

    (1) with priority over any or all administrative expenses of the kind specified in section 503(b) or 507(b) of this title;

    (2) secured by a lien on property of the estate that is not otherwise subject to a lien; or

    (3) secured by a junior lien on property of the estate that is subject to a lien.

(d)

    (1) The court, after notice and a hearing, may authorize the obtaining of credit or the incurring of debt secured by a senior or equal lien on property of the estate that is subject to a lien only if—

        (A) the trustee is unable to obtain such credit otherwise; and

        (B) there is adequate protection of the interest of the holder of the lien on the property of the estate on which such senior or equal lien is proposed to be granted.

    (2) In any hearing under this subsection, the trustee has the burden of proof on the issue of adequate protection.

(e) The reversal or modification on appeal of an authorization under this section to obtain credit or incur debt, or of a grant under this section of a priority or a lien, does not affect the validity of any debt so incurred, or any priority or lien so granted, to an entity that extended such credit in good faith, whether or not such entity knew of the pendency of the appeal, unless such authorization and the incurring of such debt, or the granting of such priority or lien, were stayed pending appeal.

(f) Except with respect to an entity that is an underwriter as defined in section 1145(b) of this title, section 5 of the Securities Act of 1933, the Trust Indenture Act of 1939, and any State or local law requiring registration for offer or sale of a security or registration or licensing of an issuer of, underwriter of, or broker or dealer in, a security does not apply to the offer or sale under this section of a security that is not an equity security.

§365. Executory contracts and unexpired leases

(a) Except as provided in sections 765 and 766 of this title and in subsections (b), (c), and (d) of this section, the trustee, subject to the court's approval, may assume or reject any executory contract or unexpired lease of the debtor.

(b)

    (1) If there has been a default in an executory contract or unexpired lease of the debtor, the trustee may not assume such contract or lease unless, at the time of assumption of such contract or lease, the trustee—

        (A) cures, or provides adequate assurance that the trustee will promptly cure, such default other than a default that is a breach of a provision relating to the satisfaction of any provision (other than a penalty rate or penalty provision) relating to a default arising from any failure to perform nonmonetary obligations under an unexpired lease of real property, if it is impossible for the trustee to cure such default by performing nonmonetary acts at and after the time of assumption, except that if such default arises from a failure to operate in accordance with a nonresidential real property lease, then such default shall be cured by performance at and after the time of assumption in accordance with such lease, and pecuniary losses resulting from such default shall be compensated in accordance with the provisions of this paragraph;

        (B) compensates, or provides adequate assurance that the trustee will promptly compensate, a party other than the debtor to such contract or lease, for any actual pecuniary loss to such party resulting from such default; and

        (C) provides adequate assurance of future performance under such contract or lease.

    (2) Paragraph (1) of this subsection does not apply to a default that is a breach of a provision relating to—

        (A) the insolvency or financial condition of the debtor at any time before the closing of the case;

        (B) the commencement of a case under this title;

        (C) the appointment of or taking possession by a trustee in a case under this title or a custodian before such commencement; or

        (D) the satisfaction of any penalty rate or penalty provision relating to a default arising from any failure by the debtor to perform nonmonetary obligations under the executory contract or unexpired lease.

    (3) For the purposes of paragraph (1) of this subsection and paragraph (2)(B) of subsection (f), adequate assurance of future performance of a lease of real property in a shopping center includes adequate assurance—

    (A) of the source of rent and other consideration due under such lease, and in the case of an assignment, that the financial condition and operating performance of the proposed assignee and its guarantors, if any, shall be similar to the financial condition and operating performance of the debtor and its guarantors, if any, as of the time the debtor became the lessee under the lease;

    (B) that any percentage rent due under such lease will not decline substantially;

    (C) that assumption or assignment of such lease is subject to all the provisions thereof, including (but not limited to) provisions such as a radius, location, use, or exclusivity provision, and will not breach any such provision contained in any other lease, financing agreement, or master agreement relating to such shopping center; and

    (D) that assumption or assignment of such lease will not disrupt any tenant mix or balance in such shopping center.

(4) Notwithstanding any other provision of this section, if there has been a default in an unexpired lease of the debtor, other than a default of a kind specified in paragraph (2) of this subsection, the trustee may not require a lessor to provide services or supplies incidental to such lease before assumption of such lease unless the lessor is compensated under the terms of such lease for any services and supplies provided under such lease before assumption of such lease.

(c) The trustee may not assume or assign any executory contract or unexpired lease of the debtor, whether or not such contract or lease prohibits or restricts assignment of rights or delegation of duties, if—

    (1)

        (A) applicable law excuses a party, other than the debtor, to such contract or lease from accepting performance from or rendering performance to an entity other than the debtor or the debtor in possession, whether or not such contract or lease prohibits or restricts assignment of rights or delegation of duties; and

        (B) such party does not consent to such assumption or assignment; or

    (2) such contract is a contract to make a loan, or extend other debt financing or financial

accommodations, to or for the benefit of the debtor, or to issue a security of the debtor; or

    (3) such lease is of nonresidential real property and has been terminated under applicable nonbankruptcy law prior to the order for relief.

(d)

    (1) In a case under chapter 7 of this title, if the trustee does not assume or reject an executory contract or unexpired lease of residential real property or of personal property of the debtor within 60 days after the order for relief, or within such additional time as the court, for cause, within such 60-day period, fixes, then such contract or lease is deemed rejected.

    (2) In a case under chapter 9, 11, 12, or 13 of this title, the trustee may assume or reject an executory contract or unexpired lease of residential real property or of personal property of the debtor at any time before the confirmation of a plan but the court, on the request of any party to such contract or lease, may order the trustee to determine within a specified period of time whether to assume or reject such contract or lease.

    (3) The trustee shall timely perform all the obligations of the debtor, except those specified in section 365(b)(2), arising from and after the order for relief under any unexpired lease of nonresidential real property, until such lease is assumed or rejected, notwithstanding section 503(b)(1) of this title. The court may extend, for cause, the time for performance of any such obligation that arises within 60 days after the date of the order for relief, but the time for performance shall not be extended beyond such 60-day period. This subsection shall not be deemed to affect the trustee's obligations under the provisions of subsection (b) or (f) of this section. Acceptance of any such performance does not constitute waiver or relinquishment of the lessor's rights under such lease or under this title.

    (4)

        (A) Subject to subparagraph (B), an unexpired lease of nonresidential real property under which the debtor is the lessee shall be deemed rejected, and the trustee shall immediately surrender that nonresidential real property to the lessor, if the trustee does not assume or reject the unexpired lease by the earlier of—

            (i) the date that is 120 days after the date of the order for relief; or

            (ii) the date of the entry of an order confirming a plan.

(B)

(i) The court may extend the period determined under subparagraph (A), prior to the expiration of the 120-day period, for 90 days on the motion of the trustee or lessor for cause.

(ii) If the court grants an extension under clause (i), the court may grant a subsequent extension only upon prior written consent of the lessor in each instance.

(5) The trustee shall timely perform all of the obligations of the debtor, except those specified in section 365(b)(2), first arising from or after 60 days after the order for relief in a case under chapter 11 of this title under an unexpired lease of personal property (other than personal property leased to an individual primarily for personal, family, or household purposes), until such lease is assumed or rejected notwithstanding section 503(b)(1) of this title, unless the court, after notice and a hearing and based on the equities of the case, orders otherwise with respect to the obligations or timely performance thereof. This subsection shall not be deemed to affect the trustee's obligations under the provisions of subsection (b) or (f). Acceptance of any such performance does not constitute waiver or relinquishment of the lessor's rights under such lease or under this title.

(e)

(1) Notwithstanding a provision in an executory contract or unexpired lease, or in applicable law, an executory contract or unexpired lease of the debtor may not be terminated or modified, and any right or obligation under such contract or lease may not be terminated or modified, at any time after the commencement of the case solely because of a provision in such contract or lease that is conditioned on—

(A) the insolvency or financial condition of the debtor at any time before the closing of the case;

(B) the commencement of a case under this title; or

(C) the appointment of or taking possession by a trustee in a case under this title or a custodian before such commencement.

(2) Paragraph (1) of this subsection does not apply to an executory contract or unexpired lease of the debtor, whether or not such contract or lease prohibits or restricts assignment of rights or delegation of duties, if—

(A)

(i) applicable law excuses a party, other than the debtor, to such contract or lease from accepting performance from or rendering performance to the trustee or to an assignee of such contract or lease, whether or not such contract or lease prohibits or restricts assignment of rights or delegation of duties; and

(ii) such party does not consent to such assumption or assignment; or

(B) such contract is a contract to make a loan, or extend other debt financing or financial accommodations, to or for the benefit of the debtor, or to issue a security of the debtor.

(f)

(1) Except as provided in subsections (b) and (c) of this section, notwithstanding a provision in an executory contract or unexpired lease of the debtor, or in applicable law, that prohibits, restricts, or conditions the assignment of such contract or lease, the trustee may assign such contract or lease under paragraph (2) of this subsection.

(2) The trustee may assign an executory contract or unexpired lease of the debtor only if—

(A) the trustee assumes such contract or lease in accordance with the provisions of this section; and

(B) adequate assurance of future performance by the assignee of such contract or lease is provided, whether or not there has been a default in such contract or lease.

(3) Notwithstanding a provision in an executory contract or unexpired lease of the debtor, or in applicable law that terminates or modifies, or permits a party other than the debtor to terminate or modify, such contract or lease or a right or obligation under such contract or lease on account of an assignment of such contract or lease, such contract, lease, right, or obligation may not be terminated or modified under such provision because of the assumption or assignment of such contract or lease by the trustee.

(g) Except as provided in subsections (h)(2) and (i)(2) of this section, the rejection of an executory contract or unexpired lease of the debtor constitutes a breach of such contract or lease—

(1) if such contract or lease has not been assumed under this section or under a plan confirmed under chapter 9, 11, 12, or 13 of this title, immediately before the date of the filing of the petition; or

(2) if such contract or lease has been assumed under this section or under a plan confirmed under chapter 9, 11, 12, or 13 of this title—

(A) if before such rejection the case has not been converted under section 1112, 1208, or 1307 of this title, at the time of such rejection; or

(B) if before such rejection the case has been converted under section 1112, 1208, or 1307 of this title—

(i) immediately before the date of such conversion, if such contract or lease was assumed before such conversion; or

(ii) at the time of such rejection, if such contract or lease was assumed after such conversion.

(h)

(1)

(A) If the trustee rejects an unexpired lease of real property under which the debtor is the lessor and—

(i) if the rejection by the trustee amounts to such a breach as would entitle the lessee to treat such lease as terminated by virtue of its terms, applicable nonbankruptcy law, or any agreement made by the lessee, then the lessee under such lease may treat such lease as terminated by the rejection; or

(ii) if the term of such lease has commenced, the lessee may retain its rights under such lease (including rights such as those relating to the amount and timing of payment of rent and other amounts payable by the lessee and any right of use, possession, quiet enjoyment, subletting, assignment, or hypothecation) that are in or appurtenant to the real property for the balance of the term of such lease and for any renewal or extension of such rights to the extent that such rights are enforceable under applicable nonbankruptcy law.

(B) If the lessee retains its rights under subparagraph (A)(ii), the lessee may offset against the rent reserved under such lease for the balance of the term after the date of the rejection of such lease and for the term of any renewal or extension of such lease, the value of any damage caused by the nonperformance after the date of such rejection, of any obligation of the debtor under such lease, but the lessee shall not have any other right against the estate or

the debtor on account of any damage occurring after such date caused by such nonperformance.

(C) The rejection of a lease of real property in a shopping center with respect to which the lessee elects to retain its rights under subparagraph (A)(ii) does not affect the enforceability under applicable nonbankruptcy law of any provision in the lease pertaining to radius, location, use, exclusivity, or tenant mix or balance.

(D) In this paragraph, "lessee" includes any successor, assign, or mortgagee permitted under the terms of such lease.

(2)

(A) If the trustee rejects a timeshare interest under a timeshare plan under which the debtor is the timeshare interest seller and—

(i) if the rejection amounts to such a breach as would entitle the timeshare interest purchaser to treat the timeshare plan as terminated under its terms, applicable nonbankruptcy law, or any agreement made by timeshare interest purchaser, the timeshare interest purchaser under the timeshare plan may treat the timeshare plan as terminated by such rejection; or

(ii) if the term of such timeshare interest has commenced, then the timeshare interest purchaser may retain its rights in such timeshare interest for the balance of such term and for any term of renewal or extension of such timeshare interest to the extent that such rights are enforceable under applicable nonbankruptcy law.

(B) If the timeshare interest purchaser retains its rights under subparagraph (A), such timeshare interest purchaser may offset against the moneys due for such timeshare interest for the balance of the term after the date of the rejection of such timeshare interest, and the term of any renewal or extension of such timeshare interest, the value of any damage caused by the nonperformance after the date of such rejection, of any obligation of the debtor under such timeshare plan, but the timeshare interest purchaser shall not have any right against the estate or the debtor on account of any damage occurring after such date caused by such nonperformance.

(i)

(1) If the trustee rejects an executory contract of the debtor for the sale of real property or for the sale of a timeshare interest under a timeshare plan, under which the purchaser is in possession, such purchaser may treat such contract as terminated, or, in the alternative, may remain in possession of such real property or timeshare interest.

(2) If such purchaser remains in possession—

    (A) such purchaser shall continue to make all payments due under such contract, but may, offset against such payments any damages occurring after the date of the rejection of such contract caused by the nonperformance of any obligation of the debtor after such date, but such purchaser does not have any rights against the estate on account of any damages arising after such date from such rejection, other than such offset; and

    (B) the trustee shall deliver title to such purchaser in accordance with the provisions of such contract, but is relieved of all other obligations to perform under such contract.

(j) A purchaser that treats an executory contract as terminated under subsection (i) of this section, or a party whose executory contract to purchase real property from the debtor is rejected and under which such party is not in possession, has a lien on the interest of the debtor in such property for the recovery of any portion of the purchase price that such purchaser or party has paid.

(k) Assignment by the trustee to an entity of a contract or lease assumed under this section relieves the trustee and the estate from any liability for any breach of such contract or lease occurring after such assignment.

(l) If an unexpired lease under which the debtor is the lessee is assigned pursuant to this section, the lessor of the property may require a deposit or other security for the performance of the debtor's obligations under the lease substantially the same as would have been required by the landlord upon the initial leasing to a similar tenant.

(m) For purposes of this section 365 and sections 541(b)(2) and 362(b)(10), leases of real property shall include any rental agreement to use real property.

(n)

    (1) If the trustee rejects an executory contract under which the debtor is a licensor of a right to intellectual property, the licensee under such contract may elect—

        (A) to treat such contract as terminated by such rejection if such rejection by the trustee amounts to such a breach as would entitle the licensee to treat such contract as terminated by virtue of its own terms, applicable nonbankruptcy law, or an

agreement made by the licensee with another entity; or

        (B) to retain its rights (including a right to enforce any exclusivity provision of such contract, but excluding any other right under applicable nonbankruptcy law to specific performance of such contract) under such contract and under any agreement supplementary to such contract, to such intellectual property (including any embodiment of such intellectual property to the extent protected by applicable nonbankruptcy law), as such rights existed immediately before the case commenced, for—

            (i) the duration of such contract; and

            (ii) any period for which such contract may be extended by the licensee as of right under applicable nonbankruptcy law.

    (2) If the licensee elects to retain its rights, as described in paragraph (1)(B) of this subsection, under such contract—

        (A) the trustee shall allow the licensee to exercise such rights;

        (B) the licensee shall make all royalty payments due under such contract for the duration of such contract and for any period described in paragraph (1)(B) of this subsection for which the licensee extends such contract; and

        (C) the licensee shall be deemed to waive—

            (i) any right of setoff it may have with respect to such contract under this title or applicable nonbankruptcy law; and

            (ii) any claim allowable under section 503(b) of this title arising from the performance of such contract.

    (3) If the licensee elects to retain its rights, as described in paragraph (1)(B) of this subsection, then on the written request of the licensee the trustee shall—

        (A) to the extent provided in such contract, or any agreement supplementary to such contract, provide to the licensee any intellectual property (including such embodiment) held by the trustee; and

        (B) not interfere with the rights of the licensee as provided in such contract, or any agreement supplementary to such contract, to such intellectual property (including such embodiment) including any right to obtain such intellectual property (or such embodiment) from another entity.

(4) Unless and until the trustee rejects such contract, on the written request of the licensee the trustee shall—

> **(A)** to the extent provided in such contract or any agreement supplementary to such contract—
>
> > **(i)** perform such contract; or
> > **(ii)** provide to the licensee such intellectual property (including any embodiment of such intellectual property to the extent protected by applicable nonbankruptcy law) held by the trustee; and
>
> **(B)** not interfere with the rights of the licensee as provided in such contract, or any agreement supplementary to such contract, to such intellectual property (including such embodiment), including any right to obtain such intellectual property (or such embodiment) from another entity.

(o) In a case under chapter 11 of this title, the trustee shall be deemed to have assumed (consistent with the debtor's other obligations under section 507), and shall immediately cure any deficit under, any commitment by the debtor to a Federal depository institutions regulatory agency (or predecessor to such agency) to maintain the capital of an insured depository institution, and any claim for a subsequent breach of the obligations thereunder shall be entitled to priority under section 507. This subsection shall not extend any commitment that would otherwise be terminated by any act of such an agency.

(p)

> **(1)** If a lease of personal property is rejected or not timely assumed by the trustee under subsection (d), the leased property is no longer property of the estate and the stay under section 362(a) is automatically terminated.
>
> **(2)**
>
> > **(A)** If the debtor in a case under chapter 7 is an individual, the debtor may notify the creditor in writing that the debtor desires to assume the lease. Upon being so notified, the creditor may, at its option, notify the debtor that it is willing to have the lease assumed by the debtor and may condition such assumption on cure of any outstanding default on terms set by the contract.
> >
> > **(B)** If, not later than 30 days after notice is provided under subparagraph (A), the debtor notifies the lessor in writing that the lease is assumed, the liability under the lease will be assumed by the debtor and not by the estate.

(C) The stay under section 362 and the injunction under section 524(a)(2) shall not be violated by notification of the debtor and negotiation of cure under this subsection.

(3) In a case under chapter 11 in which the debtor is an individual and in a case under chapter 13, if the debtor is the lessee with respect to personal property and the lease is not assumed in the plan confirmed by the court, the lease is deemed rejected as of the conclusion of the hearing on confirmation. If the lease is rejected, the stay under section 362 and any stay under section 1301 is automatically terminated with respect to the property subject to the lease.

§366. Utility service

(a) Except as provided in subsections (b) and (c) of this section, a utility may not alter, refuse, or discontinue service to, or discriminate against, the trustee or the debtor solely on the basis of the commencement of a case under this title or that a debt owed by the debtor to such utility for service rendered before the order for relief was not paid when due.

(b) Such utility may alter, refuse, or discontinue service if neither the trustee nor the debtor, within 20 days after the date of the order for relief, furnishes adequate assurance of payment, in the form of a deposit or other security, for service after such date. On request of a party in interest and after notice and a hearing, the court may order reasonable modification of the amount of the deposit or other security necessary to provide adequate assurance of payment.

(c)

> **(1)**
>
> > **(A)** For purposes of this subsection, the term "assurance of payment" means—
> >
> > > **(i)** a cash deposit;
> > > **(ii)** a letter of credit;
> > > **(iii)** a certificate of deposit;
> > > **(iv)** a surety bond;
> > > **(v)** a prepayment of utility consumption; or
> > > **(vi)** another form of security that is mutually agreed on between the utility and the debtor or the trustee.
> >
> > **(B)** For purposes of this subsection an administrative expense priority shall not constitute an assurance of payment.
>
> **(2)** Subject to paragraphs (3) and (4), with respect to a case filed under chapter 11, a utility referred to in subsection (a) may alter, refuse, or discontinue utility service, if during the 30-day period beginning on the date of the

filing of the petition, the utility does not receive from the debtor or the trustee adequate assurance of payment for utility service that is satisfactory to the utility.

(3)

    (A) On request of a party in interest and after notice and a hearing, the court may order modification of the amount of an assurance of payment under paragraph (2).

    (B) In making a determination under this paragraph whether an assurance of payment is adequate, the court may not consider—

        (i) the absence of security before the date of the filing of the petition;

        (ii) the payment by the debtor of charges for utility service in a timely manner before the date of the filing of the petition; or

        (iii) the availability of an administrative expense priority.

(4) Notwithstanding any other provision of law, with respect to a case subject to this subsection, a utility may recover or set off against a security deposit provided to the utility by the debtor before the date of the filing of the petition without notice or order of the court.

CHAPTER 5—CREDITORS, THE DEBTOR, AND THE ESTATE

SUBCHAPTER I—CREDITORS AND CLAIMS

§501. Filing of proofs of claims or interests

(a) A creditor or an indenture trustee may file a proof of claim. An equity security holder may file a proof of interest.

(b) If a creditor does not timely file a proof of such creditor's claim, an entity that is liable to such creditor with the debtor, or that has secured such creditor, may file a proof of such claim.

(c) If a creditor does not timely file a proof of such creditor's claim, the debtor or the trustee may file a proof of such claim.

(d) A claim of a kind specified in section 502(e)(2), 502(f), 502(g), 502(h) or 502(i) of this title may be filed under subsection (a), (b), or (c) of this section the same as if such claim were a claim against the debtor and had arisen before the date of the filing of the petition.

(e) A claim arising from the liability of a debtor for fuel use tax assessed consistent with the requirements of section 31705 of title 49 may be filed by the base jurisdiction designated pursuant to the International Fuel Tax Agreement (as defined in section 31701 of title 49) and, if so filed, shall be allowed as a single claim.

§502. Allowance of claims or interests

(a) A claim or interest, proof of which is filed under section 501 of this title, is deemed allowed, unless a party in interest, including a creditor of a general partner in a partnership that is a debtor in a case under chapter 7 of this title, objects.

(b) Except as provided in subsections (e)(2), (f), (g), (h) and (i) of this section, if such objection to a claim is made, the court, after notice and a hearing, shall determine the amount of such claim in lawful currency of the United States as of the date of the filing of the petition, and shall allow such claim in such amount, except to the extent that—

    (1) such claim is unenforceable against the debtor and property of the debtor, under any agreement or applicable law for a reason other than because such claim is contingent or unmatured;

    (2) such claim is for unmatured interest;

    (3) if such claim is for a tax assessed against property of the estate, such claim exceeds the value of the interest of the estate in such property;

    (4) if such claim is for services of an insider or attorney of the debtor, such claim exceeds the reasonable value of such services;

    (5) such claim is for a debt that is unmatured on the date of the filing of the petition and that is excepted from discharge under section 523(a)(5) of this title;

    (6) if such claim is the claim of a lessor for damages resulting from the termination of a lease of real property, such claim exceeds—

        (A) the rent reserved by such lease, without acceleration, for the greater of one year, or 15 percent, not to exceed three years, of the remaining term of such lease, following the earlier of—

            (i) the date of the filing of the petition; and

            (ii) the date on which such lessor repossessed, or the lessee surrendered, the leased property; plus

        (B) any unpaid rent due under such lease, without acceleration, on the earlier of such dates;

    (7) if such claim is the claim of an employee for damages resulting from the termination of an employment contract, such claim exceeds—

        (A) the compensation provided by such contract, without acceleration, for one year following the earlier of—

(i) the date of the filing of the petition; or

(ii) the date on which the employer directed the employee to terminate, or such employee terminated, performance under such contract; plus

(B) any unpaid compensation due under such contract, without acceleration, on the earlier of such dates;

(8) such claim results from a reduction, due to late payment, in the amount of an otherwise applicable credit available to the debtor in connection with an employment tax on wages, salaries, or commissions earned from the debtor; or

(9) proof of such claim is not timely filed, except to the extent tardily filed as permitted under paragraph (1), (2), or (3) of section 726(a) of this title or under the Federal Rules of Bankruptcy Procedure, except that a claim of a governmental unit shall be timely filed if it is filed before 180 days after the date of the order for relief or such later time as the Federal Rules of Bankruptcy Procedure may provide, and except that in a case under chapter 13, a claim of a governmental unit for a tax with respect to a return filed under section 1308 shall be timely if the claim is filed on or before the date that is 60 days after the date on which such return was filed as required.

(c) There shall be estimated for purpose of allowance under this section—

(1) any contingent or unliquidated claim, the fixing or liquidation of which, as the case may be, would unduly delay the administration of the case; or

(2) any right to payment arising from a right to an equitable remedy for breach of performance.

(d) Notwithstanding subsections (a) and (b) of this section, the court shall disallow any claim of any entity from which property is recoverable under section 542, 543, 550, or 553 of this title or that is a transferee of a transfer avoidable under section 522(f), 522(h), 544, 545, 547, 548, 549, or 724(a) of this title, unless such entity or transferee has paid the amount, or turned over any such property, for which such entity or transferee is liable under section 522(i), 542, 543, 550, or 553 of this title.

(e)

(1) Notwithstanding subsections (a), (b), and (c) of this section and paragraph (2) of this subsection, the court shall disallow any claim for reimbursement or contribution of an entity that is liable with the debtor on or has secured the claim of a creditor, to the extent that—

(A) such creditor's claim against the estate is disallowed;

(B) such claim for reimbursement or contribution is contingent as of the time of allowance or disallowance of such claim for reimbursement or contribution; or

(C) such entity asserts a right of subrogation to the rights of such creditor under section 509 of this title.

(2) A claim for reimbursement or contribution of such an entity that becomes fixed after the commencement of the case shall be determined, and shall be allowed under subsection (a), (b), or (c) of this section, or disallowed under subsection (d) of this section, the same as if such claim had become fixed before the date of the filing of the petition.

(f) In an involuntary case, a claim arising in the ordinary course of the debtor's business or financial affairs after the commencement of the case but before the earlier of the appointment of a trustee and the order for relief shall be determined as of the date such claim arises, and shall be allowed under subsection (a), (b), or (c) of this section or disallowed under subsection (d) or (e) of this section, the same as if such claim had arisen before the date of the filing of the petition.

(g)

(1) A claim arising from the rejection, under section 365 of this title or under a plan under chapter 9, 11, 12, or 13 of this title, of an executory contract or unexpired lease of the debtor that has not been assumed shall be determined, and shall be allowed under subsection (a), (b), or (c) of this section or disallowed under subsection (d) or (e) of this section, the same as if such claim had arisen before the date of the filing of the petition.

(2) A claim for damages calculated in accordance with section 562 shall be allowed under subsection (a), (b), or (c), or disallowed under subsection (d) or (e), as if such claim had arisen before the date of the filing of the petition.

(h) A claim arising from the recovery of property under section 522, 550, or 553 of this title shall be determined, and shall be allowed under subsection (a), (b), or (c) of this section, or disallowed under subsection (d) or (e) of this section, the same as if such claim had arisen before the date of the filing of the petition.

(i) A claim that does not arise until after the commencement of the case for a tax entitled to priority under section 507(a)(8) of this title shall be determined, and shall be allowed under subsection (a), (b), or (c) of this section, or disallowed under subsection (d) or (e) of this section, the same as if such claim had arisen before the date of the filing of the petition.

(j) A claim that has been allowed or disallowed may be reconsidered for cause. A reconsidered claim may be allowed or disallowed according to the equities of the case. Reconsideration of a claim under this subsection does not affect the validity of any payment or transfer from the estate made to a holder of an allowed claim on account of such allowed claim that is not reconsidered, but if a reconsidered claim is allowed and is of the same class as such holder's claim, such holder may not receive any additional payment or transfer from the estate on account of such holder's allowed claim until the holder of such reconsidered and allowed claim receives payment on account of such claim proportionate in value to that already received by such other holder. This subsection does not alter or modify the trustee's right to recover from a creditor any excess payment or transfer made to such creditor.

(k)

(1) The court, on the motion of the debtor and after a hearing, may reduce a claim filed under this section based in whole on an unsecured consumer debt by not more than 20 percent of the claim, if—

(A) the claim was filed by a creditor who unreasonably refused to negotiate a reasonable alternative repayment schedule proposed on behalf of the debtor by an approved nonprofit budget and credit counseling agency described in section 111;

(B) the offer of the debtor under subparagraph (A)—

(i) was made at least 60 days before the date of the filing of the petition; and

(ii) provided for payment of at least 60 percent of the amount of the debt over a period not to exceed the repayment period of the loan, or a reasonable extension thereof; and

(C) no part of the debt under the alternative repayment schedule is nondischargeable.

(2) The debtor shall have the burden of proving, by clear and convincing evidence, that—

(A) the creditor unreasonably refused to consider the debtor's proposal; and

(B) the proposed alternative repayment schedule was made prior to expiration of the 60-day period specified in paragraph (1)(B)(i).

§503. Allowance of administrative expenses

(a) An entity may timely file a request for payment of an administrative expense, or may tardily file such request if permitted by the court for cause.

(b) After notice and a hearing, there shall be allowed administrative expenses, other than claims allowed under section 502(f) of this title, including—

(1)

(A) the actual, necessary costs and expenses of preserving the estate including—

(i) wages, salaries, and commissions for services rendered after the commencement of the case; and

(ii) wages and benefits awarded pursuant to a judicial proceeding or a proceeding of the National Labor Relations Board as back pay attributable to any period of time occurring after commencement of the case under this title, as a result of a violation of Federal or State law by the debtor, without regard to the time of the occurrence of unlawful conduct on which such award is based or to whether any services were rendered, if the court determines that payment of wages and benefits by reason of the operation of this clause will not substantially increase the probability of layoff or termination of current employees, or of nonpayment of domestic support obligations, during the case under this title;

(B) any tax—

(i) incurred by the estate, whether secured or unsecured, including property taxes for which liability is in rem, in personam, or both, except a tax of a kind specified in section 507(a)(8) of this title; or

(ii) attributable to an excessive allowance of a tentative carryback adjustment that the estate received, whether the taxable year to which such adjustment relates ended before or after the commencement of the case;

(C) any fine, penalty, or reduction in credit relating to a tax of a kind specified in subparagraph (B) of this paragraph; and

(D) notwithstanding the requirements of subsection (a), a governmental unit shall not be required to file a request for the payment of an expense described in subparagraph (B) or (C), as a condition of its being an allowed administrative expense;

(2) compensation and reimbursement awarded under section 330(a) of this title;

(3) the actual, necessary expenses, other than compensation and reimbursement specified in paragraph (4) of this subsection, incurred by—

(A) a creditor that files a petition under section 303 of this title;

(B) a creditor that recovers, after the court's approval, for the benefit of the estate any property transferred or concealed by the debtor;

(C) a creditor in connection with the prosecution of a criminal offense relating to the case or to the business or property of the debtor;

(D) a creditor, an indenture trustee, an equity security holder, or a committee representing creditors or equity security holders other than a committee appointed under section 1102 of this title, in making a substantial contribution in a case under chapter 9 or 11 of this title;

(E) a custodian superseded under section 543 of this title, and compensation for the services of such custodian; or

(F) a member of a committee appointed under section 1102 of this title, if such expenses are incurred in the performance of the duties of such committee;

(4) reasonable compensation for professional services rendered by an attorney or an accountant of an entity whose expense is allowable under subparagraph (A), (B), (C), (D), or (E) of paragraph (3) of this subsection, based on the time, the nature, the extent, and the value of such services, and the cost of comparable services other than in a case under this title, and reimbursement for actual, necessary expenses incurred by such attorney or accountant;

(5) reasonable compensation for services rendered by an indenture trustee in making a substantial contribution in a case under chapter 9 or 11 of this title, based on the time, the nature, the extent, and the value of such services, and the cost of comparable services other than in a case under this title;

(6) the fees and mileage payable under chapter 119 of title 28;

(7) with respect to a nonresidential real property lease previously assumed under section 365, and subsequently rejected, a sum equal to all monetary obligations due, excluding those arising from or relating to a failure to operate or a penalty provision, for the period of 2 years following the later of the rejection date or the date of actual turnover of the premises, without reduction or setoff for any reason whatsoever except for sums actually received or to be received from an entity other than the debtor, and the claim for remaining sums due for the balance of the term of the lease shall be a claim under section 502(b)(6);

(8) the actual, necessary costs and expenses of closing a health care business incurred by a trustee or by a Federal agency (as defined in section 551(1) of title 5) or a department or agency of a State or political subdivision thereof, including any cost or expense incurred—

(A) in disposing of patient records in accordance with section 351; or

(B) in connection with transferring patients from the health care business that is in the process of being closed to another health care business; and

(9) the value of any goods received by the debtor within 20 days before the date of commencement of a case under this title in which the goods have been sold to the debtor in the ordinary course of such debtor's business.

(c) Notwithstanding subsection (b), there shall neither be allowed, nor paid—

(1) a transfer made to, or an obligation incurred for the benefit of, an insider of the debtor for the purpose of inducing such person to remain with the debtor's business, absent a finding by the court based on evidence in the record that—

(A) the transfer or obligation is essential to retention of the person because the individual has a bona fide job offer from another business at the same or greater rate of compensation;

(B) the services provided by the person are essential to the survival of the business; and

(C) either—

(i) the amount of the transfer made to, or obligation incurred for the benefit of, the person is not greater than an amount equal to 10 times the amount of the mean transfer or obligation of a similar kind given to nonmanagement employees for any purpose during the calendar year in which the transfer is made or the obligation is incurred; or

(ii) if no such similar transfers were made to, or obligations were incurred for the benefit of, such nonmanagement employees during such calendar year, the amount of the transfer or obligation is not greater than an amount equal to 25 percent of the amount of any similar transfer or obligation made to or incurred for the benefit of such insider for any purpose during the calendar year before the year in which such transfer is made or obligation is incurred;

(2) a severance payment to an insider of the debtor, unless—

(A) the payment is part of a program that is generally applicable to all full-time employees; and

(B) the amount of the payment is not greater than 10 times the amount of the mean severance pay given to nonmanagement employees during the calendar year in which the payment is made; or

(3) other transfers or obligations that are outside the ordinary course of business and not justified by the facts and circumstances of the case, including transfers made to, or obligations incurred for the benefit of, officers, managers, or consultants hired after the date of the filing of the petition.

§504. Sharing of compensation

(a) Except as provided in subsection (b) of this section, a person receiving compensation or reimbursement under section 503(b)(2) or 503(b)(4) of this title may not share or agree to share—

(1) any such compensation or reimbursement with another person; or

(2) any compensation or reimbursement received by another person under such sections.

(b)

(1) A member, partner, or regular associate in a professional association, corporation, or partnership may share compensation or reimbursement received under section 503(b)(2) or 503(b)(4) of this title with another member, partner, or regular associate in such association, corporation, or partnership, and may share in any compensation or reimbursement received under such sections by another member, partner, or regular associate in such association, corporation, or partnership.

(2) An attorney for a creditor that files a petition under section 303 of this title may share compensation and reimbursement received under section 503(b)(4) of this title with any other attorney contributing to the services rendered or expenses incurred by such creditor's attorney.

(c) This section shall not apply with respect to sharing, or agreeing to share, compensation with a bona fide public service attorney referral program that operates in accordance with non-Federal law regulating attorney referral services and with rules of professional responsibility applicable to attorney acceptance of referrals.

§505. Determination of tax liability

(a)

(1) Except as provided in paragraph (2) of this subsection, the court may determine the amount or legality of any tax, any fine or penalty relating to a tax, or any addition to tax, whether or not previously assessed, whether or not paid, and whether or not contested before and adjudicated by a judicial or administrative tribunal of competent jurisdiction.

(2) The court may not so determine—

(A) the amount or legality of a tax, fine, penalty, or addition to tax if such amount or legality was contested before and adjudicated by a judicial or administrative tribunal of competent jurisdiction before the commencement of the case under this title;

(B) any right of the estate to a tax refund, before the earlier of—

(i) 120 days after the trustee properly requests such refund from the governmental unit from which such refund is claimed; or

(ii) a determination by such governmental unit of such request; or

(C) the amount or legality of any amount arising in connection with an ad valorem tax on real or personal property of the estate, if the applicable period for contesting or redetermining that amount under applicable nonbankruptcy law has expired.

(b)

(1)

(A) The clerk shall maintain a list under which a Federal, State, or local governmental unit responsible for the collection of taxes within the district may—

(i) designate an address for service of requests under this subsection; and

(ii) describe where further information concerning additional requirements for filing such requests may be found.

(B) If such governmental unit does not designate an address and provide such address to the clerk under subparagraph (A), any request made under this subsection may be served at the address for the filing of a tax return or protest with the appropriate taxing authority of such governmental unit.

(2) A trustee may request a determination of any unpaid liability of the estate for any tax incurred during the administration of the case by submitting a tax return for such tax and a request for such a determination to the governmental unit charged with responsibility for collection or determination of such tax at the address and in the manner designated in paragraph (1). Unless such return is fraudulent, or contains a material misrepresentation, the estate, the trustee, the debtor, and any successor to the debtor are discharged from any liability for such tax—

> **(A)** upon payment of the tax shown on such return, if—
>> **(i)** such governmental unit does not notify the trustee, within 60 days after such request, that such return has been selected for examination; or
>> **(ii)** such governmental unit does not complete such an examination and notify the trustee of any tax due, within 180 days after such request or within such additional time as the court, for cause, permits;
>
> **(B)** upon payment of the tax determined by the court, after notice and a hearing, after completion by such governmental unit of such examination; or
>
> **(C)** upon payment of the tax determined by such governmental unit to be due.

(c) Notwithstanding section 362 of this title, after determination by the court of a tax under this section, the governmental unit charged with responsibility for collection of such tax may assess such tax against the estate, the debtor, or a successor to the debtor, as the case may be, subject to any otherwise applicable law.

§506. Determination of secured status

(a)

> **(1)** An allowed claim of a creditor secured by a lien on property in which the estate has an interest, or that is subject to setoff under section 553 of this title, is a secured claim to the extent of the value of such creditor's interest in the estate's interest in such property, or to the extent of the amount subject to setoff, as the case may be, and is an unsecured claim to the extent that the value of such creditor's interest or the amount so subject to setoff is less than the amount of such allowed claim.

Such value shall be determined in light of the purpose of the valuation and of the proposed disposition or use of such property, and in conjunction with any hearing on such disposition or use or on a plan affecting such creditor's interest.

> **(2)** If the debtor is an individual in a case under chapter 7 or 13, such value with respect to personal property securing an allowed claim shall be determined based on the replacement value of such property as of the date of the filing of the petition without deduction for costs of sale or marketing. With respect to property acquired for personal, family, or household purposes, replacement value shall mean the price a retail merchant would charge for property of that kind considering the age and condition of the property at the time value is determined.

(b) To the extent that an allowed secured claim is secured by property the value of which, after any recovery under subsection (c) of this section, is greater than the amount of such claim, there shall be allowed to the holder of such claim, interest on such claim, and any reasonable fees, costs, or charges provided for under the agreement or State statute under which such claim arose.

(c) The trustee may recover from property securing an allowed secured claim the reasonable, necessary costs and expenses of preserving, or disposing of, such property to the extent of any benefit to the holder of such claim, including the payment of all ad valorem property taxes with respect to the property.

(d) To the extent that a lien secures a claim against the debtor that is not an allowed secured claim, such lien is void, unless—

> **(1)** such claim was disallowed only under section 502(b)(5) or 502(e) of this title; or
>
> **(2)** such claim is not an allowed secured claim due only to the failure of any entity to file a proof of such claim under section 501 of this title.

§507. Priorities

(a) The following expenses and claims have priority in the following order:

> **(1)** First:
>> **(A)** Allowed unsecured claims for domestic support obligations that, as of the date of the filing of the petition in a case under this title, are owed to or recoverable by a spouse, former spouse, or child of the debtor, or such child's parent, legal guardian, or responsible relative, without regard to whether the claim is filed by such

person or is filed by a governmental unit on behalf of such person, on the condition that funds received under this paragraph by a governmental unit under this title after the date of the filing of the petition shall be applied and distributed in accordance with applicable nonbankruptcy law.

(B) Subject to claims under subparagraph (A), allowed unsecured claims for domestic support obligations that, as of the date of the filing of the petition, are assigned by a spouse, former spouse, child of the debtor, or such child's parent, legal guardian, or responsible relative to a governmental unit (unless such obligation is assigned voluntarily by the spouse, former spouse, child, parent, legal guardian, or responsible relative of the child for the purpose of collecting the debt) or are owed directly to or recoverable by a governmental unit under applicable nonbankruptcy law, on the condition that funds received under this paragraph by a governmental unit under this title after the date of the filing of the petition be applied and distributed in accordance with applicable nonbankruptcy law.

(C) If a trustee is appointed or elected under section 701, 702, 703, 1104, 1202, or 1302, the administrative expenses of the trustee allowed under paragraphs (1)(A), (2), and (6) of section 503(b) shall be paid before payment of claims under subparagraphs (A) and (B), to the extent that the trustee administers assets that are otherwise available for the payment of such claims.

(2) Second, administrative expenses allowed under section 503(b) of this title, unsecured claims of any Federal reserve bank related to loans made through programs or facilities authorized under section 13(3) of the Federal Reserve Act (12 U.S.C. 343), and any fees and charges assessed against the estate under chapter 123 of title 28.

(3) Third, unsecured claims allowed under section 502(f) of this title.

(4) Fourth, allowed unsecured claims, but only to the extent of $12,850 for each individual or corporation, as the case may be, earned within 180 days before the date of the filing of the petition or the date of the cessation of the debtor's business, whichever occurs first, for—

(A) wages, salaries, or commissions, including vacation, severance, and sick leave pay earned by an individual; or

(B) sales commissions earned by an individual or by a corporation with only 1 employee, acting as an independent contractor in the sale of goods or services for the debtor in the ordinary course of the debtor's business if, and only if, during the 12 months preceding that date, at least 75 percent of the amount that the individual or corporation earned by acting as an independent contractor in the sale of goods or services was earned from the debtor.

(5) Fifth, allowed unsecured claims for contributions to an employee benefit plan—

(A) arising from services rendered within 180 days before the date of the filing of the petition or the date of the cessation of the debtor's business, whichever occurs first; but only

(B) for each such plan, to the extent of—
(i) the number of employees covered by each such plan multiplied by $12,850; less
(ii) the aggregate amount paid to such employees under paragraph (4) of this subsection, plus the aggregate amount paid by the estate on behalf of such employees to any other employee benefit plan.

(6) Sixth, allowed unsecured claims of persons—

(A) engaged in the production or raising of grain, as defined in section 557(b) of this title, against a debtor who owns or operates a grain storage facility, as defined in section 557(b) of this title, for grain or the proceeds of grain, or

(B) engaged as a United States fisherman against a debtor who has acquired fish or fish produce from a fisherman through a sale or conversion, and who is engaged in operating a fish produce storage or processing facility—
but only to the extent of $6,325 for each such individual.

(7) Seventh, allowed unsecured claims of individuals, to the extent of $2,850 for each such individual, arising from the deposit, before the commencement of the case, of money in connection with the purchase, lease, or rental of property, or the purchase of services, for the personal, family, or household use of such individuals, that were not delivered or provided.

(8) Eighth, allowed unsecured claims of governmental units, only to the extent that such claims are for—

(A) a tax on or measured by income or gross receipts for a taxable year ending on or before the date of the filing of the petition—

(i) for which a return, if required, is last due, including extensions, after three years before the date of the filing of the petition;

(ii) assessed within 240 days before the date of the filing of the petition, exclusive of—

(I) any time during which an offer in compromise with respect to that tax was pending or in effect during that 240-day period, plus 30 days; and

(II) any time during which a stay of proceedings against collections was in effect in a prior case under this title during that 240-day period, plus 90 days; or

(iii) other than a tax of a kind specified in section 523(a)(1)(B) or 523(a)(1)(C) of this title, not assessed before, but assessable, under applicable law or by agreement, after, the commencement of the case;

(B) a property tax incurred before the commencement of the case and last payable without penalty after one year before the date of the filing of the petition;

(C) a tax required to be collected or withheld and for which the debtor is liable in whatever capacity;

(D) an employment tax on a wage, salary, or commission of a kind specified in paragraph (4) of this subsection earned from the debtor before the date of the filing of the petition, whether or not actually paid before such date, for which a return is last due, under applicable law or under any extension, after three years before the date of the filing of the petition;

(E) an excise tax on—

(i) a transaction occurring before the date of the filing of the petition for which a return, if required, is last due, under applicable law or under any extension, after three years before the date of the filing of the petition; or

(ii) if a return is not required, a transaction occurring during the three years immediately preceding the date of the filing of the petition;

(F) a customs duty arising out of the importation of merchandise—

(i) entered for consumption within one year before the date of the filing of the petition;

(ii) covered by an entry liquidated or reliquidated within one year before the date of the filing of the petition; or

(iii) entered for consumption within four years before the date of the filing of the petition but unliquidated on such date, if the Secretary of the Treasury certifies that failure to liquidate such entry was due to an investigation pending on such date into assessment of antidumping or countervailing duties or fraud, or if information needed for the proper appraisement or classification of such merchandise was not available to the appropriate customs officer before such date; or

(G) a penalty related to a claim of a kind specified in this paragraph and in compensation for actual pecuniary loss.

An otherwise applicable time period specified in this paragraph shall be suspended for any period during which a governmental unit is prohibited under applicable nonbankruptcy law from collecting a tax as a result of a request by the debtor for a hearing and an appeal of any collection action taken or proposed against the debtor, plus 90 days; plus any time during which the stay of proceedings was in effect in a prior case under this title or during which collection was precluded by the existence of 1 or more confirmed plans under this title, plus 90 days.

(9) Ninth, allowed unsecured claims based upon any commitment by the debtor to a Federal depository institutions regulatory agency (or predecessor to such agency) to maintain the capital of an insured depository institution.

(10) Tenth, allowed claims for death or personal injury resulting from the operation of a motor vehicle or vessel if such operation was unlawful because the debtor was intoxicated from using alcohol, a drug, or another substance.

(b) If the trustee, under section 362, 363, or 364 of this title, provides adequate protection of the interest of a holder of a claim secured by a lien on property of the debtor and if, notwithstanding such protection, such creditor has a claim allowable under subsection (a)(2) of this section arising from the stay of action against such property under section 362 of this title, from the use, sale, or lease of such property under section 363 of this title, or from the granting of a lien under section 364(d) of this title, then such creditor's claim under such subsection shall have priority over every other claim allowable under such subsection.

(c) For the purpose of subsection (a) of this section, a claim of a governmental unit arising from an erroneous refund or credit of a tax has the same priority as a claim for the tax to which such refund or credit relates.

(d) An entity that is subrogated to the rights of a holder of a claim of a kind specified in subsection (a)(1), (a)(4), (a)(5), (a)(6), (a)(7), (a)(8), or (a)(9) of this section is not subrogated to the right of the holder of such claim to priority under such subsection.

§508. Effect of distribution other than under this title

If a creditor of a partnership debtor receives, from a general partner that is not a debtor in a case under chapter 7 of this title, payment of, or a transfer of property on account of, a claim that is allowed under this title and that is not secured by a lien on property of such partner, such creditor may not receive any payment under this title on account of such claim until each of the other holders of claims on account of which such holders are entitled to share equally with such creditor under this title has received payment under this title equal in value to the consideration received by such creditor from such general partner.

§509. Claims of codebtors

(a) Except as provided in subsection (b) or (c) of this section, an entity that is liable with the debtor on, or that has secured, a claim of a creditor against the debtor, and that pays such claim, is subrogated to the rights of such creditor to the extent of such payment.

(b) Such entity is not subrogated to the rights of such creditor to the extent that—

    (1) a claim of such entity for reimbursement or contribution on account of such payment of such creditor's claim is—

        (A) allowed under section 502 of this title;

        (B) disallowed other than under section 502(e) of this title; or

        (C) subordinated under section 510 of this title; or

    (2) as between the debtor and such entity, such entity received the consideration for the claim held by such creditor.

(c) The court shall subordinate to the claim of a creditor and for the benefit of such creditor an allowed claim, by way of subrogation under this section, or for reimbursement or contribution, of an entity that is liable with the debtor on, or that has secured, such creditor's claim, until such creditor's claim is paid in full, either through payments under this title or otherwise.

§510. Subordination

(a) A subordination agreement is enforceable in a case under this title to the same extent that such agreement is enforceable under applicable nonbankruptcy law.

(b) For the purpose of distribution under this title, a claim arising from rescission of a purchase or sale of a security of the debtor or of an affiliate of the debtor, for damages arising from the purchase or sale of such a security, or for reimbursement or contribution allowed under section 502 on account of such a claim, shall be subordinated to all claims or interests that are senior to or equal the claim or interest represented by such security, except that if such security is common stock, such claim has the same priority as common stock.

(c) Notwithstanding subsections (a) and (b) of this section, after notice and a hearing, the court may—

    (1) under principles of equitable subordination, subordinate for purposes of distribution all or part of an allowed claim to all or part of another allowed claim or all or part of an allowed interest to all or part of another allowed interest; or

    (2) order that any lien securing such a subordinated claim be transferred to the estate.

§511. Rate of interest on tax claims

(a) If any provision of this title requires the payment of interest on a tax claim or on an administrative expense tax, or the payment of interest to enable a creditor to receive the present value of the allowed amount of a tax claim, the rate of interest shall be the rate determined under applicable nonbankruptcy law.

(b) In the case of taxes paid under a confirmed plan under this title, the rate of interest shall be determined as of the calendar month in which the plan is confirmed.

SUBCHAPTER II—DEBTOR'S DUTIES AND BENEFITS

§521. Debtor's duties

(a) The debtor shall—

    (1) file—

        (A) a list of creditors; and

        (B) unless the court orders otherwise—

(i) a schedule of assets and liabilities;

(ii) a schedule of current income and current expenditures;

(iii) a statement of the debtor's financial affairs and, if section 342(b) applies, a certificate—

> **(I)** of an attorney whose name is indicated on the petition as the attorney for the debtor, or a bankruptcy petition preparer signing the petition under section 110(b)(1), indicating that such attorney or the bankruptcy petition preparer delivered to the debtor the notice required by section 342(b); or
>
> **(II)** if no attorney is so indicated, and no bankruptcy petition preparer signed the petition, of the debtor that such notice was received and read by the debtor;

(iv) copies of all payment advices or other evidence of payment received within 60 days before the date of the filing of the petition, by the debtor from any employer of the debtor;

(v) a statement of the amount of monthly net income, itemized to show how the amount is calculated; and

(vi) a statement disclosing any reasonably anticipated increase in income or expenditures over the 12-month period following the date of the filing of the petition;

(2) if an individual debtor's schedule of assets and liabilities includes debts which are secured by property of the estate—

> **(A)** within thirty days after the date of the filing of a petition under chapter 7 of this title or on or before the date of the meeting of creditors, whichever is earlier, or within such additional time as the court, for cause, within such period fixes, file with the clerk a statement of his intention with respect to the retention or surrender of such property and, if applicable, specifying that such property is claimed as exempt, that the debtor intends to redeem such property, or that the debtor intends to reaffirm debts secured by such property; and
>
> **(B)** within 30 days after the first date set for the meeting of creditors under section 341(a), or within such additional time as the court, for cause, within such 30-day period fixes, perform his intention with respect to such property, as specified by subparagraph (A) of this paragraph;

except that nothing in subparagraphs (A) and (B) of this paragraph shall alter the debtor's or the trustee's rights with regard to such property under this title, except as provided in section 362(h);

(3) if a trustee is serving in the case or an auditor is serving under section 586(f) of title 28, cooperate with the trustee as necessary to enable the trustee to perform the trustee's duties under this title;

(4) if a trustee is serving in the case or an auditor is serving under section 586(f) of title 28, surrender to the trustee all property of the estate and any recorded information, including books, documents, records, and papers, relating to property of the estate, whether or not immunity is granted under section 344 of this title;

(5) appear at the hearing required under section 524(d) of this title;

(6) in a case under chapter 7 of this title in which the debtor is an individual, not retain possession of personal property as to which a creditor has an allowed claim for the purchase price secured in whole or in part by an interest in such personal property unless the debtor, not later than 45 days after the first meeting of creditors under section 341(a), either—

> **(A)** enters into an agreement with the creditor pursuant to section 524(c) with respect to the claim secured by such property; or
>
> **(B)** redeems such property from the security interest pursuant to section 722; and

(7) unless a trustee is serving in the case, continue to perform the obligations required of the administrator (as defined in section 3 of the Employee Retirement Income Security Act of 1974) of an employee benefit plan if at the time of the commencement of the case the debtor (or any entity designated by the debtor) served as such administrator.

If the debtor fails to so act within the 45-day period referred to in paragraph (6), the stay under section 362(a) is terminated with respect to the personal property of the estate or of the debtor which is affected, such property shall no longer be property of the estate, and the creditor may take whatever action as to such property as is permitted by applicable nonbankruptcy law, unless the court determines on the motion of the trustee filed before the expiration of such 45-day period, and after notice and a hearing, that such property is of consequential value or benefit to the estate, orders appropriate adequate protection of the creditor's interest, and orders the debtor to deliver any collateral in the debtor's possession to the trustee.

(b) In addition to the requirements under subsection (a), a debtor who is an individual shall file with the court—

(1) a certificate from the approved nonprofit budget and credit counseling agency that provided the debtor services under section 109(h) describing the services provided to the debtor; and

(2) a copy of the debt repayment plan, if any, developed under section 109(h) through the approved nonprofit budget and credit counseling agency referred to in paragraph (1).

(c) In addition to meeting the requirements under subsection (a), a debtor shall file with the court a record of any interest that a debtor has in an education individual retirement account (as defined in section 530(b)(1) of the Internal Revenue Code of 1986), an interest in an account in a qualified ABLE program (as defined in section 529A(b) of such Code,[1] or under a qualified State tuition program (as defined in section 529(b)(1) of such Code).

(d) If the debtor fails timely to take the action specified in subsection (a)(6) of this section, or in paragraphs (1) and (2) of section 362(h), with respect to property which a lessor or bailor owns and has leased, rented, or bailed to the debtor or as to which a creditor holds a security interest not otherwise voidable under section 522(f), 544, 545, 547, 548, or 549, nothing in this title shall prevent or limit the operation of a provision in the underlying lease or agreement that has the effect of placing the debtor in default under such lease or agreement by reason of the occurrence, pendency, or existence of a proceeding under this title or the insolvency of the debtor. Nothing in this subsection shall be deemed to justify limiting such a provision in any other circumstance.

(e)

(1) If the debtor in a case under chapter 7 or 13 is an individual and if a creditor files with the court at any time a request to receive a copy of the petition, schedules, and statement of financial affairs filed by the debtor, then the court shall make such petition, such schedules, and such statement available to such creditor.

(2)

(A) The debtor shall provide—

(i) not later than 7 days before the date first set for the first meeting of creditors, to the trustee a copy of the Federal income tax return required under applicable law (or at the election of the debtor, a transcript of such return) for the most recent tax year ending immediately before the commencement of the case and for which a Federal income tax return was filed; and

(ii) at the same time the debtor complies with clause (i), a copy of such return (or if elected under clause (i), such transcript) to any creditor that timely requests such copy.

(B) If the debtor fails to comply with clause (i) or (ii) of subparagraph (A), the court shall dismiss the case unless the debtor demonstrates that the failure to so comply is due to circumstances beyond the control of the debtor.

(C) If a creditor requests a copy of such tax return or such transcript and if the debtor fails to provide a copy of such tax return or such transcript to such creditor at the time the debtor provides such tax return or such transcript to the trustee, then the court shall dismiss the case unless the debtor demonstrates that the failure to provide a copy of such tax return or such transcript is due to circumstances beyond the control of the debtor.

(3) If a creditor in a case under chapter 13 files with the court at any time a request to receive a copy of the plan filed by the debtor, then the court shall make available to such creditor a copy of the plan—

(A) at a reasonable cost; and

(B) not later than 7 days after such request is filed.

(f) At the request of the court, the United States trustee, or any party in interest in a case under chapter 7, 11, or 13, a debtor who is an individual shall file with the court—

(1) at the same time filed with the taxing authority, a copy of each Federal income tax return required under applicable law (or at the election of the debtor, a transcript of such tax return) with respect to each tax year of the debtor ending while the case is pending under such chapter;

(2) at the same time filed with the taxing authority, each Federal income tax return required under applicable law (or at the election of the debtor, a transcript of such tax return) that had not been filed with such authority as of the date of the commencement of the case and that was subsequently filed for any tax year of the debtor ending in the 3-year period ending on the date of the commencement of the case;

(3) a copy of each amendment to any Federal income tax return or transcript filed with the court under paragraph (1) or (2); and

(4) in a case under chapter 13—

(A) on the date that is either 90 days after the end of such tax year or 1 year after the date of the commencement of the case, whichever is later, if a plan is not confirmed before such later date; and

(B) annually after the plan is confirmed and until the case is closed, not later than the date that is 45 days before the anniversary of the confirmation of the plan;

a statement, under penalty of perjury, of the income and expenditures of the debtor during the tax year of the debtor most recently concluded before such statement is filed under this paragraph, and of the monthly income of the debtor, that shows how income, expenditures, and monthly income are calculated.

(g)

(1) A statement referred to in subsection (f)(4) shall disclose—

(A) the amount and sources of the income of the debtor;

(B) the identity of any person responsible with the debtor for the support of any dependent of the debtor; and

(C) the identity of any person who contributed, and the amount contributed, to the household in which the debtor resides.

(2) The tax returns, amendments, and statement of income and expenditures described in subsections (e)(2)(A) and (f) shall be available to the United States trustee (or the bankruptcy administrator, if any), the trustee, and any party in interest for inspection and copying, subject to the requirements of section 315(c) of the Bankruptcy Abuse Prevention and Consumer Protection Act of 2005.

(h) If requested by the United States trustee or by the trustee, the debtor shall provide—

(1) a document that establishes the identity of the debtor, including a driver's license, passport, or other document that contains a photograph of the debtor; or

(2) such other personal identifying information relating to the debtor that establishes the identity of the debtor.

(i)

(1) Subject to paragraphs (2) and (4) and notwithstanding section 707(a), if an individual debtor in a voluntary case under chapter 7 or 13 fails to file all of the information required under subsection (a)(1) within 45 days after the date of the filing of the petition, the case shall be automatically dismissed effective on the 46th day after the date of the filing of the petition.

(2) Subject to paragraph (4) and with respect to a case described in paragraph (1), any party in interest may request the court to enter an order dismissing the case. If requested, the court shall enter an order of dismissal not later than 7 days after such request.

(3) Subject to paragraph (4) and upon request of the debtor made within 45 days after the date of the filing of the petition described in paragraph (1), the court may allow the debtor an additional period of not to exceed 45 days to file the information required under subsection (a)(1) if the court finds justification for extending the period for the filing.

(4) Notwithstanding any other provision of this subsection, on the motion of the trustee filed before the expiration of the applicable period of time specified in paragraph (1), (2), or (3), and after notice and a hearing, the court may decline to dismiss the case if the court finds that the debtor attempted in good faith to file all the information required by subsection (a)(1)(B)(iv) and that the best interests of creditors would be served by administration of the case.

(j)

(1) Notwithstanding any other provision of this title, if the debtor fails to file a tax return that becomes due after the commencement of the case or to properly obtain an extension of the due date for filing such return, the taxing authority may request that the court enter an order converting or dismissing the case.

(2) If the debtor does not file the required return or obtain the extension referred to in paragraph (1) within 90 days after a request is filed by the taxing authority under that paragraph, the court shall convert or dismiss the case, whichever is in the best interests of creditors and the estate.

[1] So in original. A closing parenthesis probably should precede the comma.

§522. Exemptions

(a) In this section—

(1) "dependent" includes spouse, whether or not actually dependent; and

(2) "value" means fair market value as of the date of the filing of the petition or, with respect to property that becomes property of the estate after such date, as of the date such property becomes property of the estate.

(b)

(1) Notwithstanding section 541 of this title, an individual debtor may exempt from property of the estate the property listed in either paragraph (2) or, in the alternative, paragraph (3) of this subsection. In joint cases filed under section 302 of this title and individual cases filed under section 301 or 303 of this title by or against debtors who are husband and wife, and whose estates are ordered to be jointly administered under Rule 1015(b) of the Federal Rules of Bankruptcy Procedure, one debtor may not elect to exempt property listed in paragraph (2) and the other debtor elect to exempt property listed in paragraph (3) of this subsection. If the parties cannot agree on the alternative to be elected, they shall be deemed to elect paragraph (2), where such election is permitted under the law of the jurisdiction where the case is filed.

(2) Property listed in this paragraph is property that is specified under subsection (d), unless the State law that is applicable to the debtor under paragraph (3)(A) specifically does not so authorize.

(3) Property listed in this paragraph is—

(A) subject to subsections (o) and (p), any property that is exempt under Federal law, other than subsection (d) of this section, or State or local law that is applicable on the date of the filing of the petition to the place in which the debtor's domicile has been located for the 730 days immediately preceding the date of the filing of the petition or if the debtor's domicile has not been located in a single State for such 730-day period, the place in which the debtor's domicile was located for 180 days immediately preceding the 730-day period or for a longer portion of such 180-day period than in any other place;

(B) any interest in property in which the debtor had, immediately before the commencement of the case, an interest as a tenant by the entirety or joint tenant to the extent that such interest as a tenant by the entirety or joint tenant is exempt from process under applicable nonbankruptcy law; and

(C) retirement funds to the extent that those funds are in a fund or account that is exempt from taxation under section 401, 403, 408, 408A, 414, 457, or 501(a) of the Internal Revenue Code of 1986.

If the effect of the domiciliary requirement under subparagraph (A) is to render the debtor ineligible for any exemption, the debtor may elect to exempt property that is specified under subsection (d).

(4) For purposes of paragraph (3)(C) and subsection (d)(12), the following shall apply:

(A) If the retirement funds are in a retirement fund that has received a favorable determination under section 7805 of the Internal Revenue Code of 1986, and that determination is in effect as of the date of the filing of the petition in a case under this title, those funds shall be presumed to be exempt from the estate.

(B) If the retirement funds are in a retirement fund that has not received a favorable determination under such section 7805, those funds are exempt from the estate if the debtor demonstrates that—

(i) no prior determination to the contrary has been made by a court or the Internal Revenue Service; and

(ii)

(I) the retirement fund is in substantial compliance with the applicable requirements of the Internal Revenue Code of 1986; or

(II) the retirement fund fails to be in substantial compliance with the applicable requirements of the Internal Revenue Code of 1986 and the debtor is not materially responsible for that failure.

(C) A direct transfer of retirement funds from 1 fund or account that is exempt from taxation under section 401, 403, 408, 408A, 414, 457, or 501(a) of the Internal Revenue Code of 1986, under section 401(a)(31) of the Internal Revenue Code of 1986, or otherwise, shall not cease to qualify for exemption under paragraph (3)(C) or subsection (d)(12) by reason of such direct transfer.

(D)

(i) Any distribution that qualifies as an eligible rollover distribution within the meaning of section 402(c) of the Internal Revenue Code of 1986 or that is described in clause (ii) shall not cease to qualify for exemption under paragraph (3)(C) or subsection (d)(12) by reason of such distribution.

(ii) A distribution described in this clause is an amount that—

(I) has been distributed from a fund or account that is exempt from taxation under section 401, 403, 408, 408A, 414, 457, or 501(a) of the Internal Revenue Code of 1986; and

(II) to the extent allowed by law, is deposited in such a fund or account not later than 60 days after the distribution of such amount.

(c) Unless the case is dismissed, property exempted under this section is not liable during or after the case for any debt of the debtor that arose, or that is determined under section 502 of this title as if such debt had arisen, before the commencement of the case, except—

(1) a debt of a kind specified in paragraph (1) or (5) of section 523(a) (in which case, notwithstanding any provision of applicable nonbankruptcy law to the contrary, such property shall be liable for a debt of a kind specified in such paragraph);

(2) a debt secured by a lien that is—

(A)

(i) not avoided under subsection (f) or (g) of this section or under section 544, 545, 547, 548, 549, or 724(a) of this title; and

(ii) not void under section 506(d) of this title; or

(B) a tax lien, notice of which is properly filed;

(3) a debt of a kind specified in section 523(a)(4) or 523(a)(6) of this title owed by an institution-affiliated party of an insured depository institution to a Federal depository institutions regulatory agency acting in its capacity as conservator, receiver, or liquidating agent for such institution; or

(4) a debt in connection with fraud in the obtaining or providing of any scholarship, grant, loan, tuition, discount, award, or other financial assistance for purposes of financing an education at an institution of higher education (as that term is defined in section 101 of the Higher Education Act of 1965 (20 U.S.C. 1001)).

(d) The following property may be exempted under subsection (b)(2) of this section:

(1) The debtor's aggregate interest, not to exceed $23,675 in value, in real property or personal property that the debtor or a dependent of the debtor uses as a residence, in a cooperative that owns property that the debtor or a dependent of the debtor uses as a residence, or in a burial plot for the debtor or a dependent of the debtor.

(2) The debtor's interest, not to exceed $3,775 in value, in one motor vehicle.

(3) The debtor's interest, not to exceed $600 in value in any particular item or $12,625 in aggregate value, in household furnishings, household goods, wearing apparel, appliances, books, animals, crops, or musical instruments, that are held primarily for the personal, family, or household use of the debtor or a dependent of the debtor.

(4) The debtor's aggregate interest, not to exceed $1,600 in value, in jewelry held primarily for the personal, family, or household use of the debtor or a dependent of the debtor.

(5) The debtor's aggregate interest in any property, not to exceed in value $1,250 plus up to $11,850 of any unused amount of the exemption provided under paragraph (1) of this subsection.

(6) The debtor's aggregate interest, not to exceed $2,375 in value, in any implements, professional books, or tools, of the trade of the debtor or the trade of a dependent of the debtor.

(7) Any unmatured life insurance contract owned by the debtor, other than a credit life insurance contract.

(8) The debtor's aggregate interest, not to exceed in value $12,625 less any amount of property of the estate transferred in the manner specified in section 542(d) of this title, in any accrued dividend or interest under, or loan value of, any unmatured life insurance contract owned by the debtor under which the insured is the debtor or an individual of whom the debtor is a dependent.

(9) Professionally prescribed health aids for the debtor or a dependent of the debtor.

(10) The debtor's right to receive—

(A) a social security benefit, unemployment compensation, or a local public assistance benefit;

(B) a veterans' benefit;

(C) a disability, illness, or unemployment benefit;

(D) alimony, support, or separate maintenance, to the extent reasonably necessary for the support of the debtor and any dependent of the debtor;

(E) a payment under a stock bonus, pension, profitsharing, annuity, or similar plan or contract on account of illness, disability, death, age, or length of service, to the extent reasonably necessary for the support of the debtor and any dependent of the debtor, unless—

(i) such plan or contract was established by or under the auspices of an insider that employed the debtor at the time the debtor's rights under such plan or contract arose;

(ii) such payment is on account of age or length of service; and

(iii) such plan or contract does not qualify under section 401(a), 403(a), 403(b), or 408 of the Internal Revenue Code of 1986.

(11) The debtor's right to receive, or property that is traceable to—

(A) an award under a crime victim's reparation law;

(B) a payment on account of the wrongful death of an individual of whom the debtor was a dependent, to the extent reasonably necessary for the support of the debtor and any dependent of the debtor;

(C) a payment under a life insurance contract that insured the life of an individual of whom the debtor was a dependent on the date of such individual's death, to the extent reasonably necessary for the support of the debtor and any dependent of the debtor;

(D) a payment, not to exceed $23,675, on account of personal bodily injury, not including pain and suffering or compensation for actual pecuniary loss, of the debtor or an individual of whom the debtor is a dependent; or

(E) a payment in compensation of loss of future earnings of the debtor or an individual of whom the debtor is or was a dependent, to the extent reasonably necessary for the support of the debtor and any dependent of the debtor.

(12) Retirement funds to the extent that those funds are in a fund or account that is exempt from taxation under section 401, 403, 408, 408A, 414, 457, or 501(a) of the Internal Revenue Code of 1986.

(e) A waiver of an exemption executed in favor of a creditor that holds an unsecured claim against the debtor is unenforceable in a case under this title with respect to such claim against property that the debtor may exempt under subsection (b) of this section. A waiver by the debtor of a power under subsection (f) or (h) of this section to avoid a transfer, under subsection (g) or (i) of this section to exempt property, or under subsection (i) of this section to recover property or to preserve a transfer, is unenforceable in a case under this title.

(f)

(1) Notwithstanding any waiver of exemptions but subject to paragraph (3), the debtor may avoid the fixing of a lien on an interest of the debtor in property to the extent that such lien impairs an exemption to which the debtor would have been entitled under subsection (b) of this section, if such lien is—

(A) a judicial lien, other than a judicial lien that secures a debt of a kind that is specified in section 523(a)(5); or

(B) a nonpossessory, nonpurchase-money security interest in any—

(i) household furnishings, household goods, wearing apparel, appliances, books, animals, crops, musical instruments, or jewelry that are held primarily for the personal, family, or household use of the debtor or a dependent of the debtor;

(ii) implements, professional books, or tools, of the trade of the debtor or the trade of a dependent of the debtor; or

(iii) professionally prescribed health aids for the debtor or a dependent of the debtor.

(2)

(A) For the purposes of this subsection, a lien shall be considered to impair an exemption to the extent that the sum of—

(i) the lien;

(ii) all other liens on the property; and

(iii) the amount of the exemption that the debtor could claim if there were no liens on the property;

exceeds the value that the debtor's interest in the property would have in the absence of any liens.

(B) In the case of a property subject to more than 1 lien, a lien that has been avoided shall not be considered in making the calculation under subparagraph (A) with respect to other liens.

(C) This paragraph shall not apply with respect to a judgment arising out of a mortgage foreclosure.

(3) In a case in which State law that is applicable to the debtor—

(A) permits a person to voluntarily waive a right to claim exemptions under subsection (d) or prohibits a debtor from claiming exemptions under subsection (d); and

(B) either permits the debtor to claim exemptions under State law without limitation in amount, except to the extent that the debtor has permitted the fixing of a consensual lien on any property or prohibits avoidance of a consensual lien on property otherwise eligible to be claimed as exempt property;

the debtor may not avoid the fixing of a lien on an interest of the debtor or a dependent of the debtor in property if the lien is a nonpossessory, nonpurchase-money security interest in implements, professional books, or tools of the trade of the debtor or a dependent of the debtor or farm animals or crops of the debtor or a dependent of the debtor to the extent the value of such implements, professional books, tools of the trade, animals, and crops exceeds $6,425.

(4)

(A) Subject to subparagraph (B), for purposes of paragraph (1)(B), the term "household goods" means—

(i) clothing;

(ii) furniture;

(iii) appliances;

(iv) 1 radio;

(v) 1 television;

(vi) 1 VCR;

(vii) linens;

(viii) china;

(ix) crockery;

(x) kitchenware;

(xi) educational materials and educational equipment primarily for the use of minor dependent children of the debtor;

(xii) medical equipment and supplies;

(xiii) furniture exclusively for the use of minor children, or elderly or disabled dependents of the debtor;

(xiv) personal effects (including the toys and hobby equipment of minor dependent children and wedding rings) of the debtor and the dependents of the debtor; and

(xv) 1 personal computer and related equipment.

(B) The term "household goods" does not include—

(i) works of art (unless by or of the debtor, or any relative of the debtor);

(ii) electronic entertainment equipment with a fair market value of more than $675 in the aggregate (except 1 television, 1 radio, and 1 VCR);

(iii) items acquired as antiques with a fair market value of more than $675 in the aggregate;

(iv) jewelry with a fair market value of more than $675 in the aggregate (except wedding rings); and

(v) a computer (except as otherwise provided for in this section), motor vehicle (including a tractor or lawn tractor), boat, or a motorized recreational device, conveyance, vehicle, watercraft, or aircraft.

(g) Notwithstanding sections 550 and 551 of this title, the debtor may exempt under subsection (b) of this section property that the trustee recovers under section 510(c)(2), 542, 543, 550, 551, or 553 of this title, to the extent that the debtor could have exempted such property under subsection (b) of this section if such property had not been transferred, if—

(1)

(A) such transfer was not a voluntary transfer of such property by the debtor; and

(B) the debtor did not conceal such property; or

(2) the debtor could have avoided such transfer under subsection (f)(1)(B) of this section.

(h) The debtor may avoid a transfer of property of the debtor or recover a setoff to the extent that the debtor could have exempted such property under subsection (g)(1) of this section if the trustee had avoided such transfer, if—

(1) such transfer is avoidable by the trustee under section 544, 545, 547, 548, 549, or 724(a) of this title or recoverable by the trustee under section 553 of this title; and

(2) the trustee does not attempt to avoid such transfer.

(i)

(1) If the debtor avoids a transfer or recovers a setoff under subsection (f) or (h) of this section, the debtor may recover in the manner prescribed by, and subject to the limitations of, section 550 of this title, the same as if the trustee had avoided such transfer, and may exempt any property so recovered under subsection (b) of this section.

(2) Notwithstanding section 551 of this title, a transfer avoided under section 544, 545, 547, 548, 549, or 724(a) of this title, under subsection (f) or (h) of this section, or property recovered under section 553 of this title, may be preserved for the benefit of the debtor to the extent that the debtor may exempt such property under subsection (g) of this section or paragraph (1) of this subsection.

(j) Notwithstanding subsections (g) and (i) of this section, the debtor may exempt a particular kind of property under subsections (g) and (i) of this section only to the extent that the debtor has exempted less property in value of such kind than that to which the debtor is entitled under subsection (b) of this section.

(k) Property that the debtor exempts under this section is not liable for payment of any administrative expense except—

    (1) the aliquot share of the costs and expenses of avoiding a transfer of property that the debtor exempts under subsection (g) of this section, or of recovery of such property, that is attributable to the value of the portion of such property exempted in relation to the value of the property recovered; and

    (2) any costs and expenses of avoiding a transfer under subsection (f) or (h) of this section, or of recovery of property under subsection (i)(1) of this section, that the debtor has not paid.

(l) The debtor shall file a list of property that the debtor claims as exempt under subsection (b) of this section. If the debtor does not file such a list, a dependent of the debtor may file such a list, or may claim property as exempt from property of the estate on behalf of the debtor. Unless a party in interest objects, the property claimed as exempt on such list is exempt.

(m) Subject to the limitation in subsection (b), this section shall apply separately with respect to each debtor in a joint case.

(n) For assets in individual retirement accounts described in section 408 or 408A of the Internal Revenue Code of 1986, other than a simplified employee pension under section 408(k) of such Code or a simple retirement account under section 408(p) of such Code, the aggregate value of such assets exempted under this section, without regard to amounts attributable to rollover contributions under section 402(c), 402(e)(6), 403(a)(4), 403(a)(5), and 403(b)(8) of the Internal Revenue Code of 1986, and earnings thereon, shall not exceed $1,283,025 in a case filed by a debtor who is an individual, except that such amount may be increased if the interests of justice so require.

(o) For purposes of subsection (b)(3)(A), and notwithstanding subsection (a), the value of an interest in—

    (1) real or personal property that the debtor or a dependent of the debtor uses as a residence;

    (2) a cooperative that owns property that the debtor or a dependent of the debtor uses as a residence;

    (3) a burial plot for the debtor or a dependent of the debtor; or

    (4) real or personal property that the debtor or a dependent of the debtor claims as a homestead;

shall be reduced to the extent that such value is attributable to any portion of any property that the

debtor disposed of in the 10-year period ending on the date of the filing of the petition with the intent to hinder, delay, or defraud a creditor and that the debtor could not exempt, or that portion that the debtor could not exempt, under subsection (b), if on such date the debtor had held the property so disposed of.

(p)

    (1) Except as provided in paragraph (2) of this subsection and sections 544 and 548, as a result of electing under subsection (b)(3)(A) to exempt property under State or local law, a debtor may not exempt any amount of interest that was acquired by the debtor during the 1215-day period preceding the date of the filing of the petition that exceeds in the aggregate $160,375 in value in—

        (A) real or personal property that the debtor or a dependent of the debtor uses as a residence;

        (B) a cooperative that owns property that the debtor or a dependent of the debtor uses as a residence;

        (C) a burial plot for the debtor or a dependent of the debtor; or

        (D) real or personal property that the debtor or dependent of the debtor claims as a homestead.

    (2)

        (A) The limitation under paragraph (1) shall not apply to an exemption claimed under subsection (b)(3)(A) by a family farmer for the principal residence of such farmer.

        (B) For purposes of paragraph (1), any amount of such interest does not include any interest transferred from a debtor's previous principal residence (which was acquired prior to the beginning of such 1215-day period) into the debtor's current principal residence, if the debtor's previous and current residences are located in the same State.

(q)

    (1) As a result of electing under subsection (b)(3)(A) to exempt property under State or local law, a debtor may not exempt any amount of an interest in property described in subparagraphs (A), (B), (C), and (D) of subsection (p)(1) which exceeds in the aggregate $160,375 if—

        (A) the court determines, after notice and a hearing, that the debtor has been convicted of a felony (as defined in section 3156 of title 18), which under the circumstances, demonstrates that the filing of the case was an abuse of the provisions of this title; or

(B) the debtor owes a debt arising from—

(i) any violation of the Federal securities laws (as defined in section 3(a)(47) of the Securities Exchange Act of 1934), any State securities laws, or any regulation or order issued under Federal securities laws or State securities laws;

(ii) fraud, deceit, or manipulation in a fiduciary capacity or in connection with the purchase or sale of any security registered under section 12 or 15(d) of the Securities Exchange Act of 1934 or under section 6 of the Securities Act of 1933;

(iii) any civil remedy under section 1964 of title 18; or

(iv) any criminal act, intentional tort, or willful or reckless misconduct that caused serious physical injury or death to another individual in the preceding 5 years.

(2) Paragraph (1) shall not apply to the extent the amount of an interest in property described in subparagraphs (A), (B), (C), and (D) of subsection (p)(1) is reasonably necessary for the support of the debtor and any dependent of the debtor.

§523. Exceptions to discharge

(a) A discharge under section 727, 1141, 1228(a), 1228(b), or 1328(b) of this title does not discharge an individual debtor from any debt—

(1) for a tax or a customs duty—

(A) of the kind and for the periods specified in section 507(a)(3) or 507(a)(8) of this title, whether or not a claim for such tax was filed or allowed;

(B) with respect to which a return, or equivalent report or notice, if required—

(i) was not filed or given; or

(ii) was filed or given after the date on which such return, report, or notice was last due, under applicable law or under any extension, and after two years before the date of the filing of the petition; or

(C) with respect to which the debtor made a fraudulent return or willfully attempted in any manner to evade or defeat such tax;

(2) for money, property, services, or an extension, renewal, or refinancing of credit, to the extent obtained by—

(A) false pretenses, a false representation, or actual fraud, other than a statement respecting the debtor's or an insider's financial condition;

(B) use of a statement in writing—

(i) that is materially false;

(ii) respecting the debtor's or an insider's financial condition;

(iii) on which the creditor to whom the debtor is liable for such money, property, services, or credit reasonably relied; and

(iv) that the debtor caused to be made or published with intent to deceive; or

(C)

(i) for purposes of subparagraph (A)—

(I) consumer debts owed to a single creditor and aggregating more than $675 for luxury goods or services incurred by an individual debtor on or within 90 days before the order for relief under this title are presumed to be nondischargeable; and

(II) cash advances aggregating more than $950 that are extensions of consumer credit under an open end credit plan obtained by an individual debtor on or within 70 days before the order for relief under this title, are presumed to be nondischargeable; and

(ii) for purposes of this subparagraph—

(I) the terms "consumer", "credit", and "open end credit plan" have the same meanings as in section 103 of the Truth in Lending Act; and

(II) the term "luxury goods or services" does not include goods or services reasonably necessary for the support or maintenance of the debtor or a dependent of the debtor;

(3) neither listed nor scheduled under section 521(a)(1) of this title, with the name, if known to the debtor, of the creditor to whom such debt is owed, in time to permit—

(A) if such debt is not of a kind specified in paragraph (2), (4), or (6) of this subsection, timely filing of a proof of claim, unless such creditor had notice or actual knowledge of the case in time for such timely filing; or

(B) if such debt is of a kind specified in paragraph (2), (4), or (6) of this subsection, timely filing of a proof of claim and timely request for a determination of dischargeability of such debt under one of such paragraphs, unless such creditor had notice or actual knowledge of the case in time for such timely filing and request;

(4) for fraud or defalcation while acting in a fiduciary capacity, embezzlement, or larceny;

(5) for a domestic support obligation;

(6) for willful and malicious injury by the debtor to another entity or to the property of another entity;

(7) to the extent such debt is for a fine, penalty, or forfeiture payable to and for the benefit of a governmental unit, and is not compensation for actual pecuniary loss, other than a tax penalty—

  (A) relating to a tax of a kind not specified in paragraph (1) of this subsection; or

  (B) imposed with respect to a transaction or event that occurred before three years before the date of the filing of the petition;

(8) unless excepting such debt from discharge under this paragraph would impose an undue hardship on the debtor and the debtor's dependents, for—

  (A)

   (i) an educational benefit overpayment or loan made, insured, or guaranteed by a governmental unit, or made under any program funded in whole or in part by a governmental unit or nonprofit institution; or

   (ii) an obligation to repay funds received as an educational benefit, scholarship, or stipend; or

  (B) any other educational loan that is a qualified education loan, as defined in section 221(d)(1) of the Internal Revenue Code of 1986, incurred by a debtor who is an individual;

(9) for death or personal injury caused by the debtor's operation of a motor vehicle, vessel, or aircraft if such operation was unlawful because the debtor was intoxicated from using alcohol, a drug, or another substance;

(10) that was or could have been listed or scheduled by the debtor in a prior case concerning the debtor under this title or under the Bankruptcy Act in which the debtor waived discharge, or was denied a discharge under section 727(a)(2), (3), (4), (5), (6), or (7) of this title, or under section 14c(1), (2), (3), (4), (6), or (7) of such Act;

(11) provided in any final judgment, unreviewable order, or consent order or decree entered in any court of the United States or of any State, issued by a Federal depository institutions regulatory agency, or contained in any settlement agreement entered into by the debtor, arising from any act of fraud or defalcation while acting in a fiduciary capacity committed with respect to any depository institution or insured credit union;

(12) for malicious or reckless failure to fulfill any commitment by the debtor to a Federal depository institutions regulatory agency to maintain the capital of an insured depository institution, except that this paragraph shall not extend any such commitment which would otherwise be terminated due to any act of such agency;

(13) for any payment of an order of restitution issued under title 18, United States Code;

(14) incurred to pay a tax to the United States that would be nondischargeable pursuant to paragraph (1);

(14A) incurred to pay a tax to a governmental unit, other than the United States, that would be nondischargeable under paragraph (1);

(14B) incurred to pay fines or penalties imposed under Federal election law;

(15) to a spouse, former spouse, or child of the debtor and not of the kind described in paragraph (5) that is incurred by the debtor in the course of a divorce or separation or in connection with a separation agreement, divorce decree or other order of a court of record, or a determination made in accordance with State or territorial law by a governmental unit;

(16) for a fee or assessment that becomes due and payable after the order for relief to a membership association with respect to the debtor's interest in a unit that has condominium ownership, in a share of a cooperative corporation, or a lot in a homeowners association, for as long as the debtor or the trustee has a legal, equitable, or possessory ownership interest in such unit, such corporation, or such lot, but nothing in this paragraph shall except from discharge the debt of a debtor for a membership association fee or assessment for a period arising before entry of the order for relief in a pending or subsequent bankruptcy case;

(17) for a fee imposed on a prisoner by any court for the filing of a case, motion, complaint, or appeal, or for other costs and expenses assessed with respect to such filing, regardless of an assertion of poverty by the debtor under subsection (b) or (f)(2) of section 1915 of title 28 (or a similar non-Federal law), or the debtor's status as a prisoner, as defined in section 1915(h) of title 28 (or a similar non-Federal law);

(18) owed to a pension, profit-sharing, stock bonus, or other plan established under section 401, 403, 408, 408A, 414, 457, or 501(c) of the Internal Revenue Code of 1986, under—

(A) a loan permitted under section 408(b)(1) of the Employee Retirement Income Security Act of 1974, or subject to section 72(p) of the Internal Revenue Code of 1986; or

(B) a loan from a thrift savings plan permitted under subchapter III of chapter 84 of title 5, that satisfies the requirements of section 8433(g) of such title;

but nothing in this paragraph may be construed to provide that any loan made under a governmental plan under section 414(d), or a contract or account under section 403(b), of the Internal Revenue Code of 1986 constitutes a claim or a debt under this title; or

(19) that—

(A) is for—

(i) the violation of any of the Federal securities laws (as that term is defined in section 3(a)(47) of the Securities Exchange Act of 1934), any of the State securities laws, or any regulation or order issued under such Federal or State securities laws; or

(ii) common law fraud, deceit, or manipulation in connection with the purchase or sale of any security; and

(B) results, before, on, or after the date on which the petition was filed, from—

(i) any judgment, order, consent order, or decree entered in any Federal or State judicial or administrative proceeding;

(ii) any settlement agreement entered into by the debtor; or

(iii) any court or administrative order for any damages, fine, penalty, citation, restitutionary payment, disgorgement payment, attorney fee, cost, or other payment owed by the debtor.

For purposes of this subsection, the term "return" means a return that satisfies the requirements of applicable nonbankruptcy law (including applicable filing requirements). Such term includes a return prepared pursuant to section 6020(a) of the Internal Revenue Code of 1986, or similar State or local law, or a written stipulation to a judgment or a final order entered by a nonbankruptcy tribunal, but does not include a return made pursuant to section 6020(b) of the Internal Revenue Code of 1986, or a similar State or local law.

(b) Notwithstanding subsection (a) of this section, a debt that was excepted from discharge under subsection (a)(1), (a)(3), or (a)(8) of this section, under section 17a(1), 17a(3), or 17a(5) of the Bankruptcy Act, under section 439A of the Higher Education Act of 1965, or under section 733(g) of the Public Health Service Act in a prior case concerning the debtor under this title, or under the Bankruptcy Act, is dischargeable in a case under this title unless, by the terms of subsection (a) of this section, such debt is not dischargeable in the case under this title.

(c)

(1) Except as provided in subsection (a)(3)(B) of this section, the debtor shall be discharged from a debt of a kind specified in paragraph (2), (4), or (6) of subsection (a) of this section, unless, on request of the creditor to whom such debt is owed, and after notice and a hearing, the court determines such debt to be excepted from discharge under paragraph (2), (4), or (6), as the case may be, of subsection (a) of this section.

(2) Paragraph (1) shall not apply in the case of a Federal depository institutions regulatory agency seeking, in its capacity as conservator, receiver, or liquidating agent for an insured depository institution, to recover a debt described in subsection (a)(2), (a)(4), (a)(6), or (a)(11) owed to such institution by an institution-affiliated party unless the receiver, conservator, or liquidating agent was appointed in time to reasonably comply, or for a Federal depository institutions regulatory agency acting in its corporate capacity as a successor to such receiver, conservator, or liquidating agent to reasonably comply, with subsection (a)(3)(B) as a creditor of such institution-affiliated party with respect to such debt.

(d) If a creditor requests a determination of dischargeability of a consumer debt under subsection (a)(2) of this section, and such debt is discharged, the court shall grant judgment in favor of the debtor for the costs of, and a reasonable attorney's fee for, the proceeding if the court finds that the position of the creditor was not substantially justified, except that the court shall not award such costs and fees if special circumstances would make the award unjust.

(e) Any institution-affiliated party of an insured depository institution shall be considered to be acting in a fiduciary capacity with respect to the purposes of subsection (a)(4) or (11).

§524. Effect of discharge

(a) A discharge in a case under this title—

(1) voids any judgment at any time obtained, to the extent that such judgment is a determination of the personal liability of the debtor with respect to any debt discharged under section 727, 944, 1141, 1228, or 1328 of this title, whether or not discharge of such debt is waived;

(2) operates as an injunction against the commencement or continuation of an action, the employment of process, or an act, to collect, recover or offset any such debt as a personal liability of the debtor, whether or not discharge of such debt is waived; and

(3) operates as an injunction against the commencement or continuation of an action, the employment of process, or an act, to collect or recover from, or offset against, property of the debtor of the kind specified in section 541(a)(2) of this title that is acquired after the commencement of the case, on account of any allowable community claim, except a community claim that is excepted from discharge under section 523, 1228(a)(1), or 1328(a)(1), or that would be so excepted, determined in accordance with the provisions of sections 523(c) and 523(d) of this title, in a case concerning the debtor's spouse commenced on the date of the filing of the petition in the case concerning the debtor, whether or not discharge of the debt based on such community claim is waived.

(b) Subsection (a)(3) of this section does not apply if—

(1)

(A) the debtor's spouse is a debtor in a case under this title, or a bankrupt or a debtor in a case under the Bankruptcy Act, commenced within six years of the date of the filing of the petition in the case concerning the debtor; and

(B) the court does not grant the debtor's spouse a discharge in such case concerning the debtor's spouse; or

(2)

(A) the court would not grant the debtor's spouse a discharge in a case under chapter 7 of this title concerning such spouse commenced on the date of the filing of the petition in the case concerning the debtor; and

(B) a determination that the court would not so grant such discharge is made by the bankruptcy court within the time and in the manner provided for a determination under section 727 of this title of whether a debtor is granted a discharge.

(c) An agreement between a holder of a claim and the debtor, the consideration for which, in whole or in part, is based on a debt that is dischargeable in a case under this title is enforceable only to any extent enforceable under applicable nonbankruptcy law, whether or not discharge of such debt is waived, only if—

(1) such agreement was made before the granting of the discharge under section 727, 1141, 1228, or 1328 of this title;

(2) the debtor received the disclosures described in subsection (k) at or before the time at which the debtor signed the agreement;

(3) such agreement has been filed with the court and, if applicable, accompanied by a declaration or an affidavit of the attorney that represented the debtor during the course of negotiating an agreement under this subsection, which states that—

(A) such agreement represents a fully informed and voluntary agreement by the debtor;

(B) such agreement does not impose an undue hardship on the debtor or a dependent of the debtor; and

(C) the attorney fully advised the debtor of the legal effect and consequences of—

(i) an agreement of the kind specified in this subsection; and

(ii) any default under such an agreement;

(4) the debtor has not rescinded such agreement at any time prior to discharge or within sixty days after such agreement is filed with the court, whichever occurs later, by giving notice of rescission to the holder of such claim;

(5) the provisions of subsection (d) of this section have been complied with; and

(6)

(A) in a case concerning an individual who was not represented by an attorney during the course of negotiating an agreement under this subsection, the court approves such agreement as—

(i) not imposing an undue hardship on the debtor or a dependent of the debtor; and

(ii) in the best interest of the debtor.

(B) Subparagraph (A) shall not apply to the extent that such debt is a consumer debt secured by real property.

(d) In a case concerning an individual, when the court has determined whether to grant or not to grant a discharge under section 727, 1141, 1228, or 1328 of this title, the court may hold a hearing at which the debtor shall appear in person. At any such hearing, the court shall inform the debtor that a discharge has been granted or the reason why a discharge has not been granted. If a discharge has been granted and if the debtor desires to make an agreement of the kind specified in subsection (c) of this section and was not represented by an attorney during the course of negotiating such agreement, then the court shall hold a hearing at which the debtor shall appear in person and at such hearing the court shall—

    (1) inform the debtor—

        (A) that such an agreement is not required under this title, under nonbankruptcy law, or under any agreement not made in accordance with the provisions of subsection (c) of this section; and

        (B) of the legal effect and consequences of—

            (i) an agreement of the kind specified in subsection (c) of this section; and

            (ii) a default under such an agreement; and

    (2) determine whether the agreement that the debtor desires to make complies with the requirements of subsection (c)(6) of this section, if the consideration for such agreement is based in whole or in part on a consumer debt that is not secured by real property of the debtor.

(e) Except as provided in subsection (a)(3) of this section, discharge of a debt of the debtor does not affect the liability of any other entity on, or the property of any other entity for, such debt.

(f) Nothing contained in subsection (c) or (d) of this section prevents a debtor from voluntarily repaying any debt.

(g)

    (1)

        (A) After notice and hearing, a court that enters an order confirming a plan of reorganization under chapter 11 may issue, in connection with such order, an injunction in accordance with this subsection to supplement the injunctive effect of a discharge under this section.

        (B) An injunction may be issued under subparagraph (A) to enjoin entities from taking legal action for the purpose of directly or indirectly collecting, recovering, or receiving payment or recovery with respect to any claim or demand that, under a plan of reorganization, is to be paid in whole or in part by a trust described in paragraph (2)(B)(i), except such legal actions as are expressly allowed by the injunction, the confirmation order, or the plan of reorganization.

    (2)

        (A) Subject to subsection (h), if the requirements of subparagraph (B) are met at the time an injunction described in paragraph (1) is entered, then after entry of such injunction, any proceeding that involves the validity, application, construction, or modification of such injunction, or of this subsection with respect to such injunction, may be commenced only in the district court in which such injunction was entered, and such court shall have exclusive jurisdiction over any such proceeding without regard to the amount in controversy.

        (B) The requirements of this subparagraph are that—

            (i) the injunction is to be implemented in connection with a trust that, pursuant to the plan of reorganization—

                (I) is to assume the liabilities of a debtor which at the time of entry of the order for relief has been named as a defendant in personal injury, wrongful death, or property-damage actions seeking recovery for damages allegedly caused by the presence of, or exposure to, asbestos or asbestos-containing products;

                (II) is to be funded in whole or in part by the securities of 1 or more debtors involved in such plan and by the obligation of such debtor or debtors to make future payments, including dividends;

                (III) is to own, or by the exercise of rights granted under such plan would be entitled to own if specified contingencies occur, a majority of the voting shares of—

                    (aa) each such debtor;

                    (bb) the parent corporation of each such debtor; or

                    (cc) a subsidiary of each such debtor that is also a debtor; and

                (IV) is to use its assets or income to pay claims and demands; and

            (ii) subject to subsection (h), the court determines that—

                (I) the debtor is likely to be subject to substantial future demands for payment arising out of the same or similar conduct or events that gave rise to the claims that are addressed by the injunction;

                (II) the actual amounts, numbers, and timing of such future demands cannot be determined;

                (III) pursuit of such demands outside the procedures prescribed by such plan is likely to threaten the plan's purpose to deal equitably with claims and future demands;

(IV) as part of the process of seeking confirmation of such plan—

    (aa) the terms of the injunction proposed to be issued under paragraph (1)(A), including any provisions barring actions against third parties pursuant to paragraph (4)(A), are set out in such plan and in any disclosure statement supporting the plan; and

    (bb) a separate class or classes of the claimants whose claims are to be addressed by a trust described in clause (i) is established and votes, by at least 75 percent of those voting, in favor of the plan; and

(V) subject to subsection (h), pursuant to court orders or otherwise, the trust will operate through mechanisms such as structured, periodic, or supplemental payments, pro rata distributions, matrices, or periodic review of estimates of the numbers and values of present claims and future demands, or other comparable mechanisms, that provide reasonable assurance that the trust will value, and be in a financial position to pay, present claims and future demands that involve similar claims in substantially the same manner.

(3)

(A) If the requirements of paragraph (2)(B) are met and the order confirming the plan of reorganization was issued or affirmed by the district court that has jurisdiction over the reorganization case, then after the time for appeal of the order that issues or affirms the plan—

    (i) the injunction shall be valid and enforceable and may not be revoked or modified by any court except through appeal in accordance with paragraph (6);

    (ii) no entity that pursuant to such plan or thereafter becomes a direct or indirect transferee of, or successor to any assets of, a debtor or trust that is the subject of the injunction shall be liable with respect to any claim or demand made against such entity by reason of its becoming such a transferee or successor; and

    (iii) no entity that pursuant to such plan or thereafter makes a loan to such a debtor or trust or to such a successor or

transferee shall, by reason of making the loan, be liable with respect to any claim or demand made against such entity, nor shall any pledge of assets made in connection with such a loan be upset or impaired for that reason;

(B) Subparagraph (A) shall not be construed to—

    (i) imply that an entity described in subparagraph (A)(ii) or (iii) would, if this paragraph were not applicable, necessarily be liable to any entity by reason of any of the acts described in subparagraph (A);

    (ii) relieve any such entity of the duty to comply with, or of liability under, any Federal or State law regarding the making of a fraudulent conveyance in a transaction described in subparagraph (A)(ii) or (iii); or

    (iii) relieve a debtor of the debtor's obligation to comply with the terms of the plan of reorganization, or affect the power of the court to exercise its authority under sections 1141 and 1142 to compel the debtor to do so.

(4)

  (A)

    (i) Subject to subparagraph (B), an injunction described in paragraph (1) shall be valid and enforceable against all entities that it addresses.

    (ii) Notwithstanding the provisions of section 524(e), such an injunction may bar any action directed against a third party who is identifiable from the terms of such injunction (by name or as part of an identifiable group) and is alleged to be directly or indirectly liable for the conduct of, claims against, or demands on the debtor to the extent such alleged liability of such third party arises by reason of—

      (I) the third party's ownership of a financial interest in the debtor, a past or present affiliate of the debtor, or a predecessor in interest of the debtor;

      (II) the third party's involvement in the management of the debtor or a predecessor in interest of the debtor, or service as an officer, director or employee of the debtor or a related party;

      (III) the third party's provision of insurance to the debtor or a related party; or

(IV) the third party's involvement in a transaction changing the corporate structure, or in a loan or other financial transaction affecting the financial condition, of the debtor or a related party, including but not limited to—

(aa) involvement in providing financing (debt or equity), or advice to an entity involved in such a transaction; or

(bb) acquiring or selling a financial interest in an entity as part of such a transaction.

(iii) As used in this subparagraph, the term "related party" means—

(I) a past or present affiliate of the debtor;

(II) a predecessor in interest of the debtor; or

(III) any entity that owned a financial interest in—

(aa) the debtor;

(bb) a past or present affiliate of the debtor; or

(cc) a predecessor in interest of the debtor.

(B) Subject to subsection (h), if, under a plan of reorganization, a kind of demand described in such plan is to be paid in whole or in part by a trust described in paragraph (2)(B)(i) in connection with which an injunction described in paragraph (1) is to be implemented, then such injunction shall be valid and enforceable with respect to a demand of such kind made, after such plan is confirmed, against the debtor or debtors involved, or against a third party described in subparagraph (A)(ii), if—

(i) as part of the proceedings leading to issuance of such injunction, the court appoints a legal representative for the purpose of protecting the rights of persons that might subsequently assert demands of such kind, and

(ii) the court determines, before entering the order confirming such plan, that identifying such debtor or debtors, or such third party (by name or as part of an identifiable group), in such injunction with respect to such demands for purposes of this subparagraph is fair and equitable with respect to the persons that might subsequently assert such demands, in light of the benefits provided, or to be

provided, to such trust on behalf of such debtor or debtors or such third party.

(5) In this subsection, the term "demand" means a demand for payment, present or future, that—

(A) was not a claim during the proceedings leading to the confirmation of a plan of reorganization;

(B) arises out of the same or similar conduct or events that gave rise to the claims addressed by the injunction issued under paragraph (1); and

(C) pursuant to the plan, is to be paid by a trust described in paragraph (2)(B)(i).

(6) Paragraph (3)(A)(i) does not bar an action taken by or at the direction of an appellate court on appeal of an injunction issued under paragraph (1) or of the order of confirmation that relates to the injunction.

(7) This subsection does not affect the operation of section 1144 or the power of the district court to refer a proceeding under section 157 of title 28 or any reference of a proceeding made prior to the date of the enactment of this subsection.

(h) Application to Existing Injunctions.—For purposes of subsection (g)—

(1) subject to paragraph (2), if an injunction of the kind described in subsection (g)(1)(B) was issued before the date of the enactment of this Act, as part of a plan of reorganization confirmed by an order entered before such date, then the injunction shall be considered to meet the requirements of subsection (g)(2)(B) for purposes of subsection (g)(2)(A), and to satisfy subsection (g)(4)(A)(ii), if—

(A) the court determined at the time the plan was confirmed that the plan was fair and equitable in accordance with the requirements of section 1129(b);

(B) as part of the proceedings leading to issuance of such injunction and confirmation of such plan, the court had appointed a legal representative for the purpose of protecting the rights of persons that might subsequently assert demands described in subsection (g)(4)(B) with respect to such plan; and

(C) such legal representative did not object to confirmation of such plan or issuance of such injunction; and

(2) for purposes of paragraph (1), if a trust described in subsection (g)(2)(B)(i) is subject to a court order on the date of the enactment of this Act staying such trust from settling or paying further claims—

(A) the requirements of subsection (g)(2)(B)(ii)(V) shall not apply with respect to such trust until such stay is lifted or dissolved; and

(B) if such trust meets such requirements on the date such stay is lifted or dissolved, such trust shall be considered to have met such requirements continuously from the date of the enactment of this Act.

(i) The willful failure of a creditor to credit payments received under a plan confirmed under this title, unless the order confirming the plan is revoked, the plan is in default, or the creditor has not received payments required to be made under the plan in the manner required by the plan (including crediting the amounts required under the plan), shall constitute a violation of an injunction under subsection (a)(2) if the act of the creditor to collect and failure to credit payments in the manner required by the plan caused material injury to the debtor.

(j) Subsection (a)(2) does not operate as an injunction against an act by a creditor that is the holder of a secured claim, if—

(1) such creditor retains a security interest in real property that is the principal residence of the debtor;

(2) such act is in the ordinary course of business between the creditor and the debtor; and

(3) such act is limited to seeking or obtaining periodic payments associated with a valid security interest in lieu of pursuit of in rem relief to enforce the lien.

(k)

(1) The disclosures required under subsection (c)(2) shall consist of the disclosure statement described in paragraph (3), completed as required in that paragraph, together with the agreement specified in subsection (c), statement, declaration, motion and order described, respectively, in paragraphs (4) through (8), and shall be the only disclosures required in connection with entering into such agreement.

(2) Disclosures made under paragraph (1) shall be made clearly and conspicuously and in writing. The terms "Amount Reaffirmed" and "Annual Percentage Rate" shall be disclosed more conspicuously than other terms, data or information provided in connection with this disclosure, except that the phrases "Before agreeing to reaffirm a debt, review these important disclosures" and "Summary of Reaffirmation Agreement" may be equally conspicuous. Disclosures may be made in a different order and may use terminology different from that set forth in paragraphs (2) through (8), except that the terms "Amount Reaffirmed" and "Annual Percentage Rate" must be used where indicated.

(3) The disclosure statement required under this paragraph shall consist of the following:

(A) The statement: "Part A: Before agreeing to reaffirm a debt, review these important disclosures:";

(B) Under the heading "Summary of Reaffirmation Agreement", the statement: "This Summary is made pursuant to the requirements of the Bankruptcy Code";

(C) The "Amount Reaffirmed", using that term, which shall be—

(i) the total amount of debt that the debtor agrees to reaffirm by entering into an agreement of the kind specified in subsection (c), and

(ii) the total of any fees and costs accrued as of the date of the disclosure statement, related to such total amount.

(D) In conjunction with the disclosure of the "Amount Reaffirmed", the statements—

(i) "The amount of debt you have agreed to reaffirm"; and

(ii) "Your credit agreement may obligate you to pay additional amounts which may come due after the date of this disclosure. Consult your credit agreement.".

(E) The "Annual Percentage Rate", using that term, which shall be disclosed as—

(i) if, at the time the petition is filed, the debt is an extension of credit under an open end credit plan, as the terms "credit" and "open end credit plan" are defined in section 103 of the Truth in Lending Act, then—

(I) the annual percentage rate determined under paragraphs (5) and (6) of section 127(b) of the Truth in Lending Act, as applicable, as disclosed to the debtor in the most recent periodic statement prior to entering into an agreement of the kind specified in subsection (c) or, if no such periodic statement has been given to the debtor during the prior 6 months, the annual percentage rate as it would have been so disclosed at the time the disclosure statement is given to the debtor, or to the extent this annual percentage rate is not readily available or not applicable, then

(II) the simple interest rate applicable to the amount reaffirmed as of the date the disclosure statement is given to the debtor, or if different simple interest rates apply to different balances, the simple interest rate applicable to each such balance, identifying the amount of each such balance included in the amount reaffirmed, or

(III) if the entity making the disclosure elects, to disclose the annual percentage rate under subclause (I) and the simple interest rate under subclause (II); or

(ii) if, at the time the petition is filed, the debt is an extension of credit other than under an open end credit plan, as the terms "credit" and "open end credit plan" are defined in section 103 of the Truth in Lending Act, then—

(I) the annual percentage rate under section 128(a)(4) of the Truth in Lending Act, as disclosed to the debtor in the most recent disclosure statement given to the debtor prior to the entering into an agreement of the kind specified in subsection (c) with respect to the debt, or, if no such disclosure statement was given to the debtor, the annual percentage rate as it would have been so disclosed at the time the disclosure statement is given to the debtor, or to the extent this annual percentage rate is not readily available or not applicable, then

(II) the simple interest rate applicable to the amount reaffirmed as of the date the disclosure statement is given to the debtor, or if different simple interest rates apply to different balances, the simple interest rate applicable to each such balance, identifying the amount of such balance included in the amount reaffirmed, or

(III) if the entity making the disclosure elects, to disclose the annual percentage rate under (I) and the simple interest rate under (II).

(F) If the underlying debt transaction was disclosed as a variable rate transaction on the most recent disclosure given under the Truth in Lending Act, by stating "The interest rate on your loan may be a variable interest rate which changes from time to time, so that the annual percentage rate disclosed here may be higher or lower.".

(G) If the debt is secured by a security interest which has not been waived in whole or in part or determined to be void by a final order of the court at the time of the disclosure, by disclosing that a security interest or lien in goods or property is asserted over some or all of the debts the debtor is reaffirming and listing the items and their original purchase price that are subject to the asserted security interest, or if not a purchase-money security interest then listing by items or types and the original amount of the loan.

(H) At the election of the creditor, a statement of the repayment schedule using 1 or a combination of the following—

(i) by making the statement: "Your first payment in the amount of $_____ is due on _____ but the future payment amount may be different. Consult your reaffirmation agreement or credit agreement, as applicable.", and stating the amount of the first payment and the due date of that payment in the places provided;

(ii) by making the statement: "Your payment schedule will be:", and describing the repayment schedule with the number, amount, and due dates or period of payments scheduled to repay the debts reaffirmed to the extent then known by the disclosing party; or

(iii) by describing the debtor's repayment obligations with reasonable specificity to the extent then known by the disclosing party.

(I) The following statement: "Note: When this disclosure refers to what a creditor 'may' do, it does not use the word 'may' to give the creditor specific permission. The word 'may' is used to tell you what might occur if the law permits the creditor to take the action. If you have questions about your reaffirming a debt or what the law requires, consult with the attorney who helped you negotiate this agreement reaffirming a debt. If you don't have an attorney helping you, the judge will explain the effect of your reaffirming a debt when the hearing on the reaffirmation agreement is held.".

(J)

(i) The following additional statements: "Reaffirming a debt is a serious financial decision. The law requires you to take certain steps to make sure the decision is in your best interest. If these steps are not completed, the reaffirmation agreement is not effective, even though you have signed it.

"1. Read the disclosures in this Part A carefully. Consider the decision to reaffirm carefully. Then, if you want to reaffirm, sign the reaffirmation agreement in Part B (or you may use a separate agreement you and your creditor agree on).

"2. Complete and sign Part D and be sure you can afford to make the payments you are agreeing to make and have received a copy of the disclosure statement and a completed and signed reaffirmation agreement.

"3. If you were represented by an attorney during the negotiation of your reaffirmation agreement, the attorney must have signed the certification in Part C.

"4. If you were not represented by an attorney during the negotiation of your reaffirmation agreement, you must have completed and signed Part E.

"5. The original of this disclosure must be filed with the court by you or your creditor. If a separate reaffirmation agreement (other than the one in Part B) has been signed, it must be attached.

"6. If you were represented by an attorney during the negotiation of your reaffirmation agreement, your reaffirmation agreement becomes effective upon filing with the court unless the reaffirmation is presumed to be an undue hardship as explained in Part D.

"7. If you were not represented by an attorney during the negotiation of your reaffirmation agreement, it will not be effective unless the court approves it. The court will notify you of the hearing on your reaffirmation agreement. You must attend this hearing in bankruptcy court where the judge will review your reaffirmation agreement. The bankruptcy court must approve your reaffirmation agreement as consistent with your best interests, except that no court approval is required if your reaffirmation agreement is for a consumer debt secured by a mortgage, deed of trust, security deed, or other lien on your real property, like your home.

"Your right to rescind (cancel) your reaffirmation agreement. You may rescind (cancel) your reaffirmation agreement at any time before the bankruptcy court enters a discharge order, or before the expiration of the 60-day period that begins on the date your reaffirmation agreement is filed with the court, whichever occurs later. To rescind (cancel) your reaffirmation agreement, you must notify the creditor that your reaffirmation agreement is rescinded (or canceled).

"What are your obligations if you reaffirm the debt? A reaffirmed debt remains your personal legal obligation. It is not discharged in your bankruptcy case. That means that if you default on your reaffirmed debt after your bankruptcy case is over, your creditor may be able to take your property or your wages. Otherwise, your obligations will be determined by the reaffirmation agreement which may have changed the terms of the original agreement. For example, if you are reaffirming an open end credit agreement, the creditor may be permitted by that agreement or applicable law to change the terms of that agreement in the future under certain conditions.

"Are you required to enter into a reaffirmation agreement by any law? No, you are not required to reaffirm a debt by any law. Only agree to reaffirm a debt if it is in your best interest. Be sure you can afford the payments you agree to make.

"What if your creditor has a security interest or lien? Your bankruptcy discharge does not eliminate any lien on your property. A 'lien' is often referred to as a security interest, deed of trust, mortgage or security deed. Even if you do not reaffirm and your personal liability on the debt is discharged, because of the lien your creditor may still have the right to take the property securing the lien if you do not pay the debt or default on it. If the lien is on an item of personal property that is exempt under your State's law or that the trustee has abandoned, you may be able to redeem the item rather than reaffirm the debt. To redeem, you must make a single payment to the creditor equal to the amount of the allowed secured claim, as agreed by the parties or determined by the court.".

(ii) In the case of a reaffirmation under subsection (m)(2), numbered paragraph 6 in the disclosures required by clause (i) of this subparagraph shall read as follows:

"6. If you were represented by an attorney during the negotiation of your reaffirmation agreement, your reaffirmation agreement becomes effective upon filing with the court.".

(4) The form of such agreement required under this paragraph shall consist of the following:

"Part B: Reaffirmation Agreement. I (we) agree to reaffirm the debts arising under the credit agreement described below.

"Brief description of credit agreement:

"Description of any changes to the credit agreement made as part of this reaffirmation agreement:

"Signature:　　　Date:

"Borrower:

"Co-borrower, if also reaffirming these debts:

"Accepted by creditor:

"Date of creditor acceptance:".

(5) The declaration shall consist of the following:

(A) The following certification:

"Part C: Certification by Debtor's Attorney (If Any).

"I hereby certify that (1) this agreement represents a fully informed and voluntary agreement by the debtor; (2) this agreement does not impose an undue hardship on the debtor or any dependent of the debtor; and (3) I have fully advised the debtor of the legal effect and consequences of this agreement and any default under this agreement.

"Signature of Debtor's Attorney:　　Date:".

(B) If a presumption of undue hardship has been established with respect to such agreement, such certification shall state that, in the opinion of the attorney, the debtor is able to make the payment.

(C) In the case of a reaffirmation agreement under subsection (m)(2), subparagraph (B) is not applicable.

(6)

(A) The statement in support of such agreement, which the debtor shall sign and

date prior to filing with the court, shall consist of the following:

"Part D: Debtor's Statement in Support of Reaffirmation Agreement.

"1. I believe this reaffirmation agreement will not impose an undue hardship on my dependents or me. I can afford to make the payments on the reaffirmed debt because my monthly income (take home pay plus any other income received) is $_____, and my actual current monthly expenses including monthly payments on post-bankruptcy debt and other reaffirmation agreements total $_____, leaving $_____ to make the required payments on this reaffirmed debt. I understand that if my income less my monthly expenses does not leave enough to make the payments, this reaffirmation agreement is presumed to be an undue hardship on me and must be reviewed by the court. However, this presumption may be overcome if I explain to the satisfaction of the court how I can afford to make the payments here: _____.

"2. I received a copy of the Reaffirmation Disclosure Statement in Part A and a completed and signed reaffirmation agreement.".

(B) Where the debtor is represented by an attorney and is reaffirming a debt owed to a creditor defined in section 19(b)(1)(A)(iv) of the Federal Reserve Act, the statement of support of the reaffirmation agreement, which the debtor shall sign and date prior to filing with the court, shall consist of the following:

"I believe this reaffirmation agreement is in my financial interest. I can afford to make the payments on the reaffirmed debt. I received a copy of the Reaffirmation Disclosure Statement in Part A and a completed and signed reaffirmation agreement.".

(7) The motion that may be used if approval of such agreement by the court is required in order for it to be effective, shall be signed and dated by the movant and shall consist of the following:

"Part E: Motion for Court Approval (To be completed only if the debtor is not represented by an attorney.). I (we), the debtor(s), affirm the following to be true and correct:

"I am not represented by an attorney in connection with this reaffirmation agreement.

"I believe this reaffirmation agreement is in my best interest based on the income and expenses I have disclosed in my Statement in Support of this reaffirmation agreement, and because (provide any additional relevant reasons the court should consider): "Therefore, I ask the court for an order approving this reaffirmation agreement.".

(8) The court order, which may be used to approve such agreement, shall consist of the following:

"Court Order: The court grants the debtor's motion and approves the reaffirmation agreement described above.".

(l) Notwithstanding any other provision of this title the following shall apply:

(1) A creditor may accept payments from a debtor before and after the filing of an agreement of the kind specified in subsection (c) with the court.

(2) A creditor may accept payments from a debtor under such agreement that the creditor believes in good faith to be effective.

(3) The requirements of subsections (c)(2) and (k) shall be satisfied if disclosures required under those subsections are given in good faith.

(m)

(1) Until 60 days after an agreement of the kind specified in subsection (c) is filed with the court (or such additional period as the court, after notice and a hearing and for cause, orders before the expiration of such period), it shall be presumed that such agreement is an undue hardship on the debtor if the debtor's monthly income less the debtor's monthly expenses as shown on the debtor's completed and signed statement in support of such agreement required under subsection (k)(6)(A) is less than the scheduled payments on the reaffirmed debt. This presumption shall be reviewed by the court. The presumption may be rebutted in writing by the debtor if the statement includes an explanation that identifies additional sources of funds to make the payments as agreed upon under the terms of such agreement. If the presumption is not rebutted to the satisfaction of the court, the court may disapprove such agreement. No agreement shall be disapproved without notice and a hearing to the debtor and creditor, and such hearing shall be concluded before the entry of the debtor's discharge.

(2) This subsection does not apply to reaffirmation agreements where the creditor is

a credit union, as defined in section 19(b)(1)(A)(iv) of the Federal Reserve Act.

§525. Protection against discriminatory treatment

(a) Except as provided in the Perishable Agricultural Commodities Act, 1930, the Packers and Stockyards Act, 1921, and section 1 of the Act entitled "An Act making appropriations for the Department of Agriculture for the fiscal year ending June 30, 1944, and for other purposes," approved July 12, 1943, a governmental unit may not deny, revoke, suspend, or refuse to renew a license, permit, charter, franchise, or other similar grant to, condition such a grant to, discriminate with respect to such a grant against, deny employment to, terminate the employment of, or discriminate with respect to employment against, a person that is or has been a debtor under this title or a bankrupt or a debtor under the Bankruptcy Act, or another person with whom such bankrupt or debtor has been associated, solely because such bankrupt or debtor is or has been a debtor under this title or a bankrupt or debtor under the Bankruptcy Act, has been insolvent before the commencement of the case under this title, or during the case but before the debtor is granted or denied a discharge, or has not paid a debt that is dischargeable in the case under this title or that was discharged under the Bankruptcy Act.

(b) No private employer may terminate the employment of, or discriminate with respect to employment against, an individual who is or has been a debtor under this title, a debtor or bankrupt under the Bankruptcy Act, or an individual associated with such debtor or bankrupt, solely because such debtor or bankrupt—

(1) is or has been a debtor under this title or a debtor or bankrupt under the Bankruptcy Act;

(2) has been insolvent before the commencement of a case under this title or during the case but before the grant or denial of a discharge; or

(3) has not paid a debt that is dischargeable in a case under this title or that was discharged under the Bankruptcy Act.

(c)

(1) A governmental unit that operates a student grant or loan program and a person engaged in a business that includes the making of loans guaranteed or insured under a student loan program may not deny a student grant, loan, loan guarantee, or loan insurance to a person that is or has been a debtor under this title or a bankrupt or debtor under the Bankruptcy Act, or another person with whom the debtor or bankrupt has been associated, because the debtor or bankrupt is or has been a debtor under this title or a bankrupt or debtor under the Bankruptcy Act, has been insolvent before the commencement of a case under this title or during the pendency of the case but before the debtor is granted or denied a discharge, or has not paid a debt that is dischargeable in the case under this title or that was discharged under the Bankruptcy Act.

(2) In this section, "student loan program" means any program operated under title IV of the Higher Education Act of 1965 or a similar program operated under State or local law.

§526. Restrictions on debt relief agencies

(a) A debt relief agency shall not—

(1) fail to perform any service that such agency informed an assisted person or prospective assisted person it would provide in connection with a case or proceeding under this title;

(2) make any statement, or counsel or advise any assisted person or prospective assisted person to make a statement in a document filed in a case or proceeding under this title, that is untrue or misleading, or that upon the exercise of reasonable care, should have been known by such agency to be untrue or misleading;

(3) misrepresent to any assisted person or prospective assisted person, directly or indirectly, affirmatively or by material omission, with respect to—

(A) the services that such agency will provide to such person; or

(B) the benefits and risks that may result if such person becomes a debtor in a case under this title; or

(4) advise an assisted person or prospective assisted person to incur more debt in contemplation of such person filing a case under this title or to pay an attorney or bankruptcy petition preparer a fee or charge for services performed as part of preparing for or representing a debtor in a case under this title.

(b) Any waiver by any assisted person of any protection or right provided under this section shall not be enforceable against the debtor by any Federal or State court or any other person, but may be enforced against a debt relief agency.

(c)

(1) Any contract for bankruptcy assistance between a debt relief agency and an assisted person that does not comply with the material requirements of this section, section 527, or section 528 shall be void and may not be enforced by any Federal or State court or by any other person, other than such assisted person.

(2) Any debt relief agency shall be liable to an assisted person in the amount of any fees or charges in connection with providing bankruptcy assistance to such person that such debt relief agency has received, for actual damages, and for reasonable attorneys' fees and costs if such agency is found, after notice and a hearing, to have—

(A) intentionally or negligently failed to comply with any provision of this section, section 527, or section 528 with respect to a case or proceeding under this title for such assisted person;

(B) provided bankruptcy assistance to an assisted person in a case or proceeding under this title that is dismissed or converted to a case under another chapter of this title because of such agency's intentional or negligent failure to file any required document including those specified in section 521; or

(C) intentionally or negligently disregarded the material requirements of this title or the Federal Rules of Bankruptcy Procedure applicable to such agency.

(3) In addition to such other remedies as are provided under State law, whenever the chief law enforcement officer of a State, or an official or agency designated by a State, has reason to believe that any person has violated or is violating this section, the State—

(A) may bring an action to enjoin such violation;

(B) may bring an action on behalf of its residents to recover the actual damages of assisted persons arising from such violation, including any liability under paragraph (2); and

(C) in the case of any successful action under subparagraph (A) or (B), shall be awarded the costs of the action and reasonable attorneys' fees as determined by the court.

(4) The district courts of the United States for districts located in the State shall have concurrent jurisdiction of any action under subparagraph (A) or (B) of paragraph (3).

(5) Notwithstanding any other provision of Federal law and in addition to any other remedy provided under Federal or State law, if the court, on its own motion or on the motion of the United States trustee or the debtor, finds that a person intentionally violated this section, or engaged in a clear and consistent pattern or practice of violating this section, the court may—

    (A) enjoin the violation of such section; or

    (B) impose an appropriate civil penalty against such person.

(d) No provision of this section, section 527, or section 528 shall—

    (1) annul, alter, affect, or exempt any person subject to such sections from complying with any law of any State except to the extent that such law is inconsistent with those sections, and then only to the extent of the inconsistency; or

    (2) be deemed to limit or curtail the authority or ability—

        (A) of a State or subdivision or instrumentality thereof, to determine and enforce qualifications for the practice of law under the laws of that State; or

        (B) of a Federal court to determine and enforce the qualifications for the practice of law before that court.

§527. Disclosures

(a) A debt relief agency providing bankruptcy assistance to an assisted person shall provide—

    (1) the written notice required under section 342(b)(1); and

    (2) to the extent not covered in the written notice described in paragraph (1), and not later than 3 business days after the first date on which a debt relief agency first offers to provide any bankruptcy assistance services to an assisted person, a clear and conspicuous written notice advising assisted persons that—

        (A) all information that the assisted person is required to provide with a petition and thereafter during a case under this title is required to be complete, accurate, and truthful;

        (B) all assets and all liabilities are required to be completely and accurately disclosed in the documents filed to commence the case, and the replacement value of each asset as defined in section 506 must be stated in those documents where requested after reasonable inquiry to establish such value;

        (C) current monthly income, the amounts specified in section 707(b)(2), and, in a case under chapter 13 of this title, disposable income (determined in accordance with section 707(b)(2)), are required to be stated after reasonable inquiry; and

        (D) information that an assisted person provides during their case may be audited pursuant to this title, and that failure to provide such information may result in dismissal of the case under this title or other sanction, including a criminal sanction.

(b) A debt relief agency providing bankruptcy assistance to an assisted person shall provide each assisted person at the same time as the notices required under subsection (a)(1) the following statement, to the extent applicable, or one substantially similar. The statement shall be clear and conspicuous and shall be in a single document separate from other documents or notices provided to the assisted person:

"IMPORTANT INFORMATION ABOUT BANKRUPTCY ASSISTANCE SERVICES FROM AN ATTORNEY OR BANKRUPTCY PETITION PREPARER.

"If you decide to seek bankruptcy relief, you can represent yourself, you can hire an attorney to represent you, or you can get help in some localities from a bankruptcy petition preparer who is not an attorney. THE LAW REQUIRES AN ATTORNEY OR BANKRUPTCY PETITION PREPARER TO GIVE YOU A WRITTEN CONTRACT SPECIFYING WHAT THE ATTORNEY OR BANKRUPTCY PETITION PREPARER WILL DO FOR YOU AND HOW MUCH IT WILL COST. Ask to see the contract before you hire anyone.

"The following information helps you understand what must be done in a routine bankruptcy case to help you evaluate how much service you need. Although bankruptcy can be complex, many cases are routine.

"Before filing a bankruptcy case, either you or your attorney should analyze your eligibility for different forms of debt relief available under the Bankruptcy Code and which form of relief is most likely to be beneficial for you. Be sure you understand the relief you can obtain and its limitations. To file a bankruptcy case, documents called a Petition, Schedules, and Statement of Financial Affairs, and in some cases a Statement of Intention, need to be prepared correctly and filed with the bankruptcy court. You will have to pay a filing fee to the bankruptcy court. Once your case starts, you will have to attend the required first meeting of creditors where you may be questioned by a court official called a 'trustee' and by creditors.

"If you choose to file a chapter 7 case, you may be asked by a creditor to reaffirm a debt. You may want help deciding whether to do so. A creditor is not permitted to coerce you into reaffirming your debts.

"If you choose to file a chapter 13 case in which you repay your creditors what you can afford over 3 to 5 years, you may also want help with preparing your chapter 13 plan and with the confirmation hearing on your plan which will be before a bankruptcy judge.

"If you select another type of relief under the Bankruptcy Code other than chapter 7 or chapter 13, you will want to find out what should be done from someone familiar with that type of relief.

"Your bankruptcy case may also involve litigation. You are generally permitted to represent yourself in litigation in bankruptcy court, but only attorneys, not bankruptcy petition preparers, can give you legal advice.".

(c) Except to the extent the debt relief agency provides the required information itself after reasonably diligent inquiry of the assisted person or others so as to obtain such information reasonably accurately for inclusion on the petition, schedules or statement of financial affairs, a debt relief agency providing bankruptcy assistance to an assisted person, to the extent permitted by nonbankruptcy law, shall provide each assisted person at the time required for the notice required under subsection (a)(1) reasonably sufficient information (which shall be provided in a clear and conspicuous writing) to the assisted person on how to provide all the information the assisted person is required to provide under this title pursuant to section 521, including—

    (1) how to value assets at replacement value, determine current monthly income, the amounts specified in section 707(b)(2) and, in a chapter 13 case, how to determine disposable income in accordance with section 707(b)(2) and related calculations;

    (2) how to complete the list of creditors, including how to determine what amount is owed and what address for the creditor should be shown; and

    (3) how to determine what property is exempt and how to value exempt property at replacement value as defined in section 506.

(d) A debt relief agency shall maintain a copy of the notices required under subsection (a) of this section for 2 years after the date on which the notice is given the assisted person.

§528. Requirements for debt relief agencies

(a) A debt relief agency shall—

    (1) not later than 5 business days after the first date on which such agency provides any bankruptcy assistance services to an assisted person, but prior to such assisted person's petition under this title being filed, execute a written contract with such assisted person that explains clearly and conspicuously—

        (A) the services such agency will provide to such assisted person; and

        (B) the fees or charges for such services, and the terms of payment;

    (2) provide the assisted person with a copy of the fully executed and completed contract;

    (3) clearly and conspicuously disclose in any advertisement of bankruptcy assistance services or of the benefits of bankruptcy directed to the general public (whether in general media, seminars or specific mailings, telephonic or electronic messages, or otherwise) that the services or benefits are with respect to bankruptcy relief under this title; and

    (4) clearly and conspicuously use the following statement in such advertisement: "We are a debt relief agency. We help people file for bankruptcy relief under the Bankruptcy Code." or a substantially similar statement.

(b)

    (1) An advertisement of bankruptcy assistance services or of the benefits of bankruptcy directed to the general public includes—

        (A) descriptions of bankruptcy assistance in connection with a chapter 13 plan whether or not chapter 13 is specifically mentioned in such advertisement; and

        (B) statements such as "federally supervised repayment plan" or "Federal debt restructuring help" or other similar statements that could lead a reasonable consumer to believe that debt counseling was being offered when in fact the services were directed to providing bankruptcy assistance with a chapter 13 plan or other form of bankruptcy relief under this title.

    (2) An advertisement, directed to the general public, indicating that the debt relief agency provides assistance with respect to credit defaults, mortgage foreclosures, eviction proceedings, excessive debt, debt collection pressure, or inability to pay any consumer debt shall—

        (A) disclose clearly and conspicuously in such advertisement that the assistance may involve bankruptcy relief under this title; and

(B) include the following statement: "We are a debt relief agency. We help people file for bankruptcy relief under the Bankruptcy Code." or a substantially similar statement.

SUBCHAPTER III—THE ESTATE

§541. Property of the estate

(a) The commencement of a case under section 301, 302, or 303 of this title creates an estate. Such estate is comprised of all the following property, wherever located and by whomever held:

(1) Except as provided in subsections (b) and (c)(2) of this section, all legal or equitable interests of the debtor in property as of the commencement of the case.

(2) All interests of the debtor and the debtor's spouse in community property as of the commencement of the case that is—

(A) under the sole, equal, or joint management and control of the debtor; or

(B) liable for an allowable claim against the debtor, or for both an allowable claim against the debtor and an allowable claim against the debtor's spouse, to the extent that such interest is so liable.

(3) Any interest in property that the trustee recovers under section 329(b), 363(n), 543, 550, 553, or 723 of this title.

(4) Any interest in property preserved for the benefit of or ordered transferred to the estate under section 510(c) or 551 of this title.

(5) Any interest in property that would have been property of the estate if such interest had been an interest of the debtor on the date of the filing of the petition, and that the debtor acquires or becomes entitled to acquire within 180 days after such date—

(A) by bequest, devise, or inheritance;

(B) as a result of a property settlement agreement with the debtor's spouse, or of an interlocutory or final divorce decree; or

(C) as a beneficiary of a life insurance policy or of a death benefit plan.

(6) Proceeds, product, offspring, rents, or profits of or from property of the estate, except such as are earnings from services performed by an individual debtor after the commencement of the case.

(7) Any interest in property that the estate acquires after the commencement of the case.

(b) Property of the estate does not include—

(1) any power that the debtor may exercise solely for the benefit of an entity other than the debtor;

(2) any interest of the debtor as a lessee under a lease of nonresidential real property that has terminated at the expiration of the stated term of such lease before the commencement of the case under this title, and ceases to include any interest of the debtor as a lessee under a lease of nonresidential real property that has terminated at the expiration of the stated term of such lease during the case;

(3) any eligibility of the debtor to participate in programs authorized under the Higher Education Act of 1965 (20 U.S.C. 1001 et seq.; 42 U.S.C. 2751 et seq.), or any accreditation status or State licensure of the debtor as an educational institution;

(4) any interest of the debtor in liquid or gaseous hydrocarbons to the extent that—

(A)

(i) the debtor has transferred or has agreed to transfer such interest pursuant to a farmout agreement or any written agreement directly related to a farmout agreement; and

(ii) but for the operation of this paragraph, the estate could include the interest referred to in clause (i) only by virtue of section 365 or 544(a)(3) of this title; or

(B)

(i) the debtor has transferred such interest pursuant to a written conveyance of a production payment to an entity that does not participate in the operation of the property from which such production payment is transferred; and

(ii) but for the operation of this paragraph, the estate could include the interest referred to in clause (i) only by virtue of section 365 or 542 of this title;

(5) funds placed in an education individual retirement account (as defined in section 530(b)(1) of the Internal Revenue Code of 1986) not later than 365 days before the date of the filing of the petition in a case under this title, but—

(A) only if the designated beneficiary of such account was a child, stepchild, grandchild, or stepgrandchild of the debtor for the taxable year for which funds were placed in such account;

(B) only to the extent that such funds—

(i) are not pledged or promised to any entity in connection with any extension of credit; and

(ii) are not excess contributions (as described in section 4973(e) of the Internal Revenue Code of 1986); and

(C) in the case of funds placed in all such accounts having the same designated beneficiary not earlier than 720 days nor later than 365 days before such date, only so much of such funds as does not exceed $6,425;

(6) funds used to purchase a tuition credit or certificate or contributed to an account in accordance with section 529(b)(1)(A) of the Internal Revenue Code of 1986 under a qualified State tuition program (as defined in section 529(b)(1) of such Code) not later than 365 days before the date of the filing of the petition in a case under this title, but—

(A) only if the designated beneficiary of the amounts paid or contributed to such tuition program was a child, stepchild, grandchild, or stepgrandchild of the debtor for the taxable year for which funds were paid or contributed;

(B) with respect to the aggregate amount paid or contributed to such program having the same designated beneficiary, only so much of such amount as does not exceed the total contributions permitted under section 529(b)(6) of such Code with respect to such beneficiary, as adjusted beginning on the date of the filing of the petition in a case under this title by the annual increase or decrease (rounded to the nearest tenth of 1 percent) in the education expenditure category of the Consumer Price Index prepared by the Department of Labor; and

(C) in the case of funds paid or contributed to such program having the same designated beneficiary not earlier than 720 days nor later than 365 days before such date, only so much of such funds as does not exceed $6,425;

(7) any amount—

(A) withheld by an employer from the wages of employees for payment as contributions—

(i) to—

(I) an employee benefit plan that is subject to title I of the Employee Retirement Income Security Act of 1974 or under an employee benefit plan which is a governmental plan under section 414(d) of the Internal Revenue Code of 1986;

(II) a deferred compensation plan under section 457 of the Internal Revenue Code of 1986; or

(III) a tax-deferred annuity under section 403(b) of the Internal Revenue Code of 1986;

except that such amount under this subparagraph shall not constitute disposable income as defined in section 1325(b)(2); or

(ii) to a health insurance plan regulated by State law whether or not subject to such title; or

(B) received by an employer from employees for payment as contributions—

(i) to—

(I) an employee benefit plan that is subject to title I of the Employee Retirement Income Security Act of 1974 or under an employee benefit plan which is a governmental plan under section 414(d) of the Internal Revenue Code of 1986;

(II) a deferred compensation plan under section 457 of the Internal Revenue Code of 1986; or

(III) a tax-deferred annuity under section 403(b) of the Internal Revenue Code of 1986;

except that such amount under this subparagraph shall not constitute disposable income, as defined in section 1325(b)(2); or

(ii) to a health insurance plan regulated by State law whether or not subject to such title;

(8) subject to subchapter III of chapter 5, any interest of the debtor in property where the debtor pledged or sold tangible personal property (other than securities or written or printed evidences of indebtedness or title) as collateral for a loan or advance of money given by a person licensed under law to make such loans or advances, where—

(A) the tangible personal property is in the possession of the pledgee or transferee;

(B) the debtor has no obligation to repay the money, redeem the collateral, or buy back the property at a stipulated price; and

(C) neither the debtor nor the trustee have exercised any right to redeem provided under the contract or State law, in a timely manner as provided under State law and section 108(b);

(9) any interest in cash or cash equivalents that constitute proceeds of a sale by the debtor of a money order that is made—

> **(A)** on or after the date that is 14 days prior to the date on which the petition is filed; and

> **(B)** under an agreement with a money order issuer that prohibits the commingling of such proceeds with property of the debtor (notwithstanding that, contrary to the agreement, the proceeds may have been commingled with property of the debtor),

unless the money order issuer had not taken action, prior to the filing of the petition, to require compliance with the prohibition; or

(10) funds placed in an account of a qualified ABLE program (as defined in section 529A(b) of the Internal Revenue Code of 1986) not later than 365 days before the date of the filing of the petition in a case under this title, but—

> **(A)** only if the designated beneficiary of such account was a child, stepchild, grandchild, or stepgrandchild of the debtor for the taxable year for which funds were placed in such account;

> **(B)** only to the extent that such funds—

>> **(i)** are not pledged or promised to any entity in connection with any extension of credit; and

>> **(ii)** are not excess contributions (as described in section 4973(h) of the Internal Revenue Code of 1986); and

> **(C)** in the case of funds placed in all such accounts having the same designated beneficiary not earlier than 720 days nor later than 365 days before such date, only so much of such funds as does not exceed $6,425.

Paragraph (4) shall not be construed to exclude from the estate any consideration the debtor retains, receives, or is entitled to receive for transferring an interest in liquid or gaseous hydrocarbons pursuant to a farmout agreement.

(c)

> **(1)** Except as provided in paragraph (2) of this subsection, an interest of the debtor in property becomes property of the estate under subsection (a)(1), (a)(2), or (a)(5) of this section notwithstanding any provision in an agreement, transfer instrument, or applicable nonbankruptcy law—

>> **(A)** that restricts or conditions transfer of such interest by the debtor; or

>> **(B)** that is conditioned on the insolvency or financial condition of the debtor, on the commencement of a case under this title, or

on the appointment of or taking possession by a trustee in a case under this title or a custodian before such commencement, and that effects or gives an option to effect a forfeiture, modification, or termination of the debtor's interest in property.

> **(2)** A restriction on the transfer of a beneficial interest of the debtor in a trust that is enforceable under applicable nonbankruptcy law is enforceable in a case under this title.

(d) Property in which the debtor holds, as of the commencement of the case, only legal title and not an equitable interest, such as a mortgage secured by real property, or an interest in such a mortgage, sold by the debtor but as to which the debtor retains legal title to service or supervise the servicing of such mortgage or interest, becomes property of the estate under subsection (a)(1) or (2) of this section only to the extent of the debtor's legal title to such property, but not to the extent of any equitable interest in such property that the debtor does not hold.

(e) In determining whether any of the relationships specified in paragraph (5)(A) or (6)(A) of subsection (b) exists, a legally adopted child of an individual (and a child who is a member of an individual's household, if placed with such individual by an authorized placement agency for legal adoption by such individual), or a foster child of an individual (if such child has as the child's principal place of abode the home of the debtor and is a member of the debtor's household) shall be treated as a child of such individual by blood.

(f) Notwithstanding any other provision of this title, property that is held by a debtor that is a corporation described in section 501(c)(3) of the Internal Revenue Code of 1986 and exempt from tax under section 501(a) of such Code may be transferred to an entity that is not such a corporation, but only under the same conditions as would apply if the debtor had not filed a case under this title.

§542. Turnover of property to the estate

(a) Except as provided in subsection (c) or (d) of this section, an entity, other than a custodian, in possession, custody, or control, during the case, of property that the trustee may use, sell, or lease under section 363 of this title, or that the debtor may exempt under section 522 of this title, shall deliver to the trustee, and account for, such property or the value of such property, unless such property is of inconsequential value or benefit to the estate.

(b) Except as provided in subsection (c) or (d) of this section, an entity that owes a debt that is property of the estate and that is matured, payable on demand, or payable on order, shall pay such debt to, or on the order of, the trustee, except to the extent that such debt may be offset under section 553 of this title against a claim against the debtor.

(c) Except as provided in section 362(a)(7) of this title, an entity that has neither actual notice nor actual knowledge of the commencement of the case concerning the debtor may transfer property of the estate, or pay a debt owing to the debtor, in good faith and other than in the manner specified in subsection (d) of this section, to an entity other than the trustee, with the same effect as to the entity making such transfer or payment as if the case under this title concerning the debtor had not been commenced.

(d) A life insurance company may transfer property of the estate or property of the debtor to such company in good faith, with the same effect with respect to such company as if the case under this title concerning the debtor had not been commenced, if such transfer is to pay a premium or to carry out a nonforfeiture insurance option, and is required to be made automatically, under a life insurance contract with such company that was entered into before the date of the filing of the petition and that is property of the estate.

(e) Subject to any applicable privilege, after notice and a hearing, the court may order an attorney, accountant, or other person that holds recorded information, including books, documents, records, and papers, relating to the debtor's property or financial affairs, to turn over or disclose such recorded information to the trustee.

§543. Turnover of property by a custodian

(a) A custodian with knowledge of the commencement of a case under this title concerning the debtor may not make any disbursement from, or take any action in the administration of, property of the debtor, proceeds, product, offspring, rents, or profits of such property, or property of the estate, in the possession, custody, or control of such custodian, except such action as is necessary to preserve such property.

(b) A custodian shall—

    (1) deliver to the trustee any property of the debtor held by or transferred to such custodian, or proceeds, product, offspring, rents, or profits of such property, that is in such custodian's possession, custody, or control on the date that such custodian acquires knowledge of the commencement of the case; and

    (2) file an accounting of any property of the debtor, or proceeds, product, offspring, rents, or profits of such property, that, at any time, came into the possession, custody, or control of such custodian.

(c) The court, after notice and a hearing, shall—

    (1) protect all entities to which a custodian has become obligated with respect to such property or proceeds, product, offspring, rents, or profits of such property;

    (2) provide for the payment of reasonable compensation for services rendered and costs and expenses incurred by such custodian; and

    (3) surcharge such custodian, other than an assignee for the benefit of the debtor's creditors that was appointed or took possession more than 120 days before the date of the filing of the petition, for any improper or excessive disbursement, other than a disbursement that has been made in accordance with applicable law or that has been approved, after notice and a hearing, by a court of competent jurisdiction before the commencement of the case under this title.

(d) After notice and hearing, the bankruptcy court—

    (1) may excuse compliance with subsection (a), (b), or (c) of this section if the interests of creditors and, if the debtor is not insolvent, of equity security holders would be better served by permitting a custodian to continue in possession, custody, or control of such property, and

    (2) shall excuse compliance with subsections (a) and (b)(1) of this section if the custodian is an assignee for the benefit of the debtor's creditors that was appointed or took possession more than 120 days before the date of the filing of the petition, unless compliance with such subsections is necessary to prevent fraud or injustice.

§544. Trustee as lien creditor and as successor to certain creditors and purchasers

(a) The trustee shall have, as of the commencement of the case, and without regard to any knowledge of the trustee or of any creditor, the rights and powers of, or may avoid any transfer of property of the debtor or any obligation incurred by the debtor that is voidable by—

    (1) a creditor that extends credit to the debtor at the time of the commencement of the case, and that obtains, at such time and with respect to such credit, a judicial lien on all property on which a creditor on a simple contract could have obtained such a judicial lien, whether or not such a creditor exists;

(2) a creditor that extends credit to the debtor at the time of the commencement of the case, and obtains, at such time and with respect to such credit, an execution against the debtor that is returned unsatisfied at such time, whether or not such a creditor exists; or

(3) a bona fide purchaser of real property, other than fixtures, from the debtor, against whom applicable law permits such transfer to be perfected, that obtains the status of a bona fide purchaser and has perfected such transfer at the time of the commencement of the case, whether or not such a purchaser exists.

(b)

(1) Except as provided in paragraph (2), the trustee may avoid any transfer of an interest of the debtor in property or any obligation incurred by the debtor that is voidable under applicable law by a creditor holding an unsecured claim that is allowable under section 502 of this title or that is not allowable only under section 502(e) of this title.

(2) Paragraph (1) shall not apply to a transfer of a charitable contribution (as that term is defined in section 548(d)(3)) that is not covered under section 548(a)(1)(B), by reason of section 548(a)(2). Any claim by any person to recover a transferred contribution described in the preceding sentence under Federal or State law in a Federal or State court shall be preempted by the commencement of the case.

§545. Statutory liens

The trustee may avoid the fixing of a statutory lien on property of the debtor to the extent that such lien—

(1) first becomes effective against the debtor—

(A) when a case under this title concerning the debtor is commenced;

(B) when an insolvency proceeding other than under this title concerning the debtor is commenced;

(C) when a custodian is appointed or authorized to take or takes possession;

(D) when the debtor becomes insolvent;

(E) when the debtor's financial condition fails to meet a specified standard; or

(F) at the time of an execution against property of the debtor levied at the instance of an entity other than the holder of such statutory lien;

(2) is not perfected or enforceable at the time of the commencement of the case against a bona fide purchaser that purchases such property at the time

of the commencement of the case, whether or not such a purchaser exists, except in any case in which a purchaser is a purchaser described in section 6323 of the Internal Revenue Code of 1986, or in any other similar provision of State or local law;

(3) is for rent; or

(4) is a lien of distress for rent.

§546. Limitations on avoiding powers

(a) An action or proceeding under section 544, 545, 547, 548, or 553 of this title may not be commenced after the earlier of—

(1) the later of—

(A) 2 years after the entry of the order for relief; or

(B) 1 year after the appointment or election of the first trustee under section 702, 1104, 1163, 1202, or 1302 of this title if such appointment or such election occurs before the expiration of the period specified in subparagraph (A); or

(2) the time the case is closed or dismissed.

(b)

(1) The rights and powers of a trustee under sections 544, 545, and 549 of this title are subject to any generally applicable law that—

(A) permits perfection of an interest in property to be effective against an entity that acquires rights in such property before the date of perfection; or

(B) provides for the maintenance or continuation of perfection of an interest in property to be effective against an entity that acquires rights in such property before the date on which action is taken to effect such maintenance or continuation.

(2) If—

(A) a law described in paragraph (1) requires seizure of such property or commencement of an action to accomplish such perfection, or maintenance or continuation of perfection of an interest in property; and

(B) such property has not been seized or such an action has not been commenced before the date of the filing of the petition; such interest in such property shall be perfected, or perfection of such interest shall be maintained or continued, by giving notice within the time fixed by such law for such seizure or such commencement.

(c)

(1) Except as provided in subsection (d) of this section and in section 507(c), and subject to the prior rights of a holder of a security interest in such goods or the proceeds thereof, the rights and powers of the trustee under sections 544(a), 545, 547, and 549 are subject to the right of a seller of goods that has sold goods to the debtor, in the ordinary course of such seller's business, to reclaim such goods if the debtor has received such goods while insolvent, within 45 days before the date of the commencement of a case under this title, but such seller may not reclaim such goods unless such seller demands in writing reclamation of such goods—

(A) not later than 45 days after the date of receipt of such goods by the debtor; or

(B) not later than 20 days after the date of commencement of the case, if the 45-day period expires after the commencement of the case.

(2) If a seller of goods fails to provide notice in the manner described in paragraph (1), the seller still may assert the rights contained in section 503(b)(9).

(d) In the case of a seller who is a producer of grain sold to a grain storage facility, owned or operated by the debtor, in the ordinary course of such seller's business (as such terms are defined in section 557 of this title) or in the case of a United States fisherman who has caught fish sold to a fish processing facility owned or operated by the debtor in the ordinary course of such fisherman's business, the rights and powers of the trustee under sections 544(a), 545, 547, and 549 of this title are subject to any statutory or common law right of such producer or fisherman to reclaim such grain or fish if the debtor has received such grain or fish while insolvent, but—

(1) such producer or fisherman may not reclaim any grain or fish unless such producer or fisherman demands, in writing, reclamation of such grain or fish before ten days after receipt thereof by the debtor; and

(2) the court may deny reclamation to such a producer or fisherman with a right of reclamation that has made such a demand only if the court secures such claim by a lien.

(e) Notwithstanding sections 544, 545, 547, 548(a)(1)(B), and 548(b) of this title, the trustee may not avoid a transfer that is a margin payment, as defined in section 101, 741, or 761 of this title, or settlement payment, as defined in section 101 or 741 of this title, made by or to (or for the benefit of) a commodity broker, forward contract merchant, stockbroker, financial institution, financial participant, or securities clearing agency, or that is a transfer made by or to (or for the benefit of) a commodity broker, forward contract merchant, stockbroker, financial institution, financial participant, or securities clearing agency, in connection with a securities contract, as defined in section 741(7), commodity contract, as defined in section 761(4), or forward contract, that is made before the commencement of the case, except under section 548(a)(1)(A) of this title.

(f) Notwithstanding sections 544, 545, 547, 548(a)(1)(B), and 548(b) of this title, the trustee may not avoid a transfer made by or to (or for the benefit of) a repo participant or financial participant, in connection with a repurchase agreement and that is made before the commencement of the case, except under section 548(a)(1)(A) of this title.

(g) Notwithstanding sections 544, 545, 547, 548(a)(1)(B) and 548(b) of this title, the trustee may not avoid a transfer, made by or to (or for the benefit of) a swap participant or financial participant, under or in connection with any swap agreement and that is made before the commencement of the case, except under section 548(a)(1)(A) of this title.

(h) Notwithstanding the rights and powers of a trustee under sections 544(a), 545, 547, 549, and 553, if the court determines on a motion by the trustee made not later than 120 days after the date of the order for relief in a case under chapter 11 of this title and after notice and a hearing, that a return is in the best interests of the estate, the debtor, with the consent of a creditor and subject to the prior rights of holders of security interests in such goods or the proceeds of such goods, may return goods shipped to the debtor by the creditor before the commencement of the case, and the creditor may offset the purchase price of such goods against any claim of the creditor against the debtor that arose before the commencement of the case.

(i)

(1) Notwithstanding paragraphs (2) and (3) of section 545, the trustee may not avoid a warehouseman's lien for storage, transportation, or other costs incidental to the storage and handling of goods.

(2) The prohibition under paragraph (1) shall be applied in a manner consistent with any State statute applicable to such lien that is similar to section 7–209 of the Uniform Commercial Code, as in effect on the date of enactment of the Bankruptcy Abuse Prevention and Consumer Protection Act of 2005, or any successor to such section 7–209.

(j) Notwithstanding sections 544, 545, 547, 548(a)(1)(B), and 548(b) the trustee may not avoid a transfer made by or to (or for the benefit of) a master netting agreement participant under or in connection with any master netting agreement or any individual contract covered thereby that is made before the commencement of the case, except under section 548(a)(1)(A) and except to the extent that the trustee could otherwise avoid such a transfer made under an individual contract covered by such master netting agreement.

§547. Preferences

(a) In this section—

(1) "inventory" means personal property leased or furnished, held for sale or lease, or to be furnished under a contract for service, raw materials, work in process, or materials used or consumed in a business, including farm products such as crops or livestock, held for sale or lease;

(2) "new value" means money or money's worth in goods, services, or new credit, or release by a transferee of property previously transferred to such transferee in a transaction that is neither void nor voidable by the debtor or the trustee under any applicable law, including proceeds of such property, but does not include an obligation substituted for an existing obligation;

(3) "receivable" means right to payment, whether or not such right has been earned by performance; and

(4) a debt for a tax is incurred on the day when such tax is last payable without penalty, including any extension.

(b) Except as provided in subsections (c) and (i) of this section, the trustee may avoid any transfer of an interest of the debtor in property—

(1) to or for the benefit of a creditor;

(2) for or on account of an antecedent debt owed by the debtor before such transfer was made;

(3) made while the debtor was insolvent;

(4) made—

    (A) on or within 90 days before the date of the filing of the petition; or

    (B) between ninety days and one year before the date of the filing of the petition, if such creditor at the time of such transfer was an insider; and

(5) that enables such creditor to receive more than such creditor would receive if—

    (A) the case were a case under chapter 7 of this title;

    (B) the transfer had not been made; and

    (C) such creditor received payment of such debt to the extent provided by the provisions of this title.

(c) The trustee may not avoid under this section a transfer—

(1) to the extent that such transfer was—

    (A) intended by the debtor and the creditor to or for whose benefit such transfer was made to be a contemporaneous exchange for new value given to the debtor; and

    (B) in fact a substantially contemporaneous exchange;

(2) to the extent that such transfer was in payment of a debt incurred by the debtor in the ordinary course of business or financial affairs of the debtor and the transferee, and such transfer was—

    (A) made in the ordinary course of business or financial affairs of the debtor and the transferee; or

    (B) made according to ordinary business terms;

(3) that creates a security interest in property acquired by the debtor—

    (A) to the extent such security interest secures new value that was—

        (i) given at or after the signing of a security agreement that contains a description of such property as collateral;

        (ii) given by or on behalf of the secured party under such agreement;

        (iii) given to enable the debtor to acquire such property; and

        (iv) in fact used by the debtor to acquire such property; and

    (B) that is perfected on or before 30 days after the debtor receives possession of such property;

(4) to or for the benefit of a creditor, to the extent that, after such transfer, such creditor gave new value to or for the benefit of the debtor—

    (A) not secured by an otherwise unavoidable security interest; and

    (B) on account of which new value the debtor did not make an otherwise unavoidable transfer to or for the benefit of such creditor;

(5) that creates a perfected security interest in inventory or a receivable or the proceeds of either, except to the extent that the aggregate of all such transfers to the transferee caused a reduction, as of the date of the filing of the petition and to the prejudice of other creditors holding unsecured claims, of any amount by which the debt secured by such security interest exceeded the value of all security interests for such debt on the later of—

(A)

(i) with respect to a transfer to which subsection (b)(4)(A) of this section applies, 90 days before the date of the filing of the petition; or

(ii) with respect to a transfer to which subsection (b)(4)(B) of this section applies, one year before the date of the filing of the petition; or

(B) the date on which new value was first given under the security agreement creating such security interest;

(6) that is the fixing of a statutory lien that is not avoidable under section 545 of this title;

(7) to the extent such transfer was a bona fide payment of a debt for a domestic support obligation;

(8) if, in a case filed by an individual debtor whose debts are primarily consumer debts, the aggregate value of all property that constitutes or is affected by such transfer is less than $600; or

(9) if, in a case filed by a debtor whose debts are not primarily consumer debts, the aggregate value of all property that constitutes or is affected by such transfer is less than $6,425.

(d) The trustee may avoid a transfer of an interest in property of the debtor transferred to or for the benefit of a surety to secure reimbursement of such a surety that furnished a bond or other obligation to dissolve a judicial lien that would have been avoidable by the trustee under subsection (b) of this section. The liability of such surety under such bond or obligation shall be discharged to the extent of the value of such property recovered by the trustee or the amount paid to the trustee.

(e)

(1) For the purposes of this section—

(A) a transfer of real property other than fixtures, but including the interest of a seller or purchaser under a contract for the sale of real property, is perfected when a bona fide purchaser of such property from the debtor against whom applicable law permits such transfer to be perfected cannot acquire an interest that is superior to the interest of the transferee; and

(B) a transfer of a fixture or property other than real property is perfected when a creditor on a simple contract cannot acquire a judicial lien that is superior to the interest of the transferee.

(2) For the purposes of this section, except as provided in paragraph (3) of this subsection, a transfer is made—

(A) at the time such transfer takes effect between the transferor and the transferee, if such transfer is perfected at, or within 30 days after, such time, except as provided in subsection (c)(3)(B);

(B) at the time such transfer is perfected, if such transfer is perfected after such 30 days; or

(C) immediately before the date of the filing of the petition, if such transfer is not perfected at the later of—

(i) the commencement of the case; or

(ii) 30 days after such transfer takes effect between the transferor and the transferee.

(3) For the purposes of this section, a transfer is not made until the debtor has acquired rights in the property transferred.

(f) For the purposes of this section, the debtor is presumed to have been insolvent on and during the 90 days immediately preceding the date of the filing of the petition.

(g) For the purposes of this section, the trustee has the burden of proving the avoidability of a transfer under subsection (b) of this section, and the creditor or party in interest against whom recovery or avoidance is sought has the burden of proving the nonavoidability of a transfer under subsection (c) of this section.

(h) The trustee may not avoid a transfer if such transfer was made as a part of an alternative repayment schedule between the debtor and any creditor of the debtor created by an approved nonprofit budget and credit counseling agency.

(i) If the trustee avoids under subsection (b) a transfer made between 90 days and 1 year before the date of the filing of the petition, by the debtor to an entity that is not an insider for the benefit of a creditor that is an insider, such transfer shall be considered to be avoided under this section only with respect to the creditor that is an insider.

§548. Fraudulent transfers and obligations

(a)

(1) The trustee may avoid any transfer (including any transfer to or for the benefit of an insider under an employment contract) of an interest of the debtor in property, or any obligation (including any obligation to or for the benefit of an insider under an employment contract) incurred by the debtor, that was made or incurred on or within 2 years before the date of the filing of the petition, if the debtor voluntarily or involuntarily—

(A) made such transfer or incurred such obligation with actual intent to hinder, delay, or defraud any entity to which the debtor was or became, on or after the date that such transfer was made or such obligation was incurred, indebted; or

(B)

(i) received less than a reasonably equivalent value in exchange for such transfer or obligation; and

(ii)

(I) was insolvent on the date that such transfer was made or such obligation was incurred, or became insolvent as a result of such transfer or obligation;

(II) was engaged in business or a transaction, or was about to engage in business or a transaction, for which any property remaining with the debtor was an unreasonably small capital;

(III) intended to incur, or believed that the debtor would incur, debts that would be beyond the debtor's ability to pay as such debts matured; or

(IV) made such transfer to or for the benefit of an insider, or incurred such obligation to or for the benefit of an insider, under an employment contract and not in the ordinary course of business.

(2) A transfer of a charitable contribution to a qualified religious or charitable entity or organization shall not be considered to be a transfer covered under paragraph (1)(B) in any case in which—

(A) the amount of that contribution does not exceed 15 percent of the gross annual income of the debtor for the year in which the transfer of the contribution is made; or

(B) the contribution made by a debtor exceeded the percentage amount of gross annual income specified in subparagraph (A), if the transfer was consistent with the practices of the debtor in making charitable contributions.

(b) The trustee of a partnership debtor may avoid any transfer of an interest of the debtor in property, or any obligation incurred by the debtor, that was made or incurred on or within 2 years before the date of the filing of the petition, to a general partner in the debtor, if the debtor was insolvent on the date such transfer was made or such obligation was incurred, or became insolvent as a result of such transfer or obligation.

(c) Except to the extent that a transfer or obligation voidable under this section is voidable under section 544, 545, or 547 of this title, a transferee or obligee of such a transfer or obligation that takes for value and in good faith has a lien on or may retain any interest transferred or may enforce any obligation incurred, as the case may be, to the extent that such transferee or obligee gave value to the debtor in exchange for such transfer or obligation.

(d)

(1) For the purposes of this section, a transfer is made when such transfer is so perfected that a bona fide purchaser from the debtor against whom applicable law permits such transfer to be perfected cannot acquire an interest in the property transferred that is superior to the interest in such property of the transferee, but if such transfer is not so perfected before the commencement of the case, such transfer is made immediately before the date of the filing of the petition.

(2) In this section—

(A) "value" means property, or satisfaction or securing of a present or antecedent debt of the debtor, but does not include an unperformed promise to furnish support to the debtor or to a relative of the debtor;

(B) a commodity broker, forward contract merchant, stockbroker, financial institution, financial participant, or securities clearing agency that receives a margin payment, as defined in section 101, 741, or 761 of this title, or settlement payment, as defined in section 101 or 741 of this title, takes for value to the extent of such payment;

(C) a repo participant or financial participant that receives a margin payment, as defined in section 741 or 761 of this title, or settlement payment, as defined in section 741 of this title, in connection with a repurchase agreement, takes for value to the extent of such payment;

(D) a swap participant or financial participant that receives a transfer in connection with a swap agreement takes for value to the extent of such transfer; and

(E) a master netting agreement participant that receives a transfer in connection with a master netting agreement or any individual contract covered thereby takes for value to the extent of such transfer, except that, with respect to a transfer under any individual contract covered thereby, to the extent that such master netting agreement participant otherwise did not take (or is otherwise not deemed to have taken) such transfer for value.

(3) In this section, the term "charitable contribution" means a charitable contribution, as that term is defined in section 170(c) of the Internal Revenue Code of 1986, if that contribution—

    (A) is made by a natural person; and

    (B) consists of—

        (i) a financial instrument (as that term is defined in section 731(c)(2)(C) of the Internal Revenue Code of 1986); or

        (ii) cash.

(4) In this section, the term "qualified religious or charitable entity or organization" means—

    (A) an entity described in section 170(c)(1) of the Internal Revenue Code of 1986; or

    (B) an entity or organization described in section 170(c)(2) of the Internal Revenue Code of 1986.

(e)

(1) In addition to any transfer that the trustee may otherwise avoid, the trustee may avoid any transfer of an interest of the debtor in property that was made on or within 10 years before the date of the filing of the petition, if—

    (A) such transfer was made to a self-settled trust or similar device;

    (B) such transfer was by the debtor;

    (C) the debtor is a beneficiary of such trust or similar device; and

    (D) the debtor made such transfer with actual intent to hinder, delay, or defraud any entity to which the debtor was or became, on or after the date that such transfer was made, indebted.

(2) For the purposes of this subsection, a transfer includes a transfer made in anticipation of any money judgment, settlement, civil penalty, equitable order, or criminal fine incurred by, or which the debtor believed would be incurred by—

    (A) any violation of the securities laws (as defined in section 3(a)(47) of the Securities Exchange Act of 1934 (15 U.S.C. 78c(a)(47))), any State securities laws, or any regulation or order issued under Federal securities laws or State securities laws; or

    (B) fraud, deceit, or manipulation in a fiduciary capacity or in connection with the purchase or sale of any security registered under section 12 or 15(d) of the Securities Exchange Act of 1934 (15 U.S.C. 78l and 78o(d)) or under section 6 of the Securities Act of 1933 (15 U.S.C. 77f).

§549. Postpetition transactions

(a) Except as provided in subsection (b) or (c) of this section, the trustee may avoid a transfer of property of the estate—

    (1) that occurs after the commencement of the case; and

    (2)

        (A) that is authorized only under section 303(f) or 542(c) of this title; or

        (B) that is not authorized under this title or by the court.

(b) In an involuntary case, the trustee may not avoid under subsection (a) of this section a transfer made after the commencement of such case but before the order for relief to the extent any value, including services, but not including satisfaction or securing of a debt that arose before the commencement of the case, is given after the commencement of the case in exchange for such transfer, notwithstanding any notice or knowledge of the case that the transferee has.

(c) The trustee may not avoid under subsection (a) of this section a transfer of an interest in real property to a good faith purchaser without knowledge of the commencement of the case and for present fair equivalent value unless a copy or notice of the petition was filed, where a transfer of an interest in such real property may be recorded to perfect such transfer, before such transfer is so perfected that a bona fide purchaser of such real property, against whom applicable law permits such transfer to be perfected, could not acquire an interest that is superior to such interest of such good faith purchaser. A good faith purchaser without knowledge of the commencement of the case and for less than present fair equivalent value has a lien on the property transferred to the extent of any present value given, unless a copy or notice of the petition was so filed before such transfer was so perfected.

(d) An action or proceeding under this section may not be commenced after the earlier of—

    (1) two years after the date of the transfer sought to be avoided; or

    (2) the time the case is closed or dismissed.

§550. Liability of transferee of avoided transfer

(a) Except as otherwise provided in this section, to the extent that a transfer is avoided under section 544, 545, 547, 548, 549, 553(b), or 724(a) of this title, the trustee may recover, for the benefit of the estate, the property transferred, or, if the court so orders, the value of such property, from—

(1) the initial transferee of such transfer or the entity for whose benefit such transfer was made; or

(2) any immediate or mediate transferee of such initial transferee.

(b) The trustee may not recover under section [1] (a)(2) of this section from—

(1) a transferee that takes for value, including satisfaction or securing of a present or antecedent debt, in good faith, and without knowledge of the voidability of the transfer avoided; or

(2) any immediate or mediate good faith transferee of such transferee.

(c) If a transfer made between 90 days and one year before the filing of the petition—

(1) is avoided under section 547(b) of this title; and

(2) was made for the benefit of a creditor that at the time of such transfer was an insider;

the trustee may not recover under subsection (a) from a transferee that is not an insider.

(d) The trustee is entitled to only a single satisfaction under subsection (a) of this section.

(e)

(1) A good faith transferee from whom the trustee may recover under subsection (a) of this section has a lien on the property recovered to secure the lesser of—

(A) the cost, to such transferee, of any improvement made after the transfer, less the amount of any profit realized by or accruing to such transferee from such property; and

(B) any increase in the value of such property as a result of such improvement, of the property transferred.

(2) In this subsection, "improvement" includes—

(A) physical additions or changes to the property transferred;

(B) repairs to such property;

(C) payment of any tax on such property;

(D) payment of any debt secured by a lien on such property that is superior or equal to the rights of the trustee; and

(E) preservation of such property.

(f) An action or proceeding under this section may not be commenced after the earlier of—

(1) one year after the avoidance of the transfer on account of which recovery under this section is sought; or

(2) the time the case is closed or dismissed.

---

[1] So in original. Probably should be "subsection".

§551. Automatic preservation of avoided transfer

Any transfer avoided under section 522, 544, 545, 547, 548, 549, or 724(a) of this title, or any lien void under section 506(d) of this title, is preserved for the benefit of the estate but only with respect to property of the estate.

§552. Postpetition effect of security interest

(a) Except as provided in subsection (b) of this section, property acquired by the estate or by the debtor after the commencement of the case is not subject to any lien resulting from any security agreement entered into by the debtor before the commencement of the case.

(b)

(1) Except as provided in sections 363, 506(c), 522, 544, 545, 547, and 548 of this title, if the debtor and an entity entered into a security agreement before the commencement of the case and if the security interest created by such security agreement extends to property of the debtor acquired before the commencement of the case and to proceeds, products, offspring, or profits of such property, then such security interest extends to such proceeds, products, offspring, or profits acquired by the estate after the commencement of the case to the extent provided by such security agreement and by applicable nonbankruptcy law, except to any extent that the court, after notice and a hearing and based on the equities of the case, orders otherwise.

(2) Except as provided in sections 363, 506(c), 522, 544, 545, 547, and 548 of this title, and notwithstanding section 546(b) of this title, if the debtor and an entity entered into a security agreement before the commencement of the case and if the security interest created by such security agreement extends to property of the debtor acquired before the commencement of the case and to amounts paid as rents of such property or the fees, charges, accounts, or other payments for the use or occupancy of rooms and other public facilities in hotels, motels, or other lodging properties, then such security interest extends to such rents and such fees, charges, accounts, or other payments acquired by the estate after the commencement of the case to the extent provided in such security agreement, except to any extent that the court, after notice and a hearing and based on the equities of the case, orders otherwise.

§553. Setoff

(a) Except as otherwise provided in this section and in sections 362 and 363 of this title, this title does not affect any right of a creditor to offset a mutual debt owing by such creditor to the debtor that arose before the commencement of the case under this title against a claim of such creditor against the debtor that arose before the commencement of the case, except to the extent that—

    (1) the claim of such creditor against the debtor is disallowed;

    (2) such claim was transferred, by an entity other than the debtor, to such creditor—

        (A) after the commencement of the case; or

        (B)

            (i) after 90 days before the date of the filing of the petition; and

            (ii) while the debtor was insolvent (except for a setoff of a kind described in section 362(b)(6), 362(b)(7), 362(b)(17), 362(b)(27), 555, 556, 559, 560, or 561); or

    (3) the debt owed to the debtor by such creditor was incurred by such creditor—

        (A) after 90 days before the date of the filing of the petition;

        (B) while the debtor was insolvent; and

        (C) for the purpose of obtaining a right of setoff against the debtor (except for a setoff of a kind described in section 362(b)(6), 362(b)(7), 362(b)(17), 362(b)(27), 555, 556, 559, 560, or 561).

(b)

    (1) Except with respect to a setoff of a kind described in section 362(b)(6), 362(b)(7), 362(b)(17), 362(b)(27), 555, 556, 559, 560, 561, 365(h), 546(h), or 365(i)(2) of this title, if a creditor offsets a mutual debt owing to the debtor against a claim against the debtor on or within 90 days before the date of the filing of the petition, then the trustee may recover from such creditor the amount so offset to the extent that any insufficiency on the date of such setoff is less than the insufficiency on the later of—

        (A) 90 days before the date of the filing of the petition; and

        (B) the first date during the 90 days immediately preceding the date of the filing of the petition on which there is an insufficiency.

    (2) In this subsection, "insufficiency" means amount, if any, by which a claim against the debtor exceeds a mutual debt owing to the debtor by the holder of such claim.

(c) For the purposes of this section, the debtor is presumed to have been insolvent on and during the 90 days immediately preceding the date of the filing of the petition.

§554. Abandonment of property of the estate

(a) After notice and a hearing, the trustee may abandon any property of the estate that is burdensome to the estate or that is of inconsequential value and benefit to the estate.

(b) On request of a party in interest and after notice and a hearing, the court may order the trustee to abandon any property of the estate that is burdensome to the estate or that is of inconsequential value and benefit to the estate.

(c) Unless the court orders otherwise, any property scheduled under section 521(a)(1) of this title not otherwise administered at the time of the closing of a case is abandoned to the debtor and administered for purposes of section 350 of this title.

(d) Unless the court orders otherwise, property of the estate that is not abandoned under this section and that is not administered in the case remains property of the estate.

§555. Contractual right to liquidate, terminate, or accelerate a securities contract

The exercise of a contractual right of a stockbroker, financial institution, financial participant, or securities clearing agency to cause the liquidation, termination, or acceleration of a securities contract, as defined in section 741 of this title, because of a condition of the kind specified in section 365(e)(1) of this title shall not be stayed, avoided, or otherwise limited by operation of any provision of this title or by order of a court or administrative agency in any proceeding under this title unless such order is authorized under the provisions of the Securities Investor Protection Act of 1970 or any statute administered by the Securities and Exchange Commission. As used in this section, the term "contractual right" includes a right set forth in a rule or bylaw of a derivatives clearing organization (as defined in the Commodity Exchange Act), a multilateral clearing organization (as defined in the Federal Deposit Insurance Corporation Improvement Act of 1991), a national securities exchange, a national securities association, a securities clearing agency, a contract market designated under the Commodity Exchange Act, a derivatives transaction execution facility registered under the Commodity Exchange Act, or a board of trade (as defined in the Commodity Exchange Act), or in a resolution of the governing board thereof, and a right, whether or not in writing, arising under common law, under law merchant, or by reason of normal business practice.

§556. Contractual right to liquidate, terminate, or accelerate a commodities contract or forward contract

The contractual right of a commodity broker, financial participant, or forward contract merchant to cause the liquidation, termination, or acceleration of a commodity contract, as defined in section 761 of this title, or forward contract because of a condition of the kind specified in section 365(e)(1) of this title, and the right to a variation or maintenance margin payment received from a trustee with respect to open commodity contracts or forward contracts, shall not be stayed, avoided, or otherwise limited by operation of any provision of this title or by the order of a court in any proceeding under this title. As used in this section, the term "contractual right" includes a right set forth in a rule or bylaw of a derivatives clearing organization (as defined in the Commodity Exchange Act), a multilateral clearing organization (as defined in the Federal Deposit Insurance Corporation Improvement Act of 1991), a national securities exchange, a national securities association, a securities clearing agency, a contract market designated under the Commodity Exchange Act, a derivatives transaction execution facility registered under the Commodity Exchange Act, or a board of trade (as defined in the Commodity Exchange Act) or in a resolution of the governing board thereof and a right, whether or not evidenced in writing, arising under common law, under law merchant or by reason of normal business practice.

§557. Expedited determination of interests in, and abandonment or other disposition of grain assets

(a) This section applies only in a case concerning a debtor that owns or operates a grain storage facility and only with respect to grain and the proceeds of grain. This section does not affect the application of any other section of this title to property other than grain and proceeds of grain.
(b) In this section—

(1) "grain" means wheat, corn, flaxseed, grain sorghum, barley, oats, rye, soybeans, other dry edible beans, or rice;
(2) "grain storage facility" means a site or physical structure regularly used to store grain for producers, or to store grain acquired from producers for resale; and
(3) "producer" means an entity which engages in the growing of grain.

(c)

(1) Notwithstanding sections 362, 363, 365, and 554 of this title, on the court's own motion the court may, and on the request of the trustee or an entity that claims an interest in grain or the proceeds of grain the court shall, expedite the procedures for the determination of interests in and the disposition of grain and the proceeds of grain, by shortening to the greatest extent feasible such time periods as are otherwise applicable for such procedures and by establishing, by order, a timetable having a duration of not to exceed 120 days for the completion of the applicable procedure specified in subsection (d) of this section. Such time periods and such timetable may be modified by the court, for cause, in accordance with subsection (f) of this section.
(2) The court shall determine the extent to which such time periods shall be shortened, based upon—

   (A) any need of an entity claiming an interest in such grain or the proceeds of grain for a prompt determination of such interest;
   (B) any need of such entity for a prompt disposition of such grain;
   (C) the market for such grain;
   (D) the conditions under which such grain is stored;
   (E) the costs of continued storage or disposition of such grain;
   (F) the orderly administration of the estate;
   (G) the appropriate opportunity for an entity to assert an interest in such grain; and
   (H) such other considerations as are relevant to the need to expedite such procedures in the case.
(d) The procedures that may be expedited under subsection (c) of this section include—

   (1) the filing of and response to—

      (A) a claim of ownership;
      (B) a proof of claim;
      (C) a request for abandonment;
      (D) a request for relief from the stay of action against property under section 362(a) of this title;

(E) a request for determination of secured status;

(F) a request for determination of whether such grain or the proceeds of grain—

    (i) is property of the estate;

    (ii) must be turned over to the estate; or

    (iii) may be used, sold, or leased; and

(G) any other request for determination of an interest in such grain or the proceeds of grain;

(2) the disposition of such grain or the proceeds of grain, before or after determination of interests in such grain or the proceeds of grain, by way of—

    (A) sale of such grain;

    (B) abandonment;

    (C) distribution; or

    (D) such other method as is equitable in the case;

(3) subject to sections 701, 702, 703, 1104, 1202, and 1302 of this title, the appointment of a trustee or examiner and the retention and compensation of any professional person required to assist with respect to matters relevant to the determination of interests in or disposition of such grain or the proceeds of grain; and

(4) the determination of any dispute concerning a matter specified in paragraph (1), (2), or (3) of this subsection.

(e)

(1) Any governmental unit that has regulatory jurisdiction over the operation or liquidation of the debtor or the debtor's business shall be given notice of any request made or order entered under subsection (c) of this section.

(2) Any such governmental unit may raise, and may appear and be heard on, any issue relating to grain or the proceeds of grain in a case in which a request is made, or an order is entered, under subsection (c) of this section.

(3) The trustee shall consult with such governmental unit before taking any action relating to the disposition of grain in the possession, custody, or control of the debtor or the estate.

(f) The court may extend the period for final disposition of grain or the proceeds of grain under this section beyond 120 days if the court finds that—

(1) the interests of justice so require in light of the complexity of the case; and

(2) the interests of those claimants entitled to distribution of grain or the proceeds of grain will not be materially injured by such additional delay.

(g) Unless an order establishing an expedited procedure under subsection (c) of this section, or determining any interest in or approving any disposition of grain or the proceeds of grain, is stayed pending appeal—

(1) the reversal or modification of such order on appeal does not affect the validity of any procedure, determination, or disposition that occurs before such reversal or modification, whether or not any entity knew of the pendency of the appeal; and

(2) neither the court nor the trustee may delay, due to the appeal of such order, any proceeding in the case in which such order is issued.

(h)

(1) The trustee may recover from grain and the proceeds of grain the reasonable and necessary costs and expenses allowable under section 503(b) of this title attributable to preserving or disposing of grain or the proceeds of grain, but may not recover from such grain or the proceeds of grain any other costs or expenses.

(2) Notwithstanding section 326(a) of this title, the dollar amounts of money specified in such section include the value, as of the date of disposition, of any grain that the trustee distributes in kind.

(i) In all cases where the quantity of a specific type of grain held by a debtor operating a grain storage facility exceeds ten thousand bushels, such grain shall be sold by the trustee and the assets thereof distributed in accordance with the provisions of this section.

§558. Defenses of the estate

The estate shall have the benefit of any defense available to the debtor as against any entity other than the estate, including statutes of limitation, statutes of frauds, usury, and other personal defenses. A waiver of any such defense by the debtor after the commencement of the case does not bind the estate.

§559. Contractual right to liquidate, terminate, or accelerate a repurchase agreement

The exercise of a contractual right of a repo participant or financial participant to cause the liquidation, termination, or acceleration of a repurchase agreement because of a condition of the kind specified in section 365(e)(1) of this title shall not be stayed, avoided, or otherwise limited by operation of any provision of this title or by order of a court or administrative agency in any proceeding under this title, unless, where the debtor is a stockbroker or securities clearing agency, such order is authorized under the provisions of the Securities Investor Protection Act of 1970 or any statute administered by the Securities and Exchange Commission. In the event that a repo participant or financial participant liquidates one or more repurchase agreements with a debtor and under the terms of one or more such agreements has agreed to deliver assets subject to repurchase agreements to the debtor, any excess of the market prices received on liquidation of such assets (or if any such assets are not disposed of on the date of liquidation of such repurchase agreements, at the prices available at the time of liquidation of such repurchase agreements from a generally recognized source or the most recent closing bid quotation from such a source) over the sum of the stated repurchase prices and all expenses in connection with the liquidation of such repurchase agreements shall be deemed property of the estate, subject to the available rights of setoff. As used in this section, the term "contractual right" includes a right set forth in a rule or bylaw of a derivatives clearing organization (as defined in the Commodity Exchange Act), a multilateral clearing organization (as defined in the Federal Deposit Insurance Corporation Improvement Act of 1991), a national securities exchange, a national securities association, a securities clearing agency, a contract market designated under the Commodity Exchange Act, a derivatives transaction execution facility registered under the Commodity Exchange Act, or a board of trade (as defined in the Commodity Exchange Act) or in a resolution of the governing board thereof and a right, whether or not evidenced in writing, arising under common law, under law merchant or by reason of normal business practice.

§560. Contractual right to liquidate, terminate, or accelerate a swap agreement

The exercise of any contractual right of any swap participant or financial participant to cause the liquidation, termination, or acceleration of one or more swap agreements because of a condition of the kind specified in section 365(e)(1) of this title or to offset or net out any termination values or payment amounts arising under or in connection with the termination, liquidation, or acceleration of one or more swap agreements shall not be stayed, avoided, or otherwise limited by operation of any provision of this title or by order of a court or administrative agency in any proceeding under this title. As used in this section, the term "contractual

right" includes a right set forth in a rule or bylaw of a derivatives clearing organization (as defined in the Commodity Exchange Act), a multilateral clearing organization (as defined in the Federal Deposit Insurance Corporation Improvement Act of 1991), a national securities exchange, a national securities association, a securities clearing agency, a contract market designated under the Commodity Exchange Act, a derivatives transaction execution facility registered under the Commodity Exchange Act, or a board of trade (as defined in the Commodity Exchange Act) or in a resolution of the governing board thereof and a right, whether or not evidenced in writing, arising under common law, under law merchant, or by reason of normal business practice.

§561. Contractual right to terminate, liquidate, accelerate, or offset under a master netting agreement and across contracts; proceedings under chapter 15

(a) Subject to subsection (b), the exercise of any contractual right, because of a condition of the kind specified in section 365(e)(1), to cause the termination, liquidation, or acceleration of or to offset or net termination values, payment amounts, or other transfer obligations arising under or in connection with one or more (or the termination, liquidation, or acceleration of one or more)—

(1) securities contracts, as defined in section 741(7);

(2) commodity contracts, as defined in section 761(4);

(3) forward contracts;

(4) repurchase agreements;

(5) swap agreements; or

(6) master netting agreements,

shall not be stayed, avoided, or otherwise limited by operation of any provision of this title or by any order of a court or administrative agency in any proceeding under this title.

(b)

(1) A party may exercise a contractual right described in subsection (a) to terminate, liquidate, or accelerate only to the extent that such party could exercise such a right under section 555, 556, 559, or 560 for each individual contract covered by the master netting agreement in issue.

(2) If a debtor is a commodity broker subject to subchapter IV of chapter 7—

(A) a party may not net or offset an obligation to the debtor arising under, or in connection with, a commodity contract traded on or subject to the rules of a contract market designated under the Commodity Exchange Act or a derivatives transaction execution facility registered under the Commodity Exchange Act against any claim arising under, or in connection with, other instruments, contracts, or agreements listed in subsection (a) except to the extent that the party has positive net equity in the commodity accounts at the debtor, as calculated under such subchapter; and

(B) another commodity broker may not net or offset an obligation to the debtor arising under, or in connection with, a commodity contract entered into or held on behalf of a customer of the debtor and traded on or subject to the rules of a contract market designated under the Commodity Exchange Act or a derivatives transaction execution facility registered under the Commodity Exchange Act against any claim arising under, or in connection with, other instruments, contracts, or agreements listed in subsection (a).

(3) No provision of subparagraph (A) or (B) of paragraph (2) shall prohibit the offset of claims and obligations that arise under—

(A) a cross-margining agreement or similar arrangement that has been approved by the Commodity Futures Trading Commission or submitted to the Commodity Futures Trading Commission under paragraph (1) or (2) of section 5c(c) of the Commodity Exchange Act and has not been abrogated or rendered ineffective by the Commodity Futures Trading Commission; or

(B) any other netting agreement between a clearing organization (as defined in section 761) and another entity that has been approved by the Commodity Futures Trading Commission.

(c) As used in this section, the term "contractual right" includes a right set forth in a rule or bylaw of a derivatives clearing organization (as defined in the Commodity Exchange Act), a multilateral clearing organization (as defined in the Federal Deposit Insurance Corporation Improvement Act of 1991), a national securities exchange, a national securities association, a securities clearing agency, a contract market designated under the Commodity Exchange Act, a derivatives transaction execution facility registered under the Commodity Exchange Act, or a board of trade (as defined in the Commodity Exchange Act) or in a resolution of the governing board thereof, and a right, whether

or not evidenced in writing, arising under common law, under law merchant, or by reason of normal business practice.

(d) Any provisions of this title relating to securities contracts, commodity contracts, forward contracts, repurchase agreements, swap agreements, or master netting agreements shall apply in a case under chapter 15, so that enforcement of contractual provisions of such contracts and agreements in accordance with their terms will not be stayed or otherwise limited by operation of any provision of this title or by order of a court in any case under this title, and to limit avoidance powers to the same extent as in a proceeding under chapter 7 or 11 of this title (such enforcement not to be limited based on the presence or absence of assets of the debtor in the United States).

§562. Timing of damage measurement in connection with swap agreements, securities contracts, forward contracts, commodity contracts, repurchase agreements, and master netting agreements

(a) If the trustee rejects a swap agreement, securities contract (as defined in section 741), forward contract, commodity contract (as defined in section 761), repurchase agreement, or master netting agreement pursuant to section 365(a), or if a forward contract merchant, stockbroker, financial institution, securities clearing agency, repo participant, financial participant, master netting agreement participant, or swap participant liquidates, terminates, or accelerates such contract or agreement, damages shall be measured as of the earlier of—

(1) the date of such rejection; or

(2) the date or dates of such liquidation, termination, or acceleration.

(b) If there are not any commercially reasonable determinants of value as of any date referred to in paragraph (1) or (2) of subsection (a), damages shall be measured as of the earliest subsequent date or dates on which there are commercially reasonable determinants of value.

(c) For the purposes of subsection (b), if damages are not measured as of the date or dates of rejection, liquidation, termination, or acceleration, and the forward contract merchant, stockbroker, financial institution, securities clearing agency, repo participant, financial participant, master netting agreement participant, or swap participant or the trustee objects to the timing of the measurement of damages—

(1) the trustee, in the case of an objection by a forward contract merchant, stockbroker, financial institution, securities clearing agency, repo participant, financial participant, master netting agreement participant, or swap participant; or

(2) the forward contract merchant, stockbroker, financial institution, securities clearing agency, repo participant, financial participant, master netting agreement participant, or swap participant, in the case of an objection by the trustee,

has the burden of proving that there were no commercially reasonable determinants of value as of such date or dates.

CHAPTER 7—LIQUIDATION

SUBCHAPTER I—OFFICERS AND ADMINISTRATION

§701. Interim trustee

(a)

(1) Promptly after the order for relief under this chapter, the United States trustee shall appoint one disinterested person that is a member of the panel of private trustees established under section 586(a)(1) of title 28 or that is serving as trustee in the case immediately before the order for relief under this chapter to serve as interim trustee in the case.

(2) If none of the members of such panel is willing to serve as interim trustee in the case, then the United States trustee may serve as interim trustee in the case.

(b) The service of an interim trustee under this section terminates when a trustee elected or designated under section 702 of this title to serve as trustee in the case qualifies under section 322 of this title.

(c) An interim trustee serving under this section is a trustee in a case under this title.

§702. Election of trustee

(a) A creditor may vote for a candidate for trustee only if such creditor—

(1) holds an allowable, undisputed, fixed, liquidated, unsecured claim of a kind entitled to distribution under section 726(a)(2), 726(a)(3), 726(a)(4), 752(a), 766(h), or 766(i) of this title;

(2) does not have an interest materially adverse, other than an equity interest that is not substantial in relation to such creditor's interest as a creditor, to the interest of creditors entitled to such distribution; and

(3) is not an insider.

(b) At the meeting of creditors held under section 341 of this title, creditors may elect one person to serve as trustee in the case if election of a trustee is requested by creditors that may vote under subsection (a) of this section, and that hold at least 20 percent in amount of the claims specified in subsection (a)(1) of this section that are held by creditors that may vote under subsection (a) of this section.

(c) A candidate for trustee is elected trustee if—

(1) creditors holding at least 20 percent in amount of the claims of a kind specified in subsection (a)(1) of this section that are held by creditors that may vote under subsection (a) of this section vote; and

(2) such candidate receives the votes of creditors holding a majority in amount of claims specified in subsection (a)(1) of this section that are held by creditors that vote for a trustee.

(d) If a trustee is not elected under this section, then the interim trustee shall serve as trustee in the case.

§703. Successor trustee

(a) If a trustee dies or resigns during a case, fails to qualify under section 322 of this title, or is removed under section 324 of this title, creditors may elect, in the manner specified in section 702 of this title, a person to fill the vacancy in the office of trustee.

(b) Pending election of a trustee under subsection (a) of this section, if necessary to preserve or prevent loss to the estate, the United States trustee may appoint an interim trustee in the manner specified in section 701(a).

(c) If creditors do not elect a successor trustee under subsection (a) of this section or if a trustee is needed in a case reopened under section 350 of this title, then the United States trustee—

(1) shall appoint one disinterested person that is a member of the panel of private trustees established under section 586(a)(1) of title 28 to serve as trustee in the case; or

(2) may, if none of the disinterested members of such panel is willing to serve as trustee, serve as trustee in the case.

§704. Duties of trustee

(a) The trustee shall—

(1) collect and reduce to money the property of the estate for which such trustee serves, and close such estate as expeditiously as is compatible with the best interests of parties in interest;

(2) be accountable for all property received;

(3) ensure that the debtor shall perform his intention as specified in section 521(a)(2)(B) of this title;

(4) investigate the financial affairs of the debtor;

(5) if a purpose would be served, examine proofs of claims and object to the allowance of any claim that is improper;

(6) if advisable, oppose the discharge of the debtor;

(7) unless the court orders otherwise, furnish such information concerning the estate and the estate's administration as is requested by a party in interest;

(8) if the business of the debtor is authorized to be operated, file with the court, with the United States trustee, and with any governmental unit charged with responsibility for collection or determination of any tax arising out of such operation, periodic reports and summaries of the operation of such business, including a statement of receipts and disbursements, and such other information as the United States trustee or the court requires;

(9) make a final report and file a final account of the administration of the estate with the court and with the United States trustee;

(10) if with respect to the debtor there is a claim for a domestic support obligation, provide the applicable notice specified in subsection (c);

(11) if, at the time of the commencement of the case, the debtor (or any entity designated by the debtor) served as the administrator (as defined in section 3 of the Employee Retirement Income Security Act of 1974) of an employee benefit plan, continue to perform the obligations required of the administrator; and

(12) use all reasonable and best efforts to transfer patients from a health care business that is in the process of being closed to an appropriate health care business that—

> **(A)** is in the vicinity of the health care business that is closing;
>
> **(B)** provides the patient with services that are substantially similar to those provided by the health care business that is in the process of being closed; and
>
> **(C)** maintains a reasonable quality of care.

(b)

(1) With respect to a debtor who is an individual in a case under this chapter—

> **(A)** the United States trustee (or the bankruptcy administrator, if any) shall review all materials filed by the debtor and, not later than 10 days after the date of the first meeting of creditors, file with the court a statement as to whether the debtor's case would be presumed to be an abuse under section 707(b); and
>
> **(B)** not later than 7 days after receiving a statement under subparagraph (A), the court shall provide a copy of the statement to all creditors.

(2) The United States trustee (or bankruptcy administrator, if any) shall, not later than 30 days after the date of filing a statement under paragraph (1), either file a motion to dismiss or convert under section 707(b) or file a statement setting forth the reasons the United States trustee (or the bankruptcy administrator, if any) does not consider such a motion to be appropriate, if the United States trustee (or the bankruptcy administrator, if any) determines that the debtor's case should be presumed to be an abuse under section 707(b) and the product of the debtor's current monthly income, multiplied by 12 is not less than—

> **(A)** in the case of a debtor in a household of 1 person, the median family income of the applicable State for 1 earner; or
>
> **(B)** in the case of a debtor in a household of 2 or more individuals, the highest median family income of the applicable State for a family of the same number or fewer individuals.

(c)

(1) In a case described in subsection (a)(10) to which subsection (a)(10) applies, the trustee shall—

> **(A)**
>
> > **(i)** provide written notice to the holder of the claim described in subsection (a)(10) of such claim and of the right of such holder to use the services of the State child support enforcement agency established under sections 464 and 466 of the Social Security Act for the State in which such holder resides, for assistance in collecting child support during and after the case under this title;
> >
> > **(ii)** include in the notice provided under clause (i) the address and telephone number of such State child support enforcement agency; and
> >
> > **(iii)** include in the notice provided under clause (i) an explanation of the rights of

such holder to payment of such claim under this chapter;

(B)

(i) provide written notice to such State child support enforcement agency of such claim; and

(ii) include in the notice provided under clause (i) the name, address, and telephone number of such holder; and

(C) at such time as the debtor is granted a discharge under section 727, provide written notice to such holder and to such State child support enforcement agency of—

(i) the granting of the discharge;

(ii) the last recent known address of the debtor;

(iii) the last recent known name and address of the debtor's employer; and

(iv) the name of each creditor that holds a claim that—

(I) is not discharged under paragraph (2), (4), or (14A) of section 523(a); or

(II) was reaffirmed by the debtor under section 524(c).

(2)

(A) The holder of a claim described in subsection (a)(10) or the State child support enforcement agency of the State in which such holder resides may request from a creditor described in paragraph (1)(C)(iv) the last known address of the debtor.

(B) Notwithstanding any other provision of law, a creditor that makes a disclosure of a last known address of a debtor in connection with a request made under subparagraph (A) shall not be liable by reason of making such disclosure.

§705. Creditors' committee

(a) At the meeting under section 341(a) of this title, creditors that may vote for a trustee under section 702(a) of this title may elect a committee of not fewer than three, and not more than eleven, creditors, each of whom holds an allowable unsecured claim of a kind entitled to distribution under section 726(a)(2) of this title.

(b) A committee elected under subsection (a) of this section may consult with the trustee or the United States trustee in connection with the administration of the estate, make recommendations to the trustee or the United States trustee respecting the performance of the trustee's duties, and submit to the court or the United States trustee any question affecting the administration of the estate.

§706. Conversion

(a) The debtor may convert a case under this chapter to a case under chapter 11, 12, or 13 of this title at any time, if the case has not been converted under section 1112, 1208, or 1307 of this title. Any waiver of the right to convert a case under this subsection is unenforceable.

(b) On request of a party in interest and after notice and a hearing, the court may convert a case under this chapter to a case under chapter 11 of this title at any time.

(c) The court may not convert a case under this chapter to a case under chapter 12 or 13 of this title unless the debtor requests or consents to such conversion.

(d) Notwithstanding any other provision of this section, a case may not be converted to a case under another chapter of this title unless the debtor may be a debtor under such chapter.

§707. Dismissal of a case or conversion to a case under chapter 11 or 13

(a) The court may dismiss a case under this chapter only after notice and a hearing and only for cause, including—

(1) unreasonable delay by the debtor that is prejudicial to creditors;

(2) nonpayment of any fees or charges required under chapter 123 of title 28; and

(3) failure of the debtor in a voluntary case to file, within fifteen days or such additional time as the court may allow after the filing of the petition commencing such case, the information required by paragraph (1) of section 521(a), but only on a motion by the United States trustee.

(b)

(1) After notice and a hearing, the court, on its own motion or on a motion by the United States trustee, trustee (or bankruptcy administrator, if any), or any party in interest, may dismiss a case filed by an individual debtor under this chapter whose debts are primarily consumer debts, or, with the debtor's consent, convert such a case to a case under chapter 11 or 13 of this title, if it finds that the granting of relief would be an abuse of the provisions of this chapter. In making a determination whether to dismiss a case under this section, the court may not take into consideration whether a debtor has made, or continues to make, charitable contributions (that meet the definition of "charitable contribution" under section 548(d)(3)) to any qualified religious or charitable entity or organization (as that term is defined in section 548(d)(4)).

(2)

(A)

(i) In considering under paragraph (1) whether the granting of relief would be an abuse of the provisions of this chapter, the court shall presume abuse exists if the debtor's current monthly income reduced by the amounts determined under clauses (ii), (iii), and (iv), and multiplied by 60 is not less than the lesser of—

(I) 25 percent of the debtor's nonpriority unsecured claims in the case, or $7,700, whichever is greater; or

(II) $12,850.

(ii)

(I) The debtor's monthly expenses shall be the debtor's applicable monthly expense amounts specified under the National Standards and Local Standards, and the debtor's actual monthly expenses for the categories specified as Other Necessary Expenses issued by the Internal Revenue Service for the area in which the debtor resides, as in effect on the date of the order for relief, for the debtor, the dependents of the debtor, and the spouse of the debtor in a joint case, if the spouse is not otherwise a dependent. Such expenses shall include reasonably necessary health insurance, disability insurance, and health savings account expenses for the debtor, the spouse of the debtor, or the dependents of the debtor. Notwithstanding any other provision of this clause, the monthly expenses of the debtor shall not include any payments for debts. In addition, the debtor's monthly expenses shall include the debtor's reasonably necessary expenses incurred to maintain the safety of the debtor and the family of the debtor from family violence as identified under section 302 of the Family Violence Prevention and Services Act, or other applicable Federal law. The expenses included in the debtor's monthly expenses described in the preceding sentence shall be kept confidential by the court. In addition, if it is demonstrated that it is reasonable and necessary, the debtor's monthly expenses may also include an additional allowance for food and clothing of up to 5 percent of the food and clothing categories as specified by the National Standards issued by the Internal Revenue Service.

(II) In addition, the debtor's monthly expenses may include, if applicable, the continuation of actual expenses paid by the debtor that are reasonable and necessary for care and support of an elderly, chronically ill, or disabled household member or member of the debtor's immediate family (including parents, grandparents, siblings, children, and grandchildren of the debtor, the dependents of the debtor, and the spouse of the debtor in a joint case who is not a dependent) and who is unable to pay for such reasonable and necessary expenses. Such monthly expenses may include, if applicable, contributions to an account of a qualified ABLE program to the extent such contributions are not excess contributions (as described in section 4973(h) of the Internal Revenue Code of 1986) and if the designated beneficiary of such account is a child, stepchild, grandchild, or stepgrandchild of the debtor.

(III) In addition, for a debtor eligible for chapter 13, the debtor's monthly expenses may include the actual administrative expenses of administering a chapter 13 plan for the district in which the debtor resides, up to an amount of 10 percent of the projected plan payments, as determined under schedules issued by the Executive Office for United States Trustees.

(IV) In addition, the debtor's monthly expenses may include the actual expenses for each dependent child less than 18 years of age, not to exceed $1,925 per year per child, to attend a private or public elementary or secondary school if the debtor provides documentation of such expenses and a detailed explanation of why such expenses are reasonable and necessary, and why such expenses are not already accounted for in the National Standards, Local Standards, or Other Necessary Expenses referred to in subclause (I).

(V) In addition, the debtor's monthly expenses may include an allowance for housing and utilities, in excess of the allowance specified by the Local

Standards for housing and utilities issued by the Internal Revenue Service, based on the actual expenses for home energy costs if the debtor provides documentation of such actual expenses and demonstrates that such actual expenses are reasonable and necessary.

(iii) The debtor's average monthly payments on account of secured debts shall be calculated as the sum of—

(I) the total of all amounts scheduled as contractually due to secured creditors in each month of the 60 months following the date of the filing of the petition; and

(II) any additional payments to secured creditors necessary for the debtor, in filing a plan under chapter 13 of this title, to maintain possession of the debtor's primary residence, motor vehicle, or other property necessary for the support of the debtor and the debtor's dependents, that serves as collateral for secured debts;

divided by 60.

(iv) The debtor's expenses for payment of all priority claims (including priority child support and alimony claims) shall be calculated as the total amount of debts entitled to priority, divided by 60.

(B)

(i) In any proceeding brought under this subsection, the presumption of abuse may only be rebutted by demonstrating special circumstances, such as a serious medical condition or a call or order to active duty in the Armed Forces, to the extent such special circumstances that justify additional expenses or adjustments of current monthly income for which there is no reasonable alternative.

(ii) In order to establish special circumstances, the debtor shall be required to itemize each additional expense or adjustment of income and to provide—

(I) documentation for such expense or adjustment to income; and

(II) a detailed explanation of the special circumstances that make such expenses or adjustment to income necessary and reasonable.

(iii) The debtor shall attest under oath to the accuracy of any information provided to demonstrate that additional expenses or adjustments to income are required.

(iv) The presumption of abuse may only be rebutted if the additional expenses or adjustments to income referred to in clause (i) cause the product of the debtor's current monthly income reduced by the amounts determined under clauses (ii), (iii), and (iv) of subparagraph (A) when multiplied by 60 to be less than the lesser of—

(I) 25 percent of the debtor's nonpriority unsecured claims, or $7,700, whichever is greater; or

(II) $12,850.

(C) As part of the schedule of current income and expenditures required under section 521, the debtor shall include a statement of the debtor's current monthly income, and the calculations that determine whether a presumption arises under subparagraph (A)(i), that show how each such amount is calculated.

(D) Subparagraphs (A) through (C) shall not apply, and the court may not dismiss or convert a case based on any form of means testing—

(i) if the debtor is a disabled veteran (as defined in section 3741(1) of title 38), and the indebtedness occurred primarily during a period during which he or she was—

(I) on active duty (as defined in section 101(d)(1) of title 10); or

(II) performing a homeland defense activity (as defined in section 901(1) of title 32); or

(ii) with respect to the debtor, while the debtor is—

(I) on, and during the 540-day period beginning immediately after the debtor is released from, a period of active duty (as defined in section 101(d)(1) of title 10) of not less than 90 days; or

(II) performing, and during the 540-day period beginning immediately after the debtor is no longer performing, a homeland defense activity (as defined in section 901(1) of title 32) performed for a period of not less than 90 days;

if after September 11, 2001, the debtor while a member of a reserve component of the Armed Forces or a member of the National Guard, was called to such active duty or performed such homeland defense activity.

(3) In considering under paragraph (1) whether the granting of relief would be an abuse of the provisions of this chapter in a case in which the presumption in paragraph (2)(A)(i) does not arise or is rebutted, the court shall consider—

(A) whether the debtor filed the petition in bad faith; or

(B) the totality of the circumstances (including whether the debtor seeks to reject a personal services contract and the financial need for such rejection as sought by the debtor) of the debtor's financial situation demonstrates abuse.

(4)

(A) The court, on its own initiative or on the motion of a party in interest, in accordance with the procedures described in rule 9011 of the Federal Rules of Bankruptcy Procedure, may order the attorney for the debtor to reimburse the trustee for all reasonable costs in prosecuting a motion filed under section 707(b), including reasonable attorneys' fees, if—

(i) a trustee files a motion for dismissal or conversion under this subsection; and

(ii) the court—

(I) grants such motion; and

(II) finds that the action of the attorney for the debtor in filing a case under this chapter violated rule 9011 of the Federal Rules of Bankruptcy Procedure.

(B) If the court finds that the attorney for the debtor violated rule 9011 of the Federal Rules of Bankruptcy Procedure, the court, on its own initiative or on the motion of a party in interest, in accordance with such procedures, may order—

(i) the assessment of an appropriate civil penalty against the attorney for the debtor; and

(ii) the payment of such civil penalty to the trustee, the United States trustee (or the bankruptcy administrator, if any).

(C) The signature of an attorney on a petition, pleading, or written motion shall constitute a certification that the attorney has—

(i) performed a reasonable investigation into the circumstances that gave rise to the petition, pleading, or written motion; and

(ii) determined that the petition, pleading, or written motion—

(I) is well grounded in fact; and

(II) is warranted by existing law or a good faith argument for the extension, modification, or reversal of existing law

and does not constitute an abuse under paragraph (1).

(D) The signature of an attorney on the petition shall constitute a certification that the attorney has no knowledge after an inquiry that the information in the schedules filed with such petition is incorrect.

(5)

(A) Except as provided in subparagraph (B) and subject to paragraph (6), the court, on its own initiative or on the motion of a party in interest, in accordance with the procedures described in rule 9011 of the Federal Rules of Bankruptcy Procedure, may award a debtor all reasonable costs (including reasonable attorneys' fees) in contesting a motion filed by a party in interest (other than a trustee or United States trustee (or bankruptcy administrator, if any)) under this subsection if—

(i) the court does not grant the motion; and

(ii) the court finds that—

(I) the position of the party that filed the motion violated rule 9011 of the Federal Rules of Bankruptcy Procedure; or

(II) the attorney (if any) who filed the motion did not comply with the requirements of clauses (i) and (ii) of paragraph (4)(C), and the motion was made solely for the purpose of coercing a debtor into waiving a right guaranteed to the debtor under this title.

(B) A small business that has a claim of an aggregate amount less than $1,300 shall not be subject to subparagraph (A)(ii)(I).

(C) For purposes of this paragraph—

(i) the term "small business" means an unincorporated business, partnership, corporation, association, or organization that—

(I) has fewer than 25 full-time employees as determined on the date on which the motion is filed; and

(II) is engaged in commercial or business activity; and

(ii) the number of employees of a wholly owned subsidiary of a corporation includes the employees of—

(I) a parent corporation; and

(II) any other subsidiary corporation of the parent corporation.

(6) Only the judge or United States trustee (or bankruptcy administrator, if any) may file a motion under section 707(b), if the current

monthly income of the debtor, or in a joint case, the debtor and the debtor's spouse, as of the date of the order for relief, when multiplied by 12, is equal to or less than—

(A) in the case of a debtor in a household of 1 person, the median family income of the applicable State for 1 earner;

(B) in the case of a debtor in a household of 2, 3, or 4 individuals, the highest median family income of the applicable State for a family of the same number or fewer individuals; or

(C) in the case of a debtor in a household exceeding 4 individuals, the highest median family income of the applicable State for a family of 4 or fewer individuals, plus $700 per month for each individual in excess of 4.

(7)

(A) No judge, United States trustee (or bankruptcy administrator, if any), trustee, or other party in interest may file a motion under paragraph (2) if the current monthly income of the debtor, including a veteran (as that term is defined in section 101 of title 38), and the debtor's spouse combined, as of the date of the order for relief when multiplied by 12, is equal to or less than—

(i) in the case of a debtor in a household of 1 person, the median family income of the applicable State for 1 earner;

(ii) in the case of a debtor in a household of 2, 3, or 4 individuals, the highest median family income of the applicable State for a family of the same number or fewer individuals; or

(iii) in the case of a debtor in a household exceeding 4 individuals, the highest median family income of the applicable State for a family of 4 or fewer individuals, plus $700 per month for each individual in excess of 4.

(B) In a case that is not a joint case, current monthly income of the debtor's spouse shall not be considered for purposes of subparagraph (A) if—

(i)

(I) the debtor and the debtor's spouse are separated under applicable nonbankruptcy law; or

(II) the debtor and the debtor's spouse are living separate and apart, other than for the purpose of evading subparagraph (A); and

(ii) the debtor files a statement under penalty of perjury—

(I) specifying that the debtor meets the requirement of subclause (I) or (II) of clause (i); and

(II) disclosing the aggregate, or best estimate of the aggregate, amount of any cash or money payments received from the debtor's spouse attributed to the debtor's current monthly income.

(c)

(1) In this subsection—

(A) the term "crime of violence" has the meaning given such term in section 16 of title 18; and

(B) the term "drug trafficking crime" has the meaning given such term in section 924(c)(2) of title 18.

(2) Except as provided in paragraph (3), after notice and a hearing, the court, on a motion by the victim of a crime of violence or a drug trafficking crime, may when it is in the best interest of the victim dismiss a voluntary case filed under this chapter by a debtor who is an individual if such individual was convicted of such crime.

(3) The court may not dismiss a case under paragraph (2) if the debtor establishes by a preponderance of the evidence that the filing of a case under this chapter is necessary to satisfy a claim for a domestic support obligation.

SUBCHAPTER II—COLLECTION, LIQUIDATION, AND DISTRIBUTION OF THE ESTATE

§721. Authorization to operate business

The court may authorize the trustee to operate the business of the debtor for a limited period, if such operation is in the best interest of the estate and consistent with the orderly liquidation of the estate.

§722. Redemption

An individual debtor may, whether or not the debtor has waived the right to redeem under this section, redeem tangible personal property intended primarily for personal, family, or household use, from a lien securing a dischargeable consumer debt, if such property is exempted under section 522 of this title or has been abandoned under section 554 of this title, by paying the holder of such lien the amount of the allowed secured claim of such holder that is secured by such lien in full at the time of redemption.

§723. Rights of partnership trustee against general partners

(a) If there is a deficiency of property of the estate to pay in full all claims which are allowed in a case under this chapter concerning a partnership and with respect to which a general partner of the partnership is personally liable, the trustee shall have a claim against such general partner to the extent that under applicable nonbankruptcy law such general partner is personally liable for such deficiency.

(b) To the extent practicable, the trustee shall first seek recovery of such deficiency from any general partner in such partnership that is not a debtor in a case under this title. Pending determination of such deficiency, the court may order any such partner to provide the estate with indemnity for, or assurance of payment of, any deficiency recoverable from such partner, or not to dispose of property.

(c) The trustee has a claim against the estate of each general partner in such partnership that is a debtor in a case under this title for the full amount of all claims of creditors allowed in the case concerning such partnership. Notwithstanding section 502 of this title, there shall not be allowed in such partner's case a claim against such partner on which both such partner and such partnership are liable, except to any extent that such claim is secured only by property of such partner and not by property of such partnership. The claim of the trustee under this subsection is entitled to distribution in such partner's case under section 726(a) of this title the same as any other claim of a kind specified in such section.

(d) If the aggregate that the trustee recovers from the estates of general partners under subsection (c) of this section is greater than any deficiency not recovered under subsection (b) of this section, the court, after notice and a hearing, shall determine an equitable distribution of the surplus so recovered, and the trustee shall distribute such surplus to the estates of the general partners in such partnership according to such determination.

§724. Treatment of certain liens

(a) The trustee may avoid a lien that secures a claim of a kind specified in section 726(a)(4) of this title.

(b) Property in which the estate has an interest and that is subject to a lien that is not avoidable under this title (other than to the extent that there is a properly perfected unavoidable tax lien arising in connection with an ad valorem tax on real or personal property of the estate) and that secures an allowed claim for a tax, or proceeds of such property, shall be distributed—

    (1) first, to any holder of an allowed claim secured by a lien on such property that is not avoidable under this title and that is senior to such tax lien;

    (2) second, to any holder of a claim of a kind specified in section 507(a)(1)(C) or 507(a)(2) (except that such expenses under each such section, other than claims for wages, salaries, or commissions that arise after the date of the filing of the petition, shall be limited to expenses incurred under this chapter and shall not include expenses incurred under chapter 11 of this title), 507(a)(1)(A), 507(a)(1)(B), 507(a)(3), 507(a)(4), 507(a)(5), 507(a)(6), or 507(a)(7) of this title, to the extent of the amount of such allowed tax claim that is secured by such tax lien;

    (3) third, to the holder of such tax lien, to any extent that such holder's allowed tax claim that is secured by such tax lien exceeds any amount distributed under paragraph (2) of this subsection;

    (4) fourth, to any holder of an allowed claim secured by a lien on such property that is not avoidable under this title and that is junior to such tax lien;

    (5) fifth, to the holder of such tax lien, to the extent that such holder's allowed claim secured by such tax lien is not paid under paragraph (3) of this subsection; and

    (6) sixth, to the estate.

(c) If more than one holder of a claim is entitled to distribution under a particular paragraph of subsection (b) of this section, distribution to such holders under such paragraph shall be in the same order as distribution to such holders would have been other than under this section.

(d) A statutory lien the priority of which is determined in the same manner as the priority of a tax lien under section 6323 of the Internal Revenue Code of 1986 shall be treated under subsection (b) of this section the same as if such lien were a tax lien.

(e) Before subordinating a tax lien on real or personal property of the estate, the trustee shall—

    (1) exhaust the unencumbered assets of the estate; and

    (2) in a manner consistent with section 506(c), recover from property securing an allowed secured claim the reasonable, necessary costs and expenses of preserving or disposing of such property.

(f) Notwithstanding the exclusion of ad valorem tax liens under this section and subject to the requirements of subsection (e), the following may be paid from property of the estate which secures a tax lien, or the proceeds of such property:

(1) Claims for wages, salaries, and commissions that are entitled to priority under section 507(a)(4).

(2) Claims for contributions to an employee benefit plan entitled to priority under section 507(a)(5).

§725. Disposition of certain property

After the commencement of a case under this chapter, but before final distribution of property of the estate under section 726 of this title, the trustee, after notice and a hearing, shall dispose of any property in which an entity other than the estate has an interest, such as a lien, and that has not been disposed of under another section of this title.

§726. Distribution of property of the estate

(a) Except as provided in section 510 of this title, property of the estate shall be distributed—

(1) first, in payment of claims of the kind specified in, and in the order specified in, section 507 of this title, proof of which is timely filed under section 501 of this title or tardily filed on or before the earlier of—

　(A) the date that is 10 days after the mailing to creditors of the summary of the trustee's final report; or

　(B) the date on which the trustee commences final distribution under this section;

(2) second, in payment of any allowed unsecured claim, other than a claim of a kind specified in paragraph (1), (3), or (4) of this subsection, proof of which is—

　(A) timely filed under section 501(a) of this title;

　(B) timely filed under section 501(b) or 501(c) of this title; or

　(C) tardily filed under section 501(a) of this title, if—

　　(i) the creditor that holds such claim did not have notice or actual knowledge of the case in time for timely filing of a proof of such claim under section 501(a) of this title; and

　　(ii) proof of such claim is filed in time to permit payment of such claim;

(3) third, in payment of any allowed unsecured claim proof of which is tardily filed under section 501(a) of this title, other than a claim of

the kind specified in paragraph (2)(C) of this subsection;

(4) fourth, in payment of any allowed claim, whether secured or unsecured, for any fine, penalty, or forfeiture, or for multiple, exemplary, or punitive damages, arising before the earlier of the order for relief or the appointment of a trustee, to the extent that such fine, penalty, forfeiture, or damages are not compensation for actual pecuniary loss suffered by the holder of such claim;

(5) fifth, in payment of interest at the legal rate from the date of the filing of the petition, on any claim paid under paragraph (1), (2), (3), or (4) of this subsection; and

(6) sixth, to the debtor.

(b) Payment on claims of a kind specified in paragraph (1), (2), (3), (4), (5), (6), (7), (8), (9), or (10) of section 507(a) of this title, or in paragraph (2), (3), (4), or (5) of subsection (a) of this section, shall be made pro rata among claims of the kind specified in each such particular paragraph, except that in a case that has been converted to this chapter under section 1112, 1208, or 1307 of this title, a claim allowed under section 503(b) of this title incurred under this chapter after such conversion has priority over a claim allowed under section 503(b) of this title incurred under any other chapter of this title or under this chapter before such conversion and over any expenses of a custodian superseded under section 543 of this title.

(c) Notwithstanding subsections (a) and (b) of this section, if there is property of the kind specified in section 541(a)(2) of this title, or proceeds of such property, in the estate, such property or proceeds shall be segregated from other property of the estate, and such property or proceeds and other property of the estate shall be distributed as follows:

(1) Claims allowed under section 503 of this title shall be paid either from property of the kind specified in section 541(a)(2) of this title, or from other property of the estate, as the interest of justice requires.

(2) Allowed claims, other than claims allowed under section 503 of this title, shall be paid in the order specified in subsection (a) of this section, and, with respect to claims of a kind specified in a particular paragraph of section 507 of this title or subsection (a) of this section, in the following order and manner:

　(A) First, community claims against the debtor or the debtor's spouse shall be paid from property of the kind specified in section 541(a)(2) of this title, except to the extent that such property is solely liable for debts of the debtor.

(B) Second, to the extent that community claims against the debtor are not paid under subparagraph (A) of this paragraph, such community claims shall be paid from property of the kind specified in section 541(a)(2) of this title that is solely liable for debts of the debtor.

(C) Third, to the extent that all claims against the debtor including community claims against the debtor are not paid under subparagraph (A) or (B) of this paragraph such claims shall be paid from property of the estate other than property of the kind specified in section 541(a)(2) of this title.

(D) Fourth, to the extent that community claims against the debtor or the debtor's spouse are not paid under subparagraph (A), (B), or (C) of this paragraph, such claims shall be paid from all remaining property of the estate.

§727. Discharge

(a) The court shall grant the debtor a discharge, unless—

(1) the debtor is not an individual;

(2) the debtor, with intent to hinder, delay, or defraud a creditor or an officer of the estate charged with custody of property under this title, has transferred, removed, destroyed, mutilated, or concealed, or has permitted to be transferred, removed, destroyed, mutilated, or concealed—

(A) property of the debtor, within one year before the date of the filing of the petition; or

(B) property of the estate, after the date of the filing of the petition;

(3) the debtor has concealed, destroyed, mutilated, falsified, or failed to keep or preserve any recorded information, including books, documents, records, and papers, from which the debtor's financial condition or business transactions might be ascertained, unless such act or failure to act was justified under all of the circumstances of the case;

(4) the debtor knowingly and fraudulently, in or in connection with the case—

(A) made a false oath or account;

(B) presented or used a false claim;

(C) gave, offered, received, or attempted to obtain money, property, or advantage, or a promise of money, property, or advantage, for acting or forbearing to act; or

(D) withheld from an officer of the estate entitled to possession under this title, any recorded information, including books, documents, records, and papers, relating to the debtor's property or financial affairs;

(5) the debtor has failed to explain satisfactorily, before determination of denial of discharge under this paragraph, any loss of assets or deficiency of assets to meet the debtor's liabilities;

(6) the debtor has refused, in the case—

(A) to obey any lawful order of the court, other than an order to respond to a material question or to testify;

(B) on the ground of privilege against self-incrimination, to respond to a material question approved by the court or to testify, after the debtor has been granted immunity with respect to the matter concerning which such privilege was invoked; or

(C) on a ground other than the properly invoked privilege against self-incrimination, to respond to a material question approved by the court or to testify;

(7) the debtor has committed any act specified in paragraph (2), (3), (4), (5), or (6) of this subsection, on or within one year before the date of the filing of the petition, or during the case, in connection with another case, under this title or under the Bankruptcy Act, concerning an insider;

(8) the debtor has been granted a discharge under this section, under section 1141 of this title, or under section 14, 371, or 476 of the Bankruptcy Act, in a case commenced within 8 years before the date of the filing of the petition;

(9) the debtor has been granted a discharge under section 1228 or 1328 of this title, or under section 660 or 661 of the Bankruptcy Act, in a case commenced within six years before the date of the filing of the petition, unless payments under the plan in such case totaled at least—

(A) 100 percent of the allowed unsecured claims in such case; or

(B)

(i) 70 percent of such claims; and

(ii) the plan was proposed by the debtor in good faith, and was the debtor's best effort;

(10) the court approves a written waiver of discharge executed by the debtor after the order for relief under this chapter;

(11) after filing the petition, the debtor failed to complete an instructional course concerning personal financial management described in section 111, except that this paragraph shall not apply with respect to a debtor who is a person described in section 109(h)(4) or who resides in a district for which the United States trustee (or the bankruptcy administrator, if any) determines that the approved instructional courses are not adequate to service the additional individuals who would otherwise be required to complete such instructional courses under this section (The United States trustee (or the bankruptcy administrator, if any) who makes a determination described in this paragraph shall review such determination not later than 1 year after the date of such determination, and not less frequently than annually thereafter.); or

(12) the court after notice and a hearing held not more than 10 days before the date of the entry of the order granting the discharge finds that there is reasonable cause to believe that—

(A) section 522(q)(1) may be applicable to the debtor; and

(B) there is pending any proceeding in which the debtor may be found guilty of a felony of the kind described in section 522(q)(1)(A) or liable for a debt of the kind described in section 522(q)(1)(B).

(b) Except as provided in section 523 of this title, a discharge under subsection (a) of this section discharges the debtor from all debts that arose before the date of the order for relief under this chapter, and any liability on a claim that is determined under section 502 of this title as if such claim had arisen before the commencement of the case, whether or not a proof of claim based on any such debt or liability is filed under section 501 of this title, and whether or not a claim based on any such debt or liability is allowed under section 502 of this title.

(c)

(1) The trustee, a creditor, or the United States trustee may object to the granting of a discharge under subsection (a) of this section.

(2) On request of a party in interest, the court may order the trustee to examine the acts and conduct of the debtor to determine whether a ground exists for denial of discharge.

(d) On request of the trustee, a creditor, or the United States trustee, and after notice and a hearing, the court shall revoke a discharge granted under subsection (a) of this section if—

(1) such discharge was obtained through the fraud of the debtor, and the requesting party did not know of such fraud until after the granting of such discharge;

(2) the debtor acquired property that is property of the estate, or became entitled to acquire property that would be property of the estate, and knowingly and fraudulently failed to report the acquisition of or entitlement to such property, or to deliver or surrender such property to the trustee;

(3) the debtor committed an act specified in subsection (a)(6) of this section; or

(4) the debtor has failed to explain satisfactorily—

(A) a material misstatement in an audit referred to in section 586(f) of title 28; or

(B) a failure to make available for inspection all necessary accounts, papers, documents, financial records, files, and all other papers, things, or property belonging to the debtor that are requested for an audit referred to in section 586(f) of title 28.

(e) The trustee, a creditor, or the United States trustee may request a revocation of a discharge—

(1) under subsection (d)(1) of this section within one year after such discharge is granted; or

(2) under subsection (d)(2) or (d)(3) of this section before the later of—

(A) one year after the granting of such discharge; and

(B) the date the case is closed.

SUBCHAPTER III—STOCKBROKER LIQUIDATION

§741. Definitions for this subchapter

In this subchapter—

(1) "Commission" means Securities and Exchange Commission;

(2) "customer" includes—

(A) entity with whom a person deals as principal or agent and that has a claim against such person on account of a security received, acquired, or held by such person in the ordinary course of such person's business as a stockbroker, from or for the securities account or accounts of such entity—

(i) for safekeeping;

(ii) with a view to sale;

(iii) to cover a consummated sale;

(iv) pursuant to a purchase;

(v) as collateral under a security agreement; or

(vi) for the purpose of effecting registration of transfer; and

(B) entity that has a claim against a person arising out of—

(i) a sale or conversion of a security received, acquired, or held as specified in subparagraph (A) of this paragraph; or

(ii) a deposit of cash, a security, or other property with such person for the purpose of purchasing or selling a security;

(3) "customer name security" means security—

(A) held for the account of a customer on the date of the filing of the petition by or on behalf of the debtor;

(B) registered in such customer's name on such date or in the process of being so registered under instructions from the debtor; and

(C) not in a form transferable by delivery on such date;

(4) "customer property" means cash, security, or other property, and proceeds of such cash, security, or property, received, acquired, or held by or for the account of the debtor, from or for the securities account of a customer—

(A) including—

(i) property that was unlawfully converted from and that is the lawful property of the estate;

(ii) a security held as property of the debtor to the extent such security is necessary to meet a net equity claim of a customer based on a security of the same class and series of an issuer;

(iii) resources provided through the use or realization of a customer's debit cash balance or a debit item includible in the Formula for Determination of Reserve Requirement for Brokers and Dealers as promulgated by the Commission under the Securities Exchange Act of 1934; and

(iv) other property of the debtor that any applicable law, rule, or regulation requires to be set aside or held for the benefit of a customer, unless including such property as customer property would not significantly increase customer property; but

(B) not including—

(i) a customer name security delivered to or reclaimed by a customer under section 751 of this title; or

(ii) property to the extent that a customer does not have a claim against the debtor based on such property;

(5) "margin payment" means payment or deposit of cash, a security, or other property, that is commonly known to the securities trade as original margin, initial margin, maintenance margin, or variation margin, or as a mark-to-market payment, or that secures an obligation of a participant in a securities clearing agency;

(6) "net equity" means, with respect to all accounts of a customer that such customer has in the same capacity—

(A)

(i) aggregate dollar balance that would remain in such accounts after the liquidation, by sale or purchase, at the time of the filing of the petition, of all securities positions in all such accounts, except any customer name securities of such customer; minus

(ii) any claim of the debtor against such customer in such capacity that would have been owing immediately after such liquidation; plus

(B) any payment by such customer to the trustee, within 60 days after notice under section 342 of this title, of any business related claim of the debtor against such customer in such capacity;

(7) "securities contract"—

(A) means—

(i) a contract for the purchase, sale, or loan of a security, a certificate of deposit, a mortgage loan, any interest in a mortgage loan, a group or index of securities, certificates of deposit, or mortgage loans or interests therein (including an interest therein or based on the value thereof), or option on any of the foregoing, including an option to purchase or sell any such security, certificate of deposit, mortgage loan, interest, group or index, or option, and including any repurchase or reverse repurchase transaction on any such security, certificate of deposit, mortgage loan, interest, group or index, or option (whether or not such repurchase or reverse repurchase transaction is a "repurchase agreement", as defined in section 101);

(ii) any option entered into on a national securities exchange relating to foreign currencies;

(iii) the guarantee (including by novation) by or to any securities clearing agency of a settlement of cash, securities, certificates of deposit, mortgage loans or interests therein, group or index of securities, or mortgage loans or interests therein (including any interest therein or based on the value thereof), or option on any of the foregoing, including an option to purchase or sell any such security, certificate of deposit, mortgage loan, interest, group or index, or option (whether or not such settlement is in connection with any agreement or transaction referred to in clauses (i) through (xi));

(iv) any margin loan;

(v) any extension of credit for the clearance or settlement of securities transactions;

(vi) any loan transaction coupled with a securities collar transaction, any prepaid forward securities transaction, or any total return swap transaction coupled with a securities sale transaction;

(vii) any other agreement or transaction that is similar to an agreement or transaction referred to in this subparagraph;

(viii) any combination of the agreements or transactions referred to in this subparagraph;

(ix) any option to enter into any agreement or transaction referred to in this subparagraph;

(x) a master agreement that provides for an agreement or transaction referred to in clause (i), (ii), (iii), (iv), (v), (vi), (vii), (viii), or (ix), together with all supplements to any such master agreement, without regard to whether the master agreement provides for an agreement or transaction that is not a securities contract under this subparagraph, except that such master agreement shall be considered to be a securities contract under this subparagraph only with respect to each agreement or transaction under such master agreement that is referred to in clause (i), (ii), (iii), (iv), (v), (vi), (vii), (viii), or (ix); or

(xi) any security agreement or arrangement or other credit enhancement related to any agreement or transaction referred to in this subparagraph, including any guarantee or reimbursement obligation by or to a stockbroker, securities clearing agency, financial institution, or financial participant in connection with any agreement or transaction referred to in this subparagraph, but not to exceed the damages in connection with any such agreement or transaction, measured in accordance with section 562; and

(B) does not include any purchase, sale, or repurchase obligation under a participation in a commercial mortgage loan;

(8) "settlement payment" means a preliminary settlement payment, a partial settlement payment, an interim settlement payment, a settlement payment on account, a final settlement payment, or any other similar payment commonly used in the securities trade; and

(9) "SIPC" means Securities Investor Protection Corporation.

§742. Effect of section 362 of this title in this subchapter

Notwithstanding section 362 of this title, SIPC may file an application for a protective decree under the Securities Investor Protection Act of 1970. The filing of such application stays all proceedings in the case under this title unless and until such application is dismissed. If SIPC completes the liquidation of the debtor, then the court shall dismiss the case.

§743. Notice

The clerk shall give the notice required by section 342 of this title to SIPC and to the Commission. Notwithstanding section 365(d)(1) of this title, the trustee shall assume or reject, under section 365 of this title, any executory contract of the debtor for the purchase or sale of a security in the ordinary course of the debtor's business, within a reasonable time after the date of the order for relief, but not to exceed 30 days. If the trustee does not assume such a contract within such time, such contract is rejected.

§744. Executory contracts

Notwithstanding section 365(d)(1) of this title, the trustee shall assume or reject, under section 365 of this title, any executory contract of the debtor for the purchase or sale of a security in the ordinary course of the debtor's business, within a reasonable time after the date of the order for relief, but not to exceed 30 days. If the trustee does not assume such a contract within such time, such contract is rejected.

§745. Treatment of accounts

(a) Accounts held by the debtor for a particular customer in separate capacities shall be treated as accounts of separate customers.

(b) If a stockbroker or a bank holds a customer net equity claim against the debtor that arose out of a transaction for a customer of such stockbroker or bank, each such customer of such stockbroker or bank shall be treated as a separate customer of the debtor.

(c) Each trustee's account specified as such on the debtor's books, and supported by a trust deed filed with, and qualified as such by, the Internal Revenue Service, and under the Internal Revenue Code of 1986, shall be treated as a separate customer account for each beneficiary under such trustee account.

§746. Extent of customer claims

(a) If, after the date of the filing of the petition, an entity enters into a transaction with the debtor, in a manner that would have made such entity a customer had such transaction occurred before the date of the filing of the petition, and such transaction was entered into by such entity in good faith and before the qualification under section 322 of this title of a trustee, such entity shall be deemed a customer, and the date of such transaction shall be deemed to be the date of the filing of the petition for the purpose of determining such entity's net equity.

(b) An entity does not have a claim as a customer to the extent that such entity transferred to the debtor cash or a security that, by contract, agreement, understanding, or operation of law, is—

    (1) part of the capital of the debtor; or

    (2) subordinated to the claims of any or all creditors.

§747. Subordination of certain customer claims

Except as provided in section 510 of this title, unless all other customer net equity claims have been paid in full, the trustee may not pay in full or pay in part, directly or indirectly, any net equity claim of a customer that was, on the date the transaction giving rise to such claim occurred—

    (1) an insider;

    (2) a beneficial owner of at least five percent of any class of equity securities of the debtor, other than—

        (A) nonconvertible stock having fixed preferential dividend and liquidation rights; or

        (B) interests of limited partners in a limited partnership;

    (3) a limited partner with a participation of at least five percent in the net assets or net profits of the debtor; or

    (4) an entity that, directly or indirectly, through agreement or otherwise, exercised or had the power to exercise control over the management or policies of the debtor.

§748. Reduction of securities to money

As soon as practicable after the date of the order for relief, the trustee shall reduce to money, consistent with good market practice, all securities held as property of the estate, except for customer name securities delivered or reclaimed under section 751 of this title.

§749. Voidable transfers

(a) Except as otherwise provided in this section, any transfer of property that, but for such transfer, would have been customer property, may be avoided by the trustee, and such property shall be treated as customer property, if and to the extent that the trustee avoids such transfer under section 544, 545, 547, 548, or 549 of this title. For the purpose of such sections, the property so transferred shall be deemed to have been property of the debtor and, if such transfer was made to a customer or for a customer's benefit, such customer shall be deemed, for the purposes of this section, to have been a creditor.

(b) Notwithstanding sections 544, 545, 547, 548, and 549 of this title, the trustee may not avoid a transfer made before seven days after the order for relief if such transfer is approved by the Commission by rule or order, either before or after such transfer, and if such transfer is—

    (1) a transfer of a securities contract entered into or carried by or through the debtor on behalf of a customer, and of any cash, security, or other property margining or securing such securities contract; or

    (2) the liquidation of a securities contract entered into or carried by or through the debtor on behalf of a customer.

§750. Distribution of securities

The trustee may not distribute a security except under section 751 of this title.

§751. Customer name securities

The trustee shall deliver any customer name security to or on behalf of the customer entitled to such security, unless such customer has a negative net equity. With the approval of the trustee, a customer may reclaim a customer name security after payment to the trustee, within such period as the trustee allows, of any claim of the debtor against such customer to the extent that such customer will not have a negative net equity after such payment.

§752. Customer property

(a) The trustee shall distribute customer property ratably to customers on the basis and to the extent of such customers' allowed net equity claims and in priority to all other claims, except claims of the kind specified in section 507(a)(2) of this title that are attributable to the administration of such customer property.

(b)

(1) The trustee shall distribute customer property in excess of that distributed under subsection (a) of this section in accordance with section 726 of this title.

(2) Except as provided in section 510 of this title, if a customer is not paid the full amount of such customer's allowed net equity claim from customer property, the unpaid portion of such claim is a claim entitled to distribution under section 726 of this title.

(c) Any cash or security remaining after the liquidation of a security interest created under a security agreement made by the debtor, excluding property excluded under section 741(4)(B) of this title, shall be apportioned between the general estate and customer property in the same proportion as the general estate of the debtor and customer property were subject to such security interest.

§753. Stockbroker liquidation and forward contract merchants, commodity brokers, stockbrokers, financial institutions, financial participants, securities clearing agencies, swap participants, repo participants, and master netting agreement participants

Notwithstanding any other provision of this title, the exercise of rights by a forward contract merchant, commodity broker, stockbroker, financial institution, financial participant, securities clearing agency, swap participant, repo participant, or master netting agreement participant under this title shall not affect the priority of any unsecured claim it may have after the exercise of such rights.

SUBCHAPTER IV—COMMODITY BROKER LIQUIDATION

§761. Definitions for this subchapter

In this subchapter—

(1) "Act" means Commodity Exchange Act;

(2) "clearing organization" means a derivatives clearing organization registered under the Act;

(3) "Commission" means Commodity Futures Trading Commission;

(4) "commodity contract" means—

(A) with respect to a futures commission merchant, contract for the purchase or sale of a commodity for future delivery on, or subject to the rules of, a contract market or board of trade;

(B) with respect to a foreign futures commission merchant, foreign future;

(C) with respect to a leverage transaction merchant, leverage transaction;

(D) with respect to a clearing organization, contract for the purchase or sale of a commodity for future delivery on, or subject to the rules of, a contract market or board of trade that is cleared by such clearing organization, or commodity option traded on, or subject to the rules of, a contract market or board of trade that is cleared by such clearing organization;

(E) with respect to a commodity options dealer, commodity option;

(F)

(i) any other contract, option, agreement, or transaction that is similar to a contract, option, agreement, or transaction referred to in this paragraph; and

(ii) with respect to a futures commission merchant or a clearing organization, any other contract, option, agreement, or transaction, in each case, that is cleared by a clearing organization;

(G) any combination of the agreements or transactions referred to in this paragraph;

(H) any option to enter into an agreement or transaction referred to in this paragraph;

(I) a master agreement that provides for an agreement or transaction referred to in subparagraph (A), (B), (C), (D), (E), (F), (G), or (H), together with all supplements to such master agreement, without regard to whether the master agreement provides for an agreement or transaction that is not a commodity contract under this paragraph, except that the master agreement shall be considered to be a commodity contract under this paragraph only with respect to each agreement or transaction under the master agreement that is referred to in subparagraph (A), (B), (C), (D), (E), (F), (G), or (H); or

(J) any security agreement or arrangement or other credit enhancement related to any agreement or transaction referred to in this paragraph, including any guarantee or reimbursement obligation by or to a commodity broker or financial participant in connection with any agreement or transaction referred to in this paragraph, but not to exceed the damages in connection with any such agreement or transaction, measured in accordance with section 562;

(5) "commodity option" means agreement or transaction subject to regulation under section 4c(b) of the Act;

(6) "commodity options dealer" means person that extends credit to, or that accepts cash, a security, or other property from, a customer of such person for the purchase or sale of an interest in a commodity option;

(7) "contract market" means a registered entity;

(8) "contract of sale", "commodity", "derivatives clearing organization", "future delivery", "board of trade", "registered entity", and "futures commission merchant" have the meanings assigned to those terms in the Act;

(9) "customer" means—

    (A) with respect to a futures commission merchant—

        (i) entity for or with whom such futures commission merchant deals and that holds a claim against such futures commission merchant on account of a commodity contract made, received, acquired, or held by or through such futures commission merchant in the ordinary course of such futures commission merchant's business as a futures commission merchant from or for a commodity contract account of such entity; or

        (ii) entity that holds a claim against such futures commission merchant arising out of—

            (I) the making, liquidation, or change in the value of a commodity contract of a kind specified in clause (i) of this subparagraph;

            (II) a deposit or payment of cash, a security, or other property with such futures commission merchant for the purpose of making or margining such a commodity contract; or

            (III) the making or taking of delivery on such a commodity contract;

    (B) with respect to a foreign futures commission merchant—

        (i) entity for or with whom such foreign futures commission merchant deals and that holds a claim against such foreign futures commission merchant on account of a commodity contract made, received, acquired, or held by or through such foreign futures commission merchant in the ordinary course of such foreign futures commission merchant's business as a foreign futures commission merchant from or for the foreign futures account of such entity; or

        (ii) entity that holds a claim against such foreign futures commission merchant arising out of—

            (I) the making, liquidation, or change in value of a commodity contract of a kind specified in clause (i) of this subparagraph;

            (II) a deposit or payment of cash, a security, or other property with such foreign futures commission merchant for the purpose of making or margining such a commodity contract; or

            (III) the making or taking of delivery on such a commodity contract;

    (C) with respect to a leverage transaction merchant—

        (i) entity for or with whom such leverage transaction merchant deals and that holds a claim against such leverage transaction merchant on account of a commodity contract engaged in by or with such leverage transaction merchant in the ordinary course of such leverage transaction merchant's business as a leverage transaction merchant from or for the leverage account of such entity; or

        (ii) entity that holds a claim against such leverage transaction merchant arising out of—

            (I) the making, liquidation, or change in value of a commodity contract of a kind specified in clause (i) of this subparagraph;

            (II) a deposit or payment of cash, a security, or other property with such leverage transaction merchant for the purpose of entering into or margining such a commodity contract; or

            (III) the making or taking of delivery on such a commodity contract;

    (D) with respect to a clearing organization, clearing member of such clearing organization with whom such clearing organization deals and that holds a claim against such clearing organization on account of cash, a security, or other property received by such clearing organization to margin, guarantee, or secure a commodity contract in such clearing member's proprietary account or customers' account; or

(E) with respect to a commodity options dealer—

(i) entity for or with whom such commodity options dealer deals and that holds a claim on account of a commodity contract made, received, acquired, or held by or through such commodity options dealer in the ordinary course of such commodity options dealer's business as a commodity options dealer from or for the commodity options account of such entity; or

(ii) entity that holds a claim against such commodity options dealer arising out of—

(I) the making of, liquidation of, exercise of, or a change in value of, a commodity contract of a kind specified in clause (i) of this subparagraph; or

(II) a deposit or payment of cash, a security, or other property with such commodity options dealer for the purpose of making, exercising, or margining such a commodity contract;

(10) "customer property" means cash, a security, or other property, or proceeds of such cash, security, or property, received, acquired, or held by or for the account of the debtor, from or for the account of a customer—

(A) including—

(i) property received, acquired, or held to margin, guarantee, secure, purchase, or sell a commodity contract;

(ii) profits or contractual or other rights accruing to a customer as a result of a commodity contract;

(iii) an open commodity contract;

(iv) specifically identifiable customer property;

(v) warehouse receipt or other document held by the debtor evidencing ownership of or title to property to be delivered to fulfill a commodity contract from or for the account of a customer;

(vi) cash, a security, or other property received by the debtor as payment for a commodity to be delivered to fulfill a commodity contract from or for the account of a customer;

(vii) a security held as property of the debtor to the extent such security is necessary to meet a net equity claim based on a security of the same class and series of an issuer;

(viii) property that was unlawfully converted from and that is the lawful property of the estate; and

(ix) other property of the debtor that any applicable law, rule, or regulation requires to be set aside or held for the benefit of a customer, unless including such property as customer property would not significantly increase customer property; but

(B) not including property to the extent that a customer does not have a claim against the debtor based on such property;

(11) "foreign future" means contract for the purchase or sale of a commodity for future delivery on, or subject to the rules of, a board of trade outside the United States;

(12) "foreign futures commission merchant" means entity engaged in soliciting or accepting orders for the purchase or sale of a foreign future or that, in connection with such a solicitation or acceptance, accepts cash, a security, or other property, or extends credit to margin, guarantee, or secure any trade or contract that results from such a solicitation or acceptance;

(13) "leverage transaction" means agreement that is subject to regulation under section 19 of the Commodity Exchange Act, and that is commonly known to the commodities trade as a margin account, margin contract, leverage account, or leverage contract;

(14) "leverage transaction merchant" means person in the business of engaging in leverage transactions;

(15) "margin payment" means payment or deposit of cash, a security, or other property, that is commonly known to the commodities trade as original margin, initial margin, maintenance margin, or variation margin, including mark-to-market payments, settlement payments, variation payments, daily settlement payments, and final settlement payments made as adjustments to settlement prices;

(16) "member property" means customer property received, acquired, or held by or for the account of a debtor that is a clearing organization, from or for the proprietary account of a customer that is a clearing member of the debtor; and

(17) "net equity" means, subject to such rules and regulations as the Commission promulgates under the Act, with respect to the aggregate of all of a customer's accounts that such customer has in the same capacity—

(A) the balance remaining in such customer's accounts immediately after—

(i) all commodity contracts of such customer have been transferred, liquidated, or become identified for delivery; and

(ii) all obligations of such customer in such capacity to the debtor have been offset; plus

(B) the value, as of the date of return under section 766 of this title, of any specifically identifiable customer property actually returned to such customer before the date specified in subparagraph (A) of this paragraph; plus

(C) the value, as of the date of transfer, of—

(i) any commodity contract to which such customer is entitled that is transferred to another person under section 766 of this title; and

(ii) any cash, security, or other property of such customer transferred to such other person under section 766 of this title to margin or secure such transferred commodity contract.

§762. Notice to the Commission and right to be heard

(a) The clerk shall give the notice required by section 342 of this title to the Commission.

(b) The Commission may raise and may appear and be heard on any issue in a case under this chapter.

§763. Treatment of accounts

(a) Accounts held by the debtor for a particular customer in separate capacities shall be treated as accounts of separate customers.

(b) A member of a clearing organization shall be deemed to hold such member's proprietary account in a separate capacity from such member's customers' account.

(c) The net equity in a customer's account may not be offset against the net equity in the account of any other customer.

§764. Voidable transfers

(a) Except as otherwise provided in this section, any transfer by the debtor of property that, but for such transfer, would have been customer property, may be avoided by the trustee, and such property shall be treated as customer property, if and to the extent that the trustee avoids such transfer under section 544, 545, 547, 548, 549, or 724(a) of this title. For the purpose of such sections, the property so transferred shall be deemed to have been property of the debtor, and, if such transfer was made to a customer or for a customer's benefit, such customer shall be deemed, for the purposes of this section, to have been a creditor.

(b) Notwithstanding sections 544, 545, 547, 548, 549, and 724(a) of this title, the trustee may not avoid a transfer made before seven days after the order for relief, if such transfer is approved by the Commission by rule or order, either before or after such transfer, and if such transfer is—

(1) a transfer of a commodity contract entered into or carried by or through the debtor on behalf of a customer, and of any cash, securities, or other property margining or securing such commodity contract; or

(2) the liquidation of a commodity contract entered into or carried by or through the debtor on behalf of a customer.

§765. Customer instructions

(a) The notice required by section 342 of this title to customers shall instruct each customer—

(1) to file a proof of such customer's claim promptly, and to specify in such claim any specifically identifiable security, property, or commodity contract; and

(2) to instruct the trustee of such customer's desired disposition, including transfer under section 766 of this title or liquidation, of any commodity contract specifically identified to such customer.

(b) The trustee shall comply, to the extent practicable, with any instruction received from a customer regarding such customer's desired disposition of any commodity contract specifically identified to such customer. If the trustee has transferred, under section 766 of this title, such a commodity contract, the trustee shall transmit any such instruction to the commodity broker to whom such commodity contract was so transferred.

§766. Treatment of customer property

(a) The trustee shall answer all margin calls with respect to a specifically identifiable commodity contract of a customer until such time as the trustee returns or transfers such commodity contract, but the trustee may not make a margin payment that has the effect of a distribution to such customer of more than that to which such customer is entitled under subsection (h) or (i) of this section.

(b) The trustee shall prevent any open commodity contract from remaining open after the last day of trading in such commodity contract, or into the first day on which notice of intent to deliver on such commodity contract may be tendered, whichever occurs first. With respect to any commodity contract that has remained open after the last day of trading in such commodity contract or with respect to which delivery must be made or accepted under the rules of the contract market on which such commodity contract was made, the trustee may operate the business of the debtor for the purpose of—

(1) accepting or making tender of notice of intent to deliver the physical commodity underlying such commodity contract;

(2) facilitating delivery of such commodity; or

(3) disposing of such commodity if a party to such commodity contract defaults.

(c) The trustee shall return promptly to a customer any specifically identifiable security, property, or commodity contract to which such customer is entitled, or shall transfer, on such customer's behalf, such security, property, or commodity contract to a commodity broker that is not a debtor under this title, subject to such rules or regulations as the Commission may prescribe, to the extent that the value of such security, property, or commodity contract does not exceed the amount to which such customer would be entitled under subsection (h) or (i) of this section if such security, property, or commodity contract were not returned or transferred under this subsection.

(d) If the value of a specifically identifiable security, property, or commodity contract exceeds the amount to which the customer of the debtor is entitled under subsection (h) or (i) of this section, then such customer to whom such security, property, or commodity contract is specifically identified may deposit cash with the trustee equal to the difference between the value of such security, property, or commodity contract and such amount, and the trustee then shall—

(1) return promptly such security, property, or commodity contract to such customer; or

(2) transfer, on such customer's behalf, such security, property, or commodity contract to a commodity broker that is not a debtor under this title, subject to such rules or regulations as the Commission may prescribe.

(e) Subject to subsection (b) of this section, the trustee shall liquidate any commodity contract that—

(1) is identified to a particular customer and with respect to which such customer has not timely instructed the trustee as to the desired disposition of such commodity contract;

(2) cannot be transferred under subsection (c) of this section; or

(3) cannot be identified to a particular customer.

(f) As soon as practicable after the commencement of the case, the trustee shall reduce to money, consistent with good market practice, all securities and other property, other than commodity contracts, held as property of the estate, except for specifically identifiable securities or property

distributable under subsection (h) or (i) of this section.

(g) The trustee may not distribute a security or other property except under subsection (h) or (i) of this section.

(h) Except as provided in subsection (b) of this section, the trustee shall distribute customer property ratably to customers on the basis and to the extent of such customers' allowed net equity claims, and in priority to all other claims, except claims of a kind specified in section 507(a)(2) of this title that are attributable to the administration of customer property. Such distribution shall be in the form of—

(1) cash;

(2) the return or transfer, under subsection (c) or (d) of this section, of specifically identifiable customer securities, property, or commodity contracts; or

(3) payment of margin calls under subsection (a) of this section.

Notwithstanding any other provision of this subsection, a customer net equity claim based on a proprietary account, as defined by Commission rule, regulation, or order, may not be paid either in whole or in part, directly or indirectly, out of customer property unless all other customer net equity claims have been paid in full.

(i) If the debtor is a clearing organization, the trustee shall distribute—

(1) customer property, other than member property, ratably to customers on the basis and to the extent of such customers' allowed net equity claims based on such customers' accounts other than proprietary accounts, and in priority to all other claims, except claims of a kind specified in section 507(a)(2) of this title that are attributable to the administration of such customer property; and

(2) member property ratably to customers on the basis and to the extent of such customers' allowed net equity claims based on such customers' proprietary accounts, and in priority to all other claims, except claims of a kind specified in section 507(a)(2) of this title that are attributable to the administration of member property or customer property.

(j)

(1) The trustee shall distribute customer property in excess of that distributed under subsection (h) or (i) of this section in accordance with section 726 of this title.

(2) Except as provided in section 510 of this title, if a customer is not paid the full amount of such customer's allowed net equity claim from customer property, the unpaid portion of

such claim is a claim entitled to distribution under section 726 of this title.

§767. Commodity broker liquidation and forward contract merchants, commodity brokers, stockbrokers, financial institutions, financial participants, securities clearing agencies, swap participants, repo participants, and master netting agreement participants

Notwithstanding any other provision of this title, the exercise of rights by a forward contract merchant, commodity broker, stockbroker, financial institution, financial participant, securities clearing agency, swap participant, repo participant, or master netting agreement participant under this title shall not affect the priority of any unsecured claim it may have after the exercise of such rights.

SUBCHAPTER V—CLEARING BANK LIQUIDATION

§781. Definitions

For purposes of this subchapter, the following definitions shall apply:

(1) Board.—The term "Board" means the Board of Governors of the Federal Reserve System.

(2) Depository institution.—The term "depository institution" has the same meaning as in section 3 of the Federal Deposit Insurance Act.

(3) Clearing bank.—The term "clearing bank" means an uninsured State member bank, or a corporation organized under section 25A of the Federal Reserve Act, which operates, or operates as, a multilateral clearing organization pursuant to section 409 of the Federal Deposit Insurance Corporation Improvement Act of 1991.

§782. Selection of trustee

(a) In General.—

    (1) Appointment.—Notwithstanding any other provision of this title, the conservator or receiver who files the petition shall be the trustee under this chapter, unless the Board designates an alternative trustee.

    (2) Successor.—The Board may designate a successor trustee if required.

(b) Authority of Trustee.—Whenever the Board appoints or designates a trustee, chapter 3 and sections 704 and 705 of this title shall apply to the Board in the same way and to the same extent that they apply to a United States trustee.

§783. Additional powers of trustee

(a) Distribution of Property Not of the Estate.—The trustee under this subchapter has power to distribute property not of the estate, including distributions to customers that are mandated by subchapters III and IV of this chapter.

(b) Disposition of Institution.—The trustee under this subchapter may, after notice and a hearing—

    (1) sell the clearing bank to a depository institution or consortium of depository institutions (which consortium may agree on the allocation of the clearing bank among the consortium);

    (2) merge the clearing bank with a depository institution;

    (3) transfer contracts to the same extent as could a receiver for a depository institution under paragraphs (9) and (10) of section 11(e) of the Federal Deposit Insurance Act;

    (4) transfer assets or liabilities to a depository institution; and

    (5) transfer assets and liabilities to a bridge depository institution as provided in paragraphs (1), (3)(A), (5), and (6) of section 11(n) of the Federal Deposit Insurance Act, paragraphs (9) through (13) of such section, and subparagraphs (A) through (H) and subparagraph (K) of paragraph (4) of such section 11(n), except that—

        (A) the bridge depository institution to which such assets or liabilities are transferred shall be treated as a clearing bank for the purpose of this subsection; and

        (B) any references in any such provision of law to the Federal Deposit Insurance Corporation shall be construed to be references to the appointing agency and that references to deposit insurance shall be omitted.

(c) Certain Transfers Included.—Any reference in this section to transfers of liabilities includes a ratable transfer of liabilities within a priority class.

§784. Right to be heard

The Board or a Federal reserve bank (in the case of a clearing bank that is a member of that bank) may raise and may appear and be heard on any issue in a case under this subchapter.

CHAPTER 9—ADJUSTMENT OF DEBTS OF A MUNICIPALITY

SUBCHAPTER I—GENERAL PROVISIONS

§901. Applicability of other sections of this title

(a) Sections 301, 333, 344, 347(b), 349, 350(b) 351,,[1] 361, 362, 364(c), 364(d), 364(e), 364(f), 365, 366, 501, 502, 503, 504, 506, 507(a)(2), 509, 510, 524(a)(1), 524(a)(2), 544, 545, 546, 547, 548, 549(a), 549(c), 549(d), 550, 551, 552, 553, 555, 556, 557, 559, 560, 561, 562, 1102, 1103, 1109, 1111(b), 1122, 1123(a)(1), 1123(a)(2), 1123(a)(3), 1123(a)(4), 1123(a)(5), 1123(b), 1123(d), 1124, 1125, 1126(a), 1126(b), 1126(c), 1126(e), 1126(f), 1126(g), 1127(d), 1128, 1129(a)(2), 1129(a)(3), 1129(a)(6), 1129(a)(8), 1129(a)(10), 1129(b)(1), 1129(b)(2)(A), 1129(b)(2)(B), 1142(b), 1143, 1144, and 1145 of this title apply in a case under this chapter.

(b) A term used in a section of this title made applicable in a case under this chapter by subsection (a) of this section or section 103(e) of this title has the meaning defined for such term for the purpose of such applicable section, unless such term is otherwise defined in section 902 of this title.

(c) A section made applicable in a case under this chapter by subsection (a) of this section that is operative if the business of the debtor is authorized to be operated is operative in a case under this chapter.

---

[1] So in original. The second comma probably should follow "350(b)".

§902. Definitions for this chapter

In this chapter—

(1) "property of the estate", when used in a section that is made applicable in a case under this chapter by section 103(e) or 901 of this title, means property of the debtor;

(2) "special revenues" means—

    (A) receipts derived from the ownership, operation, or disposition of projects or systems of the debtor that are primarily used or intended to be used primarily to provide transportation, utility, or other services, including the proceeds of borrowings to finance the projects or systems;

    (B) special excise taxes imposed on particular activities or transactions;

    (C) incremental tax receipts from the benefited area in the case of tax-increment financing;

    (D) other revenues or receipts derived from particular functions of the debtor, whether or not the debtor has other functions; or

    (E) taxes specifically levied to finance one or more projects or systems, excluding receipts from general property, sales, or income taxes (other than tax-increment financing) levied to finance the general purposes of the debtor;

(3) "special tax payer" means record owner or holder of legal or equitable title to real property against which a special assessment or special tax has been levied the proceeds of which are the sole source of payment of an obligation issued by the debtor to defray the cost of an improvement relating to such real property;

(4) "special tax payer affected by the plan" means special tax payer with respect to whose real property the plan proposes to increase the proportion of special assessments or special taxes referred to in paragraph (2) of this section assessed against such real property; and

(5) "trustee", when used in a section that is made applicable in a case under this chapter by section 103(e) or 901 of this title, means debtor, except as provided in section 926 of this title.

§903. Reservation of State power to control municipalities

This chapter does not limit or impair the power of a State to control, by legislation or otherwise, a municipality of or in such State in the exercise of the political or governmental powers of such municipality, including expenditures for such exercise, but—

    (1) a State law prescribing a method of composition of indebtedness of such municipality may not bind any creditor that does not consent to such composition; and

    (2) a judgment entered under such a law may not bind a creditor that does not consent to such composition.

§904. Limitation on jurisdiction and powers of court

Notwithstanding any power of the court, unless the debtor consents or the plan so provides, the court may not, by any stay, order, or decree, in the case or otherwise, interfere with—

    (1) any of the political or governmental powers of the debtor;

    (2) any of the property or revenues of the debtor; or

(3) the debtor's use or enjoyment of any income-producing property.

SUBCHAPTER II—ADMINISTRATION

§921. Petition and proceedings relating to petition

(a) Notwithstanding sections 109(d) and 301 of this title, a case under this chapter concerning an unincorporated tax or special assessment district that does not have such district's own officials is commenced by the filing under section 301 of this title of a petition under this chapter by such district's governing authority or the board or body having authority to levy taxes or assessments to meet the obligations of such district.

(b) The chief judge of the court of appeals for the circuit embracing the district in which the case is commenced shall designate the bankruptcy judge to conduct the case.

(c) After any objection to the petition, the court, after notice and a hearing, may dismiss the petition if the debtor did not file the petition in good faith or if the petition does not meet the requirements of this title.

(d) If the petition is not dismissed under subsection (c) of this section, the court shall order relief under this chapter notwithstanding section 301(b).

(e) The court may not, on account of an appeal from an order for relief, delay any proceeding under this chapter in the case in which the appeal is being taken; nor shall any court order a stay of such proceeding pending such appeal. The reversal on appeal of a finding of jurisdiction does not affect the validity of any debt incurred that is authorized by the court under section 364(c) or 364(d) of this title.

§922. Automatic stay of enforcement of claims against the debtor

(a) A petition filed under this chapter operates as a stay, in addition to the stay provided by section 362 of this title, applicable to all entities, of—

(1) the commencement or continuation, including the issuance or employment of process, of a judicial, administrative, or other action or proceeding against an officer or inhabitant of the debtor that seeks to enforce a claim against the debtor; and

(2) the enforcement of a lien on or arising out of taxes or assessments owed to the debtor.

(b) Subsections (c), (d), (e), (f), and (g) of section 362 of this title apply to a stay under subsection (a) of this section the same as such subsections apply to a stay under section 362(a) of this title.

(c) If the debtor provides, under section 362, 364, or 922 of this title, adequate protection of the interest of the holder of a claim secured by a lien on property of the debtor and if, notwithstanding such protection such creditor has a claim arising from the stay of action against such property under section 362 or 922 of this title or from the granting of a lien under section 364(d) of this title, then such claim shall be allowable as an administrative expense under section 503(b) of this title.

(d) Notwithstanding section 362 of this title and subsection (a) of this section, a petition filed under this chapter does not operate as a stay of application of pledged special revenues in a manner consistent with section 927 of this title to payment of indebtedness secured by such revenues.

§923. Notice

There shall be given notice of the commencement of a case under this chapter, notice of an order for relief under this chapter, and notice of the dismissal of a case under this chapter. Such notice shall also be published at least once a week for three successive weeks in at least one newspaper of general circulation published within the district in which the case is commenced, and in such other newspaper having a general circulation among bond dealers and bondholders as the court designates.

§924. List of creditors

The debtor shall file a list of creditors.

§925. Effect of list of claims

A proof of claim is deemed filed under section 501 of this title for any claim that appears in the list filed under section 924 of this title, except a claim that is listed as disputed, contingent, or unliquidated.

§926. Avoiding powers

(a) If the debtor refuses to pursue a cause of action under section 544, 545, 547, 548, 549(a), or 550 of this title, then on request of a creditor, the court may appoint a trustee to pursue such cause of action.

(b) A transfer of property of the debtor to or for the benefit of any holder of a bond or note, on account of such bond or note, may not be avoided under section 547 of this title.

§927. Limitation on recourse

The holder of a claim payable solely from special revenues of the debtor under applicable nonbankruptcy law shall not be treated as having recourse against the debtor on account of such claim pursuant to section 1111(b) of this title.

§928. Post petition effect of security interest

(a) Notwithstanding section 552(a) of this title and subject to subsection (b) of this section, special revenues acquired by the debtor after the commencement of the case shall remain subject to any lien resulting from any security agreement entered into by the debtor before the commencement of the case.

(b) Any such lien on special revenues, other than municipal betterment assessments, derived from a project or system shall be subject to the necessary operating expenses of such project or system, as the case may be.

§929. Municipal leases

A lease to a municipality shall not be treated as an executory contract or unexpired lease for the purposes of section 365 or 502(b)(6) of this title solely by reason of its being subject to termination in the event the debtor fails to appropriate rent.

§930. Dismissal

(a) After notice and a hearing, the court may dismiss a case under this chapter for cause, including—

    (1) want of prosecution;

    (2) unreasonable delay by the debtor that is prejudicial to creditors;

    (3) failure to propose a plan within the time fixed under section 941 of this title;

    (4) if a plan is not accepted within any time fixed by the court;

    (5) denial of confirmation of a plan under section 943(b) of this title and denial of additional time for filing another plan or a modification of a plan; or

    (6) if the court has retained jurisdiction after confirmation of a plan—

        (A) material default by the debtor with respect to a term of such plan; or

        (B) termination of such plan by reason of the occurrence of a condition specified in such plan.

(b) The court shall dismiss a case under this chapter if confirmation of a plan under this chapter is refused.

SUBCHAPTER III—THE PLAN

§941. Filing of plan

The debtor shall file a plan for the adjustment of the debtor's debts. If such a plan is not filed with the petition, the debtor shall file such a plan at such later time as the court fixes.

§942. Modification of plan

The debtor may modify the plan at any time before confirmation, but may not modify the plan so that the plan as modified fails to meet the requirements of this chapter. After the debtor files a modification, the plan as modified becomes the plan.

§943. Confirmation

(a) A special tax payer may object to confirmation of a plan.

(b) The court shall confirm the plan if—

    (1) the plan complies with the provisions of this title made applicable by sections 103(e) and 901 of this title;

    (2) the plan complies with the provisions of this chapter;

    (3) all amounts to be paid by the debtor or by any person for services or expenses in the case or incident to the plan have been fully disclosed and are reasonable;

    (4) the debtor is not prohibited by law from taking any action necessary to carry out the plan;

    (5) except to the extent that the holder of a particular claim has agreed to a different treatment of such claim, the plan provides that on the effective date of the plan each holder of a claim of a kind specified in section 507(a)(2) of this title will receive on account of such claim cash equal to the allowed amount of such claim;

    (6) any regulatory or electoral approval necessary under applicable nonbankruptcy law in order to carry out any provision of the plan has been obtained, or such provision is expressly conditioned on such approval; and

    (7) the plan is in the best interests of creditors and is feasible.

§944. Effect of confirmation

(a) The provisions of a confirmed plan bind the debtor and any creditor, whether or not—

(1) a proof of such creditor's claim is filed or deemed filed under section 501 of this title;

(2) such claim is allowed under section 502 of this title; or

(3) such creditor has accepted the plan.

(b) Except as provided in subsection (c) of this section, the debtor is discharged from all debts as of the time when—

(1) the plan is confirmed;

(2) the debtor deposits any consideration to be distributed under the plan with a disbursing agent appointed by the court; and

(3) the court has determined—

(A) that any security so deposited will constitute, after distribution, a valid legal obligation of the debtor; and

(B) that any provision made to pay or secure payment of such obligation is valid.

(c) The debtor is not discharged under subsection (b) of this section from any debt—

(1) excepted from discharge by the plan or order confirming the plan; or

(2) owed to an entity that, before confirmation of the plan, had neither notice nor actual knowledge of the case.

§945. Continuing jurisdiction and closing of the case

(a) The court may retain jurisdiction over the case for such period of time as is necessary for the successful implementation of the plan.

(b) Except as provided in subsection (a) of this section, the court shall close the case when administration of the case has been completed.

§946. Effect of exchange of securities before the date of the filing of the petition

The exchange of a new security under the plan for a claim covered by the plan, whether such exchange occurred before or after the date of the filing of the petition, does not limit or impair the effectiveness of the plan or of any provision of this chapter. The amount and number specified in section 1126(c) of this title include the amount and number of claims formerly held by a creditor that has participated in any such exchange.

CHAPTER 11—REORGANIZATION

SUBCHAPTER I—OFFICERS AND ADMINISTRATION

§1101. Definitions for this chapter

In this chapter—

(1) "debtor in possession" means debtor except when a person that has qualified under section 322 of this title is serving as trustee in the case;

(2) "substantial consummation" means—

(A) transfer of all or substantially all of the property proposed by the plan to be transferred;

(B) assumption by the debtor or by the successor to the debtor under the plan of the business or of the management of all or substantially all of the property dealt with by the plan; and

(C) commencement of distribution under the plan.

§1102. Creditors' and equity security holders' committees

(a)

(1) Except as provided in paragraph (3), as soon as practicable after the order for relief under chapter 11 of this title, the United States trustee shall appoint a committee of creditors holding unsecured claims and may appoint additional committees of creditors or of equity security holders as the United States trustee deems appropriate.

(2) On request of a party in interest, the court may order the appointment of additional committees of creditors or of equity security holders if necessary to assure adequate representation of creditors or of equity security holders. The United States trustee shall appoint any such committee.

(3) On request of a party in interest in a case in which the debtor is a small business debtor and for cause, the court may order that a committee of creditors not be appointed.

(4) On request of a party in interest and after notice and a hearing, the court may order the United States trustee to change the membership of a committee appointed under this subsection, if the court determines that the change is necessary to ensure adequate representation of creditors or equity security holders. The court may order the United States trustee to increase the number of members of a committee to include a creditor that is a small business concern (as described in section

3(a)(1) of the Small Business Act), if the court determines that the creditor holds claims (of the kind represented by the committee) the aggregate amount of which, in comparison to the annual gross revenue of that creditor, is disproportionately large.

(b)

(1) A committee of creditors appointed under subsection (a) of this section shall ordinarily consist of the persons, willing to serve, that hold the seven largest claims against the debtor of the kinds represented on such committee, or of the members of a committee organized by creditors before the commencement of the case under this chapter, if such committee was fairly chosen and is representative of the different kinds of claims to be represented.

(2) A committee of equity security holders appointed under subsection (a)(2) of this section shall ordinarily consist of the persons, willing to serve, that hold the seven largest amounts of equity securities of the debtor of the kinds represented on such committee.

(3) A committee appointed under subsection (a) shall—

(A) provide access to information for creditors who—

(i) hold claims of the kind represented by that committee; and

(ii) are not appointed to the committee;

(B) solicit and receive comments from the creditors described in subparagraph (A); and

(C) be subject to a court order that compels any additional report or disclosure to be made to the creditors described in subparagraph (A).

§1103. Powers and duties of committees

(a) At a scheduled meeting of a committee appointed under section 1102 of this title, at which a majority of the members of such committee are present, and with the court's approval, such committee may select and authorize the employment by such committee of one or more attorneys, accountants, or other agents, to represent or perform services for such committee.

(b) An attorney or accountant employed to represent a committee appointed under section 1102 of this title may not, while employed by such committee, represent any other entity having an adverse interest in connection with the case. Representation of one or more creditors of the same class as represented by the committee shall not per se constitute the representation of an adverse interest.

(c) A committee appointed under section 1102 of this title may—

(1) consult with the trustee or debtor in possession concerning the administration of the case;

(2) investigate the acts, conduct, assets, liabilities, and financial condition of the debtor, the operation of the debtor's business and the desirability of the continuance of such business, and any other matter relevant to the case or to the formulation of a plan;

(3) participate in the formulation of a plan, advise those represented by such committee of such committee's determinations as to any plan formulated, and collect and file with the court acceptances or rejections of a plan;

(4) request the appointment of a trustee or examiner under section 1104 of this title; and

(5) perform such other services as are in the interest of those represented.

(d) As soon as practicable after the appointment of a committee under section 1102 of this title, the trustee shall meet with such committee to transact such business as may be necessary and proper.

§1104. Appointment of trustee or examiner

(a) At any time after the commencement of the case but before confirmation of a plan, on request of a party in interest or the United States trustee, and after notice and a hearing, the court shall order the appointment of a trustee—

(1) for cause, including fraud, dishonesty, incompetence, or gross mismanagement of the affairs of the debtor by current management, either before or after the commencement of the case, or similar cause, but not including the number of holders of securities of the debtor or the amount of assets or liabilities of the debtor; or

(2) if such appointment is in the interests of creditors, any equity security holders, and other interests of the estate, without regard to the number of holders of securities of the debtor or the amount of assets or liabilities of the debtor.

(b)

(1) Except as provided in section 1163 of this title, on the request of a party in interest made not later than 30 days after the court orders the appointment of a trustee under subsection (a), the United States trustee shall convene a meeting of creditors for the purpose of electing one disinterested person to serve as trustee in the case. The election of a trustee shall be conducted in the manner provided in subsections (a), (b), and (c) of section 702 of this title.

(2)

    (A) If an eligible, disinterested trustee is elected at a meeting of creditors under paragraph (1), the United States trustee shall file a report certifying that election.

    (B) Upon the filing of a report under subparagraph (A)—

        (i) the trustee elected under paragraph (1) shall be considered to have been selected and appointed for purposes of this section; and

        (ii) the service of any trustee appointed under subsection (a) shall terminate.

    (C) The court shall resolve any dispute arising out of an election described in subparagraph (A).

(c) If the court does not order the appointment of a trustee under this section, then at any time before the confirmation of a plan, on request of a party in interest or the United States trustee, and after notice and a hearing, the court shall order the appointment of an examiner to conduct such an investigation of the debtor as is appropriate, including an investigation of any allegations of fraud, dishonesty, incompetence, misconduct, mismanagement, or irregularity in the management of the affairs of the debtor of or by current or former management of the debtor, if—

    (1) such appointment is in the interests of creditors, any equity security holders, and other interests of the estate; or

    (2) the debtor's fixed, liquidated, unsecured debts, other than debts for goods, services, or taxes, or owing to an insider, exceed $5,000,000.

(d) If the court orders the appointment of a trustee or an examiner, if a trustee or an examiner dies or resigns during the case or is removed under section 324 of this title, or if a trustee fails to qualify under section 322 of this title, then the United States trustee, after consultation with parties in interest, shall appoint, subject to the court's approval, one disinterested person other than the United States trustee to serve as trustee or examiner, as the case may be, in the case.

(e) The United States trustee shall move for the appointment of a trustee under subsection (a) if there are reasonable grounds to suspect that current members of the governing body of the debtor, the debtor's chief executive or chief financial officer, or members of the governing body who selected the debtor's chief executive or chief financial officer, participated in actual fraud, dishonesty, or criminal conduct in the management of the debtor or the debtor's public financial reporting.

§1105. Termination of trustee's appointment

At any time before confirmation of a plan, on request of a party in interest or the United States trustee, and after notice and a hearing, the court may terminate the trustee's appointment and restore the debtor to possession and management of the property of the estate and of the operation of the debtor's business.

§1106. Duties of trustee and examiner

(a) A trustee shall—

    (1) perform the duties of the trustee, as specified in paragraphs (2), (5), (7), (8), (9), (10), (11), and (12) of section 704(a);

    (2) if the debtor has not done so, file the list, schedule, and statement required under section 521(a)(1) of this title;

    (3) except to the extent that the court orders otherwise, investigate the acts, conduct, assets, liabilities, and financial condition of the debtor, the operation of the debtor's business and the desirability of the continuance of such business, and any other matter relevant to the case or to the formulation of a plan;

    (4) as soon as practicable—

        (A) file a statement of any investigation conducted under paragraph (3) of this subsection, including any fact ascertained pertaining to fraud, dishonesty, incompetence, misconduct, mismanagement, or irregularity in the management of the affairs of the debtor, or to a cause of action available to the estate; and

        (B) transmit a copy or a summary of any such statement to any creditors' committee or equity security holders' committee, to any indenture trustee, and to such other entity as the court designates;

    (5) as soon as practicable, file a plan under section 1121 of this title, file a report of why the trustee will not file a plan, or recommend conversion of the case to a case under chapter 7, 12, or 13 of this title or dismissal of the case;

    (6) for any year for which the debtor has not filed a tax return required by law, furnish, without personal liability, such information as may be required by the governmental unit with which such tax return was to be filed, in light of the condition of the debtor's books and records and the availability of such information;

(7) after confirmation of a plan, file such reports as are necessary or as the court orders; and

(8) if with respect to the debtor there is a claim for a domestic support obligation, provide the applicable notice specified in subsection (c).

(b) An examiner appointed under section 1104(d) of this title shall perform the duties specified in paragraphs (3) and (4) of subsection (a) of this section, and, except to the extent that the court orders otherwise, any other duties of the trustee that the court orders the debtor in possession not to perform.

(c)

(1) In a case described in subsection (a)(8) to which subsection (a)(8) applies, the trustee shall—

(A)

(i) provide written notice to the holder of the claim described in subsection (a)(8) of such claim and of the right of such holder to use the services of the State child support enforcement agency established under sections 464 and 466 of the Social Security Act for the State in which such holder resides, for assistance in collecting child support during and after the case under this title; and

(ii) include in the notice required by clause (i) the address and telephone number of such State child support enforcement agency;

(B)

(i) provide written notice to such State child support enforcement agency of such claim; and

(ii) include in the notice required by clause (i) the name, address, and telephone number of such holder; and

(C) at such time as the debtor is granted a discharge under section 1141, provide written notice to such holder and to such State child support enforcement agency of—

(i) the granting of the discharge;

(ii) the last recent known address of the debtor;

(iii) the last recent known name and address of the debtor's employer; and

(iv) the name of each creditor that holds a claim that—

(I) is not discharged under paragraph (2), (4), or (14A) of section 523(a); or

(II) was reaffirmed by the debtor under section 524(c).

(2)

(A) The holder of a claim described in subsection (a)(8) or the State child enforcement support agency of the State in which such holder resides may request from a creditor described in paragraph (1)(C)(iv) the last known address of the debtor.

(B) Notwithstanding any other provision of law, a creditor that makes a disclosure of a last known address of a debtor in connection with a request made under subparagraph (A) shall not be liable by reason of making such disclosure.

§1107. Rights, powers, and duties of debtor in possession

(a) Subject to any limitations on a trustee serving in a case under this chapter, and to such limitations or conditions as the court prescribes, a debtor in possession shall have all the rights, other than the right to compensation under section 330 of this title, and powers, and shall perform all the functions and duties, except the duties specified in sections 1106(a)(2), (3), and (4) of this title, of a trustee serving in a case under this chapter.

(b) Notwithstanding section 327(a) of this title, a person is not disqualified for employment under section 327 of this title by a debtor in possession solely because of such person's employment by or representation of the debtor before the commencement of the case.

§1108. Authorization to operate business

Unless the court, on request of a party in interest and after notice and a hearing, orders otherwise, the trustee may operate the debtor's business.

§1109. Right to be heard

(a) The Securities and Exchange Commission may raise and may appear and be heard on any issue in a case under this chapter, but the Securities and Exchange Commission may not appeal from any judgment, order, or decree entered in the case.

(b) A party in interest, including the debtor, the trustee, a creditors' committee, an equity security holders' committee, a creditor, an equity security holder, or any indenture trustee, may raise and may appear and be heard on any issue in a case under this chapter.

§1110. Aircraft equipment and vessels

(a)

(1) Except as provided in paragraph (2) and subject to subsection (b), the right of a secured party with a security interest in equipment described in paragraph (3), or of a lessor or conditional vendor of such equipment, to take possession of such equipment in compliance with a security agreement, lease, or conditional sale contract, and to enforce any of its other rights or remedies, under such security agreement, lease, or conditional sale contract, to sell, lease, or otherwise retain or dispose of such equipment, is not limited or otherwise affected by any other provision of this title or by any power of the court.

(2) The right to take possession and to enforce the other rights and remedies described in paragraph (1) shall be subject to section 362 if—

(A) before the date that is 60 days after the date of the order for relief under this chapter, the trustee, subject to the approval of the court, agrees to perform all obligations of the debtor under such security agreement, lease, or conditional sale contract; and

(B) any default, other than a default of a kind specified in section 365(b)(2), under such security agreement, lease, or conditional sale contract—

(i) that occurs before the date of the order is cured before the expiration of such 60-day period;

(ii) that occurs after the date of the order and before the expiration of such 60-day period is cured before the later of—

(I) the date that is 30 days after the date of the default; or

(II) the expiration of such 60-day period; and

(iii) that occurs on or after the expiration of such 60-day period is cured in compliance with the terms of such security agreement, lease, or conditional sale contract, if a cure is permitted under that agreement, lease, or contract.

(3) The equipment described in this paragraph—

(A) is—

(i) an aircraft, aircraft engine, propeller, appliance, or spare part (as defined in section 40102 of title 49) that is subject to a security interest granted by, leased to, or conditionally sold to a debtor that, at the time such transaction is entered into, holds an air carrier operating certificate issued pursuant to chapter 447 of title 49 for aircraft capable of carrying 10 or more individuals or 6,000 pounds or more of cargo; or

(ii) a vessel documented under chapter 121 of title 46 that is subject to a security interest granted by, leased to, or conditionally sold to a debtor that is a water carrier that, at the time such transaction is entered into, holds a certificate of public convenience and necessity or permit issued by the Department of Transportation; and

(B) includes all records and documents relating to such equipment that are required, under the terms of the security agreement, lease, or conditional sale contract, to be surrendered or returned by the debtor in connection with the surrender or return of such equipment.

(4) Paragraph (1) applies to a secured party, lessor, or conditional vendor acting in its own behalf or acting as trustee or otherwise in behalf of another party.

(b) The trustee and the secured party, lessor, or conditional vendor whose right to take possession is protected under subsection (a) may agree, subject to the approval of the court, to extend the 60-day period specified in subsection (a)(1).

(c)

(1) In any case under this chapter, the trustee shall immediately surrender and return to a secured party, lessor, or conditional vendor, described in subsection (a)(1), equipment described in subsection (a)(3), if at any time after the date of the order for relief under this chapter such secured party, lessor, or conditional vendor is entitled pursuant to subsection (a)(1) to take possession of such equipment and makes a written demand for such possession to the trustee.

(2) At such time as the trustee is required under paragraph (1) to surrender and return equipment described in subsection (a)(3), any lease of such equipment, and any security agreement or conditional sale contract relating to such equipment, if such security agreement or conditional sale contract is an executory contract, shall be deemed rejected.

(d) With respect to equipment first placed in service on or before October 22, 1994, for purposes of this section—

(1) the term "lease" includes any written agreement with respect to which the lessor and the debtor, as lessee, have expressed in the agreement or in a substantially contemporaneous writing that the agreement is to be treated as a lease for Federal income tax purposes; and

(2) the term "security interest" means a purchase-money equipment security interest.

§1111. Claims and interests

(a) A proof of claim or interest is deemed filed under section 501 of this title for any claim or interest that appears in the schedules filed under section 521(a)(1) or 1106(a)(2) of this title, except a claim or interest that is scheduled as disputed, contingent, or unliquidated.

(b)

(1)

(A) A claim secured by a lien on property of the estate shall be allowed or disallowed under section 502 of this title the same as if the holder of such claim had recourse against the debtor on account of such claim, whether or not such holder has such recourse, unless—

(i) the class of which such claim is a part elects, by at least two-thirds in amount and more than half in number of allowed claims of such class, application of paragraph (2) of this subsection; or

(ii) such holder does not have such recourse and such property is sold under section 363 of this title or is to be sold under the plan.

(B) A class of claims may not elect application of paragraph (2) of this subsection if—

(i) the interest on account of such claims of the holders of such claims in such property is of inconsequential value; or

(ii) the holder of a claim of such class has recourse against the debtor on account of such claim and such property is sold under section 363 of this title or is to be sold under the plan.

(2) If such an election is made, then notwithstanding section 506(a) of this title, such claim is a secured claim to the extent that such claim is allowed.

§1112. Conversion or dismissal

(a) The debtor may convert a case under this chapter to a case under chapter 7 of this title unless—

(1) the debtor is not a debtor in possession;

(2) the case originally was commenced as an involuntary case under this chapter; or

(3) the case was converted to a case under this chapter other than on the debtor's request.

(b)

(1) Except as provided in paragraph (2) and subsection (c), on request of a party in interest, and after notice and a hearing, the court shall convert a case under this chapter to a case under chapter 7 or dismiss a case under this chapter, whichever is in the best interests of creditors and the estate, for cause unless the court determines that the appointment under section 1104(a) of a trustee or an examiner is in the best interests of creditors and the estate.

(2) The court may not convert a case under this chapter to a case under chapter 7 or dismiss a case under this chapter if the court finds and specifically identifies unusual circumstances establishing that converting or dismissing the case is not in the best interests of creditors and the estate, and the debtor or any other party in interest establishes that—

(A) there is a reasonable likelihood that a plan will be confirmed within the timeframes established in sections 1121(e) and 1129(e) of this title, or if such sections do not apply, within a reasonable period of time; and

(B) the grounds for converting or dismissing the case include an act or omission of the debtor other than under paragraph (4)(A)—

(i) for which there exists a reasonable justification for the act or omission; and

(ii) that will be cured within a reasonable period of time fixed by the court.

(3) The court shall commence the hearing on a motion under this subsection not later than 30 days after filing of the motion, and shall decide the motion not later than 15 days after commencement of such hearing, unless the movant expressly consents to a continuance for a specific period of time or compelling circumstances prevent the court from meeting the time limits established by this paragraph.

(4) For purposes of this subsection, the term "cause" includes—

(A) substantial or continuing loss to or diminution of the estate and the absence of a reasonable likelihood of rehabilitation;

(B) gross mismanagement of the estate;

(C) failure to maintain appropriate insurance that poses a risk to the estate or to the public;

(D) unauthorized use of cash collateral substantially harmful to 1 or more creditors;

(E) failure to comply with an order of the court;

(F) unexcused failure to satisfy timely any filing or reporting requirement established by this title or by any rule applicable to a case under this chapter;

(G) failure to attend the meeting of creditors convened under section 341(a) or an examination ordered under rule 2004 of the Federal Rules of Bankruptcy Procedure without good cause shown by the debtor;

(H) failure timely to provide information or attend meetings reasonably requested by the United States trustee (or the bankruptcy administrator, if any);

(I) failure timely to pay taxes owed after the date of the order for relief or to file tax returns due after the date of the order for relief;

(J) failure to file a disclosure statement, or to file or confirm a plan, within the time fixed by this title or by order of the court;

(K) failure to pay any fees or charges required under chapter 123 of title 28;

(L) revocation of an order of confirmation under section 1144;

(M) inability to effectuate substantial consummation of a confirmed plan;

(N) material default by the debtor with respect to a confirmed plan;

(O) termination of a confirmed plan by reason of the occurrence of a condition specified in the plan; and

(P) failure of the debtor to pay any domestic support obligation that first becomes payable after the date of the filing of the petition.

(c) The court may not convert a case under this chapter to a case under chapter 7 of this title if the debtor is a farmer or a corporation that is not a moneyed, business, or commercial corporation, unless the debtor requests such conversion.

(d) The court may convert a case under this chapter to a case under chapter 12 or 13 of this title only if—

(1) the debtor requests such conversion;

(2) the debtor has not been discharged under section 1141(d) of this title; and

(3) if the debtor requests conversion to chapter 12 of this title, such conversion is equitable.

(e) Except as provided in subsections (c) and (f), the court, on request of the United States trustee, may convert a case under this chapter to a case under chapter 7 of this title or may dismiss a case under this chapter, whichever is in the best interest of creditors and the estate if the debtor in a voluntary case fails to file, within fifteen days after the filing of the petition commencing such case or such additional time as the court may allow, the information required by paragraph (1) of section 521(a), including a list containing the names and addresses of the holders of the twenty largest unsecured claims (or of all unsecured claims if there are fewer than twenty unsecured claims), and the approximate dollar amounts of each of such claims.

(f) Notwithstanding any other provision of this section, a case may not be converted to a case under another chapter of this title unless the debtor may be a debtor under such chapter.

§1113. Rejection of collective bargaining agreements

(a) The debtor in possession, or the trustee if one has been appointed under the provisions of this chapter, other than a trustee in a case covered by subchapter IV of this chapter and by title I of the Railway Labor Act, may assume or reject a collective bargaining agreement only in accordance with the provisions of this section.

(b)

(1) Subsequent to filing a petition and prior to filing an application seeking rejection of a collective bargaining agreement, the debtor in possession or trustee (hereinafter in this section "trustee" shall include a debtor in possession), shall—

(A) make a proposal to the authorized representative of the employees covered by such agreement, based on the most complete and reliable information available at the time of such proposal, which provides for those necessary modifications in the employees benefits and protections that are necessary to permit the reorganization of the debtor and assures that all creditors, the debtor and all of the affected parties are treated fairly and equitably; and

(B) provide, subject to subsection (d)(3), the representative of the employees with such relevant information as is necessary to evaluate the proposal.

(2) During the period beginning on the date of the making of a proposal provided for in paragraph (1) and ending on the date of the hearing provided for in subsection (d)(1), the trustee shall meet, at reasonable times, with the authorized representative to confer in good faith in attempting to reach mutually satisfactory modifications of such agreement.

(c) The court shall approve an application for rejection of a collective bargaining agreement only if the court finds that—

    (1) the trustee has, prior to the hearing, made a proposal that fulfills the requirements of subsection (b)(1);

    (2) the authorized representative of the employees has refused to accept such proposal without good cause; and

    (3) the balance of the equities clearly favors rejection of such agreement.

(d)

    (1) Upon the filing of an application for rejection the court shall schedule a hearing to be held not later than fourteen days after the date of the filing of such application. All interested parties may appear and be heard at such hearing. Adequate notice shall be provided to such parties at least ten days before the date of such hearing. The court may extend the time for the commencement of such hearing for a period not exceeding seven days where the circumstances of the case, and the interests of justice require such extension, or for additional periods of time to which the trustee and representative agree.

    (2) The court shall rule on such application for rejection within thirty days after the date of the commencement of the hearing. In the interests of justice, the court may extend such time for ruling for such additional period as the trustee and the employees' representative may agree to. If the court does not rule on such application within thirty days after the date of the commencement of the hearing, or within such additional time as the trustee and the employees' representative may agree to, the trustee may terminate or alter any provisions of the collective bargaining agreement pending the ruling of the court on such application.

    (3) The court may enter such protective orders, consistent with the need of the authorized representative of the employee to evaluate the trustee's proposal and the application for rejection, as may be necessary to prevent disclosure of information provided to such representative where such disclosure could compromise the position of the debtor with respect to its competitors in the industry in which it is engaged.

(e) If during a period when the collective bargaining agreement continues in effect, and if essential to the continuation of the debtor's business, or in order to avoid irreparable damage to the estate, the court, after notice and a hearing, may authorize the trustee to implement interim changes in the terms, conditions, wages, benefits, or work rules provided by a collective bargaining agreement. Any hearing under this paragraph shall be scheduled in accordance with the needs of the trustee. The implementation of such interim changes shall not render the application for rejection moot.

(f) No provision of this title shall be construed to permit a trustee to unilaterally terminate or alter any provisions of a collective bargaining agreement prior to compliance with the provisions of this section.

§1114. Payment of insurance benefits to retired employees

(a) For purposes of this section, the term "retiree benefits" means payments to any entity or person for the purpose of providing or reimbursing payments for retired employees and their spouses and dependents, for medical, surgical, or hospital care benefits, or benefits in the event of sickness, accident, disability, or death under any plan, fund, or program (through the purchase of insurance or otherwise) maintained or established in whole or in part by the debtor prior to filing a petition commencing a case under this title.

(b)

    (1) For purposes of this section, the term "authorized representative" means the authorized representative designated pursuant to subsection (c) for persons receiving any retiree benefits covered by a collective bargaining agreement or subsection (d) in the case of persons receiving retiree benefits not covered by such an agreement.

    (2) Committees of retired employees appointed by the court pursuant to this section shall have the same rights, powers, and duties as committees appointed under sections 1102 and 1103 of this title for the purpose of carrying out the purposes of sections 1114 and 1129(a)(13) and, as permitted by the court, shall have the power to enforce the rights of persons under this title as they relate to retiree benefits.

(c)

    (1) A labor organization shall be, for purposes of this section, the authorized representative of those persons receiving any retiree benefits covered by any collective bargaining agreement to which that labor organization is signatory, unless (A) such labor organization elects not to serve as the authorized representative of such persons, or (B) the court, upon a motion by any party in interest, after notice and hearing, determines that different representation of such persons is appropriate.

(2) In cases where the labor organization referred to in paragraph (1) elects not to serve as the authorized representative of those persons receiving any retiree benefits covered by any collective bargaining agreement to which that labor organization is signatory, or in cases where the court, pursuant to paragraph (1) finds different representation of such persons appropriate, the court, upon a motion by any party in interest, and after notice and a hearing, shall appoint a committee of retired employees if the debtor seeks to modify or not pay the retiree benefits or if the court otherwise determines that it is appropriate, from among such persons, to serve as the authorized representative of such persons under this section.

(d) The court, upon a motion by any party in interest, and after notice and a hearing, shall order the appointment of a committee of retired employees if the debtor seeks to modify or not pay the retiree benefits or if the court otherwise determines that it is appropriate, to serve as the authorized representative, under this section, of those persons receiving any retiree benefits not covered by a collective bargaining agreement. The United States trustee shall appoint any such committee.

(e)

(1) Notwithstanding any other provision of this title, the debtor in possession, or the trustee if one has been appointed under the provisions of this chapter (hereinafter in this section "trustee" shall include a debtor in possession), shall timely pay and shall not modify any retiree benefits, except that—

(A) the court, on motion of the trustee or authorized representative, and after notice and a hearing, may order modification of such payments, pursuant to the provisions of subsections (g) and (h) of this section, or

(B) the trustee and the authorized representative of the recipients of those benefits may agree to modification of such payments,

after which such benefits as modified shall continue to be paid by the trustee.

(2) Any payment for retiree benefits required to be made before a plan confirmed under section 1129 of this title is effective has the status of an allowed administrative expense as provided in section 503 of this title.

(f)

(1) Subsequent to filing a petition and prior to filing an application seeking modification of the retiree benefits, the trustee shall—

(A) make a proposal to the authorized representative of the retirees, based on the most complete and reliable information available at the time of such proposal, which provides for those necessary modifications in the retiree benefits that are necessary to permit the reorganization of the debtor and assures that all creditors, the debtor and all of the affected parties are treated fairly and equitably; and

(B) provide, subject to subsection (k)(3), the representative of the retirees with such relevant information as is necessary to evaluate the proposal.

(2) During the period beginning on the date of the making of a proposal provided for in paragraph (1), and ending on the date of the hearing provided for in subsection (k)(1), the trustee shall meet, at reasonable times, with the authorized representative to confer in good faith in attempting to reach mutually satisfactory modifications of such retiree benefits.

(g) The court shall enter an order providing for modification in the payment of retiree benefits if the court finds that—

(1) the trustee has, prior to the hearing, made a proposal that fulfills the requirements of subsection (f);

(2) the authorized representative of the retirees has refused to accept such proposal without good cause; and

(3) such modification is necessary to permit the reorganization of the debtor and assures that all creditors, the debtor, and all of the affected parties are treated fairly and equitably, and is clearly favored by the balance of the equities; except that in no case shall the court enter an order providing for such modification which provides for a modification to a level lower than that proposed by the trustee in the proposal found by the court to have complied with the requirements of this subsection and subsection (f): *Provided, however,* That at any time after an order is entered providing for modification in the payment of retiree benefits, or at any time after an agreement modifying such benefits is made between the trustee and the authorized representative of the recipients of such benefits, the authorized representative may apply to the court for an order increasing those benefits which order shall be granted if the increase in retiree benefits sought is consistent with the standard set forth in paragraph

(3): *Provided further,* That neither the trustee nor the authorized representative is precluded from making more than one motion for a modification order governed by this subsection.

(h)

(1) Prior to a court issuing a final order under subsection (g) of this section, if essential to the continuation of the debtor's business, or in order to avoid irreparable damage to the estate, the court, after notice and a hearing, may authorize the trustee to implement interim modifications in retiree benefits.

(2) Any hearing under this subsection shall be scheduled in accordance with the needs of the trustee.

(3) The implementation of such interim changes does not render the motion for modification moot.

(i) No retiree benefits paid between the filing of the petition and the time a plan confirmed under section 1129 of this title becomes effective shall be deducted or offset from the amounts allowed as claims for any benefits which remain unpaid, or from the amounts to be paid under the plan with respect to such claims for unpaid benefits, whether such claims for unpaid benefits are based upon or arise from a right to future unpaid benefits or from any benefits not paid as a result of modifications allowed pursuant to this section.

(j) No claim for retiree benefits shall be limited by section 502(b)(7) of this title.

(k)

(1) Upon the filing of an application for modifying retiree benefits, the court shall schedule a hearing to be held not later than fourteen days after the date of the filing of such application. All interested parties may appear and be heard at such hearing. Adequate notice shall be provided to such parties at least ten days before the date of such hearing. The court may extend the time for the commencement of such hearing for a period not exceeding seven days where the circumstances of the case, and the interests of justice require such extension, or for additional periods of time to which the trustee and the authorized representative agree.

(2) The court shall rule on such application for modification within ninety days after the date of the commencement of the hearing. In the interests of justice, the court may extend such time for ruling for such additional period as the trustee and the authorized representative may agree to. If the court does not rule on such application within ninety days after the date of the commencement of the hearing, or within such additional time as the trustee and the

authorized representative may agree to, the trustee may implement the proposed modifications pending the ruling of the court on such application.

(3) The court may enter such protective orders, consistent with the need of the authorized representative of the retirees to evaluate the trustee's proposal and the application for modification, as may be necessary to prevent disclosure of information provided to such representative where such disclosure could compromise the position of the debtor with respect to its competitors in the industry in which it is engaged.

(l) If the debtor, during the 180-day period ending on the date of the filing of the petition—

(1) modified retiree benefits; and

(2) was insolvent on the date such benefits were modified;

the court, on motion of a party in interest, and after notice and a hearing, shall issue an order reinstating as of the date the modification was made, such benefits as in effect immediately before such date unless the court finds that the balance of the equities clearly favors such modification.

(m) This section shall not apply to any retiree, or the spouse or dependents of such retiree, if such retiree's gross income for the twelve months preceding the filing of the bankruptcy petition equals or exceeds $250,000, unless such retiree can demonstrate to the satisfaction of the court that he is unable to obtain health, medical, life, and disability coverage for himself, his spouse, and his dependents who would otherwise be covered by the employer's insurance plan, comparable to the coverage provided by the employer on the day before the filing of a petition under this title.

§1115. Property of the estate

(a) In a case in which the debtor is an individual, property of the estate includes, in addition to the property specified in section 541—

(1) all property of the kind specified in section 541 that the debtor acquires after the commencement of the case but before the case is closed, dismissed, or converted to a case under chapter 7, 12, or 13, whichever occurs first; and

(2) earnings from services performed by the debtor after the commencement of the case but before the case is closed, dismissed, or converted to a case under chapter 7, 12, or 13, whichever occurs first.

(b) Except as provided in section 1104 or a confirmed plan or order confirming a plan, the debtor shall remain in possession of all property of the estate.

§1116. Duties of trustee or debtor in possession in small business cases

In a small business case, a trustee or the debtor in possession, in addition to the duties provided in this title and as otherwise required by law, shall—

(1) append to the voluntary petition or, in an involuntary case, file not later than 7 days after the date of the order for relief—

(A) its most recent balance sheet, statement of operations, cash-flow statement, and Federal income tax return; or

(B) a statement made under penalty of perjury that no balance sheet, statement of operations, or cash-flow statement has been prepared and no Federal tax return has been filed;

(2) attend, through its senior management personnel and counsel, meetings scheduled by the court or the United States trustee, including initial debtor interviews, scheduling conferences, and meetings of creditors convened under section 341 unless the court, after notice and a hearing, waives that requirement upon a finding of extraordinary and compelling circumstances;

(3) timely file all schedules and statements of financial affairs, unless the court, after notice and a hearing, grants an extension, which shall not extend such time period to a date later than 30 days after the date of the order for relief, absent extraordinary and compelling circumstances;

(4) file all postpetition financial and other reports required by the Federal Rules of Bankruptcy Procedure or by local rule of the district court;

(5) subject to section 363(c)(2), maintain insurance customary and appropriate to the industry;

(6)

(A) timely file tax returns and other required government filings; and

(B) subject to section 363(c)(2), timely pay all taxes entitled to administrative expense priority except those being contested by appropriate proceedings being diligently prosecuted; and

(7) allow the United States trustee, or a designated representative of the United States trustee, to inspect the debtor's business premises, books, and records at reasonable times, after reasonable prior written notice, unless notice is waived by the debtor.

SUBCHAPTER II—THE PLAN

§1121. Who may file a plan

(a) The debtor may file a plan with a petition commencing a voluntary case, or at any time in a voluntary case or an involuntary case.

(b) Except as otherwise provided in this section, only the debtor may file a plan until after 120 days after the date of the order for relief under this chapter.

(c) Any party in interest, including the debtor, the trustee, a creditors' committee, an equity security holders' committee, a creditor, an equity security holder, or any indenture trustee, may file a plan if and only if—

(1) a trustee has been appointed under this chapter;

(2) the debtor has not filed a plan before 120 days after the date of the order for relief under this chapter; or

(3) the debtor has not filed a plan that has been accepted, before 180 days after the date of the order for relief under this chapter, by each class of claims or interests that is impaired under the plan.

(d)

(1) Subject to paragraph (2), on request of a party in interest made within the respective periods specified in subsections (b) and (c) of this section and after notice and a hearing, the court may for cause reduce or increase the 120-day period or the 180-day period referred to in this section.

(2)

(A) The 120-day period specified in paragraph (1) may not be extended beyond a date that is 18 months after the date of the order for relief under this chapter.

(B) The 180-day period specified in paragraph (1) may not be extended beyond a date that is 20 months after the date of the order for relief under this chapter.

(e) In a small business case—

(1) only the debtor may file a plan until after 180 days after the date of the order for relief, unless that period is—

(A) extended as provided by this subsection, after notice and a hearing; or

(B) the court, for cause, orders otherwise;

(2) the plan and a disclosure statement (if any) shall be filed not later than 300 days after the date of the order for relief; and

(3) the time periods specified in paragraphs (1) and (2), and the time fixed in section 1129(e) within which the plan shall be confirmed, may be extended only if—

(A) the debtor, after providing notice to parties in interest (including the United States trustee), demonstrates by a preponderance of the evidence that it is more likely than not that the court will confirm a plan within a reasonable period of time;

(B) a new deadline is imposed at the time the extension is granted; and

(C) the order extending time is signed before the existing deadline has expired.

§1122. Classification of claims or interests

(a) Except as provided in subsection (b) of this section, a plan may place a claim or an interest in a particular class only if such claim or interest is substantially similar to the other claims or interests of such class.

(b) A plan may designate a separate class of claims consisting only of every unsecured claim that is less than or reduced to an amount that the court approves as reasonable and necessary for administrative convenience.

§1123. Contents of plan

(a) Notwithstanding any otherwise applicable nonbankruptcy law, a plan shall—

(1) designate, subject to section 1122 of this title, classes of claims, other than claims of a kind specified in section 507(a)(2), 507(a)(3), or 507(a)(8) of this title, and classes of interests;

(2) specify any class of claims or interests that is not impaired under the plan;

(3) specify the treatment of any class of claims or interests that is impaired under the plan;

(4) provide the same treatment for each claim or interest of a particular class, unless the holder of a particular claim or interest agrees to a less favorable treatment of such particular claim or interest;

(5) provide adequate means for the plan's implementation, such as—

(A) retention by the debtor of all or any part of the property of the estate;

(B) transfer of all or any part of the property of the estate to one or more entities, whether organized before or after the confirmation of such plan;

(C) merger or consolidation of the debtor with one or more persons;

(D) sale of all or any part of the property of the estate, either subject to or free of any lien, or the distribution of all or any part of the property of the estate among those having an interest in such property of the estate;

(E) satisfaction or modification of any lien;

(F) cancellation or modification of any indenture or similar instrument;

(G) curing or waiving of any default;

(H) extension of a maturity date or a change in an interest rate or other term of outstanding securities;

(I) amendment of the debtor's charter; or

(J) issuance of securities of the debtor, or of any entity referred to in subparagraph (B) or (C) of this paragraph, for cash, for property, for existing securities, or in exchange for claims or interests, or for any other appropriate purpose;

(6) provide for the inclusion in the charter of the debtor, if the debtor is a corporation, or of any corporation referred to in paragraph (5)(B) or (5)(C) of this subsection, of a provision prohibiting the issuance of nonvoting equity securities, and providing, as to the several classes of securities possessing voting power, an appropriate distribution of such power among such classes, including, in the case of any class of equity securities having a preference over another class of equity securities with respect to dividends, adequate provisions for the election of directors representing such preferred class in the event of default in the payment of such dividends;

(7) contain only provisions that are consistent with the interests of creditors and equity security holders and with public policy with respect to the manner of selection of any officer, director, or trustee under the plan and any successor to such officer, director, or trustee; and

(8) in a case in which the debtor is an individual, provide for the payment to creditors under the plan of all or such portion of earnings from personal services performed by the debtor after the commencement of the case or other future income of the debtor as is necessary for the execution of the plan.

(b) Subject to subsection (a) of this section, a plan may—

(1) impair or leave unimpaired any class of claims, secured or unsecured, or of interests;

(2) subject to section 365 of this title, provide for the assumption, rejection, or assignment of any executory contract or unexpired lease of the debtor not previously rejected under such section;

(3) provide for—

　　(A) the settlement or adjustment of any claim or interest belonging to the debtor or to the estate; or

　　(B) the retention and enforcement by the debtor, by the trustee, or by a representative of the estate appointed for such purpose, of any such claim or interest;

(4) provide for the sale of all or substantially all of the property of the estate, and the distribution of the proceeds of such sale among holders of claims or interests;

(5) modify the rights of holders of secured claims, other than a claim secured only by a security interest in real property that is the debtor's principal residence, or of holders of unsecured claims, or leave unaffected the rights of holders of any class of claims; and

(6) include any other appropriate provision not inconsistent with the applicable provisions of this title.

(c) In a case concerning an individual, a plan proposed by an entity other than the debtor may not provide for the use, sale, or lease of property exempted under section 522 of this title, unless the debtor consents to such use, sale, or lease.

(d) Notwithstanding subsection (a) of this section and sections 506(b), 1129(a)(7), and 1129(b) of this title, if it is proposed in a plan to cure a default the amount necessary to cure the default shall be determined in accordance with the underlying agreement and applicable nonbankruptcy law.

§1124. Impairment of claims or interests

Except as provided in section 1123(a)(4) of this title, a class of claims or interests is impaired under a plan unless, with respect to each claim or interest of such class, the plan—

(1) leaves unaltered the legal, equitable, and contractual rights to which such claim or interest entitles the holder of such claim or interest; or

(2) notwithstanding any contractual provision or applicable law that entitles the holder of such claim or interest to demand or receive accelerated payment of such claim or interest after the occurrence of a default—

　　(A) cures any such default that occurred before or after the commencement of the case under this title, other than a default of a kind specified in section 365(b)(2) of this title or of a kind that section 365(b)(2) expressly does not require to be cured;

　　(B) reinstates the maturity of such claim or interest as such maturity existed before such default;

　　(C) compensates the holder of such claim or interest for any damages incurred as a result of any reasonable reliance by such holder on such contractual provision or such applicable law;

　　(D) if such claim or such interest arises from any failure to perform a nonmonetary obligation, other than a default arising from failure to operate a nonresidential real property lease subject to section 365(b)(1)(A), compensates the holder of such claim or such interest (other than the debtor or an insider) for any actual pecuniary loss incurred by such holder as a result of such failure; and

　　(E) does not otherwise alter the legal, equitable, or contractual rights to which such claim or interest entitles the holder of such claim or interest.

§1125. Postpetition disclosure and solicitation

(a) In this section—

(1) "adequate information" means information of a kind, and in sufficient detail, as far as is reasonably practicable in light of the nature and history of the debtor and the condition of the debtor's books and records, including a discussion of the potential material Federal tax consequences of the plan to the debtor, any successor to the debtor, and a hypothetical investor typical of the holders of claims or interests in the case, that would enable such a hypothetical investor of the relevant class to make an informed judgment about the plan, but adequate information need not include such information about any other possible or proposed plan and in determining whether a disclosure statement provides adequate information, the court shall consider the complexity of the case, the benefit of additional information to creditors and other parties in interest, and the cost of providing additional information; and

(2) "investor typical of holders of claims or interests of the relevant class" means investor having—

　　(A) a claim or interest of the relevant class;

(B) such a relationship with the debtor as the holders of other claims or interests of such class generally have; and

(C) such ability to obtain such information from sources other than the disclosure required by this section as holders of claims or interests in such class generally have.

(b) An acceptance or rejection of a plan may not be solicited after the commencement of the case under this title from a holder of a claim or interest with respect to such claim or interest, unless, at the time of or before such solicitation, there is transmitted to such holder the plan or a summary of the plan, and a written disclosure statement approved, after notice and a hearing, by the court as containing adequate information. The court may approve a disclosure statement without a valuation of the debtor or an appraisal of the debtor's assets.

(c) The same disclosure statement shall be transmitted to each holder of a claim or interest of a particular class, but there may be transmitted different disclosure statements, differing in amount, detail, or kind of information, as between classes.

(d) Whether a disclosure statement required under subsection (b) of this section contains adequate information is not governed by any otherwise applicable nonbankruptcy law, rule, or regulation, but an agency or official whose duty is to administer or enforce such a law, rule, or regulation may be heard on the issue of whether a disclosure statement contains adequate information. Such an agency or official may not appeal from, or otherwise seek review of, an order approving a disclosure statement.

(e) A person that solicits acceptance or rejection of a plan, in good faith and in compliance with the applicable provisions of this title, or that participates, in good faith and in compliance with the applicable provisions of this title, in the offer, issuance, sale, or purchase of a security, offered or sold under the plan, of the debtor, of an affiliate participating in a joint plan with the debtor, or of a newly organized successor to the debtor under the plan, is not liable, on account of such solicitation or participation, for violation of any applicable law, rule, or regulation governing solicitation of acceptance or rejection of a plan or the offer, issuance, sale, or purchase of securities.

(f) Notwithstanding subsection (b), in a small business case—

(1) the court may determine that the plan itself provides adequate information and that a separate disclosure statement is not necessary;

(2) the court may approve a disclosure statement submitted on standard forms

approved by the court or adopted under section 2075 of title 28; and

(3)

(A) the court may conditionally approve a disclosure statement subject to final approval after notice and a hearing;

(B) acceptances and rejections of a plan may be solicited based on a conditionally approved disclosure statement if the debtor provides adequate information to each holder of a claim or interest that is solicited, but a conditionally approved disclosure statement shall be mailed not later than 25 days before the date of the hearing on confirmation of the plan; and

(C) the hearing on the disclosure statement may be combined with the hearing on confirmation of a plan.

(g) Notwithstanding subsection (b), an acceptance or rejection of the plan may be solicited from a holder of a claim or interest if such solicitation complies with applicable nonbankruptcy law and if such holder was solicited before the commencement of the case in a manner complying with applicable nonbankruptcy law.

§1126. Acceptance of plan

(a) The holder of a claim or interest allowed under section 502 of this title may accept or reject a plan. If the United States is a creditor or equity security holder, the Secretary of the Treasury may accept or reject the plan on behalf of the United States.

(b) For the purposes of subsections (c) and (d) of this section, a holder of a claim or interest that has accepted or rejected the plan before the commencement of the case under this title is deemed to have accepted or rejected such plan, as the case may be, if—

(1) the solicitation of such acceptance or rejection was in compliance with any applicable nonbankruptcy law, rule, or regulation governing the adequacy of disclosure in connection with such solicitation; or

(2) if there is not any such law, rule, or regulation, such acceptance or rejection was solicited after disclosure to such holder of adequate information, as defined in section 1125(a) of this title.

(c) A class of claims has accepted a plan if such plan has been accepted by creditors, other than any entity designated under subsection (e) of this section, that hold at least two-thirds in amount and more than one-half in number of the allowed claims of such class held by creditors, other than any entity designated under subsection (e) of this section, that have accepted or rejected such plan.

(d) A class of interests has accepted a plan if such plan has been accepted by holders of such interests, other than any entity designated under subsection (e) of this section, that hold at least two-thirds in amount of the allowed interests of such class held by holders of such interests, other than any entity designated under subsection (e) of this section, that have accepted or rejected such plan.

(e) On request of a party in interest, and after notice and a hearing, the court may designate any entity whose acceptance or rejection of such plan was not in good faith, or was not solicited or procured in good faith or in accordance with the provisions of this title.

(f) Notwithstanding any other provision of this section, a class that is not impaired under a plan, and each holder of a claim or interest of such class, are conclusively presumed to have accepted the plan, and solicitation of acceptances with respect to such class from the holders of claims or interests of such class is not required.

(g) Notwithstanding any other provision of this section, a class is deemed not to have accepted a plan if such plan provides that the claims or interests of such class do not entitle the holders of such claims or interests to receive or retain any property under the plan on account of such claims or interests.

§1127. Modification of plan

(a) The proponent of a plan may modify such plan at any time before confirmation, but may not modify such plan so that such plan as modified fails to meet the requirements of sections 1122 and 1123 of this title. After the proponent of a plan files a modification of such plan with the court, the plan as modified becomes the plan.

(b) The proponent of a plan or the reorganized debtor may modify such plan at any time after confirmation of such plan and before substantial consummation of such plan, but may not modify such plan so that such plan as modified fails to meet the requirements of sections 1122 and 1123 of this title. Such plan as modified under this subsection becomes the plan only if circumstances warrant such modification and the court, after notice and a hearing, confirms such plan as modified, under section 1129 of this title.

(c) The proponent of a modification shall comply with section 1125 of this title with respect to the plan as modified.

(d) Any holder of a claim or interest that has accepted or rejected a plan is deemed to have accepted or rejected, as the case may be, such plan as modified, unless, within the time fixed by the court, such holder changes such holder's previous acceptance or rejection.

(e) If the debtor is an individual, the plan may be modified at any time after confirmation of the plan but before the completion of payments under the plan, whether or not the plan has been substantially consummated, upon request of the debtor, the trustee, the United States trustee, or the holder of an allowed unsecured claim, to—

> **(1)** increase or reduce the amount of payments on claims of a particular class provided for by the plan;
>
> **(2)** extend or reduce the time period for such payments; or
>
> **(3)** alter the amount of the distribution to a creditor whose claim is provided for by the plan to the extent necessary to take account of any payment of such claim made other than under the plan.

(f)

> **(1)** Sections 1121 through 1128 and the requirements of section 1129 apply to any modification under subsection (e).
>
> **(2)** The plan, as modified, shall become the plan only after there has been disclosure under section 1125 as the court may direct, notice and a hearing, and such modification is approved.

§1128. Confirmation hearing

(a) After notice, the court shall hold a hearing on confirmation of a plan.

(b) A party in interest may object to confirmation of a plan.

§1129. Confirmation of plan

(a) The court shall confirm a plan only if all of the following requirements are met:

> **(1)** The plan complies with the applicable provisions of this title.
>
> **(2)** The proponent of the plan complies with the applicable provisions of this title.
>
> **(3)** The plan has been proposed in good faith and not by any means forbidden by law.
>
> **(4)** Any payment made or to be made by the proponent, by the debtor, or by a person issuing securities or acquiring property under the plan, for services or for costs and expenses in or in connection with the case, or in connection with the plan and incident to the case, has been approved by, or is subject to the approval of, the court as reasonable.
>
> **(5)**
>
>> **(A)**

(i) The proponent of the plan has disclosed the identity and affiliations of any individual proposed to serve, after confirmation of the plan, as a director, officer, or voting trustee of the debtor, an affiliate of the debtor participating in a joint plan with the debtor, or a successor to the debtor under the plan; and

(ii) the appointment to, or continuance in, such office of such individual, is consistent with the interests of creditors and equity security holders and with public policy; and

(B) the proponent of the plan has disclosed the identity of any insider that will be employed or retained by the reorganized debtor, and the nature of any compensation for such insider.

(6) Any governmental regulatory commission with jurisdiction, after confirmation of the plan, over the rates of the debtor has approved any rate change provided for in the plan, or such rate change is expressly conditioned on such approval.

(7) With respect to each impaired class of claims or interests—

(A) each holder of a claim or interest of such class—

(i) has accepted the plan; or

(ii) will receive or retain under the plan on account of such claim or interest property of a value, as of the effective date of the plan, that is not less than the amount that such holder would so receive or retain if the debtor were liquidated under chapter 7 of this title on such date; or

(B) if section 1111(b)(2) of this title applies to the claims of such class, each holder of a claim of such class will receive or retain under the plan on account of such claim property of a value, as of the effective date of the plan, that is not less than the value of such holder's interest in the estate's interest in the property that secures such claims.

(8) With respect to each class of claims or interests—

(A) such class has accepted the plan; or

(B) such class is not impaired under the plan.

(9) Except to the extent that the holder of a particular claim has agreed to a different treatment of such claim, the plan provides that—

(A) with respect to a claim of a kind specified in section 507(a)(2) or 507(a)(3)

of this title, on the effective date of the plan, the holder of such claim will receive on account of such claim cash equal to the allowed amount of such claim;

(B) with respect to a class of claims of a kind specified in section 507(a)(1), 507(a)(4), 507(a)(5), 507(a)(6), or 507(a)(7) of this title, each holder of a claim of such class will receive—

(i) if such class has accepted the plan, deferred cash payments of a value, as of the effective date of the plan, equal to the allowed amount of such claim; or

(ii) if such class has not accepted the plan, cash on the effective date of the plan equal to the allowed amount of such claim;

(C) with respect to a claim of a kind specified in section 507(a)(8) of this title, the holder of such claim will receive on account of such claim regular installment payments in cash—

(i) of a total value, as of the effective date of the plan, equal to the allowed amount of such claim;

(ii) over a period ending not later than 5 years after the date of the order for relief under section 301, 302, or 303; and

(iii) in a manner not less favorable than the most favored nonpriority unsecured claim provided for by the plan (other than cash payments made to a class of creditors under section 1122(b)); and

(D) with respect to a secured claim which would otherwise meet the description of an unsecured claim of a governmental unit under section 507(a)(8), but for the secured status of that claim, the holder of that claim will receive on account of that claim, cash payments, in the same manner and over the same period, as prescribed in subparagraph (C).

(10) If a class of claims is impaired under the plan, at least one class of claims that is impaired under the plan has accepted the plan, determined without including any acceptance of the plan by any insider.

(11) Confirmation of the plan is not likely to be followed by the liquidation, or the need for further financial reorganization, of the debtor or any successor to the debtor under the plan, unless such liquidation or reorganization is proposed in the plan.

(12) All fees payable under section 1930 of title 28, as determined by the court at the hearing on confirmation of the plan, have been paid or the plan provides for the payment of all such fees on the effective date of the plan.

(13) The plan provides for the continuation after its effective date of payment of all retiree benefits, as that term is defined in section 1114 of this title, at the level established pursuant to subsection (e)(1)(B) or (g) of section 1114 of this title, at any time prior to confirmation of the plan, for the duration of the period the debtor has obligated itself to provide such benefits.

(14) If the debtor is required by a judicial or administrative order, or by statute, to pay a domestic support obligation, the debtor has paid all amounts payable under such order or such statute for such obligation that first become payable after the date of the filing of the petition.

(15) In a case in which the debtor is an individual and in which the holder of an allowed unsecured claim objects to the confirmation of the plan—

　(A) the value, as of the effective date of the plan, of the property to be distributed under the plan on account of such claim is not less than the amount of such claim; or

　(B) the value of the property to be distributed under the plan is not less than the projected disposable income of the debtor (as defined in section 1325(b)(2)) to be received during the 5-year period beginning on the date that the first payment is due under the plan, or during the period for which the plan provides payments, whichever is longer.

(16) All transfers of property under the plan shall be made in accordance with any applicable provisions of nonbankruptcy law that govern the transfer of property by a corporation or trust that is not a moneyed, business, or commercial corporation or trust.

(b)

　(1) Notwithstanding section 510(a) of this title, if all of the applicable requirements of subsection (a) of this section other than paragraph (8) are met with respect to a plan, the court, on request of the proponent of the plan, shall confirm the plan notwithstanding the requirements of such paragraph if the plan does not discriminate unfairly, and is fair and equitable, with respect to each class of claims or interests that is impaired under, and has not accepted, the plan.

　(2) For the purpose of this subsection, the condition that a plan be fair and equitable with respect to a class includes the following requirements:

　　(A) With respect to a class of secured claims, the plan provides—

　　　(i)

　　　　(I) that the holders of such claims retain the liens securing such claims, whether the property subject to such liens is retained by the debtor or transferred to another entity, to the extent of the allowed amount of such claims; and

　　　　(II) that each holder of a claim of such class receive on account of such claim deferred cash payments totaling at least the allowed amount of such claim, of a value, as of the effective date of the plan, of at least the value of such holder's interest in the estate's interest in such property;

　　　(ii) for the sale, subject to section 363(k) of this title, of any property that is subject to the liens securing such claims, free and clear of such liens, with such liens to attach to the proceeds of such sale, and the treatment of such liens on proceeds under clause (i) or (iii) of this subparagraph; or

　　　(iii) for the realization by such holders of the indubitable equivalent of such claims.

　　(B) With respect to a class of unsecured claims—

　　　(i) the plan provides that each holder of a claim of such class receive or retain on account of such claim property of a value, as of the effective date of the plan, equal to the allowed amount of such claim; or

　　　(ii) the holder of any claim or interest that is junior to the claims of such class will not receive or retain under the plan on account of such junior claim or interest any property, except that in a case in which the debtor is an individual, the debtor may retain property included in the estate under section 1115, subject to the requirements of subsection (a)(14) of this section.

　　(C) With respect to a class of interests—

　　　(i) the plan provides that each holder of an interest of such class receive or retain on account of such interest property of a value, as of the effective date of the plan, equal to the greatest of the allowed amount of any fixed liquidation preference to which such holder is entitled, any fixed redemption price to which such holder is entitled, or the value of such interest; or

(ii) the holder of any interest that is junior to the interests of such class will not receive or retain under the plan on account of such junior interest any property.

(c) Notwithstanding subsections (a) and (b) of this section and except as provided in section 1127(b) of this title, the court may confirm only one plan, unless the order of confirmation in the case has been revoked under section 1144 of this title. If the requirements of subsections (a) and (b) of this section are met with respect to more than one plan, the court shall consider the preferences of creditors and equity security holders in determining which plan to confirm.

(d) Notwithstanding any other provision of this section, on request of a party in interest that is a governmental unit, the court may not confirm a plan if the principal purpose of the plan is the avoidance of taxes or the avoidance of the application of section 5 of the Securities Act of 1933. In any hearing under this subsection, the governmental unit has the burden of proof on the issue of avoidance.

(e) In a small business case, the court shall confirm a plan that complies with the applicable provisions of this title and that is filed in accordance with section 1121(e) not later than 45 days after the plan is filed unless the time for confirmation is extended in accordance with section 1121(e)(3).

SUBCHAPTER III— POSTCONFIRMATION MATTERS

§1141. Effect of confirmation

(a) Except as provided in subsections (d)(2) and (d)(3) of this section, the provisions of a confirmed plan bind the debtor, any entity issuing securities under the plan, any entity acquiring property under the plan, and any creditor, equity security holder, or general partner in the debtor, whether or not the claim or interest of such creditor, equity security holder, or general partner is impaired under the plan and whether or not such creditor, equity security holder, or general partner has accepted the plan.

(b) Except as otherwise provided in the plan or the order confirming the plan, the confirmation of a plan vests all of the property of the estate in the debtor.

(c) Except as provided in subsections (d)(2) and (d)(3) of this section and except as otherwise provided in the plan or in the order confirming the

plan, after confirmation of a plan, the property dealt with by the plan is free and clear of all claims and interests of creditors, equity security holders, and of general partners in the debtor.

(d)

(1) Except as otherwise provided in this subsection, in the plan, or in the order confirming the plan, the confirmation of a plan—

(A) discharges the debtor from any debt that arose before the date of such confirmation, and any debt of a kind specified in section 502(g), 502(h), or 502(i) of this title, whether or not—

(i) a proof of the claim based on such debt is filed or deemed filed under section 501 of this title;

(ii) such claim is allowed under section 502 of this title; or

(iii) the holder of such claim has accepted the plan; and

(B) terminates all rights and interests of equity security holders and general partners provided for by the plan.

(2) A discharge under this chapter does not discharge a debtor who is an individual from any debt excepted from discharge under section 523 of this title.

(3) The confirmation of a plan does not discharge a debtor if—

(A) the plan provides for the liquidation of all or substantially all of the property of the estate;

(B) the debtor does not engage in business after consummation of the plan; and

(C) the debtor would be denied a discharge under section 727(a) of this title if the case were a case under chapter 7 of this title.

(4) The court may approve a written waiver of discharge executed by the debtor after the order for relief under this chapter.

(5) In a case in which the debtor is an individual—

(A) unless after notice and a hearing the court orders otherwise for cause, confirmation of the plan does not discharge any debt provided for in the plan until the court grants a discharge on completion of all payments under the plan;

(B) at any time after the confirmation of the plan, and after notice and a hearing, the court may grant a discharge to the debtor who has not completed payments under the plan if—

(i) the value, as of the effective date of the plan, of property actually distributed under the plan on account of each allowed unsecured claim is not less than the amount that would have been paid on such claim if the estate of the debtor had been liquidated under chapter 7 on such date;

(ii) modification of the plan under section 1127 is not practicable; and

(iii) subparagraph (C) permits the court to grant a discharge; and

(C) the court may grant a discharge if, after notice and a hearing held not more than 10 days before the date of the entry of the order granting the discharge, the court finds that there is no reasonable cause to believe that—

(i) section 522(q)(1) may be applicable to the debtor; and

(ii) there is pending any proceeding in which the debtor may be found guilty of a felony of the kind described in section 522(q)(1)(A) or liable for a debt of the kind described in section 522(q)(1)(B);

and if the requirements of subparagraph (A) or (B) are met.

(6) Notwithstanding paragraph (1), the confirmation of a plan does not discharge a debtor that is a corporation from any debt—

(A) of a kind specified in paragraph (2)(A) or (2)(B) of section 523(a) that is owed to a domestic governmental unit, or owed to a person as the result of an action filed under subchapter III of chapter 37 of title 31 or any similar State statute; or

(B) for a tax or customs duty with respect to which the debtor—

(i) made a fraudulent return; or

(ii) willfully attempted in any manner to evade or to defeat such tax or such customs duty.

§1142. Implementation of plan

(a) Notwithstanding any otherwise applicable nonbankruptcy law, rule, or regulation relating to financial condition, the debtor and any entity organized or to be organized for the purpose of carrying out the plan shall carry out the plan and shall comply with any orders of the court.

(b) The court may direct the debtor and any other necessary party to execute or deliver or to join in the execution or delivery of any instrument required to effect a transfer of property dealt with by a confirmed plan, and to perform any other act, including the satisfaction of any lien, that is necessary for the consummation of the plan.

§1143. Distribution

If a plan requires presentment or surrender of a security or the performance of any other act as a condition to participation in distribution under the plan, such action shall be taken not later than five years after the date of the entry of the order of confirmation. Any entity that has not within such time presented or surrendered such entity's security or taken any such other action that the plan requires may not participate in distribution under the plan.

§1144. Revocation of an order of confirmation

On request of a party in interest at any time before 180 days after the date of the entry of the order of confirmation, and after notice and a hearing, the court may revoke such order if and only if such order was procured by fraud. An order under this section revoking an order of confirmation shall—

(1) contain such provisions as are necessary to protect any entity acquiring rights in good faith reliance on the order of confirmation; and

(2) revoke the discharge of the debtor.

§1145. Exemption from securities laws

(a) Except with respect to an entity that is an underwriter as defined in subsection (b) of this section, section 5 of the Securities Act of 1933 and any State or local law requiring registration for offer or sale of a security or registration or licensing of an issuer of, underwriter of, or broker or dealer in, a security do not apply to—

(1) the offer or sale under a plan of a security of the debtor, of an affiliate participating in a joint plan with the debtor, or of a successor to the debtor under the plan—

(A) in exchange for a claim against, an interest in, or a claim for an administrative expense in the case concerning, the debtor or such affiliate; or

(B) principally in such exchange and partly for cash or property;

(2) the offer of a security through any warrant, option, right to subscribe, or conversion privilege that was sold in the manner specified in paragraph (1) of this subsection, or the sale of a security upon the exercise of such a warrant, option, right, or privilege;

(3) the offer or sale, other than under a plan, of a security of an issuer other than the debtor or an affiliate, if—

(A) such security was owned by the debtor on the date of the filing of the petition;

(B) the issuer of such security is—

(i) required to file reports under section 13 or 15(d) of the Securities Exchange Act of 1934; and

(ii) in compliance with the disclosure and reporting provision of such applicable section; and

(C) such offer or sale is of securities that do not exceed—

(i) during the two-year period immediately following the date of the filing of the petition, four percent of the securities of such class outstanding on such date; and

(ii) during any 180-day period following such two-year period, one percent of the securities outstanding at the beginning of such 180-day period; or

(4) a transaction by a stockbroker in a security that is executed after a transaction of a kind specified in paragraph (1) or (2) of this subsection in such security and before the expiration of 40 days after the first date on which such security was bona fide offered to the public by the issuer or by or through an underwriter, if such stockbroker provides, at the time of or before such transaction by such stockbroker, a disclosure statement approved under section 1125 of this title, and, if the court orders, information supplementing such disclosure statement.

(b)

(1) Except as provided in paragraph (2) of this subsection and except with respect to ordinary trading transactions of an entity that is not an issuer, an entity is an underwriter under section 2(a)(11) of the Securities Act of 1933, if such entity—

(A) purchases a claim against, interest in, or claim for an administrative expense in the case concerning, the debtor, if such purchase is with a view to distribution of any security received or to be received in exchange for such a claim or interest;

(B) offers to sell securities offered or sold under the plan for the holders of such securities;

(C) offers to buy securities offered or sold under the plan from the holders of such securities, if such offer to buy is—

(i) with a view to distribution of such securities; and

(ii) under an agreement made in connection with the plan, with the consummation of the plan, or with the offer or sale of securities under the plan; or

(D) is an issuer, as used in such section 2(a)(11), with respect to such securities.

(2) An entity is not an underwriter under section 2(a)(11) of the Securities Act of 1933 or under paragraph (1) of this subsection with respect to an agreement that provides only for—

(A)

(i) the matching or combining of fractional interests in securities offered or sold under the plan into whole interests; or

(ii) the purchase or sale of such fractional interests from or to entities receiving such fractional interests under the plan; or

(B) the purchase or sale for such entities of such fractional or whole interests as are necessary to adjust for any remaining fractional interests after such matching.

(3) An entity other than an entity of the kind specified in paragraph (1) of this subsection is not an underwriter under section 2(a)(11) of the Securities Act of 1933 with respect to any securities offered or sold to such entity in the manner specified in subsection (a)(1) of this section.

(c) An offer or sale of securities of the kind and in the manner specified under subsection (a)(1) of this section is deemed to be a public offering.

(d) The Trust Indenture Act of 1939 does not apply to a note issued under the plan that matures not later than one year after the effective date of the plan.

§1146. Special tax provisions

(a) The issuance, transfer, or exchange of a security, or the making or delivery of an instrument of transfer under a plan confirmed under section 1129 of this title, may not be taxed under any law imposing a stamp tax or similar tax.

(b) The court may authorize the proponent of a plan to request a determination, limited to questions of law, by a State or local governmental unit charged with responsibility for collection or determination of a tax on or measured by income, of the tax effects, under section 346 of this title and under the law imposing such tax, of the plan. In the event of an actual controversy, the court may declare such effects after the earlier of—

(1) the date on which such governmental unit responds to the request under this subsection; or

(2) 270 days after such request.

SUBCHAPTER IV—RAILROAD REORGANIZATION

§1161. Inapplicability of other sections

Sections 341, 343, 1102(a)(1), 1104, 1105, 1107, 1129(a)(7), and 1129(c) of this title do not apply in a case concerning a railroad.

§1162. Definition

In this subchapter, "Board" means the "Surface Transportation Board".

§1163. Appointment of trustee

As soon as practicable after the order for relief the Secretary of Transportation shall submit a list of five disinterested persons that are qualified and willing to serve as trustees in the case. The United States trustee shall appoint one of such persons to serve as trustee in the case.

§1164. Right to be heard

The Board, the Department of Transportation, and any State or local commission having regulatory jurisdiction over the debtor may raise and may appear and be heard on any issue in a case under this chapter, but may not appeal from any judgment, order, or decree entered in the case.

§1165. Protection of the public interest

In applying sections 1166, 1167, 1169, 1170, 1171, 1172, 1173, and 1174 of this title, the court and the trustee shall consider the public interest in addition to the interests of the debtor, creditors, and equity security holders.

§1166. Effect of subtitle IV of title 49 and of Federal, State, or local regulations

Except with respect to abandonment under section 1170 of this title, or merger, modification of the financial structure of the debtor, or issuance or sale of securities under a plan, the trustee and the debtor are subject to the provisions of subtitle IV of title 49 that are applicable to railroads, and the trustee is subject to orders of any Federal, State, or local regulatory body to the same extent as the debtor would be if a petition commencing the case under this chapter had not been filed, but—

(1) any such order that would require the expenditure, or the incurring of an obligation

for the expenditure, of money from the estate is not effective unless approved by the court; and

(2) the provisions of this chapter are subject to section 601(b) of the Regional Rail Reorganization Act of 1973.

§1167. Collective bargaining agreements

Notwithstanding section 365 of this title, neither the court nor the trustee may change the wages or working conditions of employees of the debtor established by a collective bargaining agreement that is subject to the Railway Labor Act except in accordance with section 6 of such Act.

§1168. Rolling stock equipment

(a)

(1) The right of a secured party with a security interest in or of a lessor or conditional vendor of equipment described in paragraph (2) to take possession of such equipment in compliance with an equipment security agreement, lease, or conditional sale contract, and to enforce any of its other rights or remedies under such security agreement, lease, or conditional sale contract, to sell, lease, or otherwise retain or dispose of such equipment, is not limited or otherwise affected by any other provision of this title or by any power of the court, except that right to take possession and enforce those other rights and remedies shall be subject to section 362, if—

(A) before the date that is 60 days after the date of commencement of a case under this chapter, the trustee, subject to the court's approval, agrees to perform all obligations of the debtor under such security agreement, lease, or conditional sale contract; and

(B) any default, other than a default of a kind described in section 365(b)(2), under such security agreement, lease, or conditional sale contract—

(i) that occurs before the date of commencement of the case and is an event of default therewith is cured before the expiration of such 60-day period;

(ii) that occurs or becomes an event of default after the date of commencement of the case and before the expiration of such 60-day period is cured before the later of—

(I) the date that is 30 days after the date of the default or event of the default; or

(II) the expiration of such 60-day period; and

(iii) that occurs on or after the expiration of such 60-day period is cured in accordance with the terms of such security agreement, lease, or conditional sale contract, if cure is permitted under that agreement, lease, or conditional sale contract.

(2) The equipment described in this paragraph—

(A) is rolling stock equipment or accessories used on rolling stock equipment, including superstructures or racks, that is subject to a security interest granted by, leased to, or conditionally sold to a debtor; and

(B) includes all records and documents relating to such equipment that are required, under the terms of the security agreement, lease, or conditional sale contract, that is to be surrendered or returned by the debtor in connection with the surrender or return of such equipment.

(3) Paragraph (1) applies to a secured party, lessor, or conditional vendor acting in its own behalf or acting as trustee or otherwise in behalf of another party.

(b) The trustee and the secured party, lessor, or conditional vendor whose right to take possession is protected under subsection (a) may agree, subject to the court's approval, to extend the 60-day period specified in subsection (a)(1).

(c)

(1) In any case under this chapter, the trustee shall immediately surrender and return to a secured party, lessor, or conditional vendor, described in subsection (a)(1), equipment described in subsection (a)(2), if at any time after the date of commencement of the case under this chapter such secured party, lessor, or conditional vendor is entitled pursuant to subsection (a)(1) to take possession of such equipment and makes a written demand for such possession of the trustee.

(2) At such time as the trustee is required under paragraph (1) to surrender and return equipment described in subsection (a)(2), any lease of such equipment, and any security agreement or conditional sale contract relating to such equipment, if such security agreement or conditional sale contract is an executory contract, shall be deemed rejected.

(d) With respect to equipment first placed in service on or prior to October 22, 1994, for purposes of this section—

(1) the term "lease" includes any written agreement with respect to which the lessor and the debtor, as lessee, have expressed in the agreement or in a substantially contemporaneous writing that the agreement is to be treated as a lease for Federal income tax purposes; and

(2) the term "security interest" means a purchase-money equipment security interest.

(e) With respect to equipment first placed in service after October 22, 1994, for purposes of this section, the term "rolling stock equipment" includes rolling stock equipment that is substantially rebuilt and accessories used on such equipment.

§1169. Effect of rejection of lease of railroad line

(a) Except as provided in subsection (b) of this section, if a lease of a line of railroad under which the debtor is the lessee is rejected under section 365 of this title, and if the trustee, within such time as the court fixes, and with the court's approval, elects not to operate the leased line, the lessor under such lease, after such approval, shall operate the line.

(b) If operation of such line by such lessor is impracticable or contrary to the public interest, the court, on request of such lessor, and after notice and a hearing, shall order the trustee to continue operation of such line for the account of such lessor until abandonment is ordered under section 1170 of this title, or until such operation is otherwise lawfully terminated, whichever occurs first.

(c) During any such operation, such lessor is deemed a carrier subject to the provisions of subtitle IV of title 49 that are applicable to railroads.

§1170. Abandonment of railroad line

(a) The court, after notice and a hearing, may authorize the abandonment of all or a portion of a railroad line if such abandonment is—

(1)

(A) in the best interest of the estate; or

(B) essential to the formulation of a plan; and

(2) consistent with the public interest.

(b) If, except for the pendency of the case under this chapter, such abandonment would require approval by the Board under a law of the United States, the trustee shall initiate an appropriate application for such abandonment with the Board.

The court may fix a time within which the Board shall report to the court on such application.

(c) After the court receives the report of the Board, or the expiration of the time fixed under subsection (b) of this section, whichever occurs first, the court may authorize such abandonment, after notice to the Board, the Secretary of Transportation, the trustee, any party in interest that has requested notice, any affected shipper or community, and any other entity prescribed by the court, and a hearing.

(d)

（1) Enforcement of an order authorizing such abandonment shall be stayed until the time for taking an appeal has expired, or, if an appeal is timely taken, until such order has become final.

（2) If an order authorizing such abandonment is appealed, the court, on request of a party in interest, may authorize suspension of service on a line or a portion of a line pending the determination of such appeal, after notice to the Board, the Secretary of Transportation, the trustee, any party in interest that has requested notice, any affected shipper or community, and any other entity prescribed by the court, and a hearing. An appellant may not obtain a stay of the enforcement of an order authorizing such suspension by the giving of a supersedeas bond or otherwise, during the pendency of such appeal.

(e)

（1) In authorizing any abandonment of a railroad line under this section, the court shall require the rail carrier to provide a fair arrangement at least as protective of the interests of employees as that established under section 11326(a) of title 49.

（2) Nothing in this subsection shall be deemed to affect the priorities or timing of payment of employee protection which might have existed in the absence of this subsection.

§1171. Priority claims

(a) There shall be paid as an administrative expense any claim of an individual or of the personal representative of a deceased individual against the debtor or the estate, for personal injury to or death of such individual arising out of the operation of the debtor or the estate, whether such claim arose before or after the commencement of the case.

(b) Any unsecured claim against the debtor that would have been entitled to priority if a receiver in equity of the property of the debtor had been appointed by a Federal court on the date of the order for relief under this title shall be entitled to the same priority in the case under this chapter.

§1172. Contents of plan

(a) In addition to the provisions required or permitted under section 1123 of this title, a plan—

（1) shall specify the extent to and the means by which the debtor's rail service is proposed to be continued, and the extent to which any of the debtor's rail service is proposed to be terminated; and

（2) may include a provision for—

(A) the transfer of any or all of the operating railroad lines of the debtor to another operating railroad; or

(B) abandonment of any railroad line in accordance with section 1170 of this title.

(b) If, except for the pendency of the case under this chapter, transfer of, or operation of or over, any of the debtor's rail lines by an entity other than the debtor or a successor to the debtor under the plan would require approval by the Board under a law of the United States, then a plan may not propose such a transfer or such operation unless the proponent of the plan initiates an appropriate application for such a transfer or such operation with the Board and, within such time as the court may fix, not exceeding 180 days, the Board, with or without a hearing, as the Board may determine, and with or without modification or condition, approves such application, or does not act on such application. Any action or order of the Board approving, modifying, conditioning, or disapproving such application is subject to review by the court only under sections 706(2)(A), 706(2)(B), 706(2)(C), and 706(2)(D) of title 5.

(c)

（1) In approving an application under subsection (b) of this section, the Board shall require the rail carrier to provide a fair arrangement at least as protective of the interests of employees as that established under section 11326(a) of title 49.

（2) Nothing in this subsection shall be deemed to affect the priorities or timing of payment of employee protection which might have existed in the absence of this subsection.

§1173. Confirmation of plan

(a) The court shall confirm a plan if—

（1) the applicable requirements of section 1129 of this title have been met;

（2) each creditor or equity security holder will receive or retain under the plan property of a value, as of the effective date of the plan, that is not less than the value of property that each such creditor or equity security holder would so receive or retain if all of the operating railroad lines of the debtor were sold, and the proceeds of such sale, and the other property of the estate, were distributed under chapter 7 of this title on such date;

(3) in light of the debtor's past earnings and the probable prospective earnings of the reorganized debtor, there will be adequate coverage by such prospective earnings of any fixed charges, such as interest on debt, amortization of funded debt, and rent for leased railroads, provided for by the plan; and

(4) the plan is consistent with the public interest.

(b) If the requirements of subsection (a) of this section are met with respect to more than one plan, the court shall confirm the plan that is most likely to maintain adequate rail service in the public interest.

§1174. Liquidation

On request of a party in interest and after notice and a hearing, the court may, or, if a plan has not been confirmed under section 1173 of this title before five years after the date of the order for relief, the court shall, order the trustee to cease the debtor's operation and to collect and reduce to money all of the property of the estate in the same manner as if the case were a case under chapter 7 of this title.

CHAPTER 12—ADJUSTMENT OF DEBTS OF A FAMILY FARMER OR FISHERMAN WITH REGULAR ANNUAL INCOME

SUBCHAPTER I—OFFICERS, ADMINISTRATION, AND THE ESTATE

§1201. Stay of action against codebtor

(a) Except as provided in subsections (b) and (c) of this section, after the order for relief under this chapter, a creditor may not act, or commence or continue any civil action, to collect all or any part of a consumer debt of the debtor from any individual that is liable on such debt with the debtor, or that secured such debt, unless—

(1) such individual became liable on or secured such debt in the ordinary course of such individual's business; or

(2) the case is closed, dismissed, or converted to a case under chapter 7 of this title.

(b) A creditor may present a negotiable instrument, and may give notice of dishonor of such an instrument.

(c) On request of a party in interest and after notice and a hearing, the court shall grant relief from the stay provided by subsection (a) of this section with respect to a creditor, to the extent that—

(1) as between the debtor and the individual protected under subsection (a) of this section, such individual received the consideration for the claim held by such creditor;

(2) the plan filed by the debtor proposes not to pay such claim; or

(3) such creditor's interest would be irreparably harmed by continuation of such stay.

(d) Twenty days after the filing of a request under subsection (c)(2) of this section for relief from the stay provided by subsection (a) of this section, such stay is terminated with respect to the party in interest making such request, unless the debtor or any individual that is liable on such debt with the debtor files and serves upon such party in interest a written objection to the taking of the proposed action.

§1202. Trustee

(a) If the United States trustee has appointed an individual under section 586(b) of title 28 to serve as standing trustee in cases under this chapter and if such individual qualifies as a trustee under section 322 of this title, then such individual shall serve as trustee in any case filed under this chapter. Otherwise, the United States trustee shall appoint one disinterested person to serve as trustee in the case or the United States trustee may serve as trustee in the case if necessary.

(b) The trustee shall—

(1) perform the duties specified in sections 704(a)(2), 704(a)(3), 704(a)(5), 704(a)(6), 704(a)(7), and 704(a)(9) of this title;

(2) perform the duties specified in section 1106(a)(3) and 1106(a)(4) of this title if the court, for cause and on request of a party in interest, the trustee, or the United States trustee, so orders;

(3) appear and be heard at any hearing that concerns—

(A) the value of property subject to a lien;

(B) confirmation of a plan;

(C) modification of the plan after confirmation; or

(D) the sale of property of the estate;

(4) ensure that the debtor commences making timely payments required by a confirmed plan;

(5) if the debtor ceases to be a debtor in possession, perform the duties specified in sections 704(a)(8), 1106(a)(1), 1106(a)(2), 1106(a)(6), 1106(a)(7), and 1203; and

(6) if with respect to the debtor there is a claim for a domestic support obligation, provide the applicable notice specified in subsection (c).

(c)

(1) In a case described in subsection (b)(6) to which subsection (b)(6) applies, the trustee shall—

  (A)

    (i) provide written notice to the holder of the claim described in subsection (b)(6) of such claim and of the right of such holder to use the services of the State child support enforcement agency established under sections 464 and 466 of the Social Security Act for the State in which such holder resides, for assistance in collecting child support during and after the case under this title; and

    (ii) include in the notice provided under clause (i) the address and telephone number of such State child support enforcement agency;

  (B)

    (i) provide written notice to such State child support enforcement agency of such claim; and

    (ii) include in the notice provided under clause (i) the name, address, and telephone number of such holder; and

  (C) at such time as the debtor is granted a discharge under section 1228, provide written notice to such holder and to such State child support enforcement agency of—

    (i) the granting of the discharge;

    (ii) the last recent known address of the debtor;

    (iii) the last recent known name and address of the debtor's employer; and

    (iv) the name of each creditor that holds a claim that—

      (I) is not discharged under paragraph (2), (4), or (14A) of section 523(a); or

      (II) was reaffirmed by the debtor under section 524(c).

(2)

  (A) The holder of a claim described in subsection (b)(6) or the State child support enforcement agency of the State in which such holder resides may request from a creditor described in paragraph (1)(C)(iv) the last known address of the debtor.

  (B) Notwithstanding any other provision of law, a creditor that makes a disclosure of a last known address of a debtor in connection with a request made under subparagraph (A) shall not be liable by reason of making that disclosure.

§1203. Rights and powers of debtor

Subject to such limitations as the court may prescribe, a debtor in possession shall have all the rights, other than the right to compensation under section 330, and powers, and shall perform all the functions and duties, except the duties specified in paragraphs (3) and (4) of section 1106(a), of a trustee serving in a case under chapter 11, including operating the debtor's farm or commercial fishing operation.

§1204. Removal of debtor as debtor in possession

(a) On request of a party in interest, and after notice and a hearing, the court shall order that the debtor shall not be a debtor in possession for cause, including fraud, dishonesty, incompetence, or gross mismanagement of the affairs of the debtor, either before or after the commencement of the case.

(b) On request of a party in interest, and after notice and a hearing, the court may reinstate the debtor in possession.

§1205. Adequate protection

(a) Section 361 does not apply in a case under this chapter.

(b) In a case under this chapter, when adequate protection is required under section 362, 363, or 364 of this title of an interest of an entity in property, such adequate protection may be provided by—

  (1) requiring the trustee to make a cash payment or periodic cash payments to such entity, to the extent that the stay under section 362 of this title, use, sale, or lease under section 363 of this title, or any grant of a lien under section 364 of this title results in a decrease in the value of property securing a claim or of an entity's ownership interest in property;

  (2) providing to such entity an additional or replacement lien to the extent that such stay, use, sale, lease, or grant results in a decrease in the value of property securing a claim or of an entity's ownership interest in property;

(3) paying to such entity for the use of farmland the reasonable rent customary in the community where the property is located, based upon the rental value, net income, and earning capacity of the property; or

(4) granting such other relief, other than entitling such entity to compensation allowable under section 503(b)(1) of this title as an administrative expense, as will adequately protect the value of property securing a claim or of such entity's ownership interest in property.

§1206. Sales free of interests

After notice and a hearing, in addition to the authorization contained in section 363(f), the trustee in a case under this chapter may sell property under section 363(b) and (c) free and clear of any interest in such property of an entity other than the estate if the property is farmland, farm equipment, or property used to carry out a commercial fishing operation (including a commercial fishing vessel), except that the proceeds of such sale shall be subject to such interest.

§1207. Property of the estate

(a) Property of the estate includes, in addition to the property specified in section 541 of this title—

(1) all property of the kind specified in such section that the debtor acquires after the commencement of the case but before the case is closed, dismissed, or converted to a case under chapter 7 of this title, whichever occurs first; and

(2) earnings from services performed by the debtor after the commencement of the case but before the case is closed, dismissed, or converted to a case under chapter 7 of this title, whichever occurs first.

(b) Except as provided in section 1204, a confirmed plan, or an order confirming a plan, the debtor shall remain in possession of all property of the estate.

§1208. Conversion or dismissal

(a) The debtor may convert a case under this chapter to a case under chapter 7 of this title at any time. Any waiver of the right to convert under this subsection is unenforceable.

(b) On request of the debtor at any time, if the case has not been converted under section 706 or 1112

of this title, the court shall dismiss a case under this chapter. Any waiver of the right to dismiss under this subsection is unenforceable.

(c) On request of a party in interest, and after notice and a hearing, the court may dismiss a case under this chapter for cause, including—

(1) unreasonable delay, or gross mismanagement, by the debtor that is prejudicial to creditors;

(2) nonpayment of any fees and charges required under chapter 123 of title 28;

(3) failure to file a plan timely under section 1221 of this title;

(4) failure to commence making timely payments required by a confirmed plan;

(5) denial of confirmation of a plan under section 1225 of this title and denial of a request made for additional time for filing another plan or a modification of a plan;

(6) material default by the debtor with respect to a term of a confirmed plan;

(7) revocation of the order of confirmation under section 1230 of this title, and denial of confirmation of a modified plan under section 1229 of this title;

(8) termination of a confirmed plan by reason of the occurrence of a condition specified in the plan;

(9) continuing loss to or diminution of the estate and absence of a reasonable likelihood of rehabilitation; and

(10) failure of the debtor to pay any domestic support obligation that first becomes payable after the date of the filing of the petition.

(d) On request of a party in interest, and after notice and a hearing, the court may dismiss a case under this chapter or convert a case under this chapter to a case under chapter 7 of this title upon a showing that the debtor has committed fraud in connection with the case.

(e) Notwithstanding any other provision of this section, a case may not be converted to a case under another chapter of this title unless the debtor may be a debtor under such chapter.

SUBCHAPTER II—THE PLAN

§1221. Filing of plan

The debtor shall file a plan not later than 90 days after the order for relief under this chapter, except that the court may extend such period if the need for an extension is attributable to circumstances for which the debtor should not justly be held accountable.

§1222. Contents of plan

(a) The plan shall—

(1) provide for the submission of all or such portion of future earnings or other future income of the debtor to the supervision and control of the trustee as is necessary for the execution of the plan;

(2) provide for the full payment, in deferred cash payments, of all claims entitled to priority under section 507, unless—

(A) the claim is a claim owed to a governmental unit that arises as a result of the sale, transfer, exchange, or other disposition of any farm asset used in the debtor's farming operation, in which case the claim shall be treated as an unsecured claim that is not entitled to priority under section 507, but the debt shall be treated in such manner only if the debtor receives a discharge; or

(B) the holder of a particular claim agrees to a different treatment of that claim;

(3) if the plan classifies claims and interests, provide the same treatment for each claim or interest within a particular class unless the holder of a particular claim or interest agrees to less favorable treatment; and

(4) notwithstanding any other provision of this section, a plan may provide for less than full payment of all amounts owed for a claim entitled to priority under section 507(a)(1)(B) only if the plan provides that all of the debtor's projected disposable income for a 5-year period beginning on the date that the first payment is due under the plan will be applied to make payments under the plan.

(b) Subject to subsections (a) and (c) of this section, the plan may—

(1) designate a class or classes of unsecured claims, as provided in section 1122 of this title, but may not discriminate unfairly against any class so designated; however, such plan may treat claims for a consumer debt of the debtor if an individual is liable on such consumer debt with the debtor differently than other unsecured claims;

(2) modify the rights of holders of secured claims, or of holders of unsecured claims, or leave unaffected the rights of holders of any class of claims;

(3) provide for the curing or waiving of any default;

(4) provide for payments on any unsecured claim to be made concurrently with payments on any secured claim or any other unsecured claim;

(5) provide for the curing of any default within a reasonable time and maintenance of payments while the case is pending on any unsecured claim or secured claim on which the last payment is due after the date on which the final payment under the plan is due;

(6) subject to section 365 of this title, provide for the assumption, rejection, or assignment of any executory contract or unexpired lease of the debtor not previously rejected under such section;

(7) provide for the payment of all or part of a claim against the debtor from property of the estate or property of the debtor;

(8) provide for the sale of all or any part of the property of the estate or the distribution of all or any part of the property of the estate among those having an interest in such property;

(9) provide for payment of allowed secured claims consistent with section 1225(a)(5) of this title, over a period exceeding the period permitted under section 1222(c);

(10) provide for the vesting of property of the estate, on confirmation of the plan or at a later time, in the debtor or in any other entity;

(11) provide for the payment of interest accruing after the date of the filing of the petition on unsecured claims that are nondischargeable under section 1228(a), except that such interest may be paid only to the extent that the debtor has disposable income available to pay such interest after making provision for full payment of all allowed claims; and

(12) include any other appropriate provision not inconsistent with this title.

(c) Except as provided in subsections (b)(5) and (b)(9), the plan may not provide for payments over a period that is longer than three years unless the court for cause approves a longer period, but the court may not approve a period that is longer than five years.

(d) Notwithstanding subsection (b)(2) of this section and sections 506(b) and 1225(a)(5) of this title, if it is proposed in a plan to cure a default, the amount necessary to cure the default, shall be determined in accordance with the underlying agreement and applicable nonbankruptcy law.

§1223. Modification of plan before confirmation

(a) The debtor may modify the plan at any time before confirmation, but may not modify the plan so that the plan as modified fails to meet the requirements of section 1222 of this title.

(b) After the debtor files a modification under this section, the plan as modified becomes the plan.

(c) Any holder of a secured claim that has accepted or rejected the plan is deemed to have accepted or rejected, as the case may be, the plan as modified, unless the modification provides for a change in the rights of such holder from what such rights were under the plan before modification, and such holder changes such holder's previous acceptance or rejection.

§1224. Confirmation hearing

After expedited notice, the court shall hold a hearing on confirmation of the plan. A party in interest, the trustee, or the United States trustee may object to the confirmation of the plan. Except for cause, the hearing shall be concluded not later than 45 days after the filing of the plan.

§1225. Confirmation of plan

(a) Except as provided in subsection (b), the court shall confirm a plan if—

(1) the plan complies with the provisions of this chapter and with the other applicable provisions of this title;

(2) any fee, charge, or amount required under chapter 123 of title 28, or by the plan, to be paid before confirmation, has been paid;

(3) the plan has been proposed in good faith and not by any means forbidden by law;

(4) the value, as of the effective date of the plan, of property to be distributed under the plan on account of each allowed unsecured claim is not less than the amount that would be paid on such claim if the estate of the debtor were liquidated under chapter 7 of this title on such date;

(5) with respect to each allowed secured claim provided for by the plan—

(A) the holder of such claim has accepted the plan;

(B)

(i) the plan provides that the holder of such claim retain the lien securing such claim; and

(ii) the value, as of the effective date of the plan, of property to be distributed by the trustee or the debtor under the plan on account of such claim is not less than the allowed amount of such claim; or

(C) the debtor surrenders the property securing such claim to such holder;

(6) the debtor will be able to make all payments under the plan and to comply with the plan; and

(7) the debtor has paid all amounts that are required to be paid under a domestic support obligation and that first become payable after the date of the filing of the petition if the debtor is required by a judicial or administrative order, or by statute, to pay such domestic support obligation.

(b)

(1) If the trustee or the holder of an allowed unsecured claim objects to the confirmation of the plan, then the court may not approve the plan unless, as of the effective date of the plan—

(A) the value of the property to be distributed under the plan on account of such claim is not less than the amount of such claim;

(B) the plan provides that all of the debtor's projected disposable income to be received in the three-year period, or such longer period as the court may approve under section 1222(c), beginning on the date that the first payment is due under the plan will be applied to make payments under the plan; or

(C) the value of the property to be distributed under the plan in the 3-year period, or such longer period as the court may approve under section 1222(c), beginning on the date that the first distribution is due under the plan is not less than the debtor's projected disposable income for such period.

(2) For purposes of this subsection, "disposable income" means income which is received by the debtor and which is not reasonably necessary to be expended—

(A) for the maintenance or support of the debtor or a dependent of the debtor or for a domestic support obligation that first becomes payable after the date of the filing of the petition; or

(B) for the payment of expenditures necessary for the continuation, preservation, and operation of the debtor's business.

(c) After confirmation of a plan, the court may order any entity from whom the debtor receives income to pay all or any part of such income to the trustee.

§1226. Payments

(a) Payments and funds received by the trustee shall be retained by the trustee until confirmation or denial of confirmation of a plan. If a plan is confirmed, the trustee shall distribute any such payment in accordance with the plan. If a plan is not confirmed, the trustee shall return any such payments to the debtor, after deducting—

    (1) any unpaid claim allowed under section 503(b) of this title; and

    (2) if a standing trustee is serving in the case, the percentage fee fixed for such standing trustee.

(b) Before or at the time of each payment to creditors under the plan, there shall be paid—

    (1) any unpaid claim of the kind specified in section 507(a)(2) of this title; and

    (2) if a standing trustee appointed under section 1202(c) of this title is serving in the case, the percentage fee fixed for such standing trustee under section 1202(d) of this title.

(c) Except as otherwise provided in the plan or in the order confirming the plan, the trustee shall make payments to creditors under the plan.

§1227. Effect of confirmation

(a) Except as provided in section 1228(a) of this title, the provisions of a confirmed plan bind the debtor, each creditor, each equity security holder, and each general partner in the debtor, whether or not the claim of such creditor, such equity security holder, or such general partner in the debtor is provided for by the plan, and whether or not such creditor, such equity security holder, or such general partner in the debtor has objected to, has accepted, or has rejected the plan.

(b) Except as otherwise provided in the plan or the order confirming the plan, the confirmation of a plan vests all of the property of the estate in the debtor.

(c) Except as provided in section 1228(a) of this title and except as otherwise provided in the plan or in the order confirming the plan, the property vesting in the debtor under subsection (b) of this section is free and clear of any claim or interest of any creditor provided for by the plan.

§1228. Discharge

(a) Subject to subsection (d), as soon as practicable after completion by the debtor of all payments under the plan, and in the case of a debtor who is required by a judicial or administrative order, or by statute, to pay a domestic support obligation, after such debtor certifies that all amounts payable under such order or such statute that are due on or before the date of the certification (including amounts due before the petition was filed, but only to the extent provided for by the plan) have been paid, other than payments to holders of allowed claims provided for under section 1222(b)(5) or 1222(b)(9) of this title, unless the court approves a written waiver of discharge executed by the debtor after the order for relief under this chapter, the court shall grant the debtor a discharge of all debts provided for by the plan allowed under section 503 of this title or disallowed under section 502 of this title, except any debt—

    (1) provided for under section 1222(b)(5) or 1222(b)(9) of this title; or

    (2) of the kind specified in section 523(a) of this title.

(b) Subject to subsection (d), at any time after the confirmation of the plan and after notice and a hearing, the court may grant a discharge to a debtor that has not completed payments under the plan only if—

    (1) the debtor's failure to complete such payments is due to circumstances for which the debtor should not justly be held accountable;

    (2) the value, as of the effective date of the plan, of property actually distributed under the plan on account of each allowed unsecured claim is not less than the amount that would have been paid on such claim if the estate of the debtor had been liquidated under chapter 7 of this title on such date; and

    (3) modification of the plan under section 1229 of this title is not practicable.

(c) A discharge granted under subsection (b) of this section discharges the debtor from all unsecured debts provided for by the plan or disallowed under section 502 of this title, except any debt—

    (1) provided for under section 1222(b)(5) or 1222(b)(9) of this title; or

    (2) of a kind specified in section 523(a) of this title.

(d) On request of a party in interest before one year after a discharge under this section is granted, and after notice and a hearing, the court may revoke such discharge only if—

    (1) such discharge was obtained by the debtor through fraud; and

    (2) the requesting party did not know of such fraud until after such discharge was granted.

(e) After the debtor is granted a discharge, the court shall terminate the services of any trustee serving in the case.

(f) The court may not grant a discharge under this chapter unless the court after notice and a hearing held not more than 10 days before the date of the entry of the order granting the discharge finds that there is no reasonable cause to believe that—

(1) section 522(q)(1) may be applicable to the debtor; and

(2) there is pending any proceeding in which the debtor may be found guilty of a felony of the kind described in section 522(q)(1)(A) or liable for a debt of the kind described in section 522(q)(1)(B).

§1229. Modification of plan after confirmation

(a) At any time after confirmation of the plan but before the completion of payments under such plan, the plan may be modified, on request of the debtor, the trustee, or the holder of an allowed unsecured claim, to—

(1) increase or reduce the amount of payments on claims of a particular class provided for by the plan;

(2) extend or reduce the time for such payments; or

(3) alter the amount of the distribution to a creditor whose claim is provided for by the plan to the extent necessary to take account of any payment of such claim other than under the plan.

(b)

(1) Sections 1222(a), 1222(b), and 1223(c) of this title and the requirements of section 1225(a) of this title apply to any modification under subsection (a) of this section.

(2) The plan as modified becomes the plan unless, after notice and a hearing, such modification is disapproved.

(c) A plan modified under this section may not provide for payments over a period that expires after three years after the time that the first payment under the original confirmed plan was due, unless the court, for cause, approves a longer period, but the court may not approve a period that expires after five years after such time.

(d) A plan may not be modified under this section—

(1) to increase the amount of any payment due before the plan as modified becomes the plan;

(2) by anyone except the debtor, based on an increase in the debtor's disposable income, to increase the amount of payments to unsecured creditors required for a particular month so that the aggregate of such payments exceeds the debtor's disposable income for such month; or

(3) in the last year of the plan by anyone except the debtor, to require payments that would leave the debtor with insufficient funds to carry on the farming operation after the plan is completed.

§1230. Revocation of an order of confirmation

(a) On request of a party in interest at any time within 180 days after the date of the entry of an order of confirmation under section 1225 of this title, and after notice and a hearing, the court may revoke such order if such order was procured by fraud.

(b) If the court revokes an order of confirmation under subsection (a) of this section, the court shall dispose of the case under section 1207 of this title, unless, within the time fixed by the court, the debtor proposes and the court confirms a modification of the plan under section 1229 of this title.

§1231. Special tax provisions

(a) The issuance, transfer, or exchange of a security, or the making or delivery of an instrument of transfer under a plan confirmed under section 1225 of this title, may not be taxed under any law imposing a stamp tax or similar tax.

(b) The court may authorize the proponent of a plan to request a determination, limited to questions of law, by any governmental unit charged with responsibility for collection or determination of a tax on or measured by income, of the tax effects, under section 346 of this title and under the law imposing such tax, of the plan. In the event of an actual controversy, the court may declare such effects after the earlier of—

(1) the date on which such governmental unit responds to the request under this subsection; or

(2) 270 days after such request.

CHAPTER 13—ADJUSTMENT OF DEBTS OF AN INDIVIDUAL WITH REGULAR INCOME

SUBCHAPTER I—OFFICERS, ADMINISTRATION, AND THE ESTATE

§1301. Stay of action against codebtor

(a) Except as provided in subsections (b) and (c) of this section, after the order for relief under this chapter, a creditor may not act, or commence or continue any civil action, to collect all or any part of a consumer debt of the debtor from any individual that is liable on such debt with the debtor, or that secured such debt, unless—

(1) such individual became liable on or secured such debt in the ordinary course of such individual's business; or

(2) the case is closed, dismissed, or converted to a case under chapter 7 or 11 of this title.

(b) A creditor may present a negotiable instrument, and may give notice of dishonor of such an instrument.

(c) On request of a party in interest and after notice and a hearing, the court shall grant relief from the stay provided by subsection (a) of this section with respect to a creditor, to the extent that—

(1) as between the debtor and the individual protected under subsection (a) of this section, such individual received the consideration for the claim held by such creditor;

(2) the plan filed by the debtor proposes not to pay such claim; or

(3) such creditor's interest would be irreparably harmed by continuation of such stay.

(d) Twenty days after the filing of a request under subsection (c)(2) of this section for relief from the stay provided by subsection (a) of this section, such stay is terminated with respect to the party in interest making such request, unless the debtor or any individual that is liable on such debt with the debtor files and serves upon such party in interest a written objection to the taking of the proposed action.

§1302. Trustee

(a) If the United States trustee appoints an individual under section 586(b) of title 28 to serve as standing trustee in cases under this chapter and if such individual qualifies under section 322 of this title, then such individual shall serve as trustee in the case. Otherwise, the United States trustee shall appoint one disinterested person to serve as trustee in the case or the United States trustee may serve as a trustee in the case.

(b) The trustee shall—

(1) perform the duties specified in sections 704(a)(2), 704(a)(3), 704(a)(4), 704(a)(5), 704(a)(6), 704(a)(7), and 704(a)(9) of this title;

(2) appear and be heard at any hearing that concerns—

(A) the value of property subject to a lien;

(B) confirmation of a plan; or

(C) modification of the plan after confirmation;

(3) dispose of, under regulations issued by the Director of the Administrative Office of the United States Courts, moneys received or to be received in a case under chapter XIII of the Bankruptcy Act;

(4) advise, other than on legal matters, and assist the debtor in performance under the plan;

(5) ensure that the debtor commences making timely payments under section 1326 of this title; and

(6) if with respect to the debtor there is a claim for a domestic support obligation, provide the applicable notice specified in subsection (d).

(c) If the debtor is engaged in business, then in addition to the duties specified in subsection (b) of this section, the trustee shall perform the duties specified in sections 1106(a)(3) and 1106(a)(4) of this title.

(d)

(1) In a case described in subsection (b)(6) to which subsection (b)(6) applies, the trustee shall—

(A)

(i) provide written notice to the holder of the claim described in subsection (b)(6) of such claim and of the right of such holder to use the services of the State child support enforcement agency established under sections 464 and 466 of the Social Security Act for the State in which such holder resides, for assistance in collecting child support during and after the case under this title; and

(ii) include in the notice provided under clause (i) the address and telephone number of such State child support enforcement agency;

(B)

(i) provide written notice to such State child support enforcement agency of such claim; and

(ii) include in the notice provided under clause (i) the name, address, and telephone number of such holder; and

(C) at such time as the debtor is granted a discharge under section 1328, provide written notice to such holder and to such State child support enforcement agency of—

(i) the granting of the discharge;

(ii) the last recent known address of the debtor;

(iii) the last recent known name and address of the debtor's employer; and

(iv) the name of each creditor that holds a claim that—

(I) is not discharged under paragraph (2) or (4) of section 523(a); or

(II) was reaffirmed by the debtor under section 524(c).

(2)

(A) The holder of a claim described in subsection (b)(6) or the State child support enforcement agency of the State in which such holder resides may request from a creditor described in paragraph (1)(C)(iv) the last known address of the debtor.

(B) Notwithstanding any other provision of law, a creditor that makes a disclosure of a last known address of a debtor in connection with a request made under subparagraph (A) shall not be liable by reason of making that disclosure.

§1303. Rights and powers of debtor

Subject to any limitations on a trustee under this chapter, the debtor shall have, exclusive of the trustee, the rights and powers of a trustee under sections 363(b), 363(d), 363(e), 363(f), and 363(l), of this title.

§1304. Debtor engaged in business

(a) A debtor that is self-employed and incurs trade credit in the production of income from such employment is engaged in business.

(b) Unless the court orders otherwise, a debtor engaged in business may operate the business of the debtor and, subject to any limitations on a trustee under sections 363(c) and 364 of this title and to such limitations or conditions as the court prescribes, shall have, exclusive of the trustee, the rights and powers of the trustee under such sections.

(c) A debtor engaged in business shall perform the duties of the trustee specified in section 704(a)(8) of this title.

§1305. Filing and allowance of postpetition claims

(a) A proof of claim may be filed by any entity that holds a claim against the debtor—

(1) for taxes that become payable to a governmental unit while the case is pending; or

(2) that is a consumer debt, that arises after the date of the order for relief under this chapter, and that is for property or services necessary for the debtor's performance under the plan.

(b) Except as provided in subsection (c) of this section, a claim filed under subsection (a) of this section shall be allowed or disallowed under section 502 of this title, but shall be determined as of the date such claim arises, and shall be allowed under section 502(a), 502(b), or 502(c) of this title, or disallowed under section 502(d) or 502(e) of this title, the same as if such claim had arisen before the date of the filing of the petition.

(c) A claim filed under subsection (a)(2) of this section shall be disallowed if the holder of such claim knew or should have known that prior approval by the trustee of the debtor's incurring the obligation was practicable and was not obtained.

§1306. Property of the estate

(a) Property of the estate includes, in addition to the property specified in section 541 of this title—

(1) all property of the kind specified in such section that the debtor acquires after the commencement of the case but before the case is closed, dismissed, or converted to a case under chapter 7, 11, or 12 of this title, whichever occurs first; and

(2) earnings from services performed by the debtor after the commencement of the case but before the case is closed, dismissed, or converted to a case under chapter 7, 11, or 12 of this title, whichever occurs first.

(b) Except as provided in a confirmed plan or order confirming a plan, the debtor shall remain in possession of all property of the estate.

§1307. Conversion or dismissal

(a) The debtor may convert a case under this chapter to a case under chapter 7 of this title at any time. Any waiver of the right to convert under this subsection is unenforceable.

(b) On request of the debtor at any time, if the case has not been converted under section 706, 1112, or 1208 of this title, the court shall dismiss a case under this chapter. Any waiver of the right to dismiss under this subsection is unenforceable.

(c) Except as provided in subsection (f) of this section, on request of a party in interest or the United States trustee and after notice and a hearing, the court may convert a case under this chapter to a case under chapter 7 of this title, or may dismiss a case under this chapter, whichever is in the best interests of creditors and the estate, for cause, including—

(1) unreasonable delay by the debtor that is prejudicial to creditors;

(2) nonpayment of any fees and charges required under chapter 123 of title 28;

(3) failure to file a plan timely under section 1321 of this title;

(4) failure to commence making timely payments under section 1326 of this title;

(5) denial of confirmation of a plan under section 1325 of this title and denial of a request made for additional time for filing another plan or a modification of a plan;

(6) material default by the debtor with respect to a term of a confirmed plan;

(7) revocation of the order of confirmation under section 1330 of this title, and denial of confirmation of a modified plan under section 1329 of this title;

(8) termination of a confirmed plan by reason of the occurrence of a condition specified in the plan other than completion of payments under the plan;

(9) only on request of the United States trustee, failure of the debtor to file, within fifteen days, or such additional time as the court may allow, after the filing of the petition commencing such case, the information required by paragraph (1) of section 521(a);

(10) only on request of the United States trustee, failure to timely file the information required by paragraph (2) of section 521(a); or

(11) failure of the debtor to pay any domestic support obligation that first becomes payable after the date of the filing of the petition.

(d) Except as provided in subsection (f) of this section, at any time before the confirmation of a plan under section 1325 of this title, on request of a party in interest or the United States trustee and after notice and a hearing, the court may convert a case under this chapter to a case under chapter 11 or 12 of this title.

(e) Upon the failure of the debtor to file a tax return under section 1308, on request of a party in interest or the United States trustee and after notice and a hearing, the court shall dismiss a case or convert a case under this chapter to a case under chapter 7 of this title, whichever is in the best interest of the creditors and the estate.

(f) The court may not convert a case under this chapter to a case under chapter 7, 11, or 12 of this title if the debtor is a farmer, unless the debtor requests such conversion.

(g) Notwithstanding any other provision of this section, a case may not be converted to a case under another chapter of this title unless the debtor may be a debtor under such chapter.

§1308. Filing of prepetition tax returns

(a) Not later than the day before the date on which the meeting of the creditors is first scheduled to be held under section 341(a), if the debtor was required to file a tax return under applicable nonbankruptcy law, the debtor shall file with appropriate tax authorities all tax returns for all taxable periods ending during the 4-year period ending on the date of the filing of the petition.

(b)

(1) Subject to paragraph (2), if the tax returns required by subsection (a) have not been filed by the date on which the meeting of creditors is first scheduled to be held under section 341(a), the trustee may hold open that meeting for a reasonable period of time to allow the debtor an additional period of time to file any unfiled returns, but such additional period of time shall not extend beyond—

(A) for any return that is past due as of the date of the filing of the petition, the date that is 120 days after the date of that meeting; or

(B) for any return that is not past due as of the date of the filing of the petition, the later of—

(i) the date that is 120 days after the date of that meeting; or

(ii) the date on which the return is due under the last automatic extension of time for filing that return to which the debtor is entitled, and for which request is timely made, in accordance with applicable nonbankruptcy law.

(2) After notice and a hearing, and order entered before the tolling of any applicable filing period determined under paragraph (1), if the debtor demonstrates by a preponderance of the evidence that the failure to file a return as required under paragraph (1) is attributable to circumstances beyond the control of the debtor, the court may extend the filing period established by the trustee under paragraph (1) for—

(A) a period of not more than 30 days for returns described in paragraph (1)(A); and

(B) a period not to extend after the applicable extended due date for a return described in paragraph (1)(B).

(c) For purposes of this section, the term "return" includes a return prepared pursuant to subsection (a) or (b) of section 6020 of the Internal Revenue Code of 1986, or a similar State or local law, or a written stipulation to a judgment or a final order entered by a nonbankruptcy tribunal.

SUBCHAPTER II—THE PLAN

§1321. Filing of plan

The debtor shall file a plan.

§1322. Contents of plan

(a) The plan—

(1) shall provide for the submission of all or such portion of future earnings or other future income of the debtor to the supervision and control of the trustee as is necessary for the execution of the plan;

(2) shall provide for the full payment, in deferred cash payments, of all claims entitled to priority under section 507 of this title, unless the holder of a particular claim agrees to a different treatment of such claim;

(3) if the plan classifies claims, shall provide the same treatment for each claim within a particular class; and

(4) notwithstanding any other provision of this section, may provide for less than full payment of all amounts owed for a claim entitled to priority under section 507(a)(1)(B) only if the plan provides that all of the debtor's projected disposable income for a 5-year period beginning on the date that the first payment is due under the plan will be applied to make payments under the plan.

(b) Subject to subsections (a) and (c) of this section, the plan may—

(1) designate a class or classes of unsecured claims, as provided in section 1122 of this title, but may not discriminate unfairly against any class so designated; however, such plan may treat claims for a consumer debt of the debtor if an individual is liable on such consumer debt with the debtor differently than other unsecured claims;

(2) modify the rights of holders of secured claims, other than a claim secured only by a security interest in real property that is the debtor's principal residence, or of holders of unsecured claims, or leave unaffected the rights of holders of any class of claims;

(3) provide for the curing or waiving of any default;

(4) provide for payments on any unsecured claim to be made concurrently with payments on any secured claim or any other unsecured claim;

(5) notwithstanding paragraph (2) of this subsection, provide for the curing of any default within a reasonable time and maintenance of payments while the case is pending on any unsecured claim or secured claim on which the last payment is due after the date on which the final payment under the plan is due;

(6) provide for the payment of all or any part of any claim allowed under section 1305 of this title;

(7) subject to section 365 of this title, provide for the assumption, rejection, or assignment of any executory contract or unexpired lease of the debtor not previously rejected under such section;

(8) provide for the payment of all or part of a claim against the debtor from property of the estate or property of the debtor;

(9) provide for the vesting of property of the estate, on confirmation of the plan or at a later time, in the debtor or in any other entity;

(10) provide for the payment of interest accruing after the date of the filing of the petition on unsecured claims that are nondischargeable under section 1328(a), except that such interest may be paid only to the extent that the debtor has disposable income available to pay such interest after making provision for full payment of all allowed claims; and

(11) include any other appropriate provision not inconsistent with this title.

(c) Notwithstanding subsection (b)(2) and applicable nonbankruptcy law—

(1) a default with respect to, or that gave rise to, a lien on the debtor's principal residence may be cured under paragraph (3) or (5) of subsection (b) until such residence is sold at a foreclosure sale that is conducted in accordance with applicable nonbankruptcy law; and

(2) in a case in which the last payment on the original payment schedule for a claim secured only by a security interest in real property that is the debtor's principal residence is due before the date on which the final payment under the plan is due, the plan may provide for the payment of the claim as modified pursuant to section 1325(a)(5) of this title.

(d)

(1) If the current monthly income of the debtor and the debtor's spouse combined, when multiplied by 12, is not less than—

(A) in the case of a debtor in a household of 1 person, the median family income of the applicable State for 1 earner;

(B) in the case of a debtor in a household of 2, 3, or 4 individuals, the highest median family income of the applicable State for a family of the same number or fewer individuals; or

(C) in the case of a debtor in a household exceeding 4 individuals, the highest median family income of the applicable State for a family of 4 or fewer individuals, plus $700 per month for each individual in excess of 4,

the plan may not provide for payments over a period that is longer than 5 years.

(2) If the current monthly income of the debtor and the debtor's spouse combined, when multiplied by 12, is less than—

(A) in the case of a debtor in a household of 1 person, the median family income of the applicable State for 1 earner;

(B) in the case of a debtor in a household of 2, 3, or 4 individuals, the highest median family income of the applicable State for a family of the same number or fewer individuals; or

(C) in the case of a debtor in a household exceeding 4 individuals, the highest median family income of the applicable State for a family of 4 or fewer individuals, plus $700 per month for each individual in excess of 4,

the plan may not provide for payments over a period that is longer than 3 years, unless the court, for cause, approves a longer period, but the court may not approve a period that is longer than 5 years.

(e) Notwithstanding subsection (b)(2) of this section and sections 506(b) and 1325(a)(5) of this title, if it is proposed in a plan to cure a default, the amount necessary to cure the default, shall be determined in accordance with the underlying agreement and applicable nonbankruptcy law.

(f) A plan may not materially alter the terms of a loan described in section 362(b)(19) and any amounts required to repay such loan shall not constitute "disposable income" under section 1325.

§1323. Modification of plan before confirmation

(a) The debtor may modify the plan at any time before confirmation, but may not modify the plan so that the plan as modified fails to meet the requirements of section 1322 of this title.

(b) After the debtor files a modification under this section, the plan as modified becomes the plan.

(c) Any holder of a secured claim that has accepted or rejected the plan is deemed to have accepted or rejected, as the case may be, the plan as modified, unless the modification provides for a change in the rights of such holder from what such rights were under the plan before modification, and such

holder changes such holder's previous acceptance or rejection.

§1324. Confirmation hearing

(a) Except as provided in subsection (b) and after notice, the court shall hold a hearing on confirmation of the plan. A party in interest may object to confirmation of the plan.

(b) The hearing on confirmation of the plan may be held not earlier than 20 days and not later than 45 days after the date of the meeting of creditors under section 341(a), unless the court determines that it would be in the best interests of the creditors and the estate to hold such hearing at an earlier date and there is no objection to such earlier date.

§1325. Confirmation of plan

(a) Except as provided in subsection (b), the court shall confirm a plan if—

(1) The plan complies with the provisions of this chapter and with the other applicable provisions of this title;

(2) any fee, charge, or amount required under chapter 123 of title 28, or by the plan, to be paid before confirmation, has been paid;

(3) the plan has been proposed in good faith and not by any means forbidden by law;

(4) the value, as of the effective date of the plan, of property to be distributed under the plan on account of each allowed unsecured claim is not less than the amount that would be paid on such claim if the estate of the debtor were liquidated under chapter 7 of this title on such date;

(5) with respect to each allowed secured claim provided for by the plan—

(A) the holder of such claim has accepted the plan;

(B)

(i) the plan provides that—

(I) the holder of such claim retain the lien securing such claim until the earlier of—

(aa) the payment of the underlying debt determined under nonbankruptcy law; or

(bb) discharge under section 1328; and

(II) if the case under this chapter is dismissed or converted without completion of the plan, such lien shall also be retained by such holder to the extent recognized by applicable nonbankruptcy law;

(ii) the value, as of the effective date of the plan, of property to be distributed under the plan on account of such claim is not less than the allowed amount of such claim; and

(iii) if—

(I) property to be distributed pursuant to this subsection is in the form of periodic payments, such payments shall be in equal monthly amounts; and

(II) the holder of the claim is secured by personal property, the amount of such payments shall not be less than an amount sufficient to provide to the holder of such claim adequate protection during the period of the plan; or

(C) the debtor surrenders the property securing such claim to such holder;

(6) the debtor will be able to make all payments under the plan and to comply with the plan;

(7) the action of the debtor in filing the petition was in good faith;

(8) the debtor has paid all amounts that are required to be paid under a domestic support obligation and that first become payable after the date of the filing of the petition if the debtor is required by a judicial or administrative order, or by statute, to pay such domestic support obligation; and

(9) the debtor has filed all applicable Federal, State, and local tax returns as required by section 1308.

For purposes of paragraph (5), section 506 shall not apply to a claim described in that paragraph if the creditor has a purchase money security interest securing the debt that is the subject of the claim, the debt was incurred within the 910-day period preceding the date of the filing of the petition, and the collateral for that debt consists of a motor vehicle (as defined in section 30102 of title 49) acquired for the personal use of the debtor, or if collateral for that debt consists of any other thing of value, if the debt was incurred during the 1-year period preceding that filing.

(b)

(1) If the trustee or the holder of an allowed unsecured claim objects to the confirmation of the plan, then the court may not approve the plan unless, as of the effective date of the plan—

(A) the value of the property to be distributed under the plan on account of such claim is not less than the amount of such claim; or

(B) the plan provides that all of the debtor's projected disposable income to be received in the applicable commitment period beginning on the date that the first payment is due under the plan will be applied to make payments to unsecured creditors under the plan.

(2) For purposes of this subsection, the term "disposable income" means current monthly income received by the debtor (other than child support payments, foster care payments, or disability payments for a dependent child made in accordance with applicable nonbankruptcy law to the extent reasonably necessary to be expended for such child) less amounts reasonably necessary to be expended—

(A)

(i) for the maintenance or support of the debtor or a dependent of the debtor, or for a domestic support obligation, that first becomes payable after the date the petition is filed; and

(ii) for charitable contributions (that meet the definition of "charitable contribution" under section 548(d)(3)) to a qualified religious or charitable entity or organization (as defined in section 548(d)(4)) in an amount not to exceed 15 percent of gross income of the debtor for the year in which the contributions are made; and

(B) if the debtor is engaged in business, for the payment of expenditures necessary for the continuation, preservation, and operation of such business.

(3) Amounts reasonably necessary to be expended under paragraph (2), other than subparagraph (A)(ii) of paragraph (2), shall be determined in accordance with subparagraphs (A) and (B) of section 707(b)(2), if the debtor has current monthly income, when multiplied by 12, greater than—

(A) in the case of a debtor in a household of 1 person, the median family income of the applicable State for 1 earner;

(B) in the case of a debtor in a household of 2, 3, or 4 individuals, the highest median family income of the applicable State for a family of the same number or fewer individuals; or

(C) in the case of a debtor in a household exceeding 4 individuals, the highest median family income of the applicable State for a family of 4 or fewer individuals, plus $700 per month for each individual in excess of 4.

(4) For purposes of this subsection, the "applicable commitment period"—

    (A) subject to subparagraph (B), shall be—

        (i) 3 years; or

        (ii) not less than 5 years, if the current monthly income of the debtor and the debtor's spouse combined, when multiplied by 12, is not less than—

            (I) in the case of a debtor in a household of 1 person, the median family income of the applicable State for 1 earner;

            (II) in the case of a debtor in a household of 2, 3, or 4 individuals, the highest median family income of the applicable State for a family of the same number or fewer individuals; or

            (III) in the case of a debtor in a household exceeding 4 individuals, the highest median family income of the applicable State for a family of 4 or fewer individuals, plus $700 per month for each individual in excess of 4; and

    (B) may be less than 3 or 5 years, whichever is applicable under subparagraph (A), but only if the plan provides for payment in full of all allowed unsecured claims over a shorter period.

(c) After confirmation of a plan, the court may order any entity from whom the debtor receives income to pay all or any part of such income to the trustee.

§1326. Payments

(a)

    (1) Unless the court orders otherwise, the debtor shall commence making payments not later than 30 days after the date of the filing of the plan or the order for relief, whichever is earlier, in the amount—

        (A) proposed by the plan to the trustee;

        (B) scheduled in a lease of personal property directly to the lessor for that portion of the obligation that becomes due after the order for relief, reducing the payments under subparagraph (A) by the amount so paid and providing the trustee with evidence of such payment, including the amount and date of payment; and

        (C) that provides adequate protection directly to a creditor holding an allowed claim secured by personal property to the extent the claim is attributable to the purchase of such property by the debtor for that portion of the obligation that becomes due after the order for relief, reducing the payments under subparagraph (A) by the amount so paid and providing the trustee with evidence of such payment, including the amount and date of payment.

    (2) A payment made under paragraph (1)(A) shall be retained by the trustee until confirmation or denial of confirmation. If a plan is confirmed, the trustee shall distribute any such payment in accordance with the plan as soon as is practicable. If a plan is not confirmed, the trustee shall return any such payments not previously paid and not yet due and owing to creditors pursuant to paragraph (3) to the debtor, after deducting any unpaid claim allowed under section 503(b).

    (3) Subject to section 363, the court may, upon notice and a hearing, modify, increase, or reduce the payments required under this subsection pending confirmation of a plan.

    (4) Not later than 60 days after the date of filing of a case under this chapter, a debtor retaining possession of personal property subject to a lease or securing a claim attributable in whole or in part to the purchase price of such property shall provide the lessor or secured creditor reasonable evidence of the maintenance of any required insurance coverage with respect to the use or ownership of such property and continue to do so for so long as the debtor retains possession of such property.

(b) Before or at the time of each payment to creditors under the plan, there shall be paid—

    (1) any unpaid claim of the kind specified in section 507(a)(2) of this title;

    (2) if a standing trustee appointed under section 586(b) of title 28 is serving in the case, the percentage fee fixed for such standing trustee under section 586(e)(1)(B) of title 28; and

    (3) if a chapter 7 trustee has been allowed compensation due to the conversion or dismissal of the debtor's prior case pursuant to section 707(b), and some portion of that compensation remains unpaid in a case converted to this chapter or in the case dismissed under section 707(b) and refiled under this chapter, the amount of any such unpaid compensation, which shall be paid monthly—

        (A) by prorating such amount over the remaining duration of the plan; and

        (B) by monthly payments not to exceed the greater of—

            (i) $25; or

            (ii) the amount payable to unsecured nonpriority creditors, as provided by the plan, multiplied by 5 percent, and the result divided by the number of months in the plan.

(c) Except as otherwise provided in the plan or in the order confirming the plan, the trustee shall make payments to creditors under the plan.

(d) Notwithstanding any other provision of this title—

 (1) compensation referred to in subsection (b)(3) is payable and may be collected by the trustee under that paragraph, even if such amount has been discharged in a prior case under this title; and

 (2) such compensation is payable in a case under this chapter only to the extent permitted by subsection (b)(3).

§1327. Effect of confirmation

(a) The provisions of a confirmed plan bind the debtor and each creditor, whether or not the claim of such creditor is provided for by the plan, and whether or not such creditor has objected to, has accepted, or has rejected the plan.

(b) Except as otherwise provided in the plan or the order confirming the plan, the confirmation of a plan vests all of the property of the estate in the debtor.

(c) Except as otherwise provided in the plan or in the order confirming the plan, the property vesting in the debtor under subsection (b) of this section is free and clear of any claim or interest of any creditor provided for by the plan.

§1328. Discharge

(a) Subject to subsection (d), as soon as practicable after completion by the debtor of all payments under the plan, and in the case of a debtor who is required by a judicial or administrative order, or by statute, to pay a domestic support obligation, after such debtor certifies that all amounts payable under such order or such statute that are due on or before the date of the certification (including amounts due before the petition was filed, but only to the extent provided for by the plan) have been paid, unless the court approves a written waiver of discharge executed by the debtor after the order for relief under this chapter, the court shall grant the debtor a discharge of all debts provided for by the plan or disallowed under section 502 of this title, except any debt—

 (1) provided for under section 1322(b)(5);

 (2) of the kind specified in section 507(a)(8)(C) or in paragraph (1)(B), (1)(C), (2), (3), (4), (5), (8), or (9) of section 523(a);

 (3) for restitution, or a criminal fine, included in a sentence on the debtor's conviction of a crime; or

 (4) for restitution, or damages, awarded in a civil action against the debtor as a result of willful or malicious injury by the debtor that caused personal injury to an individual or the death of an individual.

(b) Subject to subsection (d), at any time after the confirmation of the plan and after notice and a hearing, the court may grant a discharge to a debtor that has not completed payments under the plan only if—

 (1) the debtor's failure to complete such payments is due to circumstances for which the debtor should not justly be held accountable;

 (2) the value, as of the effective date of the plan, of property actually distributed under the plan on account of each allowed unsecured claim is not less than the amount that would have been paid on such claim if the estate of the debtor had been liquidated under chapter 7 of this title on such date; and

 (3) modification of the plan under section 1329 of this title is not practicable.

(c) A discharge granted under subsection (b) of this section discharges the debtor from all unsecured debts provided for by the plan or disallowed under section 502 of this title, except any debt—

 (1) provided for under section 1322(b)(5) of this title; or

 (2) of a kind specified in section 523(a) of this title.

(d) Notwithstanding any other provision of this section, a discharge granted under this section does not discharge the debtor from any debt based on an allowed claim filed under section 1305(a)(2) of this title if prior approval by the trustee of the debtor's incurring such debt was practicable and was not obtained.

(e) On request of a party in interest before one year after a discharge under this section is granted, and after notice and a hearing, the court may revoke such discharge only if—

 (1) such discharge was obtained by the debtor through fraud; and

 (2) the requesting party did not know of such fraud until after such discharge was granted.

(f) Notwithstanding subsections (a) and (b), the court shall not grant a discharge of all debts provided for in the plan or disallowed under section 502, if the debtor has received a discharge—

 (1) in a case filed under chapter 7, 11, or 12 of this title during the 4-year period preceding the date of the order for relief under this chapter, or

(2) in a case filed under chapter 13 of this title during the 2-year period preceding the date of such order.

(g)

(1) The court shall not grant a discharge under this section to a debtor unless after filing a petition the debtor has completed an instructional course concerning personal financial management described in section 111.

(2) Paragraph (1) shall not apply with respect to a debtor who is a person described in section 109(h)(4) or who resides in a district for which the United States trustee (or the bankruptcy administrator, if any) determines that the approved instructional courses are not adequate to service the additional individuals who would otherwise be required to complete such instructional course by reason of the requirements of paragraph (1).

(3) The United States trustee (or the bankruptcy administrator, if any) who makes a determination described in paragraph (2) shall review such determination not later than 1 year after the date of such determination, and not less frequently than annually thereafter.

(h) The court may not grant a discharge under this chapter unless the court after notice and a hearing held not more than 10 days before the date of the entry of the order granting the discharge finds that there is no reasonable cause to believe that—

(1) section 522(q)(1) may be applicable to the debtor; and

(2) there is pending any proceeding in which the debtor may be found guilty of a felony of the kind described in section 522(q)(1)(A) or liable for a debt of the kind described in section 522(q)(1)(B).

§1329. Modification of plan after confirmation

(a) At any time after confirmation of the plan but before the completion of payments under such plan, the plan may be modified, upon request of the debtor, the trustee, or the holder of an allowed unsecured claim, to—

(1) increase or reduce the amount of payments on claims of a particular class provided for by the plan;

(2) extend or reduce the time for such payments;

(3) alter the amount of the distribution to a creditor whose claim is provided for by the plan to the extent necessary to take account of

any payment of such claim other than under the plan; or

(4) reduce amounts to be paid under the plan by the actual amount expended by the debtor to purchase health insurance for the debtor (and for any dependent of the debtor if such dependent does not otherwise have health insurance coverage) if the debtor documents the cost of such insurance and demonstrates that—

(A) such expenses are reasonable and necessary;

(B)

(i) if the debtor previously paid for health insurance, the amount is not materially larger than the cost the debtor previously paid or the cost necessary to maintain the lapsed policy; or

(ii) if the debtor did not have health insurance, the amount is not materially larger than the reasonable cost that would be incurred by a debtor who purchases health insurance, who has similar income, expenses, age, and health status, and who lives in the same geographical location with the same number of dependents who do not otherwise have health insurance coverage; and

(C) the amount is not otherwise allowed for purposes of determining disposable income under section 1325(b) of this title;

and upon request of any party in interest, files proof that a health insurance policy was purchased.

(b)

(1) Sections 1322(a), 1322(b), and 1323(c) of this title and the requirements of section 1325(a) of this title apply to any modification under subsection (a) of this section.

(2) The plan as modified becomes the plan unless, after notice and a hearing, such modification is disapproved.

(c) A plan modified under this section may not provide for payments over a period that expires after the applicable commitment period under section 1325(b)(1)(B) after the time that the first payment under the original confirmed plan was due, unless the court, for cause, approves a longer period, but the court may not approve a period that expires after five years after such time.

§1330. Revocation of an order of confirmation

(a) On request of a party in interest at any time within 180 days after the date of the entry of an order of confirmation under section 1325 of this title, and after notice and a hearing, the court may revoke such order if such order was procured by fraud.

(b) If the court revokes an order of confirmation under subsection (a) of this section, the court shall dispose of the case under section 1307 of this title, unless, within the time fixed by the court, the debtor proposes and the court confirms a modification of the plan under section 1329 of this title.

CHAPTER 15—ANCILLARY AND OTHER CROSS-BORDER CASES

§1501. Purpose and scope of application

(a) The purpose of this chapter is to incorporate the Model Law on Cross-Border Insolvency so as to provide effective mechanisms for dealing with cases of cross-border insolvency with the objectives of—

    (1) cooperation between—

        (A) courts of the United States, United States trustees, trustees, examiners, debtors, and debtors in possession; and

        (B) the courts and other competent authorities of foreign countries involved in cross-border insolvency cases;

    (2) greater legal certainty for trade and investment;

    (3) fair and efficient administration of cross-border insolvencies that protects the interests of all creditors, and other interested entities, including the debtor;

    (4) protection and maximization of the value of the debtor's assets; and

    (5) facilitation of the rescue of financially troubled businesses, thereby protecting investment and preserving employment.

(b) This chapter applies where—

    (1) assistance is sought in the United States by a foreign court or a foreign representative in connection with a foreign proceeding;

    (2) assistance is sought in a foreign country in connection with a case under this title;

    (3) a foreign proceeding and a case under this title with respect to the same debtor are pending concurrently; or

    (4) creditors or other interested persons in a foreign country have an interest in requesting the commencement of, or participating in, a case or proceeding under this title.

(c) This chapter does not apply to—

    (1) a proceeding concerning an entity, other than a foreign insurance company, identified by exclusion in section 109(b);

    (2) an individual, or to an individual and such individual's spouse, who have debts within the limits specified in section 109(e) and who are citizens of the United States or aliens lawfully admitted for permanent residence in the United States; or

    (3) an entity subject to a proceeding under the Securities Investor Protection Act of 1970, a stockbroker subject to subchapter III of chapter 7 of this title, or a commodity broker subject to subchapter IV of chapter 7 of this title.

(d) The court may not grant relief under this chapter with respect to any deposit, escrow, trust fund, or other security required or permitted under any applicable State insurance law or regulation for the benefit of claim holders in the United States.

SUBCHAPTER I—GENERAL PROVISIONS

§1502. Definitions

For the purposes of this chapter, the term—

    (1) "debtor" means an entity that is the subject of a foreign proceeding;

    (2) "establishment" means any place of operations where the debtor carries out a nontransitory economic activity;

    (3) "foreign court" means a judicial or other authority competent to control or supervise a foreign proceeding;

    (4) "foreign main proceeding" means a foreign proceeding pending in the country where the debtor has the center of its main interests;

    (5) "foreign nonmain proceeding" means a foreign proceeding, other than a foreign main proceeding, pending in a country where the debtor has an establishment;

    (6) "trustee" includes a trustee, a debtor in possession in a case under any chapter of this title, or a debtor under chapter 9 of this title;

    (7) "recognition" means the entry of an order granting recognition of a foreign main proceeding or foreign nonmain proceeding under this chapter; and

    (8) "within the territorial jurisdiction of the United States", when used with reference to property of a debtor, refers to tangible property located within the territory of the United States and intangible property deemed under applicable nonbankruptcy law to be located within that territory, including any property subject to attachment or garnishment that may properly be seized or garnished by an action in a Federal or State court in the United States.

§1503. International obligations of the United States

To the extent that this chapter conflicts with an obligation of the United States arising out of any treaty or other form of agreement to which it is a party with one or more other countries, the requirements of the treaty or agreement prevail.

§1504. Commencement of ancillary case

A case under this chapter is commenced by the filing of a petition for recognition of a foreign proceeding under section 1515.

§1505. Authorization to act in a foreign country

A trustee or another entity (including an examiner) may be authorized by the court to act in a foreign country on behalf of an estate created under section 541. An entity authorized to act under this section may act in any way permitted by the applicable foreign law.

§1506. Public policy exception

Nothing in this chapter prevents the court from refusing to take an action governed by this chapter if the action would be manifestly contrary to the public policy of the United States.

§1507. Additional assistance

(a) Subject to the specific limitations stated elsewhere in this chapter the court, if recognition is granted, may provide additional assistance to a foreign representative under this title or under other laws of the United States.
(b) In determining whether to provide additional assistance under this title or under other laws of the United States, the court shall consider whether such additional assistance, consistent with the principles of comity, will reasonably assure—
   (1) just treatment of all holders of claims against or interests in the debtor's property;
   (2) protection of claim holders in the United States against prejudice and inconvenience in the processing of claims in such foreign proceeding;
   (3) prevention of preferential or fraudulent dispositions of property of the debtor;
   (4) distribution of proceeds of the debtor's property substantially in accordance with the order prescribed by this title; and

(5) if appropriate, the provision of an opportunity for a fresh start for the individual that such foreign proceeding concerns.

§1508. Interpretation

In interpreting this chapter, the court shall consider its international origin, and the need to promote an application of this chapter that is consistent with the application of similar statutes adopted by foreign jurisdictions.

SUBCHAPTER II—ACCESS OF FOREIGN REPRESENTATIVES AND CREDITORS TO THE COURT

§1509. Right of direct access

(a) A foreign representative may commence a case under section 1504 by filing directly with the court a petition for recognition of a foreign proceeding under section 1515.
(b) If the court grants recognition under section 1517, and subject to any limitations that the court may impose consistent with the policy of this chapter—
   (1) the foreign representative has the capacity to sue and be sued in a court in the United States;
   (2) the foreign representative may apply directly to a court in the United States for appropriate relief in that court; and
   (3) a court in the United States shall grant comity or cooperation to the foreign representative.
(c) A request for comity or cooperation by a foreign representative in a court in the United States other than the court which granted recognition shall be accompanied by a certified copy of an order granting recognition under section 1517.
(d) If the court denies recognition under this chapter, the court may issue any appropriate order necessary to prevent the foreign representative from obtaining comity or cooperation from courts in the United States.
(e) Whether or not the court grants recognition, and subject to sections 306 and 1510, a foreign representative is subject to applicable nonbankruptcy law.
(f) Notwithstanding any other provision of this section, the failure of a foreign representative to commence a case or to obtain recognition under this chapter does not affect any right the foreign representative may have to sue in a court in the

United States to collect or recover a claim which is the property of the debtor.

§1510. Limited jurisdiction

The sole fact that a foreign representative files a petition under section 1515 does not subject the foreign representative to the jurisdiction of any court in the United States for any other purpose.

§1511. Commencement of case under section 301, 302, or 303

(a) Upon recognition, a foreign representative may commence—
>**(1)** an involuntary case under section 303; or
>**(2)** a voluntary case under section 301 or 302, if the foreign proceeding is a foreign main proceeding.

(b) The petition commencing a case under subsection (a) must be accompanied by a certified copy of an order granting recognition. The court where the petition for recognition has been filed must be advised of the foreign representative's intent to commence a case under subsection (a) prior to such commencement.

§1512. Participation of a foreign representative in a case under this title

Upon recognition of a foreign proceeding, the foreign representative in the recognized proceeding is entitled to participate as a party in interest in a case regarding the debtor under this title.

§1513. Access of foreign creditors to a case under this title

(a) Foreign creditors have the same rights regarding the commencement of, and participation in, a case under this title as domestic creditors.

(b)
>**(1)** Subsection (a) does not change or codify present law as to the priority of claims under section 507 or 726, except that the claim of a foreign creditor under those sections shall not be given a lower priority than that of general unsecured claims without priority solely because the holder of such claim is a foreign creditor.
>**(2)**
>>**(A)** Subsection (a) and paragraph (1) do not change or codify present law as to the allowability of foreign revenue claims or other foreign public law claims in a proceeding under this title.

>>**(B)** Allowance and priority as to a foreign tax claim or other foreign public law claim shall be governed by any applicable tax treaty of the United States, under the conditions and circumstances specified therein.

§1514. Notification to foreign creditors concerning a case under this title

(a) Whenever in a case under this title notice is to be given to creditors generally or to any class or category of creditors, such notice shall also be given to the known creditors generally, or to creditors in the notified class or category, that do not have addresses in the United States. The court may order that appropriate steps be taken with a view to notifying any creditor whose address is not yet known.

(b) Such notification to creditors with foreign addresses described in subsection (a) shall be given individually, unless the court considers that, under the circumstances, some other form of notification would be more appropriate. No letter or other formality is required.

(c) When a notification of commencement of a case is to be given to foreign creditors, such notification shall—
>**(1)** indicate the time period for filing proofs of claim and specify the place for filing such proofs of claim;
>**(2)** indicate whether secured creditors need to file proofs of claim; and
>**(3)** contain any other information required to be included in such notification to creditors under this title and the orders of the court.

(d) Any rule of procedure or order of the court as to notice or the filing of a proof of claim shall provide such additional time to creditors with foreign addresses as is reasonable under the circumstances.

SUBCHAPTER III—RECOGNITION OF A FOREIGN PROCEEDING AND RELIEF

§1515. Application for recognition

(a) A foreign representative applies to the court for recognition of a foreign proceeding in which the foreign representative has been appointed by filing a petition for recognition.

(b) A petition for recognition shall be accompanied by—

(1) a certified copy of the decision commencing such foreign proceeding and appointing the foreign representative;

(2) a certificate from the foreign court affirming the existence of such foreign proceeding and of the appointment of the foreign representative; or

(3) in the absence of evidence referred to in paragraphs (1) and (2), any other evidence acceptable to the court of the existence of such foreign proceeding and of the appointment of the foreign representative.

(c) A petition for recognition shall also be accompanied by a statement identifying all foreign proceedings with respect to the debtor that are known to the foreign representative.

(d) The documents referred to in paragraphs (1) and (2) of subsection (b) shall be translated into English. The court may require a translation into English of additional documents.

§1516. Presumptions concerning recognition

(a) If the decision or certificate referred to in section 1515(b) indicates that the foreign proceeding is a foreign proceeding and that the person or body is a foreign representative, the court is entitled to so presume.

(b) The court is entitled to presume that documents submitted in support of the petition for recognition are authentic, whether or not they have been legalized.

(c) In the absence of evidence to the contrary, the debtor's registered office, or habitual residence in the case of an individual, is presumed to be the center of the debtor's main interests.

§1517. Order granting recognition

(a) Subject to section 1506, after notice and a hearing, an order recognizing a foreign proceeding shall be entered if—

(1) such foreign proceeding for which recognition is sought is a foreign main proceeding or foreign nonmain proceeding within the meaning of section 1502;

(2) the foreign representative applying for recognition is a person or body; and

(3) the petition meets the requirements of section 1515.

(b) Such foreign proceeding shall be recognized—

(1) as a foreign main proceeding if it is pending in the country where the debtor has the center of its main interests; or

(2) as a foreign nonmain proceeding if the debtor has an establishment within the meaning of section 1502 in the foreign country where the proceeding is pending.

(c) A petition for recognition of a foreign proceeding shall be decided upon at the earliest possible time. Entry of an order recognizing a foreign proceeding constitutes recognition under this chapter.

(d) The provisions of this subchapter do not prevent modification or termination of recognition if it is shown that the grounds for granting it were fully or partially lacking or have ceased to exist, but in considering such action the court shall give due weight to possible prejudice to parties that have relied upon the order granting recognition. A case under this chapter may be closed in the manner prescribed under section 350.

§1518. Subsequent information

From the time of filing the petition for recognition of a foreign proceeding, the foreign representative shall file with the court promptly a notice of change of status concerning—

(1) any substantial change in the status of such foreign proceeding or the status of the foreign representative's appointment; and

(2) any other foreign proceeding regarding the debtor that becomes known to the foreign representative.

§1519. Relief that may be granted upon filing petition for recognition

(a) From the time of filing a petition for recognition until the court rules on the petition, the court may, at the request of the foreign representative, where relief is urgently needed to protect the assets of the debtor or the interests of the creditors, grant relief of a provisional nature, including—

(1) staying execution against the debtor's assets;

(2) entrusting the administration or realization of all or part of the debtor's assets located in the United States to the foreign representative or another person authorized by the court, including an examiner, in order to protect and preserve the value of assets that, by their nature or because of other circumstances, are perishable, susceptible to devaluation or otherwise in jeopardy; and

(3) any relief referred to in paragraph (3), (4), or (7) of section 1521(a).

(b) Unless extended under section 1521(a)(6), the relief granted under this section terminates when the petition for recognition is granted.

(c) It is a ground for denial of relief under this section that such relief would interfere with the administration of a foreign main proceeding.

(d) The court may not enjoin a police or regulatory act of a governmental unit, including a criminal action or proceeding, under this section.

(e) The standards, procedures, and limitations applicable to an injunction shall apply to relief under this section.

(f) The exercise of rights not subject to the stay arising under section 362(a) pursuant to paragraph (6), (7), (17), or (27) of section 362(b) or pursuant to section 362(o) shall not be stayed by any order of a court or administrative agency in any proceeding under this chapter.

§1520. Effects of recognition of a foreign main proceeding

(a) Upon recognition of a foreign proceeding that is a foreign main proceeding—

(1) sections 361 and 362 apply with respect to the debtor and the property of the debtor that is within the territorial jurisdiction of the United States;

(2) sections 363, 549, and 552 apply to a transfer of an interest of the debtor in property that is within the territorial jurisdiction of the United States to the same extent that the sections would apply to property of an estate;

(3) unless the court orders otherwise, the foreign representative may operate the debtor's business and may exercise the rights and powers of a trustee under and to the extent provided by sections 363 and 552; and

(4) section 552 applies to property of the debtor that is within the territorial jurisdiction of the United States.

(b) Subsection (a) does not affect the right to commence an individual action or proceeding in a foreign country to the extent necessary to preserve a claim against the debtor.

(c) Subsection (a) does not affect the right of a foreign representative or an entity to file a petition commencing a case under this title or the right of any party to file claims or take other proper actions in such a case.

§1521. Relief that may be granted upon recognition

(a) Upon recognition of a foreign proceeding, whether main or nonmain, where necessary to effectuate the purpose of this chapter and to protect the assets of the debtor or the interests of the creditors, the court may, at the request of the foreign representative, grant any appropriate relief, including—

(1) staying the commencement or continuation of an individual action or proceeding concerning the debtor's assets, rights, obligations or liabilities to the extent they have not been stayed under section 1520(a);

(2) staying execution against the debtor's assets to the extent it has not been stayed under section 1520(a);

(3) suspending the right to transfer, encumber or otherwise dispose of any assets of the debtor to the extent this right has not been suspended under section 1520(a);

(4) providing for the examination of witnesses, the taking of evidence or the delivery of information concerning the debtor's assets, affairs, rights, obligations or liabilities;

(5) entrusting the administration or realization of all or part of the debtor's assets within the territorial jurisdiction of the United States to the foreign representative or another person, including an examiner, authorized by the court;

(6) extending relief granted under section 1519(a); and

(7) granting any additional relief that may be available to a trustee, except for relief available under sections 522, 544, 545, 547, 548, 550, and 724(a).

(b) Upon recognition of a foreign proceeding, whether main or nonmain, the court may, at the request of the foreign representative, entrust the distribution of all or part of the debtor's assets located in the United States to the foreign representative or another person, including an examiner, authorized by the court, provided that the court is satisfied that the interests of creditors in the United States are sufficiently protected.

(c) In granting relief under this section to a representative of a foreign nonmain proceeding, the court must be satisfied that the relief relates to assets that, under the law of the United States, should be administered in the foreign nonmain proceeding or concerns information required in that proceeding.

(d) The court may not enjoin a police or regulatory act of a governmental unit, including a criminal action or proceeding, under this section.

(e) The standards, procedures, and limitations applicable to an injunction shall apply to relief under paragraphs (1), (2), (3), and (6) of subsection (a).

(f) The exercise of rights not subject to the stay arising under section 362(a) pursuant to paragraph (6), (7), (17), or (27) of section 362(b) or pursuant to section 362(o) shall not be stayed by any order of a court or administrative agency in any proceeding under this chapter.

§1522. Protection of creditors and other interested persons

(a) The court may grant relief under section 1519 or 1521, or may modify or terminate relief under subsection (c), only if the interests of the creditors and other interested entities, including the debtor, are sufficiently protected.

(b) The court may subject relief granted under section 1519 or 1521, or the operation of the debtor's business under section 1520(a)(3), to conditions it considers appropriate, including the giving of security or the filing of a bond.

(c) The court may, at the request of the foreign representative or an entity affected by relief granted under section 1519 or 1521, or at its own motion, modify or terminate such relief.

(d) Section 1104(d) shall apply to the appointment of an examiner under this chapter. Any examiner shall comply with the qualification requirements imposed on a trustee by section 322.

§1523. Actions to avoid acts detrimental to creditors

(a) Upon recognition of a foreign proceeding, the foreign representative has standing in a case concerning the debtor pending under another chapter of this title to initiate actions under sections 522, 544, 545, 547, 548, 550, 553, and 724(a).

(b) When a foreign proceeding is a foreign nonmain proceeding, the court must be satisfied that an action under subsection (a) relates to assets that, under United States law, should be administered in the foreign nonmain proceeding.

§1524. Intervention by a foreign representative

Upon recognition of a foreign proceeding, the foreign representative may intervene in any proceedings in a State or Federal court in the United States in which the debtor is a party.

SUBCHAPTER IV—COOPERATION WITH FOREIGN COURTS AND FOREIGN REPRESENTATIVES

§1525. Cooperation and direct communication between the court and foreign courts or foreign representatives

(a) Consistent with section 1501, the court shall cooperate to the maximum extent possible with a foreign court or a foreign representative, either directly or through the trustee.

(b) The court is entitled to communicate directly with, or to request information or assistance directly from, a foreign court or a foreign representative, subject to the rights of a party in interest to notice and participation.

§1526. Cooperation and direct communication between the trustee and foreign courts or foreign representatives

(a) Consistent with section 1501, the trustee or other person, including an examiner, authorized by the court, shall, subject to the supervision of the court, cooperate to the maximum extent possible with a foreign court or a foreign representative.

(b) The trustee or other person, including an examiner, authorized by the court is entitled, subject to the supervision of the court, to communicate directly with a foreign court or a foreign representative.

§1527. Forms of cooperation

Cooperation referred to in sections 1525 and 1526 may be implemented by any appropriate means, including—

(1) appointment of a person or body, including an examiner, to act at the direction of the court;

(2) communication of information by any means considered appropriate by the court;

(3) coordination of the administration and supervision of the debtor's assets and affairs;

(4) approval or implementation of agreements concerning the coordination of proceedings; and

(5) coordination of concurrent proceedings regarding the same debtor.

SUBCHAPTER V—CONCURRENT PROCEEDINGS

§1528. Commencement of a case under this title after recognition of a foreign main proceeding

After recognition of a foreign main proceeding, a case under another chapter of this title may be commenced only if the debtor has assets in the

United States. The effects of such case shall be restricted to the assets of the debtor that are within the territorial jurisdiction of the United States and, to the extent necessary to implement cooperation and coordination under sections 1525, 1526, and 1527, to other assets of the debtor that are within the jurisdiction of the court under sections 541(a) of this title, and 1334(e) of title 28, to the extent that such other assets are not subject to the jurisdiction and control of a foreign proceeding that has been recognized under this chapter.

§1529. Coordination of a case under this title and a foreign proceeding

If a foreign proceeding and a case under another chapter of this title are pending concurrently regarding the same debtor, the court shall seek cooperation and coordination under sections 1525, 1526, and 1527, and the following shall apply:

(1) If the case in the United States is pending at the time the petition for recognition of such foreign proceeding is filed—

(A) any relief granted under section 1519 or 1521 must be consistent with the relief granted in the case in the United States; and

(B) section 1520 does not apply even if such foreign proceeding is recognized as a foreign main proceeding.

(2) If a case in the United States under this title commences after recognition, or after the date of the filing of the petition for recognition, of such foreign proceeding—

(A) any relief in effect under section 1519 or 1521 shall be reviewed by the court and shall be modified or terminated if inconsistent with the case in the United States; and

(B) if such foreign proceeding is a foreign main proceeding, the stay and suspension referred to in section 1520(a) shall be modified or terminated if inconsistent with the relief granted in the case in the United States.

(3) In granting, extending, or modifying relief granted to a representative of a foreign nonmain proceeding, the court must be satisfied that the relief relates to assets that, under the laws of the United States, should be administered in the foreign nonmain proceeding or concerns information required in that proceeding.

(4) In achieving cooperation and coordination under sections 1528 and 1529, the court may grant any of the relief authorized under section 305.

§1530. Coordination of more than 1 foreign proceeding

In matters referred to in section 1501, with respect to more than 1 foreign proceeding regarding the debtor, the court shall seek cooperation and coordination under sections 1525, 1526, and 1527, and the following shall apply:

(1) Any relief granted under section 1519 or 1521 to a representative of a foreign nonmain proceeding after recognition of a foreign main proceeding must be consistent with the foreign main proceeding.

(2) If a foreign main proceeding is recognized after recognition, or after the filing of a petition for recognition, of a foreign nonmain proceeding, any relief in effect under section 1519 or 1521 shall be reviewed by the court and shall be modified or terminated if inconsistent with the foreign main proceeding.

(3) If, after recognition of a foreign nonmain proceeding, another foreign nonmain proceeding is recognized, the court shall grant, modify, or terminate relief for the purpose of facilitating coordination of the proceedings.

§1531. Presumption of insolvency based on recognition of a foreign main proceeding

In the absence of evidence to the contrary, recognition of a foreign main proceeding is, for the purpose of commencing a proceeding under section 303, proof that the debtor is generally not paying its debts as such debts become due.

§1532. Rule of payment in concurrent proceedings

Without prejudice to secured claims or rights in rem, a creditor who has received payment with respect to its claim in a foreign proceeding pursuant to a law relating to insolvency may not receive a payment for the same claim in a case under any other chapter of this title regarding the debtor, so long as the payment to other creditors of the same class is proportionately less than the payment the creditor has already received.

CPSIA information can be obtained
at www.ICGtesting.com
Printed in the USA
FFHW01n1424190718
47473731-50747FF